BINGE PARENTING

Other Baby Blues® Books from Andrews McMeel Publishing

Guess Who Didn't Take a Nap?
I Thought Labor Ended When the Baby Was Born
We Are Experiencing Parental Difficulties . . . Please Stand By
Night of the Living Dad
I Saw Elvis in My Ultrasound
One More and We're Outnumbered!
Check, Please . . .
threats, bribes & videotape
If I'm a Stay-at-Home Mom, Why Am I Always in the Car?
Lift and Separate
I Shouldn't Have to Scream More Than Once!
Motherhood Is Not for Wimps
Baby Blues®: Unplugged
Dad to the Bone
Never a Dry Moment
Two Plus One Is Enough
Playdate: Category 5
Our Server Is Down
Something Chocolate This Way Comes
Briefcase Full of Baby Blues®
Night Shift
The Day Phonics Kicked In
My Space
The Natural Disorder of Things
We Were Here First
Ambushed! In the Family Room
Cut!
Eat, Cry, Poop
Scribbles at an Exhibition
Bedlam
Wetter, Louder, Stickier
No Yelling!
Gross!

Treasuries

The Super-Absorbent Biodegradable Family-Size Baby Blues®
Baby Blues®: Ten Years and Still in Diapers
Butt-Naked Baby Blues®
Wall-to-Wall Baby Blues®
Driving Under the Influence of Children
Framed!
X-Treme Parenting
BBXX: Baby Blues: Decades 1 and 2

Gift Books

It's a Boy
It's a Girl

BINGE PARENTING

rick kirkman
jerry scott

Scrapbook

NO.
34

Andrews McMeel
PUBLISHING®

To my team, Kim, Abbey, and Cady Lane.

—J.S.

To the service men and women of the U.S.—and their families—
many of whom spend long stretches apart. Thank you.

—R.K.

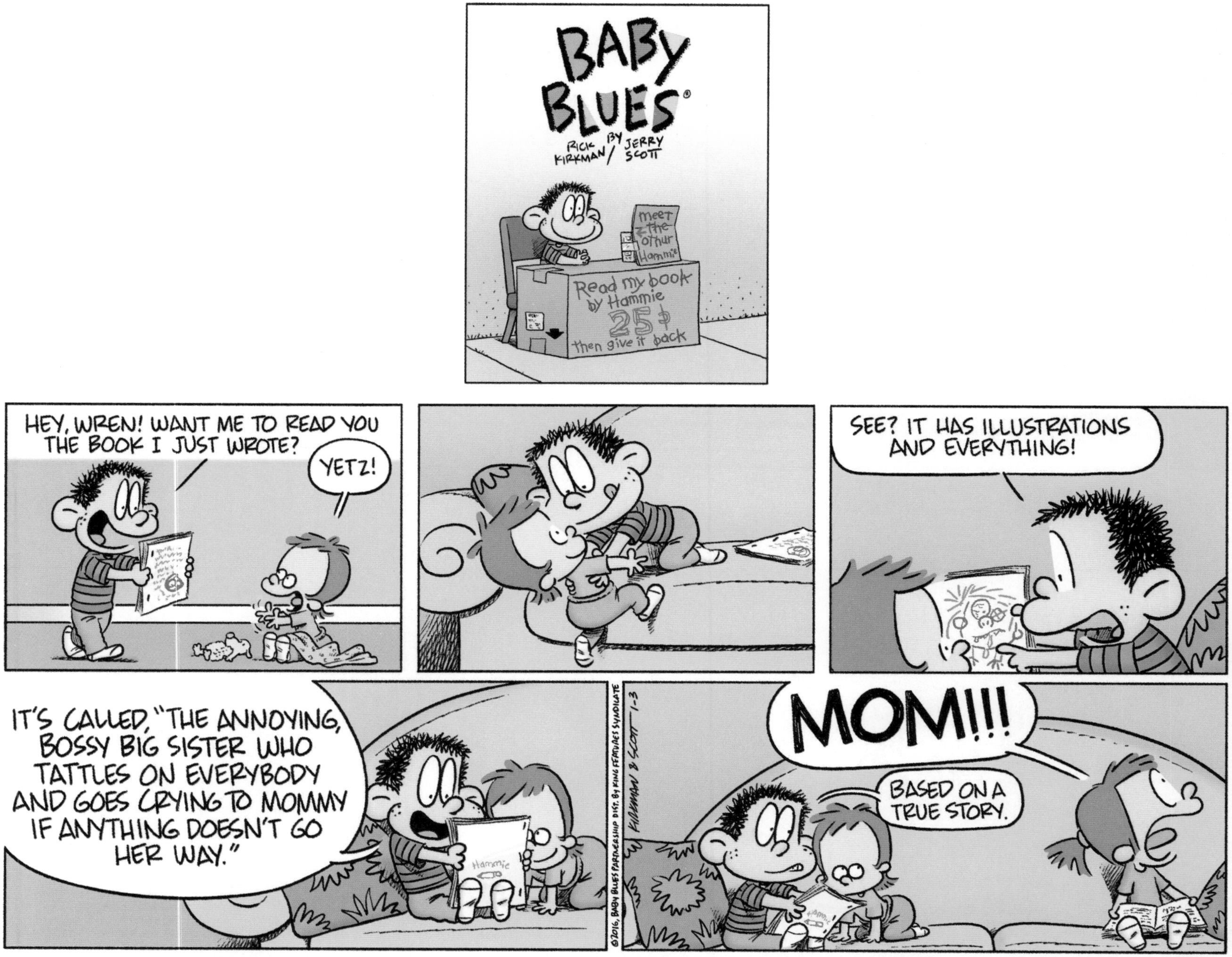
BABY BLUES®
BY RICK KIRKMAN / JERRY SCOTT
meet the othur Hammie
Read my book by Hammie 25¢ then give it back
HEY, WREN! WANT ME TO READ YOU THE BOOK I JUST WROTE?
YETZ!
SEE? IT HAS ILLUSTRATIONS AND EVERYTHING!
IT'S CALLED, "THE ANNOYING, BOSSY BIG SISTER WHO TATTLES ON EVERYBODY AND GOES CRYING TO MOMMY IF ANYTHING DOESN'T GO HER WAY."
Hammie
©2016, BABY BLUES PARTNERSHIP DIST. BY KING FEATURES SYNDICATE
KIRKMAN & SCOTT 1-3
MOM!!!
BASED ON A TRUE STORY.

Rick: This title panel is inspired by an event that happened in eighth grade: A friend and I created a parody of *MAD* magazine, called *MUD* (we were comic geniuses). Since we had no way to print multiple copies, we charged our friends and neighbors twenty-five cents each to read it and then return it, so we could charge someone else to read it. When the other kids' parents found out their kids paid for something they couldn't keep, we were forced to refund everyone's money. When you think about it, we were actually decades ahead of our time. We were not only geniuses but visionaries!

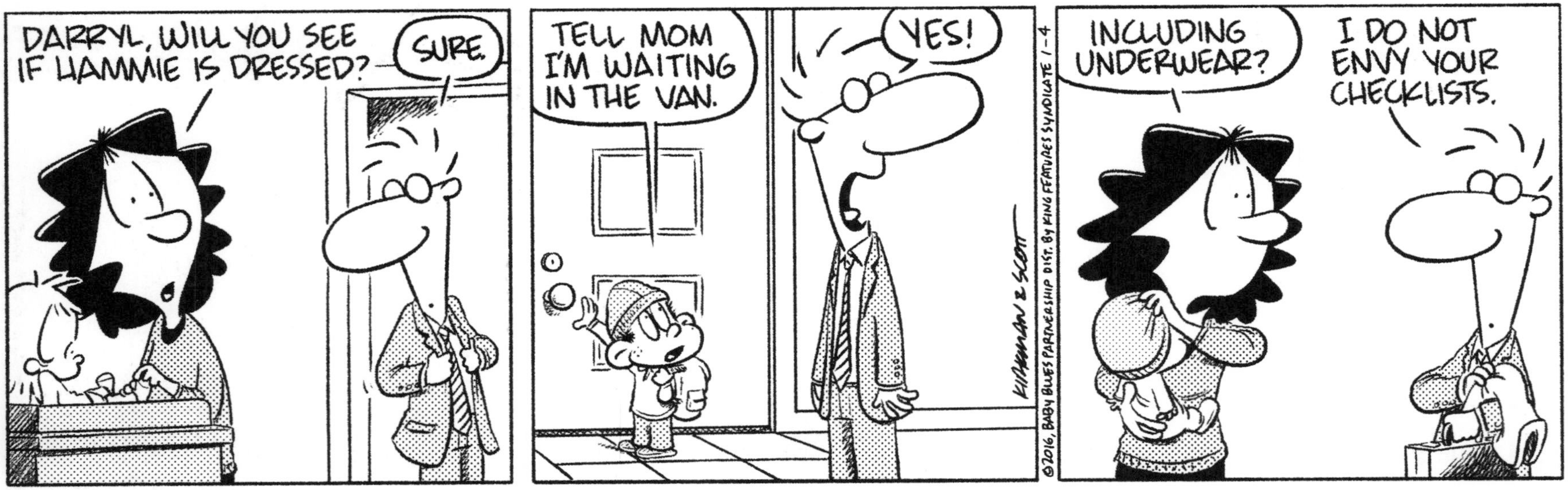
DARRYL, WILL YOU SEE IF HAMMIE IS DRESSED?
SURE.
TELL MOM I'M WAITING IN THE VAN.
YES!
INCLUDING UNDERWEAR?
I DO NOT ENVY YOUR CHECKLISTS.
KIRKMAN & SCOTT
©2016, BABY BLUES PARTNERSHIP DIST. BY KING FEATURES SYNDICATE 1-4

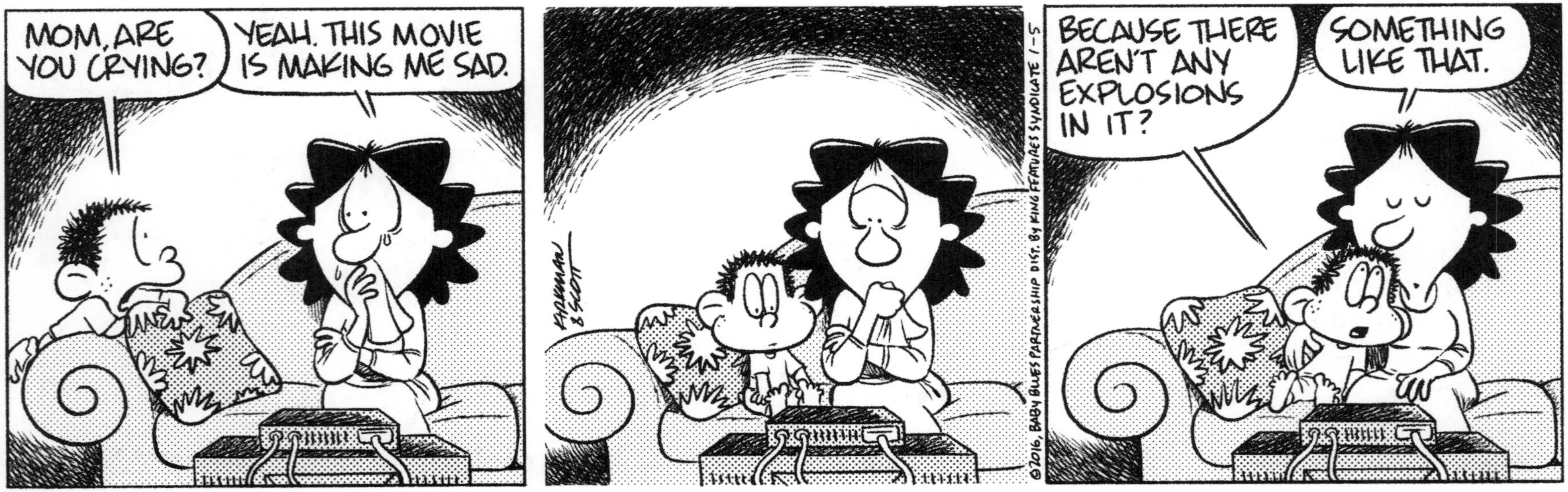
MOM, ARE YOU CRYING?
YEAH. THIS MOVIE IS MAKING ME SAD.
BECAUSE THERE AREN'T ANY EXPLOSIONS IN IT?
SOMETHING LIKE THAT.
KIRKMAN & SCOTT
©2016, BABY BLUES PARTNERSHIP DIST. BY KING FEATURES SYNDICATE 1-5

Rick: Funny, I never saw in a *Peanuts* book: "Happiness is an explosion on TV."

Jerry: I like to see the kids express their sweet, sympathetic sides once in a while, with a little ornery on the side.

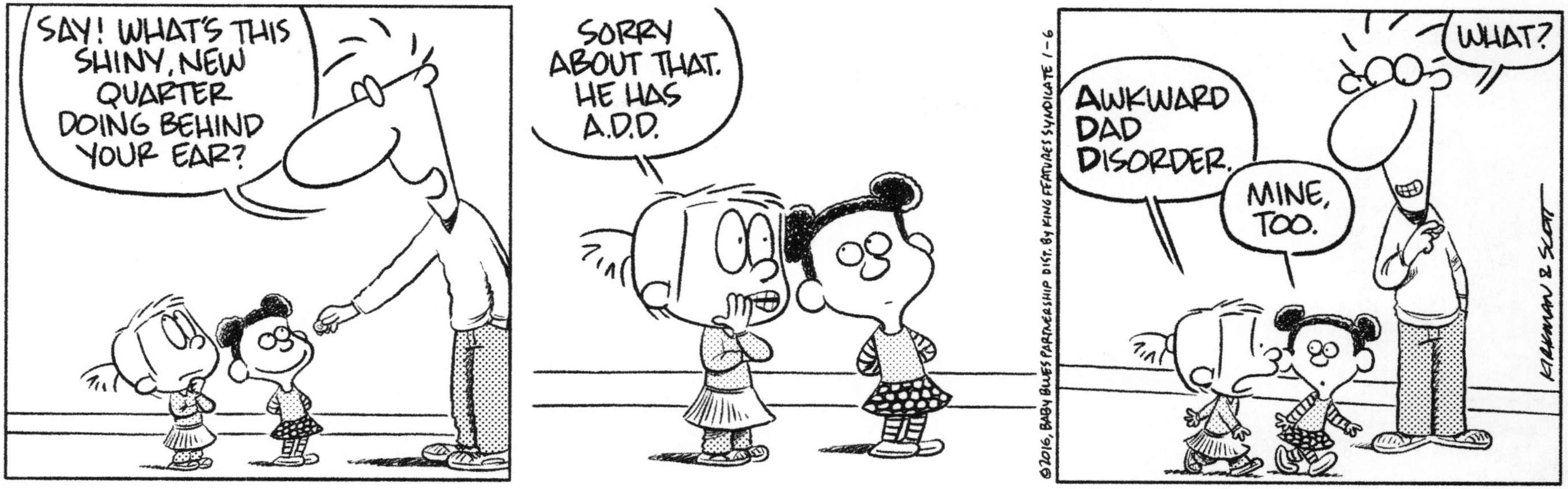
SAY! WHAT'S THIS SHINY, NEW QUARTER DOING BEHIND YOUR EAR?
SORRY ABOUT THAT. HE HAS A.D.D.
©2016, BABY BLUES PARTNERSHIP DIST. BY KING FEATURES SYNDICATE 1-6
AWKWARD DAD DISORDER.
MINE, TOO.
WHAT?
KIRKMAN & SCOTT

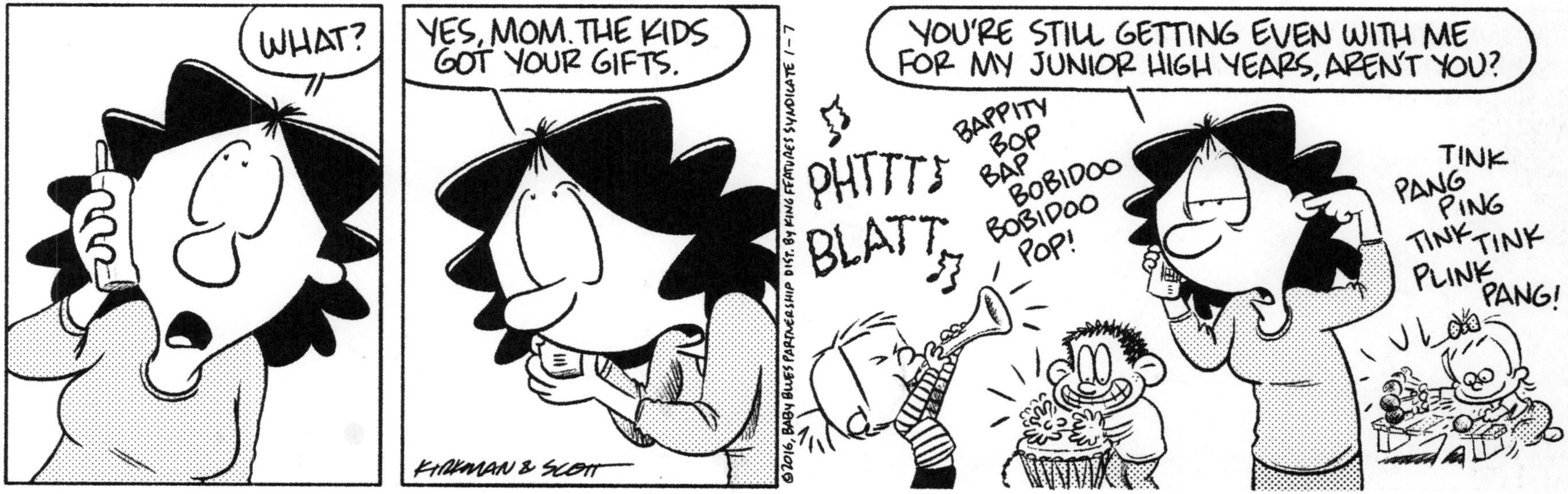
WHAT?
YES, MOM. THE KIDS GOT YOUR GIFTS.
KIRKMAN & SCOTT
©2016, BABY BLUES PARTNERSHIP DIST. BY KING FEATURES SYNDICATE 1-7
YOU'RE STILL GETTING EVEN WITH ME FOR MY JUNIOR HIGH YEARS, AREN'T YOU?
PHTTTT
BLATT
BAPPITY BOP BAP BOBIDOO BOBIDOO POP!
TINK PANG PING TINK TINK PLINK PANG!

Rick: Early musical instrument training is painful but, to me, an essential part of growing up.

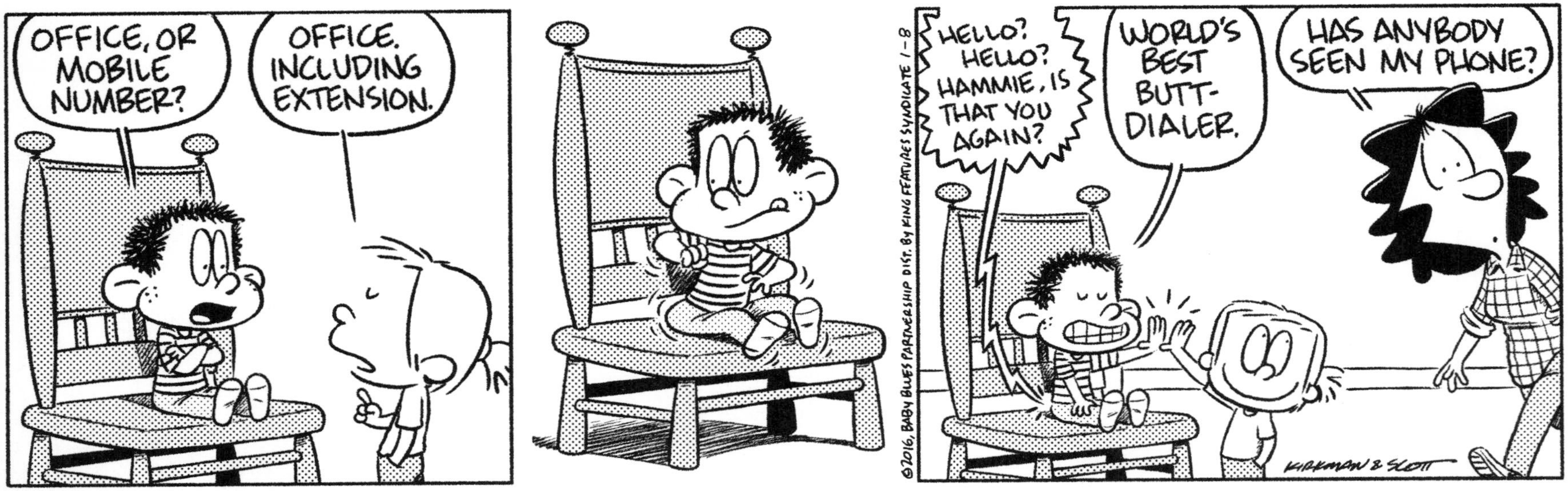
OFFICE, OR MOBILE NUMBER?
OFFICE. INCLUDING EXTENSION.
HELLO? HELLO? HAMMIE, IS THAT YOU AGAIN?
WORLD'S BEST BUTT-DIALER.
HAS ANYBODY SEEN MY PHONE?
©2016, BABY BLUES PARTNERSHIP DIST. BY KING FEATURES SYNDICATE 1-8
KIRKMAN & SCOTT

Jerry: My older sister butt-dials me regularly. It makes me wonder about her opinion of me.

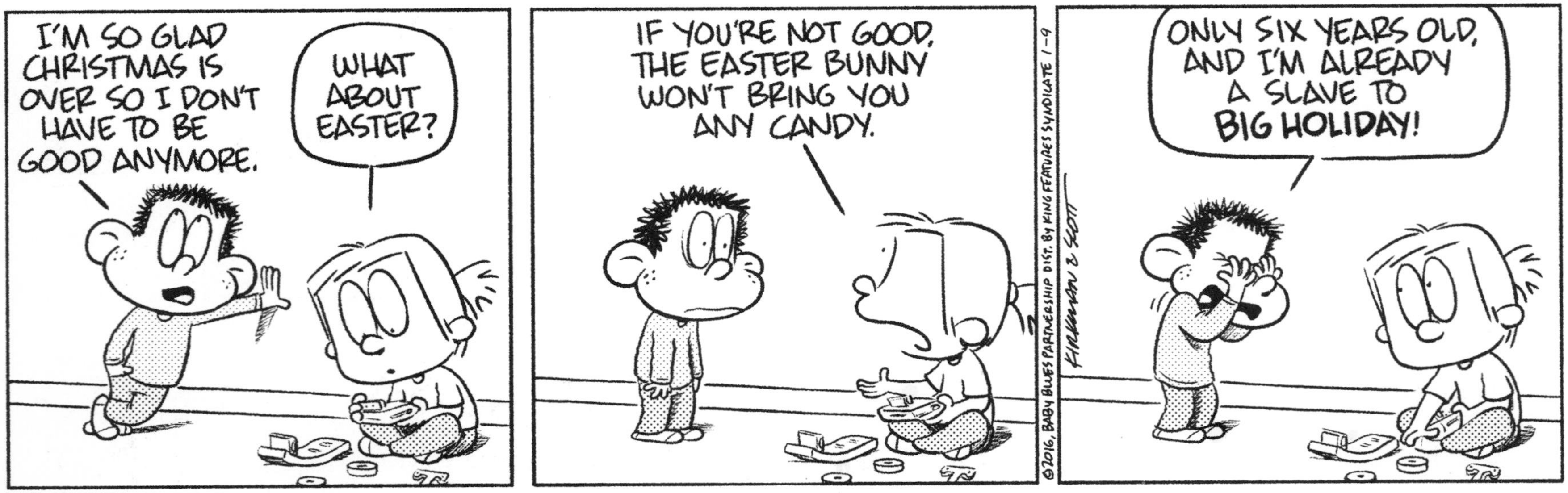
I'M SO GLAD CHRISTMAS IS OVER SO I DON'T HAVE TO BE GOOD ANYMORE.
WHAT ABOUT EASTER?
IF YOU'RE NOT GOOD, THE EASTER BUNNY WON'T BRING YOU ANY CANDY.
©2016, BABY BLUES PARTNERSHIP DIST. BY KING FEATURES SYNDICATE 1-9
KIRKMAN & SCOTT
ONLY SIX YEARS OLD, AND I'M ALREADY A SLAVE TO BIG HOLIDAY!

BABY BLUES®
RICK KIRKMAN / BY JERRY SCOTT

WHAT IS THAT STUFF?
KALE.
KALE?? I'M NOT EATING KALE!
©2015, BABY BLUES PARTNERSHIP DIST. BY KING FEATURES SYNDICATE
IT'S FULL OF ALL THAT GUNK THAT ATHLETES LIKE. DO I LOOK LIKE I WANT HUGE MUSCLES? FORGET IT!
1-10
KIRKMAN & SCOTT
I WON'T EAT KALE, AND I WON'T HANG AROUND ANYBODY WHO WILL!
LIPS THAT TOUCH KALE, WILL NEVER TOUCH MINE!
I'LL HAVE THE KALE.
IF YOU INSIST.
$

Rick: A little nod to the late Jack LaLanne, a fixture in my childhood.

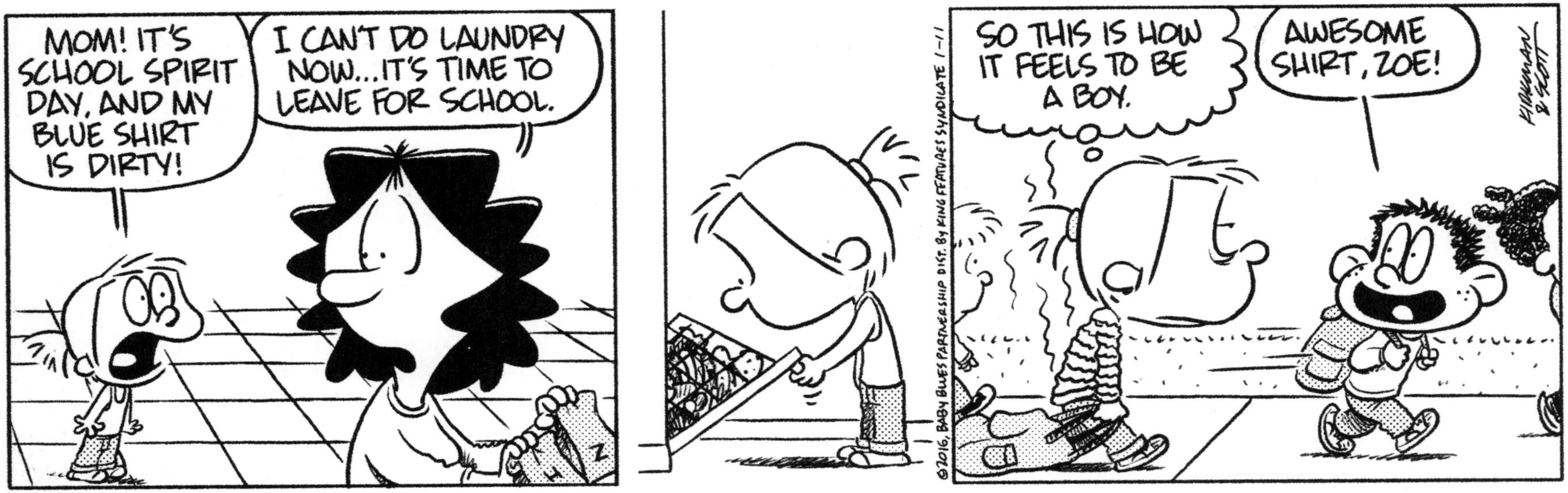
MOM! IT'S SCHOOL SPIRIT DAY, AND MY BLUE SHIRT IS DIRTY!
I CAN'T DO LAUNDRY NOW... IT'S TIME TO LEAVE FOR SCHOOL.
SO THIS IS HOW IT FEELS TO BE A BOY.
AWESOME SHIRT, ZOE!
KIRKMAN & SCOTT
©2016, BABY BLUES PARTNERSHIP DIST. BY KING FEATURES SYNDICATE 1-11

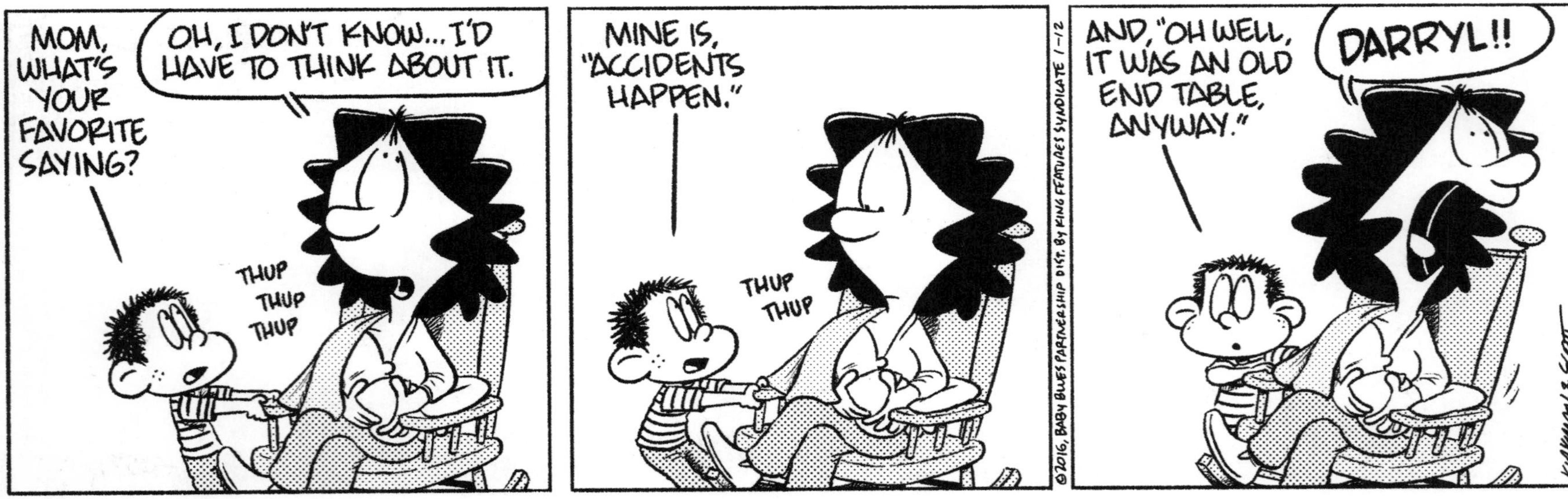
MOM, WHAT'S YOUR FAVORITE SAYING?
OH, I DON'T KNOW... I'D HAVE TO THINK ABOUT IT.
THUP THUP THUP
MINE IS, "ACCIDENTS HAPPEN."
THUP THUP
AND, "OH WELL, IT WAS AN OLD END TABLE, ANYWAY."
DARRYL!!
KIRKMAN & SCOTT
©2016, BABY BLUES PARTNERSHIP DIST. BY KING FEATURES SYNDICATE 1-12

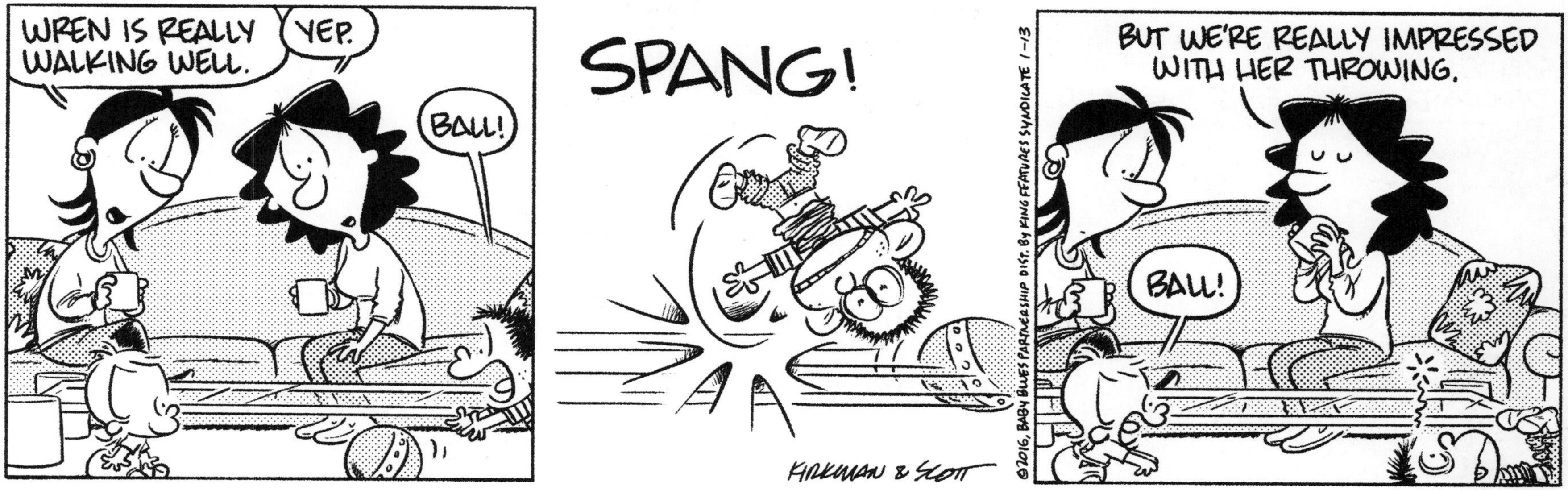
WREN IS REALLY WALKING WELL.
YEP.
BALL!
SPANG!
KIRKMAN & SCOTT
©2016, BABY BLUES PARTNERSHIP DIST. BY KING FEATURES SYNDICATE 1-13
BUT WE'RE REALLY IMPRESSED WITH HER THROWING.
BALL!

Rick: Jerry supplied the "SPANG!" sound effect in this, and it has become one of my favorites.

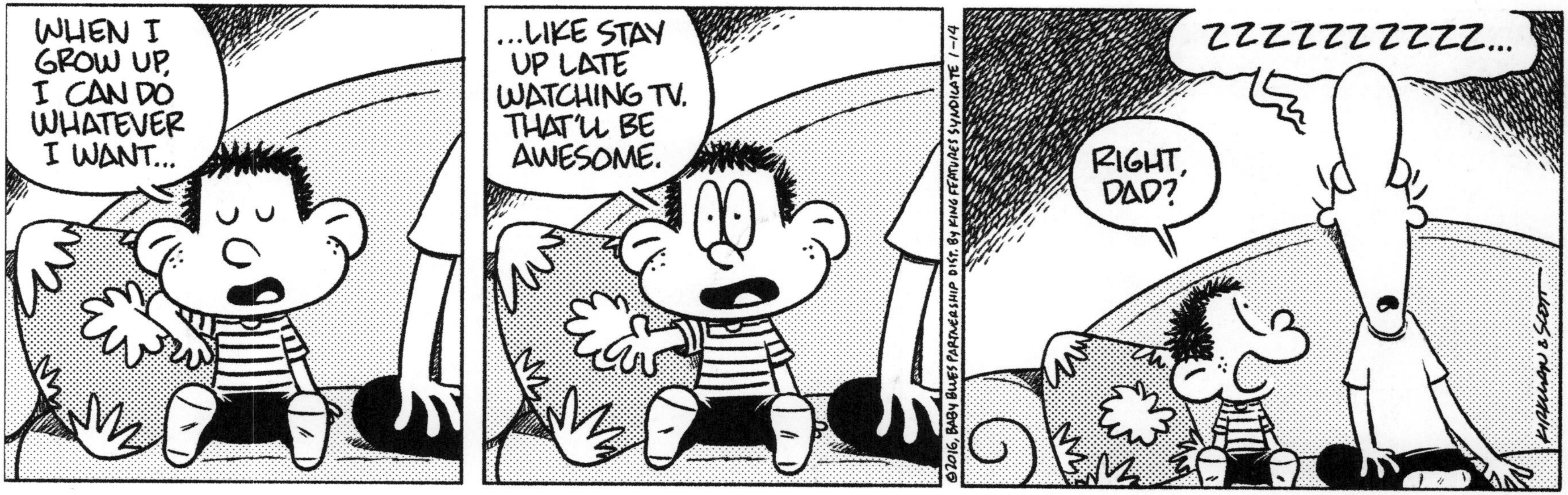
WHEN I GROW UP, I CAN DO WHATEVER I WANT...
...LIKE STAY UP LATE WATCHING TV. THAT'LL BE AWESOME.
©2016, BABY BLUES PARTNERSHIP DIST. BY KING FEATURES SYNDICATE 1-14
ZZZZZZZZZZ...
RIGHT, DAD?
KIRKMAN & SCOTT

Jerry: When I was a kid, I thought all adults watched TV with their heads tipped back and mouths open. Turns out that I was right.

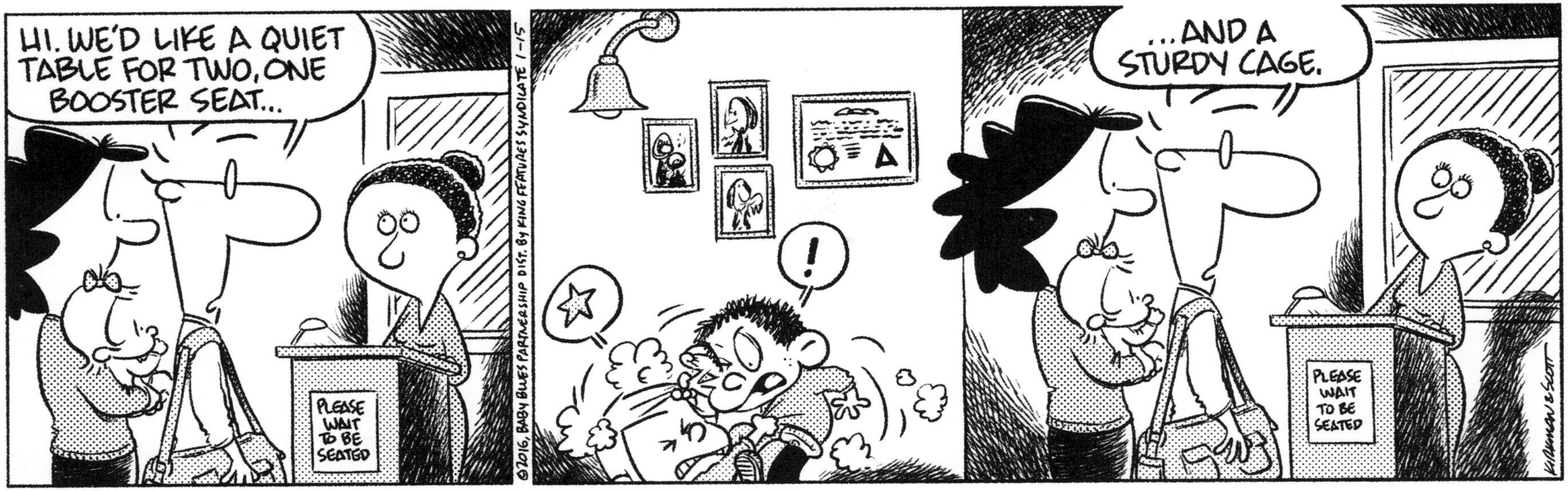
HI. WE'D LIKE A QUIET TABLE FOR TWO, ONE BOOSTER SEAT...
PLEASE WAIT TO BE SEATED
©2016, BABY BLUES PARTNERSHIP DIST. BY KING FEATURES SYNDICATE 1-15
!
...AND A STURDY CAGE.
PLEASE WAIT TO BE SEATED
KIRKMAN & SCOTT

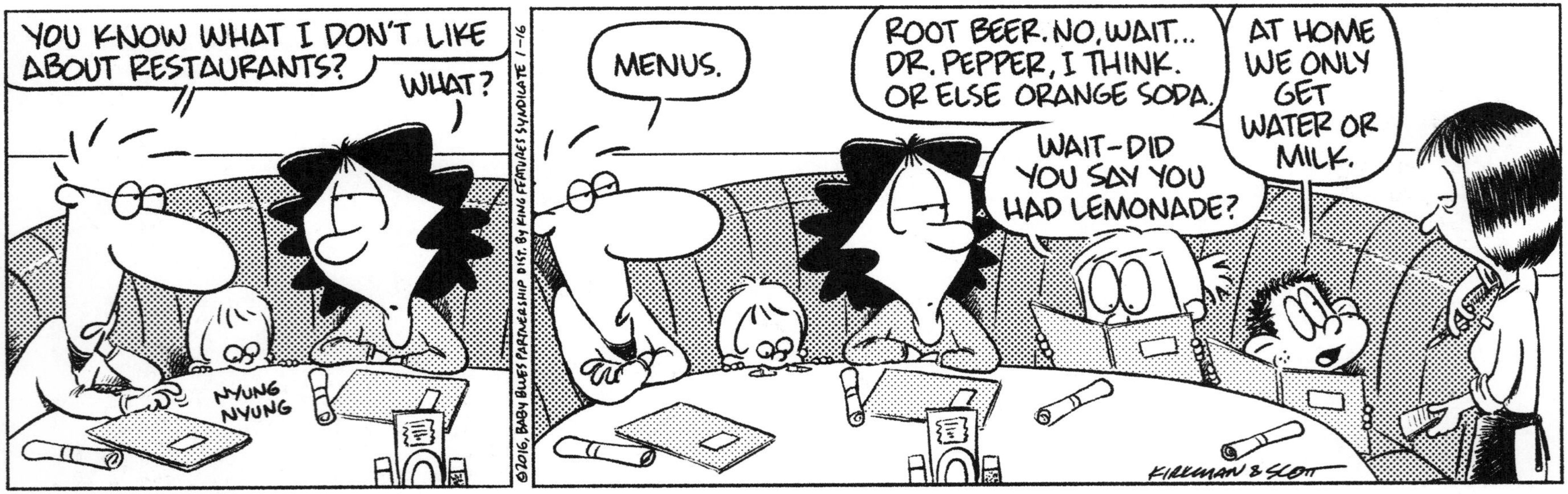
YOU KNOW WHAT I DON'T LIKE ABOUT RESTAURANTS?
WHAT?
NYUNG NYUNG
©2016, BABY BLUES PARTNERSHIP DIST. BY KING FEATURES SYNDICATE 1-16
MENUS.
ROOT BEER. NO, WAIT... DR. PEPPER, I THINK. OR ELSE ORANGE SODA.
WAIT-DID YOU SAY YOU HAD LEMONADE?
AT HOME WE ONLY GET WATER OR MILK.
KIRKMAN & SCOTT

BABY BLUES®

THE FANTASY
I'M GOING TO PUT THESE CLOTHES IN THE WASHER NOW.
THEN I'LL GET UP REALLY EARLY AND COOK A HEARTY BREAKFAST WHILE THEY'RE IN THE DRYER.
WHEN THE KIDS WAKE UP, THERE WILL BE FRESH WAFFLES ON THE TABLE AND TOASTY-WARM JEANS TO WEAR ON A COLD WINTER DAY!
THAT SOUNDS GREAT!
©2016, BABY BLUES PARTNERSHIP DIST. BY KING FEATURES SYNDICATE 1-17
THE REALITY
YOU OVERSLEPT, WE'RE OUT OF CEREAL, AND OUR JEANS ARE WET.
THAT SOUNDS NORMAL.
KIRKMAN & SCOTT

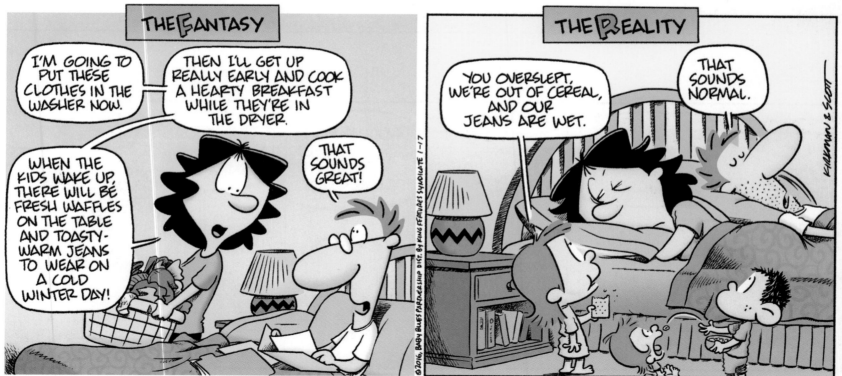

Jerry: My job is coming up with the ideas for *Baby Blues*, but Rick often tosses in extra visual gems that make the strip so much better. Did you notice Hammie tossing cereal into Wren's mouth in the second panel?

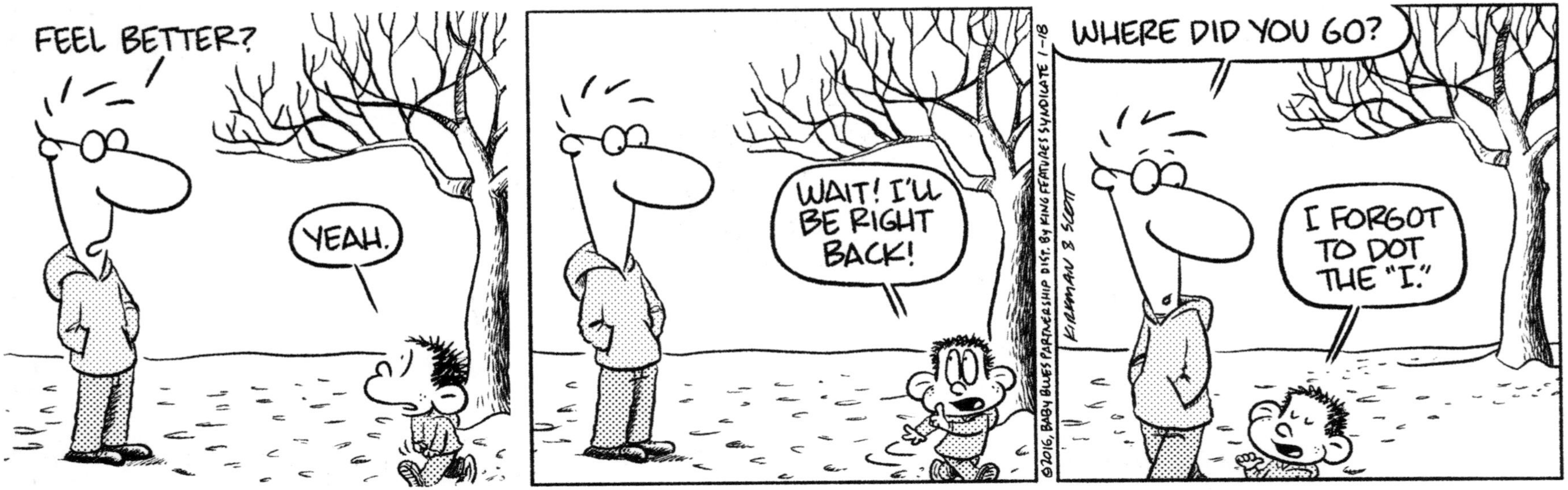
FEEL BETTER?
YEAH.
WAIT! I'LL BE RIGHT BACK!
WHERE DID YOU GO?
I FORGOT TO DOT THE "I."
©2016, BABY BLUES PARTNERSHIP DIST. BY KING FEATURES SYNDICATE 1-18
KIRKMAN & SCOTT

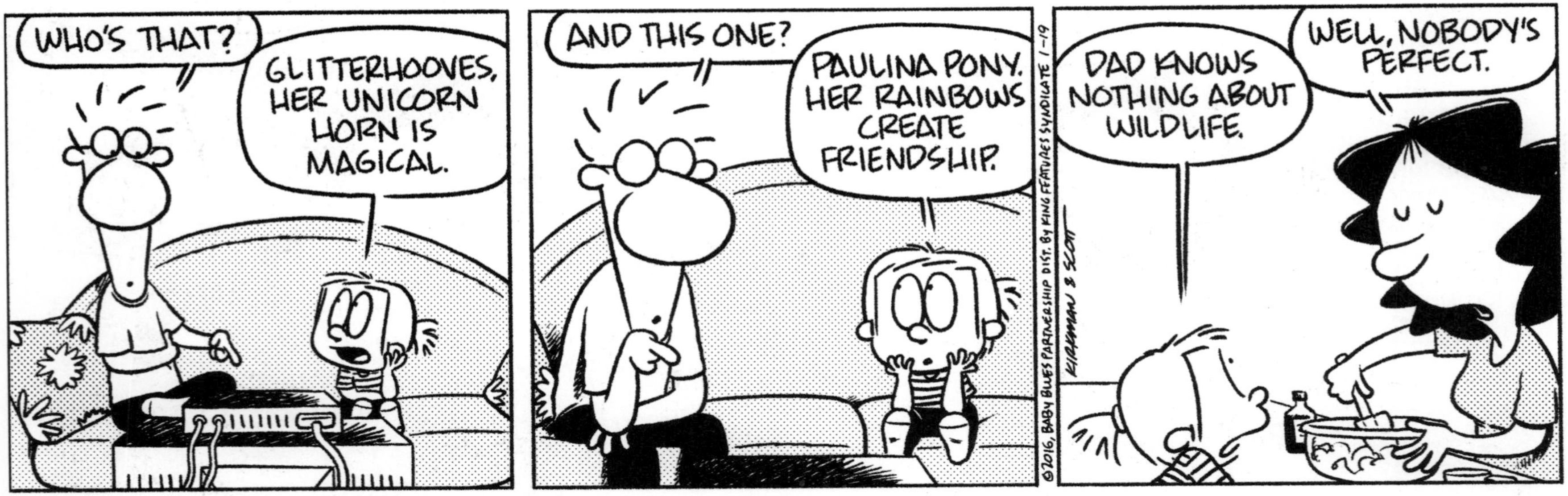
WHO'S THAT?
GLITTERHOOVES. HER UNICORN HORN IS MAGICAL.
AND THIS ONE?
PAULINA PONY. HER RAINBOWS CREATE FRIENDSHIP.
DAD KNOWS NOTHING ABOUT WILDLIFE.
WELL, NOBODY'S PERFECT.
©2016, BABY BLUES PARTNERSHIP DIST. BY KING FEATURES SYNDICATE 1-19
KIRKMAN & SCOTT

Jerry: Being the father of two horse-obsessed girls, I had to keep up on my unicornology.

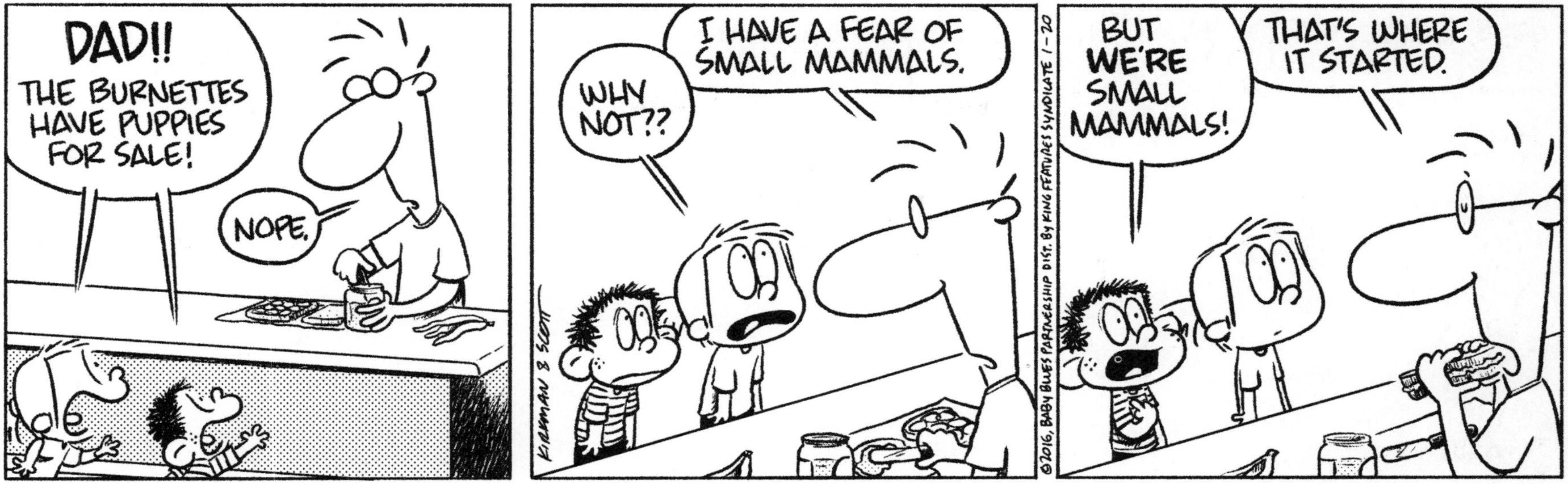
DAD!! THE BURNETTES HAVE PUPPIES FOR SALE!
NOPE.
KIRKMAN & SCOTT
WHY NOT??
I HAVE A FEAR OF SMALL MAMMALS.
©2016, BABY BLUES PARTNERSHIP DIST. BY KING FEATURES SYNDICATE 1-20
BUT **WE'RE** SMALL MAMMALS!
THAT'S WHERE IT STARTED.

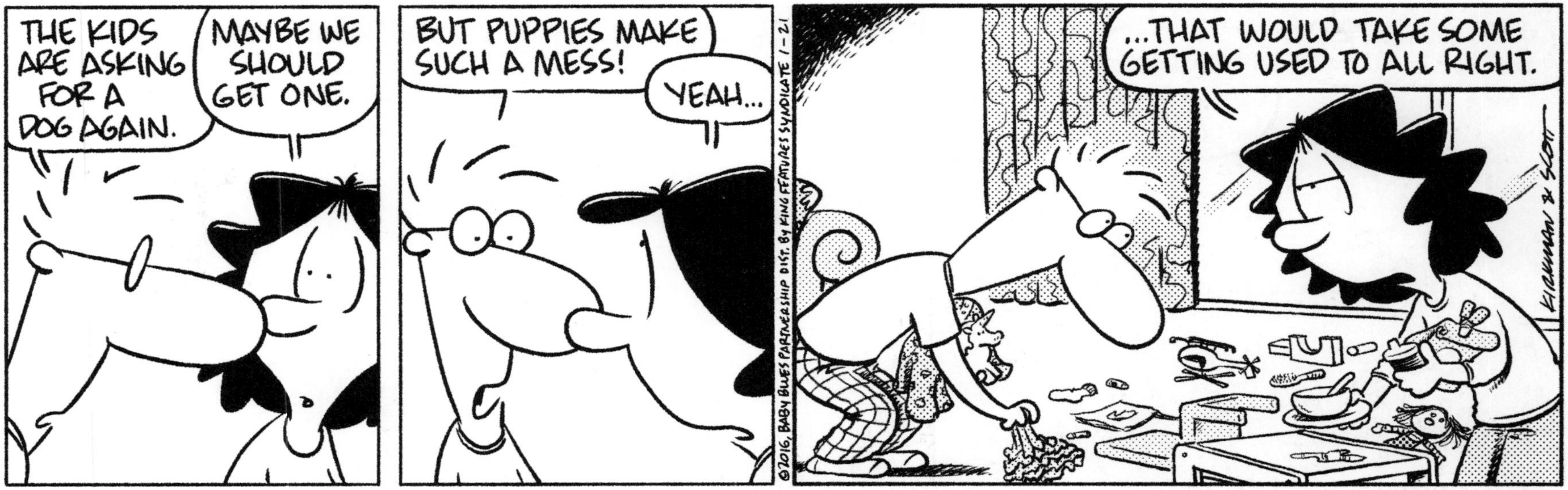
THE KIDS ARE ASKING FOR A DOG AGAIN.
MAYBE WE SHOULD GET ONE.
BUT PUPPIES MAKE SUCH A MESS!
YEAH...
©2016, BABY BLUES PARTNERSHIP DIST. BY KING FEATURES SYNDICATE 1-21
...THAT WOULD TAKE SOME GETTING USED TO ALL RIGHT.
KIRKMAN & SCOTT

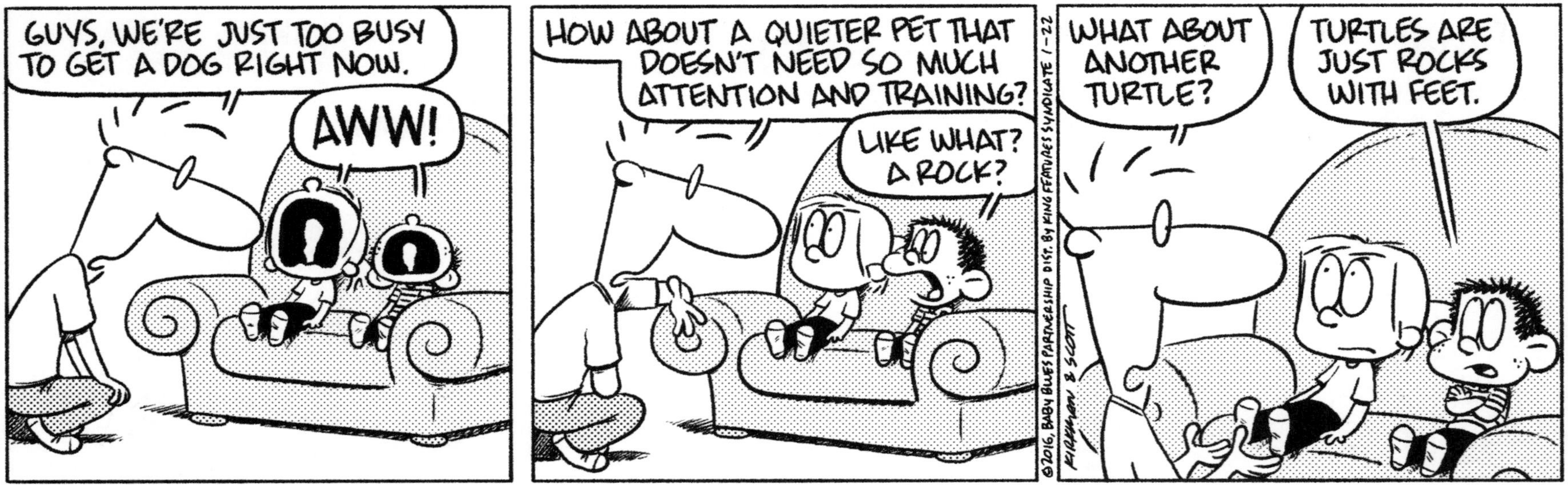
GUYS, WE'RE JUST TOO BUSY TO GET A DOG RIGHT NOW.
AWW!
HOW ABOUT A QUIETER PET THAT DOESN'T NEED SO MUCH ATTENTION AND TRAINING?
LIKE WHAT? A ROCK?
©2016, BABY BLUES PARTNERSHIP DIST. BY KING FEATURES SYNDICATE 1-22
KIRKMAN & SCOTT
WHAT ABOUT ANOTHER TURTLE?
TURTLES ARE JUST ROCKS WITH FEET.

Jerry: My apologies to turtle lovers. The views expressed by the characters in this comic strip do not necessarily reflect the views of its creators.

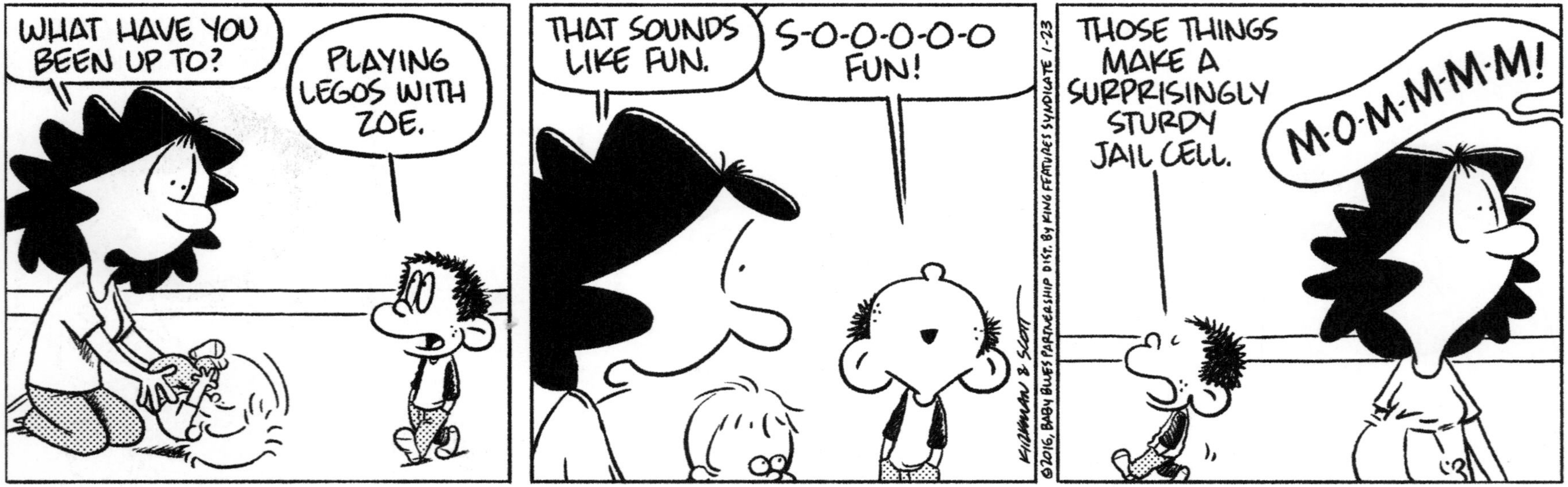
WHAT HAVE YOU BEEN UP TO?
PLAYING LEGOS WITH ZOE.
THAT SOUNDS LIKE FUN.
S-O-O-O-O-O FUN!
KIRKMAN & SCOTT
©2016, BABY BLUES PARTNERSHIP DIST. BY KING FEATURES SYNDICATE 1-23
THOSE THINGS MAKE A SURPRISINGLY STURDY JAIL CELL.
M-O-M-M-M-M!

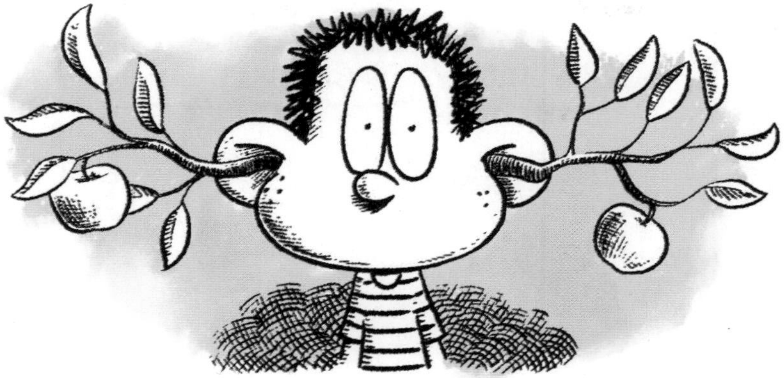

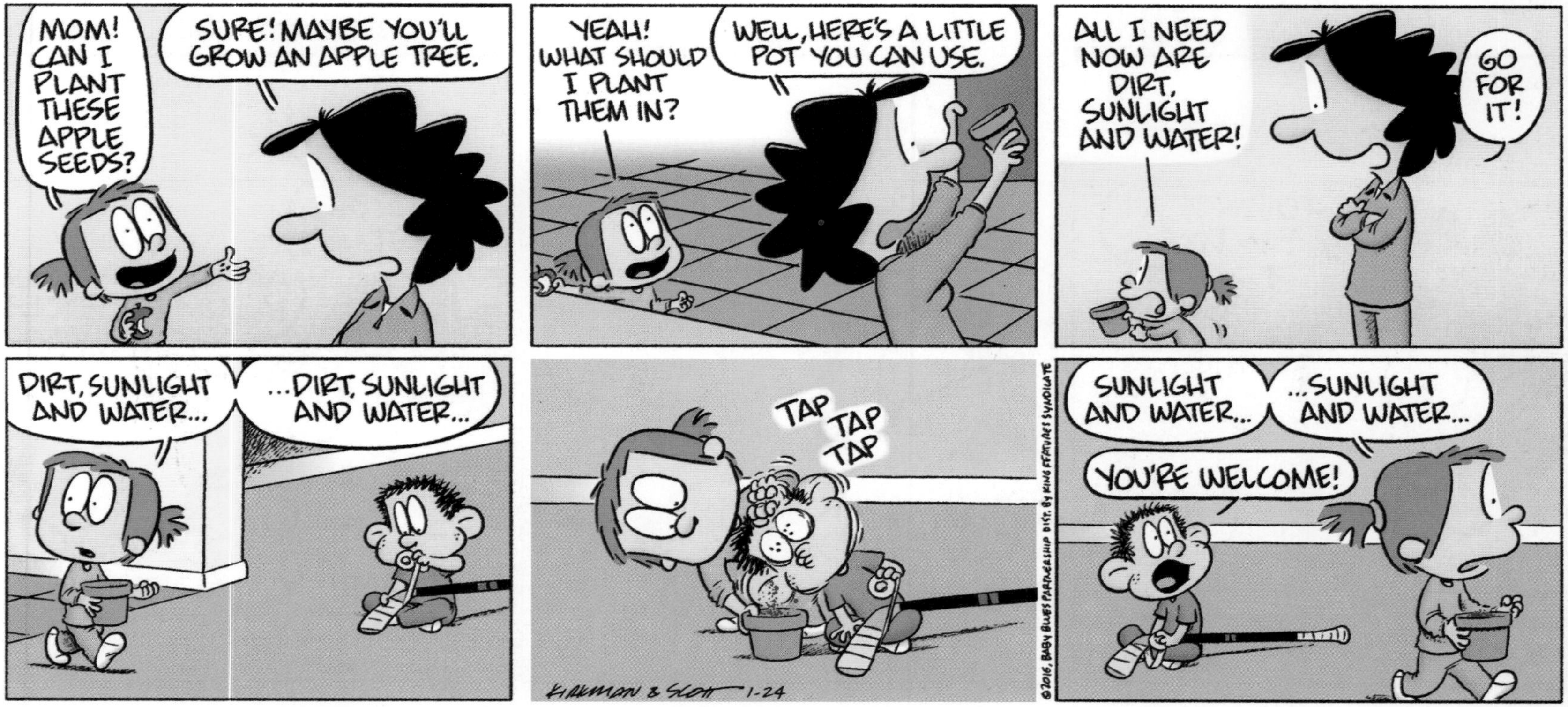
MOM! CAN I PLANT THESE APPLE SEEDS?
SURE! MAYBE YOU'LL GROW AN APPLE TREE.
YEAH! WHAT SHOULD I PLANT THEM IN?
WELL, HERE'S A LITTLE POT YOU CAN USE.
ALL I NEED NOW ARE DIRT, SUNLIGHT AND WATER!
GO FOR IT!
DIRT, SUNLIGHT AND WATER...
...DIRT, SUNLIGHT AND WATER...
TAP
TAP
TAP
KIRKMAN & SCOTT 1-24
©2016, BABY BLUES PARTNERSHIP DIST. BY KING FEATURES SYNDICATE
SUNLIGHT AND WATER...
...SUNLIGHT AND WATER...
YOU'RE WELCOME!

Jerry: My grandma used to say that she could grow potatoes with the dirt in my ears. Grandma was always a little weird.

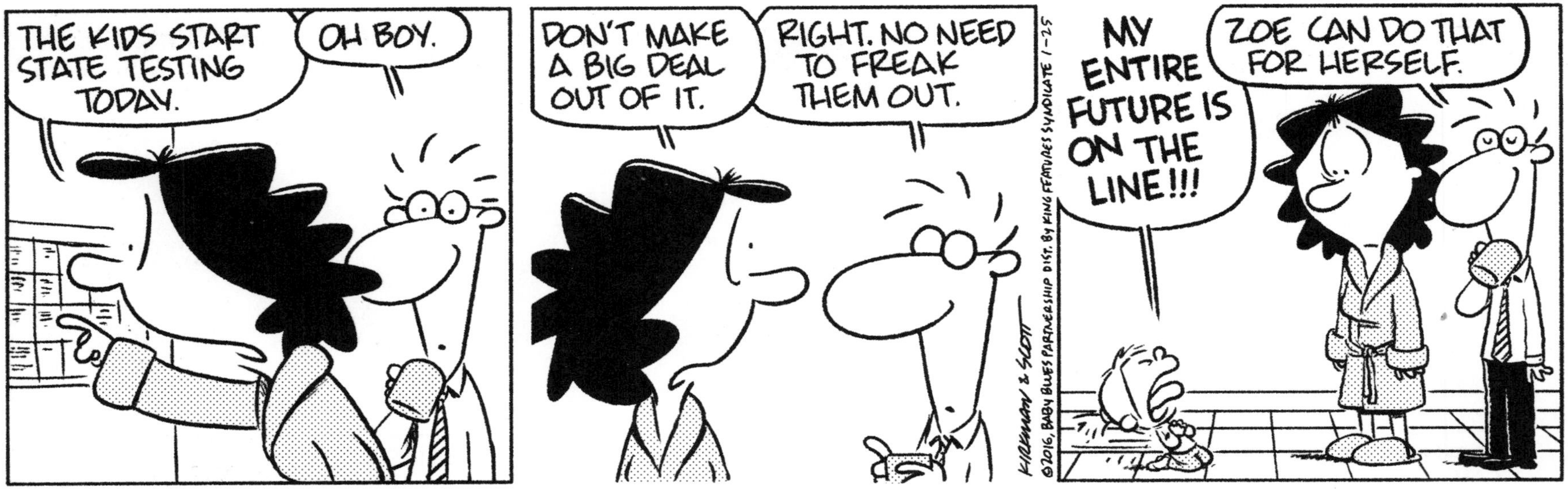
THE KIDS START STATE TESTING TODAY.
OH BOY.
DON'T MAKE A BIG DEAL OUT OF IT.
RIGHT. NO NEED TO FREAK THEM OUT.
KIRKMAN & SCOTT
©2016, BABY BLUES PARTNERSHIP DIST. BY KING FEATURES SYNDICATE 1-25
MY ENTIRE FUTURE IS ON THE LINE!!!
ZOE CAN DO THAT FOR HERSELF.

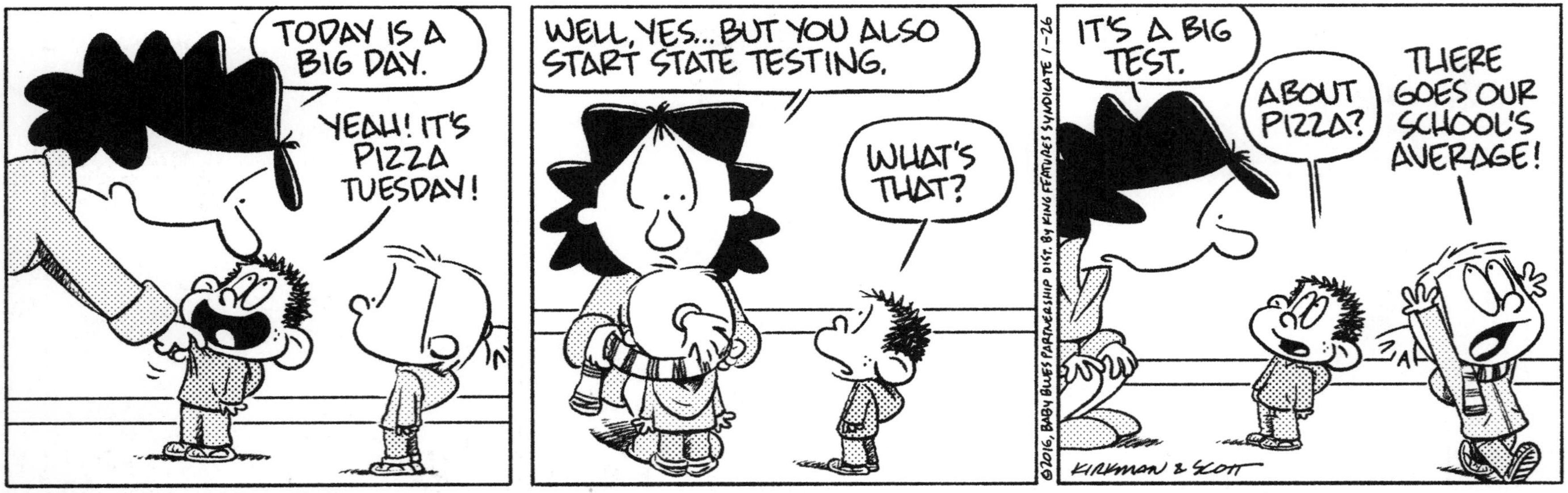
TODAY IS A BIG DAY.
YEAH! IT'S PIZZA TUESDAY!
WELL, YES... BUT YOU ALSO START STATE TESTING.
WHAT'S THAT?
©2016, BABY BLUES PARTNERSHIP DIST. BY KING FEATURES SYNDICATE 1-26
IT'S A BIG TEST.
ABOUT PIZZA?
THERE GOES OUR SCHOOL'S AVERAGE!
KIRKMAN & SCOTT

Jerry: Some people are freaked out by standardized testing, and some people are Hammie.

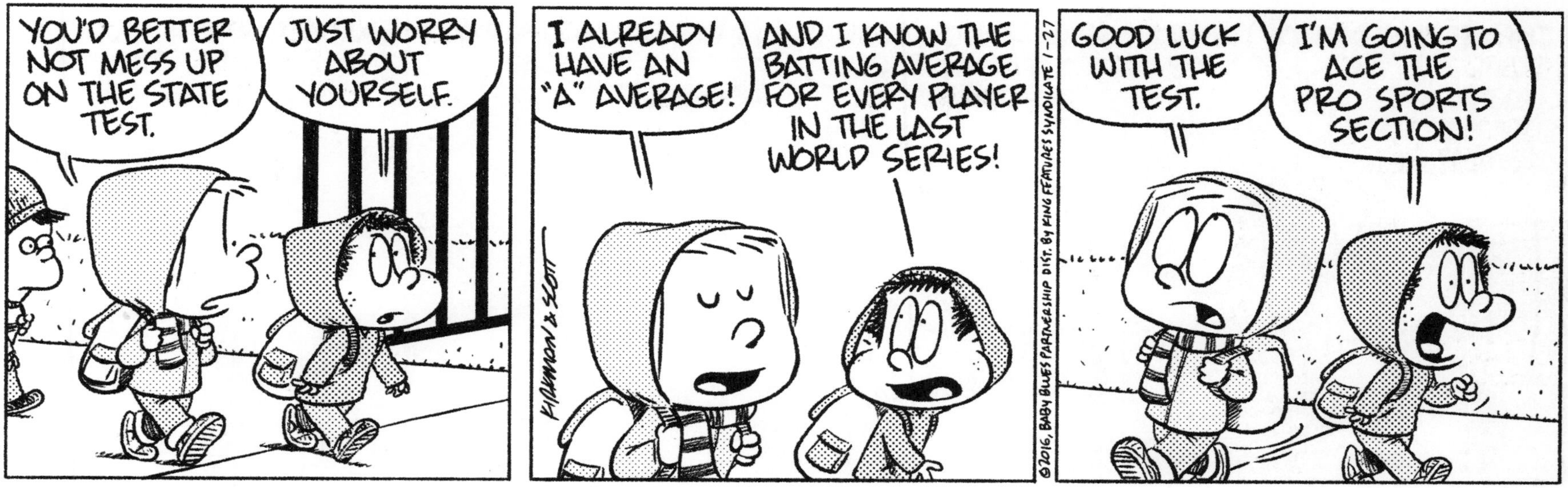
YOU'D BETTER NOT MESS UP ON THE STATE TEST.
JUST WORRY ABOUT YOURSELF.
I ALREADY HAVE AN "A" AVERAGE!
AND I KNOW THE BATTING AVERAGE FOR EVERY PLAYER IN THE LAST WORLD SERIES!
KIRKMAN & SCOTT
©2016, BABY BLUES PARTNERSHIP DIST. BY KING FEATURES SYNDICATE 1-27
GOOD LUCK WITH THE TEST.
I'M GOING TO ACE THE PRO SPORTS SECTION!

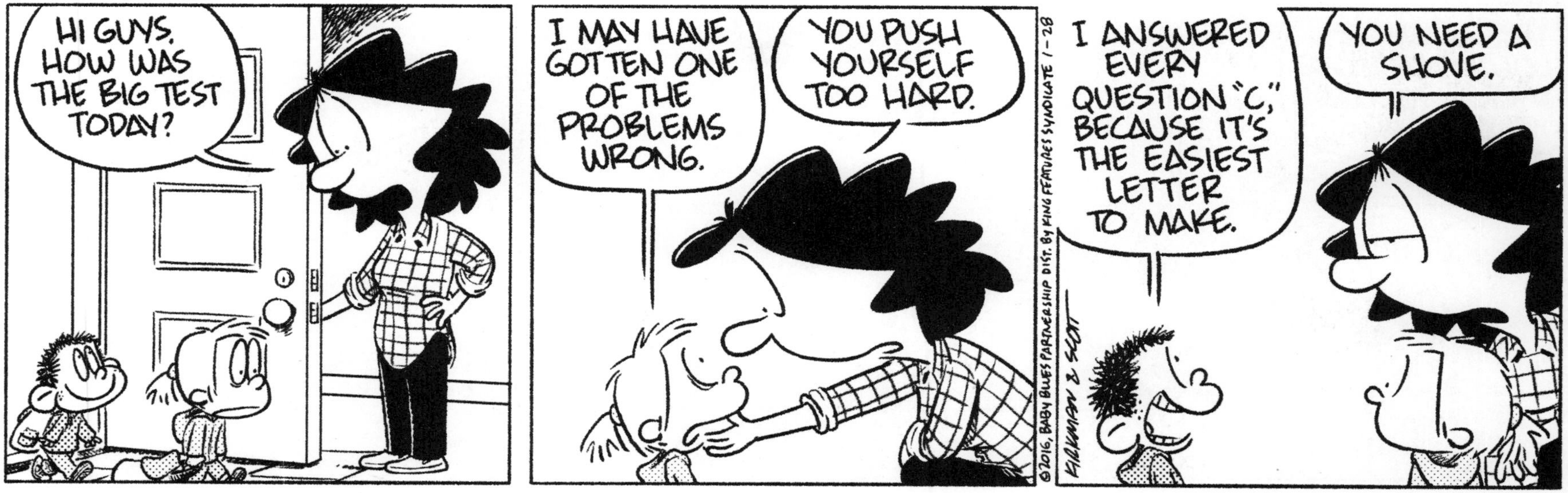
HI GUYS. HOW WAS THE BIG TEST TODAY?
I MAY HAVE GOTTEN ONE OF THE PROBLEMS WRONG.
YOU PUSH YOURSELF TOO HARD.
©2016, BABY BLUES PARTNERSHIP DIST. BY KING FEATURES SYNDICATE 1-28
I ANSWERED EVERY QUESTION "C," BECAUSE IT'S THE EASIEST LETTER TO MAKE.
KIRKMAN & SCOTT
YOU NEED A SHOVE.

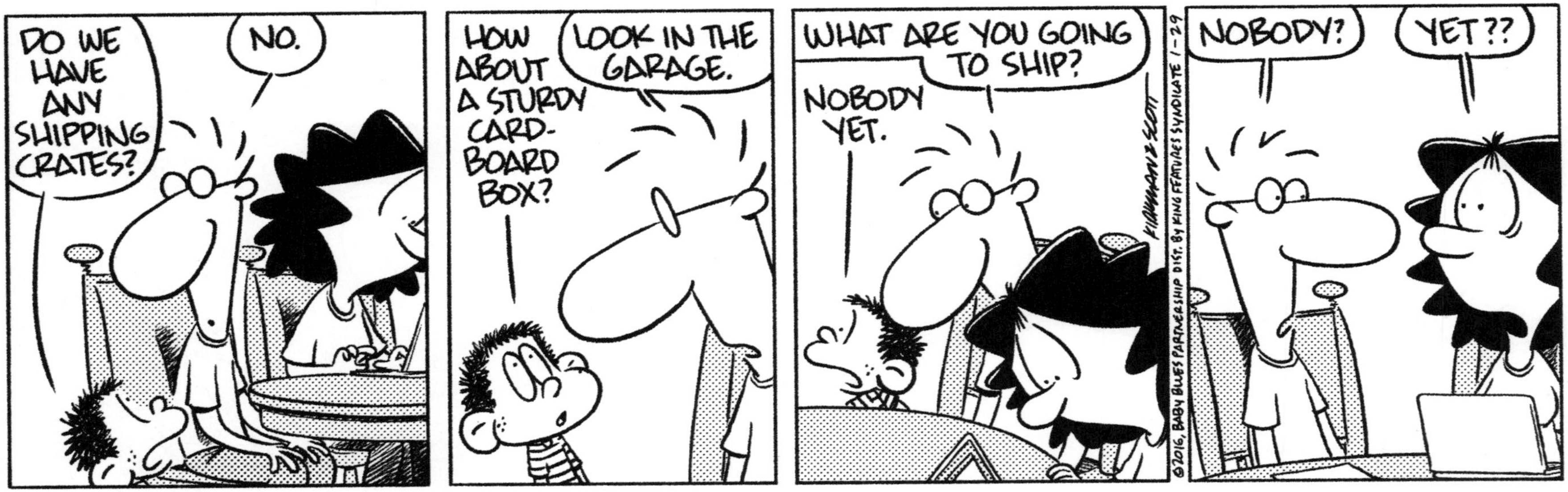
DO WE HAVE ANY SHIPPING CRATES?
NO.
HOW ABOUT A STURDY CARD-BOARD BOX?
LOOK IN THE GARAGE.
WHAT ARE YOU GOING TO SHIP?
NOBODY YET.
NOBODY?
YET??
©2016, BABY BLUES PARTNERSHIP DIST. BY KING FEATURES SYNDICATE 1-29
KIRKMAN & SCOTT

Rick: Two red flags in a two-word sentence.

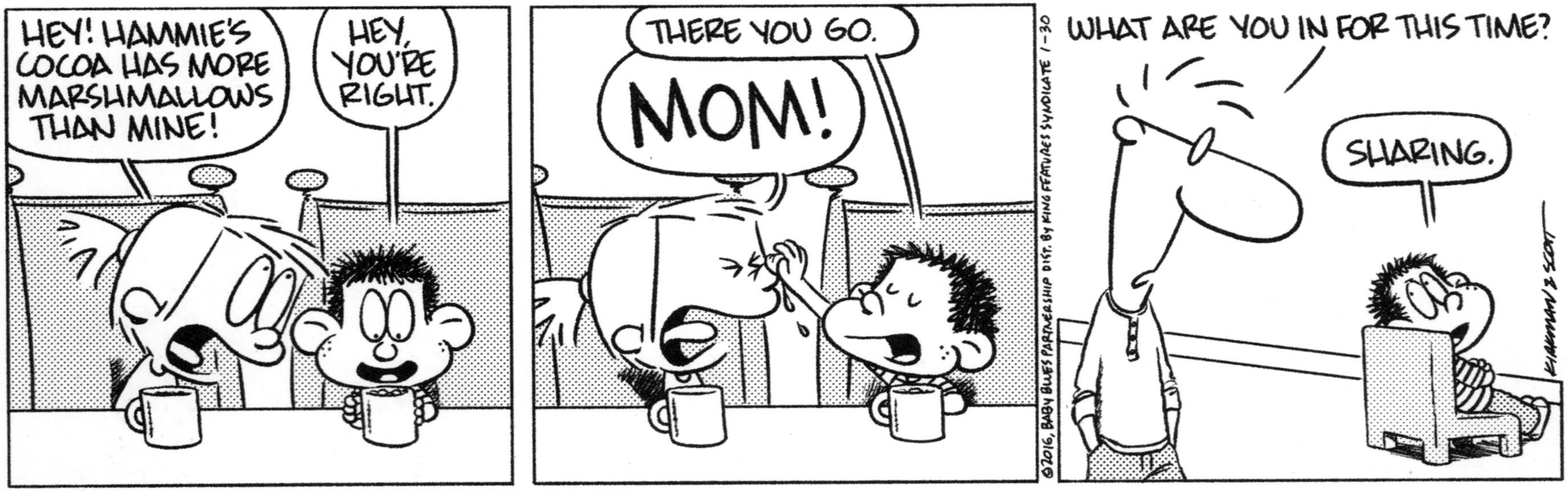
HEY! HAMMIE'S COCOA HAS MORE MARSHMALLOWS THAN MINE!
HEY, YOU'RE RIGHT.
THERE YOU GO.
MOM!
WHAT ARE YOU IN FOR THIS TIME?
SHARING.
©2016, BABY BLUES PARTNERSHIP DIST. BY KING FEATURES SYNDICATE 1-30
KIRKMAN & SCOTT

Jerry: Technically true.

BABY BLUES®
BY RICK KIRKMAN / JERRY SCOTT

YOU'RE WORKING OUT PRETTY HARD THERE, WANDA.
I KNOW.
I HAVE TO
IF I
WANT TO
BE READY FOR
VALENTINE'S DAY.
KIRKMAN & SCOTT
©2016, BABY BLUES PARTNERSHIP DIST. BY KING FEATURES SYNDICATE 1-31
OH.
OHHH!

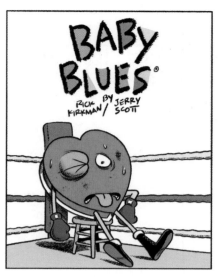

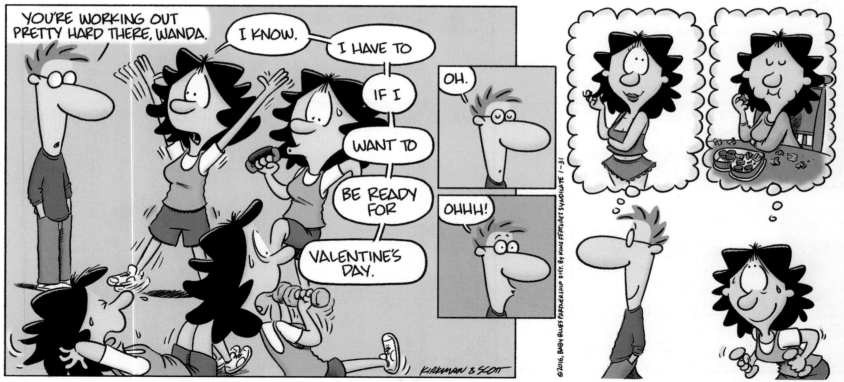

Rick: The only way they're on the same page is that they are both here on page 23.

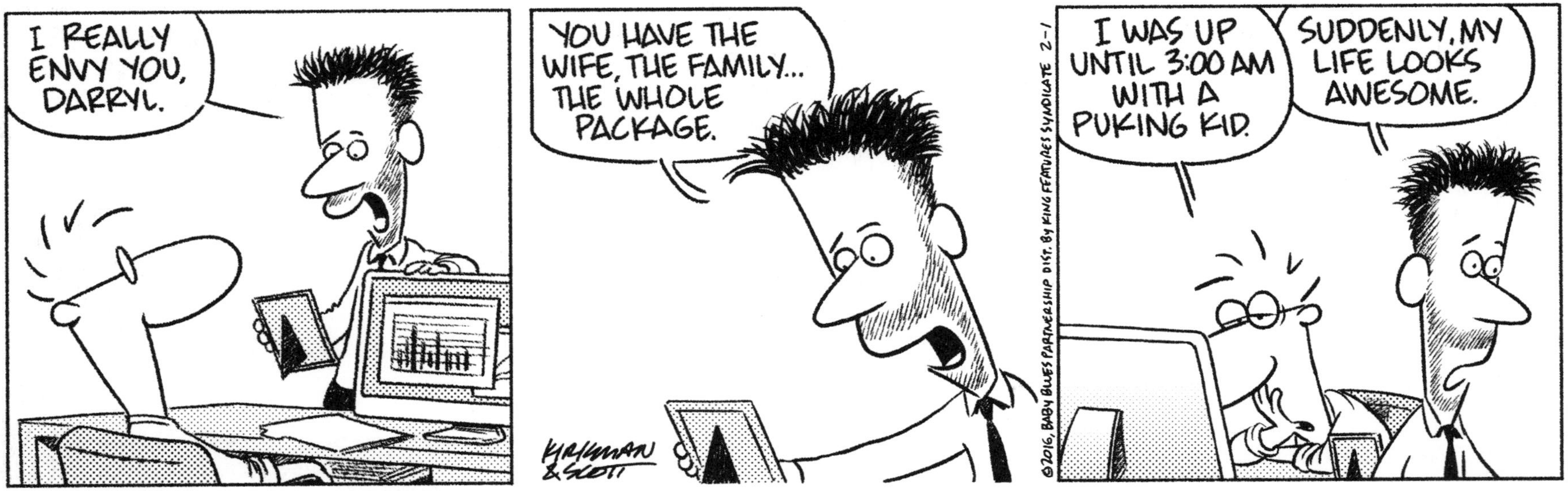
I REALLY ENVY YOU, DARRYL.
YOU HAVE THE WIFE, THE FAMILY... THE WHOLE PACKAGE.
KIRKMAN & SCOTT
©2016, BABY BLUES PARTNERSHIP DIST. BY KING FEATURES SYNDICATE 2-1
I WAS UP UNTIL 3:00 AM WITH A PUKING KID.
SUDDENLY, MY LIFE LOOKS AWESOME.

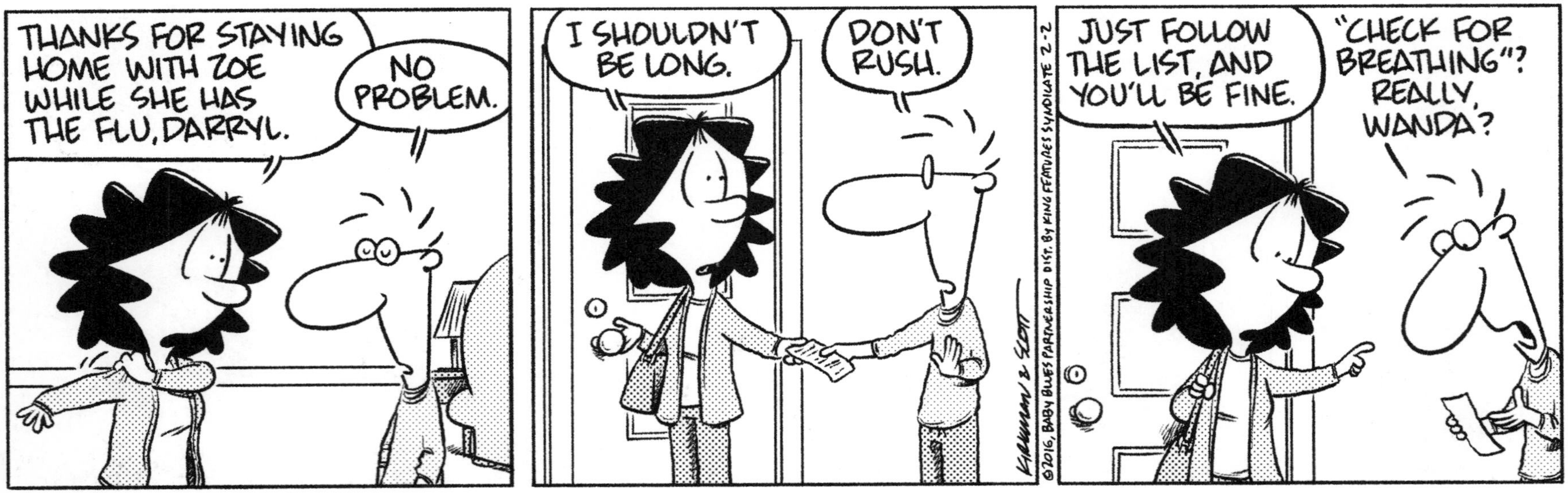
THANKS FOR STAYING HOME WITH ZOE WHILE SHE HAS THE FLU, DARRYL.
NO PROBLEM.
I SHOULDN'T BE LONG.
DON'T RUSH.
KIRKMAN & SCOTT
©2016, BABY BLUES PARTNERSHIP DIST. BY KING FEATURES SYNDICATE 2-2
JUST FOLLOW THE LIST, AND YOU'LL BE FINE.
"CHECK FOR BREATHING"? REALLY, WANDA?

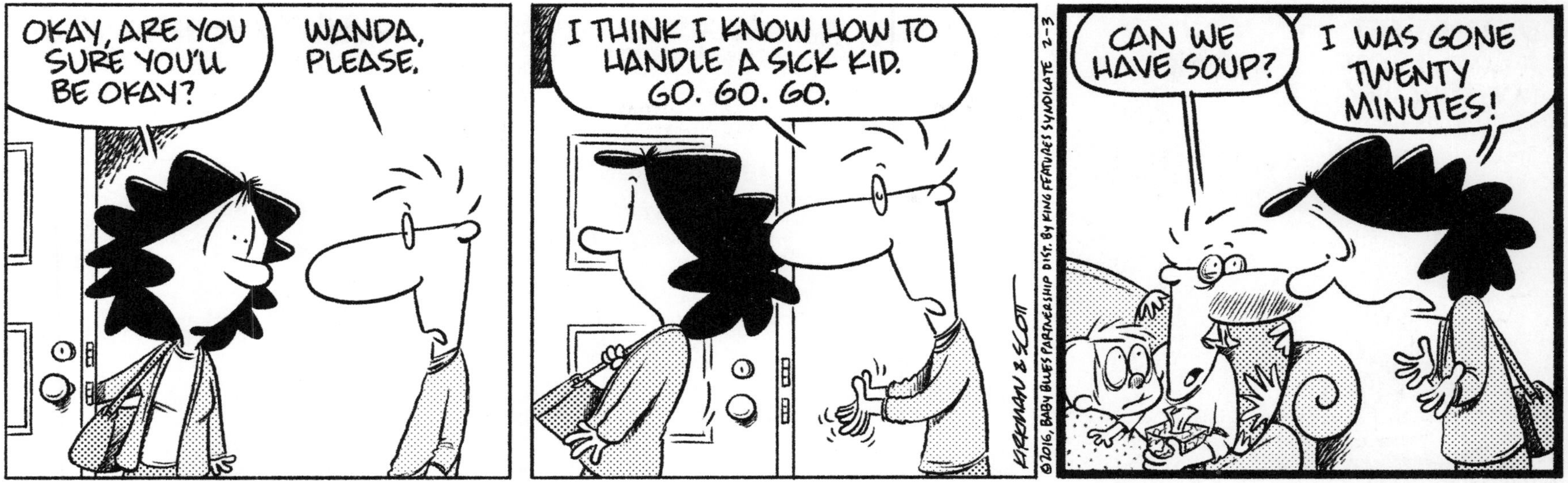
OKAY, ARE YOU SURE YOU'LL BE OKAY?
WANDA, PLEASE.
I THINK I KNOW HOW TO HANDLE A SICK KID. GO. GO. GO.
KIRKMAN & SCOTT
©2016, BABY BLUES PARTNERSHIP DIST. BY KING FEATURES SYNDICATE 2-3
CAN WE HAVE SOUP?
I WAS GONE TWENTY MINUTES!

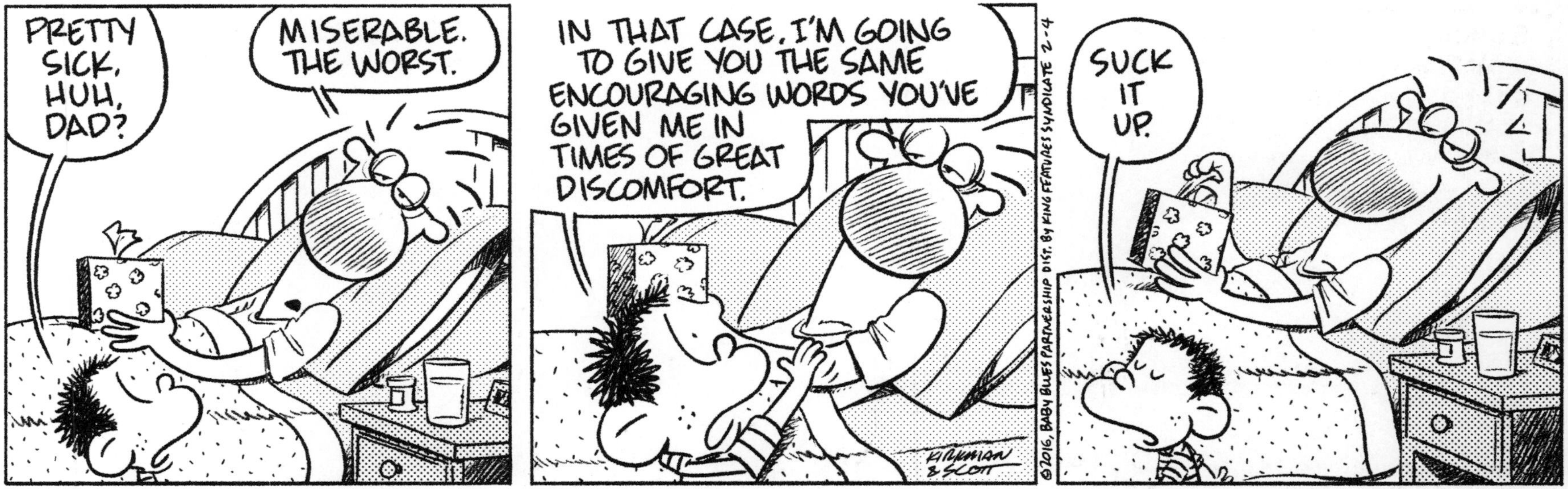
PRETTY SICK, HUH, DAD?
MISERABLE. THE WORST.
IN THAT CASE, I'M GOING TO GIVE YOU THE SAME ENCOURAGING WORDS YOU'VE GIVEN ME IN TIMES OF GREAT DISCOMFORT.
KIRKMAN & SCOTT
©2016, BABY BLUES PARTNERSHIP DIST. BY KING FEATURES SYNDICATE 2-4
SUCK IT UP.

Jerry: Don't you love it when the stuff you say to your kids boomerangs back at you? Me either.

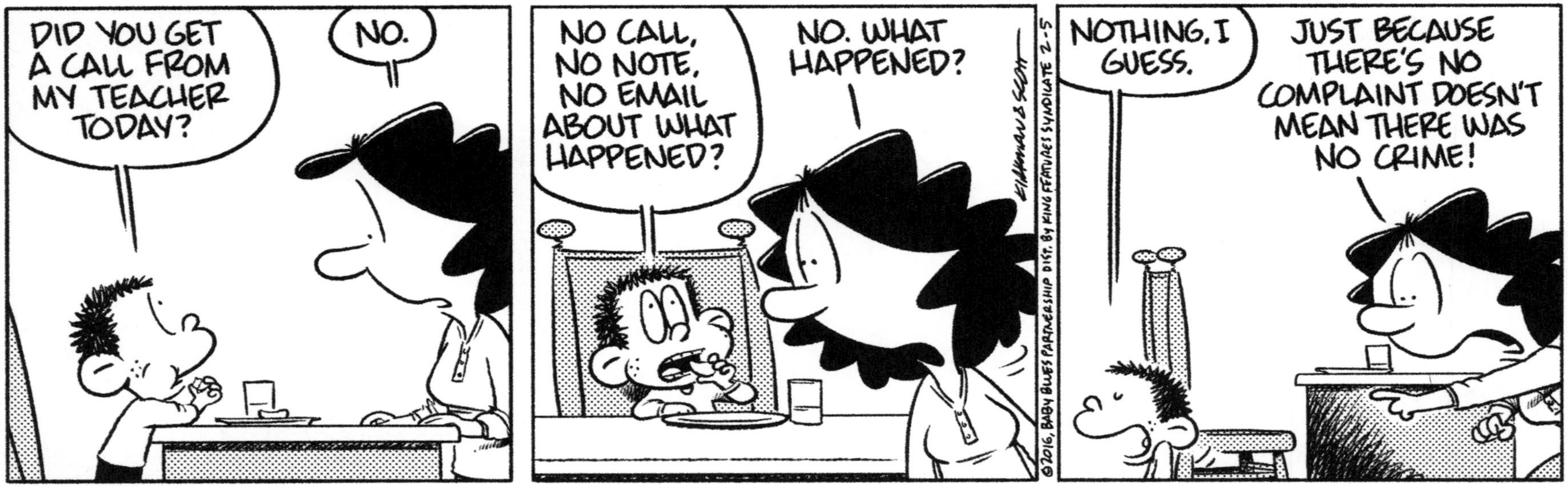
DID YOU GET A CALL FROM MY TEACHER TODAY?
NO.
NO CALL, NO NOTE, NO EMAIL ABOUT WHAT HAPPENED?
NO. WHAT HAPPENED?
©2016, BABY BLUES PARTNERSHIP DIST. BY KING FEATURES SYNDICATE 2-5
NOTHING, I GUESS.
JUST BECAUSE THERE'S NO COMPLAINT DOESN'T MEAN THERE WAS NO CRIME!

Jerry: No body, no crime.

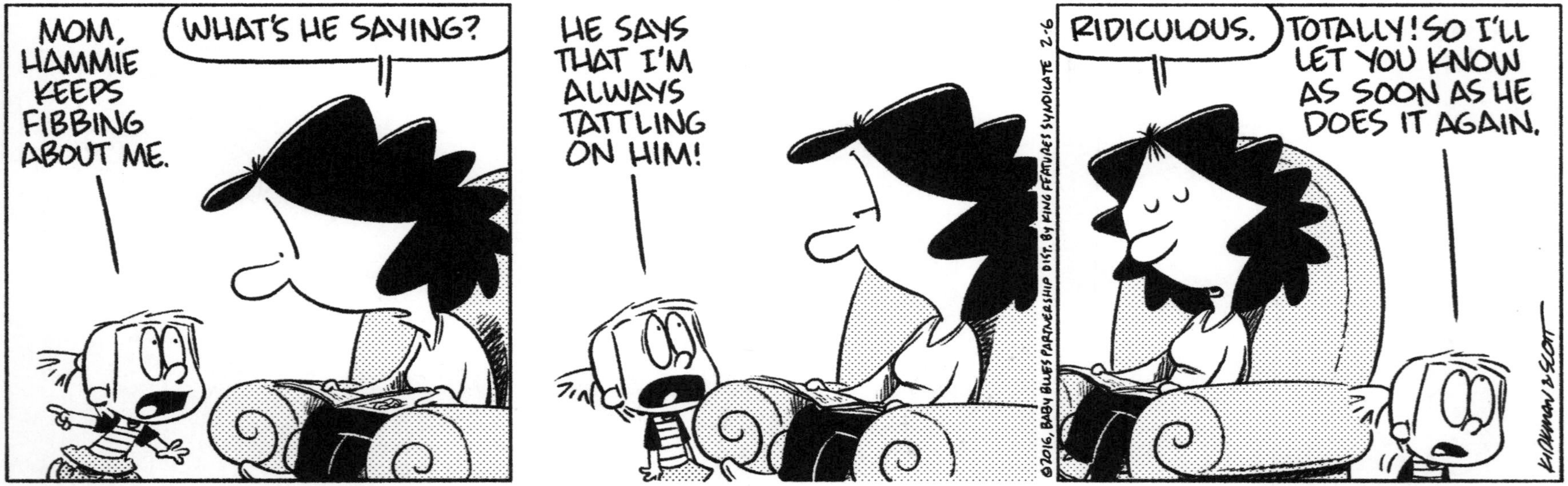
MOM, HAMMIE KEEPS FIBBING ABOUT ME.
WHAT'S HE SAYING?
HE SAYS THAT I'M ALWAYS TATTLING ON HIM!
©2016, BABY BLUES PARTNERSHIP DIST. BY KING FEATURES SYNDICATE 2-6
RIDICULOUS.
TOTALLY! SO I'LL LET YOU KNOW AS SOON AS HE DOES IT AGAIN.

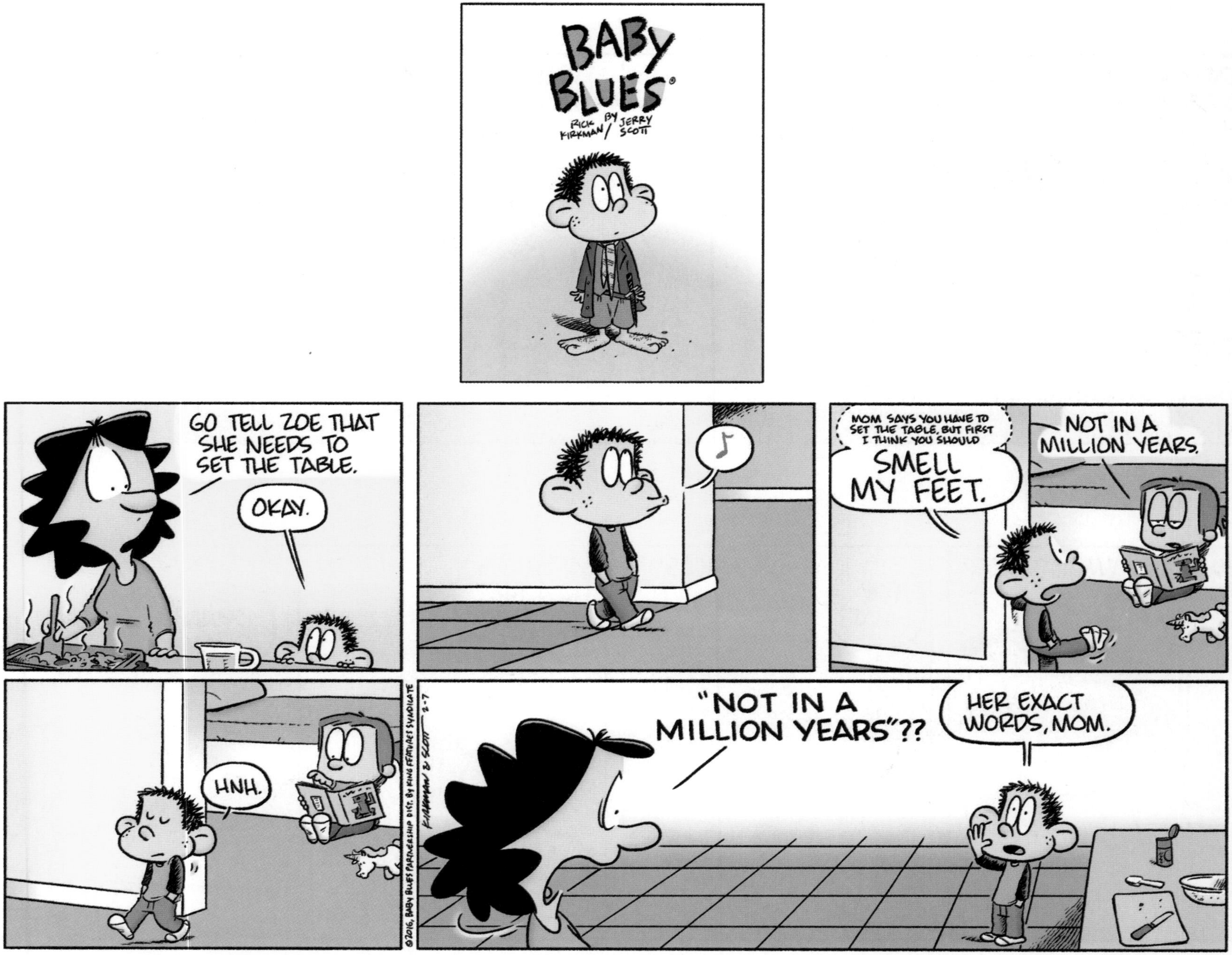
BABY BLUES®
BY RICK KIRKMAN / JERRY SCOTT
GO TELL ZOE THAT SHE NEEDS TO SET THE TABLE.
OKAY.
♪
MOM SAYS YOU HAVE TO SET THE TABLE, BUT FIRST I THINK YOU SHOULD
SMELL MY FEET.
NOT IN A MILLION YEARS.
HNH.
©2016, BABY BLUES PARTNERSHIP DIST. BY KING FEATURES SYNDICATE
KIRKMAN & SCOTT 2-7
"NOT IN A MILLION YEARS"??
HER EXACT WORDS, MOM.

Rick: Why is it kids always want their siblings to smell their feet? Note the title panel debut of Hammie Baggins.

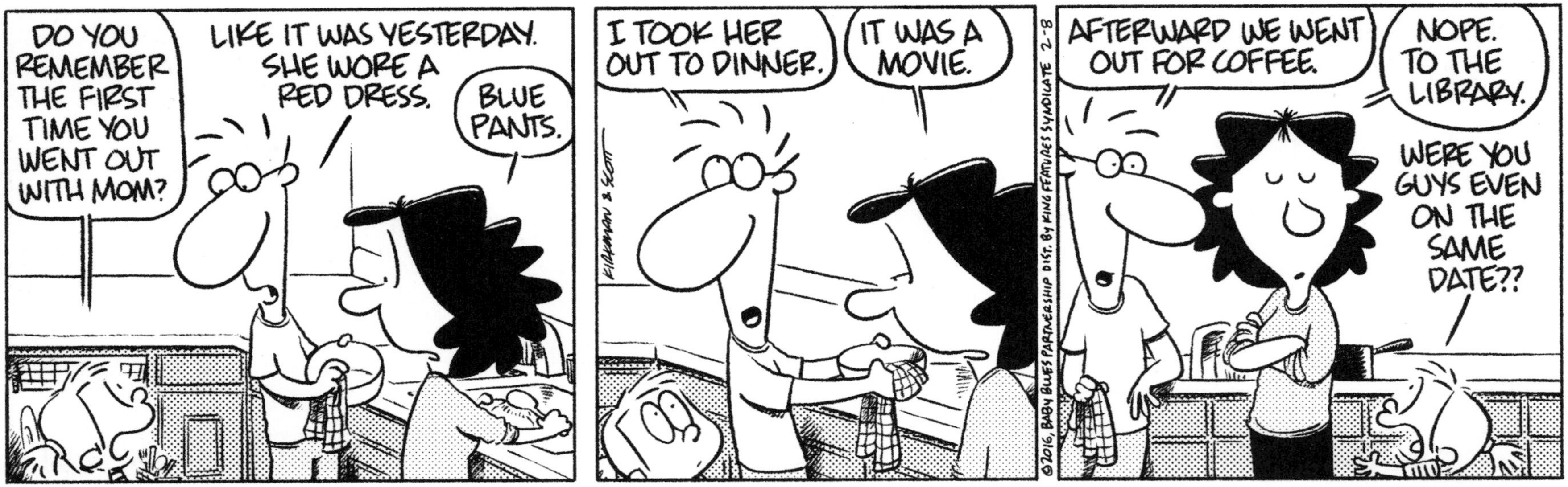
DO YOU REMEMBER THE FIRST TIME YOU WENT OUT WITH MOM?
LIKE IT WAS YESTERDAY. SHE WORE A RED DRESS.
BLUE PANTS.
KIRKMAN & SCOTT
I TOOK HER OUT TO DINNER.
IT WAS A MOVIE.
©2016, BABY BLUES PARTNERSHIP DIST. BY KING FEATURES SYNDICATE 2-8
AFTERWARD WE WENT OUT FOR COFFEE.
NOPE. TO THE LIBRARY.
WERE YOU GUYS EVEN ON THE SAME DATE??

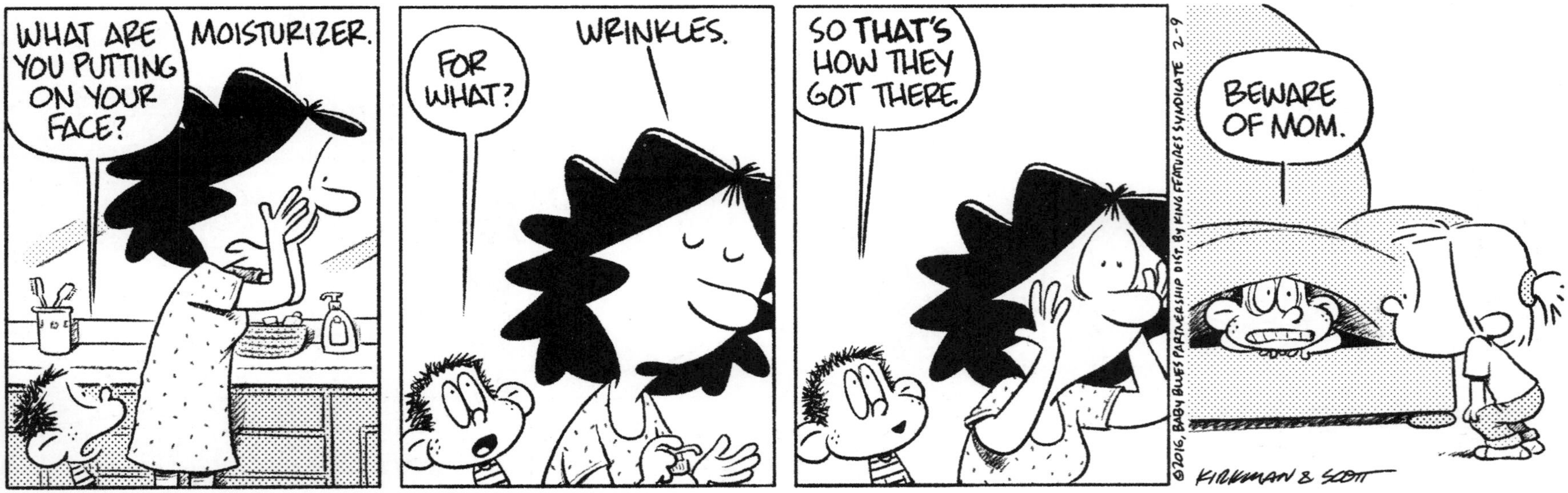
WHAT ARE YOU PUTTING ON YOUR FACE?
MOISTURIZER.
FOR WHAT?
WRINKLES.
SO THAT'S HOW THEY GOT THERE.
©2016, BABY BLUES PARTNERSHIP DIST. BY KING FEATURES SYNDICATE 2-9
BEWARE OF MOM.
KIRKMAN & SCOTT

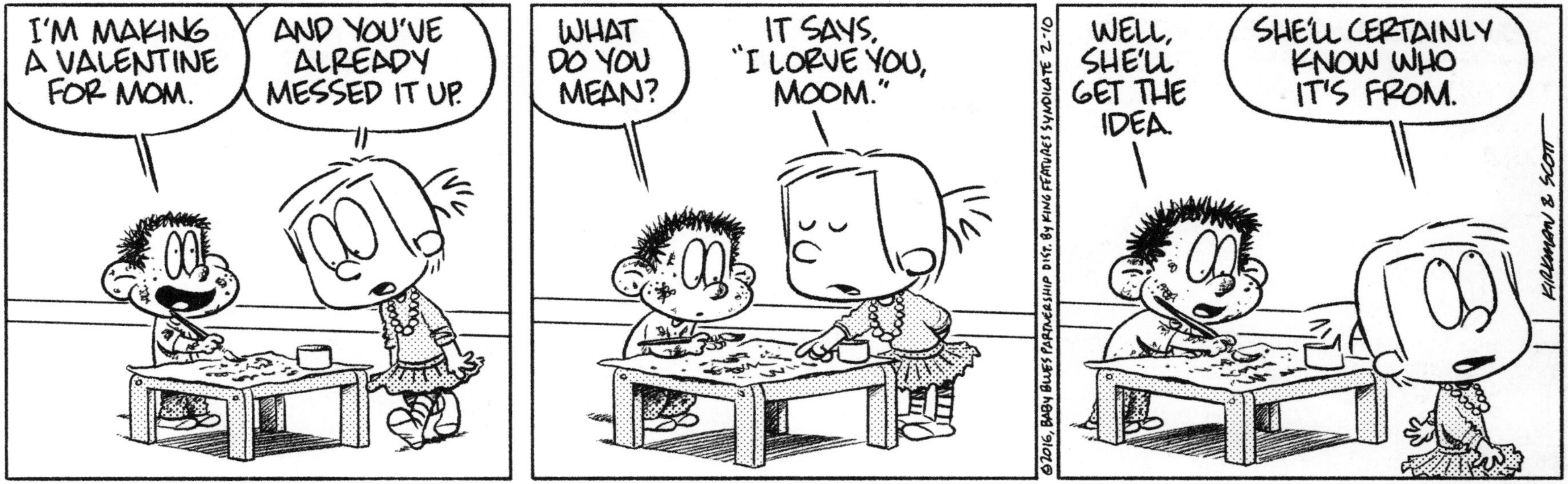
I'M MAKING A VALENTINE FOR MOM.
AND YOU'VE ALREADY MESSED IT UP.
WHAT DO YOU MEAN?
IT SAYS, "I LORVE YOU, MOOM."
WELL, SHE'LL GET THE IDEA.
SHE'LL CERTAINLY KNOW WHO IT'S FROM.
©2016, BABY BLUES PARTNERSHIP DIST. BY KING FEATURES SYNDICATE 2-10
KIRKMAN & SCOTT

Jerry: One of the cool things about Wanda is that she doesn't always sweat the details.

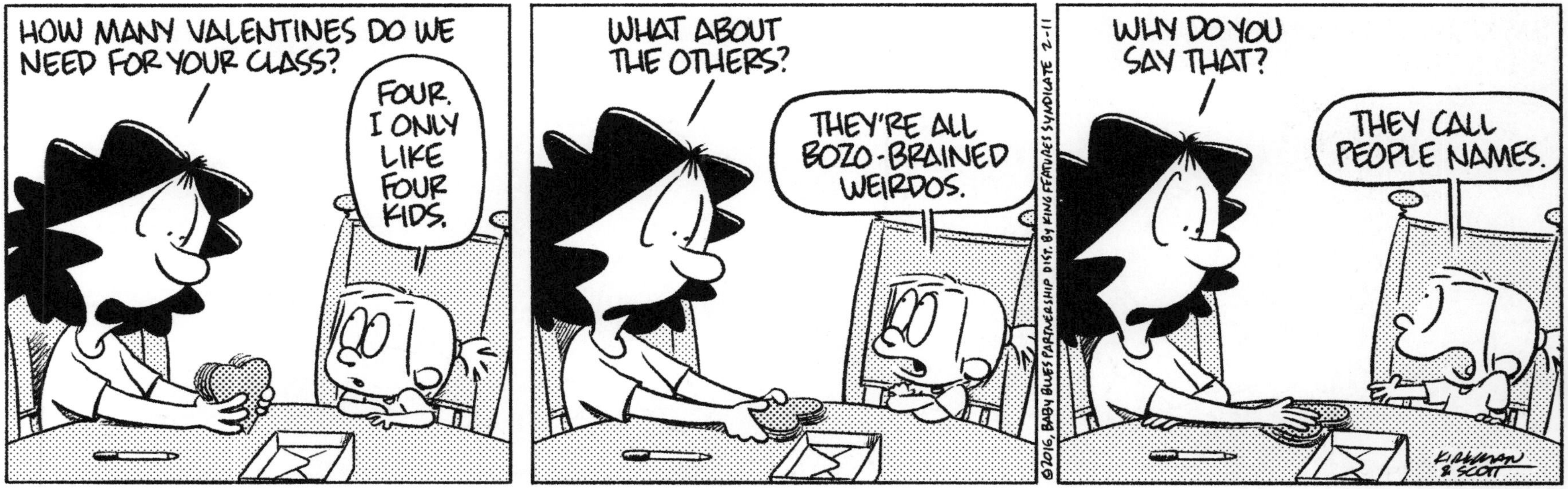
HOW MANY VALENTINES DO WE NEED FOR YOUR CLASS?
FOUR. I ONLY LIKE FOUR KIDS.
WHAT ABOUT THE OTHERS?
THEY'RE ALL BOZO-BRAINED WEIRDOS.
WHY DO YOU SAY THAT?
THEY CALL PEOPLE NAMES.
©2016, BABY BLUES PARTNERSHIP DIST. BY KING FEATURES SYNDICATE 2-11
KIRKMAN & SCOTT

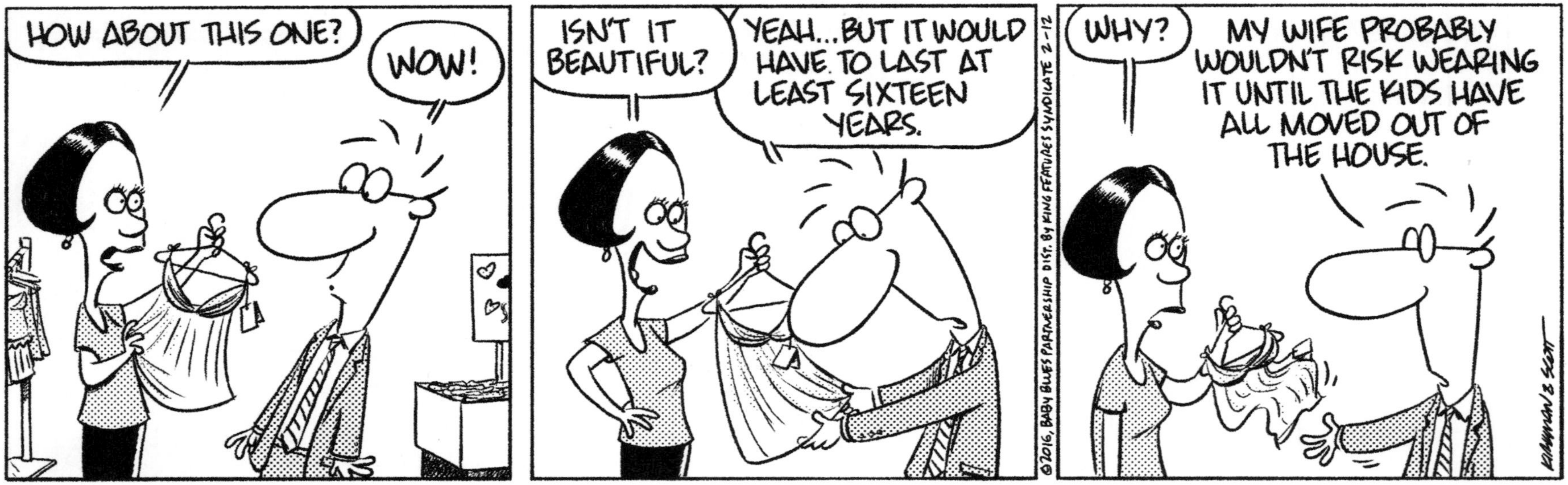
HOW ABOUT THIS ONE?
WOW!
ISN'T IT BEAUTIFUL?
YEAH...BUT IT WOULD HAVE TO LAST AT LEAST SIXTEEN YEARS.
WHY?
MY WIFE PROBABLY WOULDN'T RISK WEARING IT UNTIL THE KIDS HAVE ALL MOVED OUT OF THE HOUSE.
©2016, BABY BLUES PARTNERSHIP DIST. BY KING FEATURES SYNDICATE 2-12
KIRKMAN & SCOTT

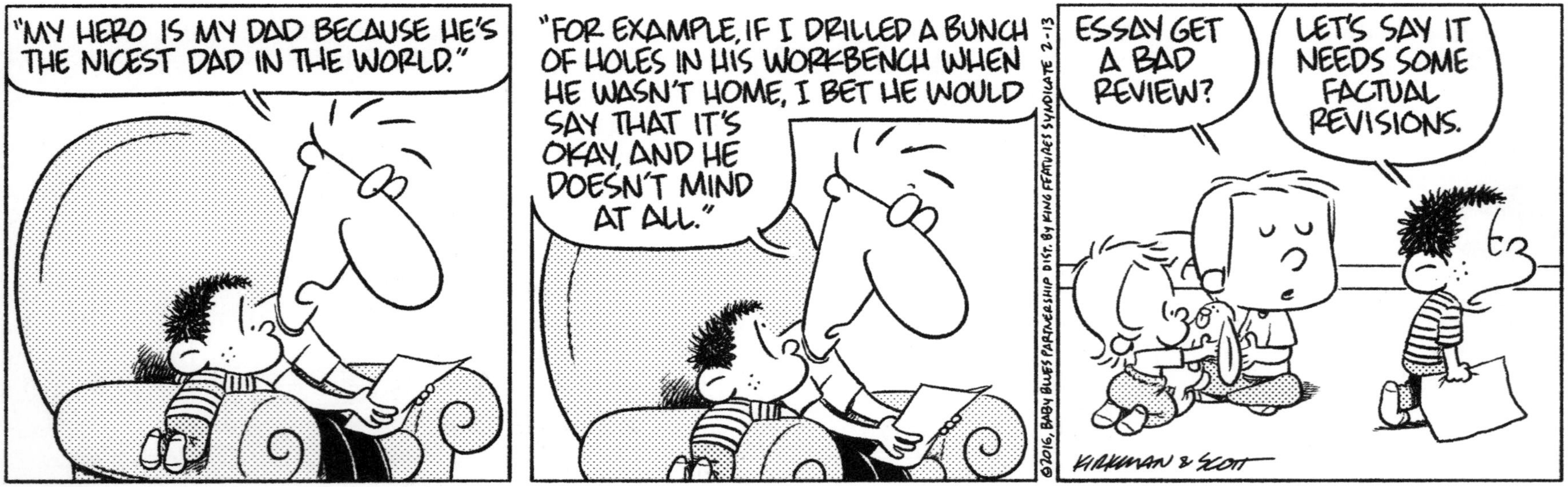
"MY HERO IS MY DAD BECAUSE HE'S THE NICEST DAD IN THE WORLD."
"FOR EXAMPLE, IF I DRILLED A BUNCH OF HOLES IN HIS WORKBENCH WHEN HE WASN'T HOME, I BET HE WOULD SAY THAT IT'S OKAY, AND HE DOESN'T MIND AT ALL."
ESSAY GET A BAD REVIEW?
LET'S SAY IT NEEDS SOME FACTUAL REVISIONS.
©2016, BABY BLUES PARTNERSHIP DIST. BY KING FEATURES SYNDICATE 2-13
KIRKMAN & SCOTT

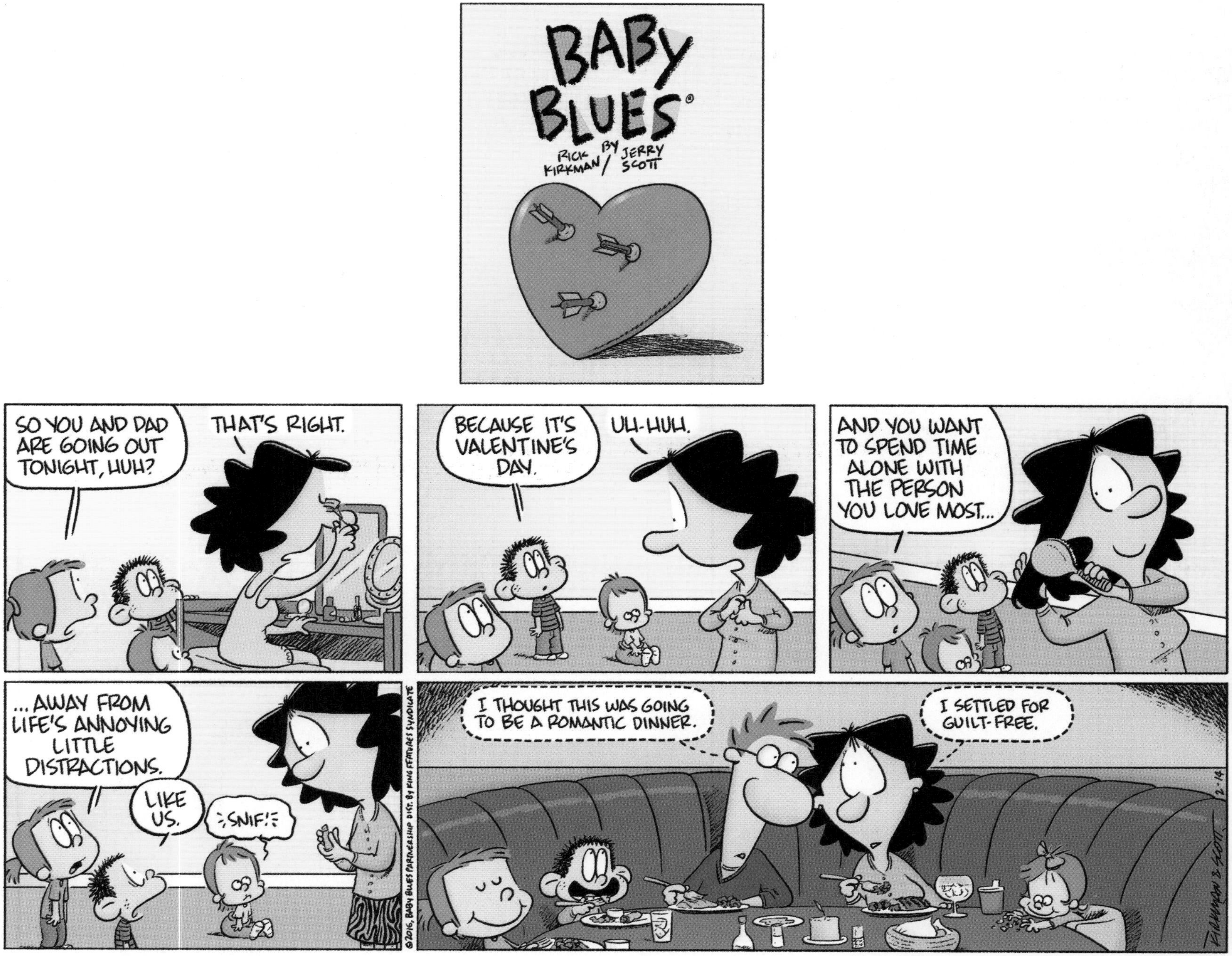
BABY BLUES®
BY RICK KIRKMAN / JERRY SCOTT
SO YOU AND DAD ARE GOING OUT TONIGHT, HUH?
THAT'S RIGHT.
BECAUSE IT'S VALENTINE'S DAY.
UH-HUH.
AND YOU WANT TO SPEND TIME ALONE WITH THE PERSON YOU LOVE MOST...
...AWAY FROM LIFE'S ANNOYING LITTLE DISTRACTIONS.
LIKE US.
SNIF!
©2016, BABY BLUES PARTNERSHIP DIST. BY KING FEATURES SYNDICATE
I THOUGHT THIS WAS GOING TO BE A ROMANTIC DINNER.
I SETTLED FOR GUILT-FREE.
2-14
KIRKMAN & SCOTT

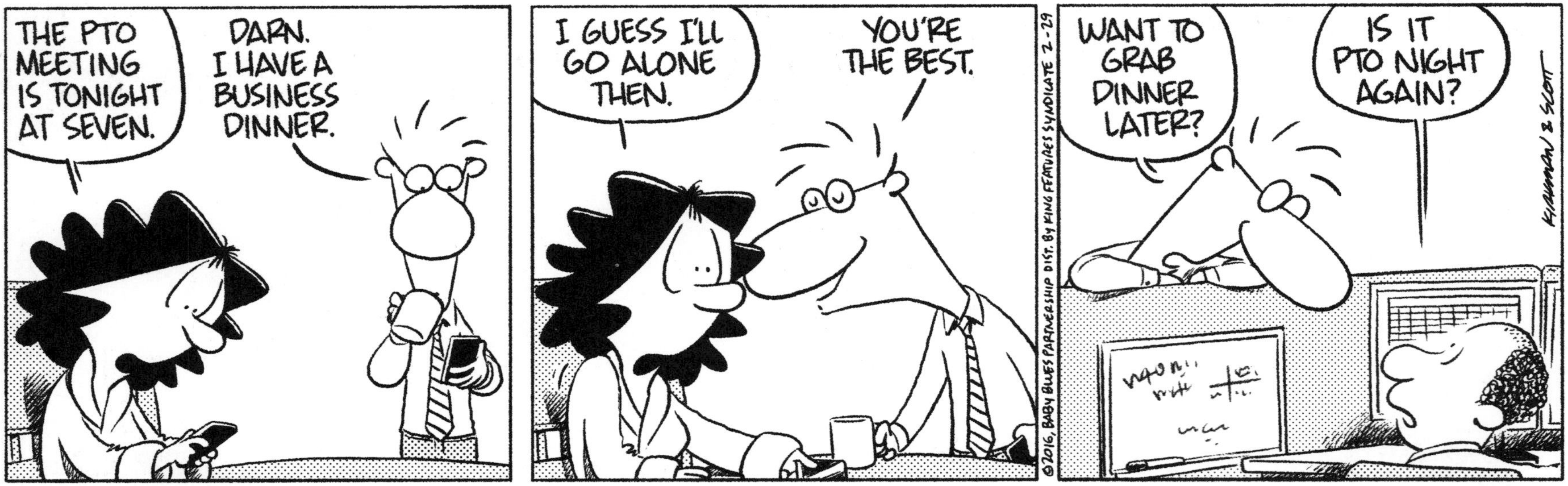
THE PTO MEETING IS TONIGHT AT SEVEN.
DARN. I HAVE A BUSINESS DINNER.
I GUESS I'LL GO ALONE THEN.
YOU'RE THE BEST.
©2016, BABY BLUES PARTNERSHIP DIST. BY KING FEATURES SYNDICATE 2-29
WANT TO GRAB DINNER LATER?
IS IT PTO NIGHT AGAIN?
KIRKMAN & SCOTT

Rick: All I have to say is "Shame on you, Darryl." And, "Why didn't I ever think of that?"

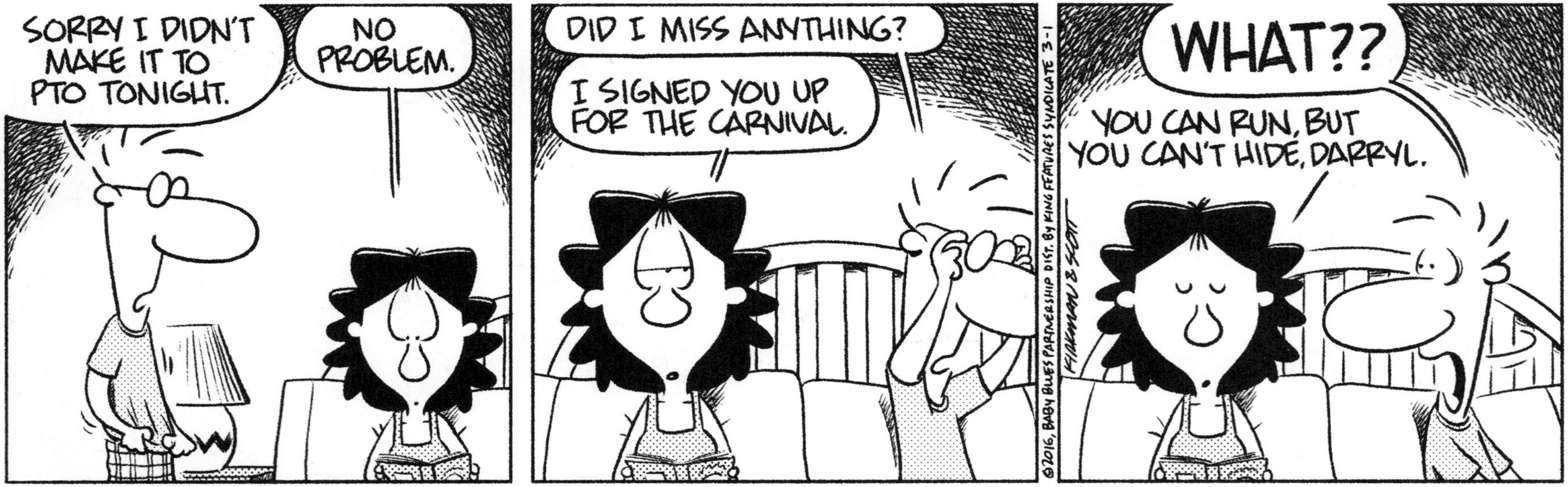
SORRY I DIDN'T MAKE IT TO PTO TONIGHT.
NO PROBLEM.
DID I MISS ANYTHING?
I SIGNED YOU UP FOR THE CARNIVAL.
©2016, BABY BLUES PARTNERSHIP DIST. BY KING FEATURES SYNDICATE 3-1
KIRKMAN & SCOTT
WHAT??
YOU CAN RUN, BUT YOU CAN'T HIDE, DARRYL.

Jerry: "Absentee volunteer" was my identity during my kids' elementary school years. I put away a lot of folding chairs.

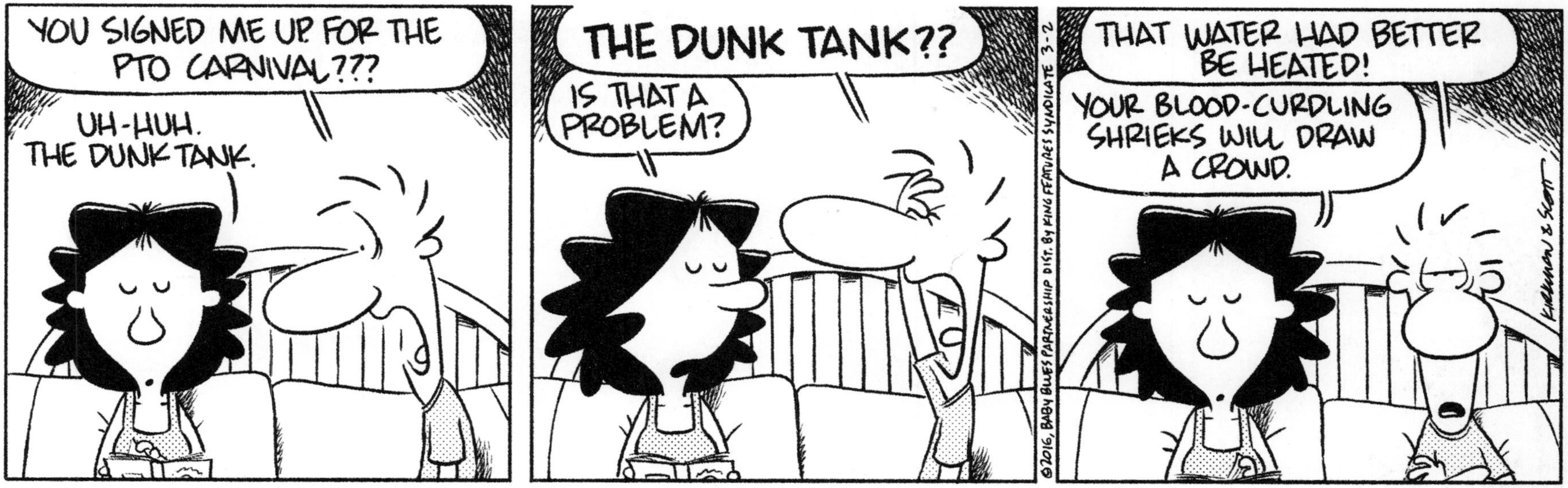
YOU SIGNED ME UP FOR THE PTO CARNIVAL???
UH-HUH. THE DUNK TANK.
THE DUNK TANK??
IS THAT A PROBLEM?
©2016, BABY BLUES PARTNERSHIP DIST. BY KING FEATURES SYNDICATE 3-2
THAT WATER HAD BETTER BE HEATED!
YOUR BLOOD-CURDLING SHRIEKS WILL DRAW A CROWD.
KIRKMAN & SCOTT

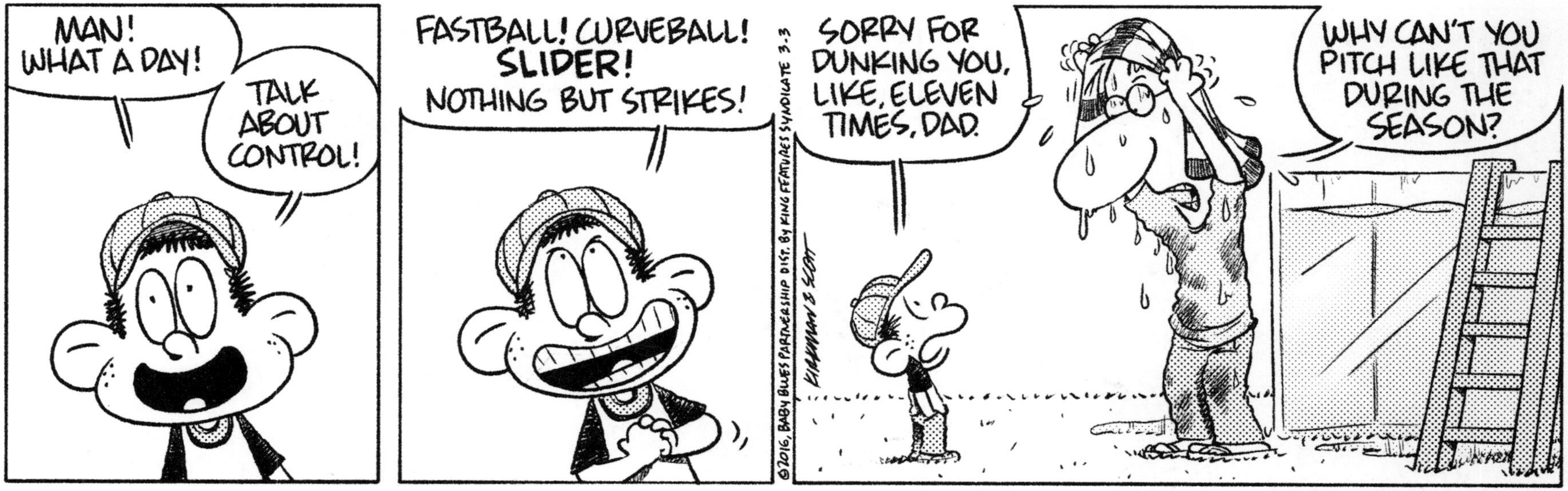
MAN! WHAT A DAY!
TALK ABOUT CONTROL!
FASTBALL! CURVEBALL! SLIDER! NOTHING BUT STRIKES!
©2016, BABY BLUES PARTNERSHIP DIST. BY KING FEATURES SYNDICATE 3-3
KIRKMAN & SCOTT
SORRY FOR DUNKING YOU, LIKE, ELEVEN TIMES, DAD.
WHY CAN'T YOU PITCH LIKE THAT DURING THE SEASON?

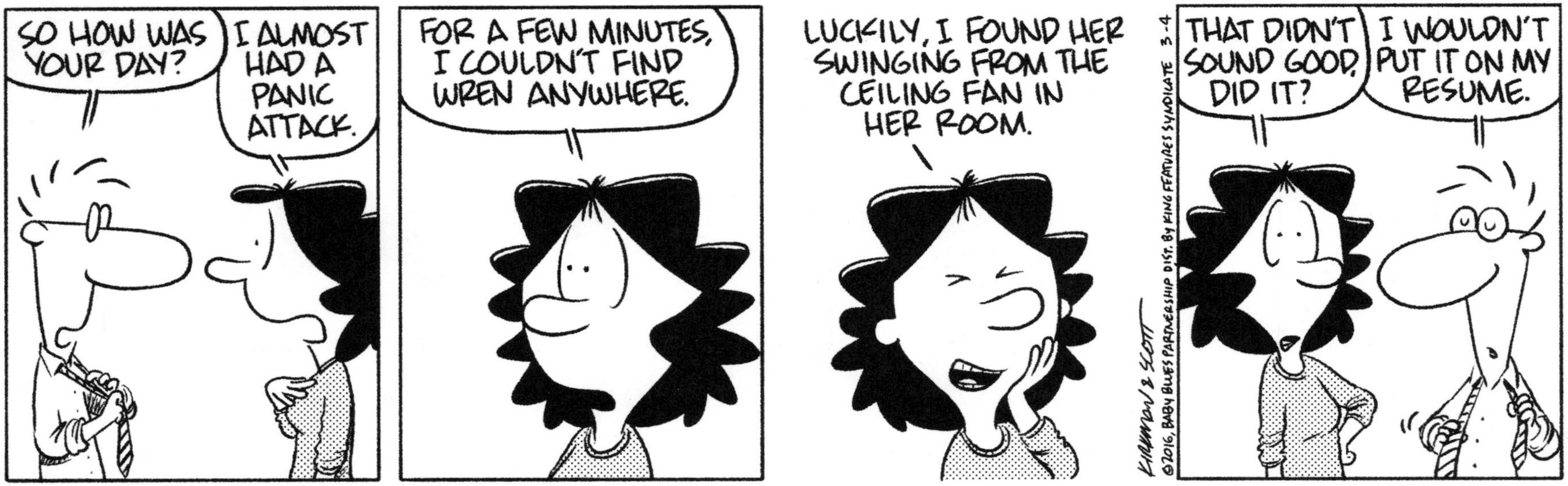
SO HOW WAS YOUR DAY?
I ALMOST HAD A PANIC ATTACK.
FOR A FEW MINUTES, I COULDN'T FIND WREN ANYWHERE.
LUCKILY, I FOUND HER SWINGING FROM THE CEILING FAN IN HER ROOM.
KIRKMAN & SCOTT
©2016, BABY BLUES PARTNERSHIP DIST. BY KING FEATURES SYNDICATE 3-4
THAT DIDN'T SOUND GOOD, DID IT?
I WOULDN'T PUT IT ON MY RESUME.

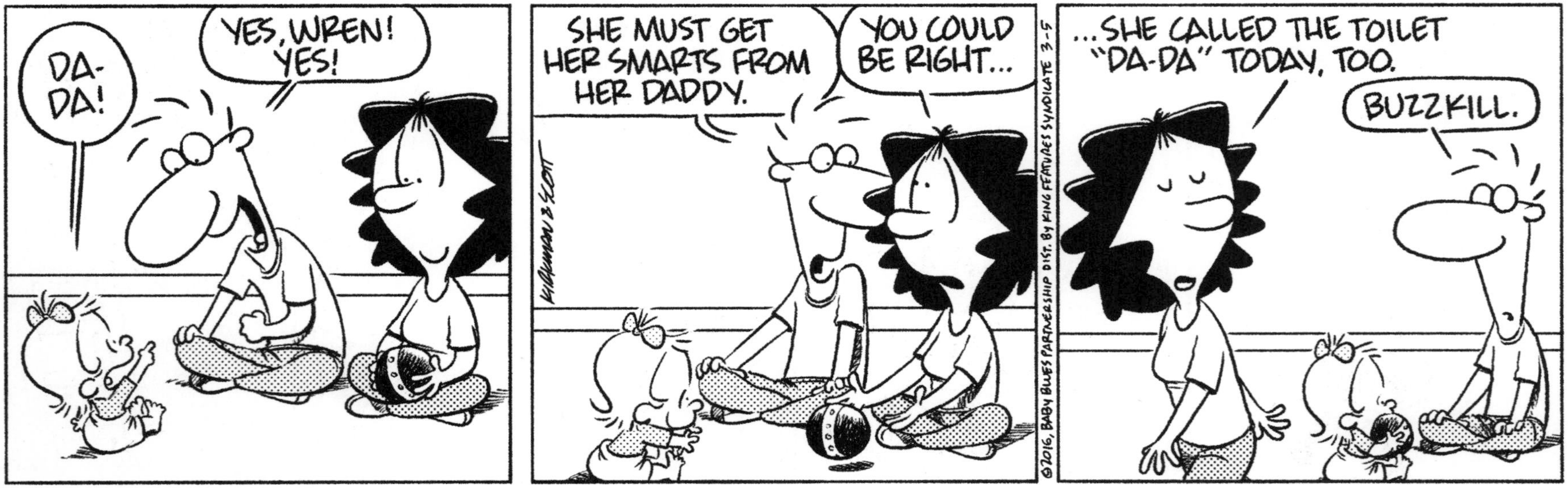
DA-DA!
YES, WREN! YES!
KIRKMAN & SCOTT
SHE MUST GET HER SMARTS FROM HER DADDY.
YOU COULD BE RIGHT...
©2016, BABY BLUES PARTNERSHIP DIST. BY KING FEATURES SYNDICATE 3-5
...SHE CALLED THE TOILET "DA-DA" TODAY, TOO.
BUZZKILL.

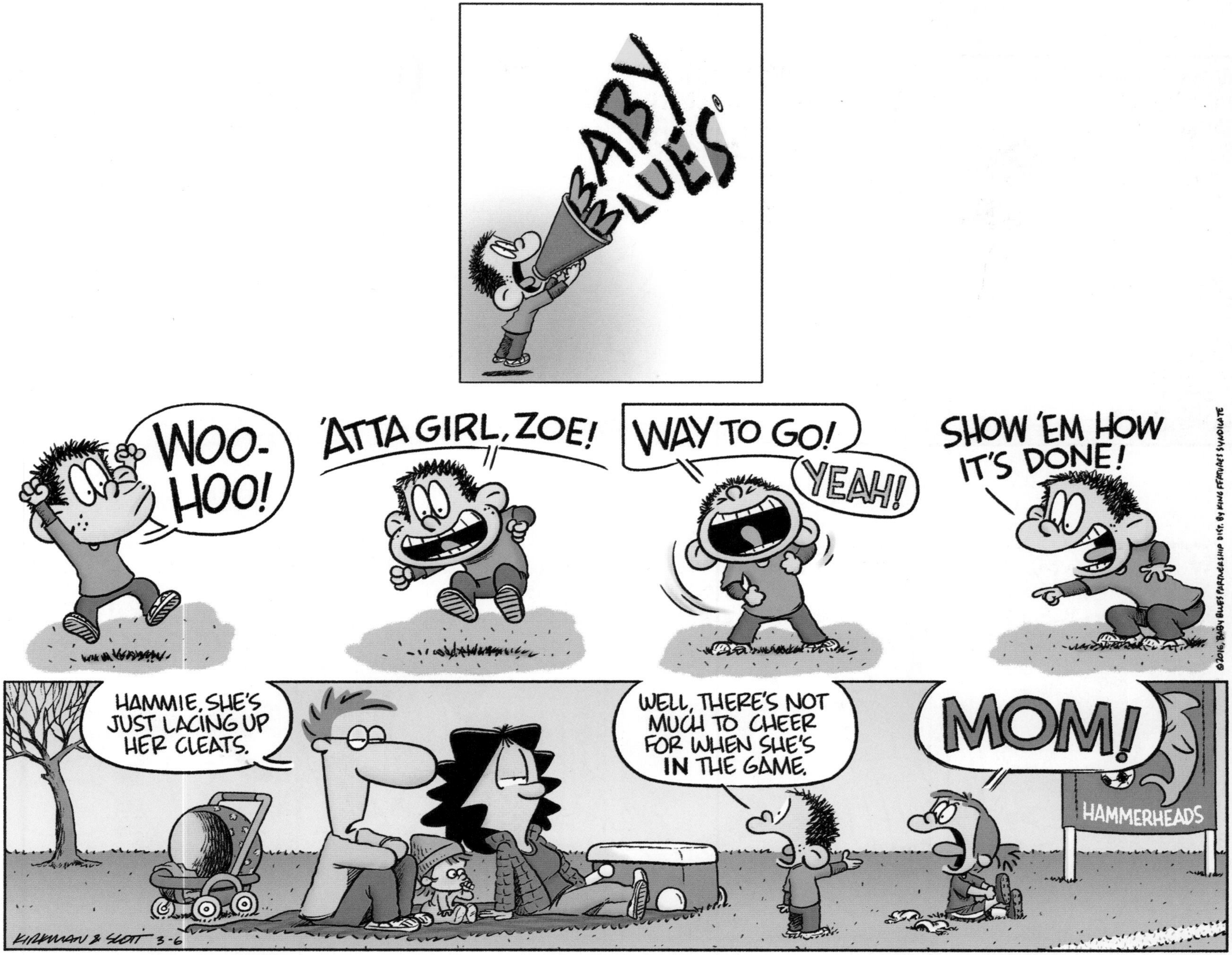
BABY BLUES®
WOO-HOO!
'ATTA GIRL, ZOE!
WAY TO GO!
YEAH!
SHOW 'EM HOW IT'S DONE!
HAMMIE, SHE'S JUST LACING UP HER CLEATS.
WELL, THERE'S NOT MUCH TO CHEER FOR WHEN SHE'S IN THE GAME.
MOM!
HAMMERHEADS
KIRKMAN & SCOTT 3-6

Jerry: That team banner in the last panel is the logo Rick designed for his daughter's soccer team. His kid played for The Hammerheads, and mine played for The Killer Ladybugs. The teams might not have been great, but the banners were awesome!

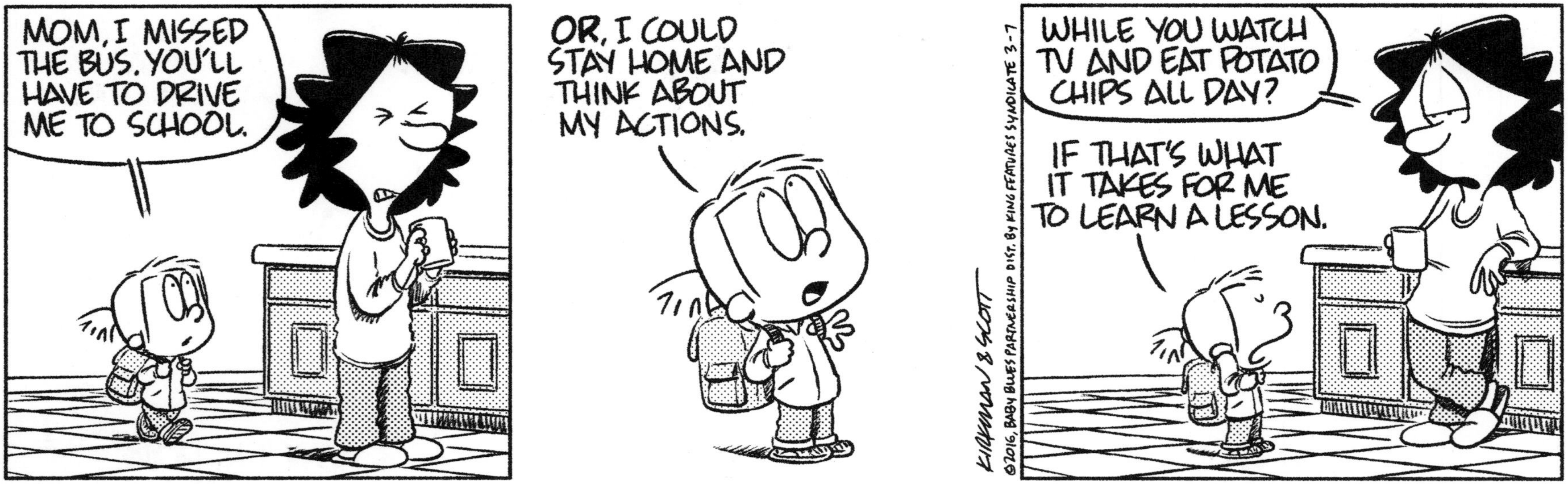
MOM, I MISSED THE BUS. YOU'LL HAVE TO DRIVE ME TO SCHOOL.
OR, I COULD STAY HOME AND THINK ABOUT MY ACTIONS.
WHILE YOU WATCH TV AND EAT POTATO CHIPS ALL DAY?
IF THAT'S WHAT IT TAKES FOR ME TO LEARN A LESSON.
KIRKMAN & SCOTT
©2016, BABY BLUES PARTNERSHIP DIST. BY KING FEATURES SYNDICATE 3-7

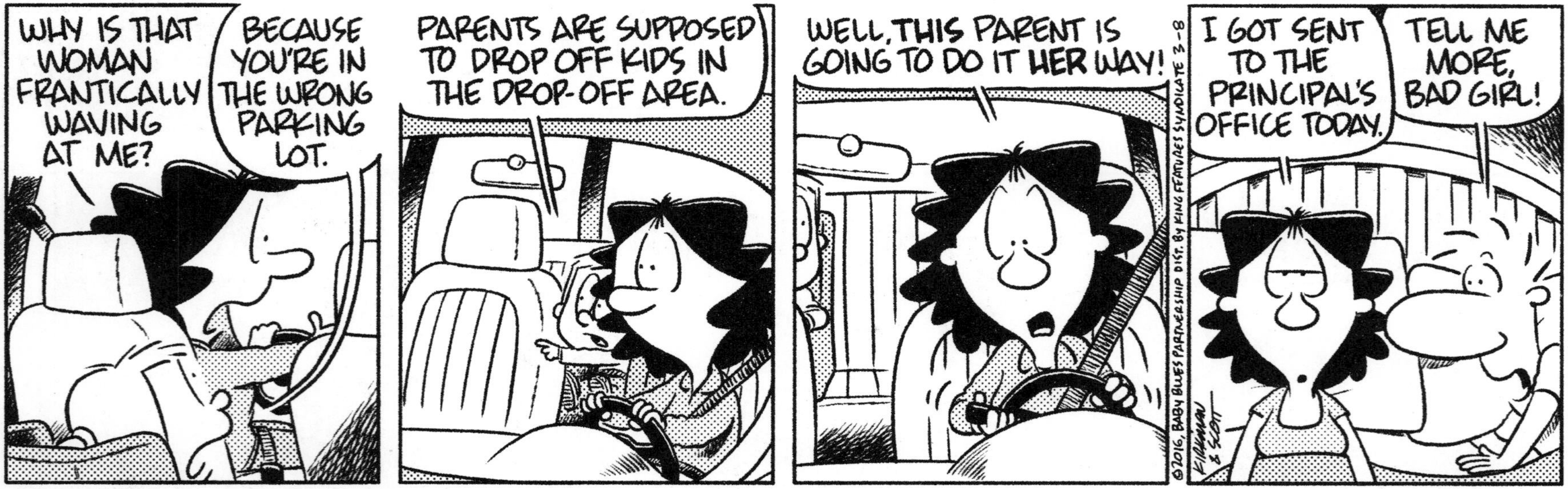
WHY IS THAT WOMAN FRANTICALLY WAVING AT ME?
BECAUSE YOU'RE IN THE WRONG PARKING LOT.
PARENTS ARE SUPPOSED TO DROP OFF KIDS IN THE DROP-OFF AREA.
WELL, THIS PARENT IS GOING TO DO IT HER WAY!
I GOT SENT TO THE PRINCIPAL'S OFFICE TODAY.
TELL ME MORE, BAD GIRL!
©2016, BABY BLUES PARTNERSHIP DIST. BY KING FEATURES SYNDICATE 3-8
KIRKMAN & SCOTT

Jerry: I'm not going to say this idea was based on something someone's wife did. I'm smarter than that.

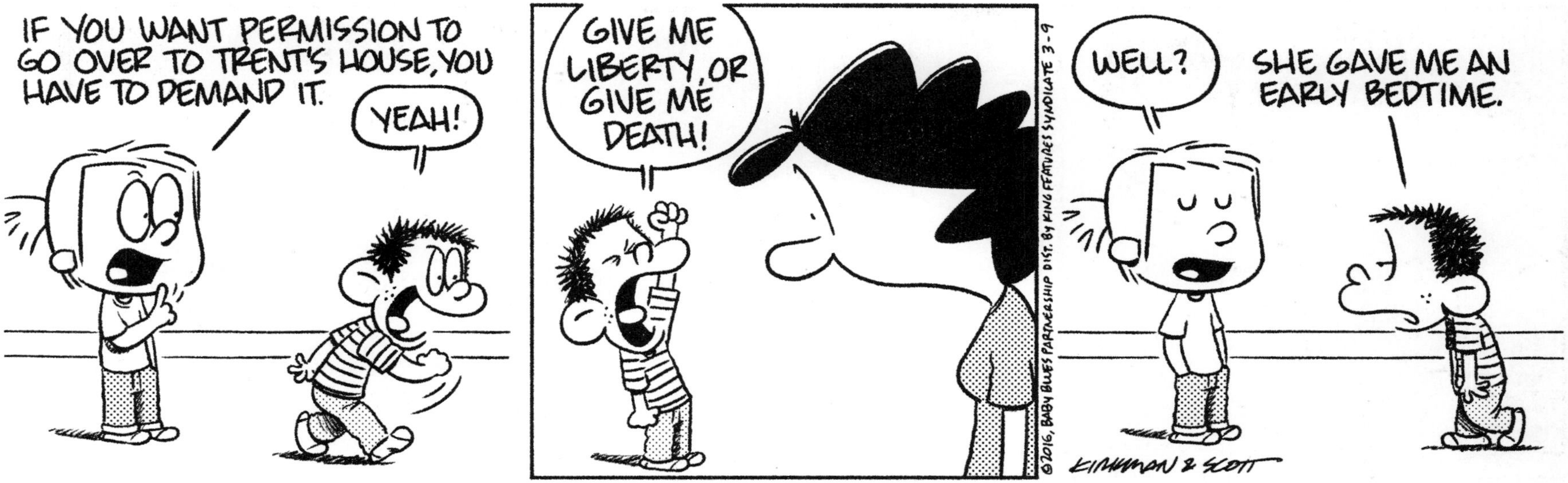
IF YOU WANT PERMISSION TO GO OVER TO TRENT'S HOUSE, YOU HAVE TO DEMAND IT.
YEAH!
GIVE ME LIBERTY, OR GIVE ME DEATH!
©2016, BABY BLUES PARTNERSHIP DIST. BY KING FEATURES SYNDICATE 3-9
WELL?
SHE GAVE ME AN EARLY BEDTIME.
KIRKMAN & SCOTT

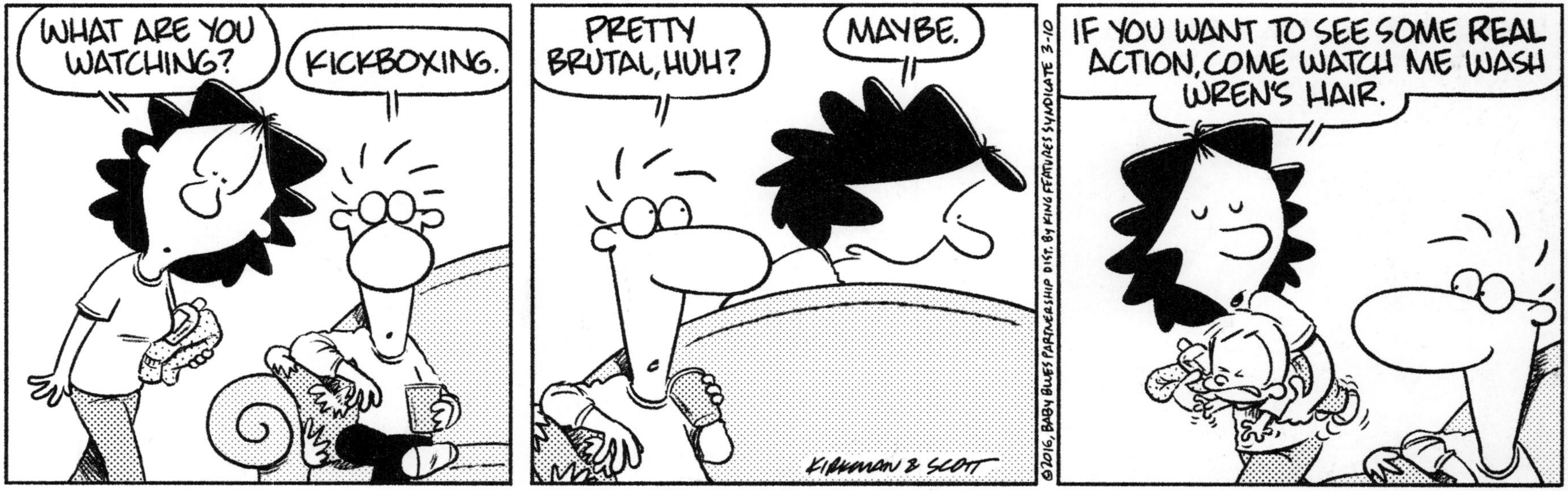
WHAT ARE YOU WATCHING?
KICKBOXING.
PRETTY BRUTAL, HUH?
MAYBE.
KIRKMAN & SCOTT
©2016, BABY BLUES PARTNERSHIP DIST. BY KING FEATURES SYNDICATE 3-10
IF YOU WANT TO SEE SOME REAL ACTION, COME WATCH ME WASH WREN'S HAIR.

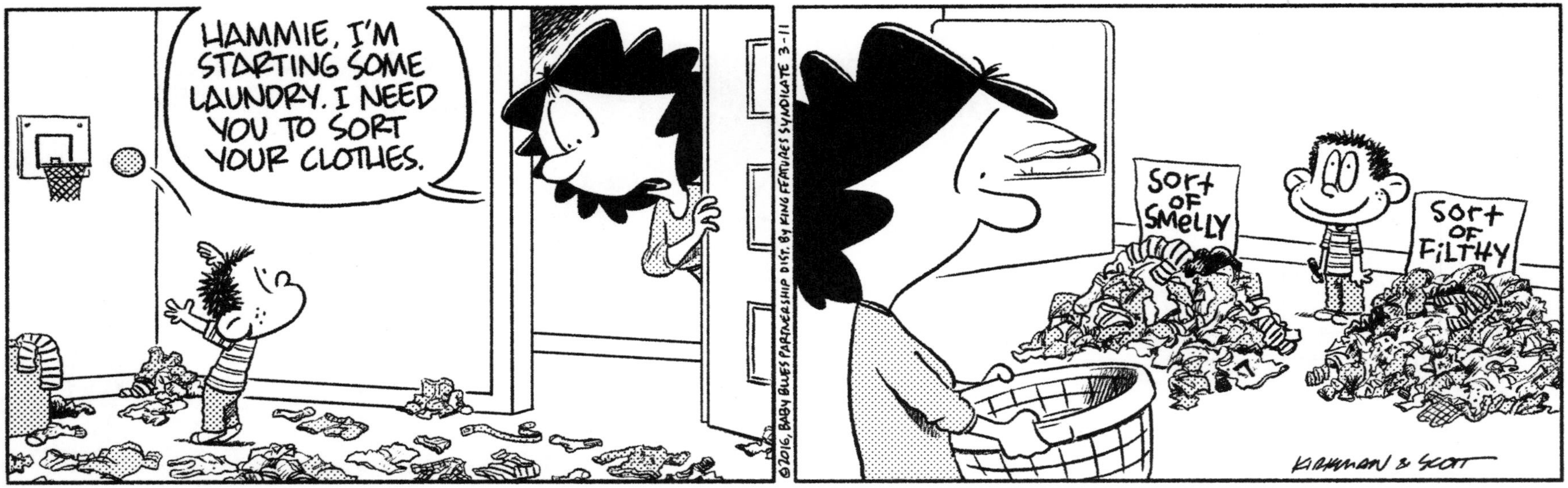
HAMMIE, I'M STARTING SOME LAUNDRY. I NEED YOU TO SORT YOUR CLOTHES.
©2016, BABY BLUES PARTNERSHIP DIST. BY KING FEATURES SYNDICATE 3-11
Sort OF Smelly
Sort OF FiLTHY
KIRKMAN & SCOTT

Rick: That's called "Thinking Outside the Hamper."

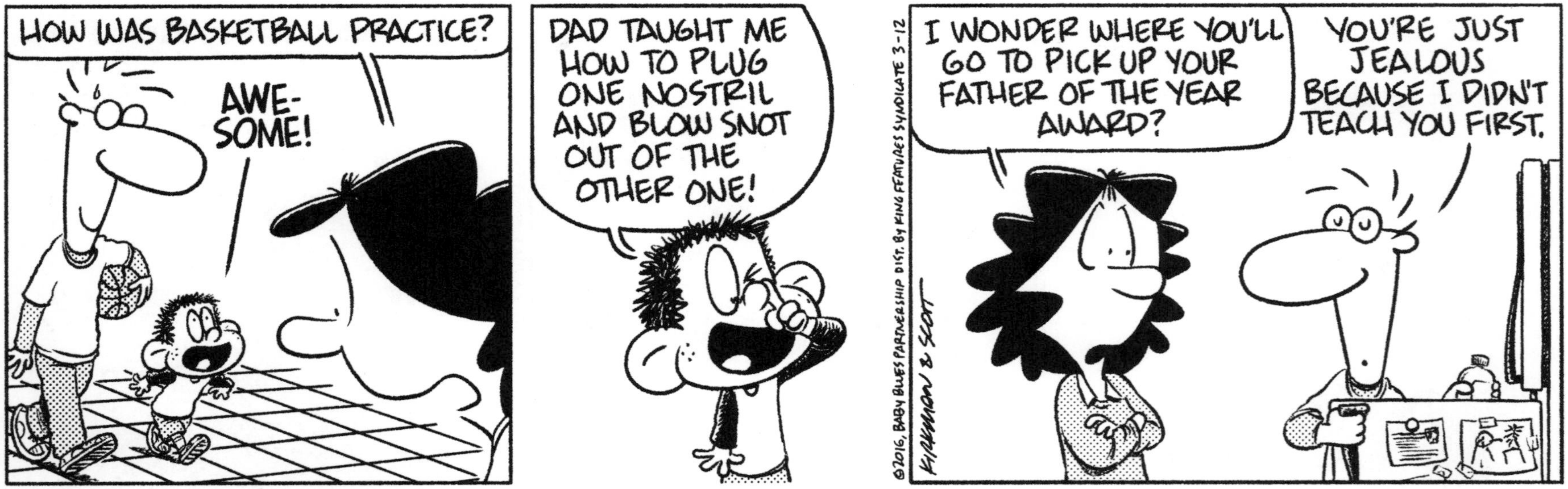
HOW WAS BASKETBALL PRACTICE?
AWE-SOME!
DAD TAUGHT ME HOW TO PLUG ONE NOSTRIL AND BLOW SNOT OUT OF THE OTHER ONE!
©2016, BABY BLUES PARTNERSHIP DIST. BY KING FEATURES SYNDICATE 3-12
KIRKMAN & SCOTT
I WONDER WHERE YOU'LL GO TO PICK UP YOUR FATHER OF THE YEAR AWARD?
YOU'RE JUST JEALOUS BECAUSE I DIDN'T TEACH YOU FIRST.

Rick: Eww. I've always hated seeing athletes do that on TV.

Jerry: Little League Baseball was tough for me because I never learned to spit well.

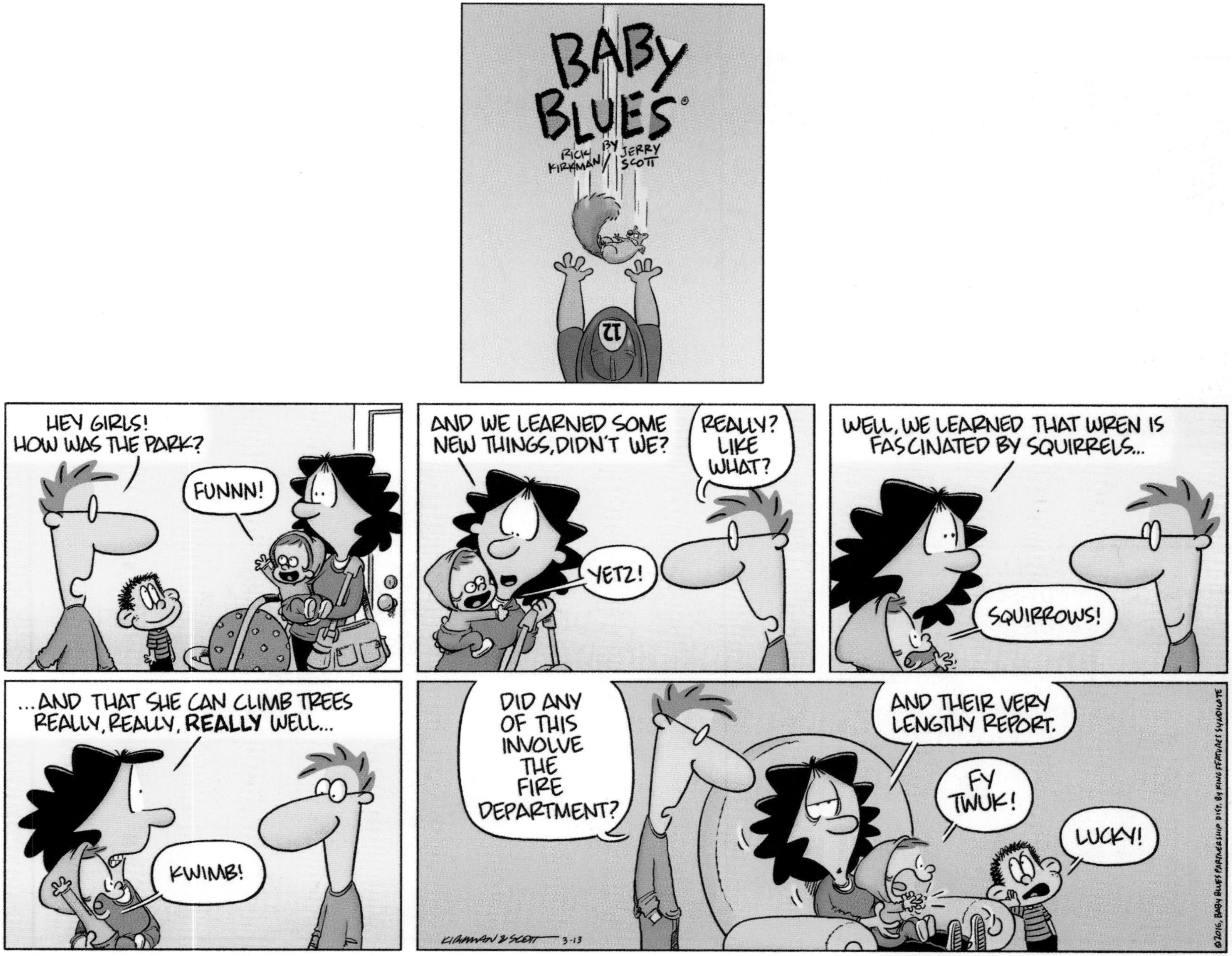
BABY BLUES®
BY RICK KIRKMAN / JERRY SCOTT
HEY GIRLS! HOW WAS THE PARK?
FUNNN!
AND WE LEARNED SOME NEW THINGS, DIDN'T WE?
YETZ!
REALLY? LIKE WHAT?
WELL, WE LEARNED THAT WREN IS FASCINATED BY SQUIRRELS...
SQUIRROWS!
...AND THAT SHE CAN CLIMB TREES REALLY, REALLY, **REALLY** WELL...
KWIMB!
DID ANY OF THIS INVOLVE THE FIRE DEPARTMENT?
AND THEIR VERY LENGTHY REPORT.
FY TWUK!
LUCKY!
KIRKMAN & SCOTT 3-13
©2016, BABY BLUES PARTNERSHIP DIST. BY KING FEATURES SYNDICATE

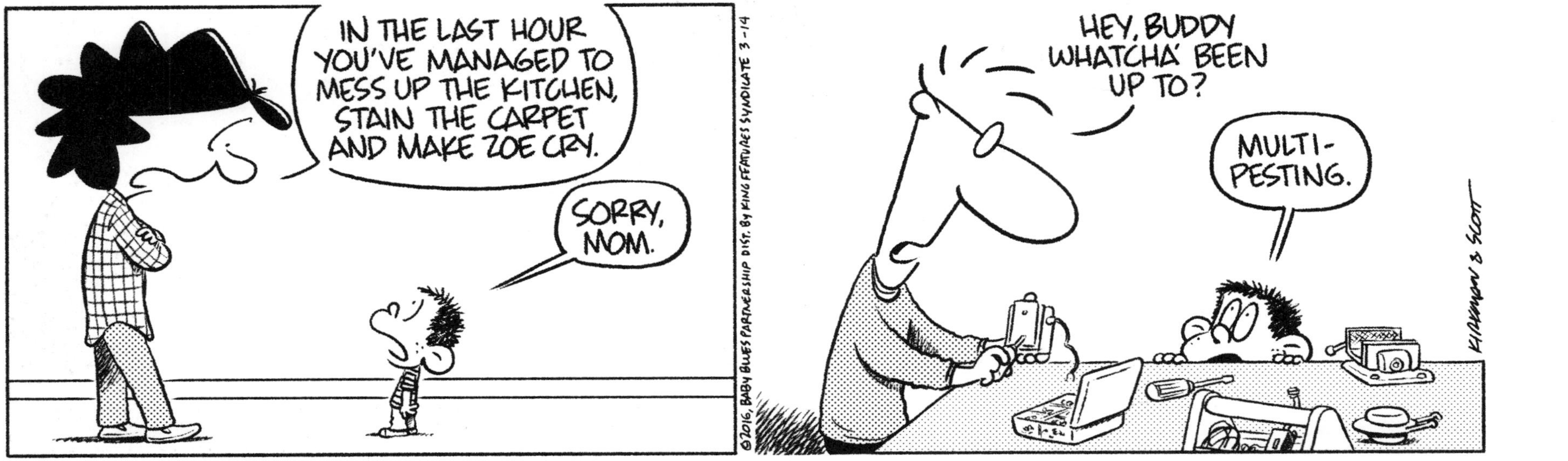
IN THE LAST HOUR YOU'VE MANAGED TO MESS UP THE KITCHEN, STAIN THE CARPET AND MAKE ZOE CRY.
SORRY, MOM.
©2016, BABY BLUES PARTNERSHIP DIST. BY KING FEATURES SYNDICATE 3-14
HEY, BUDDY WHATCHA' BEEN UP TO?
MULTI-PESTING.
KIRKMAN & SCOTT

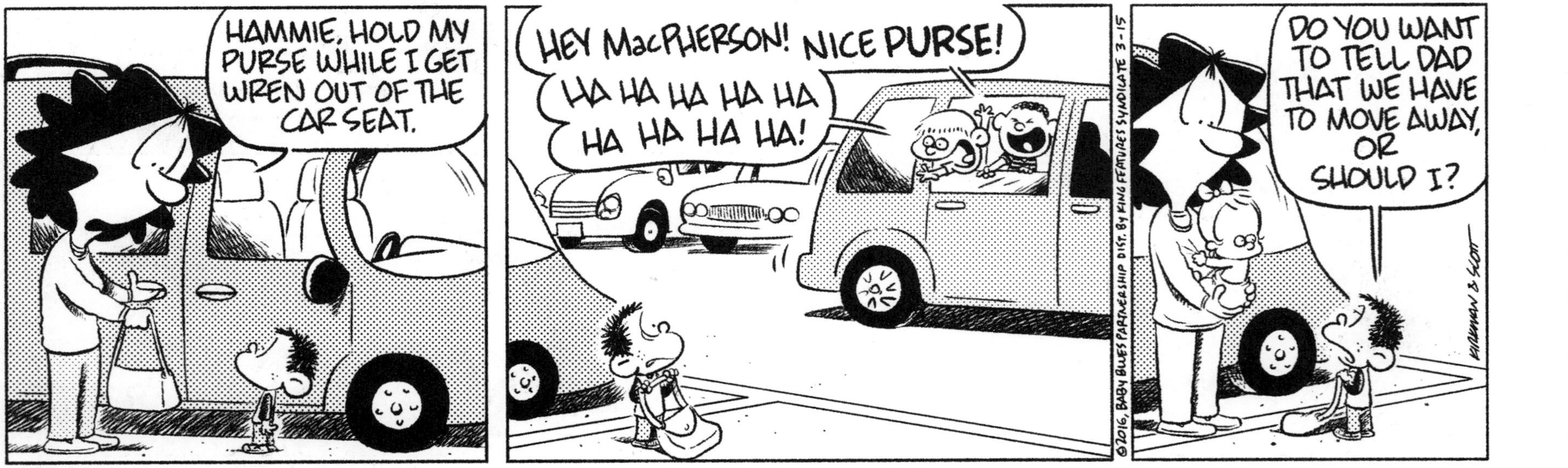
HAMMIE, HOLD MY PURSE WHILE I GET WREN OUT OF THE CAR SEAT.
HEY MacPHERSON!
NICE PURSE!
HA HA HA HA HA HA HA HA HA!
©2016, BABY BLUES PARTNERSHIP DIST. BY KING FEATURES SYNDICATE 3-15
DO YOU WANT TO TELL DAD THAT WE HAVE TO MOVE AWAY, OR SHOULD I?
KIRKMAN & SCOTT

Rick: I can still feel the cringe when things like that happened.

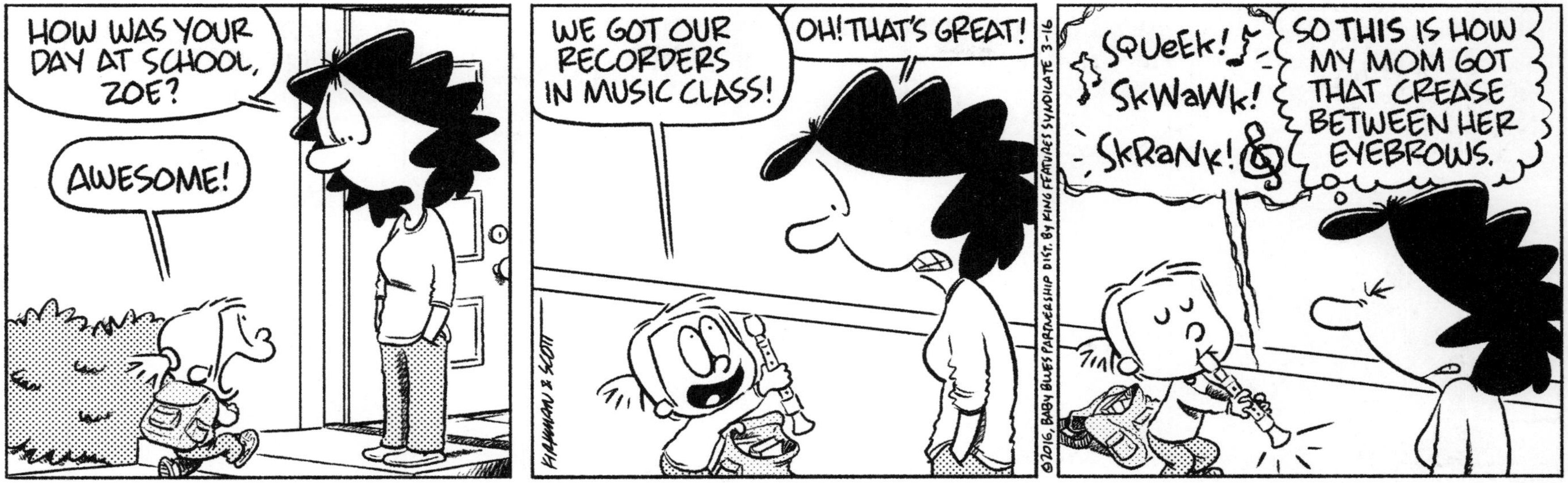
HOW WAS YOUR DAY AT SCHOOL, ZOE?
AWESOME!
WE GOT OUR RECORDERS IN MUSIC CLASS!
OH! THAT'S GREAT!
KIRKMAN & SCOTT
©2016, BABY BLUES PARTNERSHIP DIST. BY KING FEATURES SYNDICATE 3-16
SQUEEK!
SKWAWK!
SKRANK!
SO THIS IS HOW MY MOM GOT THAT CREASE BETWEEN HER EYEBROWS.

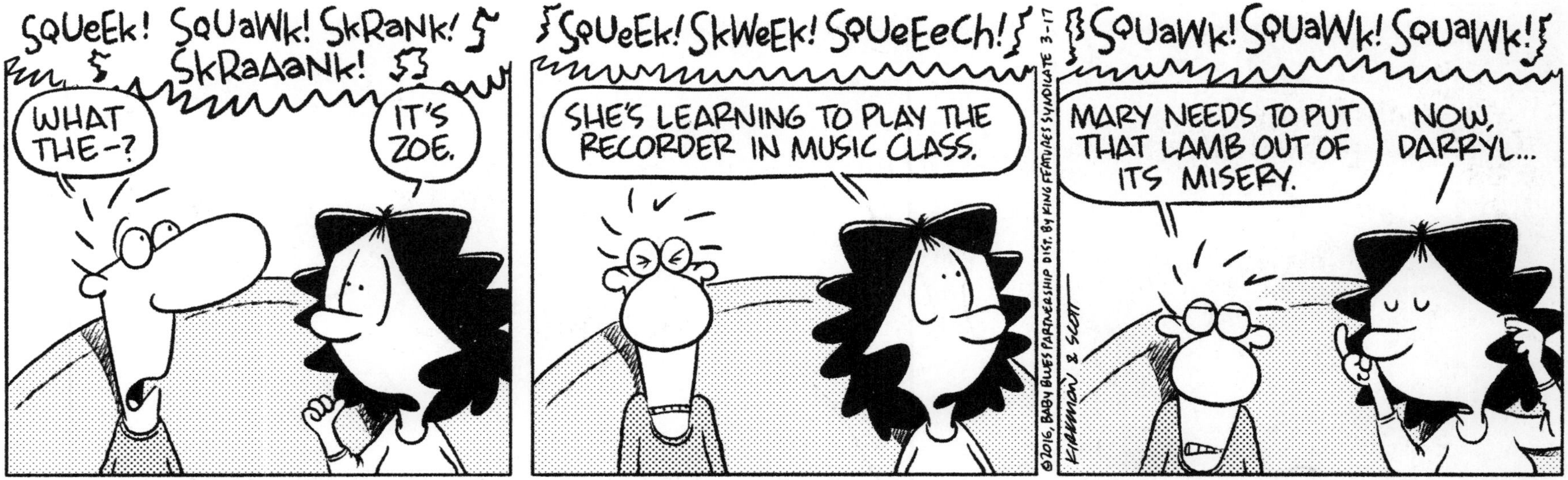
SQUEEK! SQUAWK! SKRANK!
SKRAAANK!
WHAT THE–?
IT'S ZOE.
SQUEEK! SKWEEK! SQUEEECH!
SHE'S LEARNING TO PLAY THE RECORDER IN MUSIC CLASS.
©2016, BABY BLUES PARTNERSHIP DIST. BY KING FEATURES SYNDICATE 3-17
KIRKMAN & SCOTT
SQUAWK! SQUAWK! SQUAWK!
MARY NEEDS TO PUT THAT LAMB OUT OF ITS MISERY.
NOW, DARRYL...

Jerry: Recorders are great for teaching kids the fundamentals of music, and parents the fundamentals of headache remedies.

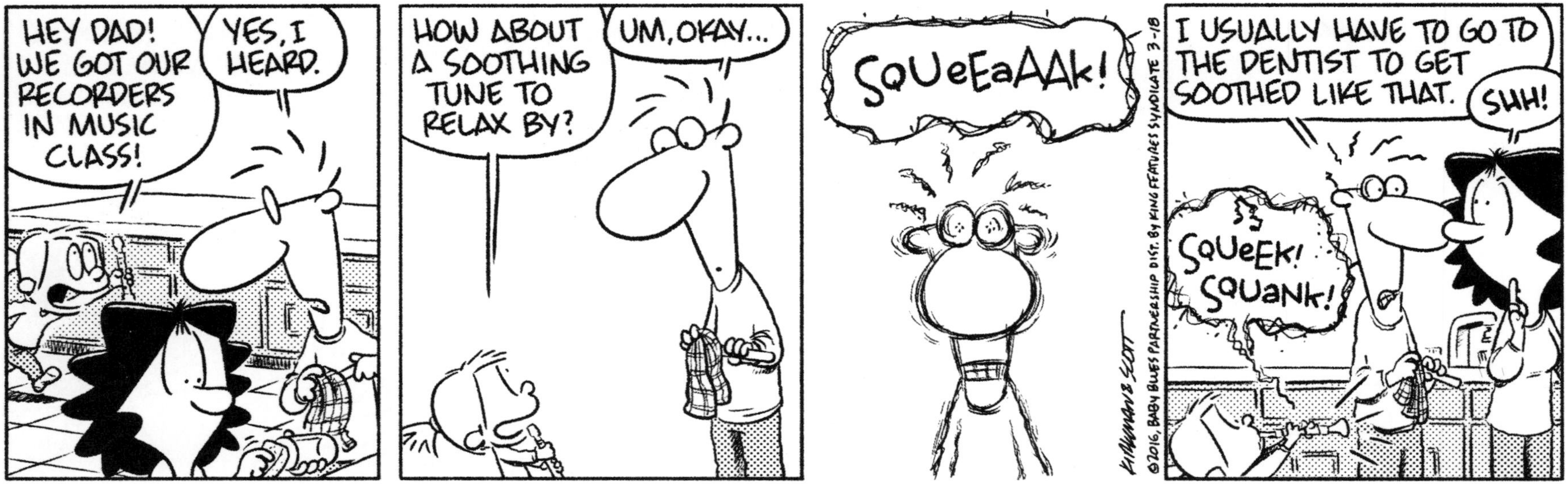
HEY DAD! WE GOT OUR RECORDERS IN MUSIC CLASS!
YES, I HEARD.
HOW ABOUT A SOOTHING TUNE TO RELAX BY?
UM, OKAY...
SQUeEaAAk!
KIRKMAN & SCOTT
©2016, BABY BLUES PARTNERSHIP DIST. BY KING FEATURES SYNDICATE 3-18
I USUALLY HAVE TO GO TO THE DENTIST TO GET SOOTHED LIKE THAT.
SHH!
SQUeEK! SQUanK!

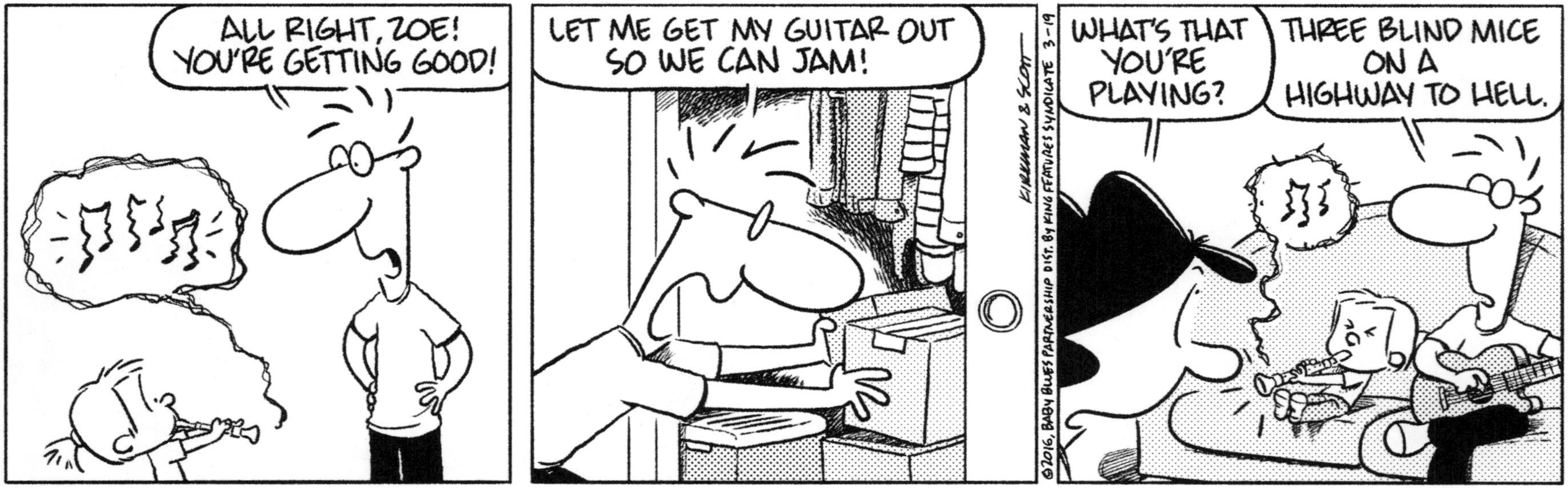
ALL RIGHT, ZOE! YOU'RE GETTING GOOD!
LET ME GET MY GUITAR OUT SO WE CAN JAM!
KIRKMAN & SCOTT 3-19
©2016, BABY BLUES PARTNERSHIP DIST. BY KING FEATURES SYNDICATE
WHAT'S THAT YOU'RE PLAYING?
THREE BLIND MICE ON A HIGHWAY TO HELL.

Rick: I wanna hear that song.

Jerry: This is a joke you will not see in *The Family Circus*. Go ahead and check. I'll wait.

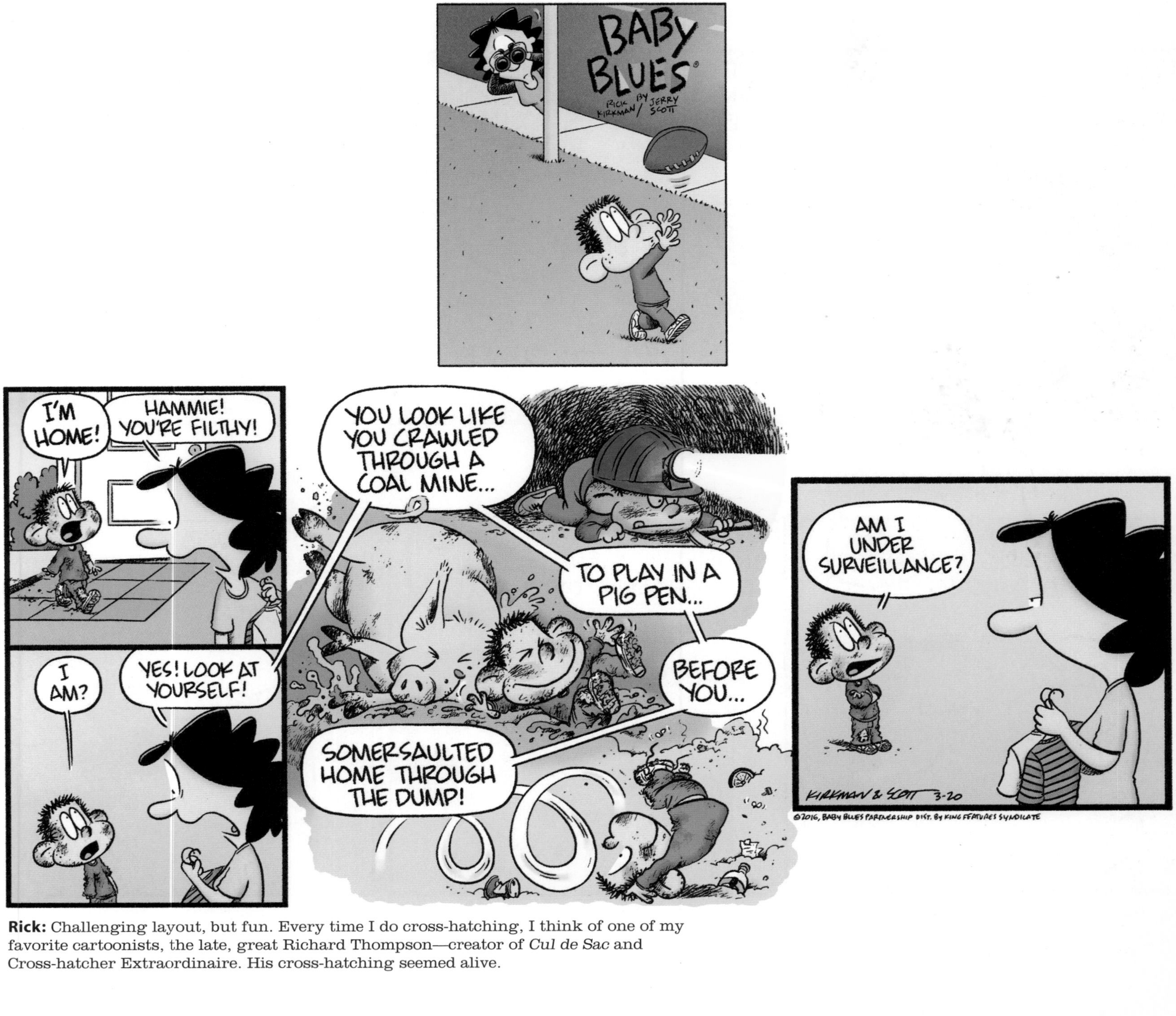
BABY BLUES®
RICK KIRKMAN / BY JERRY SCOTT
I'M HOME!
HAMMIE! YOU'RE FILTHY!
I AM?
YES! LOOK AT YOURSELF!
YOU LOOK LIKE YOU CRAWLED THROUGH A COAL MINE...
TO PLAY IN A PIG PEN...
BEFORE YOU...
SOMERSAULTED HOME THROUGH THE DUMP!
AM I UNDER SURVEILLANCE?
KIRKMAN & SCOTT 3-20
©2016, BABY BLUES PARTNERSHIP DIST. BY KING FEATURES SYNDICATE

Rick: Challenging layout, but fun. Every time I do cross-hatching, I think of one of my favorite cartoonists, the late, great Richard Thompson—creator of *Cul de Sac* and Cross-hatcher Extraordinaire. His cross-hatching seemed alive.

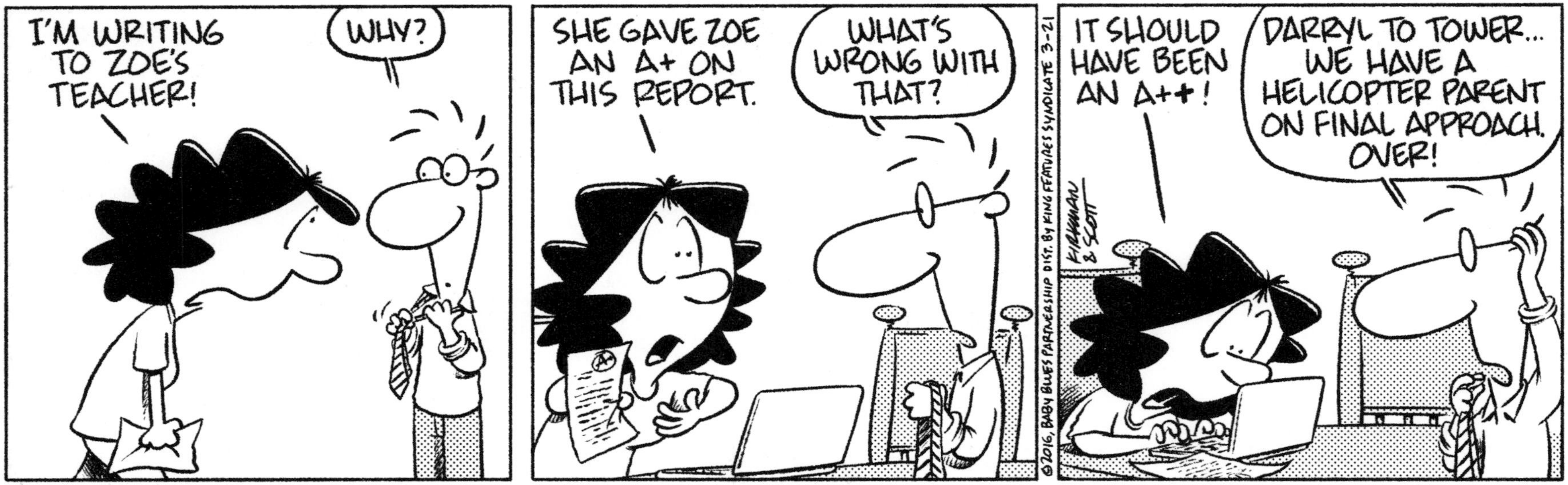
I'M WRITING TO ZOE'S TEACHER!
WHY?
SHE GAVE ZOE AN A+ ON THIS REPORT.
WHAT'S WRONG WITH THAT?
©2016, BABY BLUES PARTNERSHIP DIST. BY KING FEATURES SYNDICATE 3-21
IT SHOULD HAVE BEEN AN A++!
KIRKMAN & SCOTT
DARRYL TO TOWER... WE HAVE A HELICOPTER PARENT ON FINAL APPROACH. OVER!

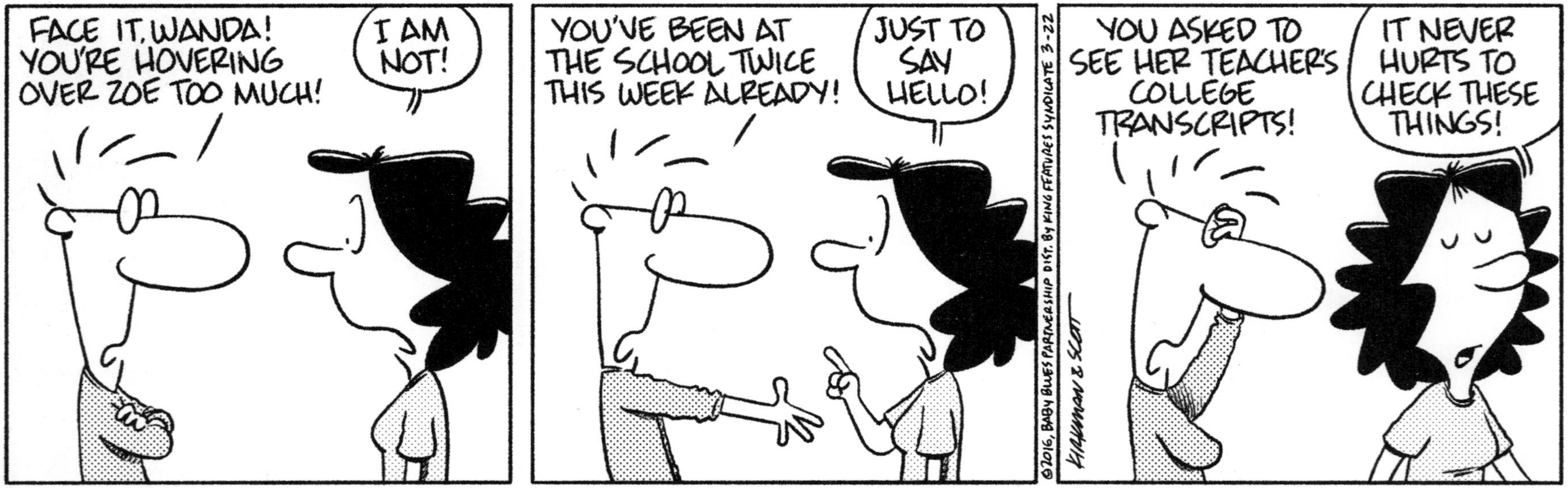
FACE IT, WANDA! YOU'RE HOVERING OVER ZOE TOO MUCH!
I AM NOT!
YOU'VE BEEN AT THE SCHOOL TWICE THIS WEEK ALREADY!
JUST TO SAY HELLO!
©2016, BABY BLUES PARTNERSHIP DIST. BY KING FEATURES SYNDICATE 3-22
YOU ASKED TO SEE HER TEACHER'S COLLEGE TRANSCRIPTS!
IT NEVER HURTS TO CHECK THESE THINGS!
KIRKMAN & SCOTT

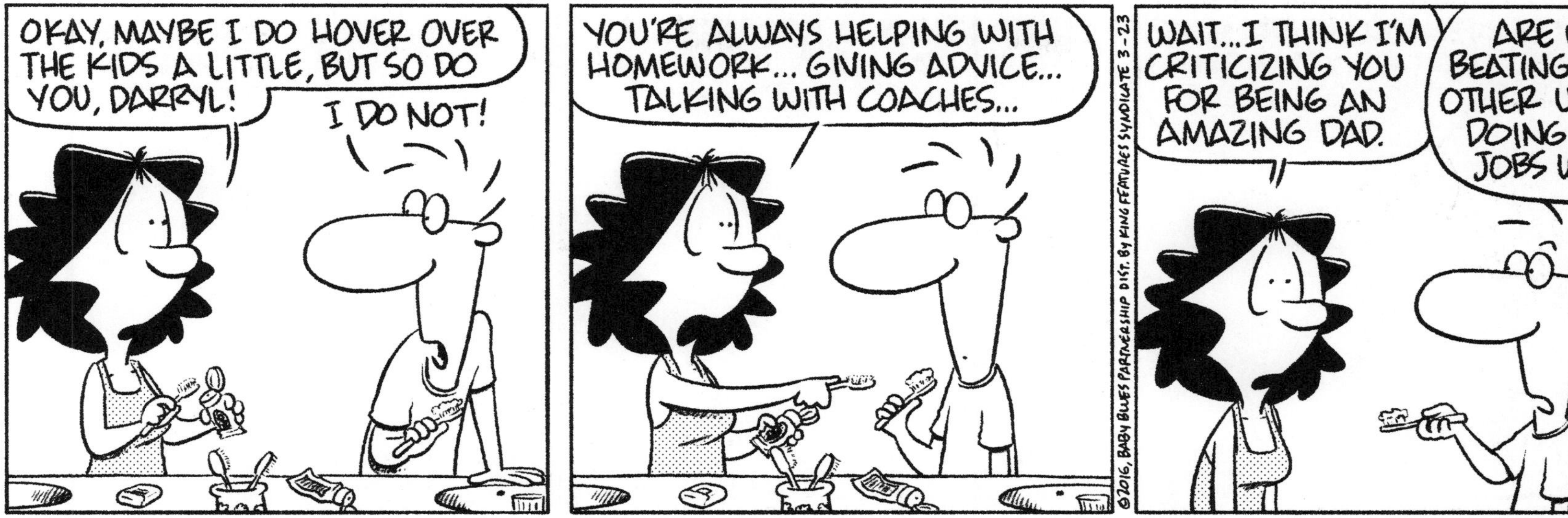
OKAY, MAYBE I DO HOVER OVER THE KIDS A LITTLE, BUT SO DO YOU, DARRYL!
I DO NOT!
YOU'RE ALWAYS HELPING WITH HOMEWORK... GIVING ADVICE... TALKING WITH COACHES...
©2016, BABY BLUES PARTNERSHIP DIST. BY KING FEATURES SYNDICATE 3-23
WAIT...I THINK I'M CRITICIZING YOU FOR BEING AN AMAZING DAD.
ARE WE BEATING EACH OTHER UP FOR DOING OUR JOBS WELL?
KIRKMAN & SCOTT

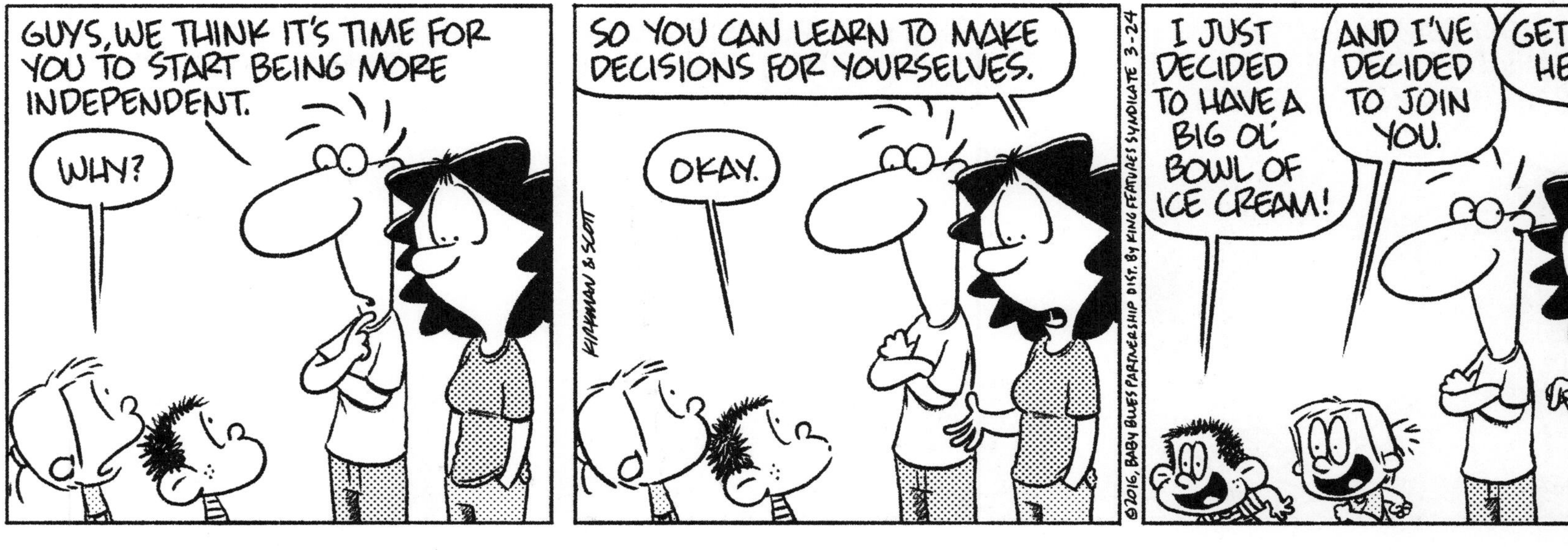
GUYS, WE THINK IT'S TIME FOR YOU TO START BEING MORE INDEPENDENT.
WHY?
KIRKMAN & SCOTT
SO YOU CAN LEARN TO MAKE DECISIONS FOR YOURSELVES.
OKAY.
©2016, BABY BLUES PARTNERSHIP DIST. BY KING FEATURES SYNDICATE 3-24
I JUST DECIDED TO HAVE A BIG OL' BOWL OF ICE CREAM!
AND I'VE DECIDED TO JOIN YOU.
GET BACK HERE!

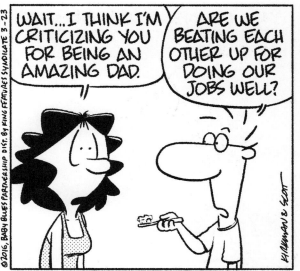

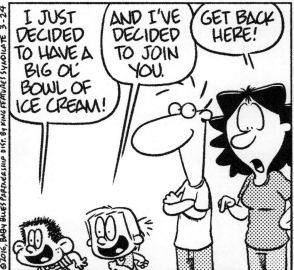

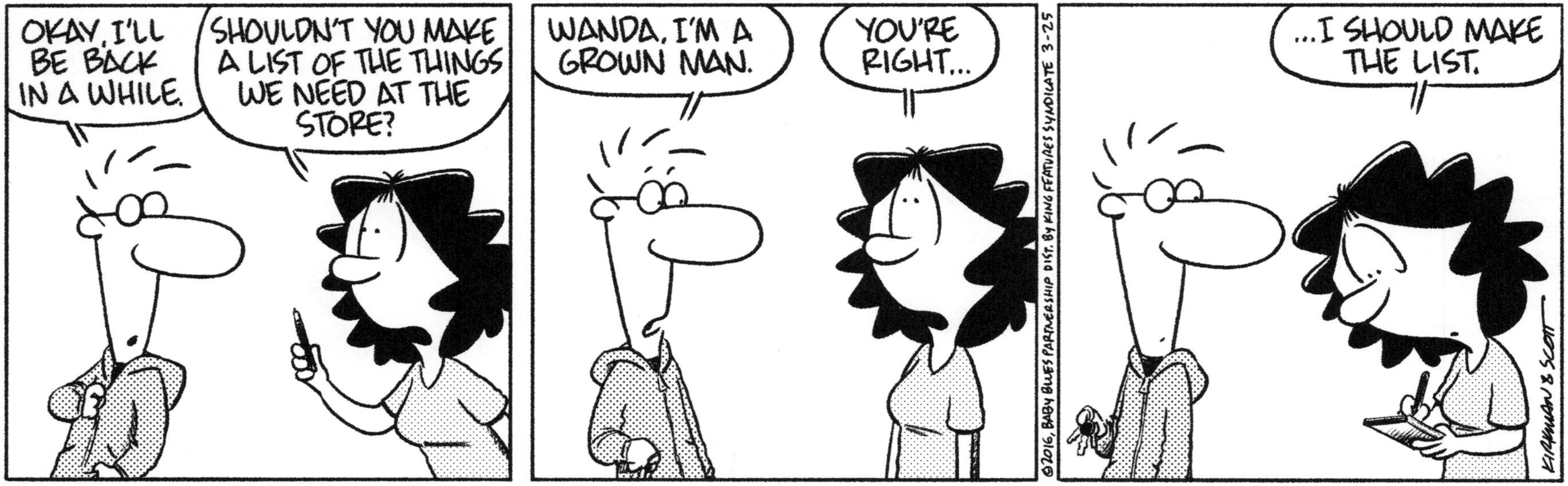
OKAY, I'LL BE BACK IN A WHILE.
SHOULDN'T YOU MAKE A LIST OF THE THINGS WE NEED AT THE STORE?
WANDA, I'M A GROWN MAN.
YOU'RE RIGHT...
©2016, BABY BLUES PARTNERSHIP DIST. BY KING FEATURES SYNDICATE 3-25
...I SHOULD MAKE THE LIST.
KIRKMAN & SCOTT

Rick: If I'm not mistaken, I believe this was a conversation between my wife and me. I can't remember.

Jerry: Yeah, it was you. I could never be that forgetful about whatever it is we were just talking about.

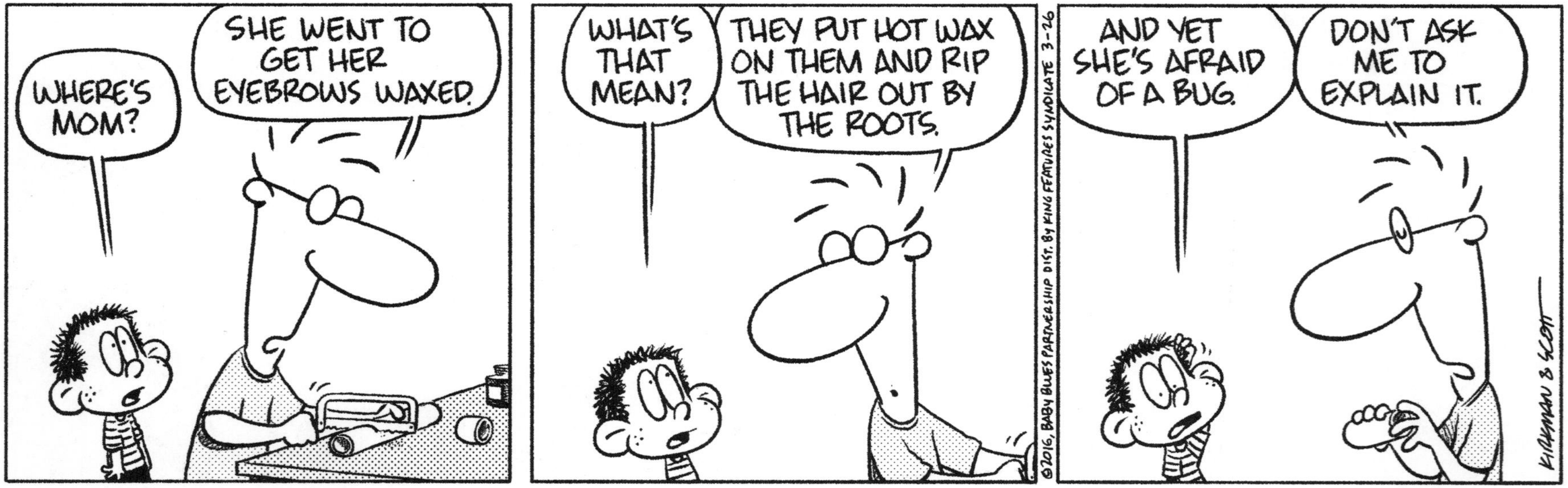
WHERE'S MOM?
SHE WENT TO GET HER EYEBROWS WAXED.
WHAT'S THAT MEAN?
THEY PUT HOT WAX ON THEM AND RIP THE HAIR OUT BY THE ROOTS.
©2016, BABY BLUES PARTNERSHIP DIST. BY KING FEATURES SYNDICATE 3-26
AND YET SHE'S AFRAID OF A BUG.
DON'T ASK ME TO EXPLAIN IT.
KIRKMAN & SCOTT

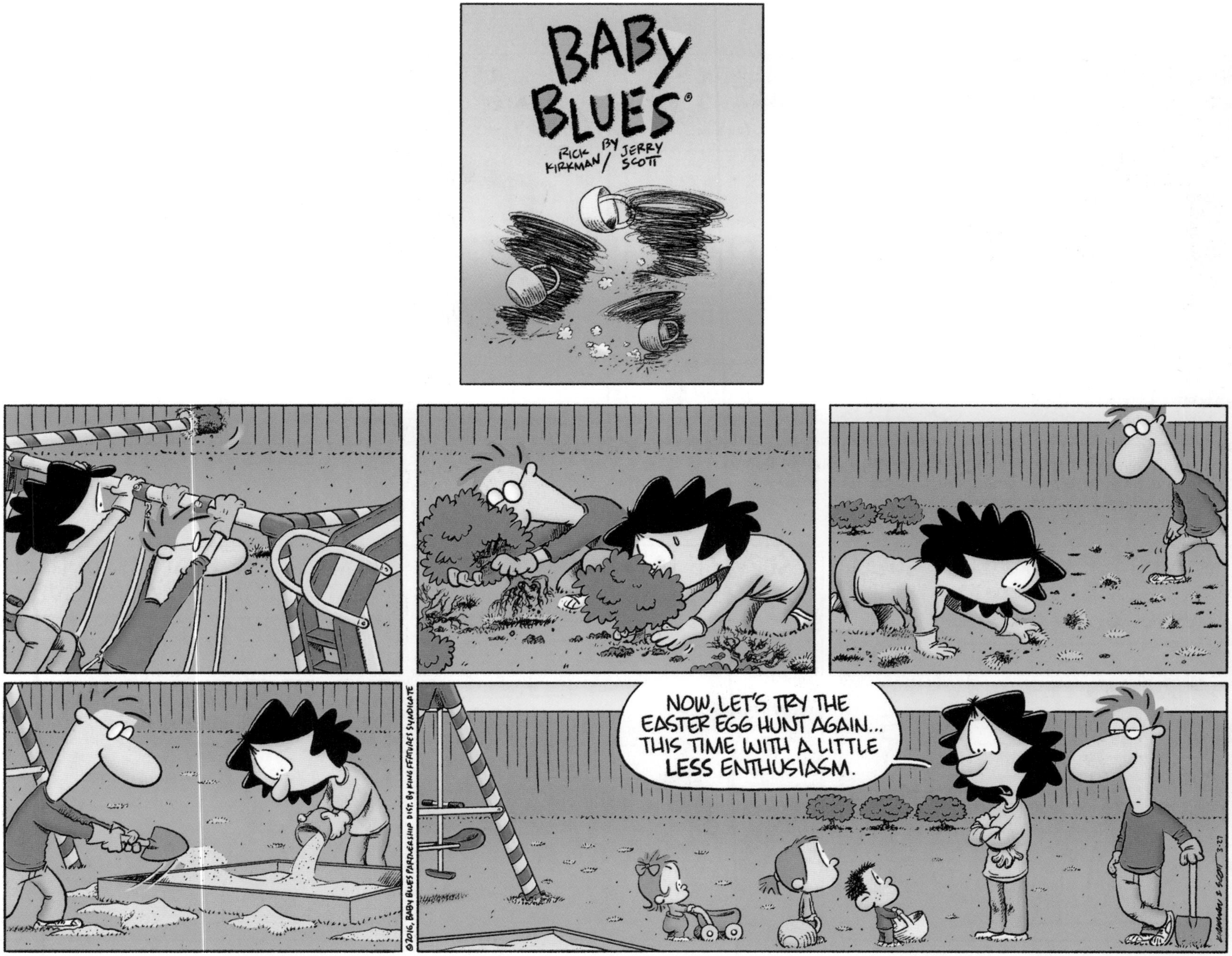
BABY BLUES®
BY RICK KIRKMAN / JERRY SCOTT
©2016, BABY BLUES PARTNERSHIP DIST. BY KING FEATURES SYNDICATE
NOW, LET'S TRY THE EASTER EGG HUNT AGAIN... THIS TIME WITH A LITTLE LESS ENTHUSIASM.

Rick: My favorite part of this is that we didn't actually show anything happen.

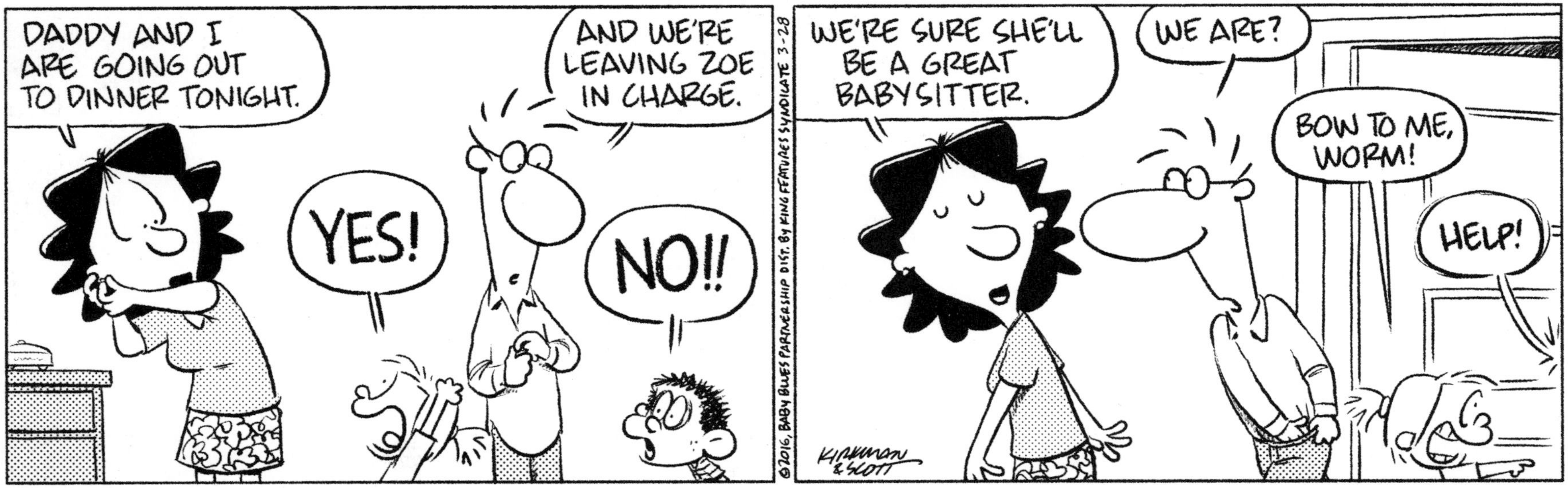
DADDY AND I ARE GOING OUT TO DINNER TONIGHT.
AND WE'RE LEAVING ZOE IN CHARGE.
YES!
NO!!
©2016, BABY BLUES PARTNERSHIP DIST. BY KING FEATURES SYNDICATE 3-28
WE'RE SURE SHE'LL BE A GREAT BABYSITTER.
WE ARE?
BOW TO ME, WORM!
HELP!
KIRKMAN & SCOTT

Jerry: I'm pretty sure that my parents never knew what a monster I was when my sister babysat me. I plan to keep it that way.

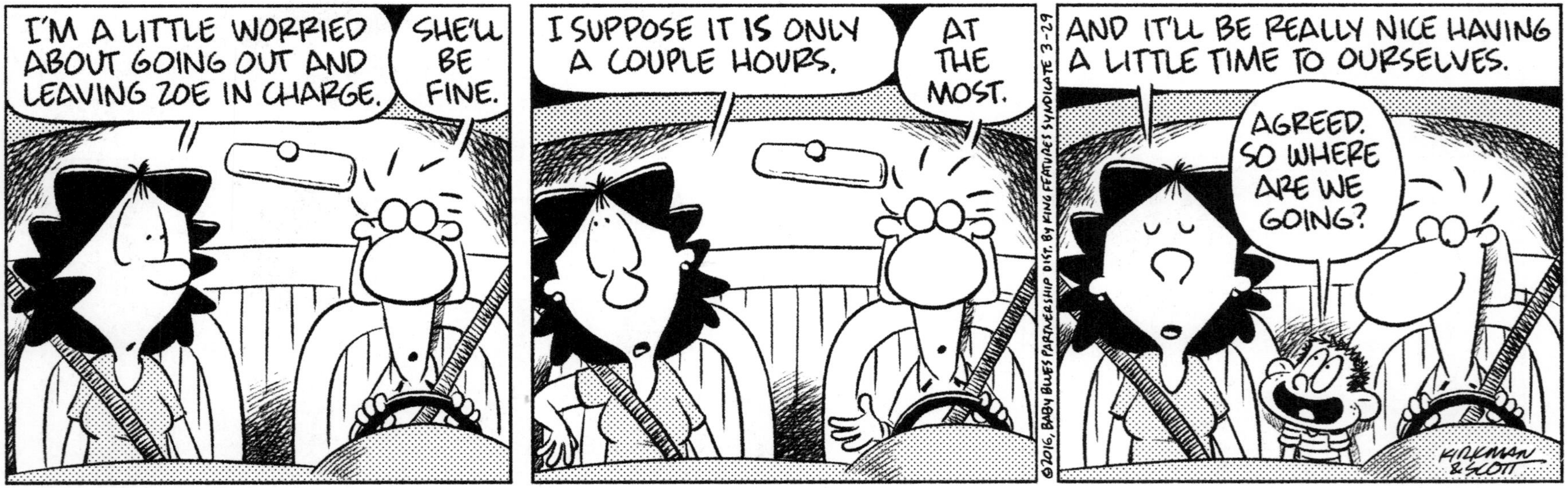
I'M A LITTLE WORRIED ABOUT GOING OUT AND LEAVING ZOE IN CHARGE.
SHE'LL BE FINE.
I SUPPOSE IT IS ONLY A COUPLE HOURS.
AT THE MOST.
©2016, BABY BLUES PARTNERSHIP DIST. BY KING FEATURES SYNDICATE 3-29
AND IT'LL BE REALLY NICE HAVING A LITTLE TIME TO OURSELVES.
AGREED. SO WHERE ARE WE GOING?
KIRKMAN & SCOTT

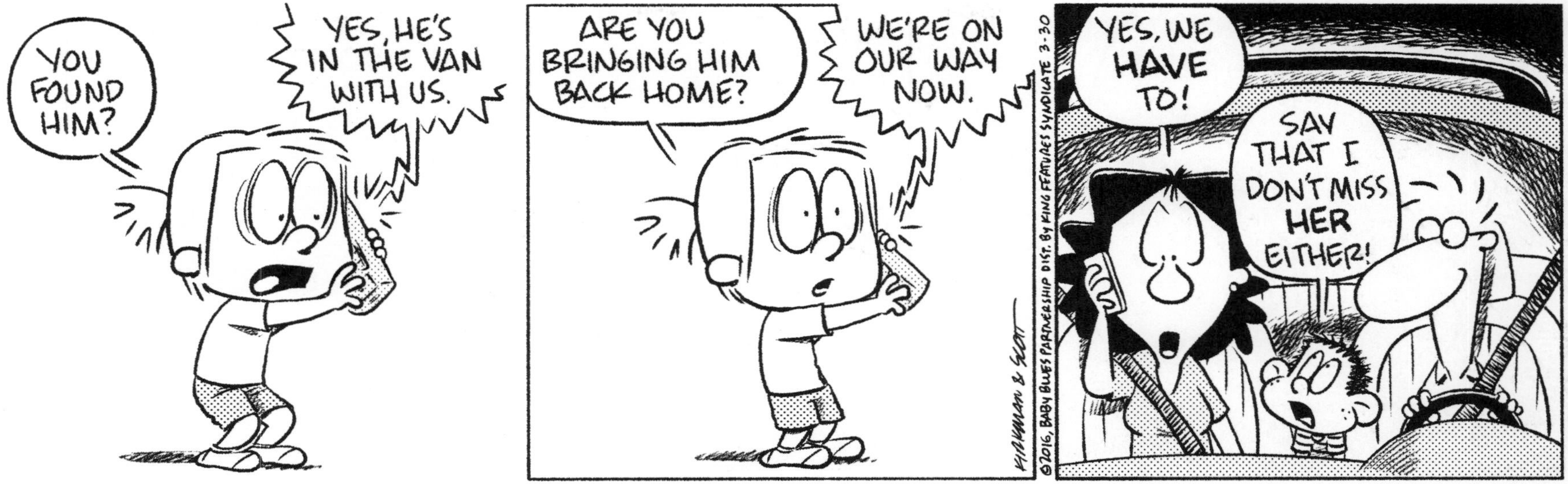
YOU FOUND HIM?
YES, HE'S IN THE VAN WITH US.
ARE YOU BRINGING HIM BACK HOME?
WE'RE ON OUR WAY NOW.
KIRKMAN & SCOTT
©2016, BABY BLUES PARTNERSHIP DIST. BY KING FEATURES SYNDICATE 3-30
YES, WE **HAVE** TO!
SAY THAT I DON'T MISS **HER** EITHER!

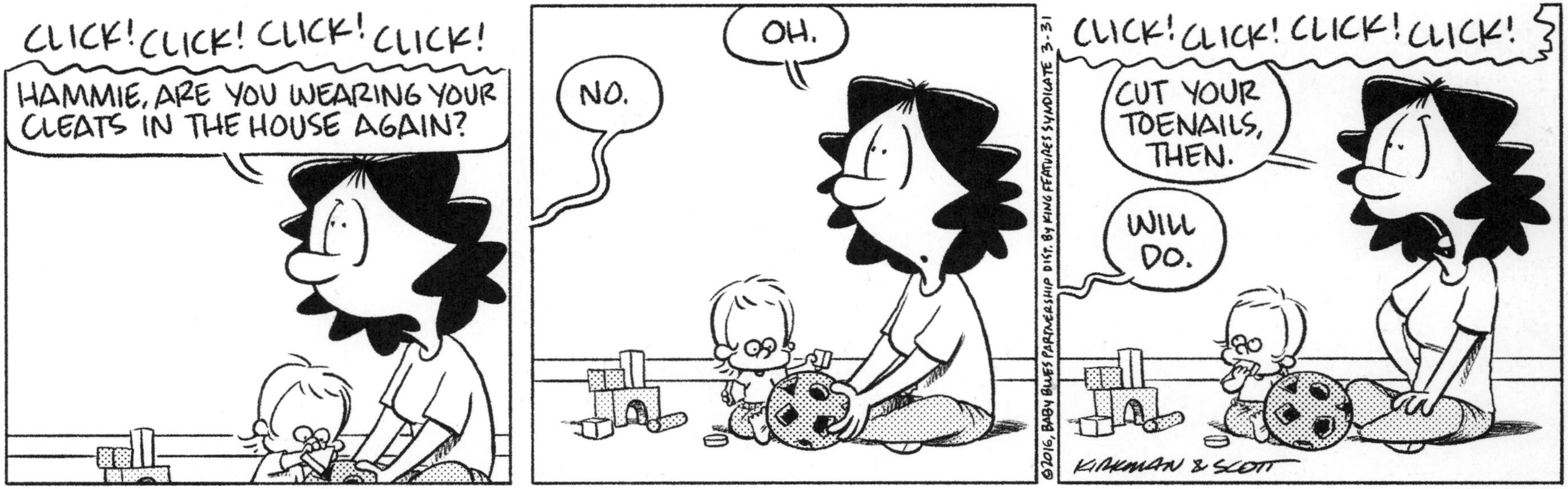
CLICK! CLICK! CLICK! CLICK!
HAMMIE, ARE YOU WEARING YOUR CLEATS IN THE HOUSE AGAIN?
NO.
OH.
©2016, BABY BLUES PARTNERSHIP DIST. BY KING FEATURES SYNDICATE 3-31
CLICK! CLICK! CLICK! CLICK!
CUT YOUR TOENAILS, THEN.
WILL DO.
KIRKMAN & SCOTT

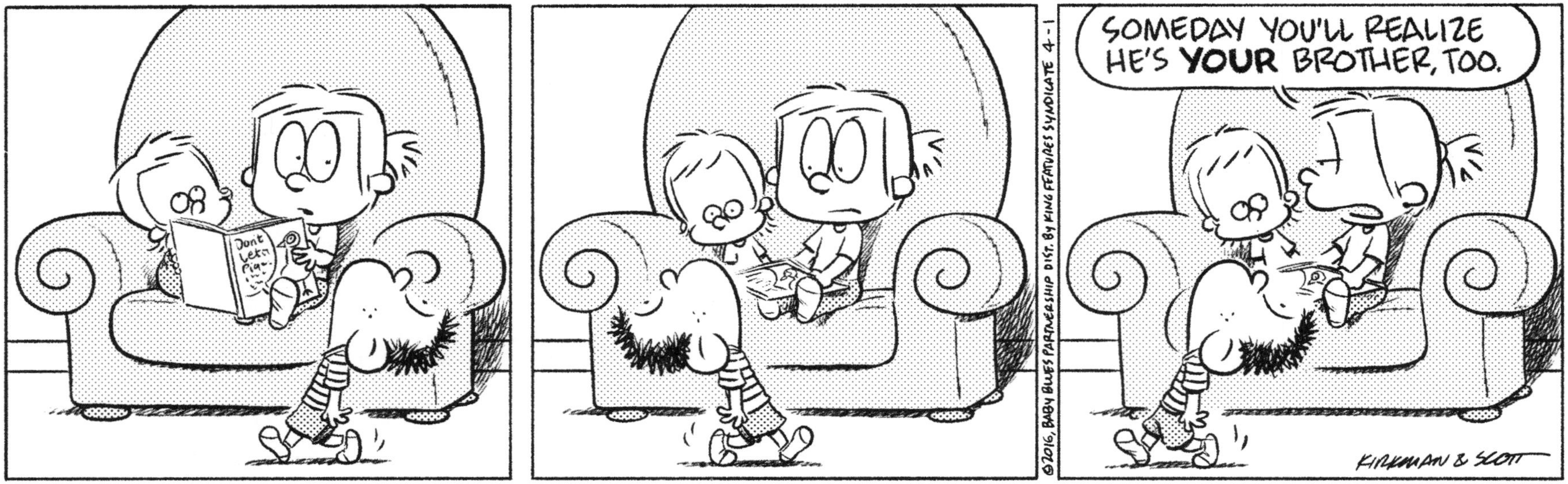
SOMEDAY YOU'LL REALIZE HE'S **YOUR** BROTHER, TOO.
©2016, BABY BLUES PARTNERSHIP DIST. BY KING FEATURES SYNDICATE 4-1
KIRKMAN & SCOTT

Rick: I saw a kid doing this in the waiting room of a doctor's office. I just had to draw it in a gag.

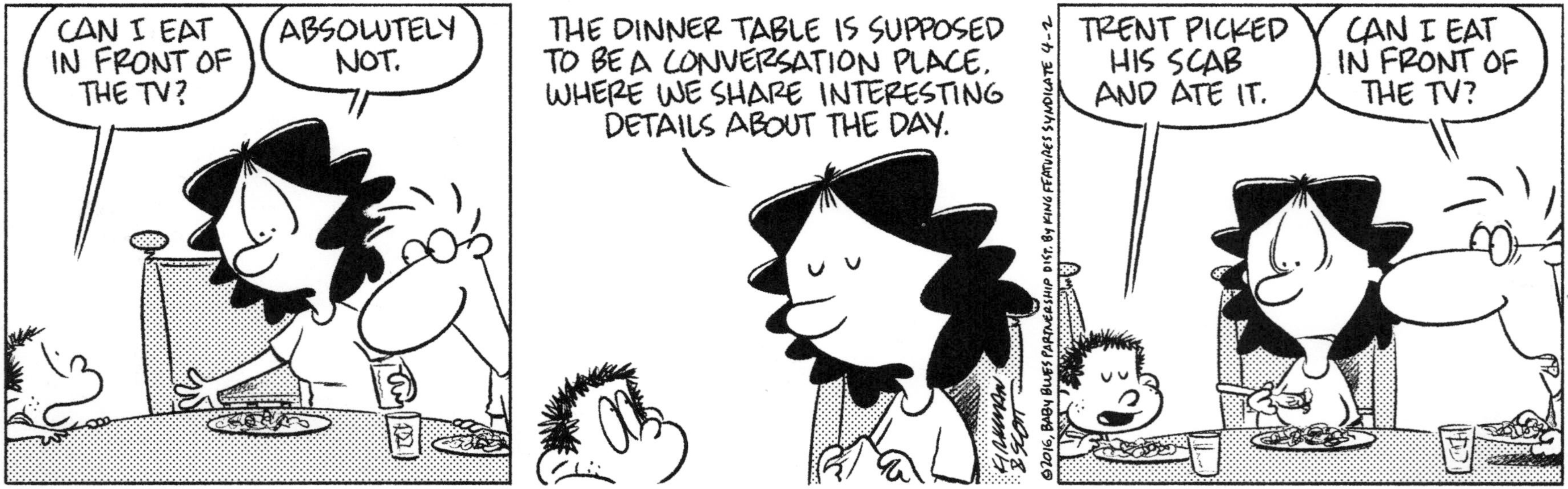
CAN I EAT IN FRONT OF THE TV?
ABSOLUTELY NOT.
THE DINNER TABLE IS SUPPOSED TO BE A CONVERSATION PLACE, WHERE WE SHARE INTERESTING DETAILS ABOUT THE DAY.
KIRKMAN & SCOTT
©2016, BABY BLUES PARTNERSHIP DIST. BY KING FEATURES SYNDICATE 4-2
TRENT PICKED HIS SCAB AND ATE IT.
CAN I EAT IN FRONT OF THE TV?

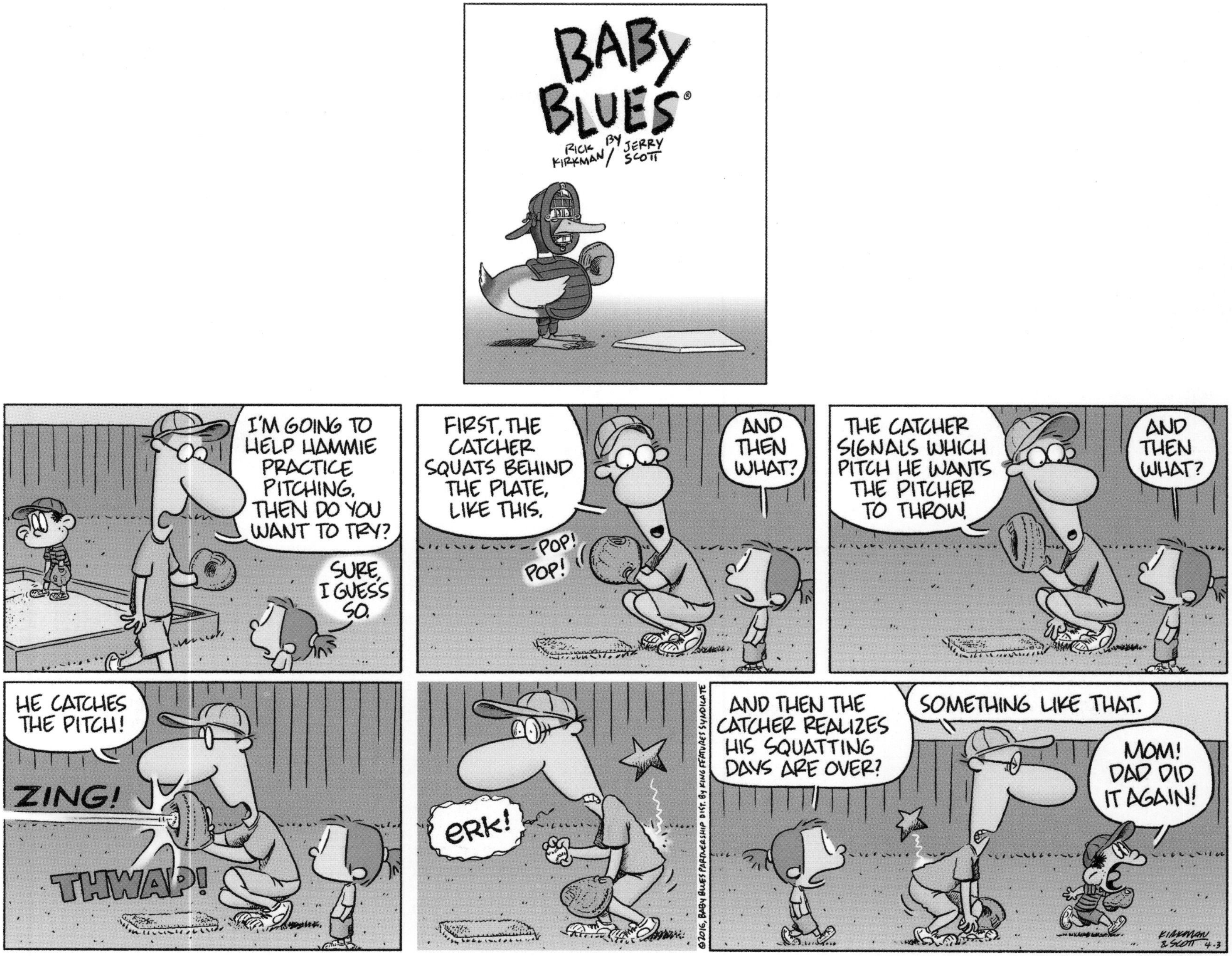
BABY BLUES®
BY RICK KIRKMAN / JERRY SCOTT
I'M GOING TO HELP HAMMIE PRACTICE PITCHING, THEN DO YOU WANT TO TRY?
SURE, I GUESS SO.
FIRST, THE CATCHER SQUATS BEHIND THE PLATE, LIKE THIS.
POP! POP!
AND THEN WHAT?
THE CATCHER SIGNALS WHICH PITCH HE WANTS THE PITCHER TO THROW.
AND THEN WHAT?
HE CATCHES THE PITCH!
ZING!
THWAP!
ERK!
©2016, BABY BLUES PARTNERSHIP DIST. BY KING FEATURES SYNDICATE
AND THEN THE CATCHER REALIZES HIS SQUATTING DAYS ARE OVER?
SOMETHING LIKE THAT.
MOM! DAD DID IT AGAIN!
KIRKMAN & SCOTT 4-3

Rick: I live Darryl's pain.

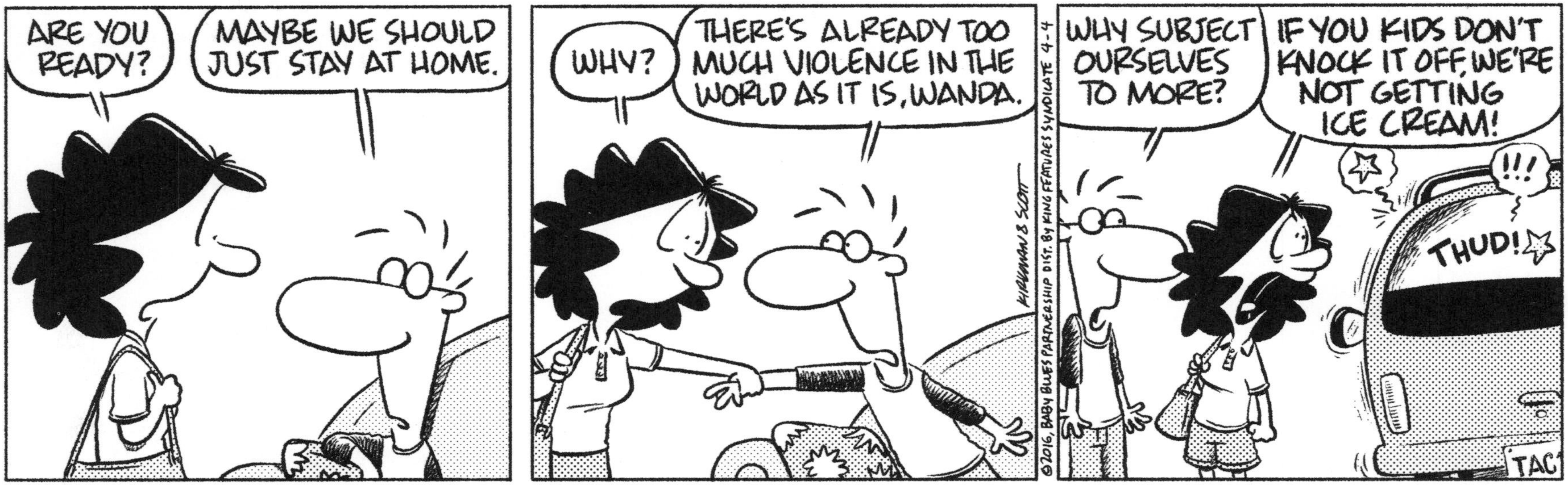
ARE YOU READY?
MAYBE WE SHOULD JUST STAY AT HOME.
WHY?
THERE'S ALREADY TOO MUCH VIOLENCE IN THE WORLD AS IT IS, WANDA.
KIRKMAN & SCOTT
©2016, BABY BLUES PARTNERSHIP DIST. BY KING FEATURES SYNDICATE 4-4
WHY SUBJECT OURSELVES TO MORE?
IF YOU KIDS DON'T KNOCK IT OFF, WE'RE NOT GETTING ICE CREAM!
!!!
THUD!

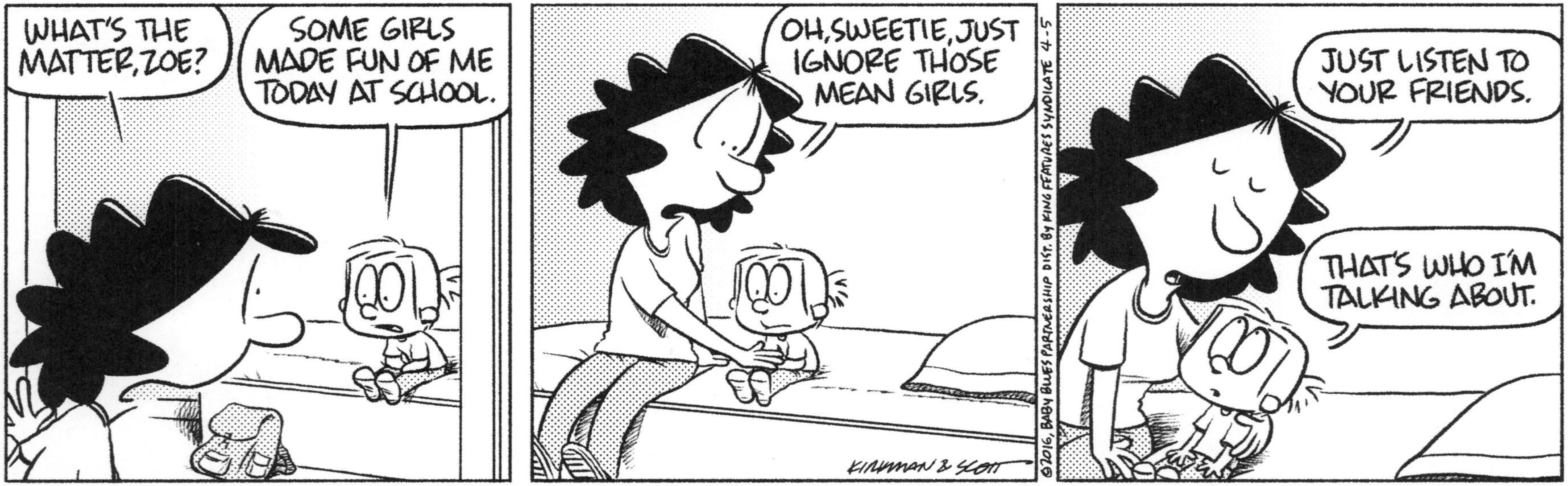
WHAT'S THE MATTER, ZOE?
SOME GIRLS MADE FUN OF ME TODAY AT SCHOOL.
OH, SWEETIE, JUST IGNORE THOSE MEAN GIRLS.
KIRKMAN & SCOTT
©2016, BABY BLUES PARTNERSHIP DIST. BY KING FEATURES SYNDICATE 4-5
JUST LISTEN TO YOUR FRIENDS.
THAT'S WHO I'M TALKING ABOUT.

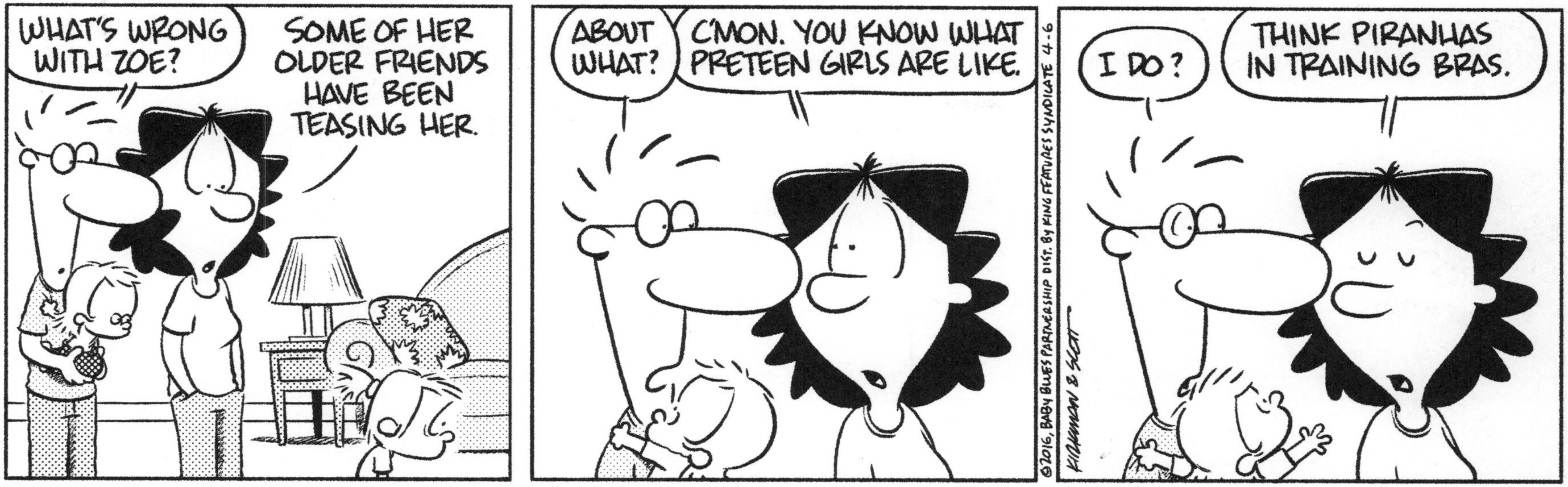
WHAT'S WRONG WITH ZOE?
SOME OF HER OLDER FRIENDS HAVE BEEN TEASING HER.
ABOUT WHAT?
C'MON. YOU KNOW WHAT PRETEEN GIRLS ARE LIKE.
©2016, BABY BLUES PARTNERSHIP DIST. BY KING FEATURES SYNDICATE 4-6
KIRKMAN & SCOTT
I DO?
THINK PIRANHAS IN TRAINING BRAS.

Jerry: Piranhas in training bras. There's an image that'll haunt you for a while.

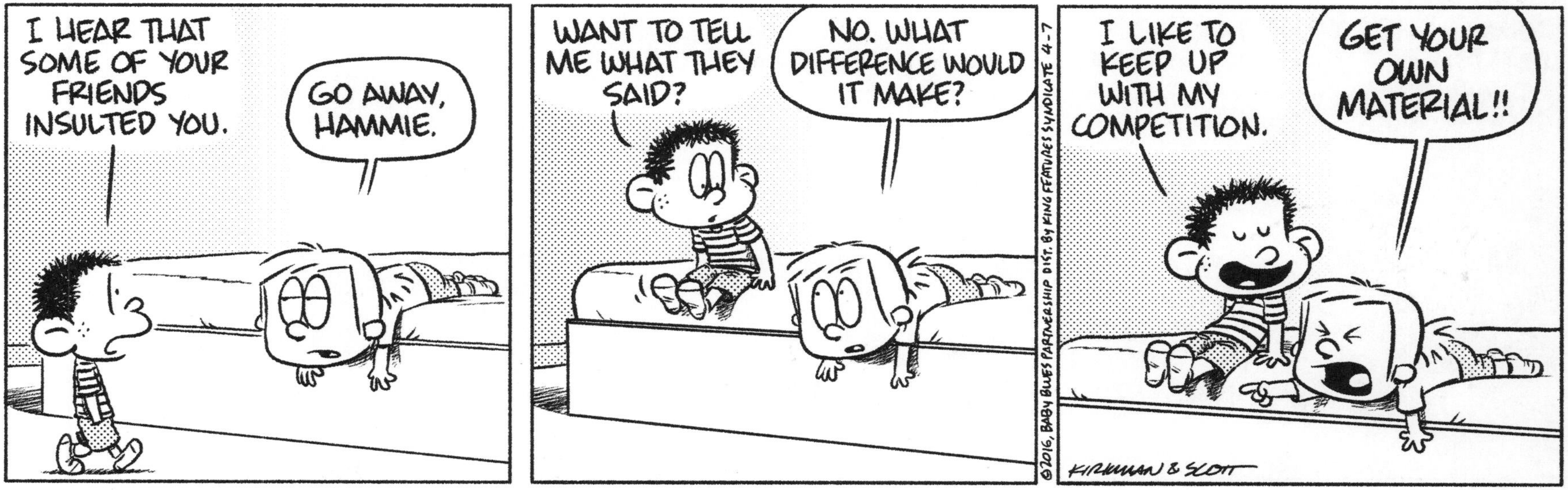
I HEAR THAT SOME OF YOUR FRIENDS INSULTED YOU.
GO AWAY, HAMMIE.
WANT TO TELL ME WHAT THEY SAID?
NO. WHAT DIFFERENCE WOULD IT MAKE?
©2016, BABY BLUES PARTNERSHIP DIST. BY KING FEATURES SYNDICATE 4-7
I LIKE TO KEEP UP WITH MY COMPETITION.
GET YOUR OWN MATERIAL!!
KIRKMAN & SCOTT

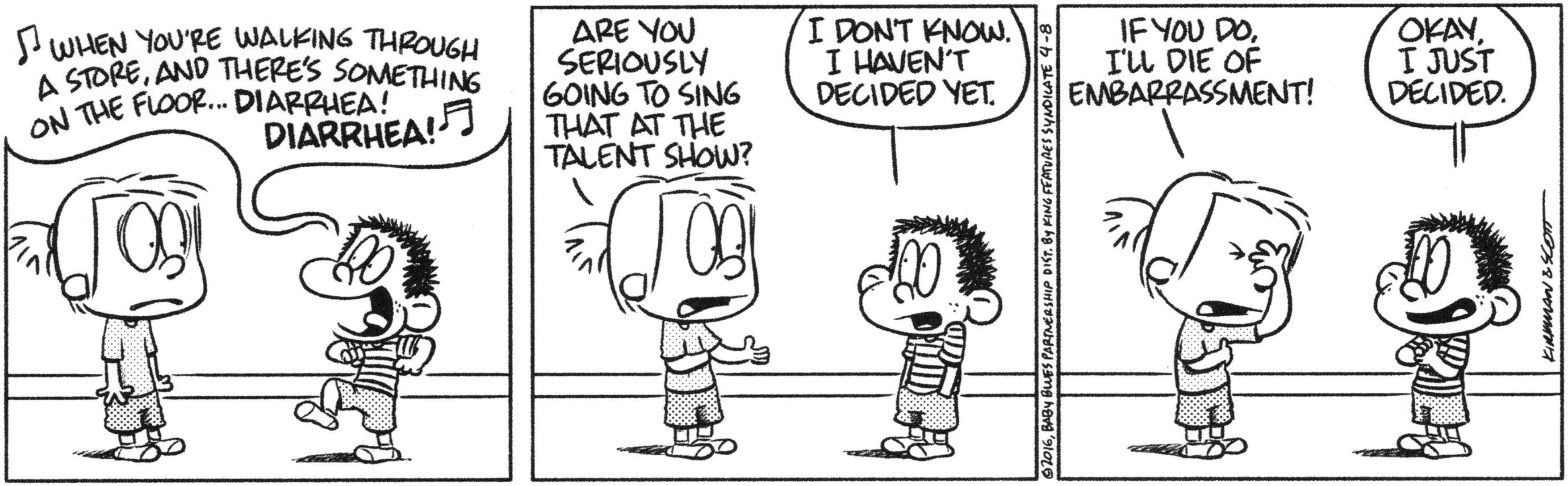
♫ WHEN YOU'RE WALKING THROUGH A STORE, AND THERE'S SOMETHING ON THE FLOOR... DIARRHEA! DIARRHEA! ♫
ARE YOU SERIOUSLY GOING TO SING THAT AT THE TALENT SHOW?
I DON'T KNOW. I HAVEN'T DECIDED YET.
©2016, BABY BLUES PARTNERSHIP DIST. BY KING FEATURES SYNDICATE 4-8
IF YOU DO, I'LL DIE OF EMBARRASSMENT!
OKAY, I JUST DECIDED.
KIRKMAN & SCOTT

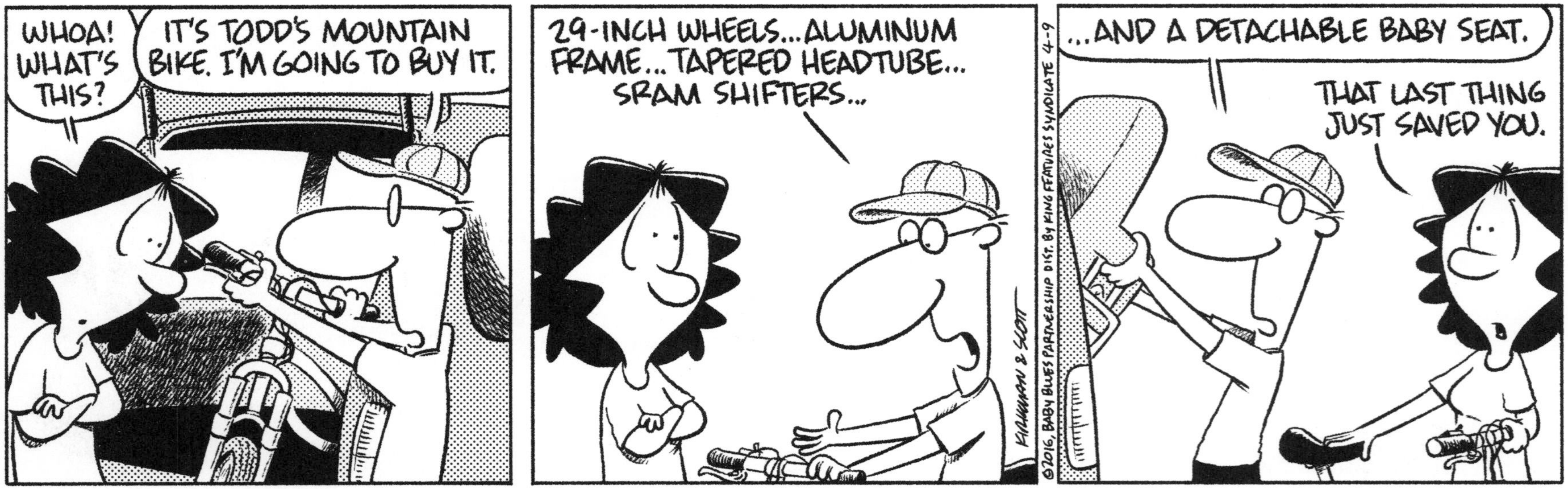
WHOA! WHAT'S THIS?
IT'S TODD'S MOUNTAIN BIKE. I'M GOING TO BUY IT.
29-INCH WHEELS... ALUMINUM FRAME... TAPERED HEADTUBE... SRAM SHIFTERS...
KIRKMAN & SCOTT
©2016, BABY BLUES PARTNERSHIP DIST. BY KING FEATURES SYNDICATE 4-9
...AND A DETACHABLE BABY SEAT.
THAT LAST THING JUST SAVED YOU.

Jerry: Rick HATES to draw bicycles. He almost had to draw this one.

WE GOT A LETTER FROM DAVID AND VIOLAINE.

OH YEAH? WHAT ARE THEY UP TO?

WELL, THEY'VE BEEN TO PARIS TWICE IN THE PAST SIX MONTHS.

THEY'RE STILL COLLECTING ART AND WINE AND HAVE PLANS TO TAKE A COOKING COURSE AT LE CORDON BLEU THIS SUMMER.

WOW.

WHAT SHOULD I WRITE BACK TO THEM?

JUST SAY THAT OUR KIDS ARE ACTIVE AND THAT WE'RE KEEPING OUR HEADS ABOVE WATER AS WE PLUNGE INTO THE FUTURE.

YEAH! AND I'LL PUT "PLUNGE" IN ITALICS.

KIRKMAN & SCOTT 4-10

© 2010 BABY BLUES PARTNERSHIP DIST. BY KING FEATURES SYNDICATE

Rick: David and Violaine are a delightful couple I met at a charity auction for the Wyakin Foundation.
They very generously bought the right to have their names in a *Baby Blues* strip and get the original art.
It's the only strip I've done on paper in over two years. Thanks, David and Violaine!

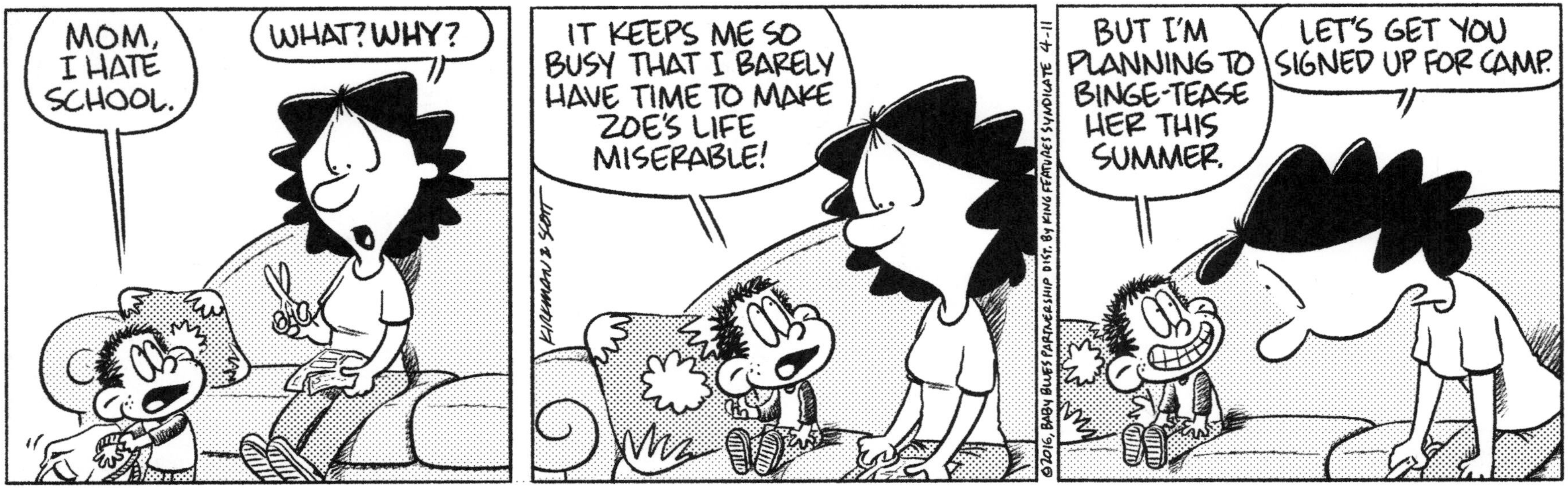
MOM, I HATE SCHOOL.
WHAT? WHY?
IT KEEPS ME SO BUSY THAT I BARELY HAVE TIME TO MAKE ZOE'S LIFE MISERABLE!
KIRKMAN & SCOTT
©2016, BABY BLUES PARTNERSHIP DIST. BY KING FEATURES SYNDICATE 4-11
BUT I'M PLANNING TO BINGE-TEASE HER THIS SUMMER.
LET'S GET YOU SIGNED UP FOR CAMP.

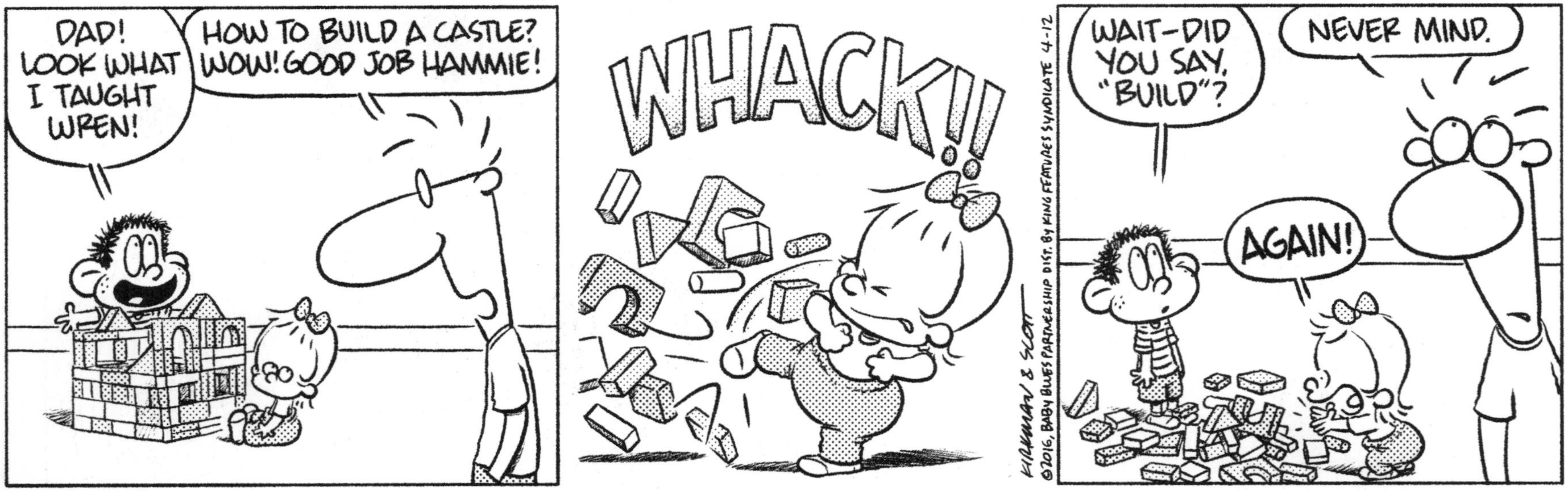
DAD! LOOK WHAT I TAUGHT WREN!
HOW TO BUILD A CASTLE? WOW! GOOD JOB HAMMIE!
WHACK!!
KIRKMAN & SCOTT
©2016, BABY BLUES PARTNERSHIP DIST. BY KING FEATURES SYNDICATE 4-12
WAIT-DID YOU SAY, "BUILD"?
NEVER MIND.
AGAIN!

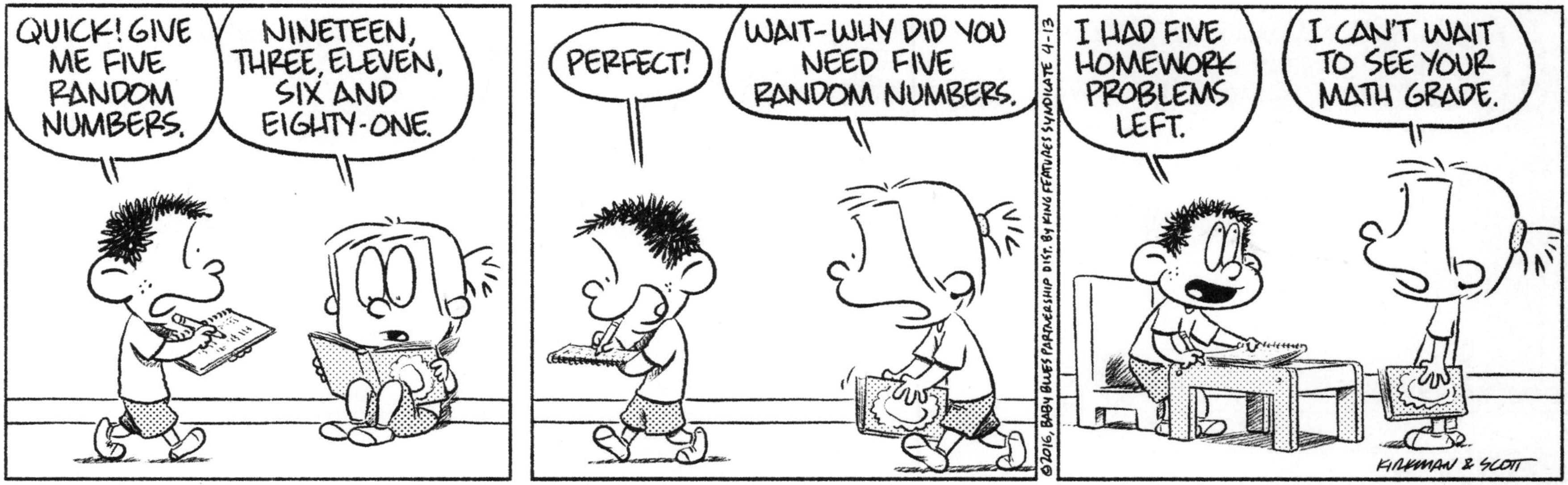
QUICK! GIVE ME FIVE RANDOM NUMBERS.
NINETEEN, THREE, ELEVEN, SIX AND EIGHTY-ONE.
PERFECT!
WAIT- WHY DID YOU NEED FIVE RANDOM NUMBERS.
©2016, BABY BLUES PARTNERSHIP DIST. BY KING FEATURES SYNDICATE 4-13
I HAD FIVE HOMEWORK PROBLEMS LEFT.
I CAN'T WAIT TO SEE YOUR MATH GRADE.
KIRKMAN & SCOTT

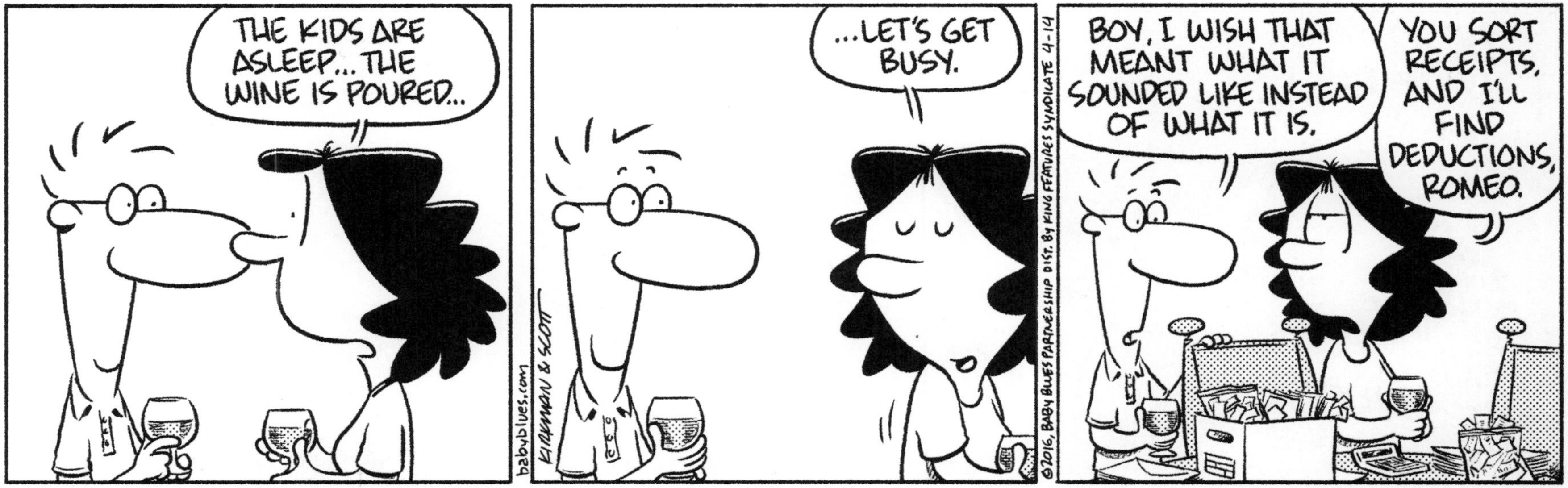
THE KIDS ARE ASLEEP... THE WINE IS POURED...
babyblues.com
KIRKMAN & SCOTT
...LET'S GET BUSY.
©2016, BABY BLUES PARTNERSHIP DIST. BY KING FEATURES SYNDICATE 4-14
BOY, I WISH THAT MEANT WHAT IT SOUNDED LIKE INSTEAD OF WHAT IT IS.
YOU SORT RECEIPTS, AND I'LL FIND DEDUCTIONS, ROMEO.

Jerry: Tax time . . . the most romantic time of the year.

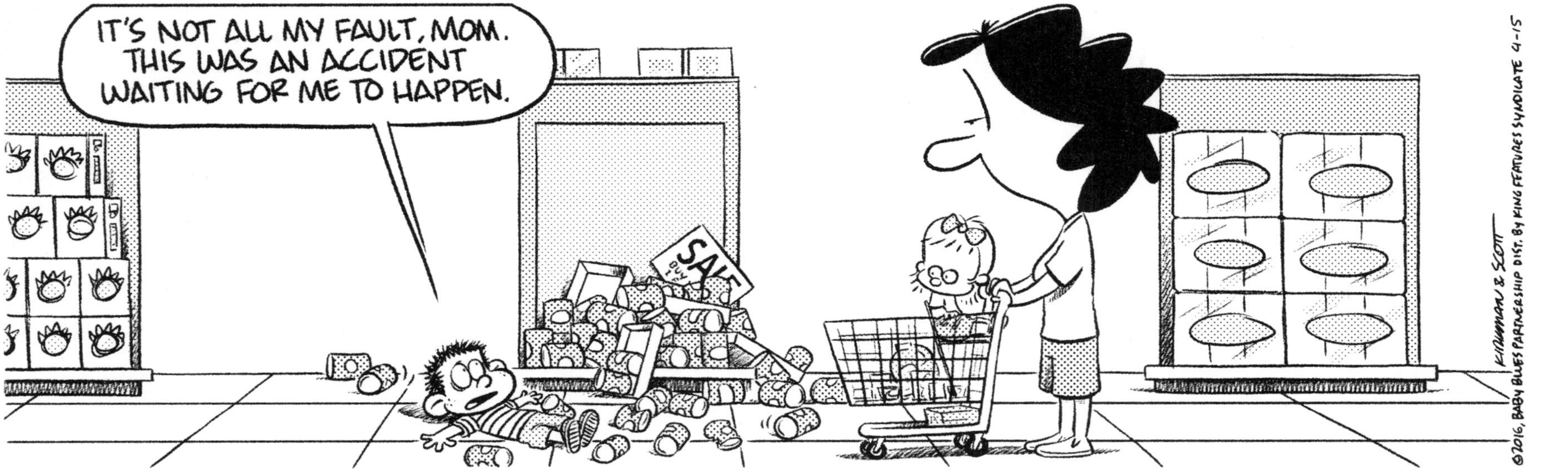
IT'S NOT ALL MY FAULT, MOM. THIS WAS AN ACCIDENT WAITING FOR ME TO HAPPEN.
SALE
KIRKMAN & SCOTT
©2016, BABY BLUES PARTNERSHIP DIST. BY KING FEATURES SYNDICATE 4-15

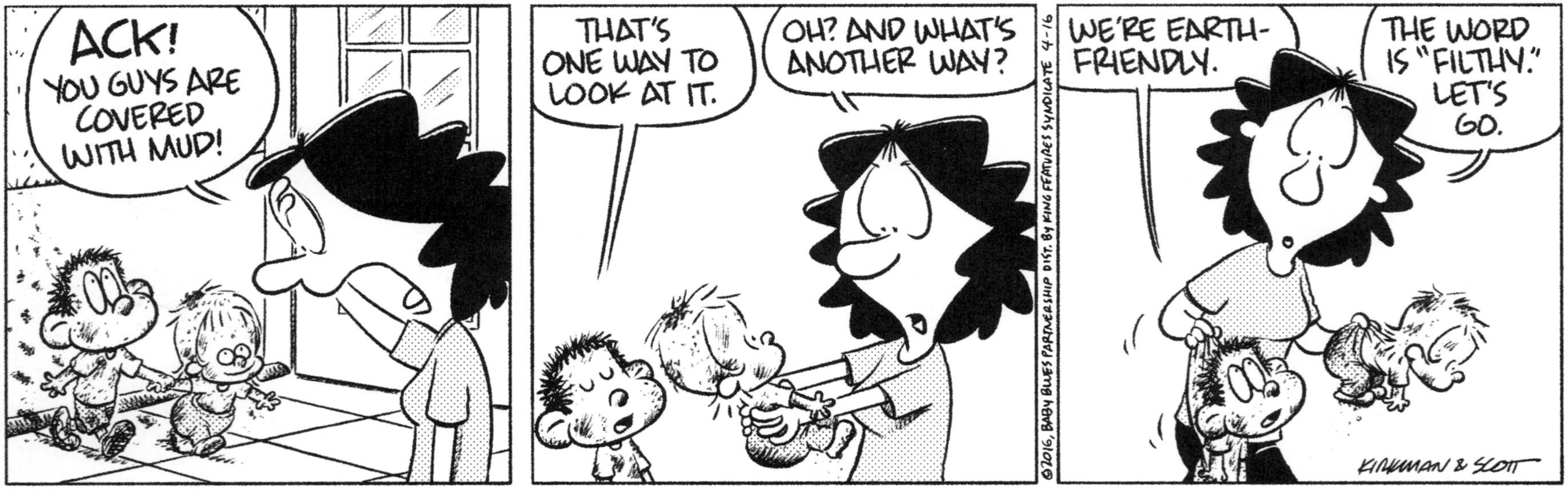
ACK! YOU GUYS ARE COVERED WITH MUD!
THAT'S ONE WAY TO LOOK AT IT.
OH? AND WHAT'S ANOTHER WAY?
©2016, BABY BLUES PARTNERSHIP DIST. BY KING FEATURES SYNDICATE 4-16
WE'RE EARTH-FRIENDLY.
THE WORD IS "FILTHY." LET'S GO.
KIRKMAN & SCOTT

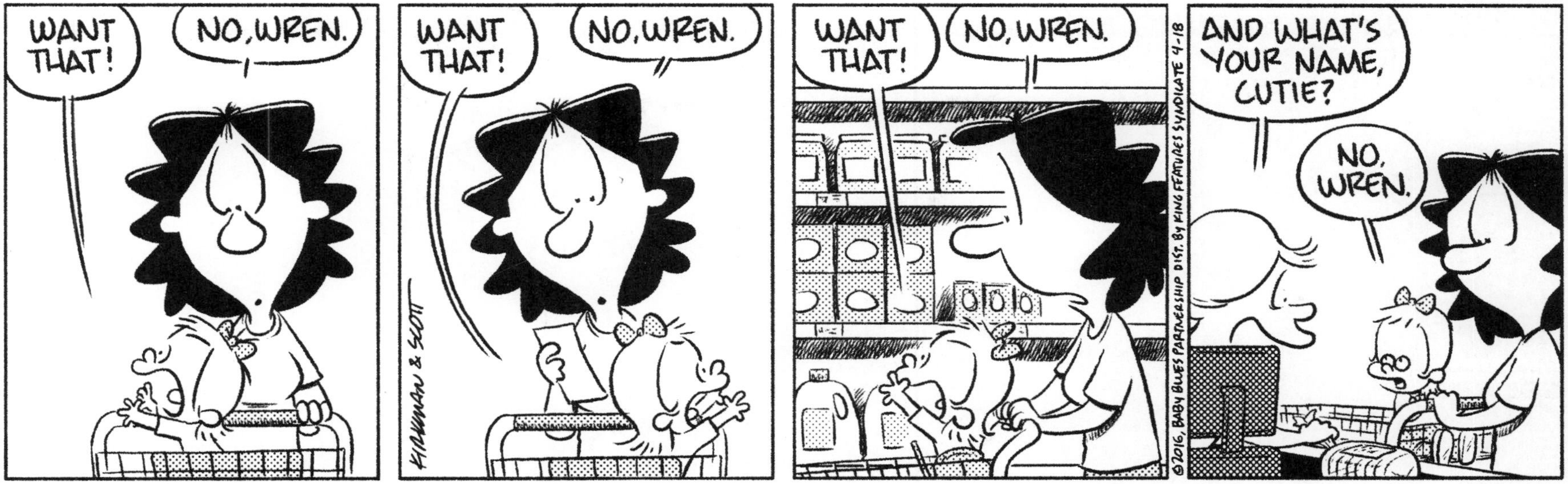
WANT THAT!
NO, WREN.
WANT THAT!
NO, WREN.
KIRKMAN & SCOTT
WANT THAT!
NO, WREN.
©2016, BABY BLUES PARTNERSHIP DIST. BY KING FEATURES SYNDICATE 4-18
AND WHAT'S YOUR NAME, CUTIE?
NO, WREN.

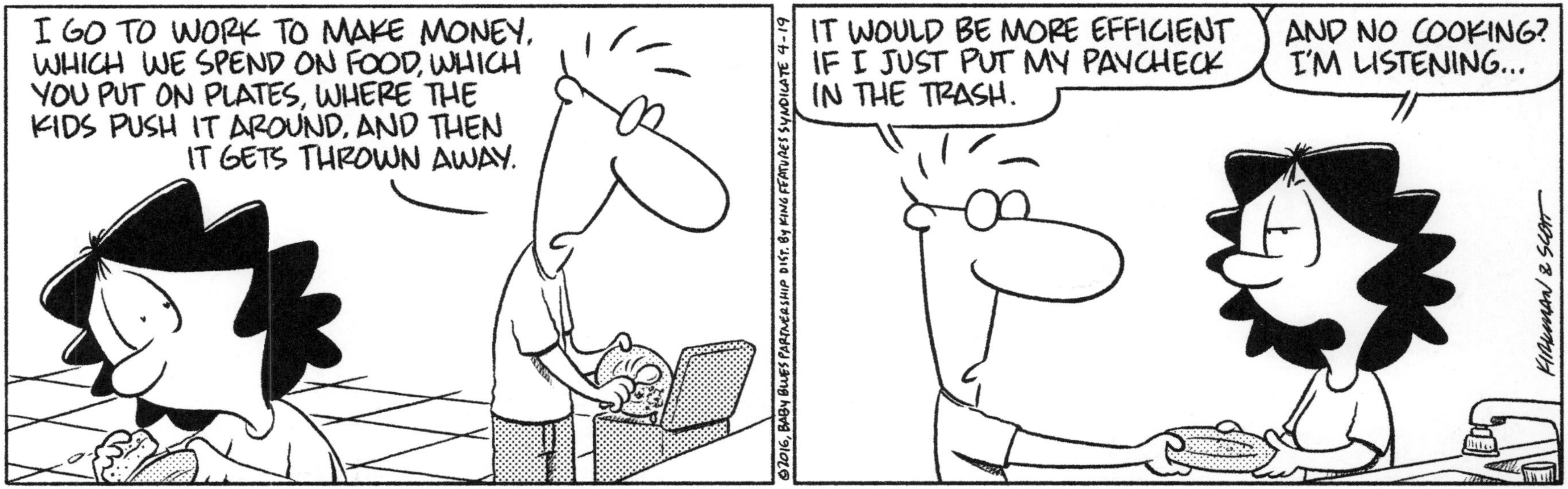
I GO TO WORK TO MAKE MONEY, WHICH WE SPEND ON FOOD, WHICH YOU PUT ON PLATES, WHERE THE KIDS PUSH IT AROUND, AND THEN IT GETS THROWN AWAY.
©2016, BABY BLUES PARTNERSHIP DIST. BY KING FEATURES SYNDICATE 4-19
IT WOULD BE MORE EFFICIENT IF I JUST PUT MY PAYCHECK IN THE TRASH.
AND NO COOKING? I'M LISTENING...
KIRKMAN & SCOTT

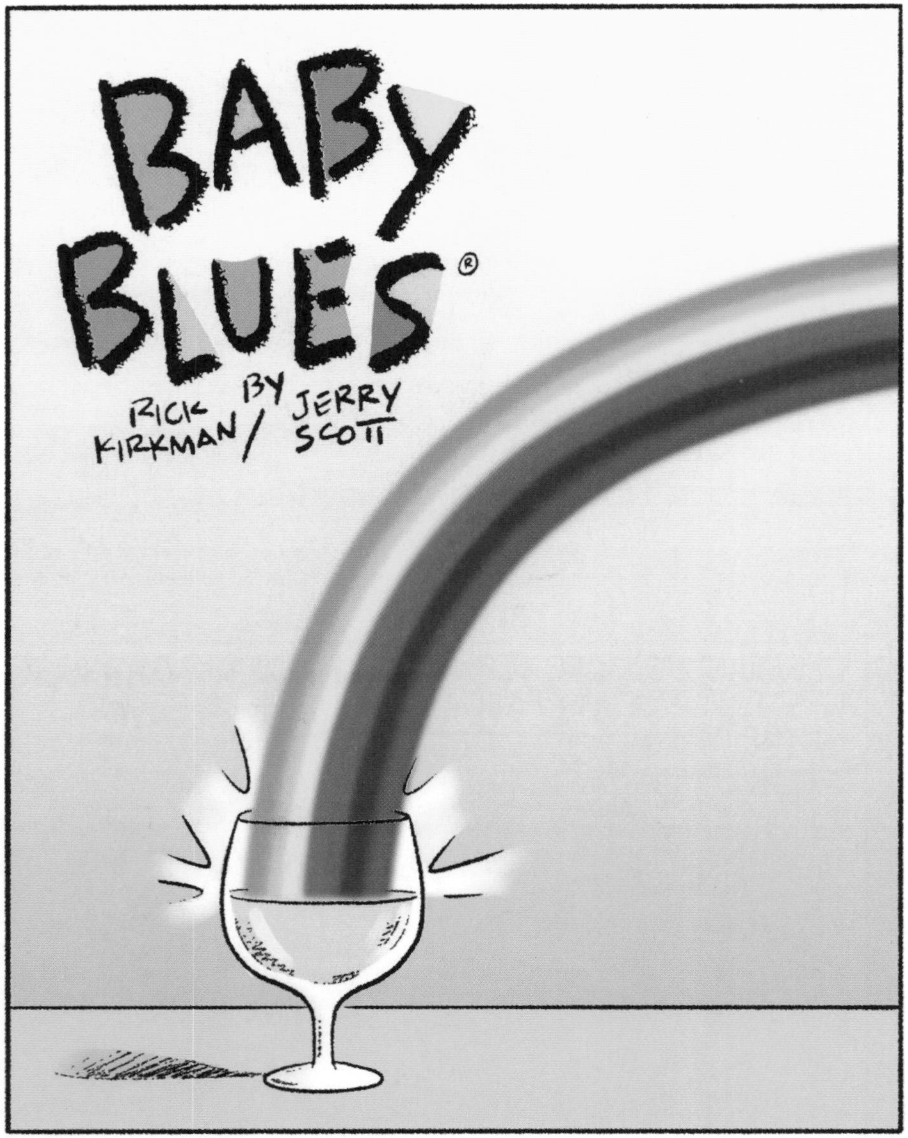
BABY BLUES®
BY
RICK KIRKMAN / JERRY SCOTT

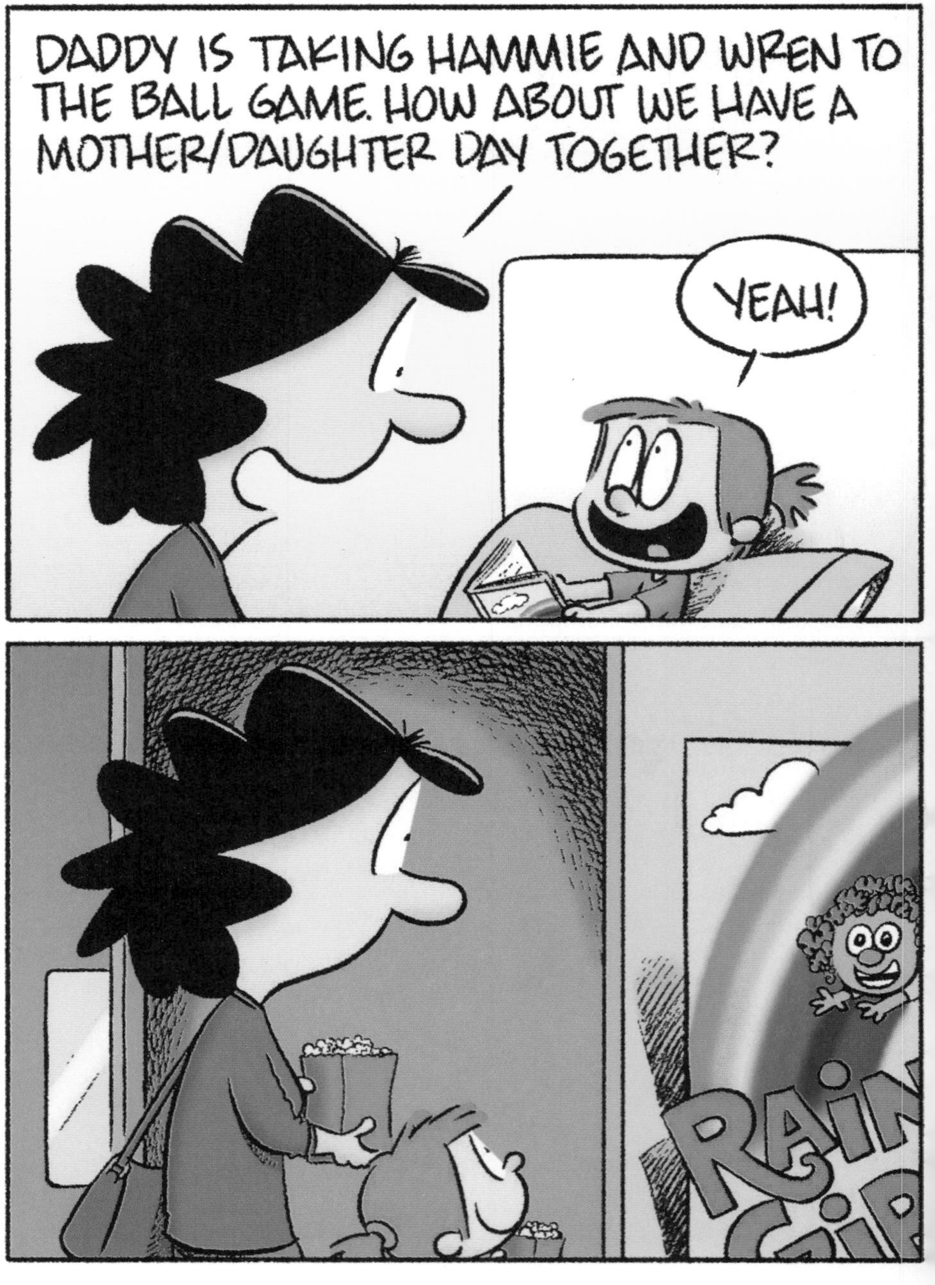
DADDY IS TAKING HAMMIE AND WREN TO THE BALL GAME. HOW ABOUT WE HAVE A MOTHER/DAUGHTER DAY TOGETHER?
YEAH!

Rick: I'm with Wanda after having to figure out a way to do so many rainbows on the computer.

Jerry: My younger daughter went through a rainbow phase for a while. I drew the line at rainbow toilet paper.

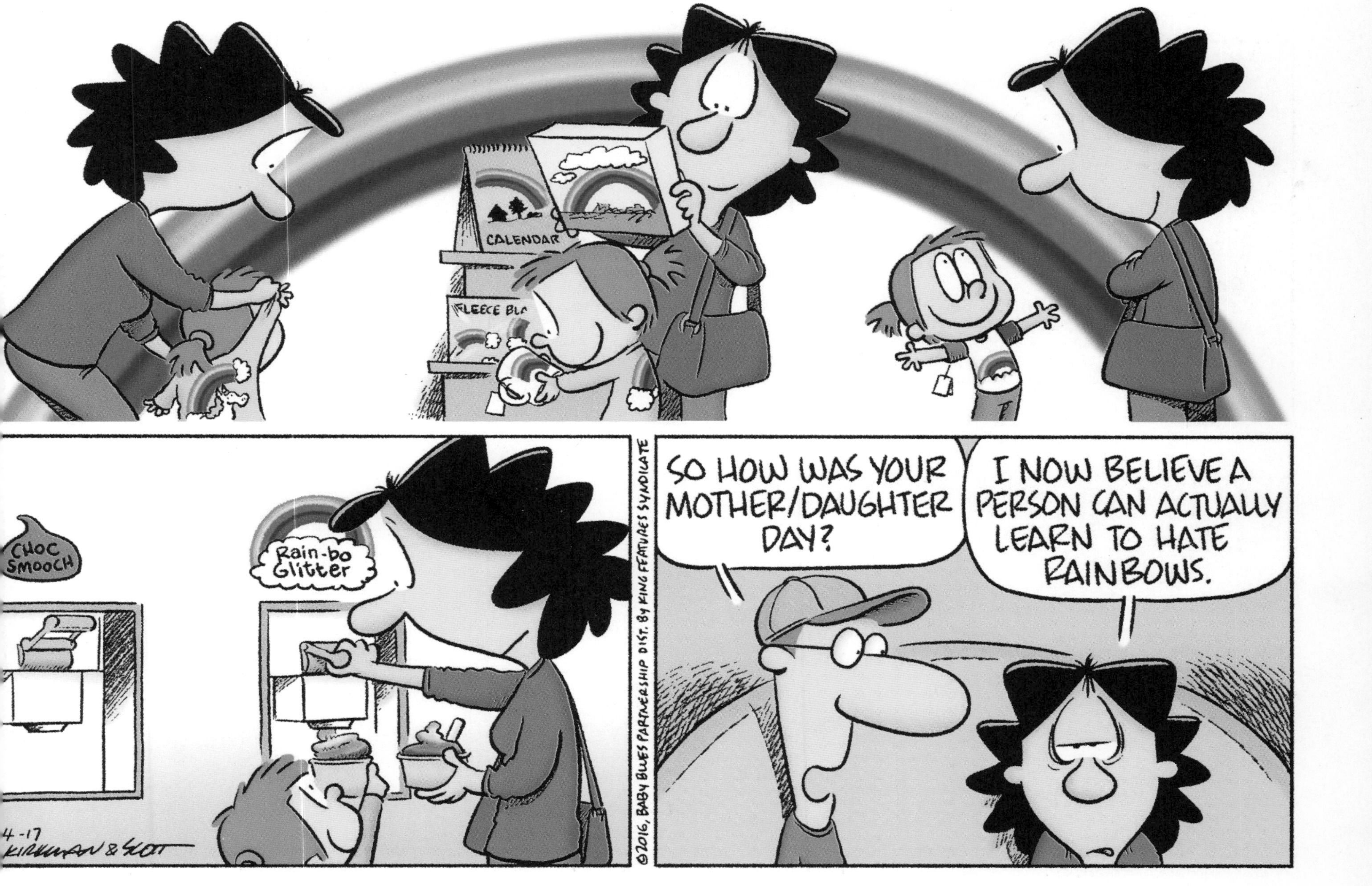
CALENDAR
FLEECE
CHOC SMOOCH
Rain-bo Glitter
4-17 KIRKMAN & SCOTT
©2016, BABY BLUES PARTNERSHIP DIST. BY KING FEATURES SYNDICATE
SO HOW WAS YOUR MOTHER/DAUGHTER DAY?
I NOW BELIEVE A PERSON CAN ACTUALLY LEARN TO HATE RAINBOWS.

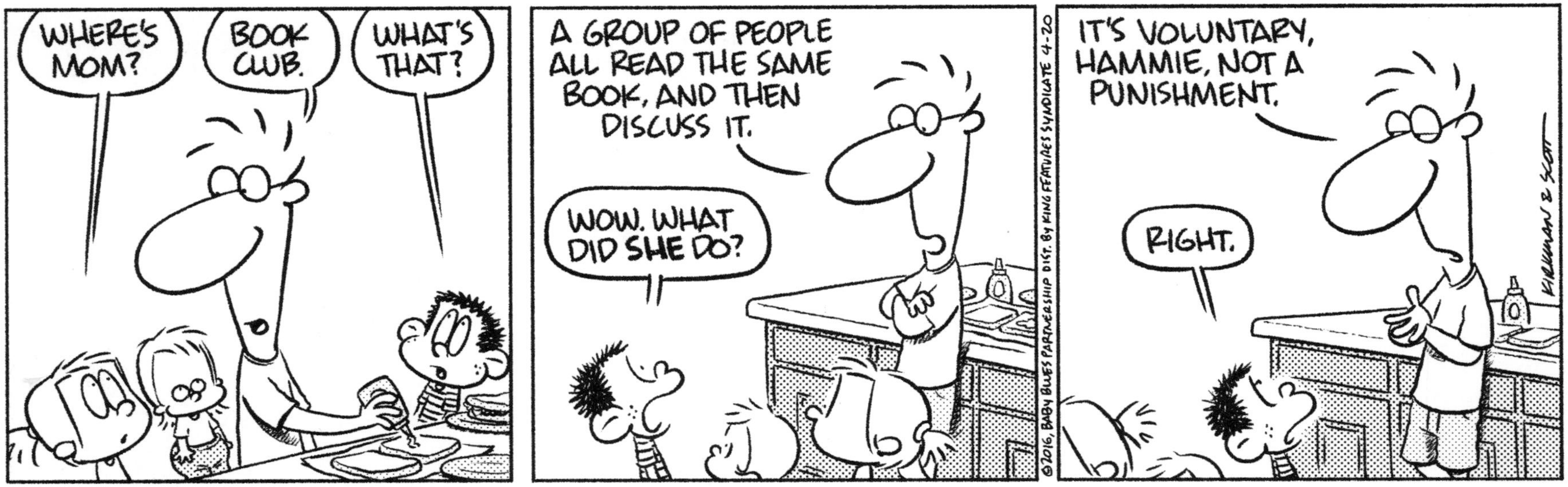
WHERE'S MOM?
BOOK CLUB.
WHAT'S THAT?
A GROUP OF PEOPLE ALL READ THE SAME BOOK, AND THEN DISCUSS IT.
WOW. WHAT DID SHE DO?
©2016, BABY BLUES PARTNERSHIP DIST. BY KING FEATURES SYNDICATE 4-20
IT'S VOLUNTARY, HAMMIE, NOT A PUNISHMENT.
RIGHT.
KIRKMAN & SCOTT

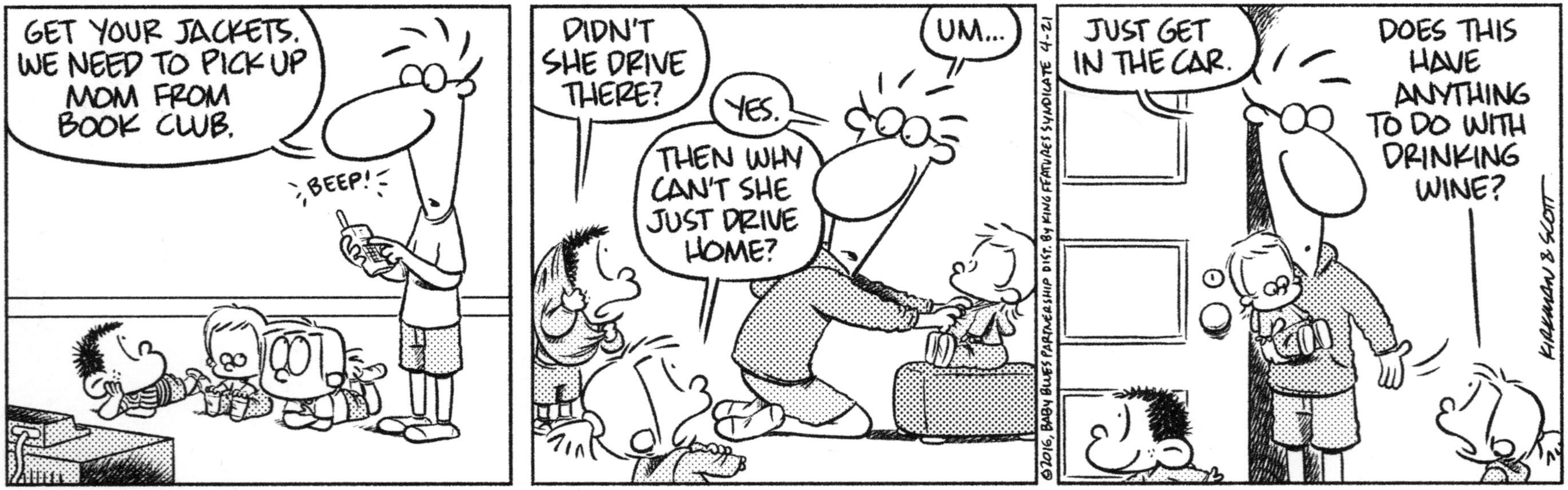
GET YOUR JACKETS. WE NEED TO PICK UP MOM FROM BOOK CLUB.
BEEP!
DIDN'T SHE DRIVE THERE?
YES.
UM...
THEN WHY CAN'T SHE JUST DRIVE HOME?
©2016, BABY BLUES PARTNERSHIP DIST. BY KING FEATURES SYNDICATE 4-21
JUST GET IN THE CAR.
DOES THIS HAVE ANYTHING TO DO WITH DRINKING WINE?
KIRKMAN & SCOTT

Jerry: This series upset a few people because Wanda drank a little too much wine at a book club meeting. Some folks sure take their comic strips seriously.

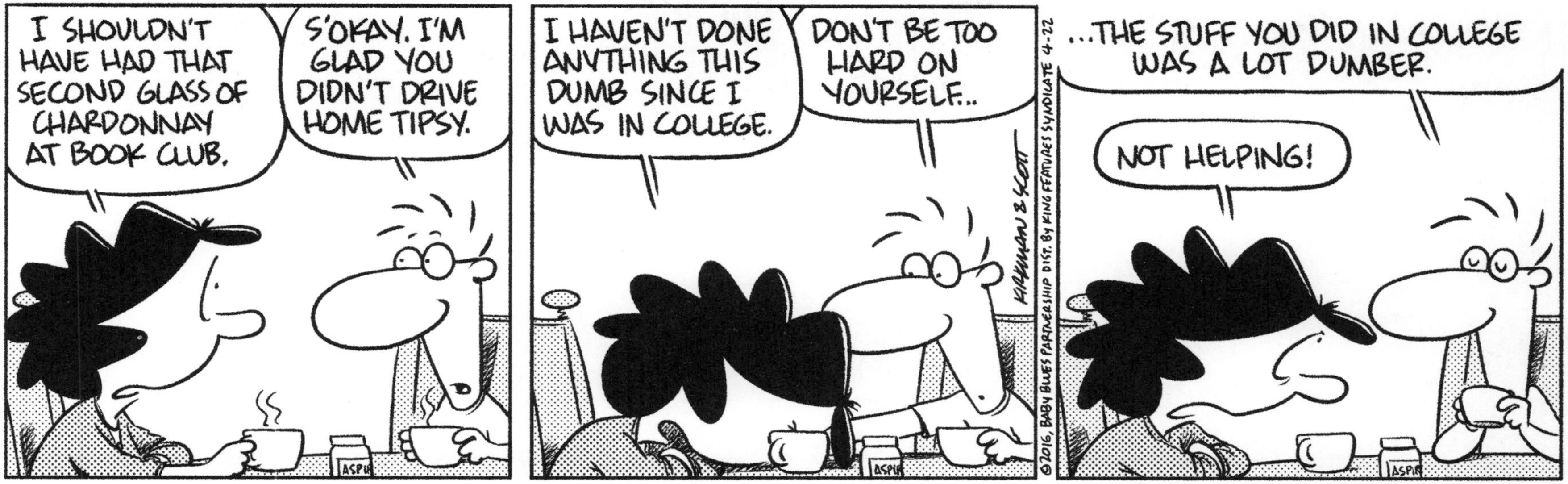
I SHOULDN'T HAVE HAD THAT SECOND GLASS OF CHARDONNAY AT BOOK CLUB.
S'OKAY. I'M GLAD YOU DIDN'T DRIVE HOME TIPSY.
I HAVEN'T DONE ANYTHING THIS DUMB SINCE I WAS IN COLLEGE.
DON'T BE TOO HARD ON YOURSELF...
...THE STUFF YOU DID IN COLLEGE WAS A LOT DUMBER.
NOT HELPING!
KIRKMAN & SCOTT
©2016, BABY BLUES PARTNERSHIP DIST. BY KING FEATURES SYNDICATE 4-22

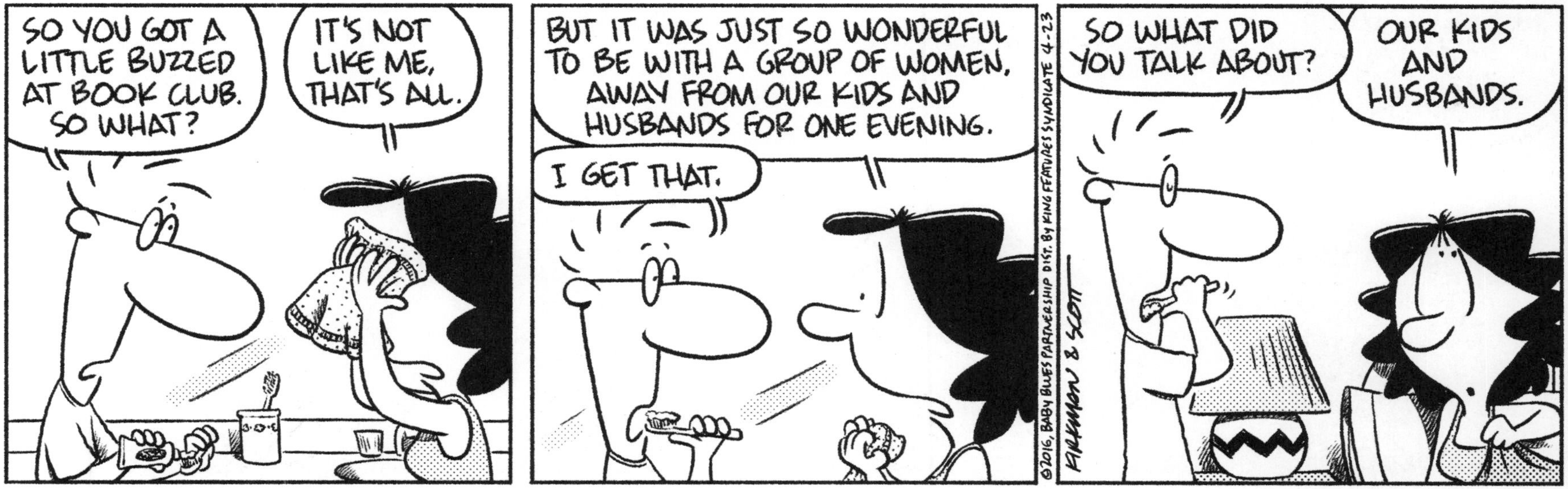
SO YOU GOT A LITTLE BUZZED AT BOOK CLUB. SO WHAT?
IT'S NOT LIKE ME, THAT'S ALL.
BUT IT WAS JUST SO WONDERFUL TO BE WITH A GROUP OF WOMEN, AWAY FROM OUR KIDS AND HUSBANDS FOR ONE EVENING.
I GET THAT.
SO WHAT DID YOU TALK ABOUT?
OUR KIDS AND HUSBANDS.
KIRKMAN & SCOTT
©2016, BABY BLUES PARTNERSHIP DIST. BY KING FEATURES SYNDICATE 4-23

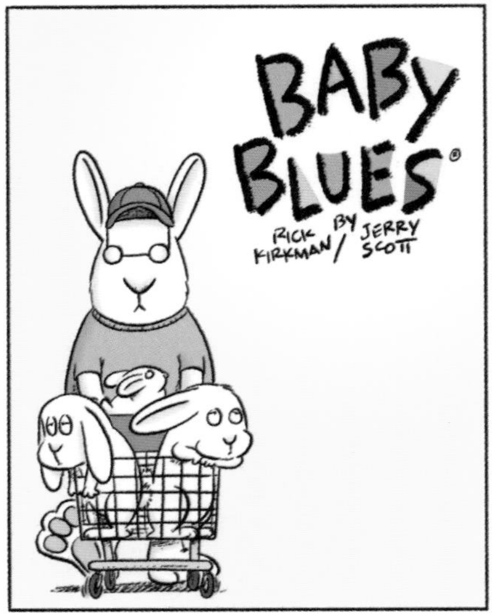
BABY BLUES®
BY RICK KIRKMAN / JERRY SCOTT

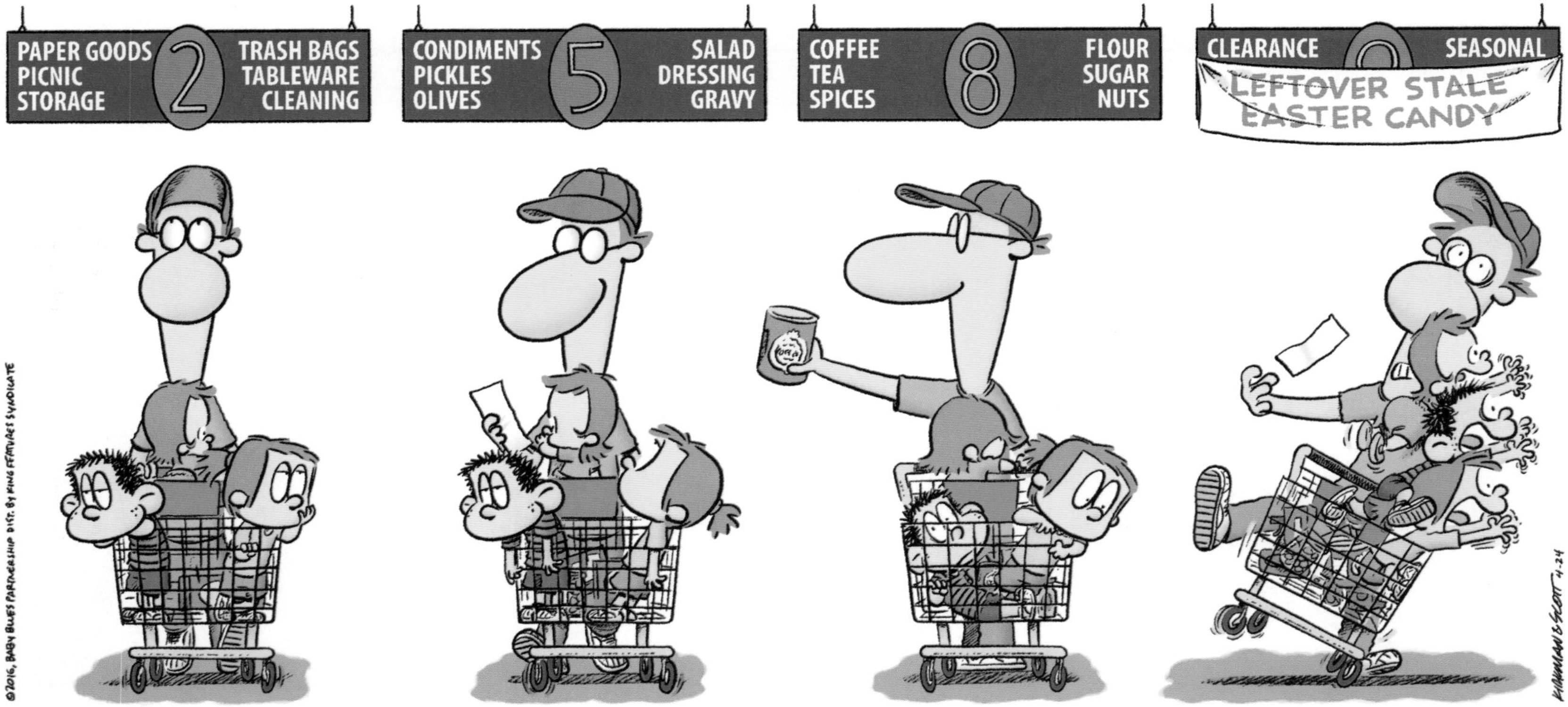
PAPER GOODS PICNIC STORAGE 2 TRASH BAGS TABLEWARE CLEANING
CONDIMENTS PICKLES OLIVES 5 SALAD DRESSING GRAVY
COFFEE TEA SPICES 8 FLOUR SUGAR NUTS
CLEARANCE SEASONAL
LEFTOVER STALE EASTER CANDY
©2016, BABY BLUES PARTNERSHIP DIST. BY KING FEATURES SYNDICATE
KIRKMAN & SCOTT 4-24

Rick: This gag posed the challenge of getting across Jerry's gag without cluttering the background with tons of store junk. Reducing it down to its barest elements kept the focus on the kids in the cart so the last panel had more impact.

Jerry: Some of my favorite strips are wordless. Nicely drawn, Rick!

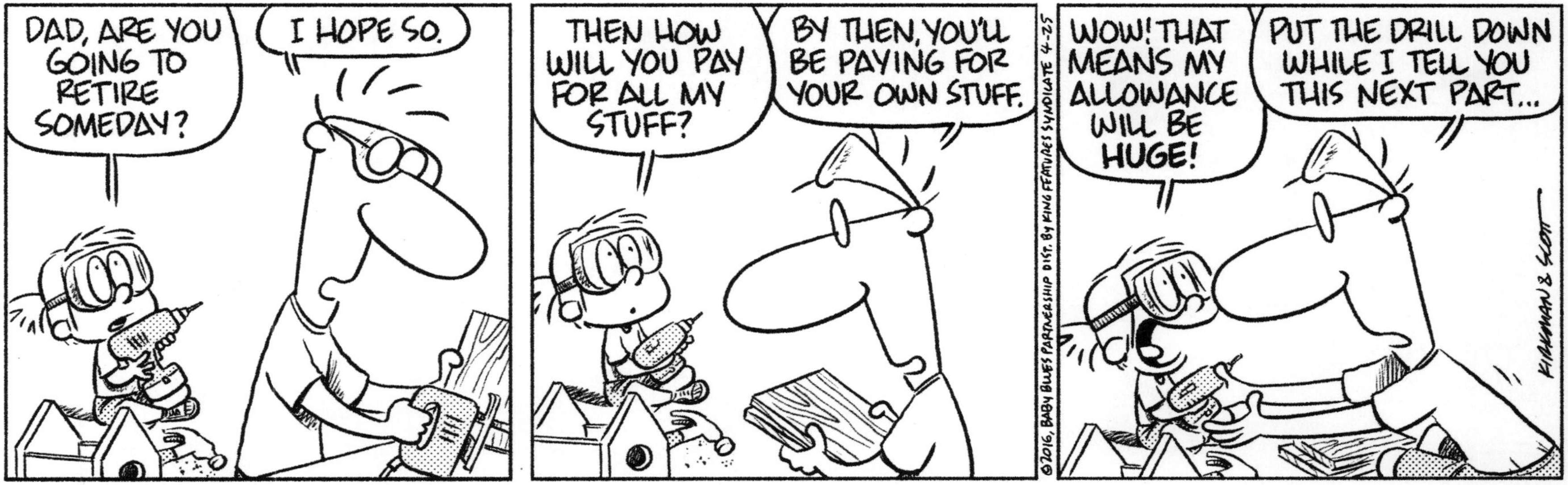
DAD, ARE YOU GOING TO RETIRE SOMEDAY?
I HOPE SO.
THEN HOW WILL YOU PAY FOR ALL MY STUFF?
BY THEN, YOU'LL BE PAYING FOR YOUR OWN STUFF.
©2016, BABY BLUES PARTNERSHIP DIST. BY KING FEATURES SYNDICATE 4-25
WOW! THAT MEANS MY ALLOWANCE WILL BE HUGE!
PUT THE DRILL DOWN WHILE I TELL YOU THIS NEXT PART...
KIRKMAN & SCOTT

Jerry: Right. Never explain economics to a person holding power tools.

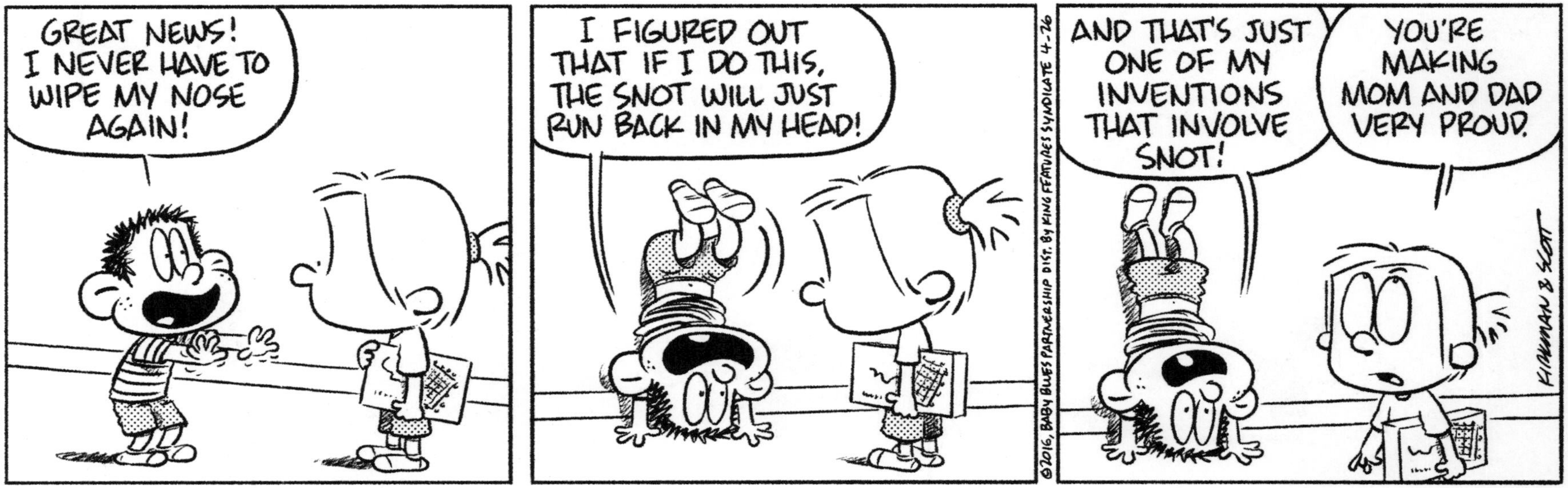
GREAT NEWS! I NEVER HAVE TO WIPE MY NOSE AGAIN!
I FIGURED OUT THAT IF I DO THIS, THE SNOT WILL JUST RUN BACK IN MY HEAD!
©2016, BABY BLUES PARTNERSHIP DIST. BY KING FEATURES SYNDICATE 4-26
AND THAT'S JUST ONE OF MY INVENTIONS THAT INVOLVE SNOT!
YOU'RE MAKING MOM AND DAD VERY PROUD.
KIRKMAN & SCOTT

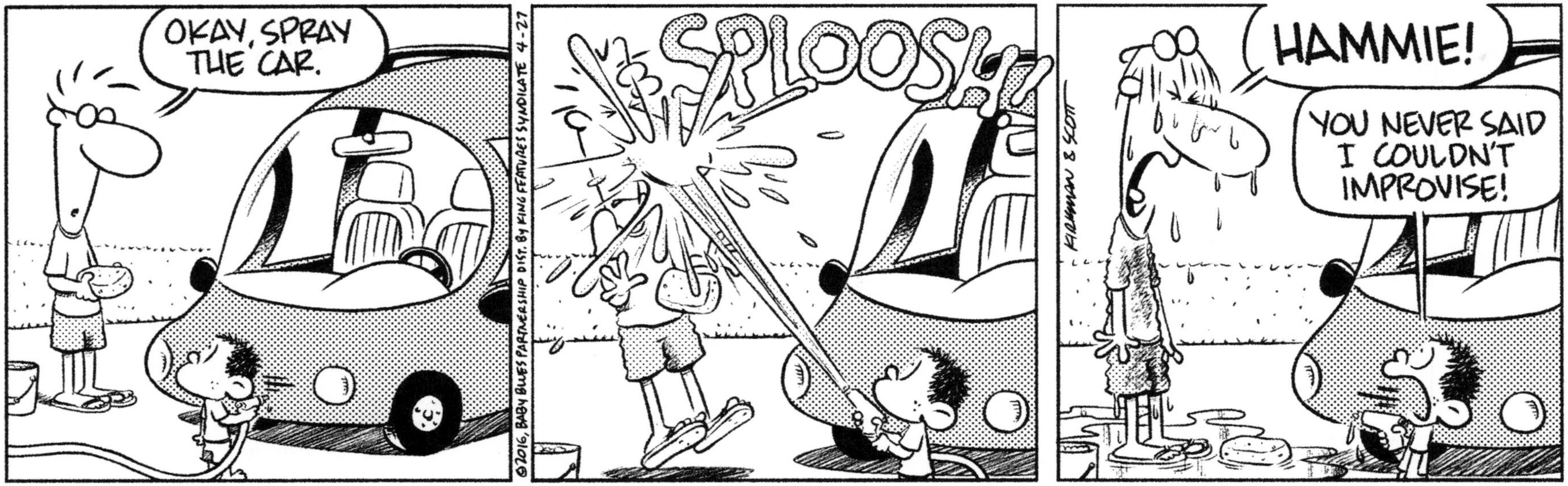
OKAY, SPRAY THE CAR.
©2016, BABY BLUES PARTNERSHIP DIST. BY KING FEATURES SYNDICATE 4-27
SPLOOSH!!
KIRKMAN & SCOTT
HAMMIE!
YOU NEVER SAID I COULDN'T IMPROVISE!

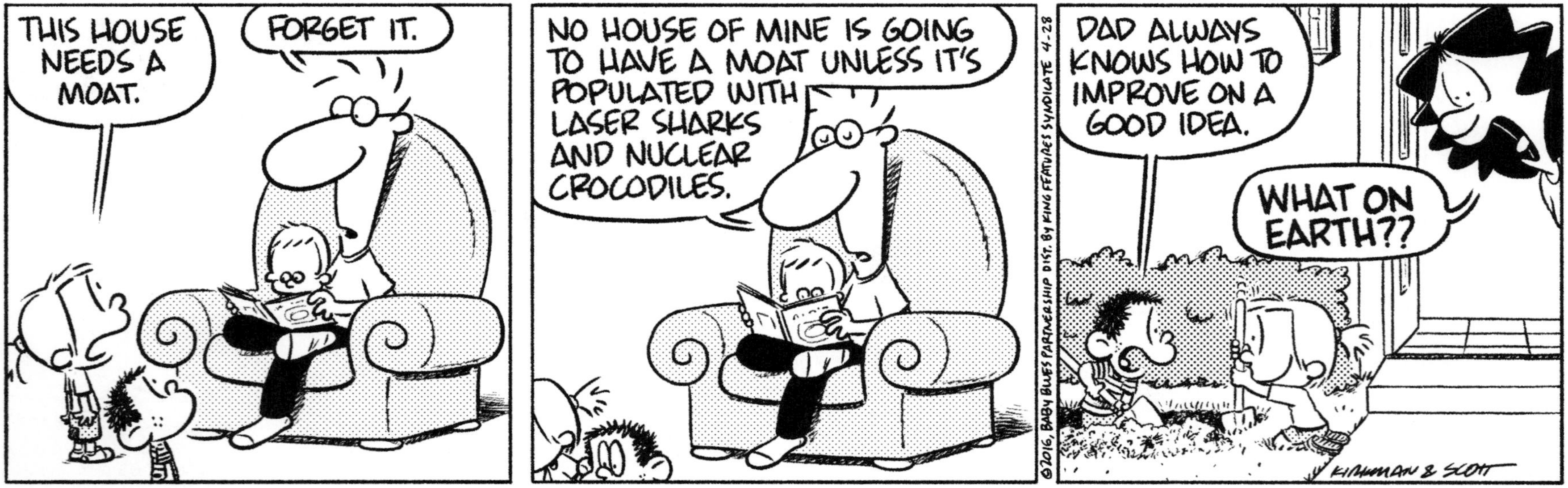
THIS HOUSE NEEDS A MOAT.
FORGET IT.
NO HOUSE OF MINE IS GOING TO HAVE A MOAT UNLESS IT'S POPULATED WITH LASER SHARKS AND NUCLEAR CROCODILES.
©2016, BABY BLUES PARTNERSHIP DIST. BY KING FEATURES SYNDICATE 4-28
DAD ALWAYS KNOWS HOW TO IMPROVE ON A GOOD IDEA.
WHAT ON EARTH??
KIRKMAN & SCOTT

Jerry: This should be standard moat policy, if you ask me.

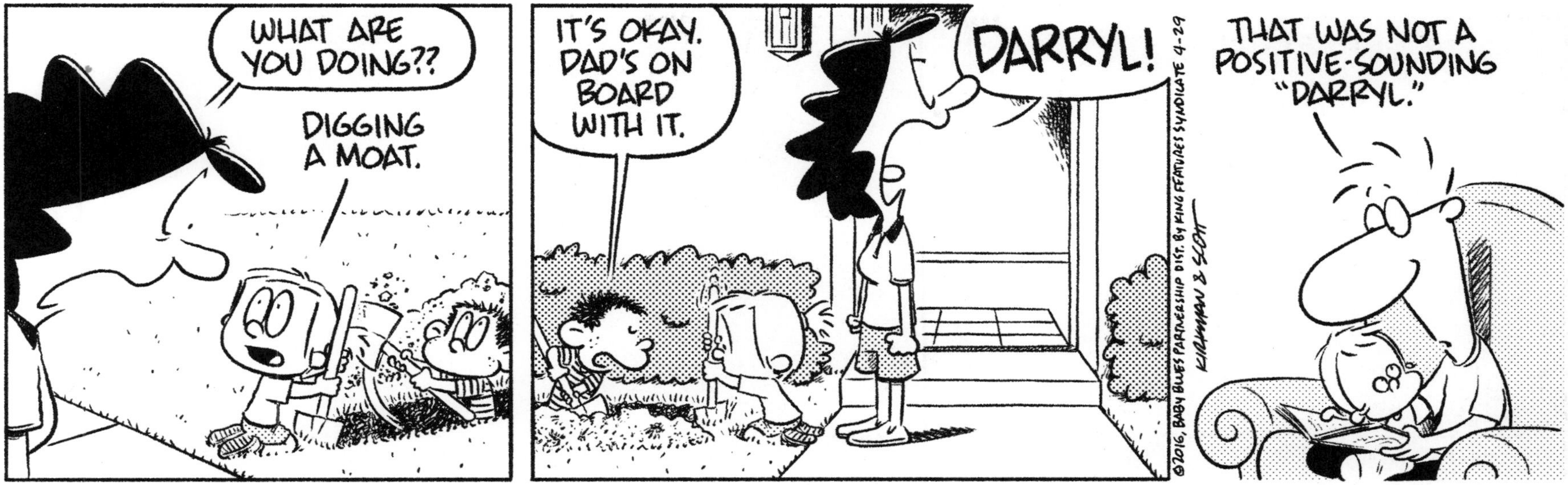
WHAT ARE YOU DOING??
DIGGING A MOAT.
IT'S OKAY. DAD'S ON BOARD WITH IT.
DARRYL!
THAT WAS NOT A POSITIVE-SOUNDING "DARRYL."
©2016, BABY BLUES PARTNERSHIP DIST. BY KING FEATURES SYNDICATE 4-29
KIRKMAN & SCOTT

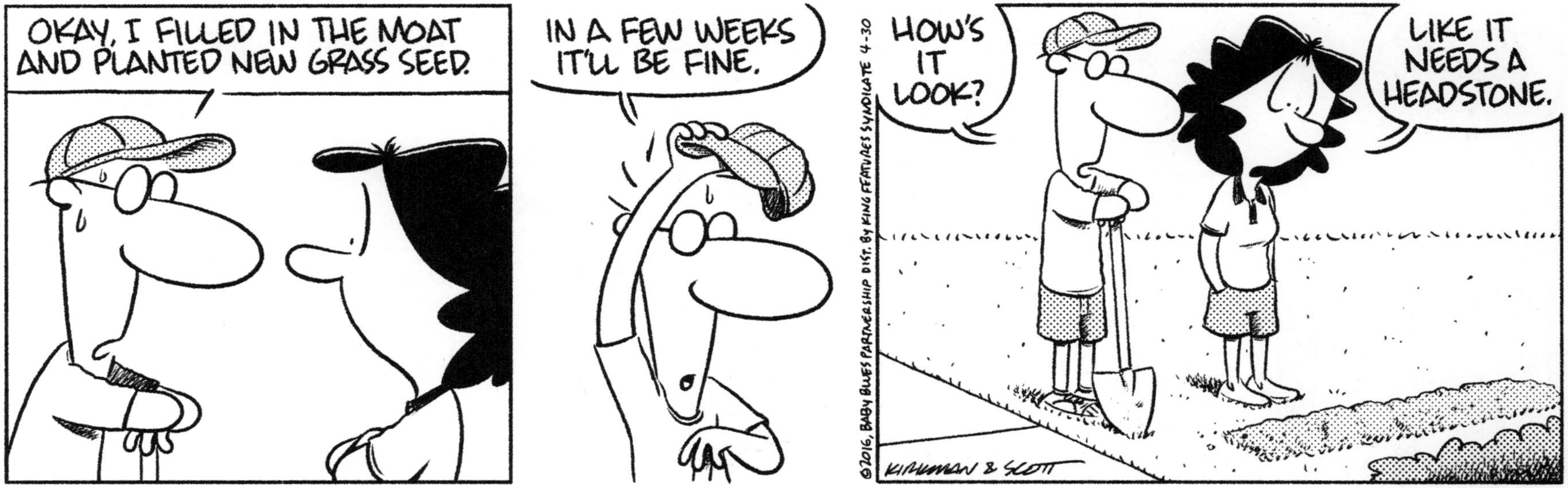
OKAY, I FILLED IN THE MOAT AND PLANTED NEW GRASS SEED.
IN A FEW WEEKS IT'LL BE FINE.
HOW'S IT LOOK?
LIKE IT NEEDS A HEADSTONE.
©2016, BABY BLUES PARTNERSHIP DIST. BY KING FEATURES SYNDICATE 4-30
KIRKMAN & SCOTT

PBBTH! PBBTH!
BLAAT!
BOSS
BABY BLUES
HEY HAMMIE! WANT TO PLAY M—
MOOLAH $TREET
NOT NOW, I HAVE TO PRACTICE.
PRACTICE WHAT?
SKILLS.
SKILLS?
YEAH. DAD SAYS THAT THE TALENTS I DEVELOP NOW WILL HELP ME IN THE FUTURE, WHEN I START COMPETING FOR JOBS.
©2016, BABY BLUES PARTNERSHIP DIST. BY KING FEATURES SYNDICATE
FOOP! BLAT! PPBBTH! PBBTH! PBBTH!
WHAT'S THAT SOUND?
HAMMIE IS IN THERE WORKING ON HIS RÉSUMÉ.

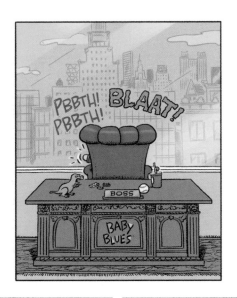

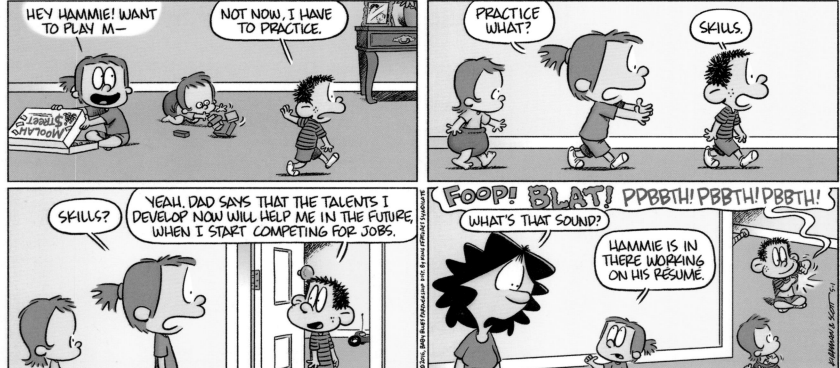

Rick: I don't know, that title panel art might be a little too subtle with just that tiny part of Hammie's arm sticking out. Did you even notice?

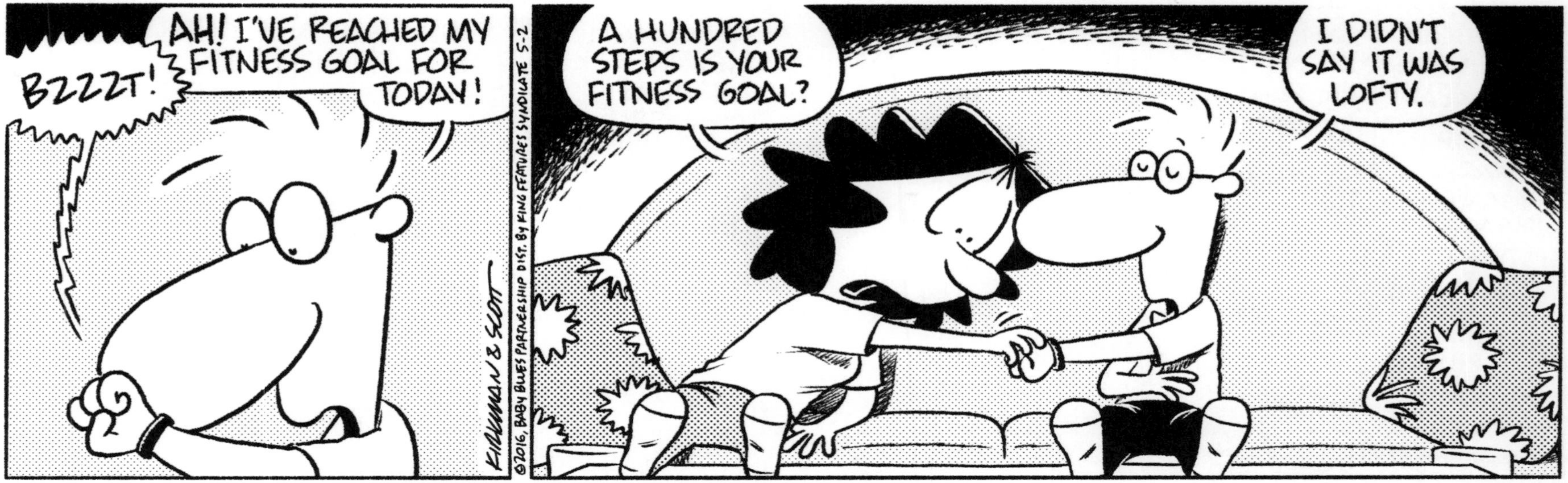
BZZZT!
AH! I'VE REACHED MY FITNESS GOAL FOR TODAY!
KIRKMAN & SCOTT
©2016, BABY BLUES PARTNERSHIP DIST. BY KING FEATURES SYNDICATE 5-2
A HUNDRED STEPS IS YOUR FITNESS GOAL?
I DIDN'T SAY IT WAS LOFTY.

Jerry: I stopped wearing a Fitbit when it started showing negative numbers.

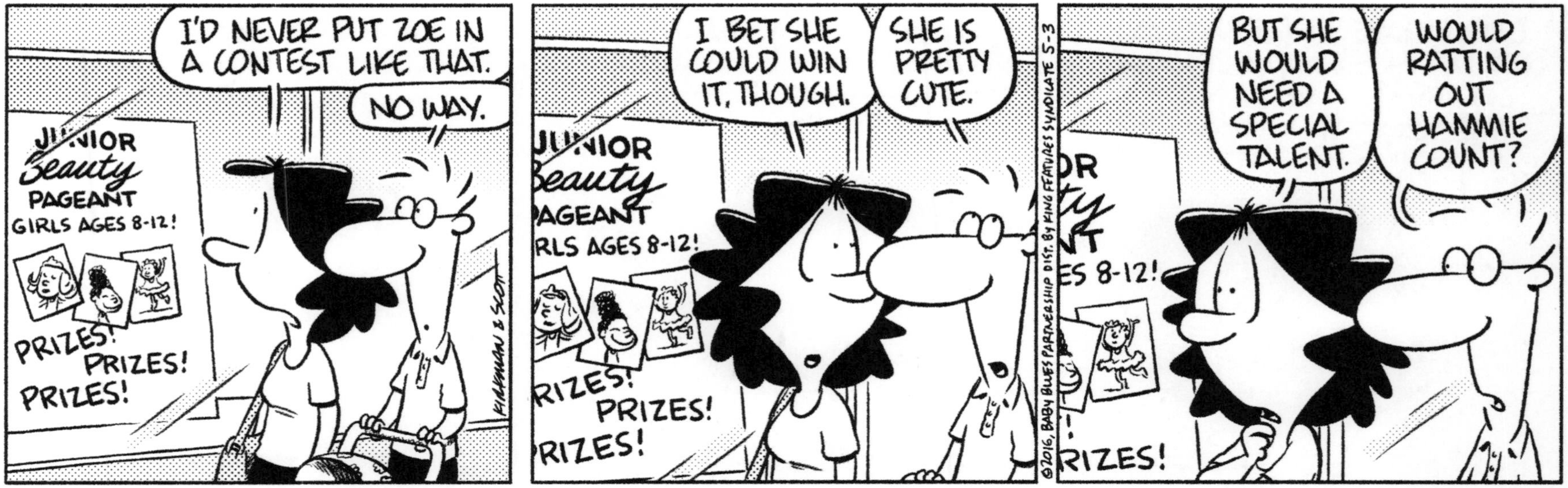
JUNIOR Beauty PAGEANT GIRLS AGES 8-12! PRIZES! PRIZES! PRIZES!
I'D NEVER PUT ZOE IN A CONTEST LIKE THAT.
NO WAY.
KIRKMAN & SCOTT
I BET SHE COULD WIN IT, THOUGH.
SHE IS PRETTY CUTE.
©2016, BABY BLUES PARTNERSHIP DIST. BY KING FEATURES SYNDICATE 5-3
BUT SHE WOULD NEED A SPECIAL TALENT.
WOULD RATTING OUT HAMMIE COUNT?

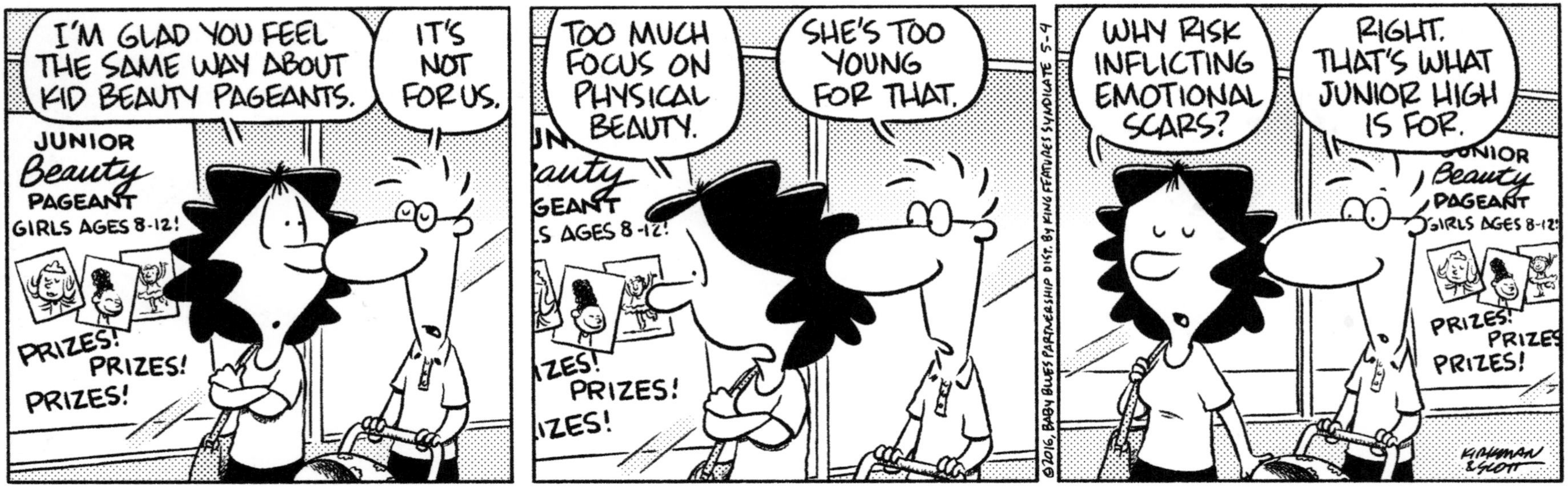
I'M GLAD YOU FEEL THE SAME WAY ABOUT KID BEAUTY PAGEANTS.
IT'S NOT FOR US.
JUNIOR Beauty PAGEANT GIRLS AGES 8-12!
PRIZES! PRIZES! PRIZES!
TOO MUCH FOCUS ON PHYSICAL BEAUTY.
SHE'S TOO YOUNG FOR THAT.
©2016, BABY BLUES PARTNERSHIP DIST. BY KING FEATURES SYNDICATE 5-4
WHY RISK INFLICTING EMOTIONAL SCARS?
RIGHT. THAT'S WHAT JUNIOR HIGH IS FOR.
KIRKMAN & SCOTT

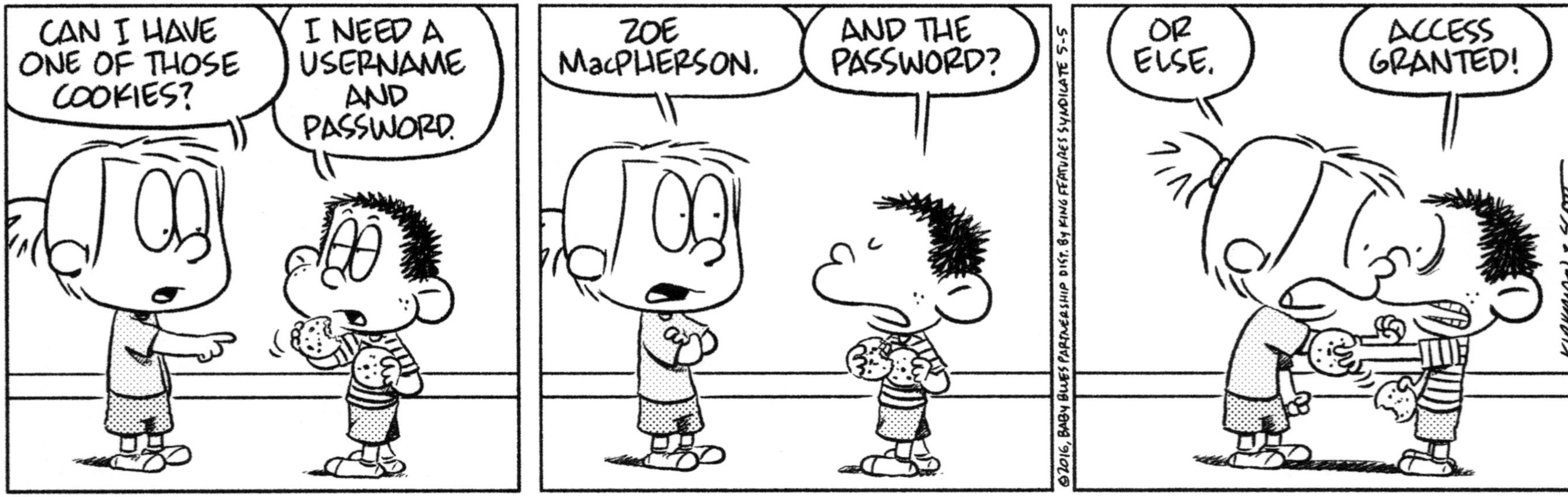
CAN I HAVE ONE OF THOSE COOKIES?
I NEED A USERNAME AND PASSWORD.
ZOE MacPHERSON.
AND THE PASSWORD?
©2016, BABY BLUES PARTNERSHIP DIST. BY KING FEATURES SYNDICATE 5-5
OR ELSE.
ACCESS GRANTED!
KIRKMAN & SCOTT

Rick: At least it wasn't PASSWORD. **Jerry:** Easy password to remember.

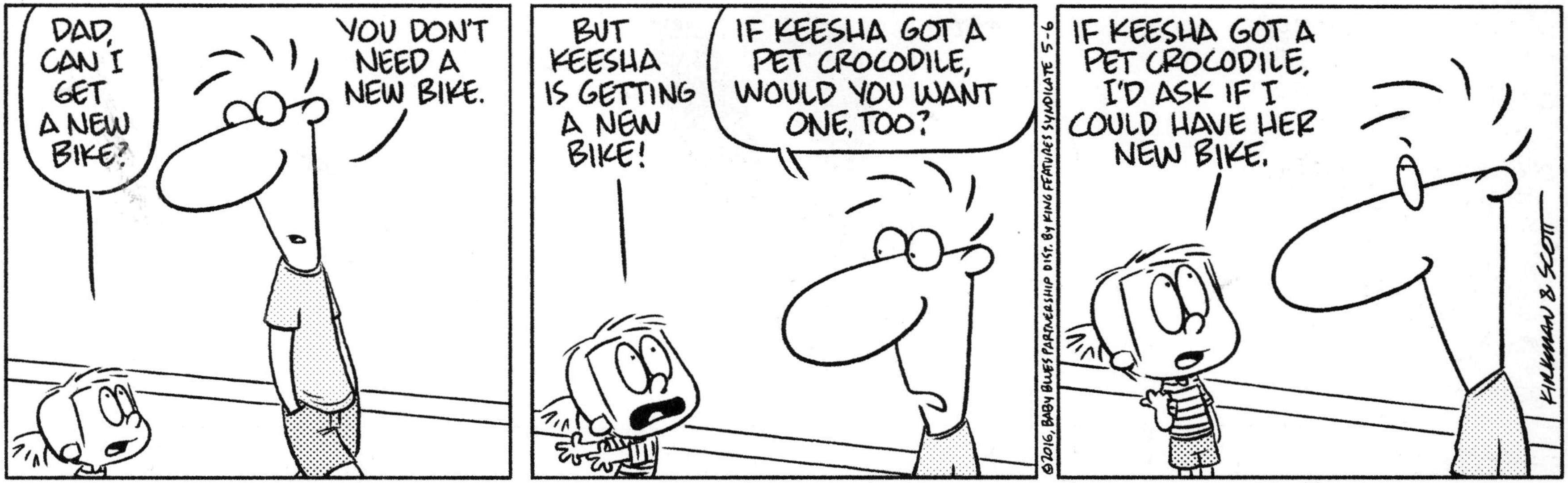
DAD, CAN I GET A NEW BIKE?
YOU DON'T NEED A NEW BIKE.
BUT KEESHA IS GETTING A NEW BIKE!
IF KEESHA GOT A PET CROCODILE, WOULD YOU WANT ONE, TOO?
©2016, BABY BLUES PARTNERSHIP DIST. BY KING FEATURES SYNDICATE 5-6
IF KEESHA GOT A PET CROCODILE, I'D ASK IF I COULD HAVE HER NEW BIKE.
KIRKMAN & SCOTT

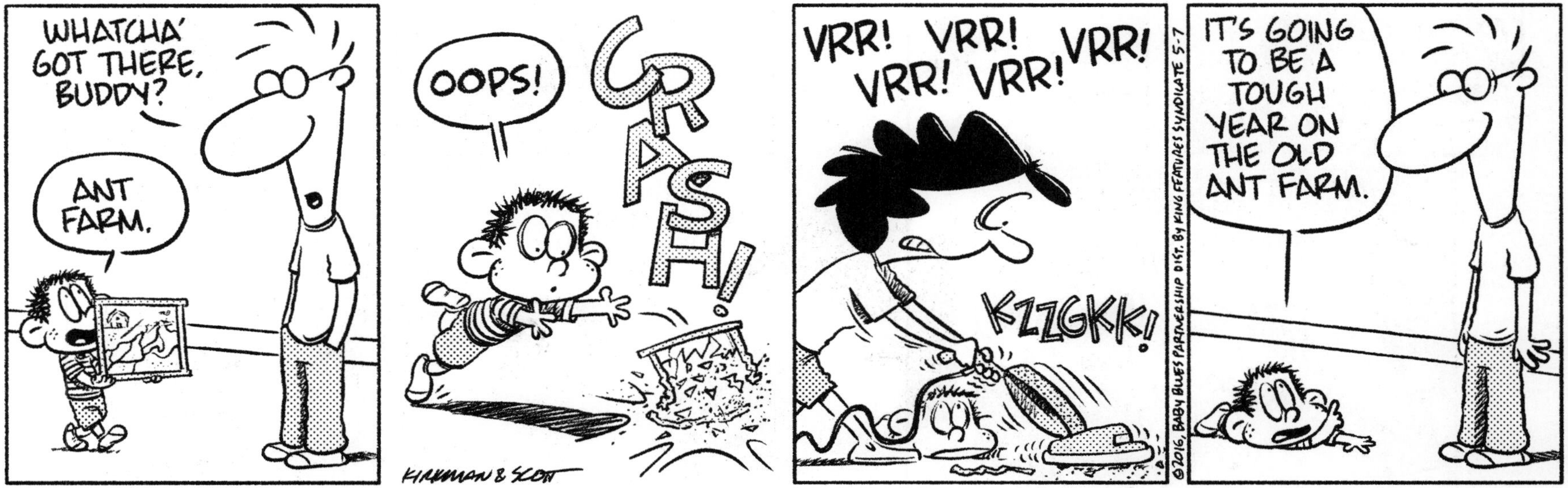
WHATCHA' GOT THERE, BUDDY?
ANT FARM.
OOPS!
CRASH!
KIRKMAN & SCOTT
VRR! VRR! VRR! VRR! VRR!
KZZGKK!
©2016, BABY BLUES PARTNERSHIP DIST. BY KING FEATURES SYNDICATE 5-7
IT'S GOING TO BE A TOUGH YEAR ON THE OLD ANT FARM.

Rick: That's what *I* think it sounds like when you vacuum up a shattered ant farm.

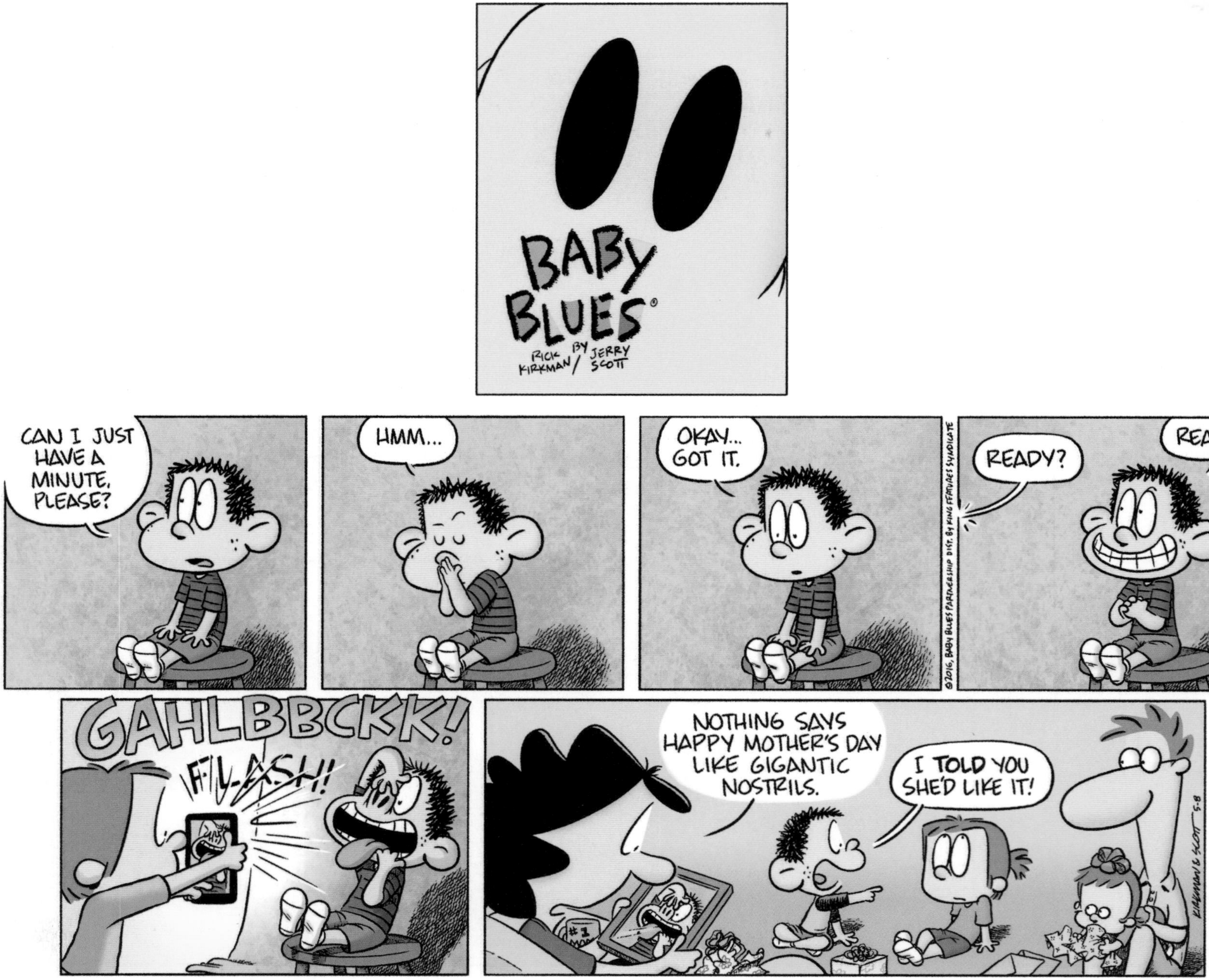
BABY BLUES®
BY RICK KIRKMAN / JERRY SCOTT
CAN I JUST HAVE A MINUTE, PLEASE?
HMM...
OKAY... GOT IT.
READY?
READY.
©2016, BABY BLUES PARTNERSHIP DIST. BY KING FEATURES SYNDICATE
GAHLBBCKK!
FLASH!
NOTHING SAYS HAPPY MOTHER'S DAY LIKE GIGANTIC NOSTRILS.
I TOLD YOU SHE'D LIKE IT!
KIRKMAN & SCOTT 5-8

Jerry: Like they say, it's the thought that counts. And the face.

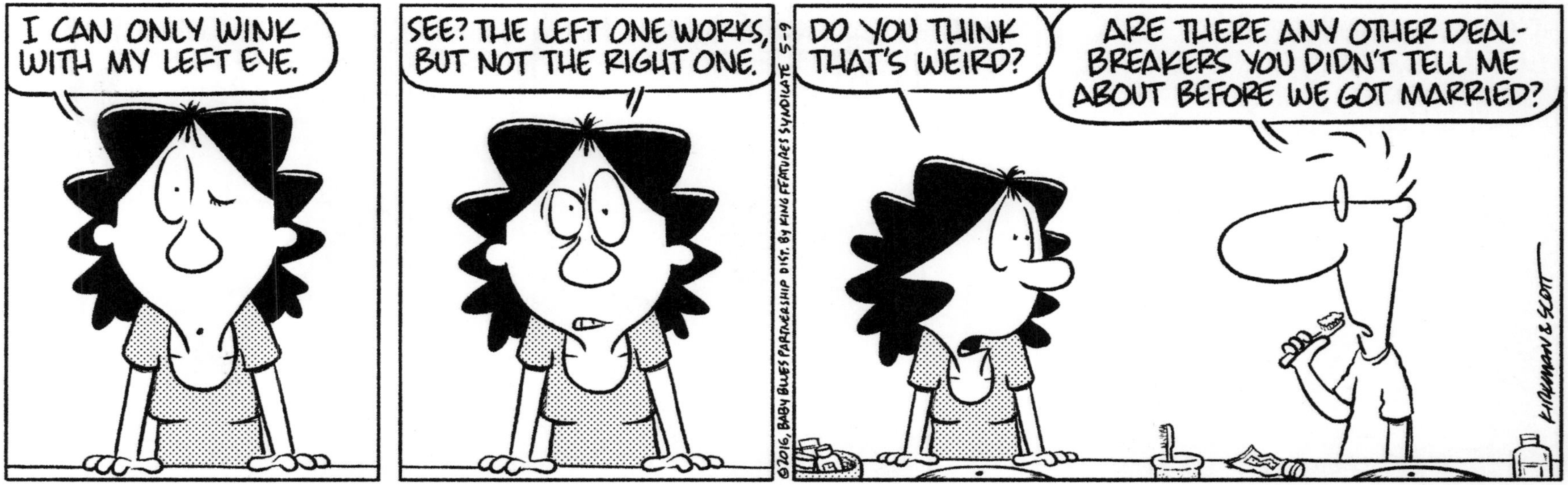
I CAN ONLY WINK WITH MY LEFT EYE.
SEE? THE LEFT ONE WORKS, BUT NOT THE RIGHT ONE.
©2016, BABY BLUES PARTNERSHIP DIST. BY KING FEATURES SYNDICATE 5-9
DO YOU THINK THAT'S WEIRD?
ARE THERE ANY OTHER DEAL-BREAKERS YOU DIDN'T TELL ME ABOUT BEFORE WE GOT MARRIED?
KIRKMAN & SCOTT

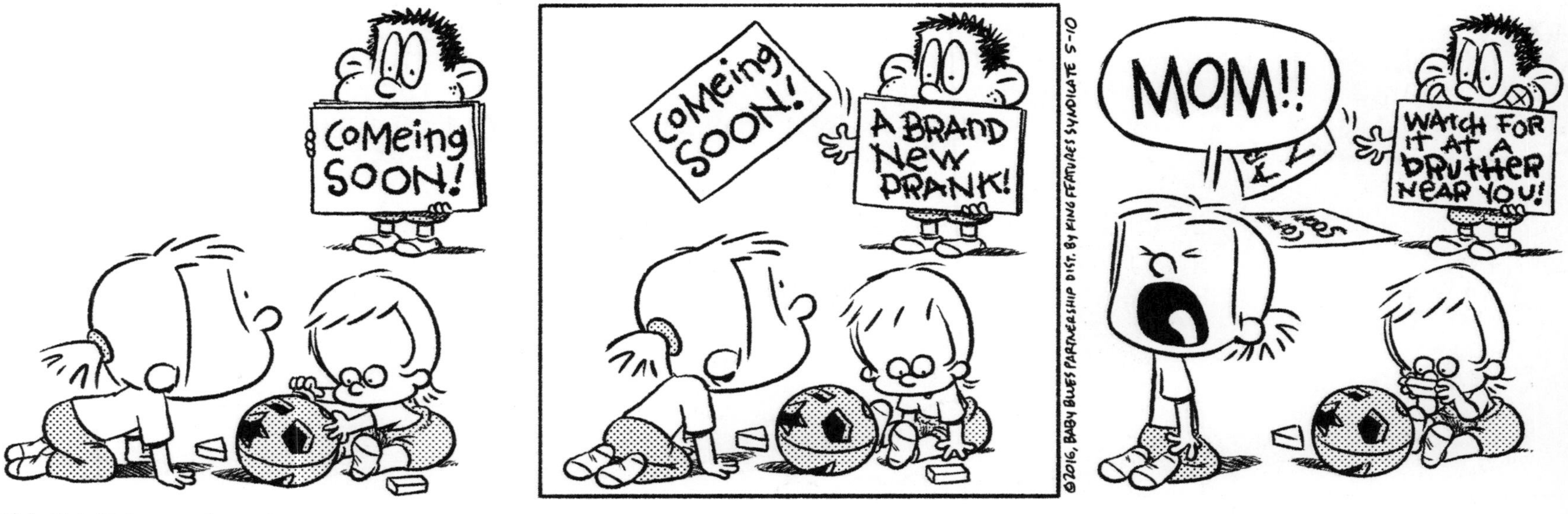
COMeing SOON!
COMeing SOON!
A BRAND NEW PRANK!
©2016, BABY BLUES PARTNERSHIP DIST. BY KING FEATURES SYNDICATE 5-10
MOM!!
WATCH FOR IT AT A BRUTHER NEAR YOU!
KIRKMAN & SCOTT

Rick: Bob Dylan, you're not.

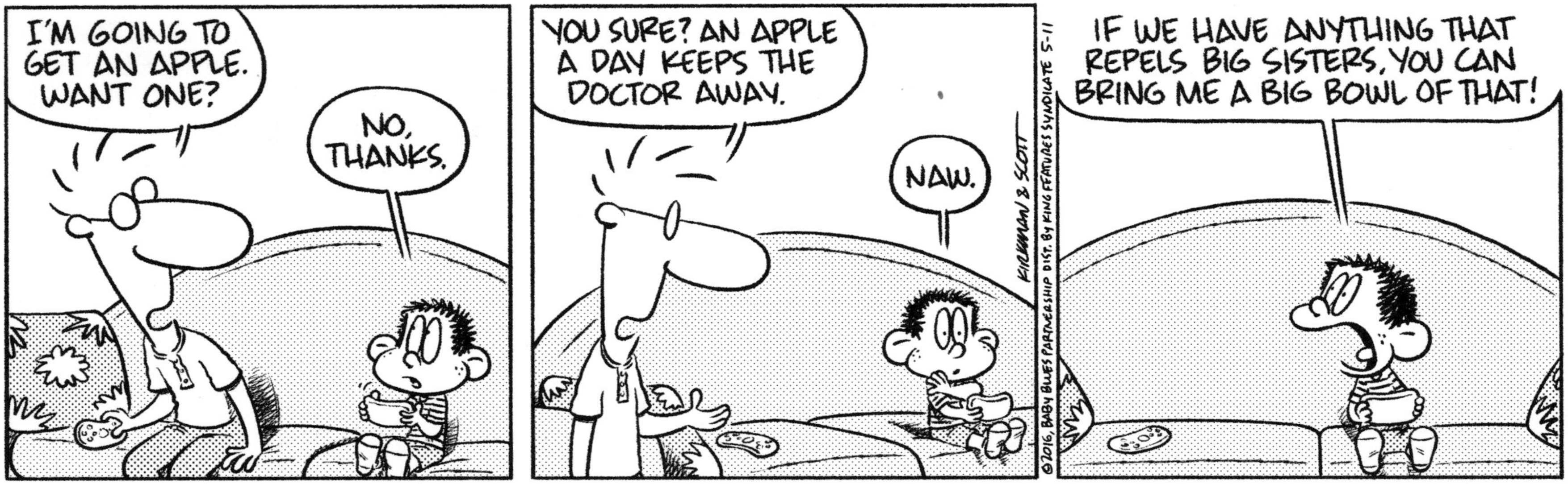
I'M GOING TO GET AN APPLE. WANT ONE?
NO, THANKS.
YOU SURE? AN APPLE A DAY KEEPS THE DOCTOR AWAY.
NAW.
KIRKMAN & SCOTT
©2016, BABY BLUES PARTNERSHIP DIST. BY KING FEATURES SYNDICATE 5-11
IF WE HAVE ANYTHING THAT REPELS BIG SISTERS, YOU CAN BRING ME A BIG BOWL OF THAT!

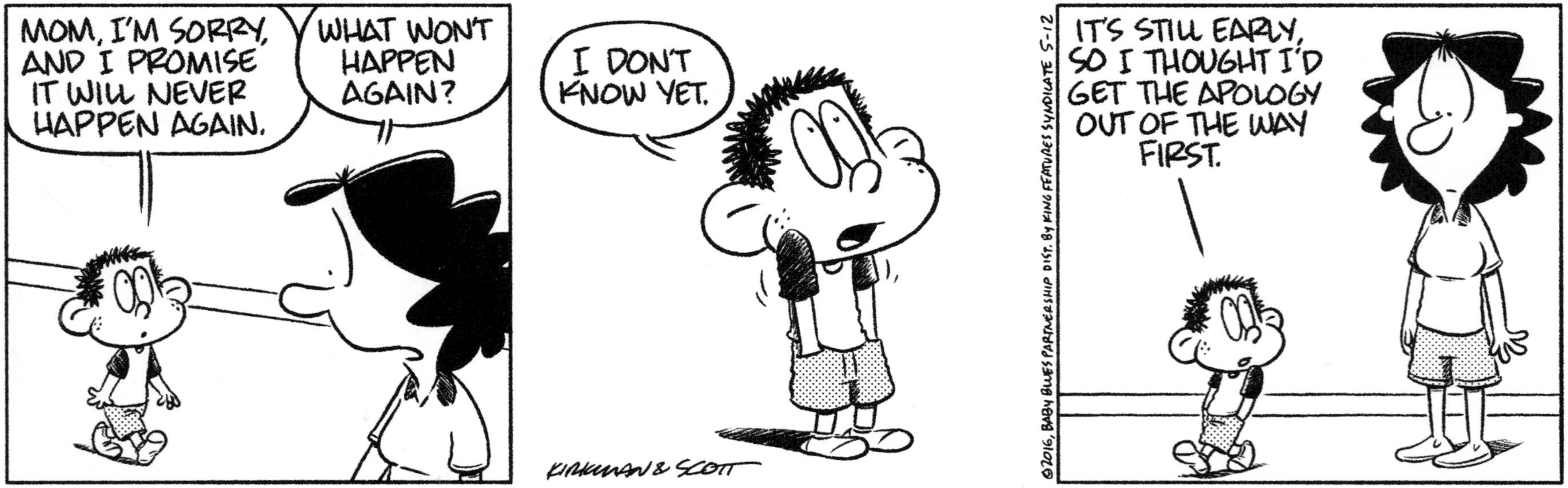
MOM, I'M SORRY, AND I PROMISE IT WILL NEVER HAPPEN AGAIN.
WHAT WON'T HAPPEN AGAIN?
I DON'T KNOW YET.
KIRKMAN & SCOTT
©2016, BABY BLUES PARTNERSHIP DIST. BY KING FEATURES SYNDICATE 5-12
IT'S STILL EARLY, SO I THOUGHT I'D GET THE APOLOGY OUT OF THE WAY FIRST.

Jerry: It's a good policy to start every day with a blanket apology.

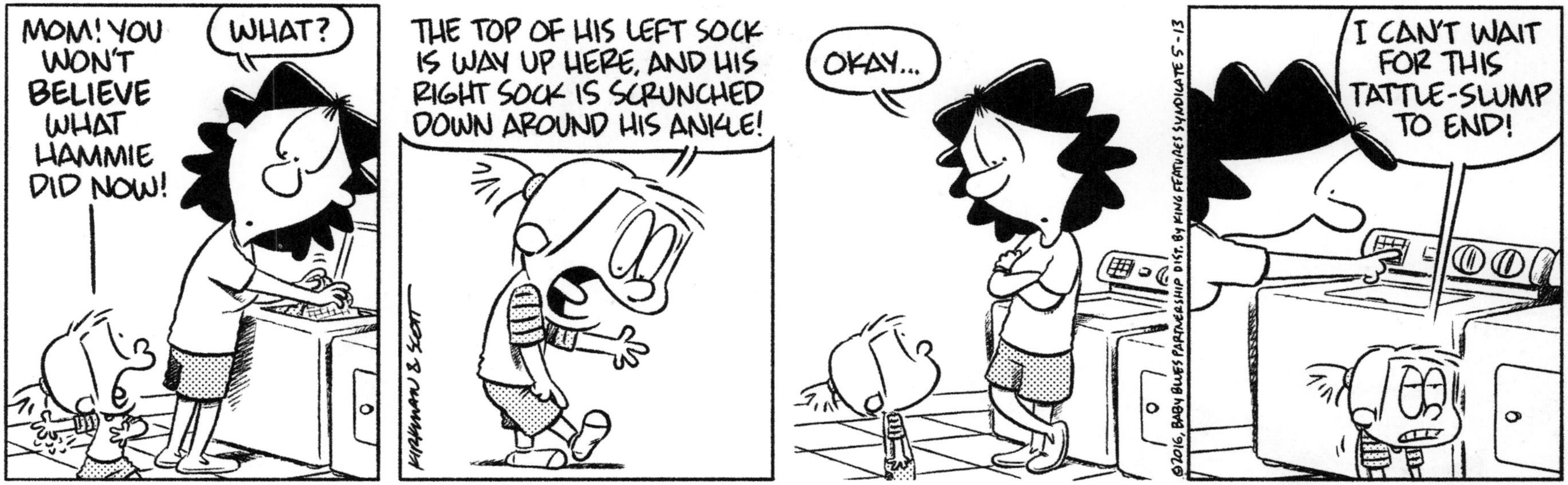
MOM! YOU WON'T BELIEVE WHAT HAMMIE DID NOW!
WHAT?
THE TOP OF HIS LEFT SOCK IS WAY UP HERE, AND HIS RIGHT SOCK IS SCRUNCHED DOWN AROUND HIS ANKLE!
KIRKMAN & SCOTT
OKAY...
©2016, BABY BLUES PARTNERSHIP DIST. BY KING FEATURES SYNDICATE 5-13
I CAN'T WAIT FOR THIS TATTLE-SLUMP TO END!

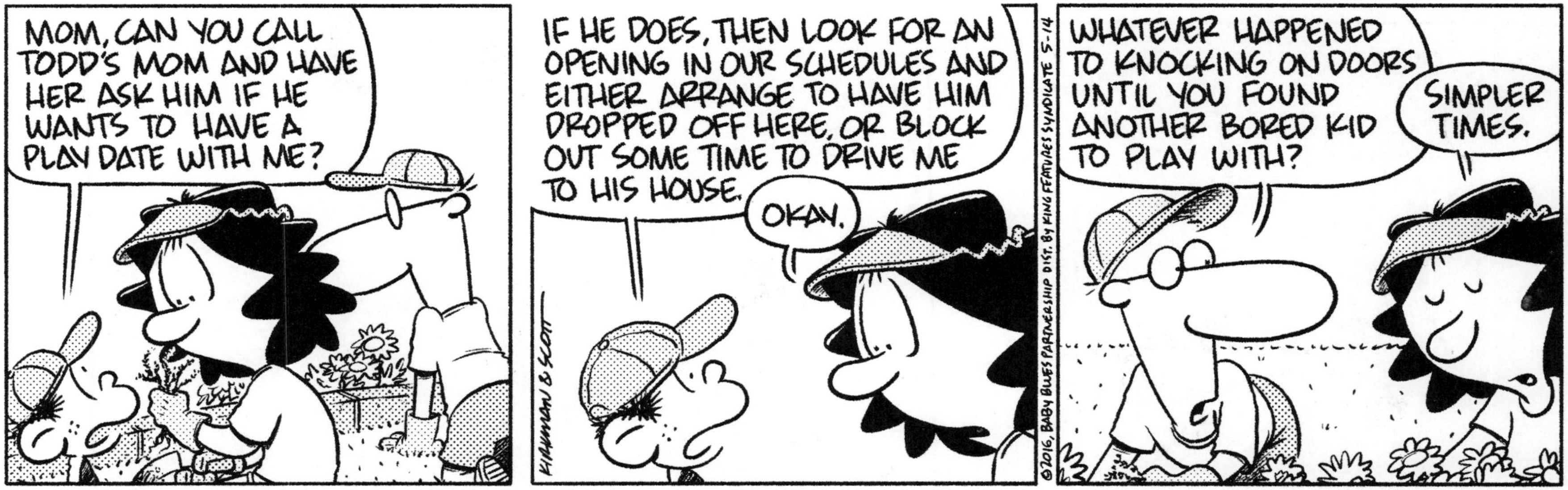
MOM, CAN YOU CALL TODD'S MOM AND HAVE HER ASK HIM IF HE WANTS TO HAVE A PLAY DATE WITH ME?
IF HE DOES, THEN LOOK FOR AN OPENING IN OUR SCHEDULES AND EITHER ARRANGE TO HAVE HIM DROPPED OFF HERE, OR BLOCK OUT SOME TIME TO DRIVE ME TO HIS HOUSE.
OKAY.
KIRKMAN & SCOTT
©2016, BABY BLUES PARTNERSHIP DIST. BY KING FEATURES SYNDICATE 5-14
WHATEVER HAPPENED TO KNOCKING ON DOORS UNTIL YOU FOUND ANOTHER BORED KID TO PLAY WITH?
SIMPLER TIMES.

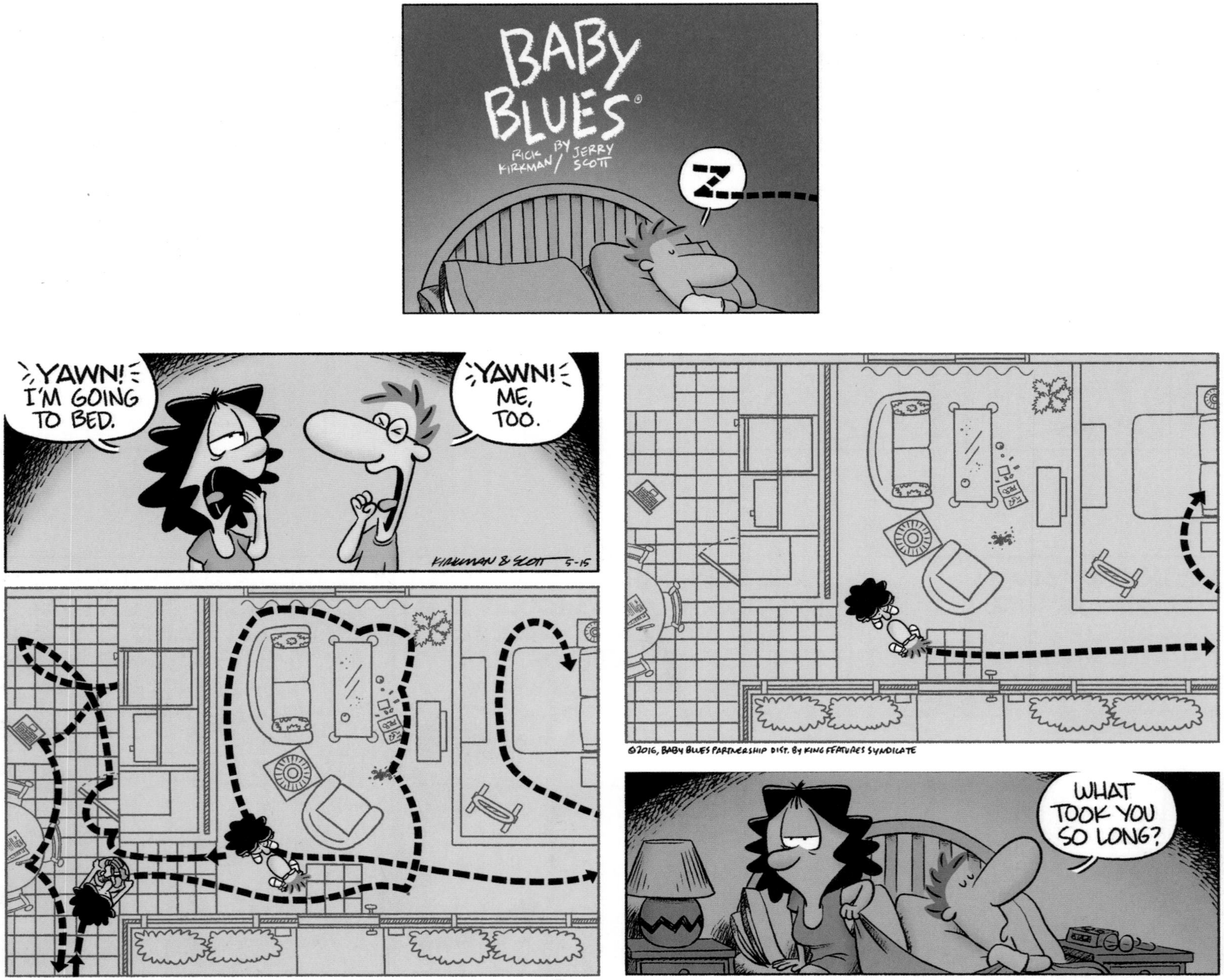
BABY BLUES®
BY RICK KIRKMAN / JERRY SCOTT
Z
YAWN! I'M GOING TO BED.
YAWN! ME, TOO.
KIRKMAN & SCOTT 5-15
©2016, BABY BLUES PARTNERSHIP DIST. BY KING FEATURES SYNDICATE
WHAT TOOK YOU SO LONG?

Rick: This gag, in its written form, had this instruction for two panels: "Show an aerial view (no roof) or a (partial) floor plan of the house." If that weren't enough, there was supposed to be a label for every stop along Wanda's route. Well, that's where I draw the dotted line—there's just no room for all that. It still might have benefitted from labels, but they would've been so small, you would've needed a magnifying glass to read them. Great idea, but maybe a bit ambitious for my skill level.

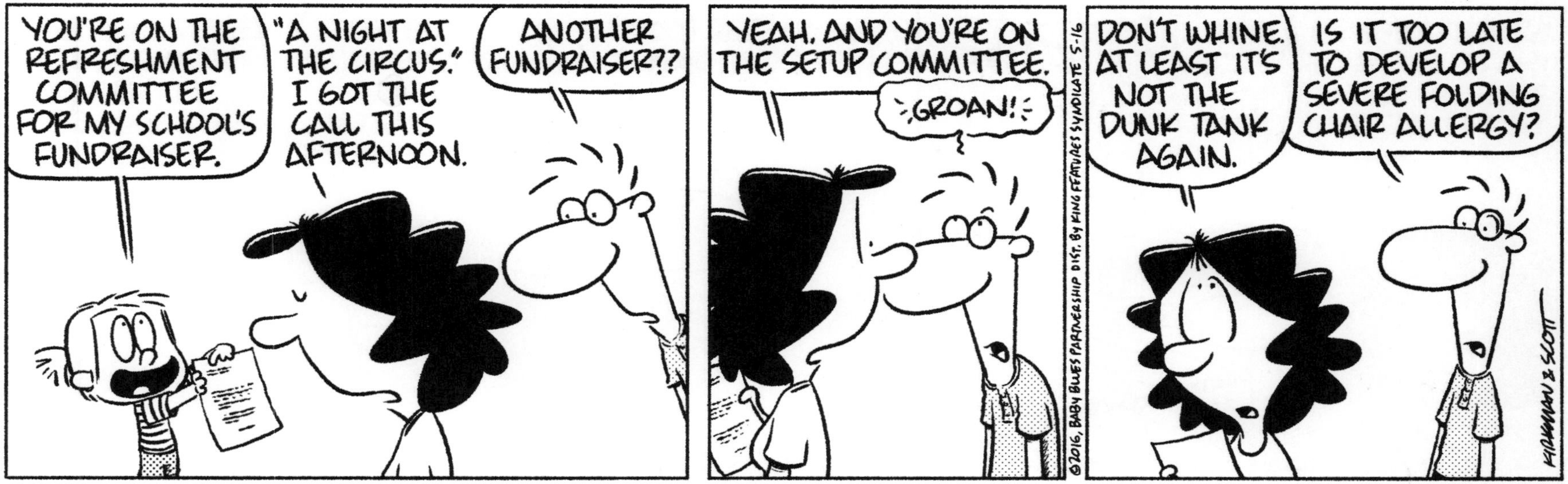
YOU'RE ON THE REFRESHMENT COMMITTEE FOR MY SCHOOL'S FUNDRAISER.
"A NIGHT AT THE CIRCUS." I GOT THE CALL THIS AFTERNOON.
ANOTHER FUNDRAISER??
YEAH. AND YOU'RE ON THE SETUP COMMITTEE.
GROAN!
©2016, BABY BLUES PARTNERSHIP DIST. BY KING FEATURES SYNDICATE 5-16
DON'T WHINE. AT LEAST IT'S NOT THE DUNK TANK AGAIN.
IS IT TOO LATE TO DEVELOP A SEVERE FOLDING CHAIR ALLERGY?
KIRKMAN & SCOTT

Jerry: I wasn't kidding on page 32 about all the folding chairs I have put away at school events.

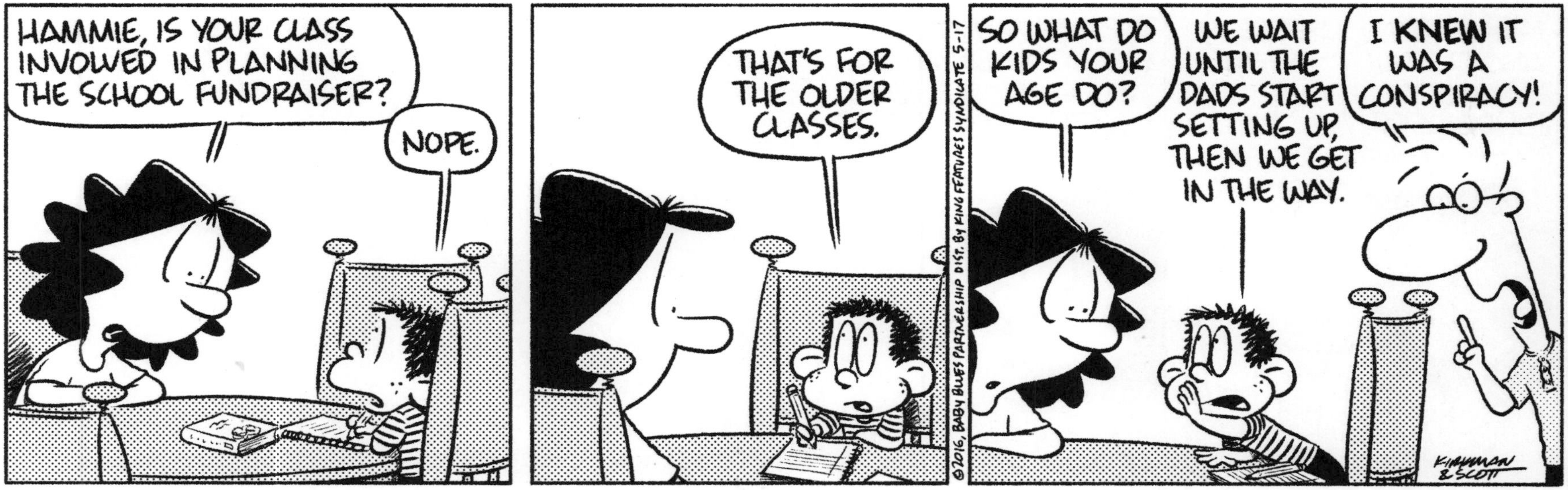
HAMMIE, IS YOUR CLASS INVOLVED IN PLANNING THE SCHOOL FUNDRAISER?
NOPE.
THAT'S FOR THE OLDER CLASSES.
©2016, BABY BLUES PARTNERSHIP DIST. BY KING FEATURES SYNDICATE 5-17
SO WHAT DO KIDS YOUR AGE DO?
WE WAIT UNTIL THE DADS START SETTING UP, THEN WE GET IN THE WAY.
I KNEW IT WAS A CONSPIRACY!
KIRKMAN & SCOTT

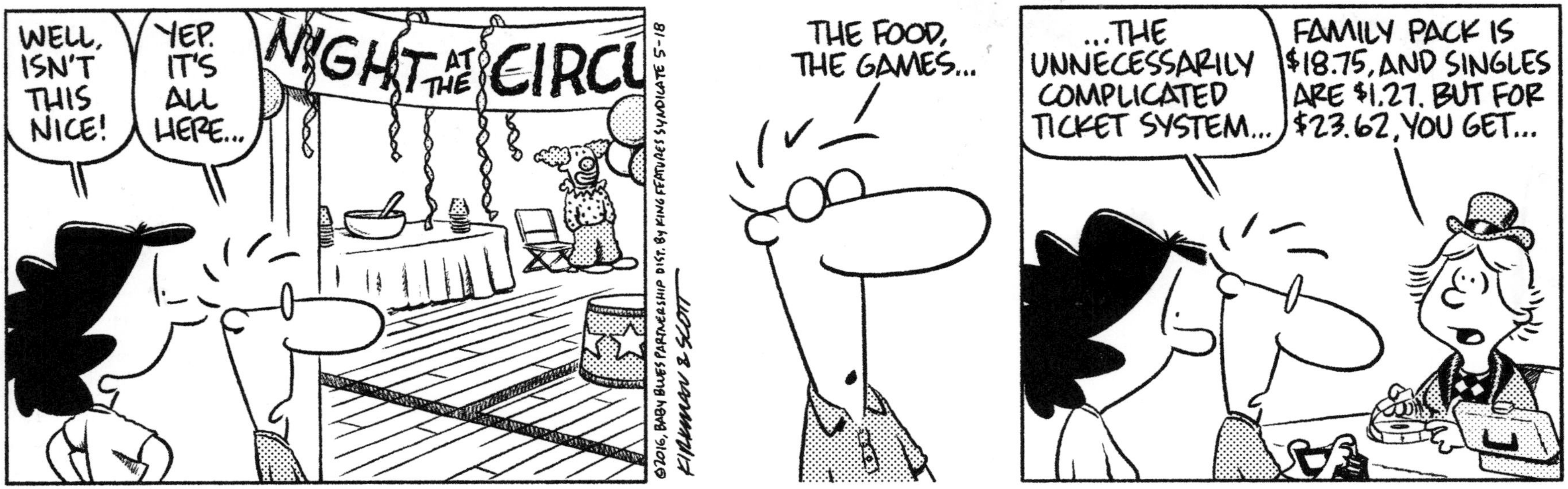
WELL, ISN'T THIS NICE!
YEP. IT'S ALL HERE...
NIGHT AT THE CIRCU
THE FOOD, THE GAMES...
...THE UNNECESSARILY COMPLICATED TICKET SYSTEM...
FAMILY PACK IS $18.75, AND SINGLES ARE $1.27. BUT FOR $23.62, YOU GET...
©2016, BABY BLUES PARTNERSHIP DIST. BY KING FEATURES SYNDICATE 5-18
KIRKMAN & SCOTT

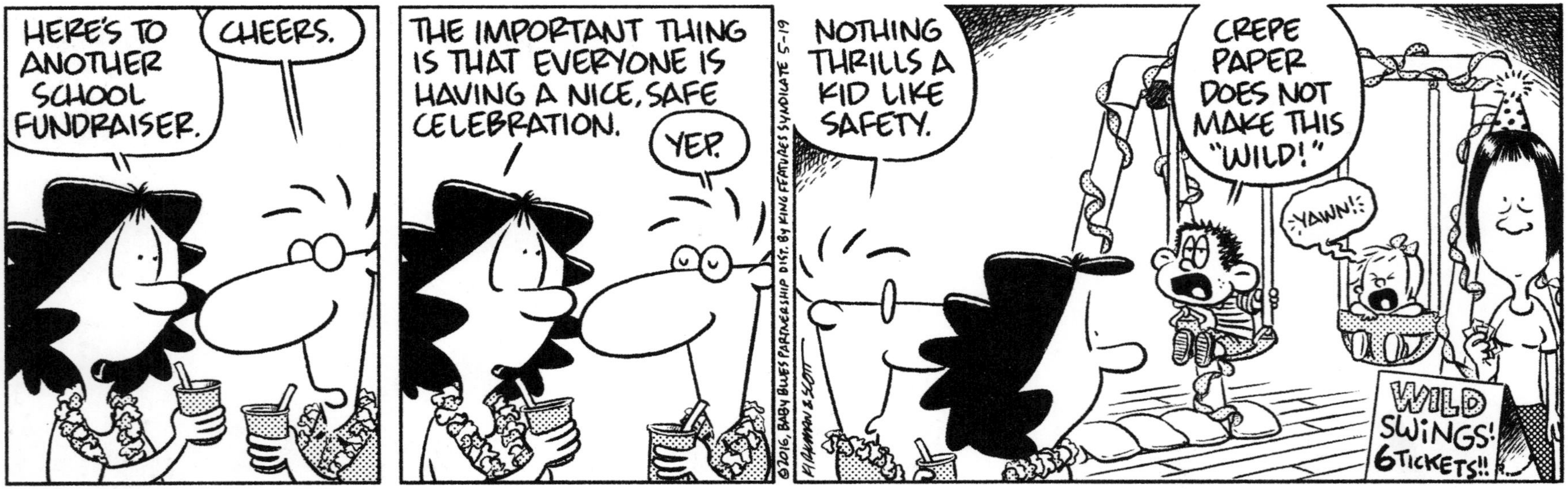
HERE'S TO ANOTHER SCHOOL FUNDRAISER.
CHEERS.
THE IMPORTANT THING IS THAT EVERYONE IS HAVING A NICE, SAFE CELEBRATION.
YEP.
NOTHING THRILLS A KID LIKE SAFETY.
CREPE PAPER DOES NOT MAKE THIS "WILD!"
YAWN!
WILD SWINGS! 6 TICKETS!!
©2016, BABY BLUES PARTNERSHIP DIST. BY KING FEATURES SYNDICATE 5-19
KIRKMAN & SCOTT

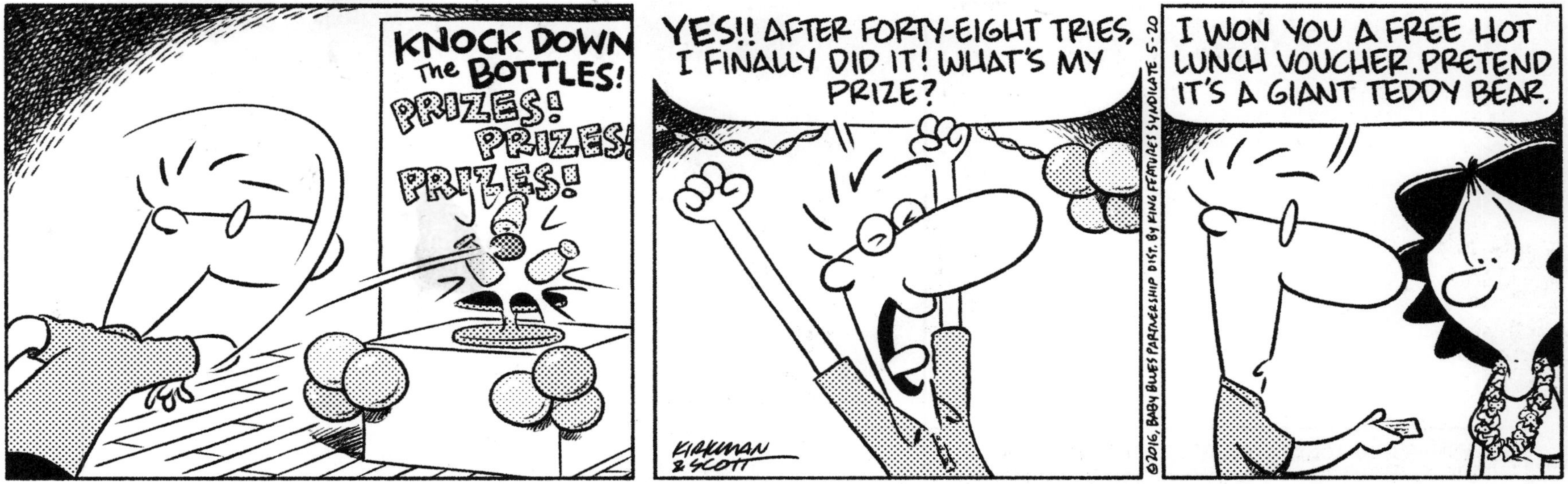
KNOCK DOWN The BOTTLES!
PRIZES! PRIZES! PRIZES!
YES!! AFTER FORTY-EIGHT TRIES, I FINALLY DID IT! WHAT'S MY PRIZE?
KIRKMAN & SCOTT
©2016, BABY BLUES PARTNERSHIP DIST. BY KING FEATURES SYNDICATE 5-20
I WON YOU A FREE HOT LUNCH VOUCHER. PRETEND IT'S A GIANT TEDDY BEAR.

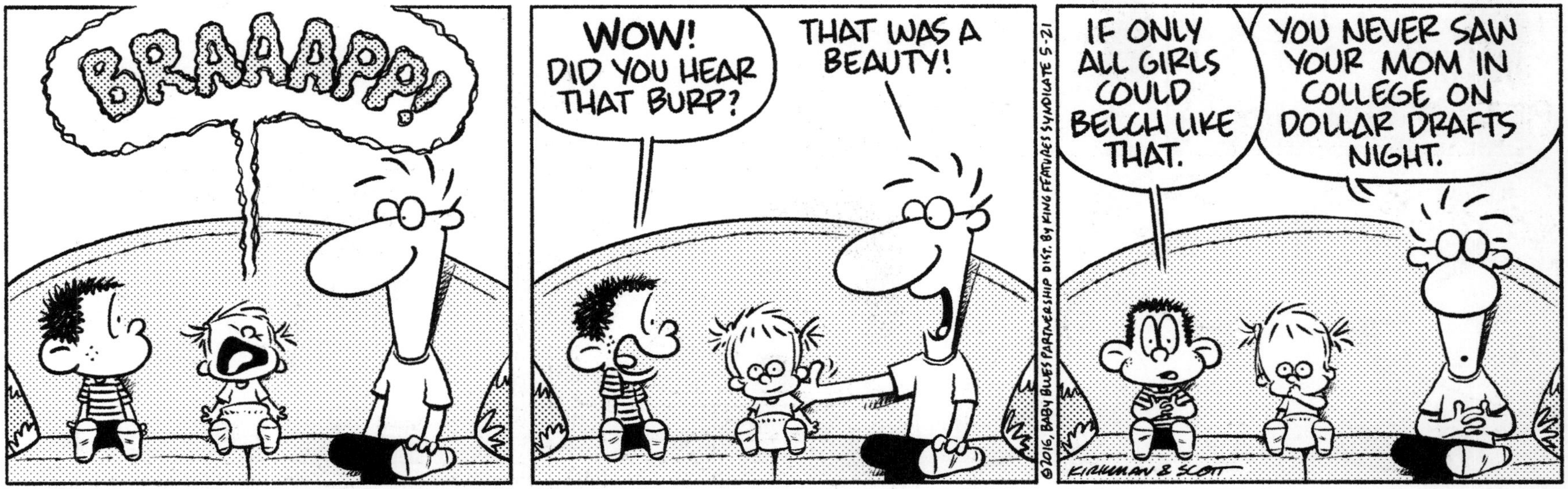
BRAAAPP!
WOW! DID YOU HEAR THAT BURP?
THAT WAS A BEAUTY!
©2016, BABY BLUES PARTNERSHIP DIST. BY KING FEATURES SYNDICATE 5-21
IF ONLY ALL GIRLS COULD BELCH LIKE THAT.
YOU NEVER SAW YOUR MOM IN COLLEGE ON DOLLAR DRAFTS NIGHT.
KIRKMAN & SCOTT

Jerry: Kinda wish I'd known Wanda in college.

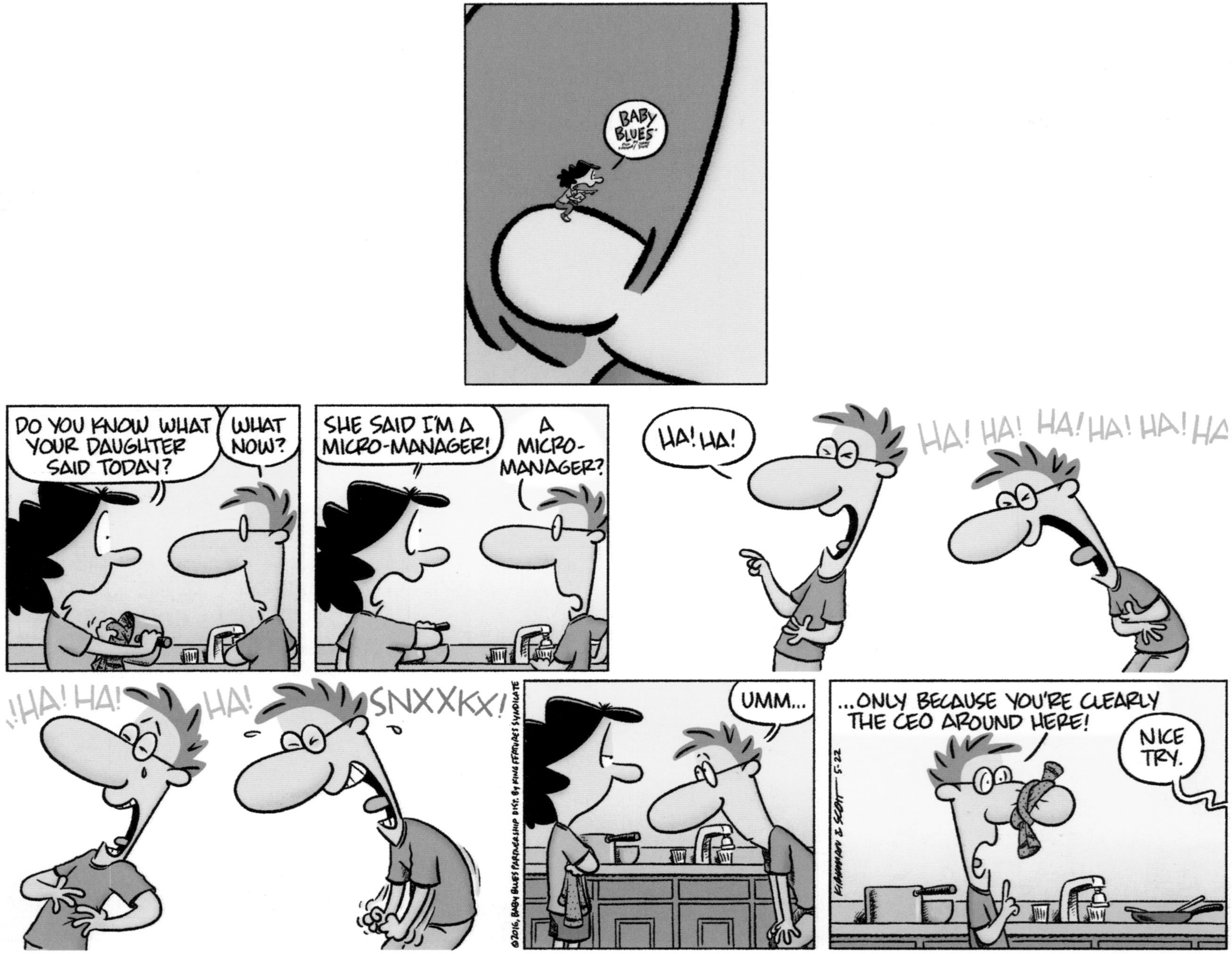
BABY BLUES
DO YOU KNOW WHAT YOUR DAUGHTER SAID TODAY?
WHAT NOW?
SHE SAID I'M A MICRO-MANAGER!
A MICRO-MANAGER?
HA! HA!
HA! HA! HA! HA! HA! HA
HA! HA!
HA!
SNXXKX!
©2016, BABY BLUES PARTNERSHIP DIST. BY KING FEATURES SYNDICATE
UMM...
KIRKMAN & SCOTT 5-22
...ONLY BECAUSE YOU'RE CLEARLY THE CEO AROUND HERE!
NICE TRY.

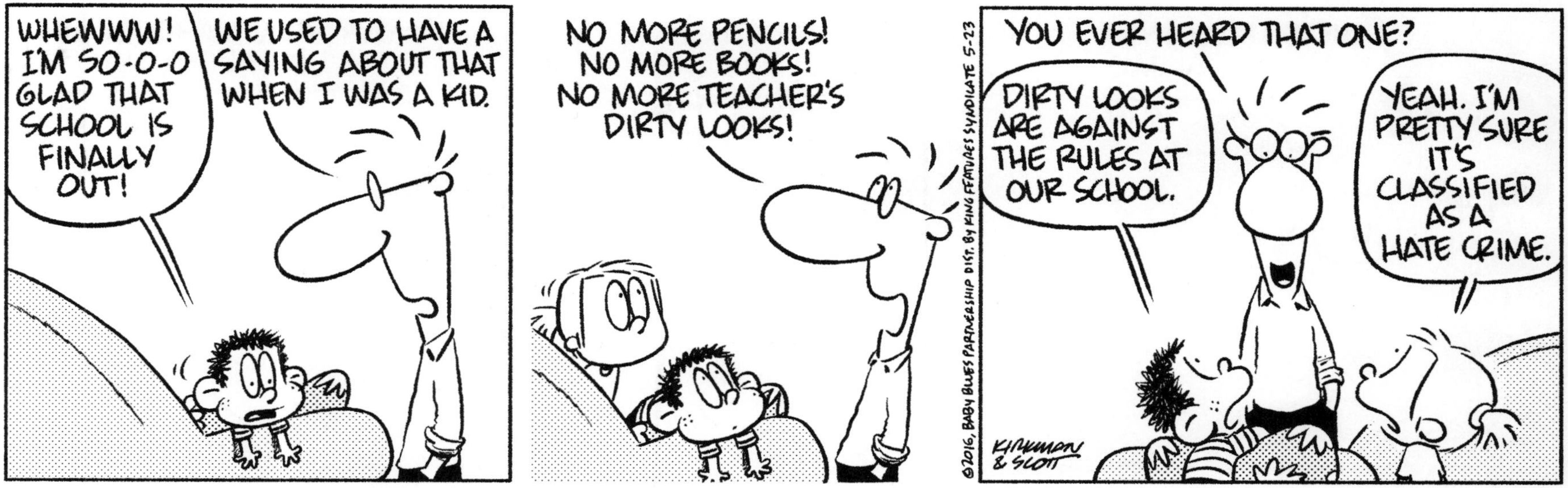
WHEWWW! I'M SO-O-O GLAD THAT SCHOOL IS FINALLY OUT!
WE USED TO HAVE A SAYING ABOUT THAT WHEN I WAS A KID.
NO MORE PENCILS! NO MORE BOOKS! NO MORE TEACHER'S DIRTY LOOKS!
©2016, BABY BLUES PARTNERSHIP DIST. BY KING FEATURES SYNDICATE 5-23
YOU EVER HEARD THAT ONE?
DIRTY LOOKS ARE AGAINST THE RULES AT OUR SCHOOL.
YEAH. I'M PRETTY SURE IT'S CLASSIFIED AS A HATE CRIME.
KIRKMAN & SCOTT

Rick: Without that rhyme, Alice Cooper would've been stuck for more lyrics.

Jerry: Simpler times, these are not.

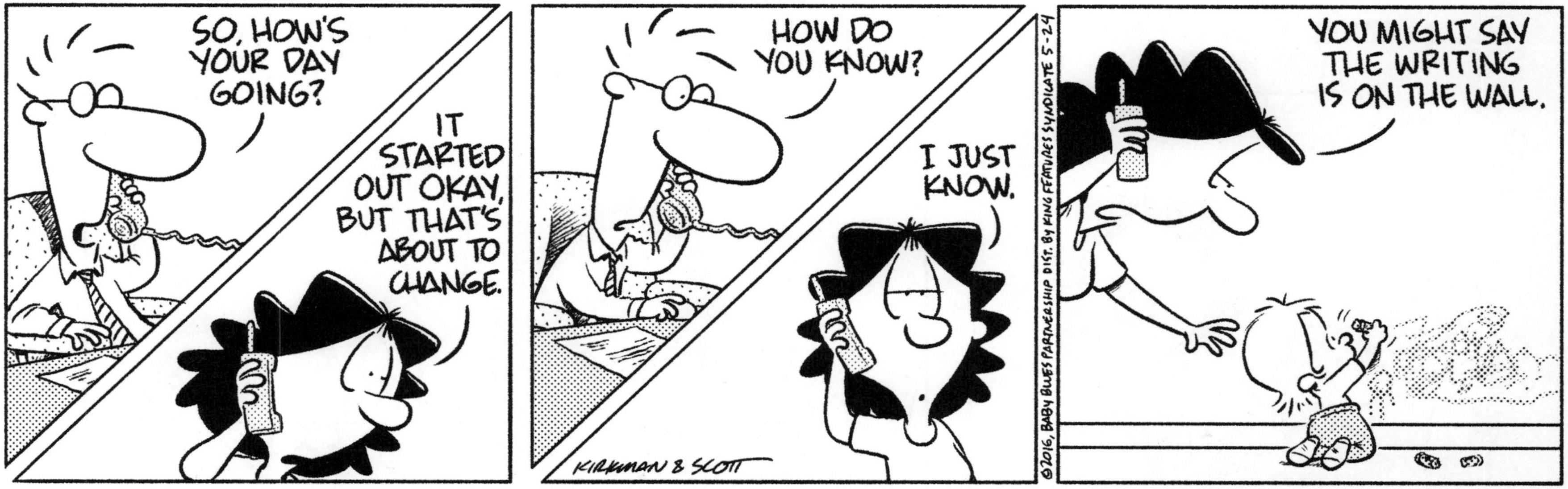
SO, HOW'S YOUR DAY GOING?
IT STARTED OUT OKAY, BUT THAT'S ABOUT TO CHANGE.
HOW DO YOU KNOW?
I JUST KNOW.
KIRKMAN & SCOTT
©2016, BABY BLUES PARTNERSHIP DIST. BY KING FEATURES SYNDICATE 5-24
YOU MIGHT SAY THE WRITING IS ON THE WALL.

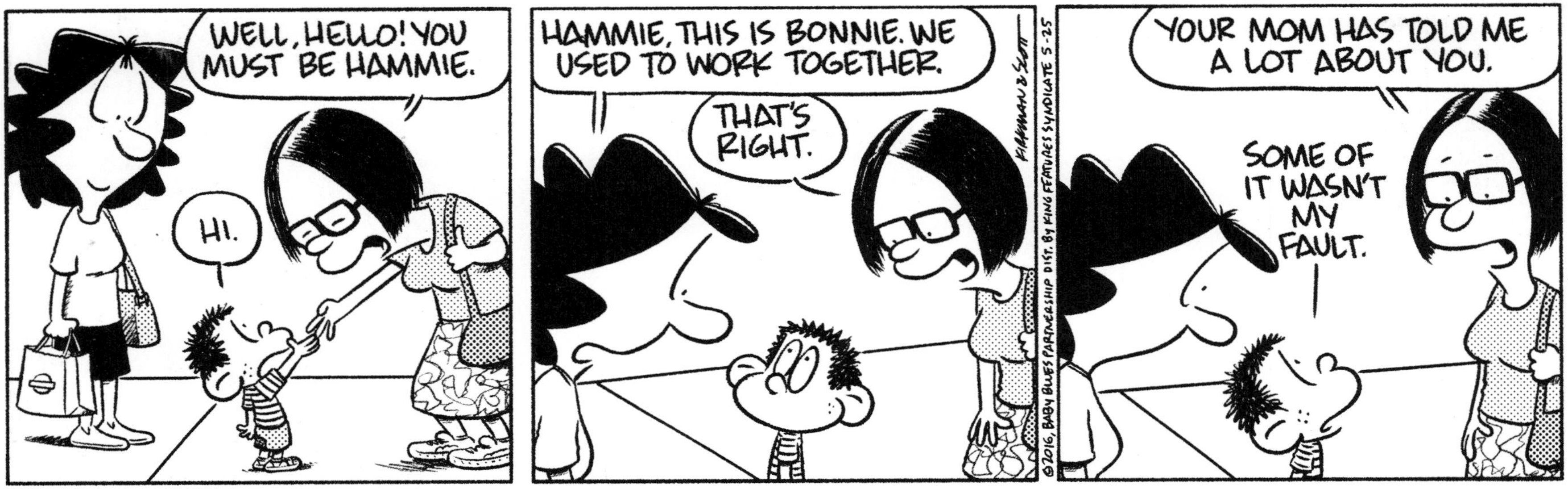
WELL, HELLO! YOU MUST BE HAMMIE.
HI.
HAMMIE, THIS IS BONNIE. WE USED TO WORK TOGETHER.
THAT'S RIGHT.
YOUR MOM HAS TOLD ME A LOT ABOUT YOU.
SOME OF IT WASN'T MY FAULT.

Jerry: What else are you supposed to say to grown-ups in this situation?

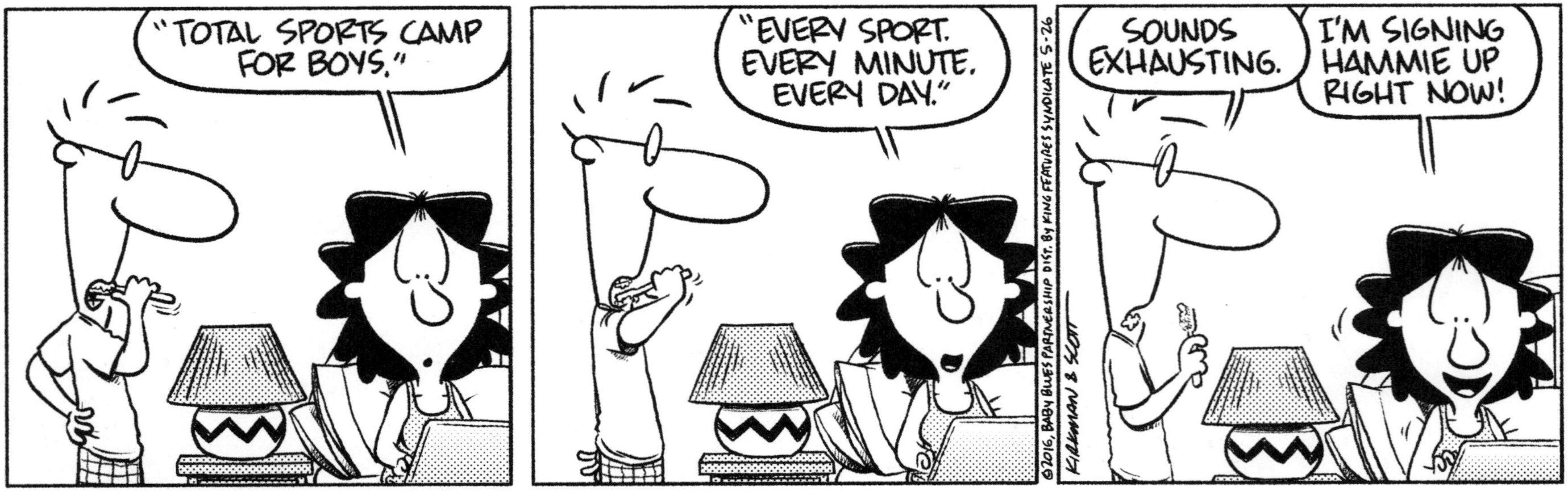
"TOTAL SPORTS CAMP FOR BOYS."
"EVERY SPORT. EVERY MINUTE. EVERY DAY."
SOUNDS EXHAUSTING.
I'M SIGNING HAMMIE UP RIGHT NOW!

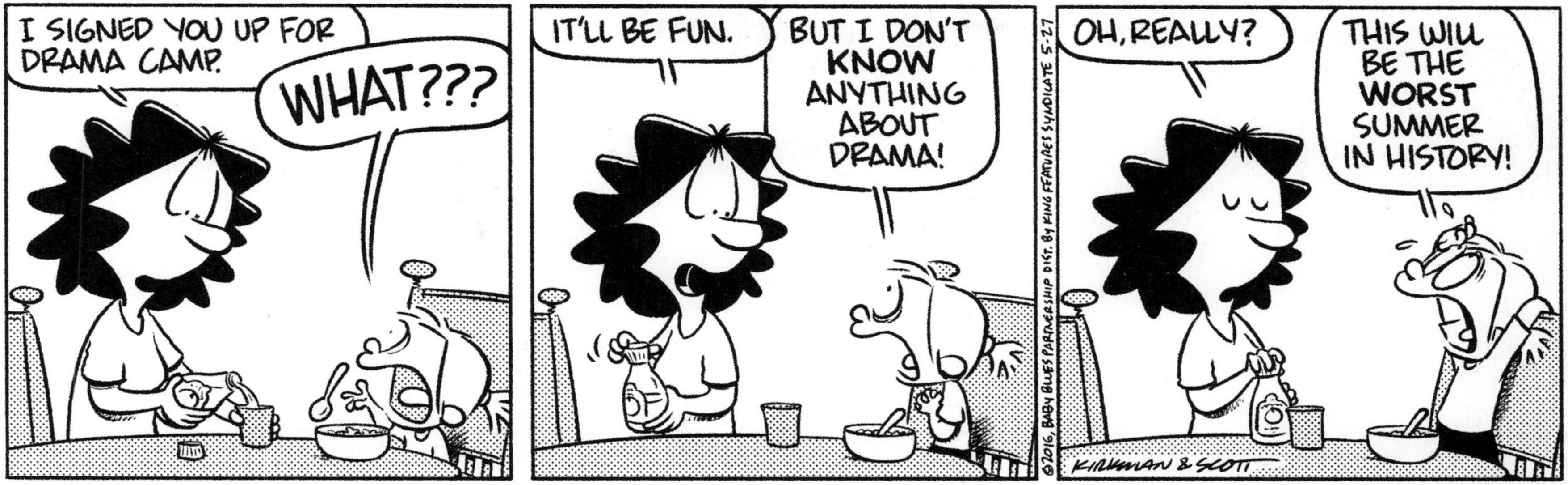
I SIGNED YOU UP FOR DRAMA CAMP.
WHAT???
IT'LL BE FUN.
BUT I DON'T KNOW ANYTHING ABOUT DRAMA!
©2016, BABY BLUES PARTNERSHIP DIST. BY KING FEATURES SYNDICATE 5-27
OH, REALLY?
THIS WILL BE THE WORST SUMMER IN HISTORY!
KIRKMAN & SCOTT

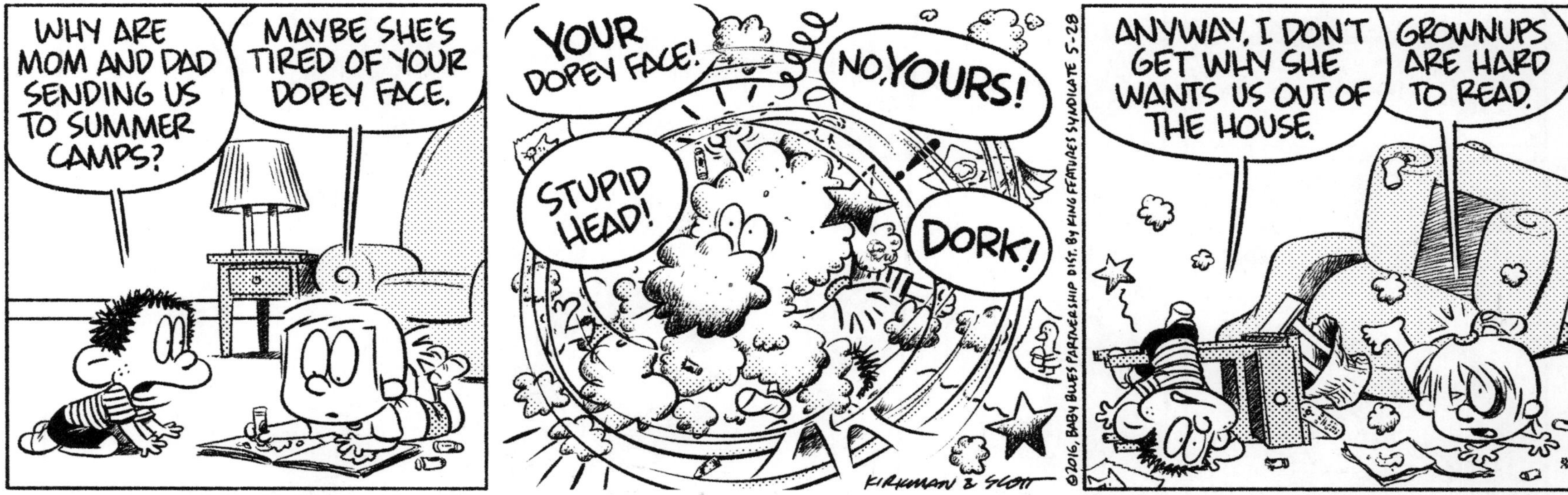
WHY ARE MOM AND DAD SENDING US TO SUMMER CAMPS?
MAYBE SHE'S TIRED OF YOUR DOPEY FACE.
YOUR DOPEY FACE!
NO, YOURS!
STUPID HEAD!
DORK!
KIRKMAN & SCOTT
©2016, BABY BLUES PARTNERSHIP DIST. BY KING FEATURES SYNDICATE 5-28
ANYWAY, I DON'T GET WHY SHE WANTS US OUT OF THE HOUSE.
GROWNUPS ARE HARD TO READ.

Rick: The only time I think fights are fun—when you're drawing them.

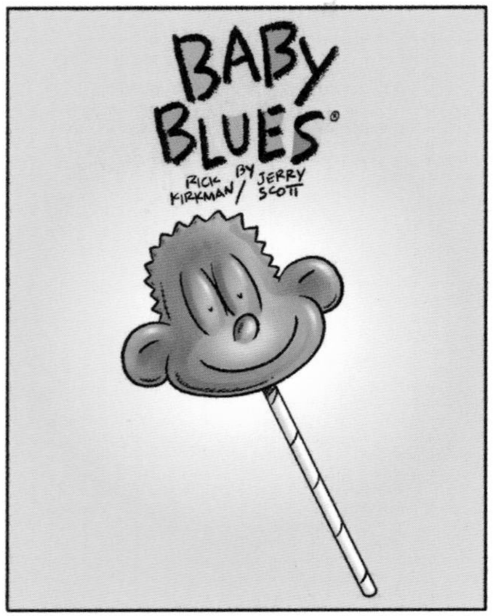
BABY BLUES®
BY RICK KIRKMAN / JERRY SCOTT

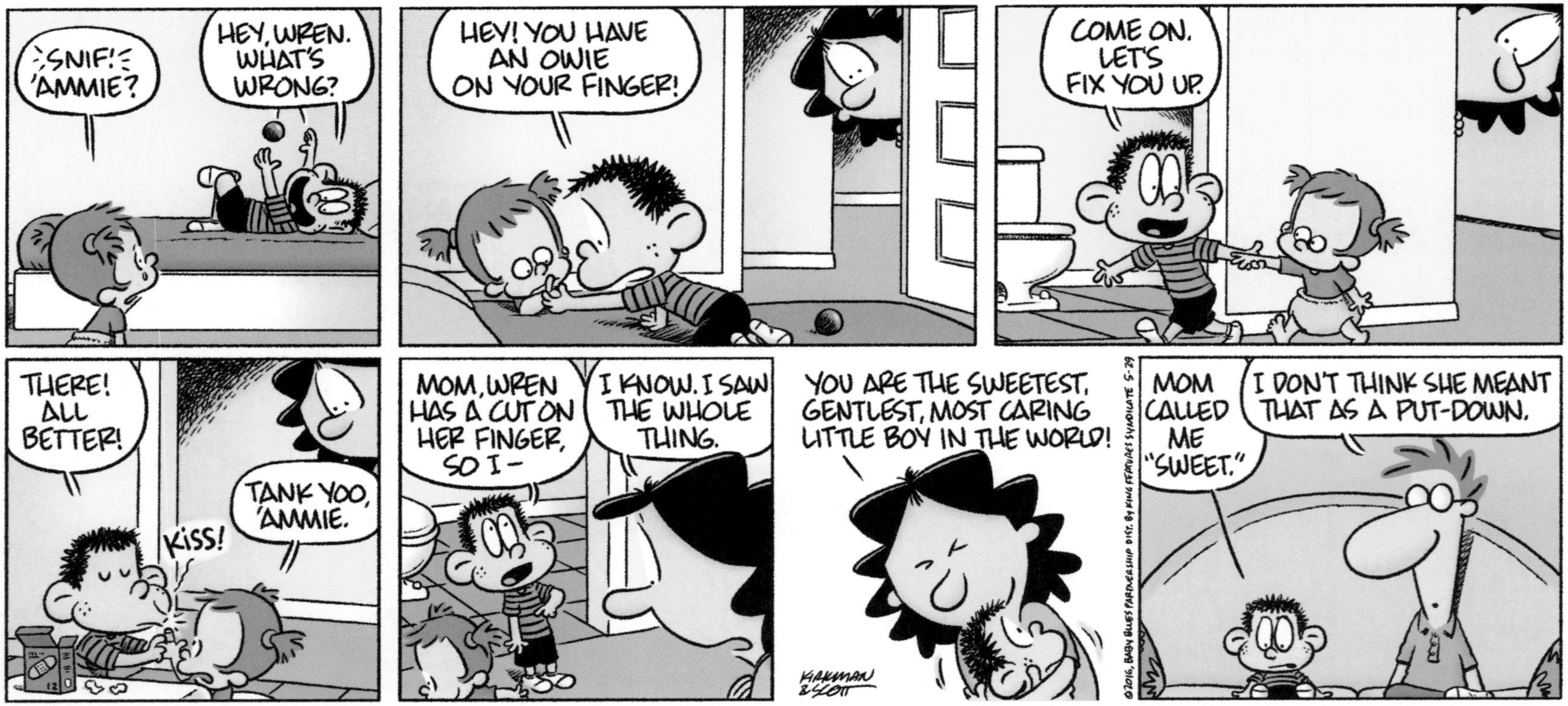
SNIF! 'AMMIE?
HEY, WREN. WHAT'S WRONG?
HEY! YOU HAVE AN OWIE ON YOUR FINGER!
COME ON. LET'S FIX YOU UP.
THERE! ALL BETTER!
KISS!
TANK YOO, 'AMMIE.
MOM, WREN HAS A CUT ON HER FINGER, SO I–
I KNOW. I SAW THE WHOLE THING.
YOU ARE THE SWEETEST, GENTLEST, MOST CARING LITTLE BOY IN THE WORLD!
KIRKMAN & SCOTT
©2016, BABY BLUES PARTNERSHIP DIST. BY KING FEATURES SYNDICATE 5-29
MOM CALLED ME "SWEET."
I DON'T THINK SHE MEANT THAT AS A PUT-DOWN.

Jerry: Call him kind, call him caring . . . just don't use the "s" word.

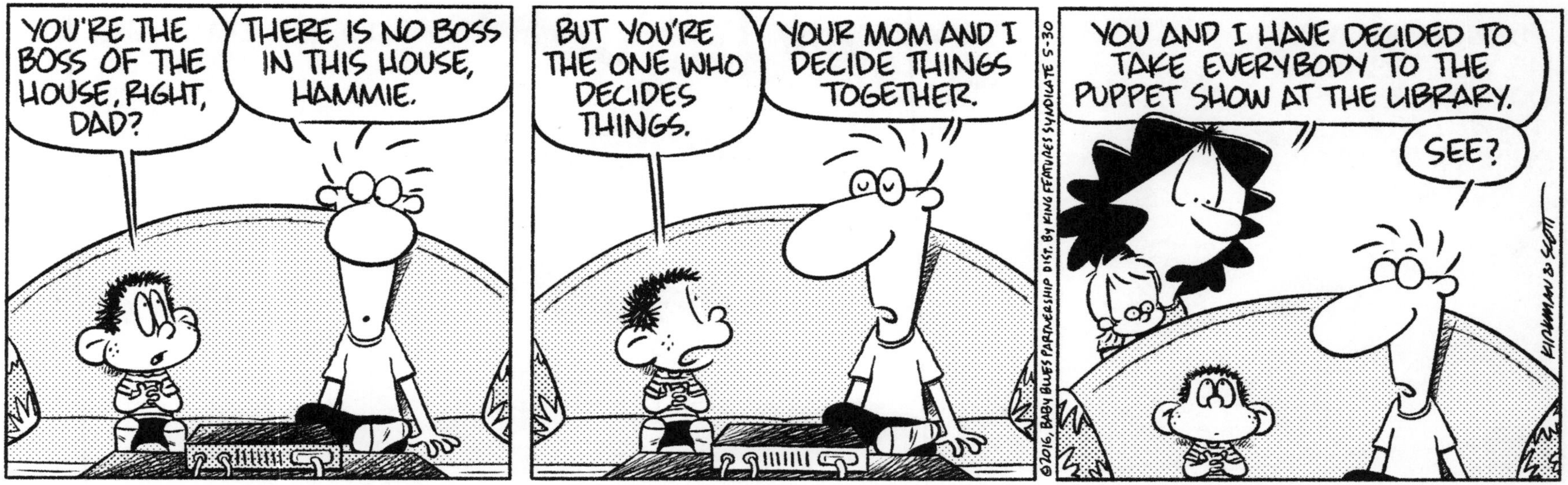
YOU'RE THE BOSS OF THE HOUSE, RIGHT, DAD?
THERE IS NO BOSS IN THIS HOUSE, HAMMIE.
BUT YOU'RE THE ONE WHO DECIDES THINGS.
YOUR MOM AND I DECIDE THINGS TOGETHER.
©2016, BABY BLUES PARTNERSHIP DIST. BY KING FEATURES SYNDICATE 5-30
YOU AND I HAVE DECIDED TO TAKE EVERYBODY TO THE PUPPET SHOW AT THE LIBRARY.
SEE?
KIRKMAN & SCOTT

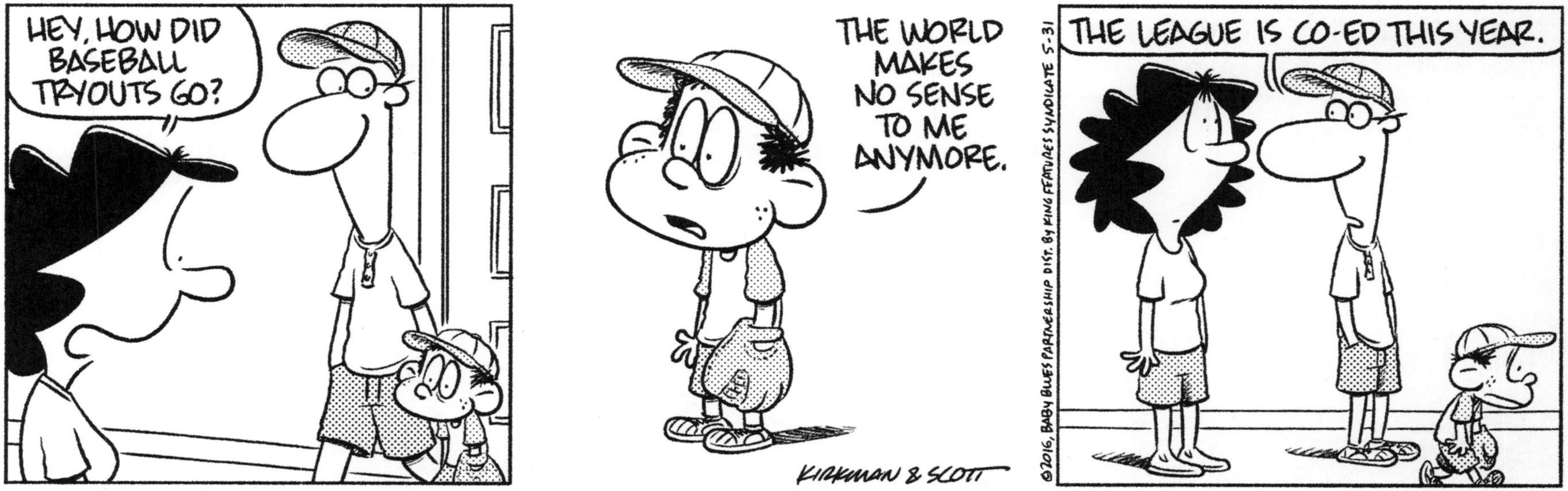
HEY, HOW DID BASEBALL TRYOUTS GO?
THE WORLD MAKES NO SENSE TO ME ANYMORE.
KIRKMAN & SCOTT
©2016, BABY BLUES PARTNERSHIP DIST. BY KING FEATURES SYNDICATE 5-31
THE LEAGUE IS CO-ED THIS YEAR.

Rick: I'm sure this gag was not meant to be social commentary at the time, but it seems to have gained relevance lately.

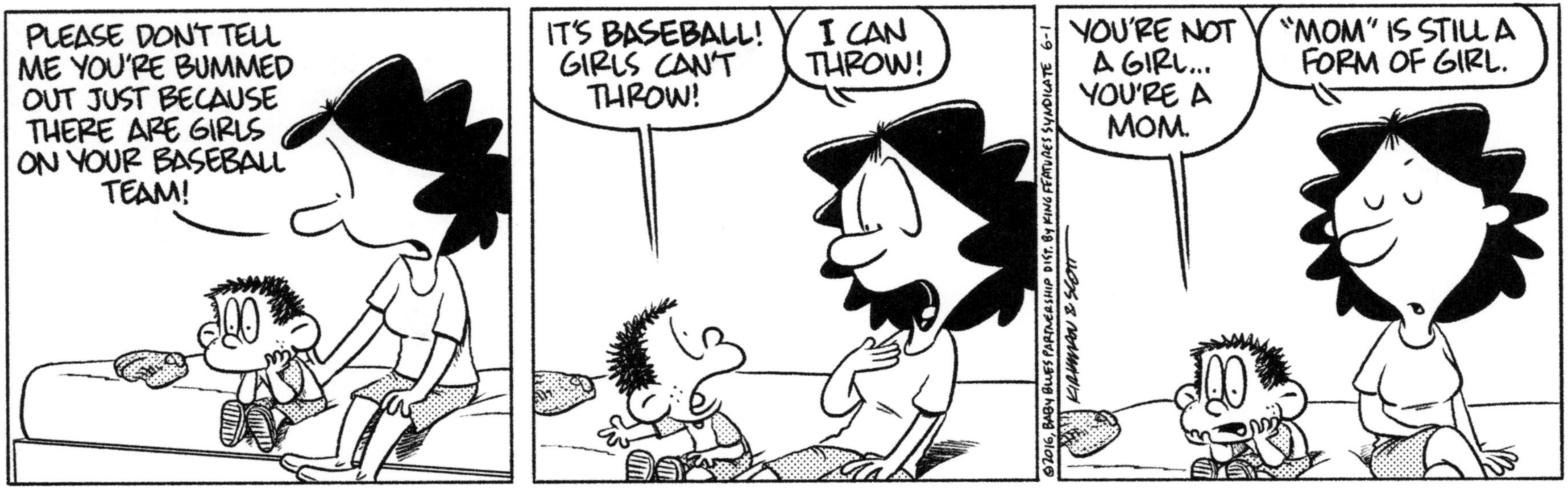
PLEASE DON'T TELL ME YOU'RE BUMMED OUT JUST BECAUSE THERE ARE GIRLS ON YOUR BASEBALL TEAM!
IT'S BASEBALL! GIRLS CAN'T THROW!
I CAN THROW!
YOU'RE NOT A GIRL... YOU'RE A MOM.
"MOM" IS STILL A FORM OF GIRL.
©2016, BABY BLUES PARTNERSHIP DIST. BY KING FEATURES SYNDICATE 6-1
KIRKMAN & SCOTT

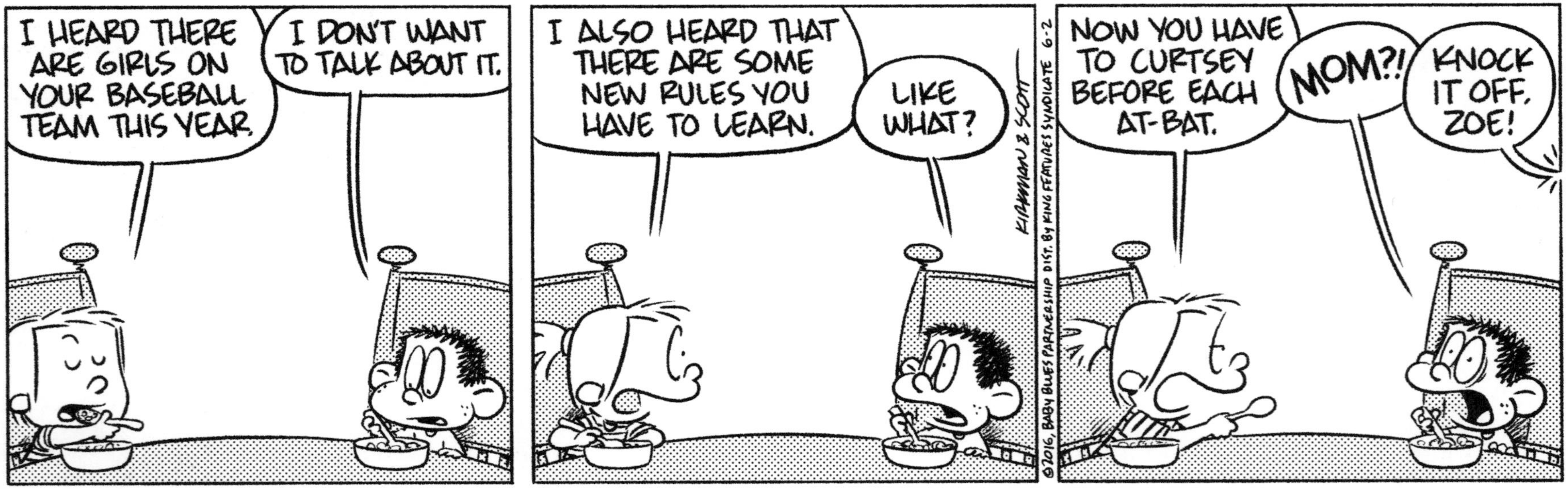
I HEARD THERE ARE GIRLS ON YOUR BASEBALL TEAM THIS YEAR.
I DON'T WANT TO TALK ABOUT IT.
I ALSO HEARD THAT THERE ARE SOME NEW RULES YOU HAVE TO LEARN.
LIKE WHAT?
NOW YOU HAVE TO CURTSEY BEFORE EACH AT-BAT.
MOM?!
KNOCK IT OFF, ZOE!
©2016, BABY BLUES PARTNERSHIP DIST. BY KING FEATURES SYNDICATE 6-2
KIRKMAN & SCOTT

Jerry: Nothing like a big sister to make a bad situation even worse.

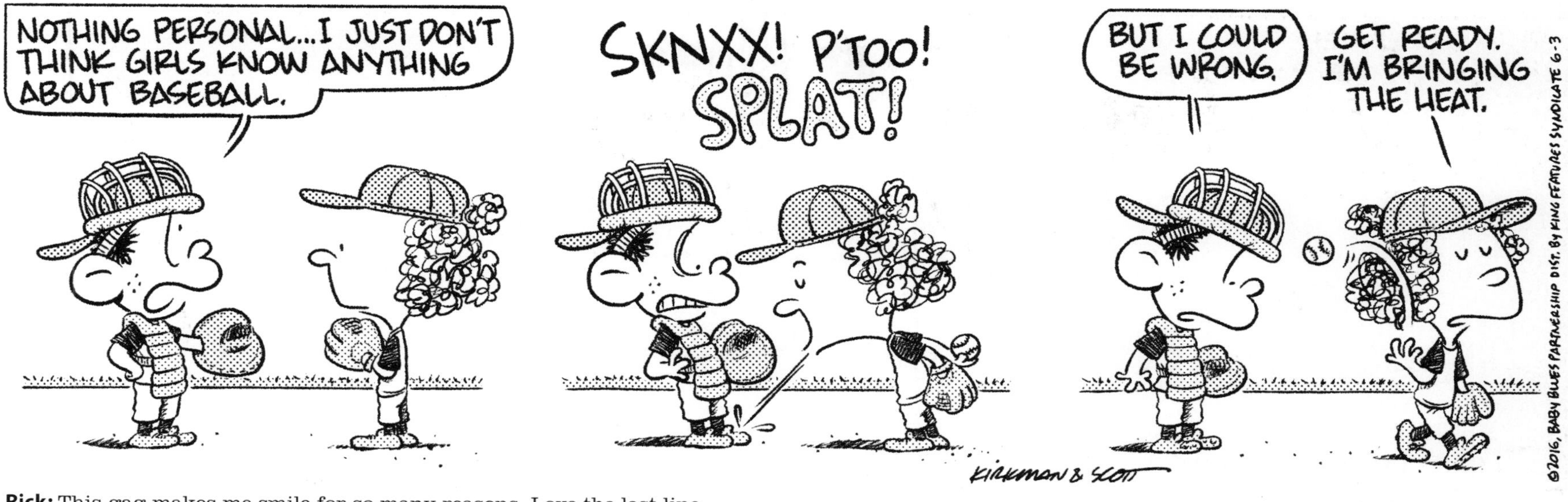
NOTHING PERSONAL...I JUST DON'T THINK GIRLS KNOW ANYTHING ABOUT BASEBALL.
SKNXX! P'TOO!
SPLAT!
BUT I COULD BE WRONG.
GET READY. I'M BRINGING THE HEAT.
©2016, BABY BLUES PARTNERSHIP DIST. BY KING FEATURES SYNDICATE 6-3
KIRKMAN & SCOTT

Rick: This gag makes me smile for so many reasons. Love the last line.

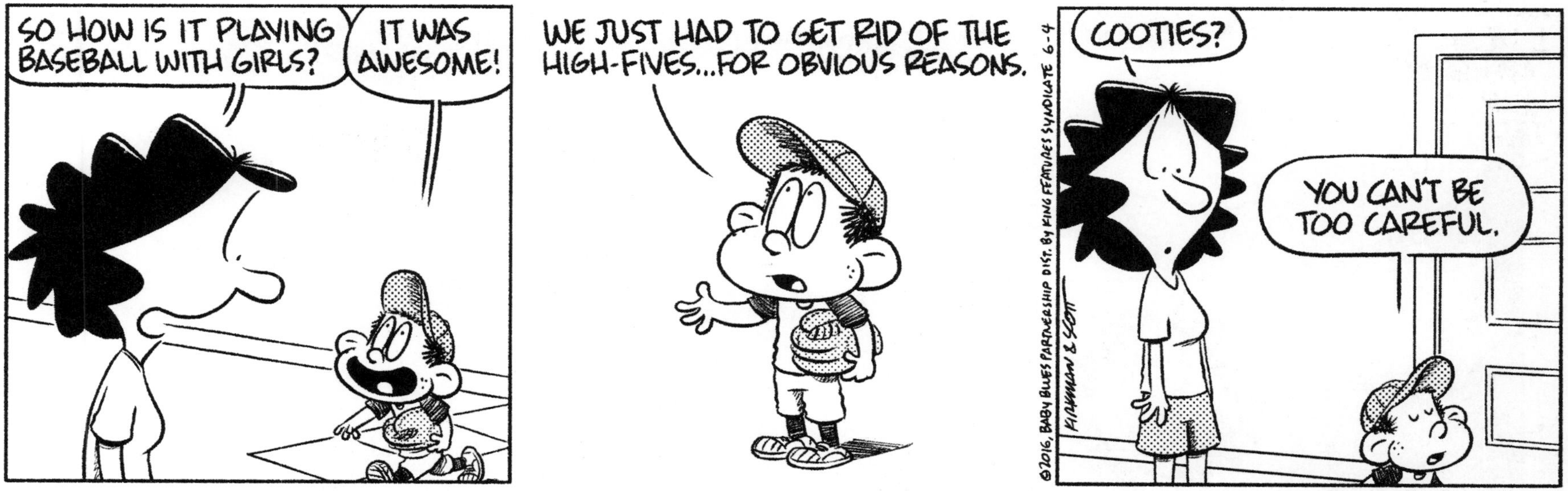
SO HOW IS IT PLAYING BASEBALL WITH GIRLS?
IT WAS AWESOME!
WE JUST HAD TO GET RID OF THE HIGH-FIVES...FOR OBVIOUS REASONS.
COOTIES?
YOU CAN'T BE TOO CAREFUL.
©2016, BABY BLUES PARTNERSHIP DIST. BY KING FEATURES SYNDICATE 6-4
KIRKMAN & SCOTT

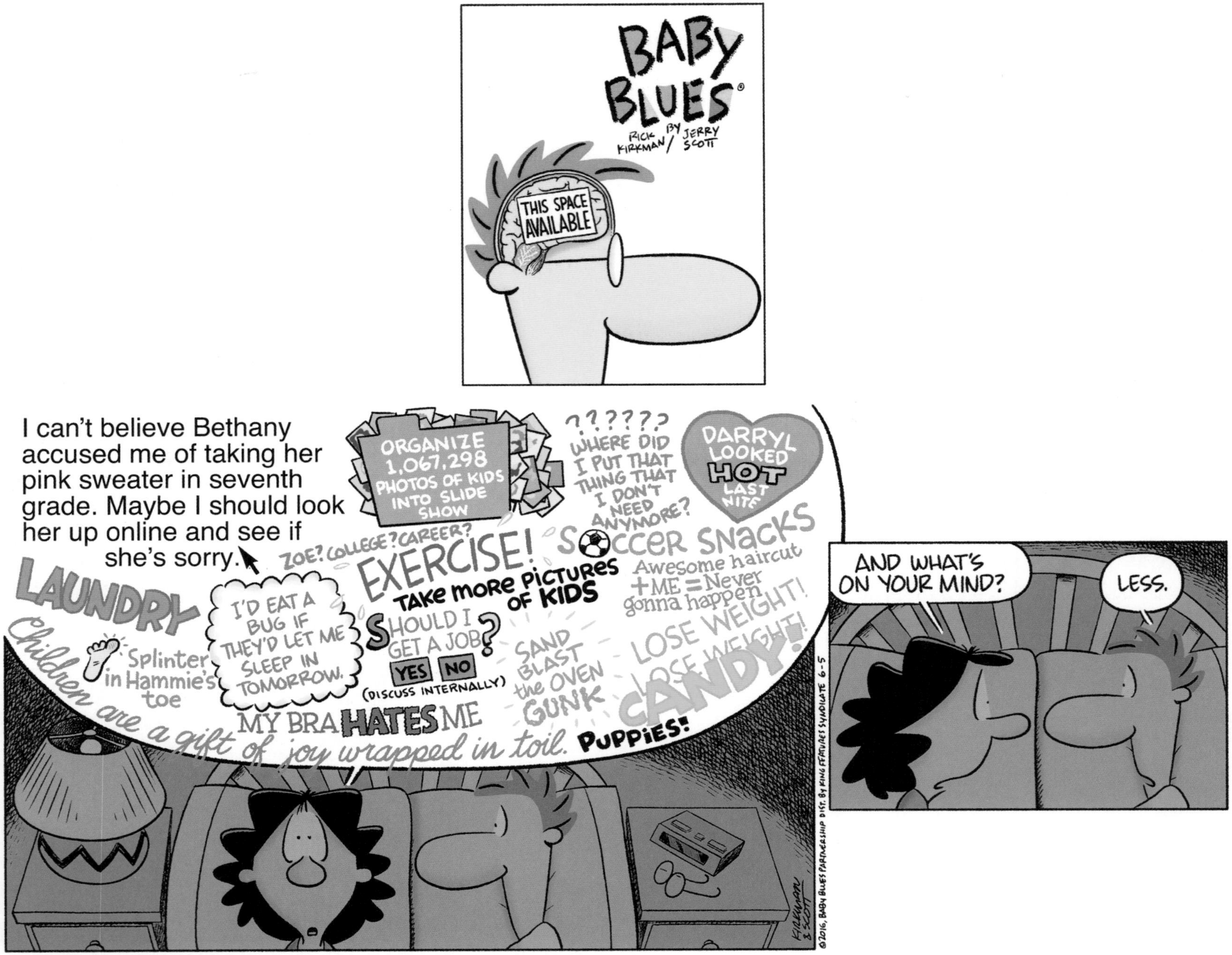
BABY BLUES®
BY RICK KIRKMAN / JERRY SCOTT
THIS SPACE AVAILABLE
I can't believe Bethany accused me of taking her pink sweater in seventh grade. Maybe I should look her up online and see if she's sorry.
ORGANIZE 1,067,298 PHOTOS OF KIDS INTO SLIDE SHOW
??????
WHERE DID I PUT THAT THING THAT I DON'T NEED ANYMORE?
DARRYL LOOKED HOT LAST NITE
LAUNDRY
ZOE? COLLEGE? CAREER?
EXERCISE!
SOCCER SNACKS
Awesome haircut + ME = Never gonna happen
TAKE MORE PICTURES OF KIDS
I'D EAT A BUG IF THEY'D LET ME SLEEP IN TOMORROW.
SHOULD I GET A JOB?
YES NO
(DISCUSS INTERNALLY)
Splinter in Hammie's toe
SAND BLAST the OVEN GUNK
LOSE WEIGHT!
LOSE WEIGHT!
CANDY!
MY BRA HATES ME
Children are a gift of joy wrapped in toil.
PUPPIES!
AND WHAT'S ON YOUR MIND?
LESS.
KIRKMAN & SCOTT
©2016, BABY BLUES PARTNERSHIP DIST. BY KING FEATURES SYNDICATE 6-5

Rick: I have to admit, this setup was sparked by a blog post, although our version is more family-newspaper friendly.

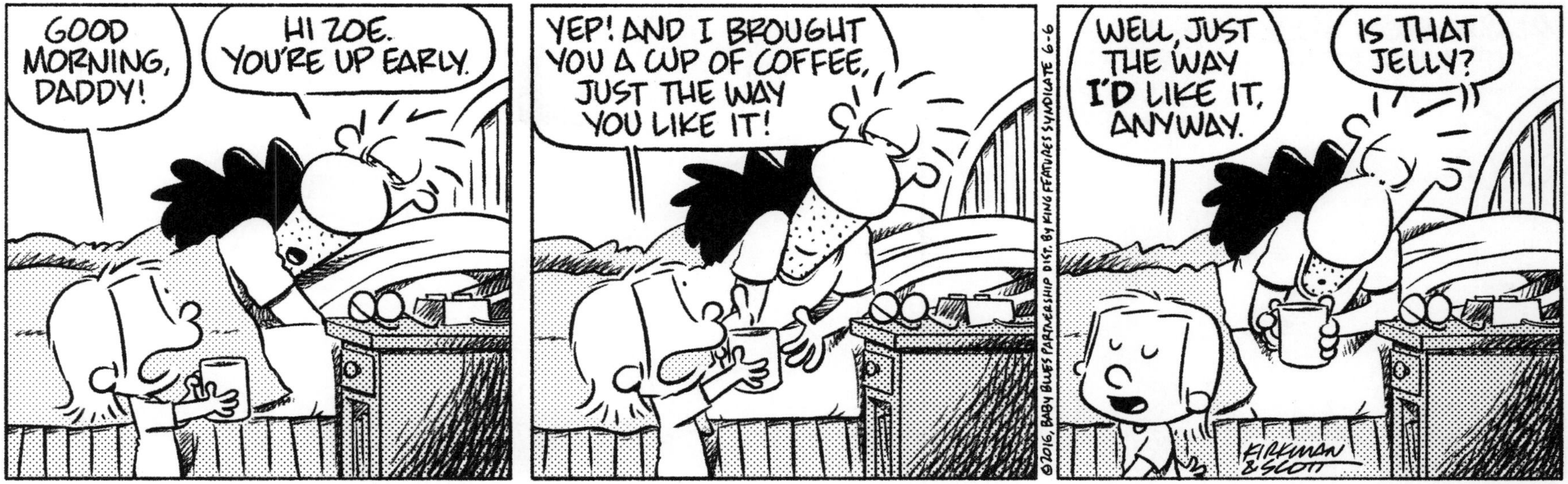
GOOD MORNING, DADDY!
HI ZOE. YOU'RE UP EARLY.
YEP! AND I BROUGHT YOU A CUP OF COFFEE, JUST THE WAY YOU LIKE IT!
©2016, BABY BLUES PARTNERSHIP DIST. BY KING FEATURES SYNDICATE 6-6
WELL, JUST THE WAY I'D LIKE IT, ANYWAY.
IS THAT JELLY?
KIRKMAN & SCOTT

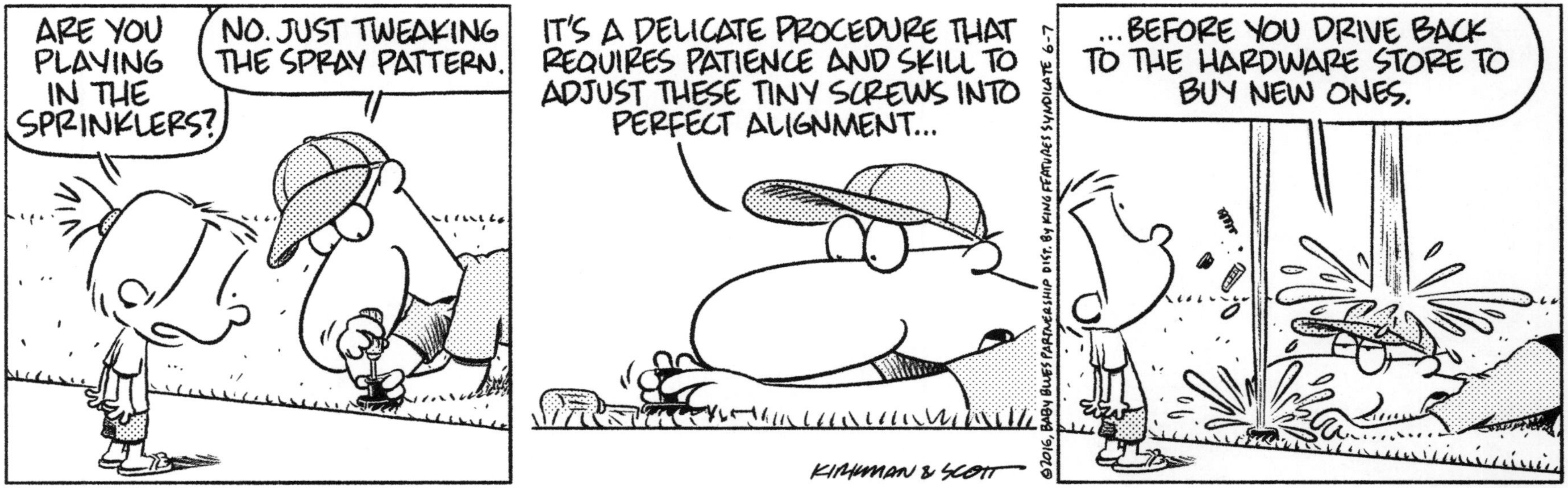
ARE YOU PLAYING IN THE SPRINKLERS?
NO. JUST TWEAKING THE SPRAY PATTERN.
IT'S A DELICATE PROCEDURE THAT REQUIRES PATIENCE AND SKILL TO ADJUST THESE TINY SCREWS INTO PERFECT ALIGNMENT...
KIRKMAN & SCOTT
©2016, BABY BLUES PARTNERSHIP DIST. BY KING FEATURES SYNDICATE 6-7
...BEFORE YOU DRIVE BACK TO THE HARDWARE STORE TO BUY NEW ONES.

Jerry: If you don't make at least three trips to the hardware store for every weekend project, you're not trying hard enough.

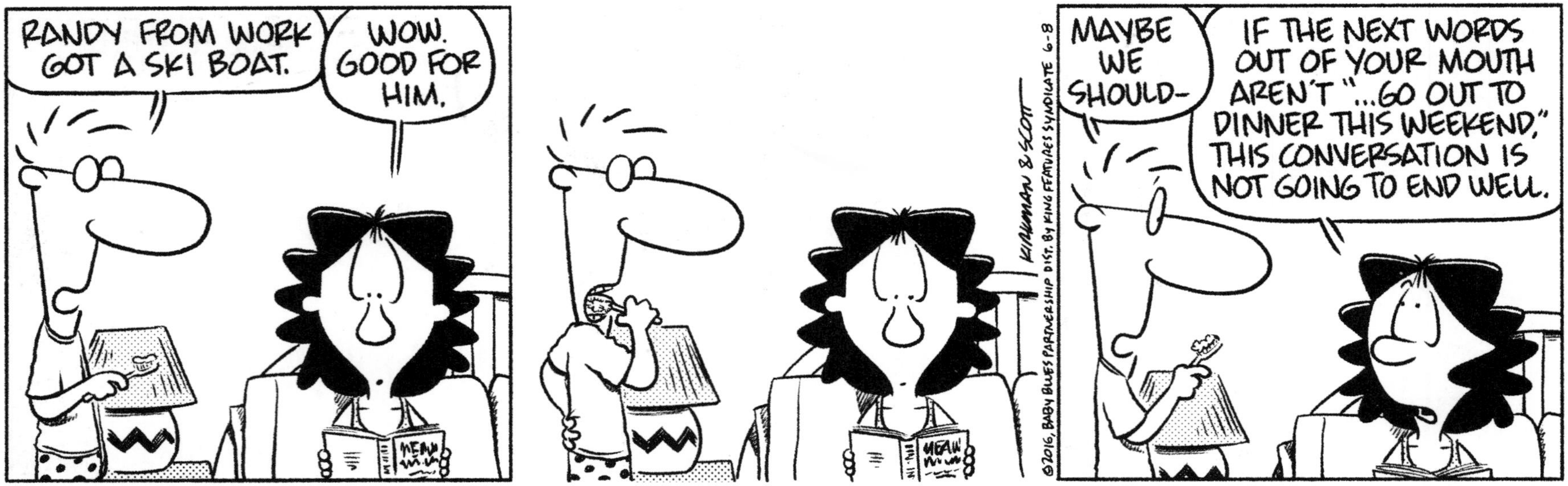
RANDY FROM WORK GOT A SKI BOAT.
WOW. GOOD FOR HIM.
KIRKMAN & SCOTT
©2016, BABY BLUES PARTNERSHIP DIST. BY KING FEATURES SYNDICATE 6-8
MAYBE WE SHOULD-
IF THE NEXT WORDS OUT OF YOUR MOUTH AREN'T "...GO OUT TO DINNER THIS WEEKEND," THIS CONVERSATION IS NOT GOING TO END WELL.

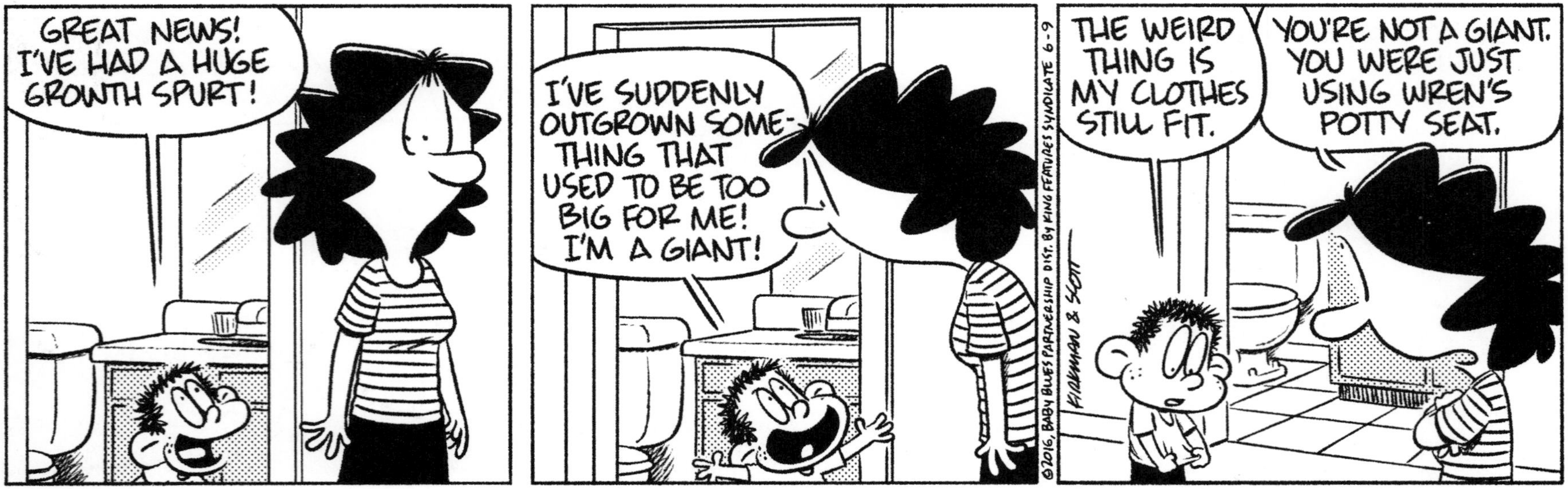
GREAT NEWS! I'VE HAD A HUGE GROWTH SPURT!
I'VE SUDDENLY OUTGROWN SOME-THING THAT USED TO BE TOO BIG FOR ME! I'M A GIANT!
©2016, BABY BLUES PARTNERSHIP DIST. BY KING FEATURES SYNDICATE 6-9
KIRKMAN & SCOTT
THE WEIRD THING IS MY CLOTHES STILL FIT.
YOU'RE NOT A GIANT. YOU WERE JUST USING WREN'S POTTY SEAT.

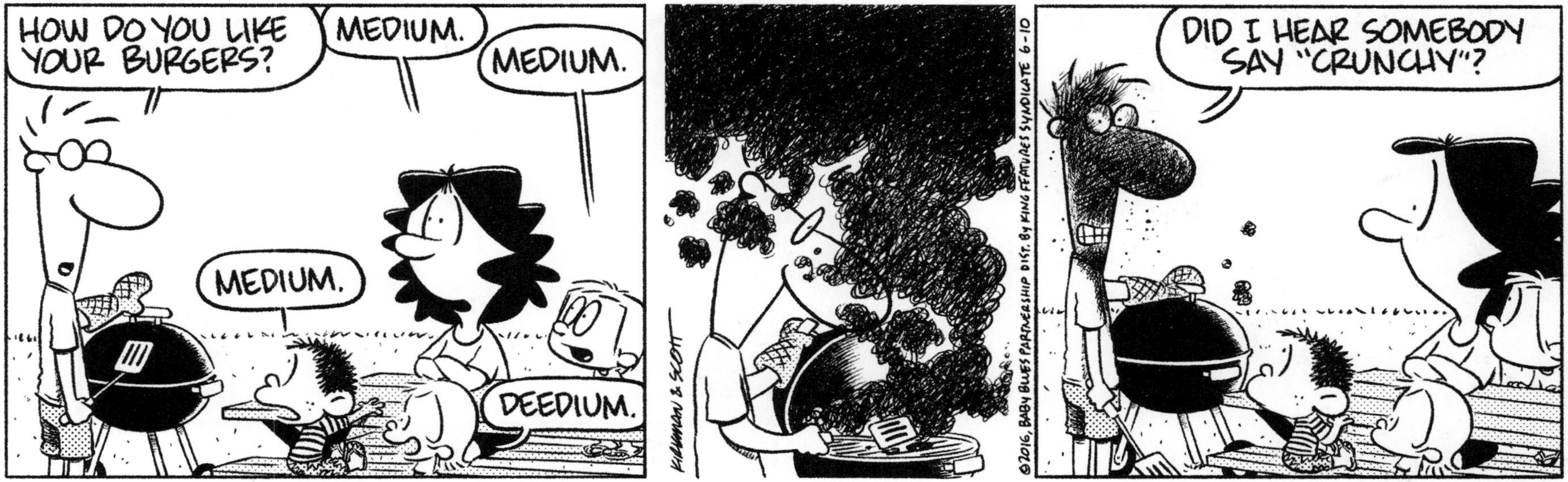
HOW DO YOU LIKE YOUR BURGERS?
MEDIUM.
MEDIUM.
MEDIUM.
DEEDIUM.
KIRKMAN & SCOTT
©2016, BABY BLUES PARTNERSHIP DIST. BY KING FEATURES SYNDICATE 6-10
DID I HEAR SOMEBODY SAY "CRUNCHY"?

Rick: It's nice that every now and then there's a strip that gives me a chance to scribble.

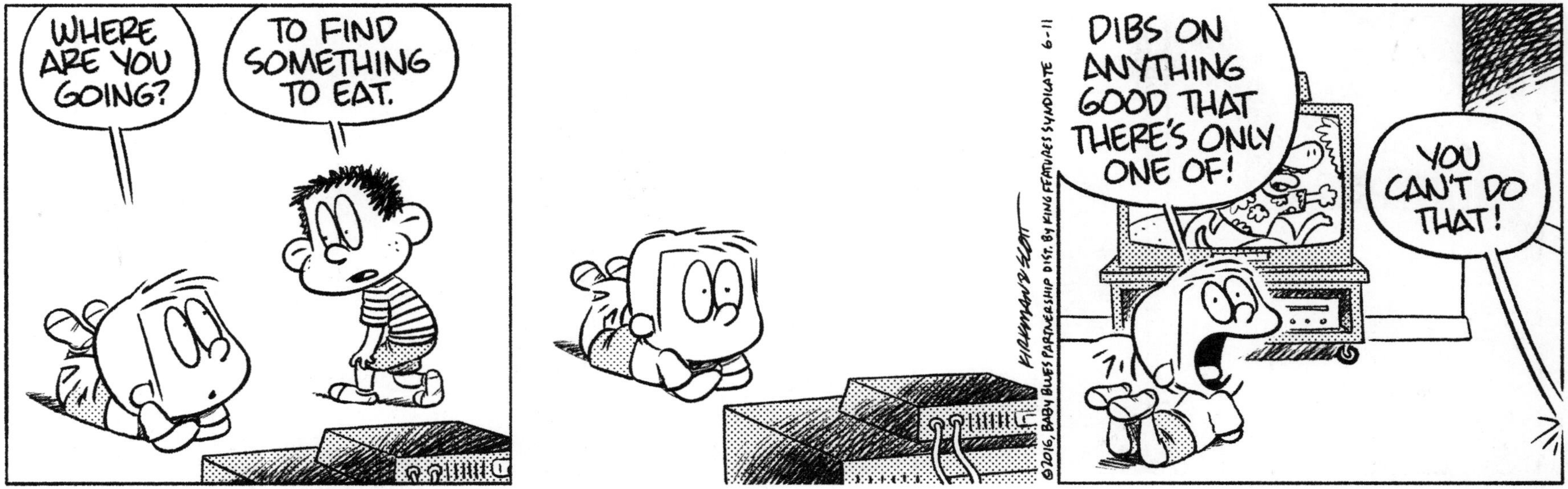
WHERE ARE YOU GOING?
TO FIND SOMETHING TO EAT.
KIRKMAN & SCOTT
©2016, BABY BLUES PARTNERSHIP DIST. BY KING FEATURES SYNDICATE 6-11
DIBS ON ANYTHING GOOD THAT THERE'S ONLY ONE OF!
YOU CAN'T DO THAT!

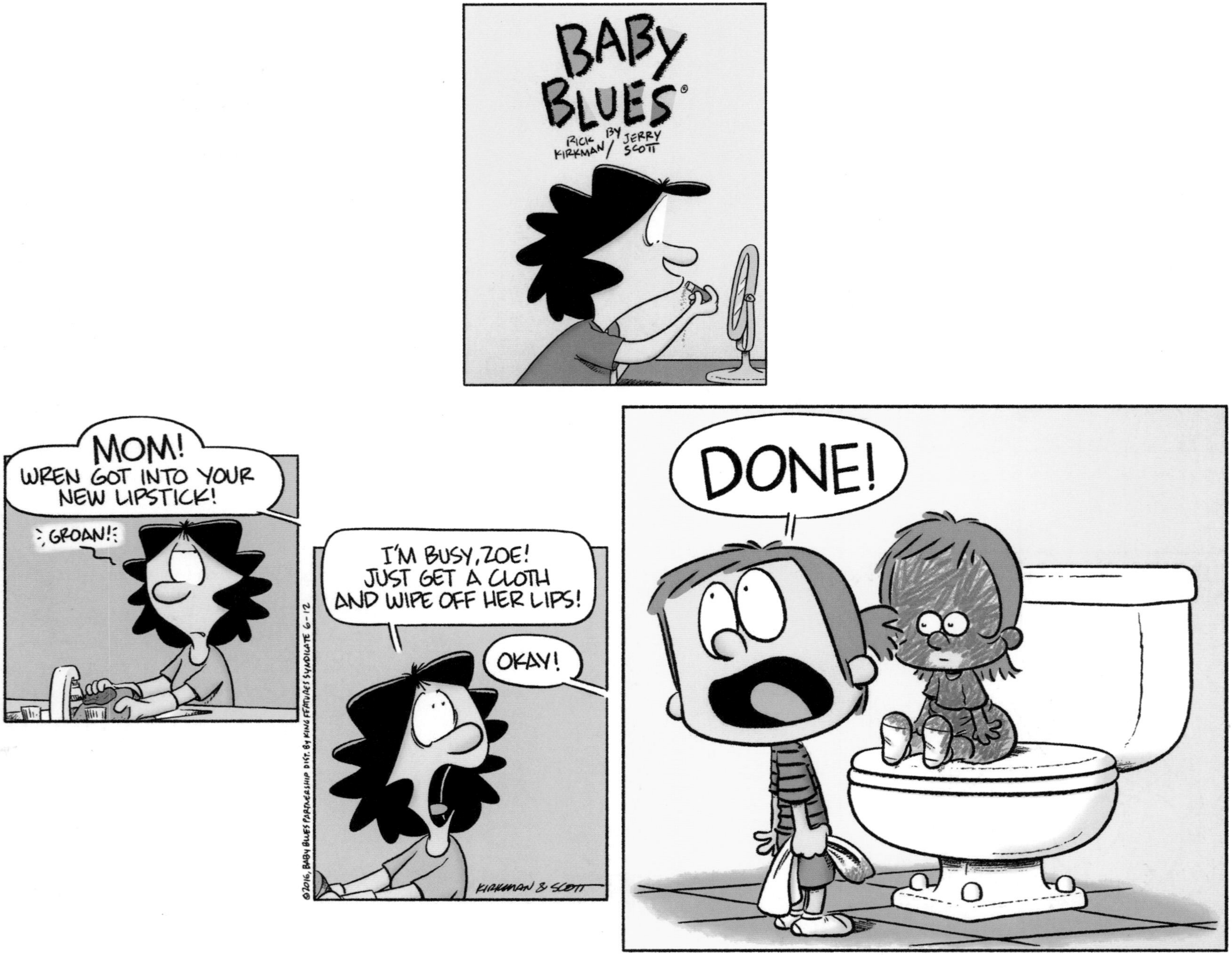
BABY BLUES®
BY RICK KIRKMAN / JERRY SCOTT
MOM! WREN GOT INTO YOUR NEW LIPSTICK!
GROAN!
I'M BUSY, ZOE! JUST GET A CLOTH AND WIPE OFF HER LIPS!
OKAY!
©2016, BABY BLUES PARTNERSHIP DIST. BY KING FEATURES SYNDICATE 6-12
KIRKMAN & SCOTT
DONE!

Jerry: The setting in this last panel could have been anywhere, but the toilet adds just the right amount of funny. Plus, Rick draws funny toilets.

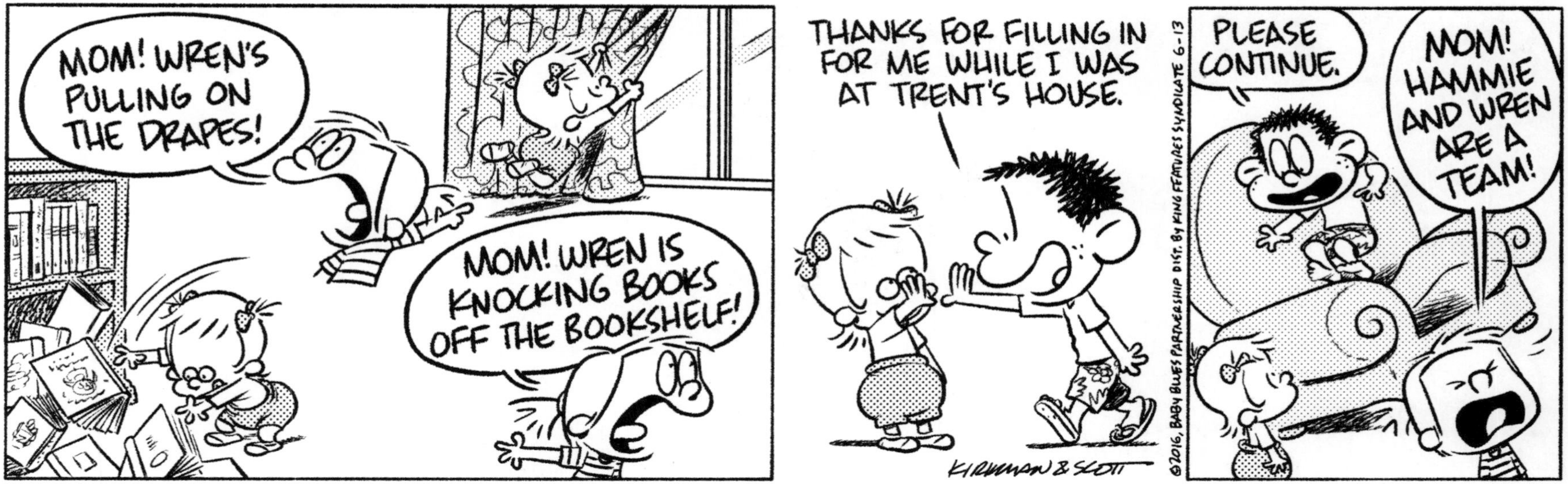
MOM! WREN'S PULLING ON THE DRAPES!
MOM! WREN IS KNOCKING BOOKS OFF THE BOOKSHELF!
THANKS FOR FILLING IN FOR ME WHILE I WAS AT TRENT'S HOUSE.
PLEASE CONTINUE.
MOM! HAMMIE AND WREN ARE A TEAM!
KIRKMAN & SCOTT
©2016, BABY BLUES PARTNERSHIP DIST. BY KING FEATURES SYNDICATE 6-13

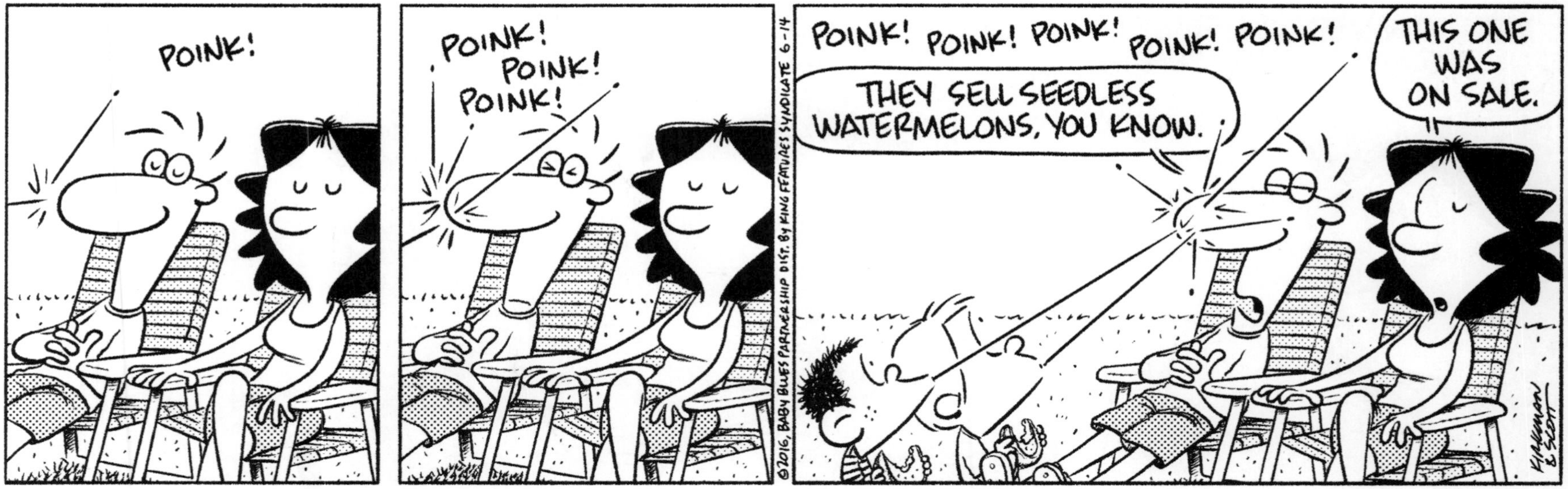
POINK!
POINK! POINK! POINK!
©2016, BABY BLUES PARTNERSHIP DIST. BY KING FEATURES SYNDICATE 6-14
POINK! POINK! POINK! POINK! POINK!
THEY SELL SEEDLESS WATERMELONS, YOU KNOW.
THIS ONE WAS ON SALE.
KIRKMAN & SCOTT

Rick: This is one that made me laugh, just reading it, as I imagined the drawing.

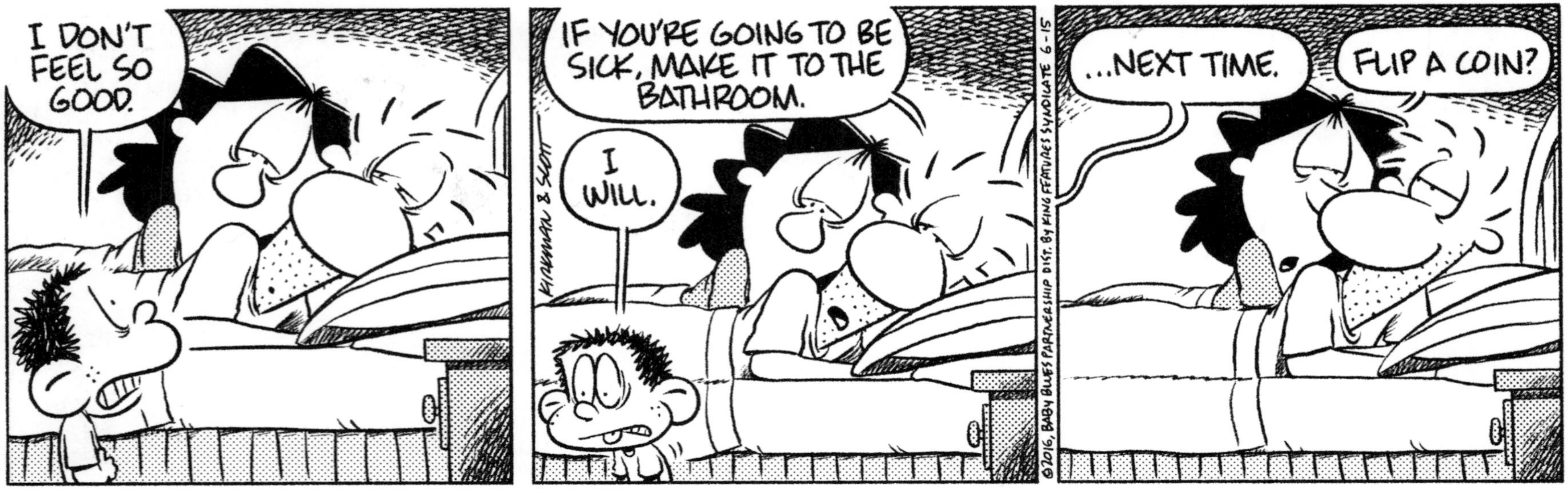
I DON'T FEEL SO GOOD.
IF YOU'RE GOING TO BE SICK, MAKE IT TO THE BATHROOM.
I WILL.
KIRKMAN & SCOTT
©2016, BABY BLUES PARTNERSHIP DIST. BY KING FEATURES SYNDICATE 6-15
...NEXT TIME.
FLIP A COIN?

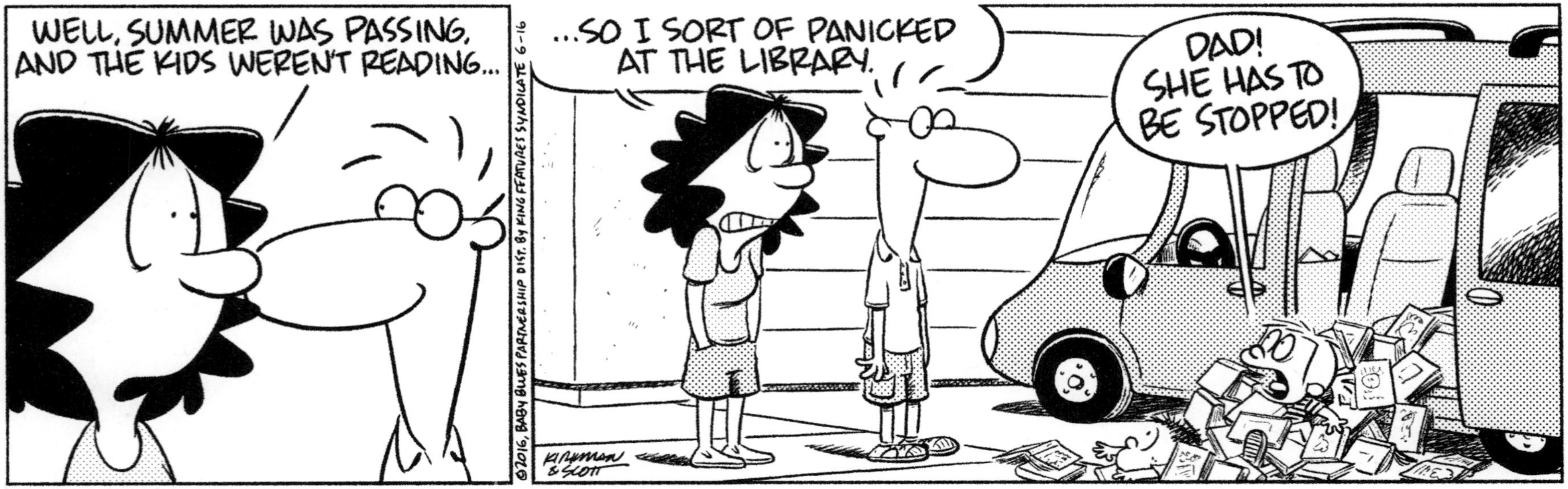
WELL, SUMMER WAS PASSING, AND THE KIDS WEREN'T READING...
©2016, BABY BLUES PARTNERSHIP DIST. BY KING FEATURES SYNDICATE 6-16
...SO I SORT OF PANICKED AT THE LIBRARY.
DAD! SHE HAS TO BE STOPPED!
KIRKMAN & SCOTT

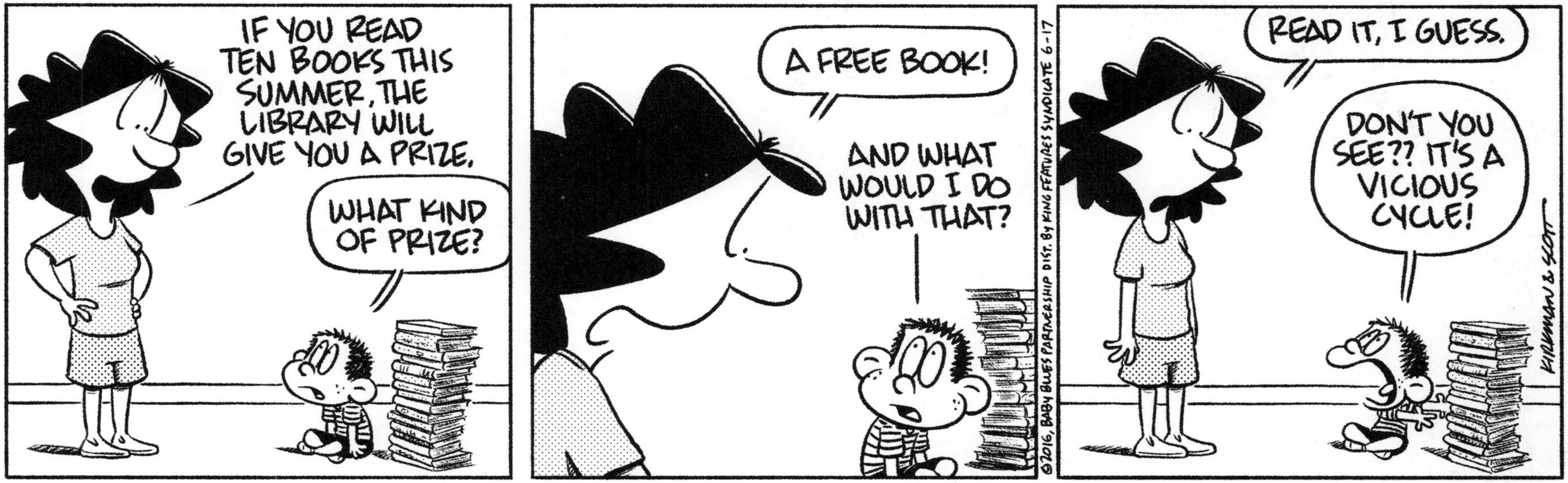
IF YOU READ TEN BOOKS THIS SUMMER, THE LIBRARY WILL GIVE YOU A PRIZE.
WHAT KIND OF PRIZE?
A FREE BOOK!
AND WHAT WOULD I DO WITH THAT?
©2016, BABY BLUES PARTNERSHIP DIST. BY KING FEATURES SYNDICATE 6-17
READ IT, I GUESS.
DON'T YOU SEE?? IT'S A VICIOUS CYCLE!
KIRKMAN & SCOTT

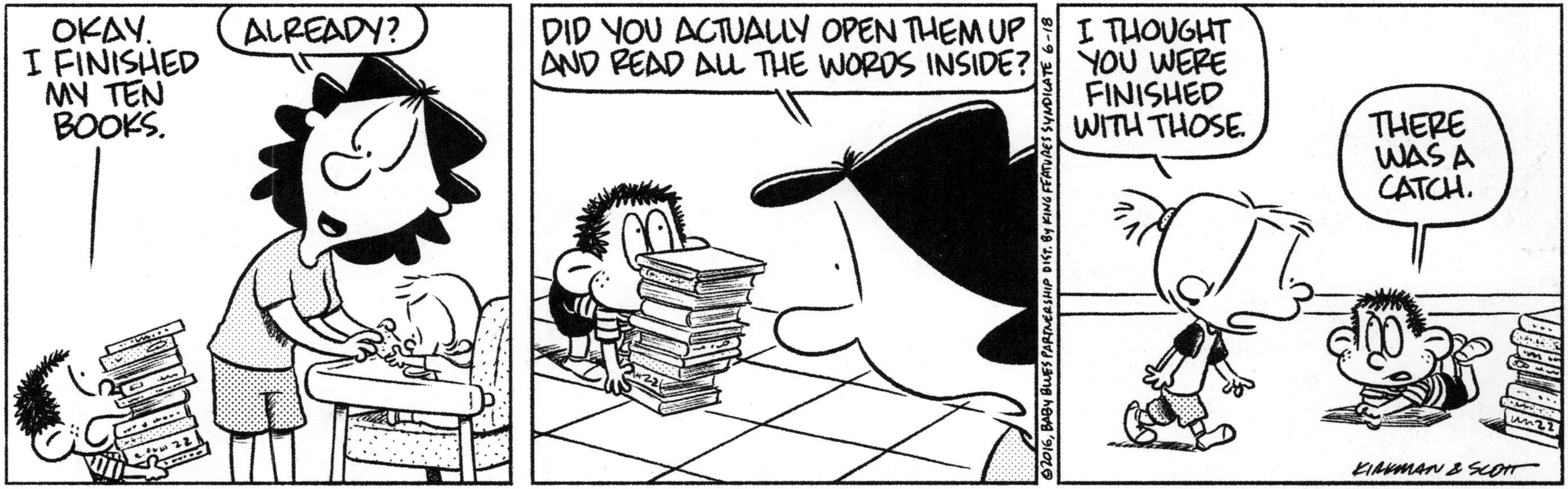
OKAY. I FINISHED MY TEN BOOKS.
ALREADY?
DID YOU ACTUALLY OPEN THEM UP AND READ ALL THE WORDS INSIDE?
©2016, BABY BLUES PARTNERSHIP DIST. BY KING FEATURES SYNDICATE 6-18
I THOUGHT YOU WERE FINISHED WITH THOSE.
THERE WAS A CATCH.
KIRKMAN & SCOTT

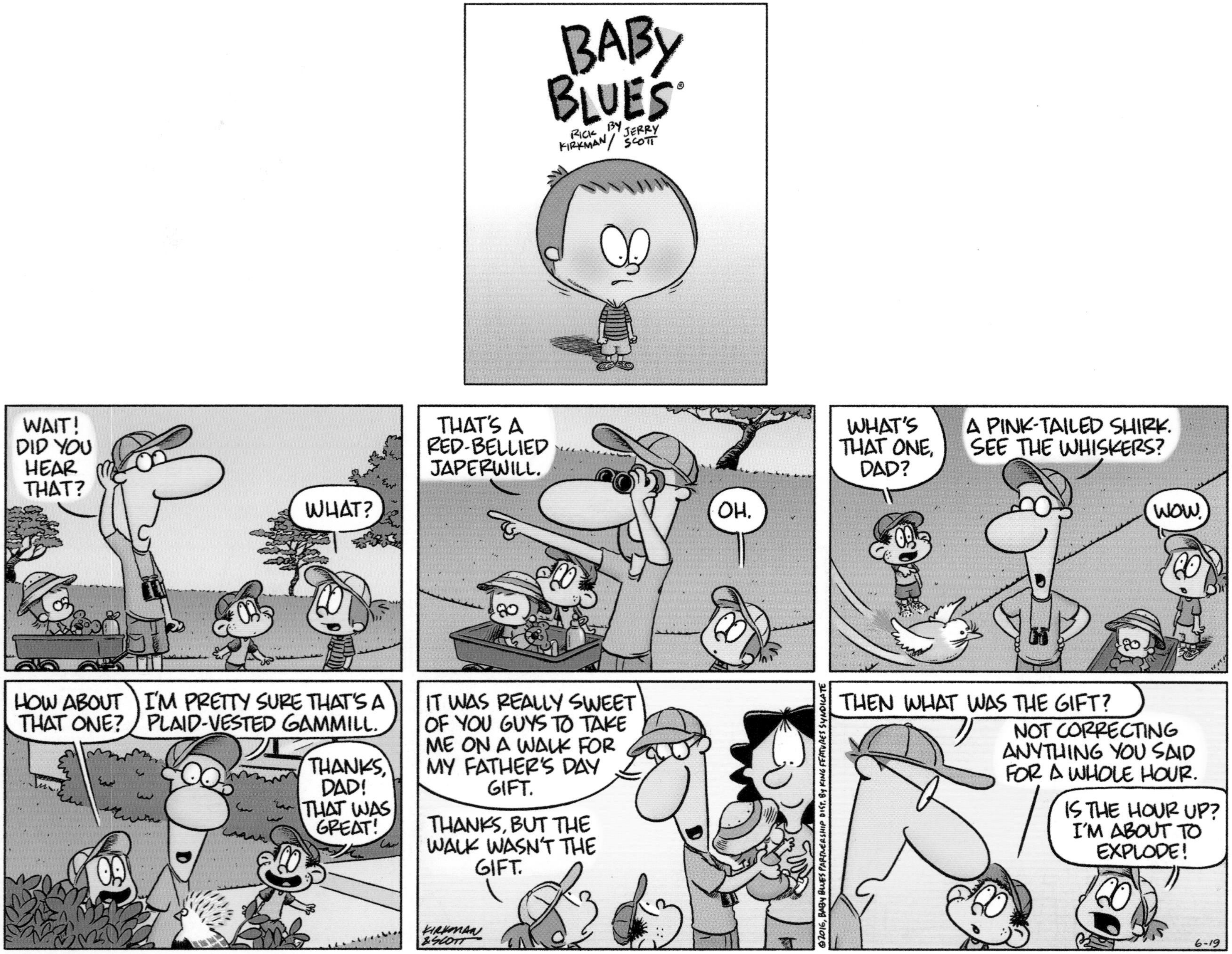
BABY BLUES®
BY RICK KIRKMAN / JERRY SCOTT
WAIT! DID YOU HEAR THAT?
WHAT?
THAT'S A RED-BELLIED JAPERWILL.
OH.
WHAT'S THAT ONE, DAD?
A PINK-TAILED SHIRK. SEE THE WHISKERS?
WOW.
HOW ABOUT THAT ONE?
I'M PRETTY SURE THAT'S A PLAID-VESTED GAMMILL.
THANKS, DAD! THAT WAS GREAT!
IT WAS REALLY SWEET OF YOU GUYS TO TAKE ME ON A WALK FOR MY FATHER'S DAY GIFT.
THANKS, BUT THE WALK WASN'T THE GIFT.
KIRKMAN & SCOTT
©2016, BABY BLUES PARTNERSHIP DIST. BY KING FEATURES SYNDICATE
THEN WHAT WAS THE GIFT?
NOT CORRECTING ANYTHING YOU SAID FOR A WHOLE HOUR.
IS THE HOUR UP? I'M ABOUT TO EXPLODE!
6-19

Rick: Hee-hee—"Plaid-vested Gammill."

Jerry: So named for our famous comedy-writer friend, the inimitable Tom Gammill. Hi, Tom!

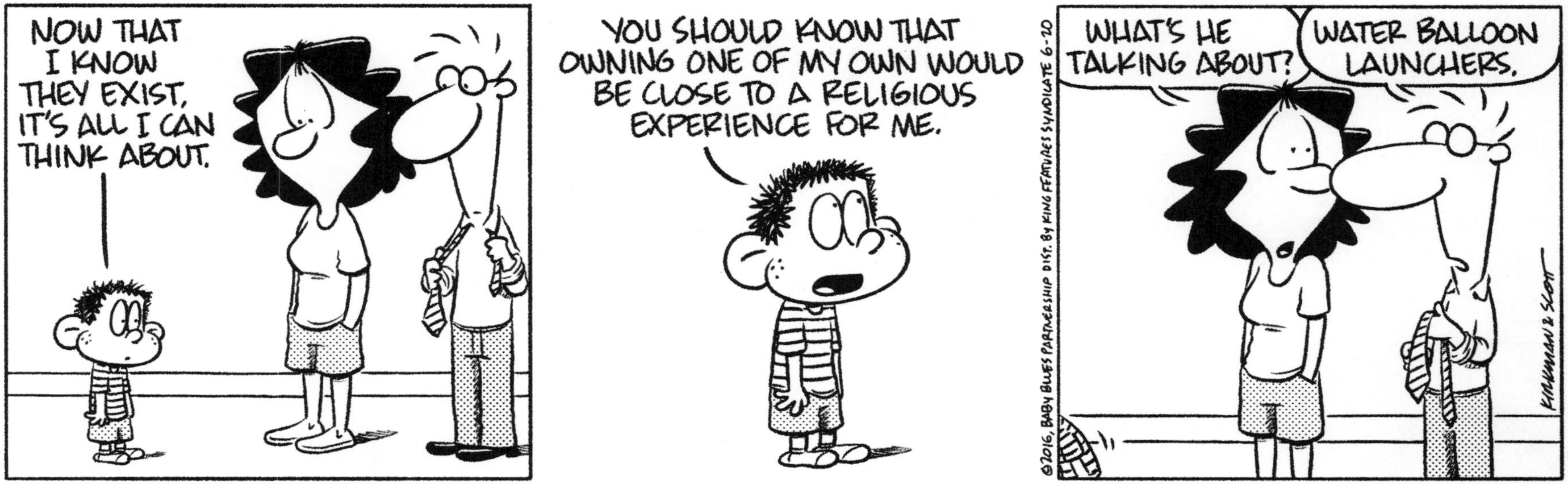
NOW THAT I KNOW THEY EXIST, IT'S ALL I CAN THINK ABOUT.
YOU SHOULD KNOW THAT OWNING ONE OF MY OWN WOULD BE CLOSE TO A RELIGIOUS EXPERIENCE FOR ME.
WHAT'S HE TALKING ABOUT?
WATER BALLOON LAUNCHERS.
©2016, BABY BLUES PARTNERSHIP DIST. BY KING FEATURES SYNDICATE 6-20
KIRKMAN & SCOTT

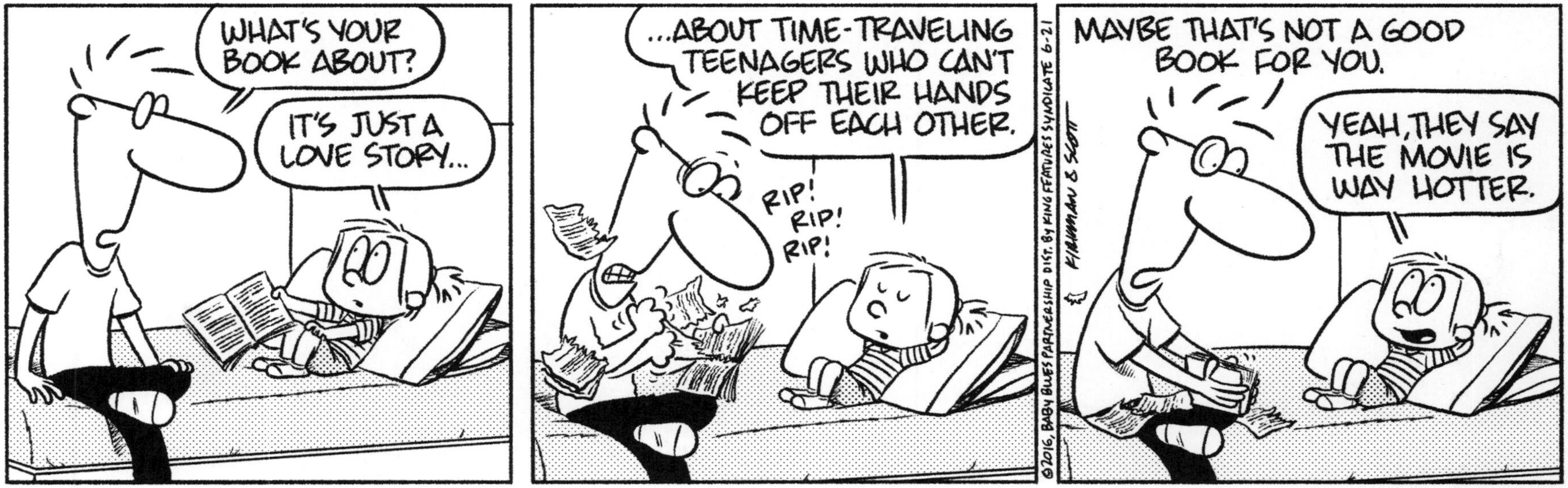
WHAT'S YOUR BOOK ABOUT?
IT'S JUST A LOVE STORY...
...ABOUT TIME-TRAVELING TEENAGERS WHO CAN'T KEEP THEIR HANDS OFF EACH OTHER.
RIP! RIP! RIP!
MAYBE THAT'S NOT A GOOD BOOK FOR YOU.
YEAH, THEY SAY THE MOVIE IS WAY HOTTER.
©2016, BABY BLUES PARTNERSHIP DIST. BY KING FEATURES SYNDICATE 6-21
KIRKMAN & SCOTT

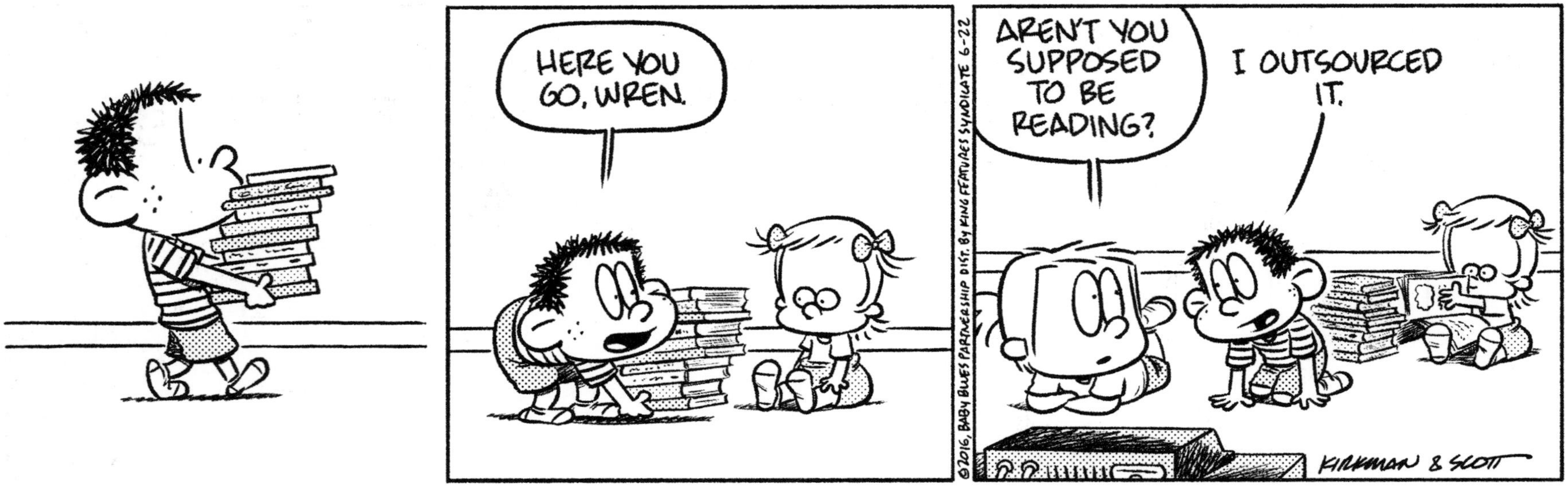
HERE YOU GO, WREN.
©2016, BABY BLUES PARTNERSHIP DIST. BY KING FEATURES SYNDICATE 6-22
AREN'T YOU SUPPOSED TO BE READING?
I OUTSOURCED IT.
KIRKMAN & SCOTT

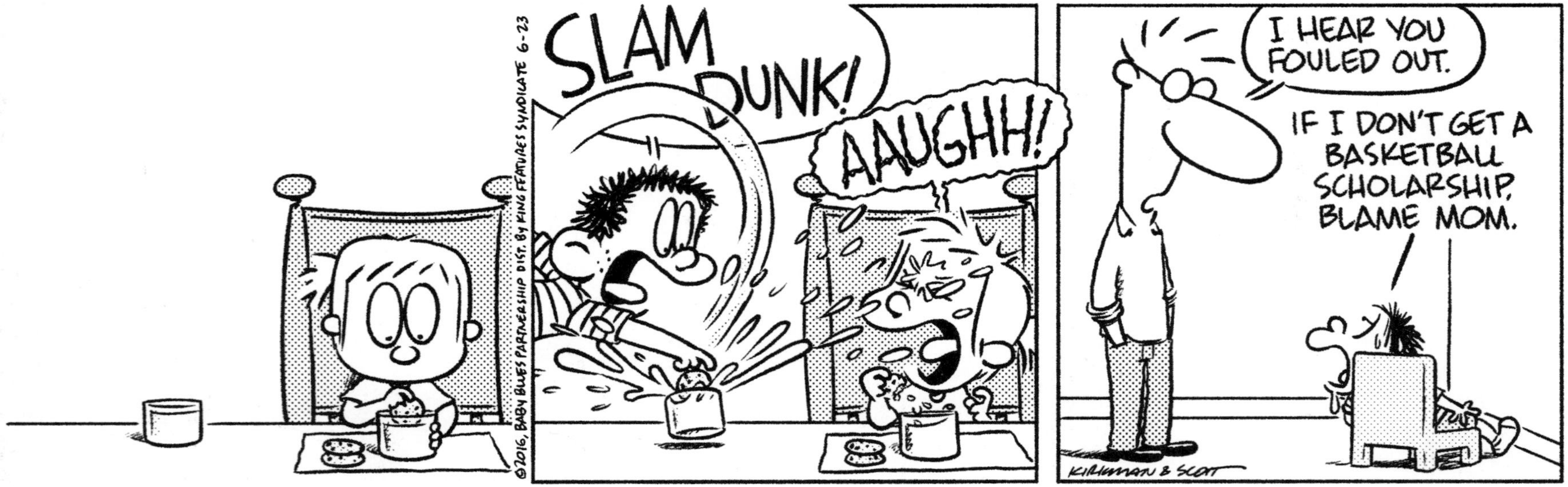
©2016, BABY BLUES PARTNERSHIP DIST. BY KING FEATURES SYNDICATE 6-23
SLAM DUNK!
AAUGHH!
I HEAR YOU FOULED OUT.
IF I DON'T GET A BASKETBALL SCHOLARSHIP, BLAME MOM.
KIRKMAN & SCOTT

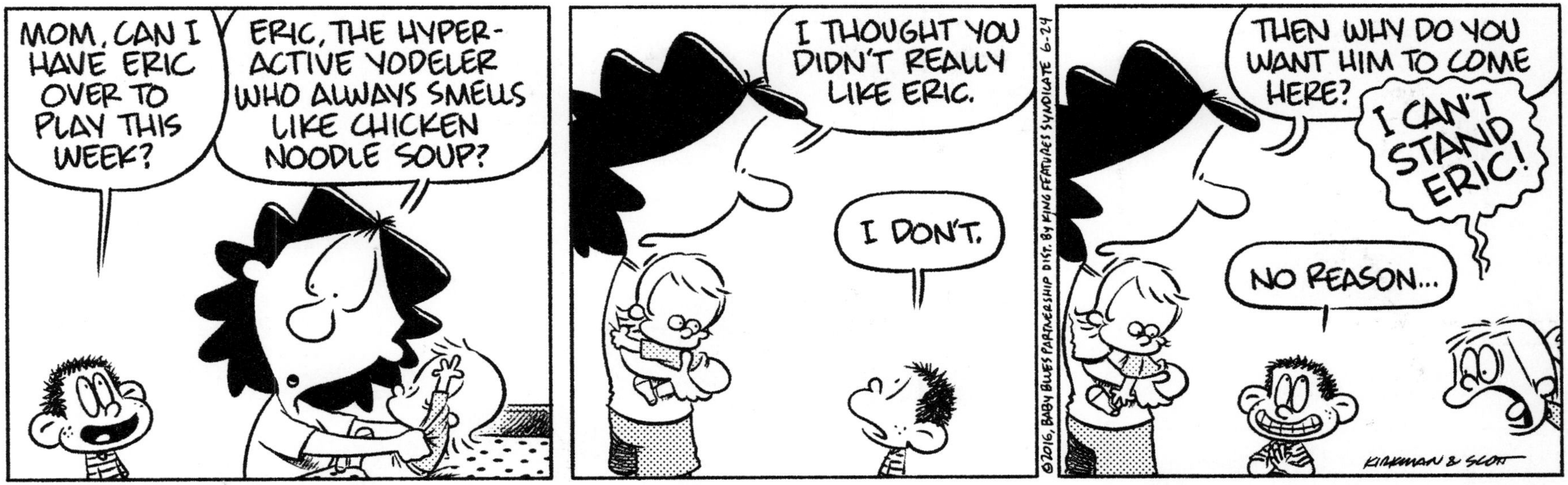
MOM, CAN I HAVE ERIC OVER TO PLAY THIS WEEK?
ERIC, THE HYPER-ACTIVE YODELER WHO ALWAYS SMELLS LIKE CHICKEN NOODLE SOUP?
I THOUGHT YOU DIDN'T REALLY LIKE ERIC.
I DON'T.
©2016, BABY BLUES PARTNERSHIP DIST. BY KING FEATURES SYNDICATE 6-24
THEN WHY DO YOU WANT HIM TO COME HERE?
I CAN'T STAND ERIC!
NO REASON...
KIRKMAN & SCOTT

Jerry: I had a hyperactive friend named Eric who always smelled like chicken noodle soup. He wasn't a yodeler, though. I made that part up.

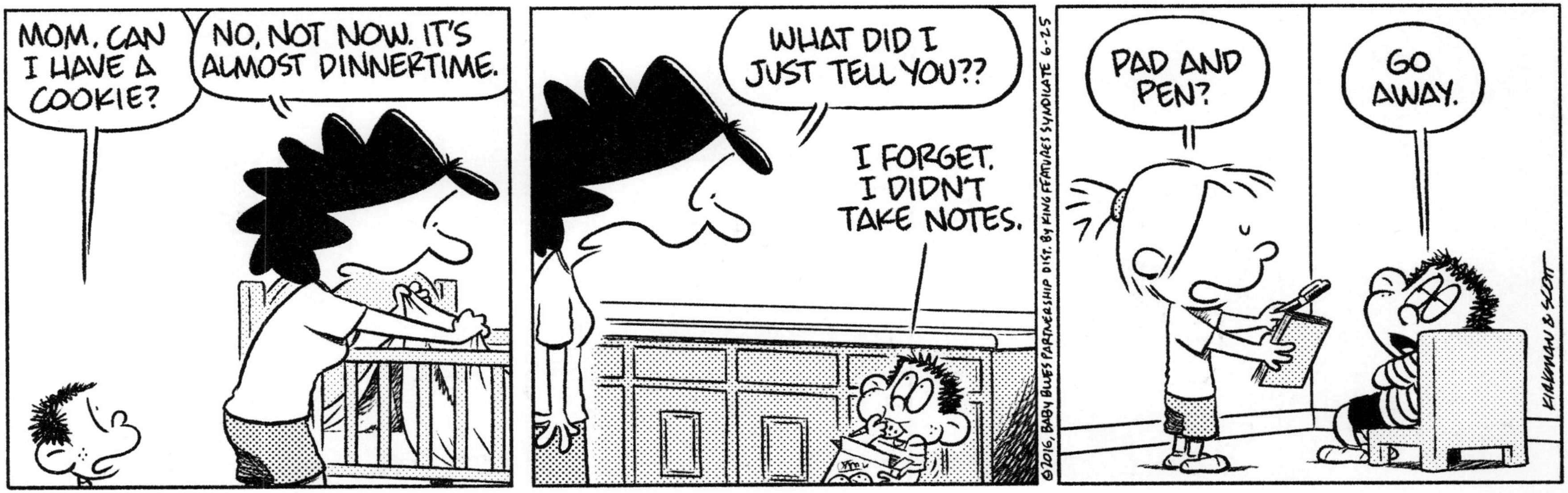
MOM, CAN I HAVE A COOKIE?
NO, NOT NOW. IT'S ALMOST DINNERTIME.
WHAT DID I JUST TELL YOU??
I FORGET. I DIDN'T TAKE NOTES.
©2016, BABY BLUES PARTNERSHIP DIST. BY KING FEATURES SYNDICATE 6-25
PAD AND PEN?
GO AWAY.
KIRKMAN & SCOTT

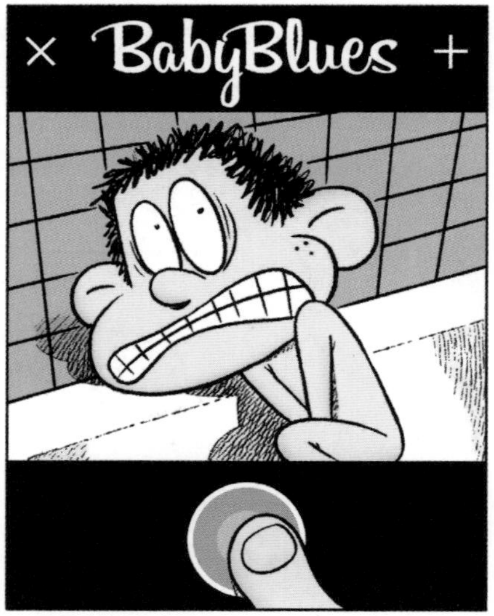
BabyBlues

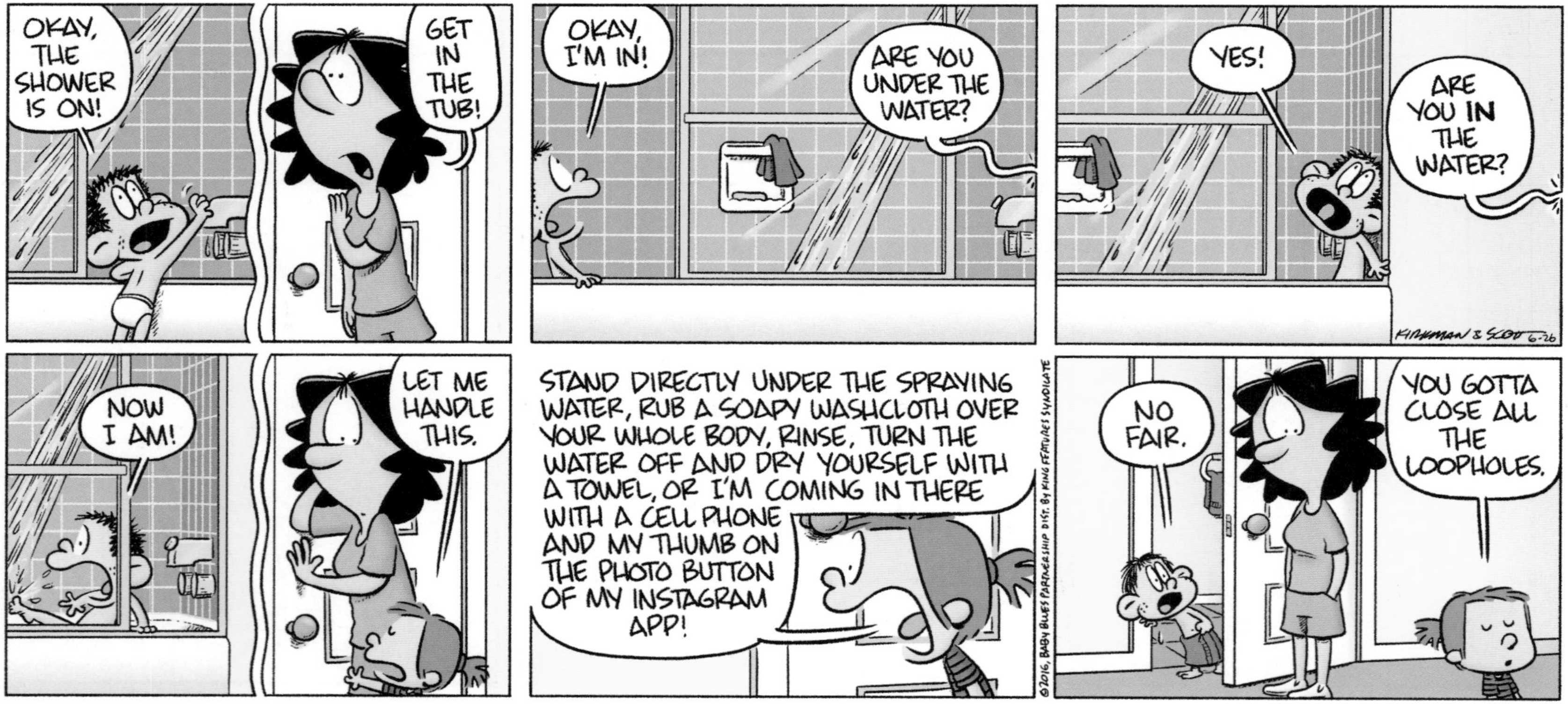
OKAY, THE SHOWER IS ON!
GET IN THE TUB!
OKAY, I'M IN!
ARE YOU UNDER THE WATER?
YES!
ARE YOU **IN** THE WATER?
KIRKMAN & SCOTT 6-26
NOW I AM!
LET ME HANDLE THIS.
STAND DIRECTLY UNDER THE SPRAYING WATER, RUB A SOAPY WASHCLOTH OVER YOUR WHOLE BODY, RINSE, TURN THE WATER OFF AND DRY YOURSELF WITH A TOWEL, OR I'M COMING IN THERE WITH A CELL PHONE AND MY THUMB ON THE PHOTO BUTTON OF MY INSTAGRAM APP!
©2016, BABY BLUES PARTNERSHIP DIST. BY KING FEATURES SYNDICATE
NO FAIR.
YOU GOTTA CLOSE ALL THE LOOPHOLES.

Jerry: Technology improves discipline. Who knew?

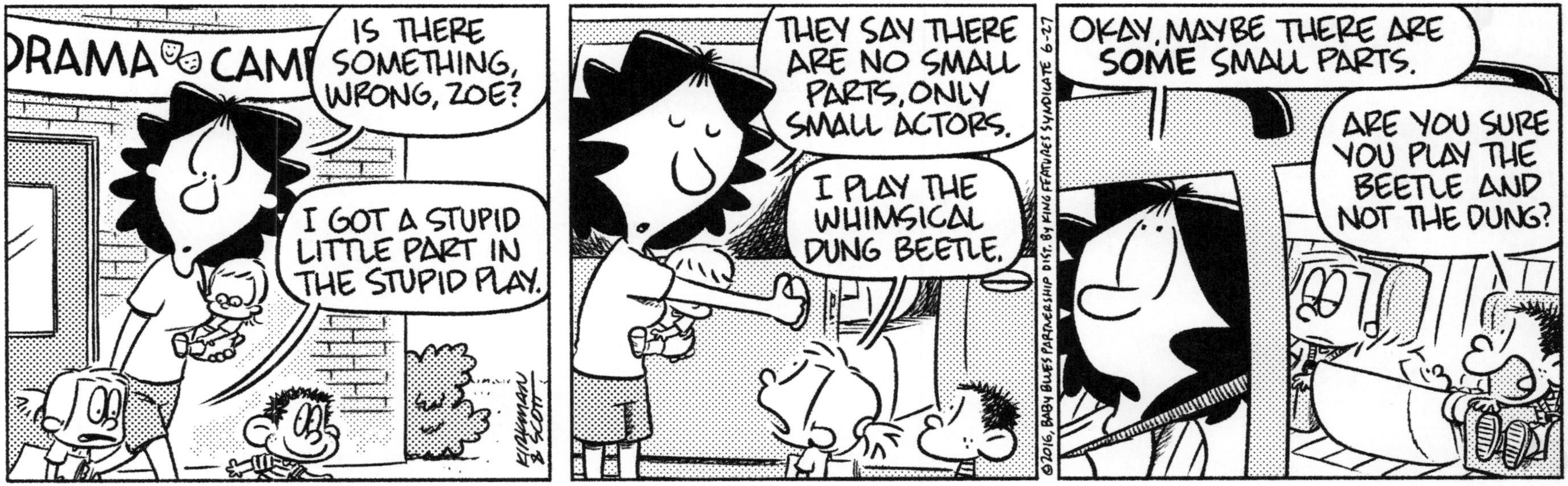
IS THERE SOMETHING, WRONG, ZOE?
I GOT A STUPID LITTLE PART IN THE STUPID PLAY.
THEY SAY THERE ARE NO SMALL PARTS, ONLY SMALL ACTORS.
I PLAY THE WHIMSICAL DUNG BEETLE.
OKAY, MAYBE THERE ARE SOME SMALL PARTS.
ARE YOU SURE YOU PLAY THE BEETLE AND NOT THE DUNG?
KIRKMAN & SCOTT
©2016, BABY BLUES PARTNERSHIP DIST. BY KING FEATURES SYNDICATE 6-27

Jerry: Once Hammie played the part of the colon in a school play, and now Zoe is going to be a dung beetle. I should see a therapist.

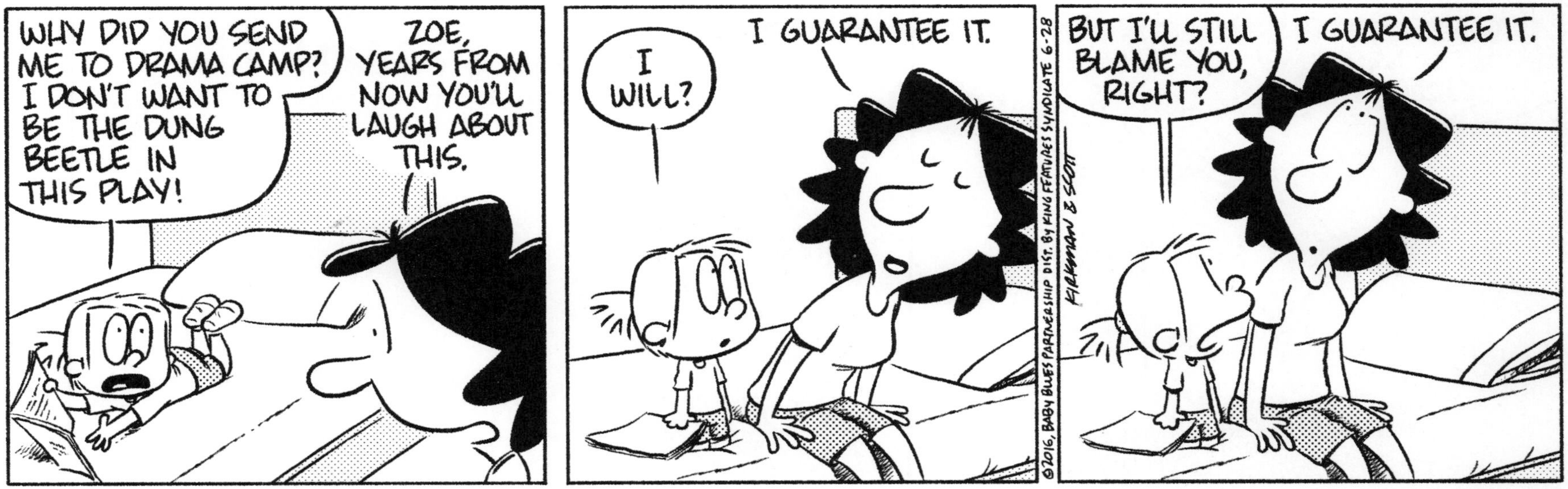
WHY DID YOU SEND ME TO DRAMA CAMP? I DON'T WANT TO BE THE DUNG BEETLE IN THIS PLAY!
ZOE, YEARS FROM NOW YOU'LL LAUGH ABOUT THIS.
I WILL?
I GUARANTEE IT.
BUT I'LL STILL BLAME YOU, RIGHT?
I GUARANTEE IT.
KIRKMAN & SCOTT
©2016, BABY BLUES PARTNERSHIP DIST. BY KING FEATURES SYNDICATE 6-28

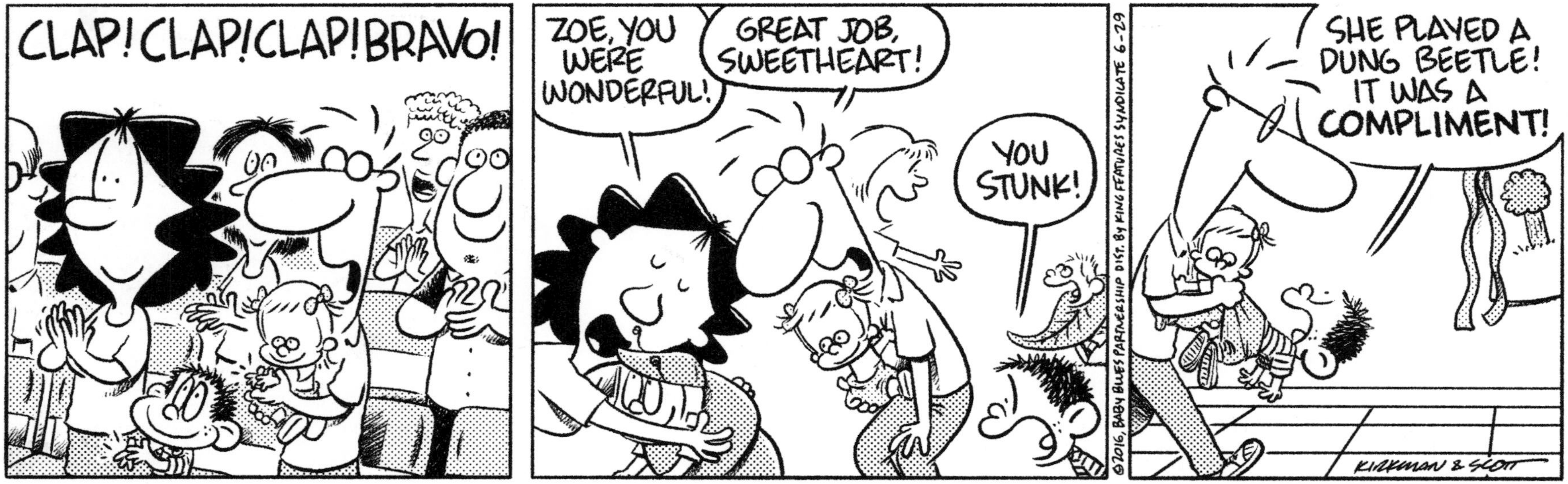
CLAP! CLAP! CLAP! BRAVO!
ZOE, YOU WERE WONDERFUL!
GREAT JOB, SWEETHEART!
YOU STUNK!
©2016, BABY BLUES PARTNERSHIP DIST. BY KING FEATURES SYNDICATE 6-29
SHE PLAYED A DUNG BEETLE! IT WAS A COMPLIMENT!
KIRKMAN & SCOTT

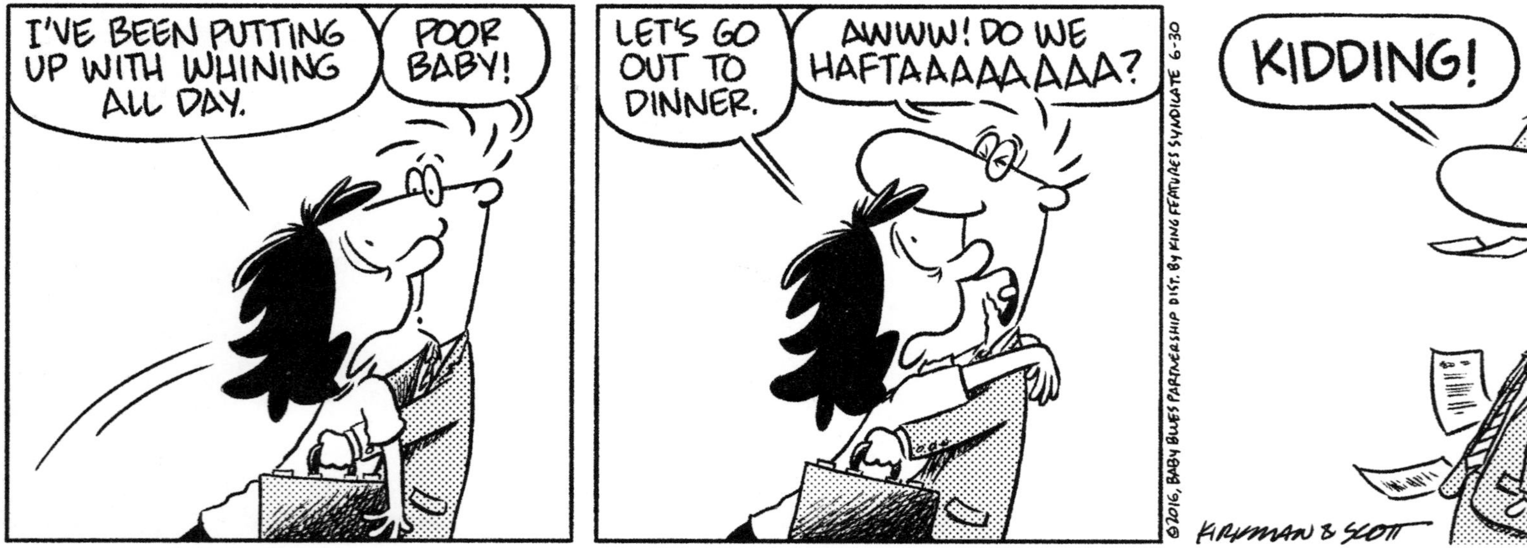
I'VE BEEN PUTTING UP WITH WHINING ALL DAY.
POOR BABY!
LET'S GO OUT TO DINNER.
AWWW! DO WE HAFTAAAAAAAAA?
©2016, BABY BLUES PARTNERSHIP DIST. BY KING FEATURES SYNDICATE 6-30
KIDDING!
KIRKMAN & SCOTT

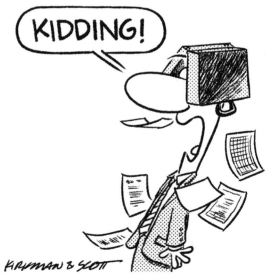

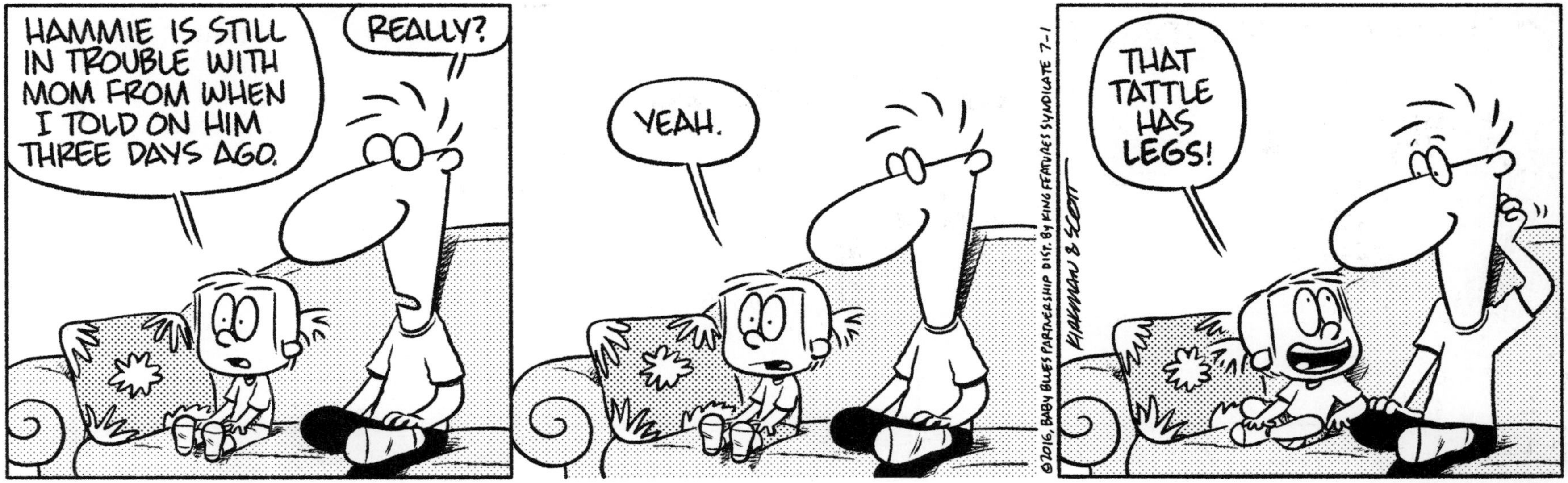
HAMMIE IS STILL IN TROUBLE WITH MOM FROM WHEN I TOLD ON HIM THREE DAYS AGO.
REALLY?
YEAH.
THAT TATTLE HAS LEGS!
©2016, BABY BLUES PARTNERSHIP DIST. BY KING FEATURES SYNDICATE 7-1
KIRKMAN & SCOTT

Jerry: Good work is its own reward.

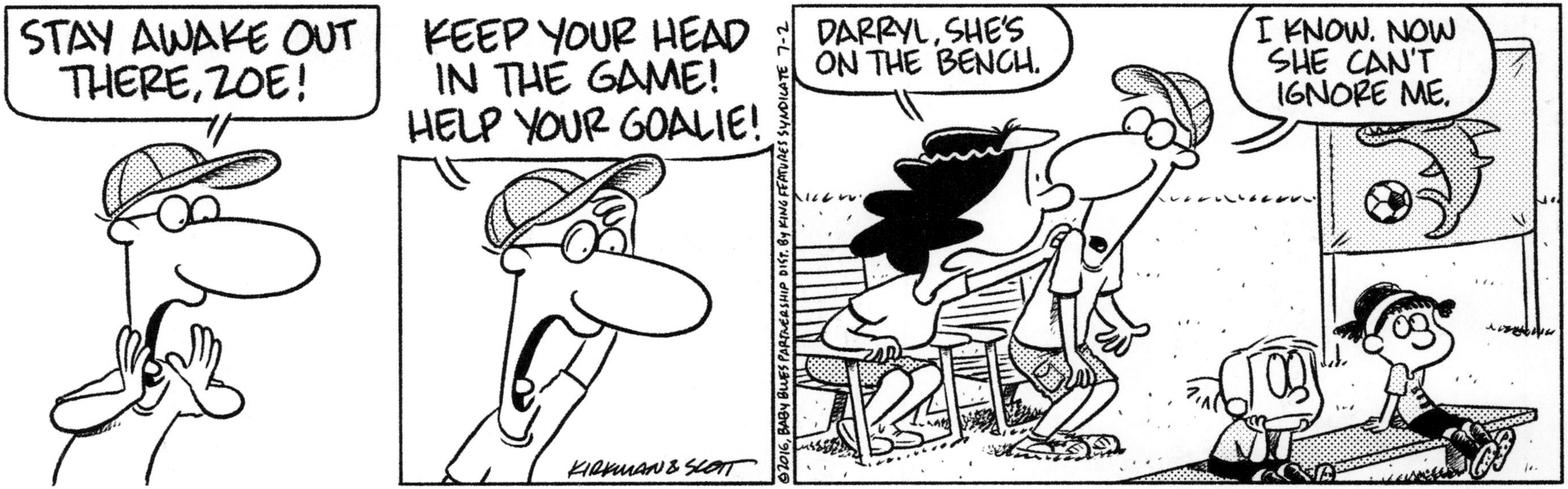
STAY AWAKE OUT THERE, ZOE!
KEEP YOUR HEAD IN THE GAME! HELP YOUR GOALIE!
KIRKMAN & SCOTT
©2016, BABY BLUES PARTNERSHIP DIST. BY KING FEATURES SYNDICATE 7-2
DARRYL, SHE'S ON THE BENCH.
I KNOW. NOW SHE CAN'T IGNORE ME.

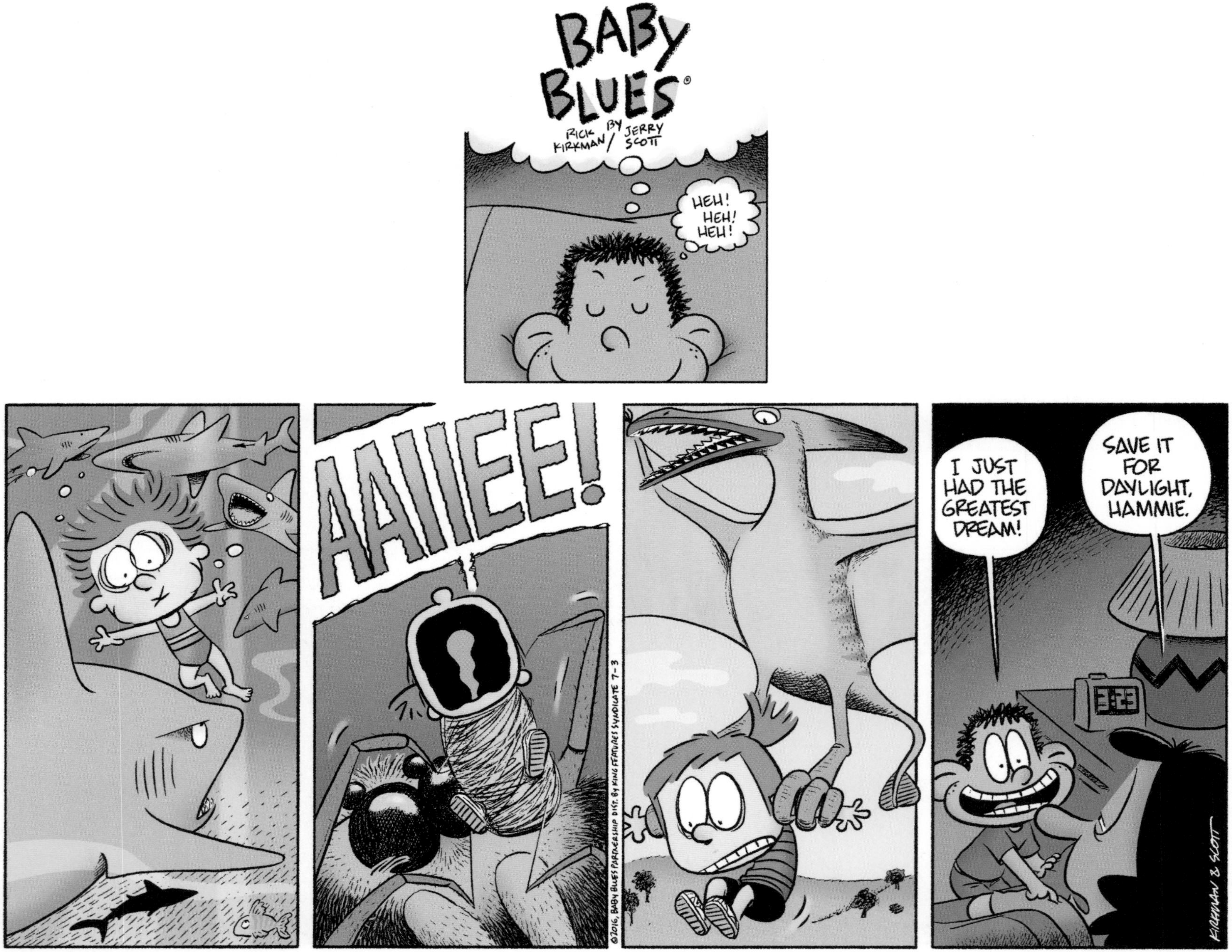
BABY BLUES®
BY RICK KIRKMAN / JERRY SCOTT
HEH! HEH! HEH!
AAIIEE!
©2016, BABY BLUES PARTNERSHIP DIST. BY KING FEATURES SYNDICATE 7-3
I JUST HAD THE GREATEST DREAM!
SAVE IT FOR DAYLIGHT, HAMMIE.
KIRKMAN & SCOTT

Rick: An ambitious Sunday strip—Google research to the rescue.

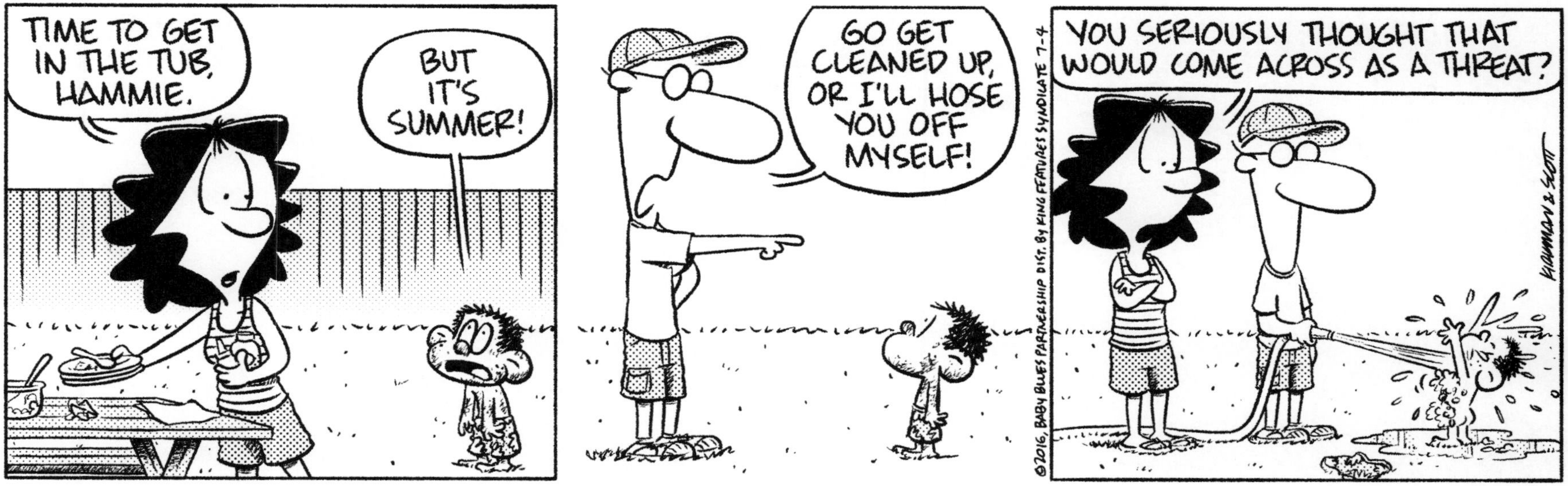
TIME TO GET IN THE TUB, HAMMIE.
BUT IT'S SUMMER!
GO GET CLEANED UP, OR I'LL HOSE YOU OFF MYSELF!
YOU SERIOUSLY THOUGHT THAT WOULD COME ACROSS AS A THREAT?
©2016, BABY BLUES PARTNERSHIP DIST. BY KING FEATURES SYNDICATE 7-4
KIRKMAN & SCOTT

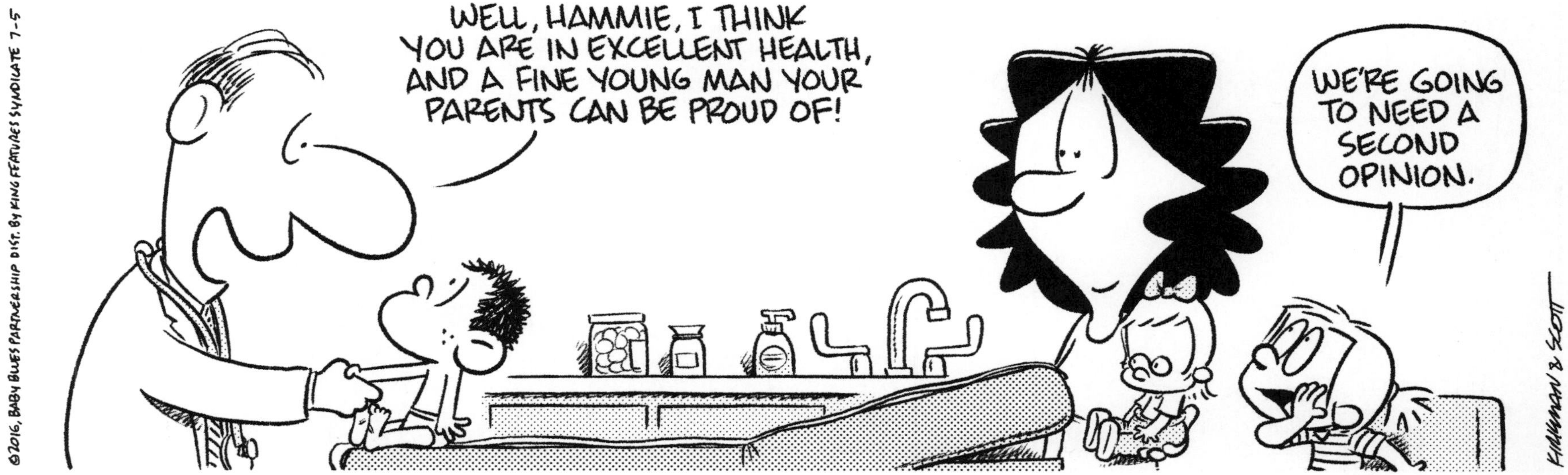
WELL, HAMMIE, I THINK YOU ARE IN EXCELLENT HEALTH, AND A FINE YOUNG MAN YOUR PARENTS CAN BE PROUD OF!
WE'RE GOING TO NEED A SECOND OPINION.
©2016, BABY BLUES PARTNERSHIP DIST. BY KING FEATURES SYNDICATE 7-5
KIRKMAN & SCOTT

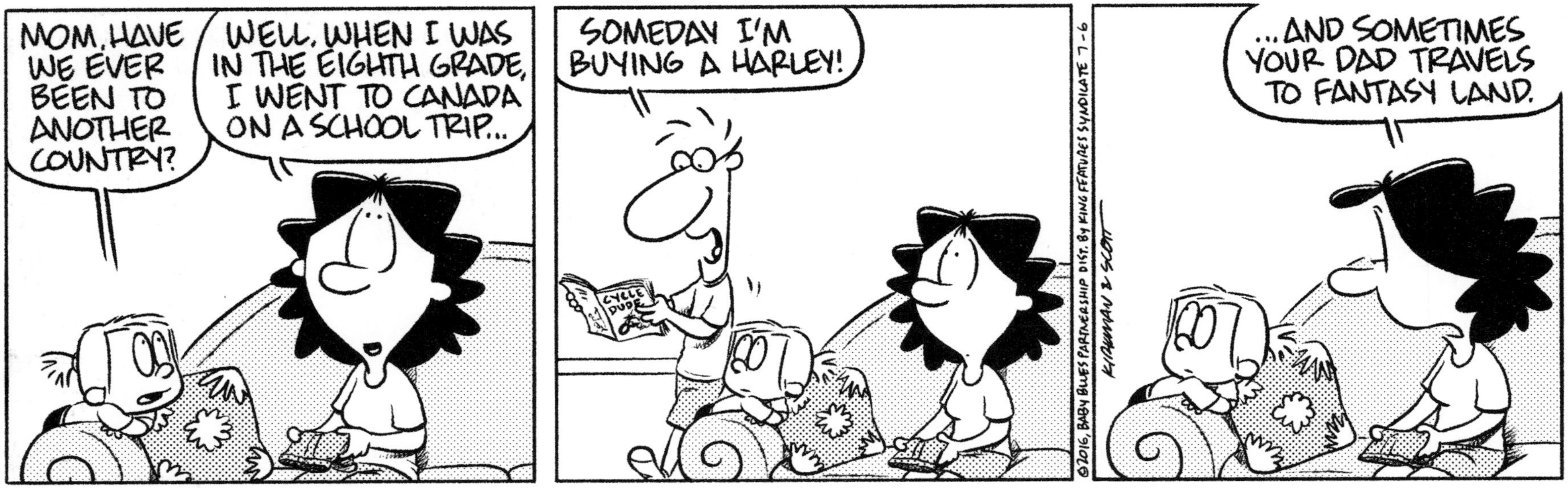
MOM, HAVE WE EVER BEEN TO ANOTHER COUNTRY?
WELL, WHEN I WAS IN THE EIGHTH GRADE, I WENT TO CANADA ON A SCHOOL TRIP...
SOMEDAY I'M BUYING A HARLEY!
CYCLE DUDE
©2016, BABY BLUES PARTNERSHIP DIST. BY KING FEATURES SYNDICATE 7-6
KIRKMAN & SCOTT
...AND SOMETIMES YOUR DAD TRAVELS TO FANTASY LAND.

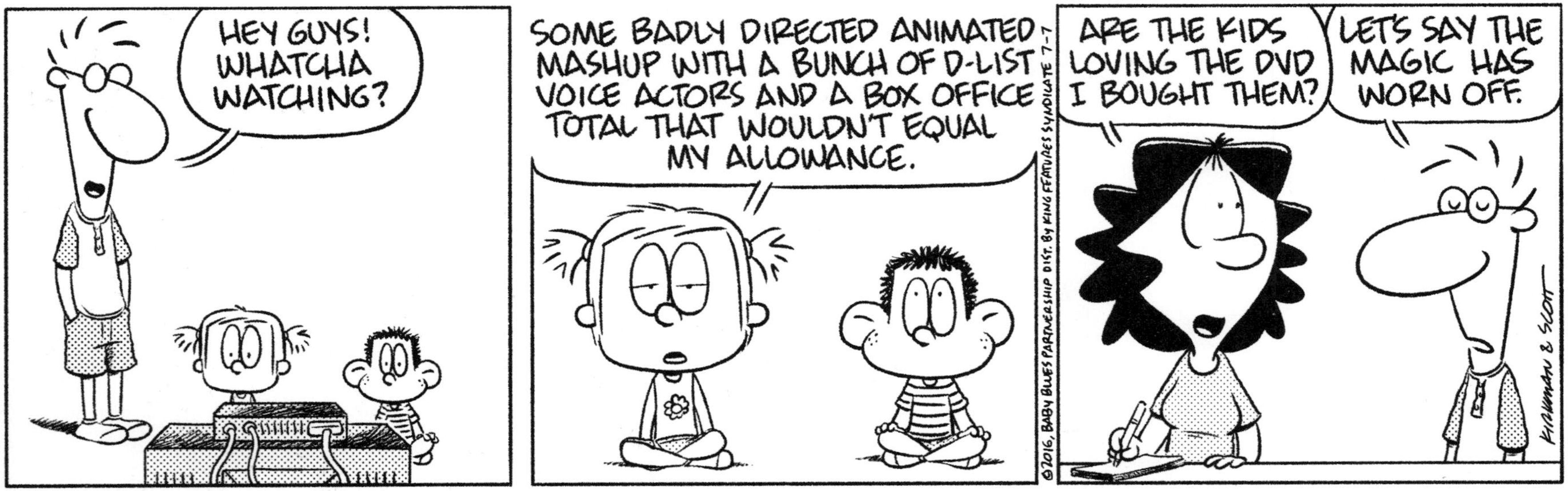
HEY GUYS! WHATCHA WATCHING?
SOME BADLY DIRECTED ANIMATED MASHUP WITH A BUNCH OF D-LIST VOICE ACTORS AND A BOX OFFICE TOTAL THAT WOULDN'T EQUAL MY ALLOWANCE.
©2016, BABY BLUES PARTNERSHIP DIST. BY KING FEATURES SYNDICATE 7-7
ARE THE KIDS LOVING THE DVD I BOUGHT THEM?
LET'S SAY THE MAGIC HAS WORN OFF.
KIRKMAN & SCOTT

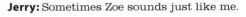

Jerry: Sometimes Zoe sounds just like me.

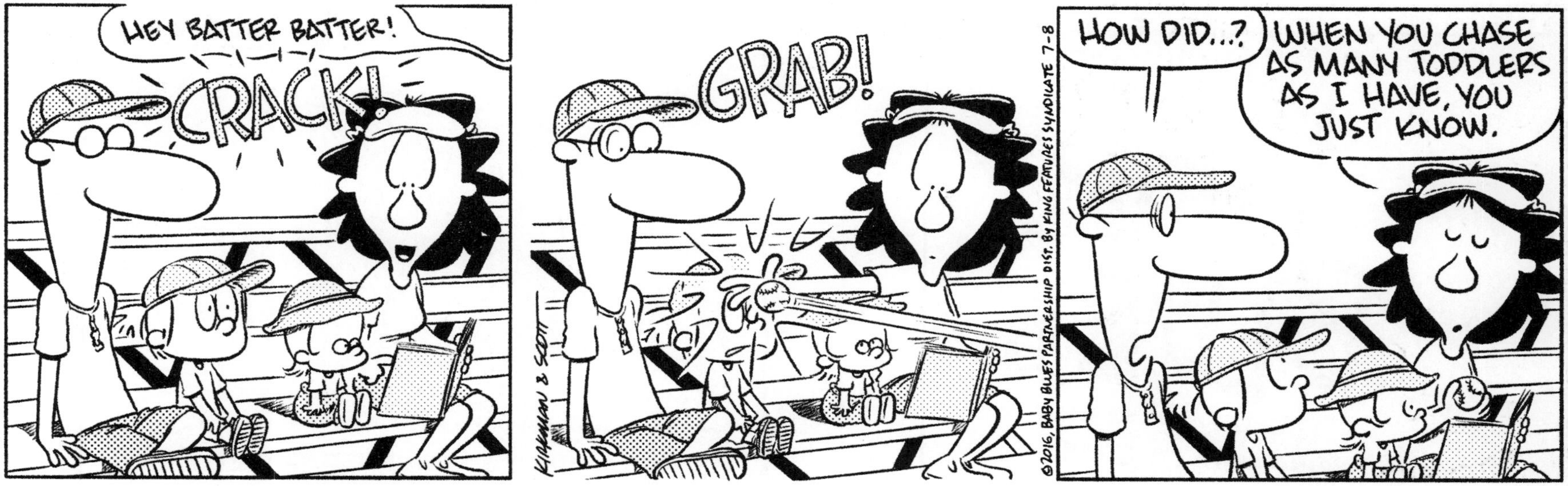
HEY BATTER BATTER!
CRACK!
GRAB!
KIRKMAN & SCOTT
©2016, BABY BLUES PARTNERSHIP DIST. BY KING FEATURES SYNDICATE 7-8
HOW DID...?
WHEN YOU CHASE AS MANY TODDLERS AS I HAVE, YOU JUST KNOW.

Rick: Along with bicycles, horses, and piles of toys, drawing bleachers is racing to the Top 10 of Things I Don't Like to Draw.

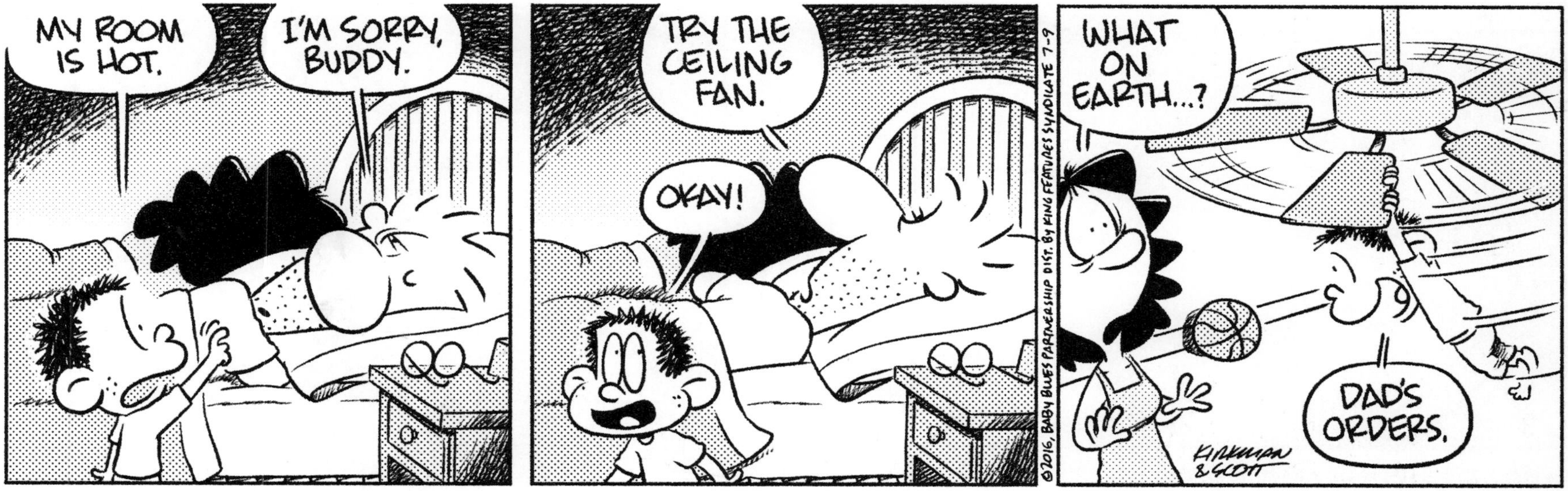
MY ROOM IS HOT.
I'M SORRY, BUDDY.
TRY THE CEILING FAN.
OKAY!
©2016, BABY BLUES PARTNERSHIP DIST. BY KING FEATURES SYNDICATE 7-9
WHAT ON EARTH...?
DAD'S ORDERS.
KIRKMAN & SCOTT

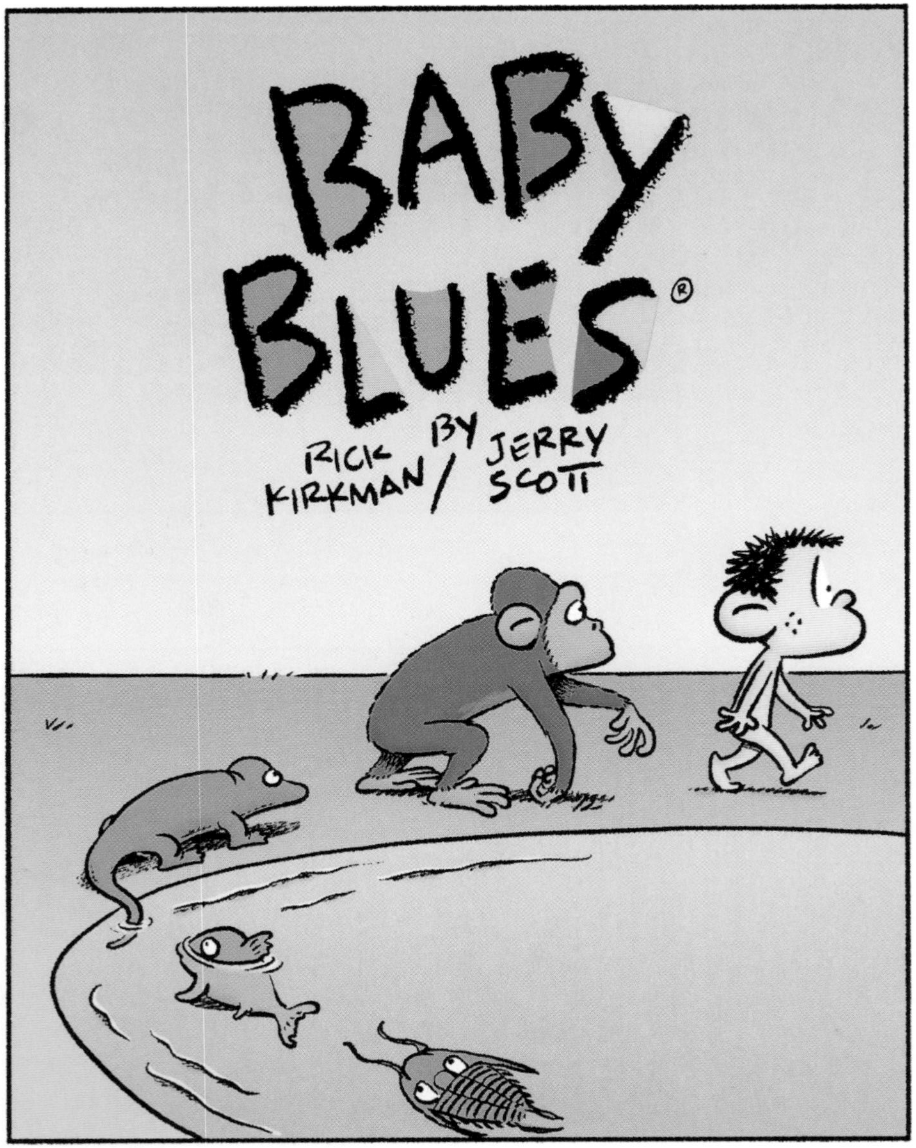
BABY BLUES®
BY
RICK KIRKMAN / JERRY SCOTT

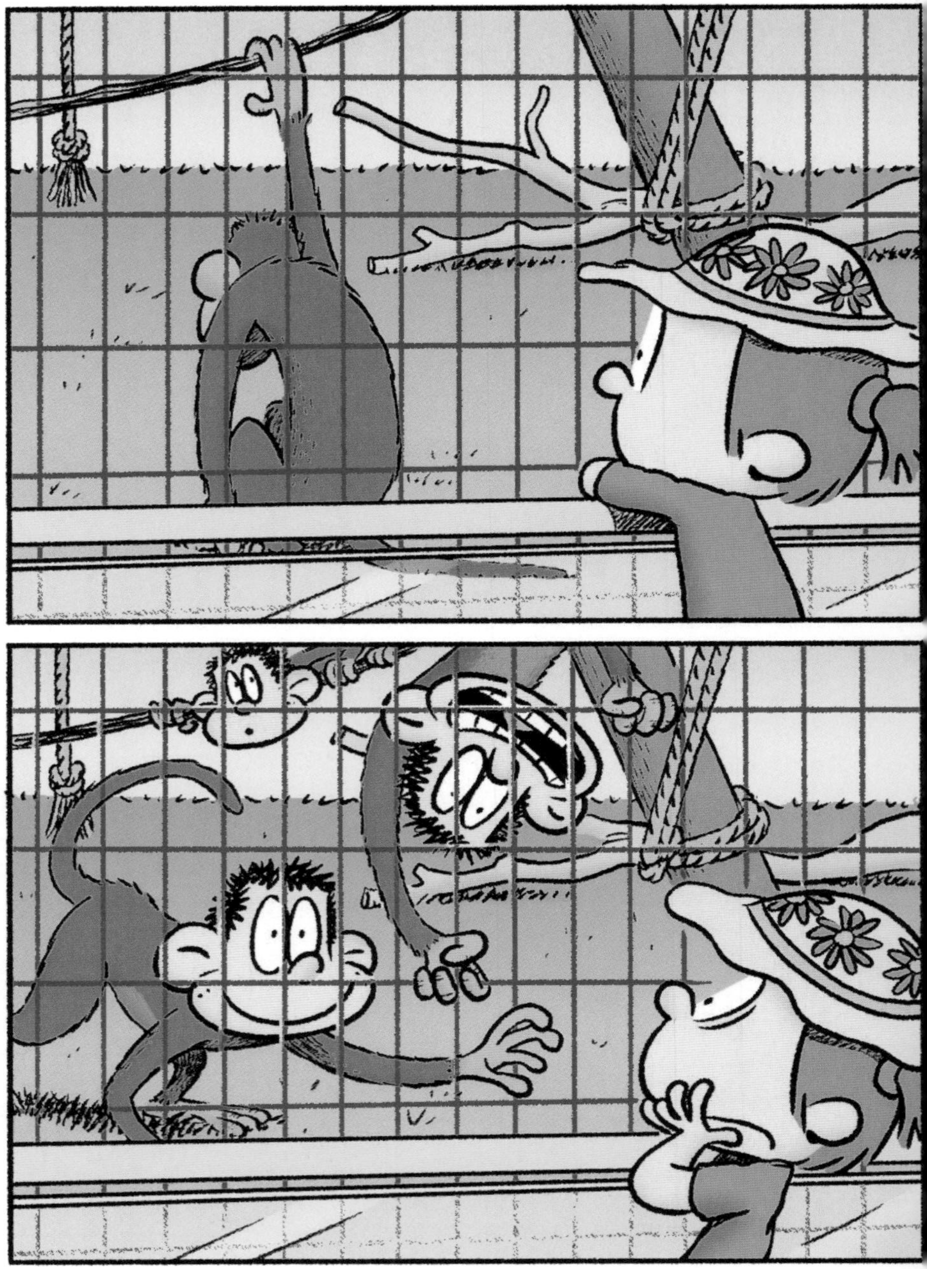

Rick: The idea of drawing a bunch of monkeys with Hammie's face was really fun. Not so fun, trying to figure out how to manage all the wire caging in color so it didn't distract from the drawing.

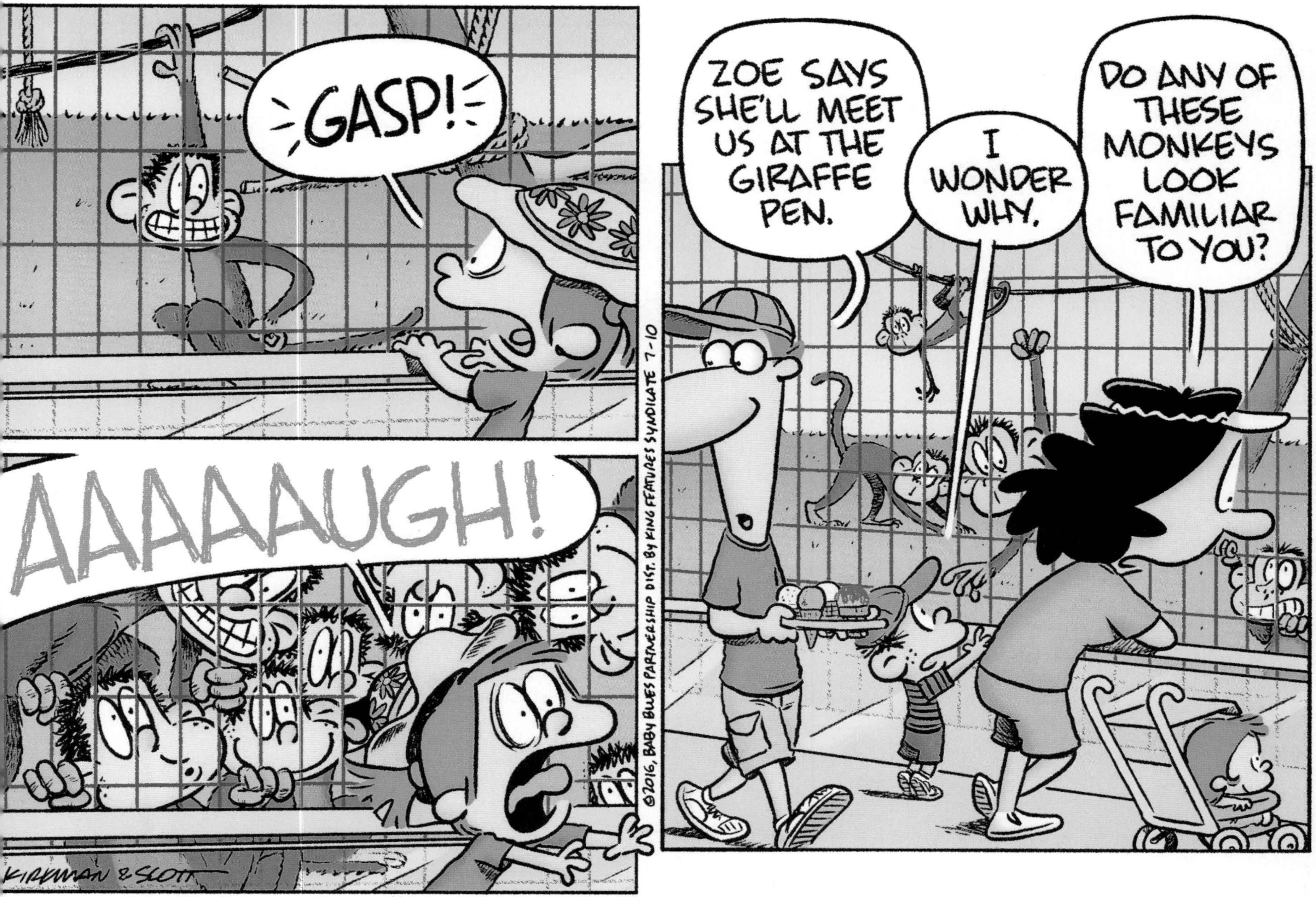
GASP!
AAAAAUGH!
©2016, BABY BLUES PARTNERSHIP DIST. BY KING FEATURES SYNDICATE 7-10
KIRKMAN & SCOTT
ZOE SAYS SHE'LL MEET US AT THE GIRAFFE PEN.
I WONDER WHY.
DO ANY OF THESE MONKEYS LOOK FAMILIAR TO YOU?

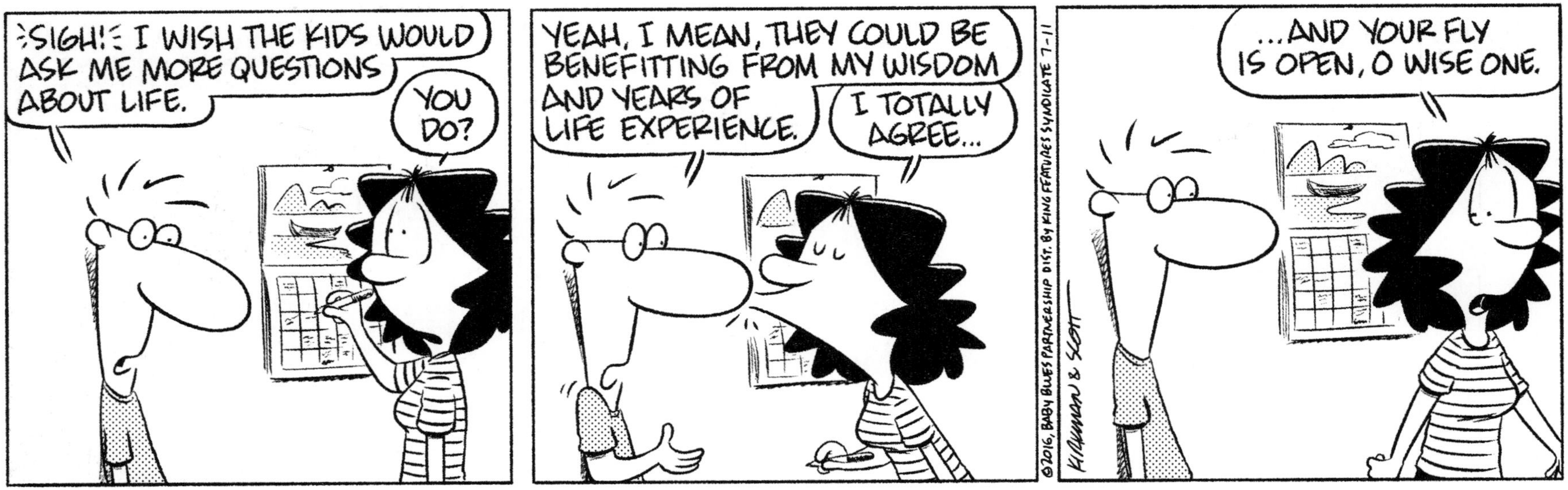

SIGH! I WISH THE KIDS WOULD ASK ME MORE QUESTIONS ABOUT LIFE.
YOU DO?
YEAH, I MEAN, THEY COULD BE BENEFITTING FROM MY WISDOM AND YEARS OF LIFE EXPERIENCE.
I TOTALLY AGREE...
...AND YOUR FLY IS OPEN, O WISE ONE.
©2016, BABY BLUES PARTNERSHIP DIST. BY KING FEATURES SYNDICATE 7-11
KIRKMAN & SCOTT

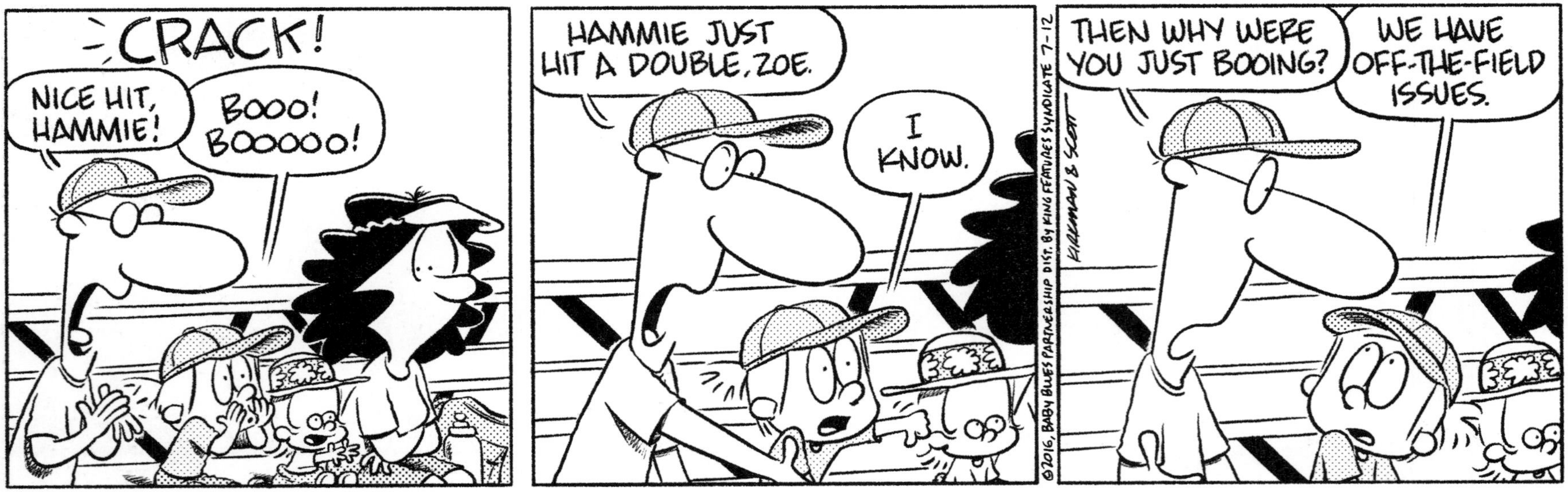

CRACK!
NICE HIT, HAMMIE!
BOOO! BOOOOOO!
HAMMIE JUST HIT A DOUBLE, ZOE.
I KNOW.
THEN WHY WERE YOU JUST BOOING?
WE HAVE OFF-THE-FIELD ISSUES.
©2016, BABY BLUES PARTNERSHIP DIST. BY KING FEATURES SYNDICATE 7-12
KIRKMAN & SCOTT

Rick: Grrr. Bleachers.

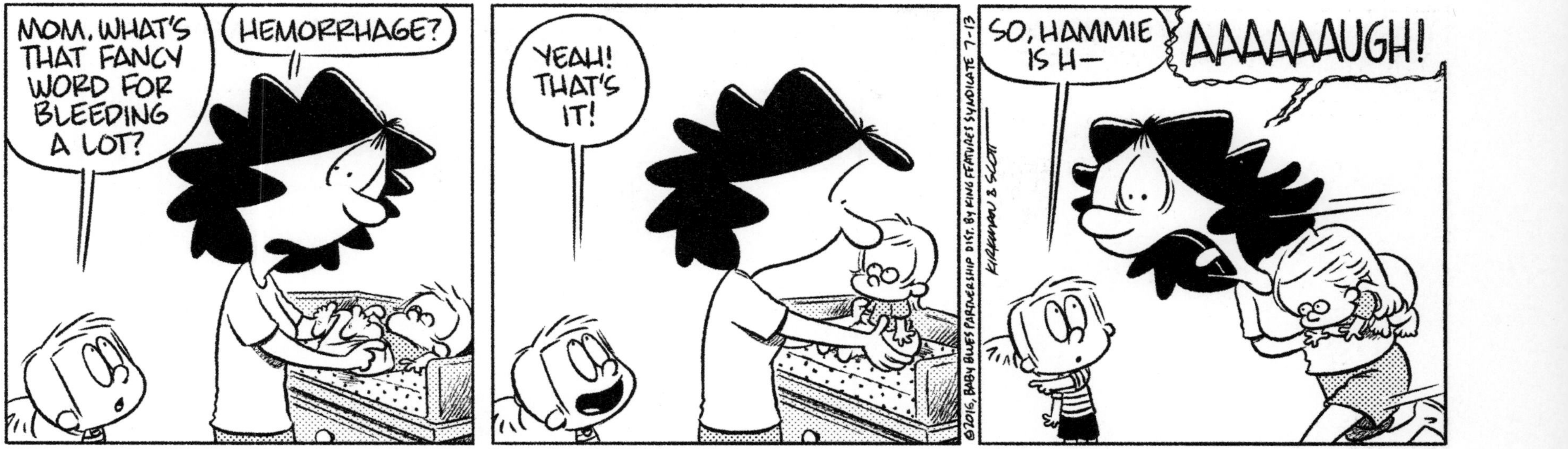
MOM, WHAT'S THAT FANCY WORD FOR BLEEDING A LOT?
HEMORRHAGE?
YEAH! THAT'S IT!
©2016, BABY BLUES PARTNERSHIP DIST. BY KING FEATURES SYNDICATE 7-13
KIRKMAN & SCOTT
SO, HAMMIE IS H—
AAAAAAUGH!

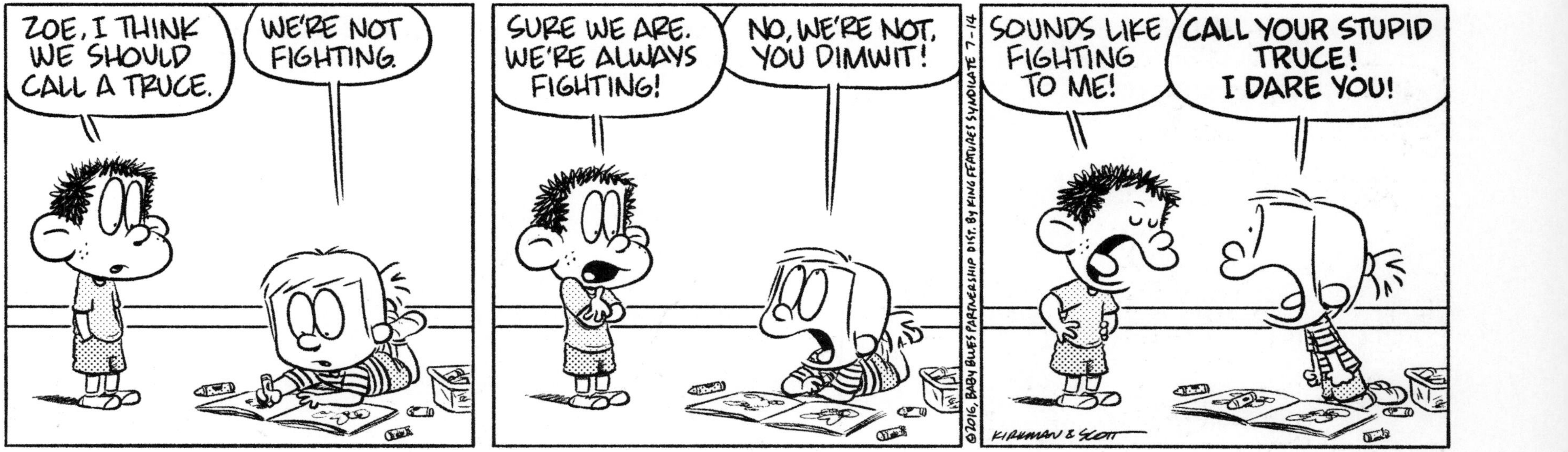
ZOE, I THINK WE SHOULD CALL A TRUCE.
WE'RE NOT FIGHTING.
SURE WE ARE. WE'RE ALWAYS FIGHTING!
NO, WE'RE NOT, YOU DIMWIT!
©2016, BABY BLUES PARTNERSHIP DIST. BY KING FEATURES SYNDICATE 7-14
SOUNDS LIKE FIGHTING TO ME!
CALL YOUR STUPID TRUCE! I DARE YOU!
KIRKMAN & SCOTT

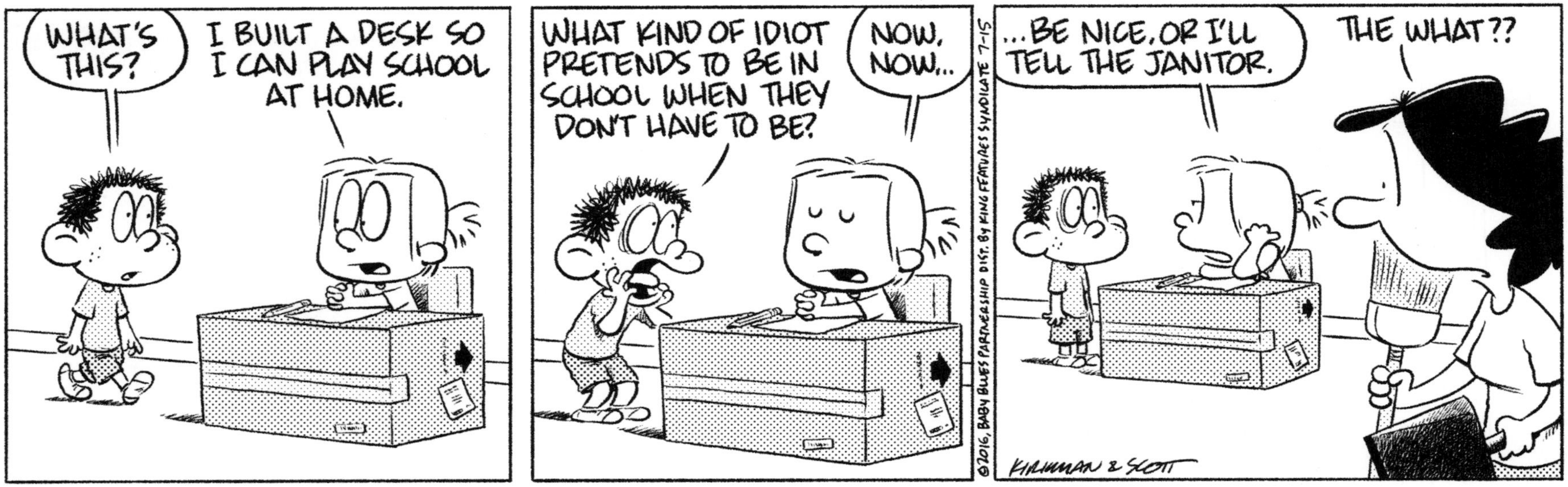
WHAT'S THIS?
I BUILT A DESK SO I CAN PLAY SCHOOL AT HOME.
WHAT KIND OF IDIOT PRETENDS TO BE IN SCHOOL WHEN THEY DON'T HAVE TO BE?
NOW, NOW...
...BE NICE, OR I'LL TELL THE JANITOR.
THE WHAT??
©2016, BABY BLUES PARTNERSHIP DIST. BY KING FEATURES SYNDICATE 7-15
KIRKMAN & SCOTT

Jerry: "That's CUSTODIAN to you, missy!"

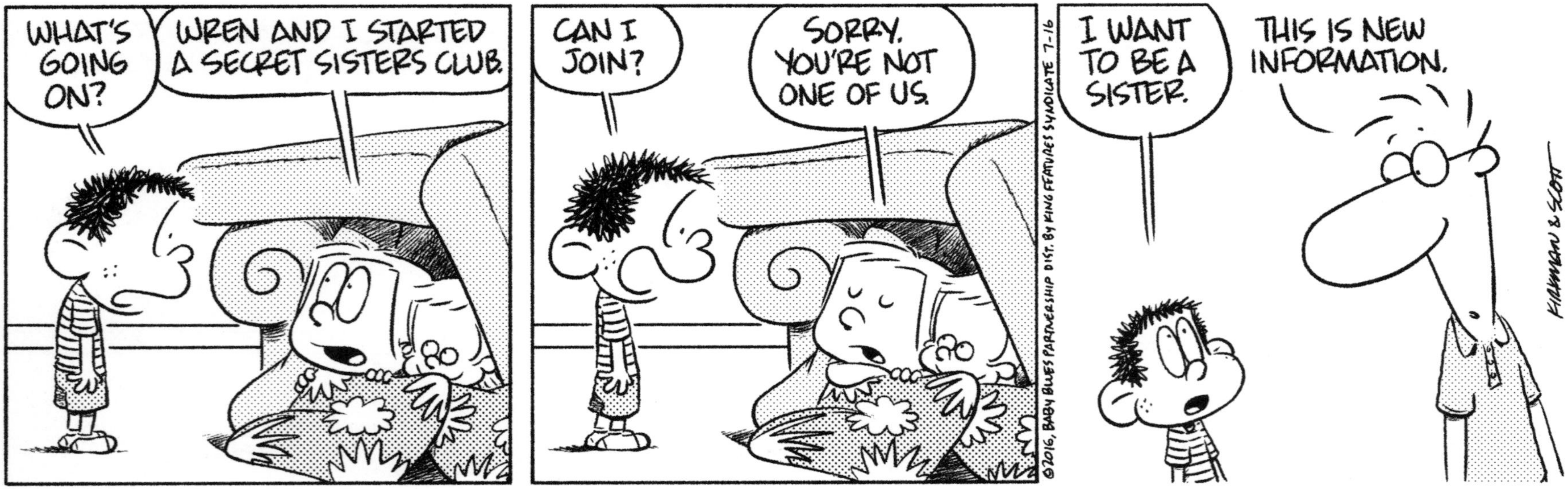
WHAT'S GOING ON?
WREN AND I STARTED A SECRET SISTERS CLUB.
CAN I JOIN?
SORRY. YOU'RE NOT ONE OF US.
I WANT TO BE A SISTER.
THIS IS NEW INFORMATION.
©2016, BABY BLUES PARTNERSHIP DIST. BY KING FEATURES SYNDICATE 7-16
KIRKMAN & SCOTT

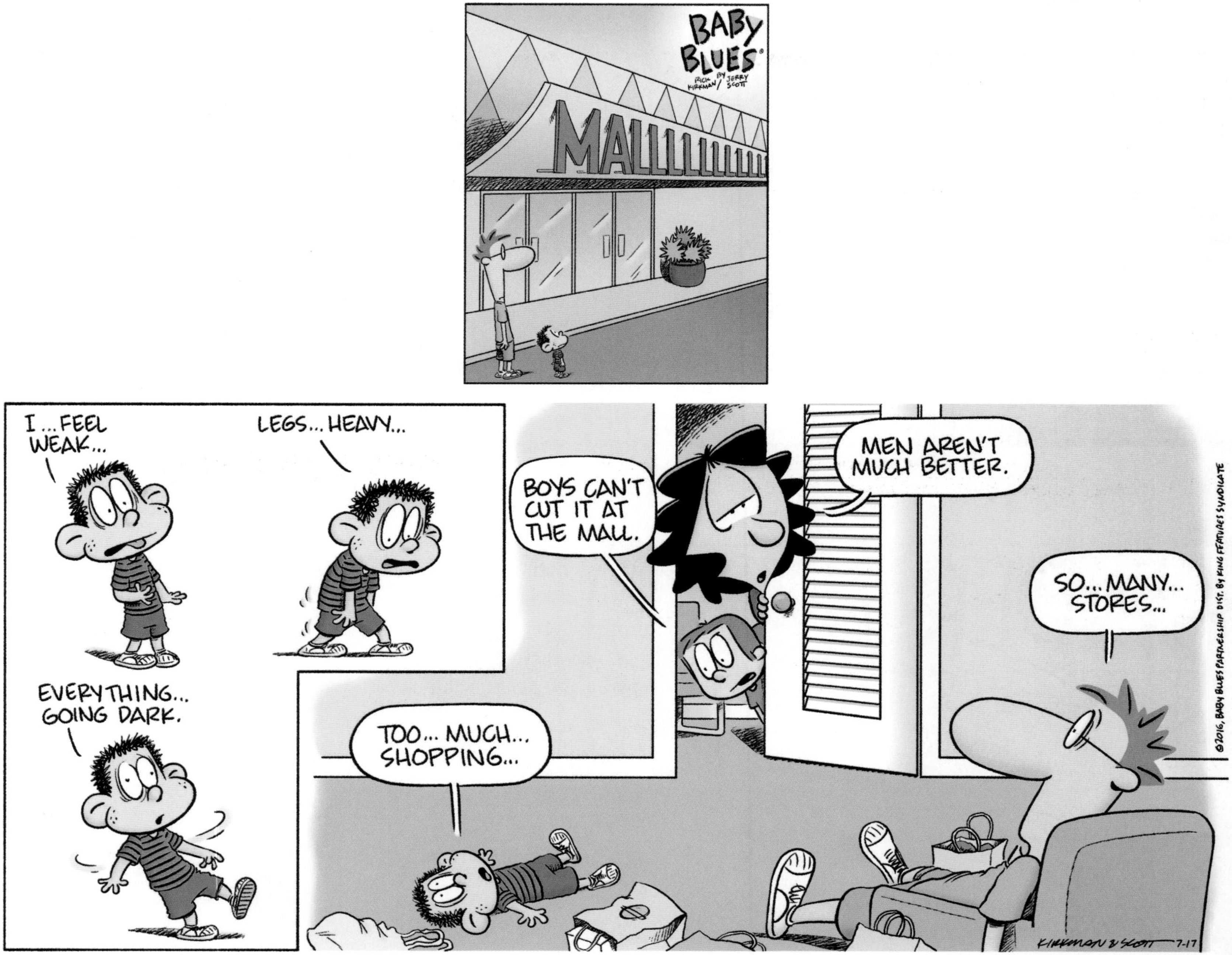
BABY BLUES
RICK KIRKMAN / BY JERRY SCOTT
MALLLLLLLLLL
I ... FEEL WEAK...
LEGS... HEAVY...
EVERYTHING... GOING DARK.
TOO... MUCH... SHOPPING...
BOYS CAN'T CUT IT AT THE MALL.
MEN AREN'T MUCH BETTER.
SO... MANY... STORES...
©2016, BABY BLUES PARTNERSHIP DIST. BY KING FEATURES SYNDICATE
KIRKMAN & SCOTT 7-17

Jerry: Shopping wipes me out, and I lose all sense of direction. My wife thinks it's hilarious to watch me try to find the car afterward.

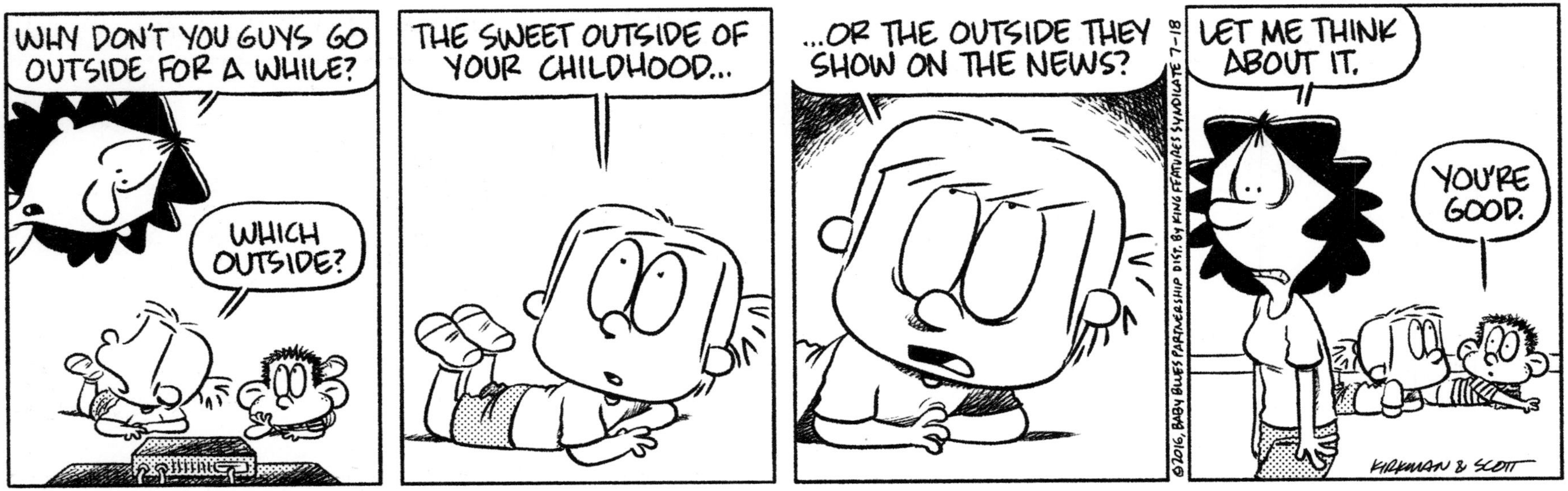
WHY DON'T YOU GUYS GO OUTSIDE FOR A WHILE?
WHICH OUTSIDE?
THE SWEET OUTSIDE OF YOUR CHILDHOOD...
...OR THE OUTSIDE THEY SHOW ON THE NEWS?
©2016, BABY BLUES PARTNERSHIP DIST. BY KING FEATURES SYNDICATE 7-18
LET ME THINK ABOUT IT.
YOU'RE GOOD.
KIRKMAN & SCOTT

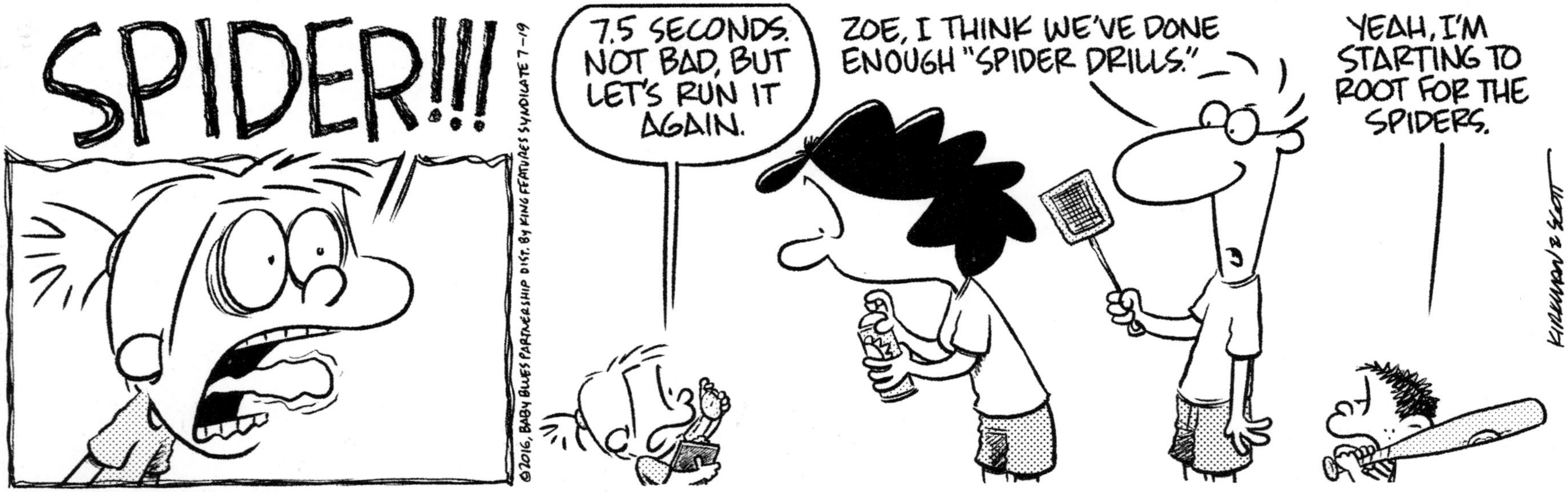
SPIDER!!!
©2016, BABY BLUES PARTNERSHIP DIST. BY KING FEATURES SYNDICATE 7-19
7.5 SECONDS. NOT BAD, BUT LET'S RUN IT AGAIN.
ZOE, I THINK WE'VE DONE ENOUGH "SPIDER DRILLS."
YEAH, I'M STARTING TO ROOT FOR THE SPIDERS.
KIRKMAN & SCOTT

Rick: There's not much that is more fun to draw than fear. I really like gags like this, where the characters kind of provide panels of their own while still in one drawing.

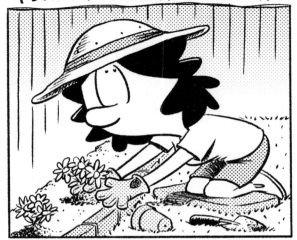

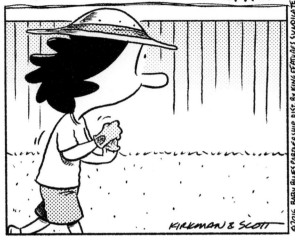

PSHHHHHHHHHHHHHHHH
PSHHHHHHHHHHHHHHHH
©2016, BABY BLUES PARTNERSHIP DIST. BY KING FEATURES SYNDICATE 7-20
KIRKMAN & SCOTT
PSHHHHHHHHHHHHHHHH
I THINK YOU GOT HIM.
YOU CAN'T BE TOO CAREFUL WITH MOSQUITOES.

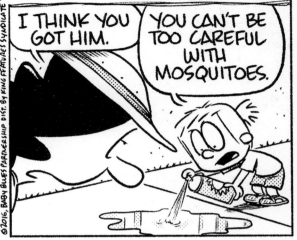

ZOE, YOU NEED TO GET OVER YOUR FEAR OF BUGS.
I DON'T HAVE A FEAR OF BUGS.
HATRED, THEN.
I DON'T HATE BUGS.
©2016, BABY BLUES PARTNERSHIP DIST. BY KING FEATURES SYNDICATE 7-21
KIRKMAN & SCOTT
WHITE-HOT, VENOMOUS LOATHING, BENT ON TOTAL ANNIHILATION?
YOU'RE GETTING WARMER.

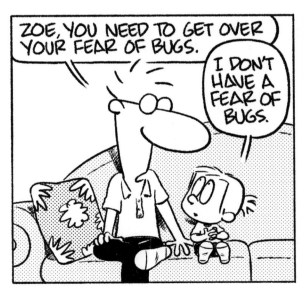

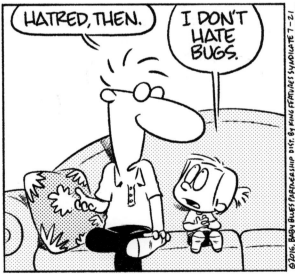

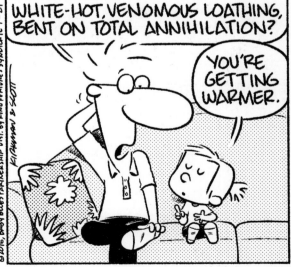

Jerry: Health care costs keep going up, and the price of flatscreen TVs keeps going down. Maybe those two industries should swap CEOs for a while.

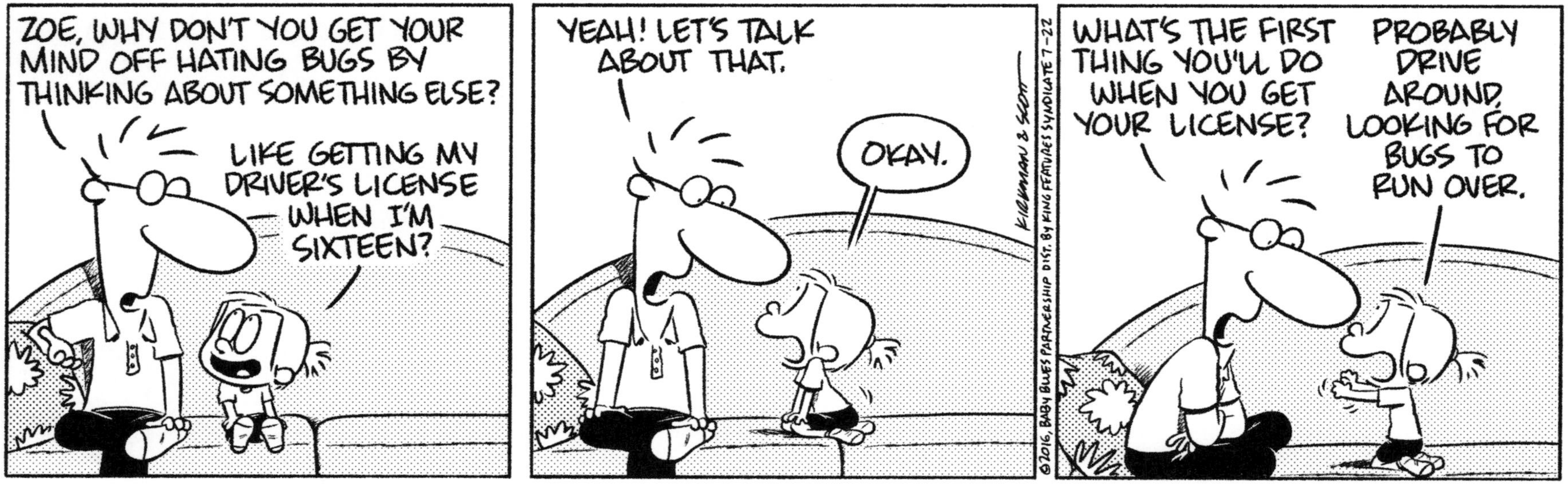
ZOE, WHY DON'T YOU GET YOUR MIND OFF HATING BUGS BY THINKING ABOUT SOMETHING ELSE?
LIKE GETTING MY DRIVER'S LICENSE WHEN I'M SIXTEEN?
YEAH! LET'S TALK ABOUT THAT.
OKAY.
KIRKMAN & SCOTT
©2016, BABY BLUES PARTNERSHIP DIST. BY KING FEATURES SYNDICATE 7-22
WHAT'S THE FIRST THING YOU'LL DO WHEN YOU GET YOUR LICENSE?
PROBABLY DRIVE AROUND, LOOKING FOR BUGS TO RUN OVER.

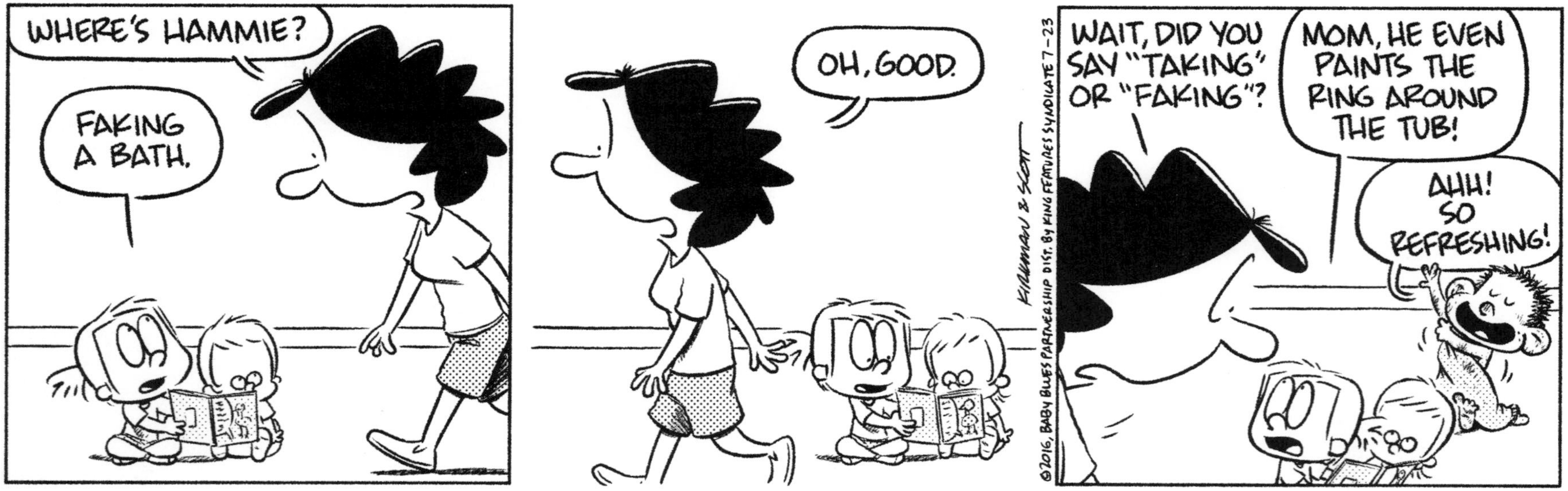
WHERE'S HAMMIE?
FAKING A BATH.
OH, GOOD.
KIRKMAN & SCOTT
©2016, BABY BLUES PARTNERSHIP DIST. BY KING FEATURES SYNDICATE 7-23
WAIT, DID YOU SAY "TAKING" OR "FAKING"?
MOM, HE EVEN PAINTS THE RING AROUND THE TUB!
AHH! SO REFRESHING!

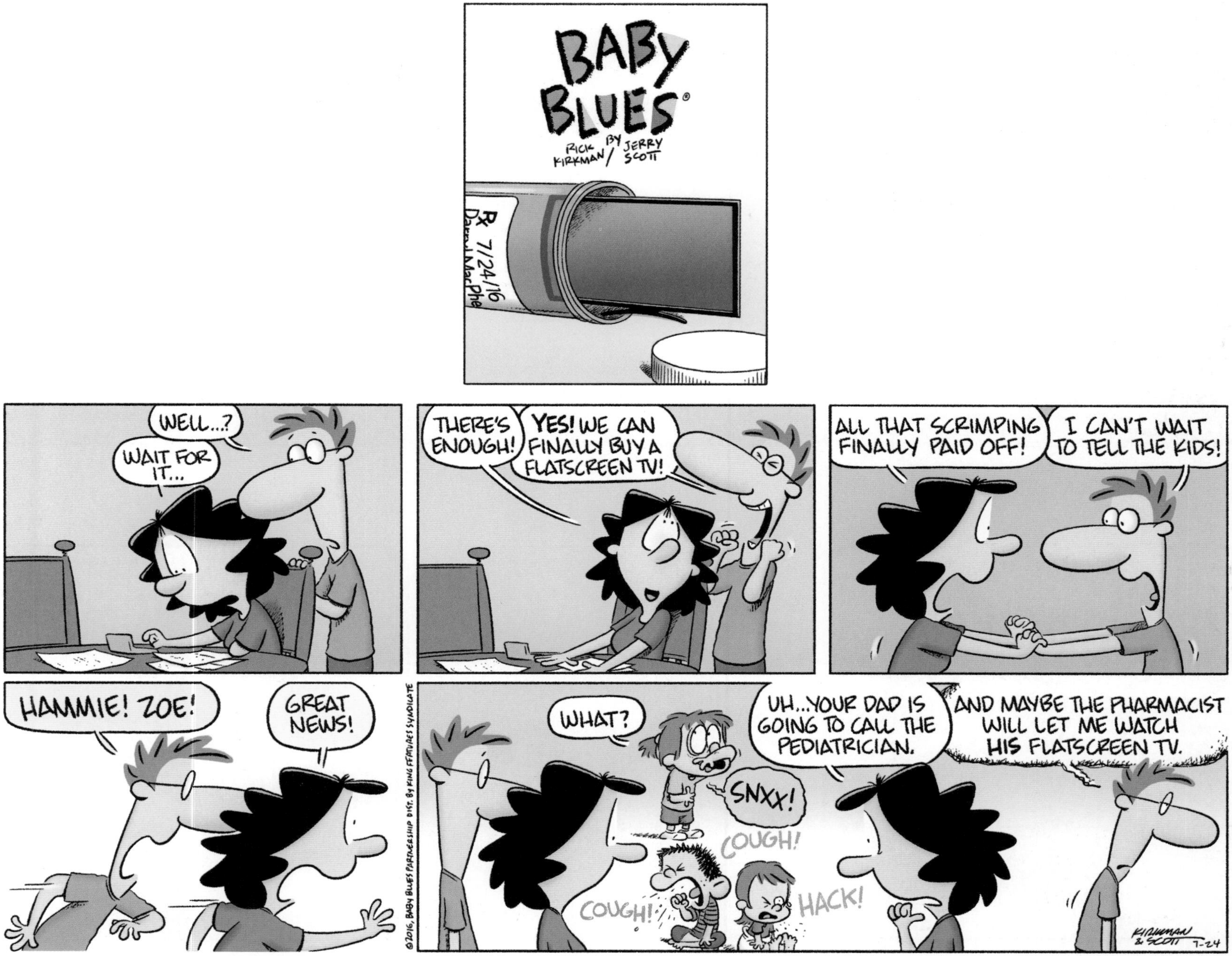
BABY BLUES®
BY RICK KIRKMAN / JERRY SCOTT
Rx 7/24/16
WELL...?
WAIT FOR IT...
THERE'S ENOUGH!
YES! WE CAN FINALLY BUY A FLATSCREEN TV!
ALL THAT SCRIMPING FINALLY PAID OFF!
I CAN'T WAIT TO TELL THE KIDS!
HAMMIE! ZOE!
GREAT NEWS!
©2016, BABY BLUES PARTNERSHIP DIST. BY KING FEATURES SYNDICATE
WHAT?
SNXX!
COUGH!
COUGH!
HACK!
UH...YOUR DAD IS GOING TO CALL THE PEDIATRICIAN.
AND MAYBE THE PHARMACIST WILL LET ME WATCH HIS FLATSCREEN TV.
KIRKMAN & SCOTT 7-24

Rick: It's about time they limped into the 21st century. But, alas . . .

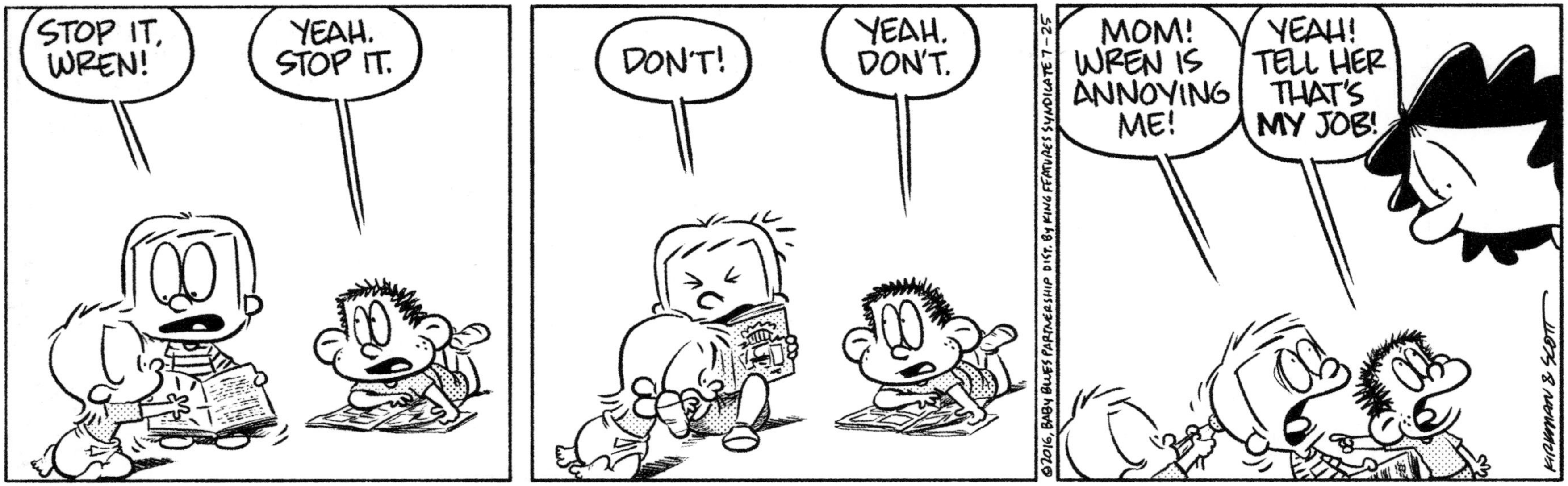
STOP IT, WREN!
YEAH. STOP IT.
DON'T!
YEAH. DON'T.
©2016, BABY BLUES PARTNERSHIP DIST. BY KING FEATURES SYNDICATE 7-25
MOM! WREN IS ANNOYING ME!
YEAH! TELL HER THAT'S MY JOB!
KIRKMAN & SCOTT

Jerry: Division of labor is important in any household.

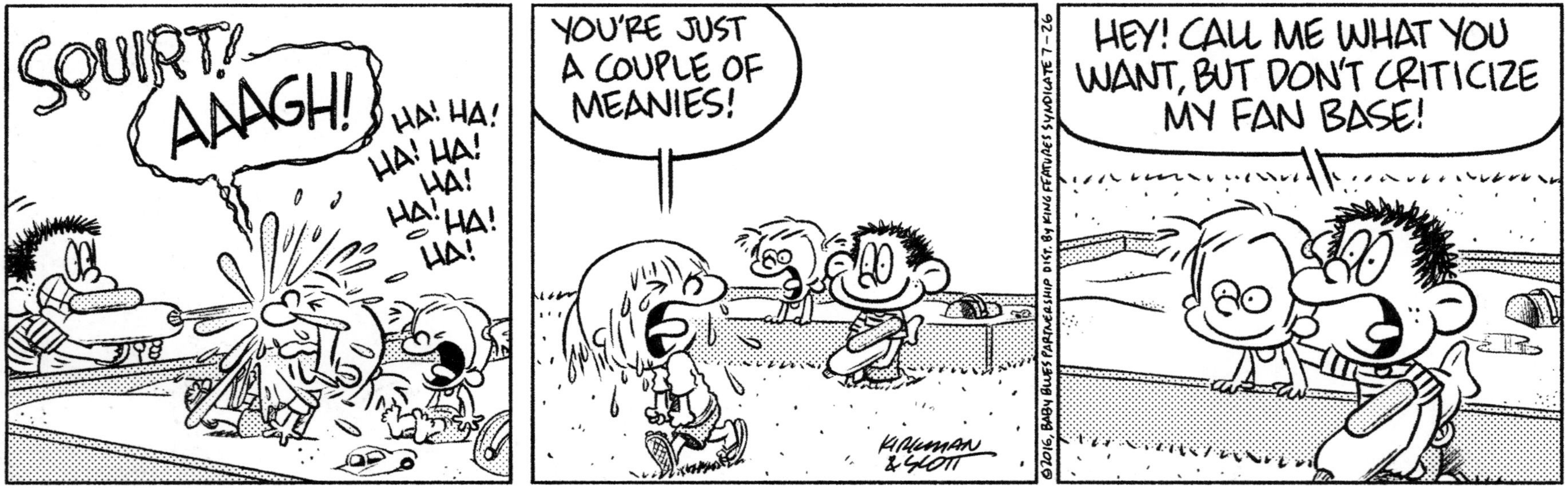
SQUIRT!
AAAGH!
HA! HA! HA! HA! HA! HA! HA! HA!
YOU'RE JUST A COUPLE OF MEANIES!
KIRKMAN & SCOTT
©2016, BABY BLUES PARTNERSHIP DIST. BY KING FEATURES SYNDICATE 7-26
HEY! CALL ME WHAT YOU WANT, BUT DON'T CRITICIZE MY FAN BASE!

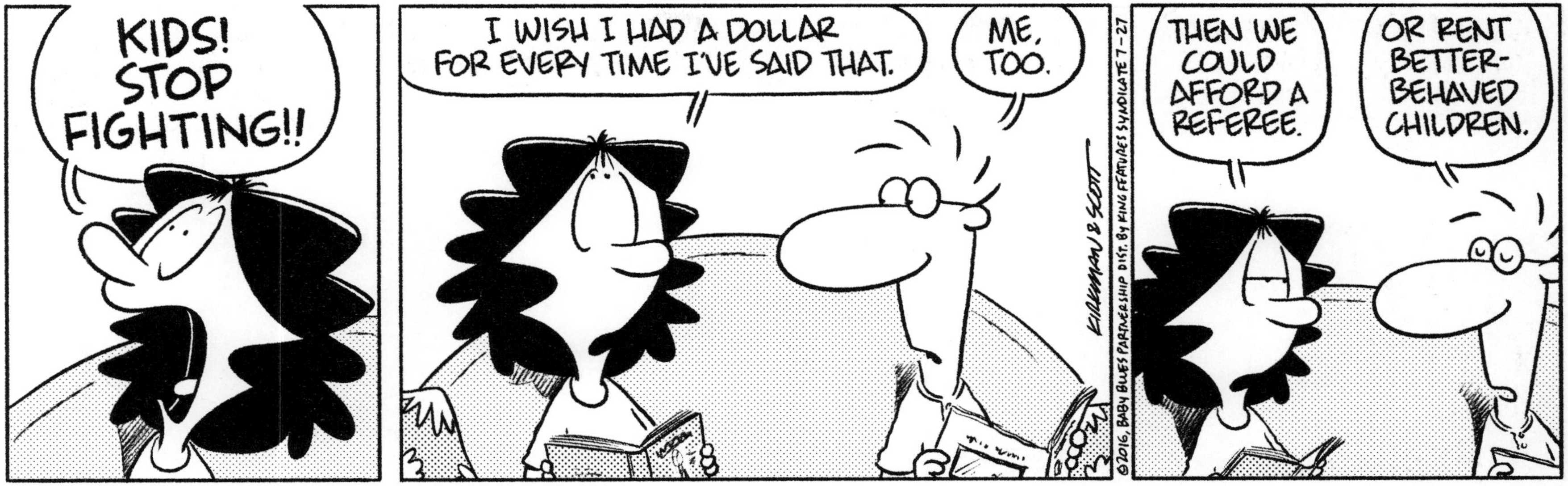
KIDS! STOP FIGHTING!!
I WISH I HAD A DOLLAR FOR EVERY TIME I'VE SAID THAT.
ME, TOO.
THEN WE COULD AFFORD A REFEREE.
OR RENT BETTER-BEHAVED CHILDREN.
KIRKMAN & SCOTT
©2016, BABY BLUES PARTNERSHIP DIST. BY KING FEATURES SYNDICATE 7-27

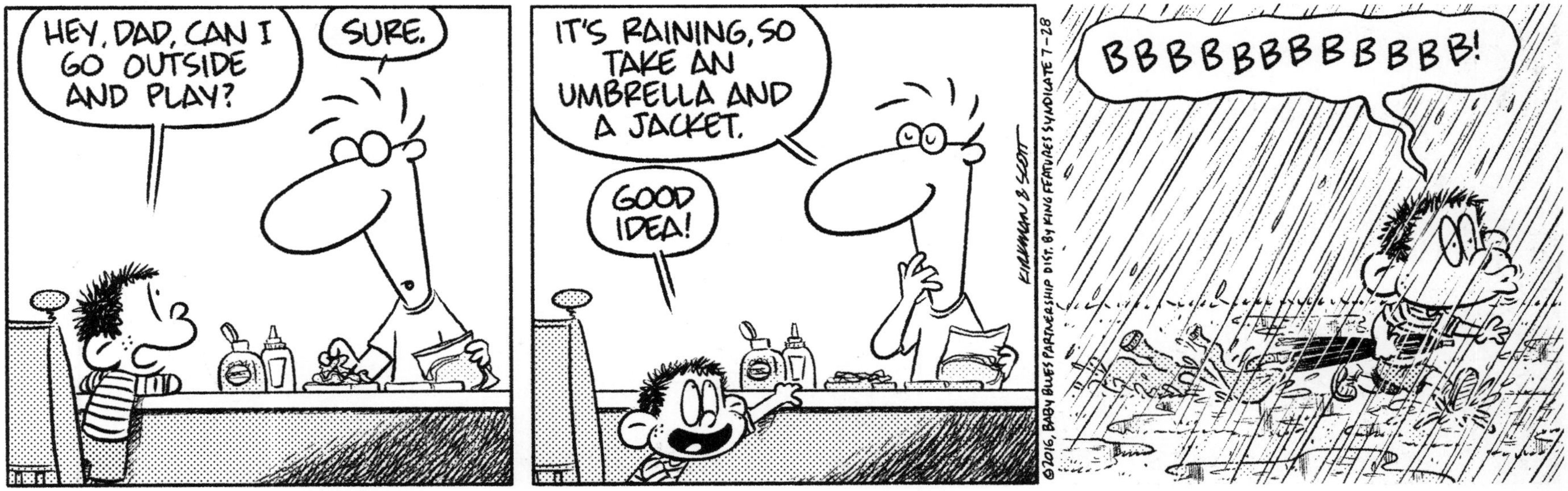
HEY, DAD, CAN I GO OUTSIDE AND PLAY?
SURE.
IT'S RAINING, SO TAKE AN UMBRELLA AND A JACKET.
GOOD IDEA!
BBBBBBBBBBBB!
KIRKMAN & SCOTT
©2016, BABY BLUES PARTNERSHIP DIST. BY KING FEATURES SYNDICATE 7-28

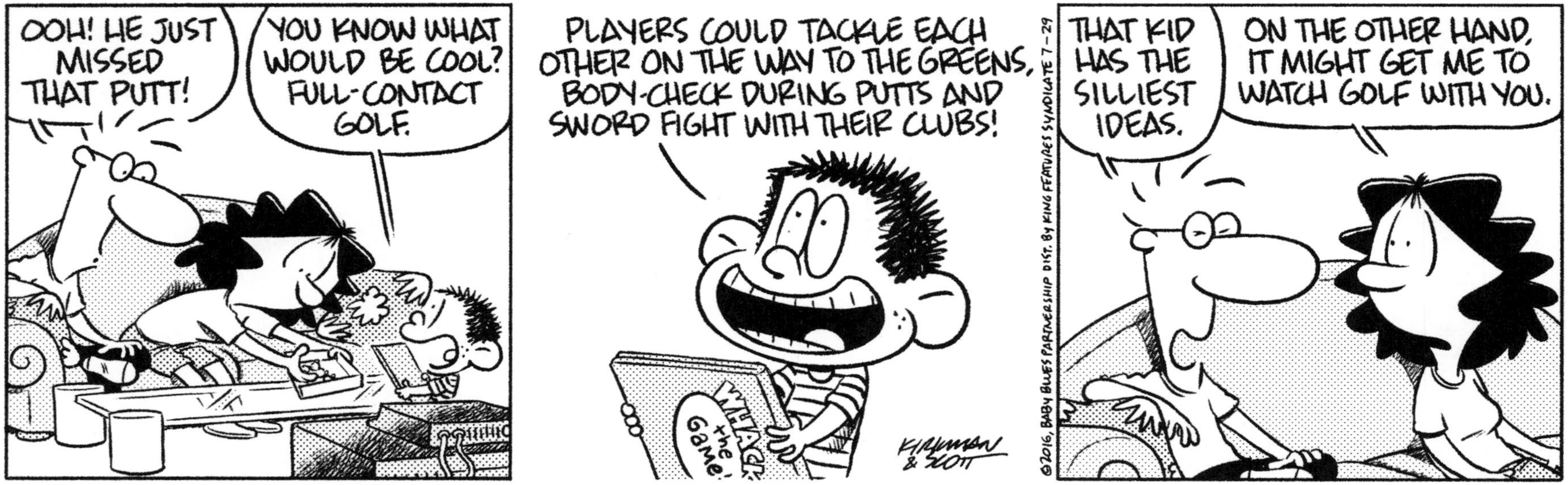
OOH! HE JUST MISSED THAT PUTT!
YOU KNOW WHAT WOULD BE COOL? FULL-CONTACT GOLF.
PLAYERS COULD TACKLE EACH OTHER ON THE WAY TO THE GREENS, BODY-CHECK DURING PUTTS AND SWORD FIGHT WITH THEIR CLUBS!
WHACK! the Game
KIRKMAN & SCOTT
©2016, BABY BLUES PARTNERSHIP DIST. BY KING FEATURES SYNDICATE 7-29
THAT KID HAS THE SILLIEST IDEAS.
ON THE OTHER HAND, IT MIGHT GET ME TO WATCH GOLF WITH YOU.

Jerry: They'd have to get rid of the whispering golf commentators, but Hammie's idea is worth exploring.

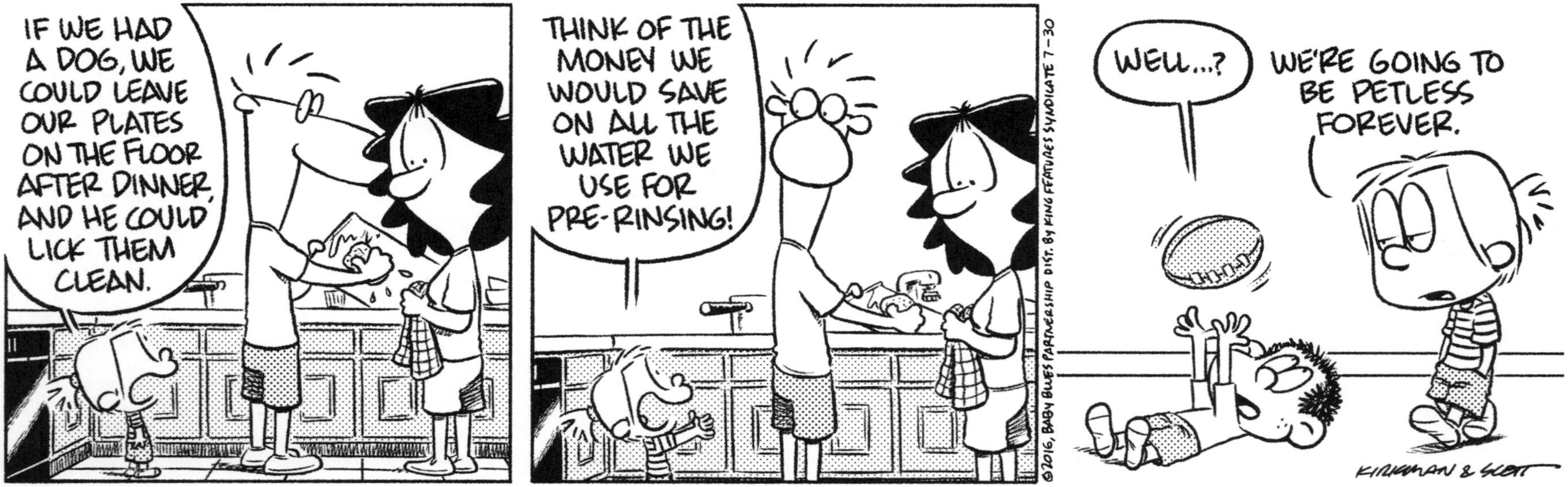
IF WE HAD A DOG, WE COULD LEAVE OUR PLATES ON THE FLOOR AFTER DINNER, AND HE COULD LICK THEM CLEAN.
THINK OF THE MONEY WE WOULD SAVE ON ALL THE WATER WE USE FOR PRE-RINSING!
©2016, BABY BLUES PARTNERSHIP DIST. BY KING FEATURES SYNDICATE 7-30
WELL...?
WE'RE GOING TO BE PETLESS FOREVER.
KIRKMAN & SCOTT

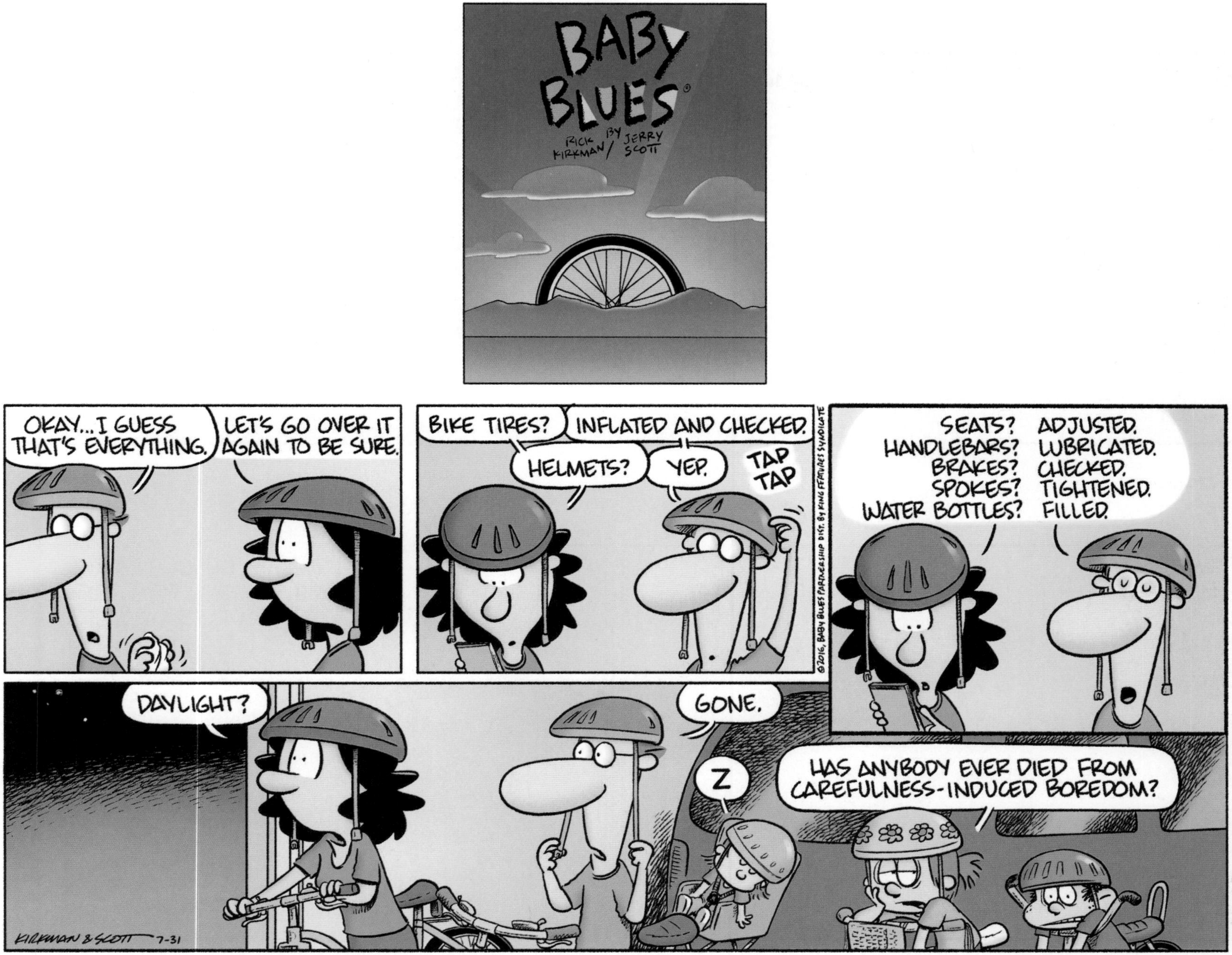
BABY BLUES®
BY RICK KIRKMAN / JERRY SCOTT
OKAY... I GUESS THAT'S EVERYTHING.
LET'S GO OVER IT AGAIN TO BE SURE.
BIKE TIRES?
INFLATED AND CHECKED.
HELMETS?
YEP.
TAP TAP
SEATS? ADJUSTED.
HANDLEBARS? LUBRICATED.
BRAKES? CHECKED.
SPOKES? TIGHTENED.
WATER BOTTLES? FILLED.
DAYLIGHT?
GONE.
Z
HAS ANYBODY EVER DIED FROM CAREFULNESS-INDUCED BOREDOM?
KIRKMAN & SCOTT 7-31
©2016, BABY BLUES PARTNERSHIP DIST. BY KING FEATURES SYNDICATE

Rick: This is us going bike riding, and we don't even have kids to take anymore. Pathetic, now that I see it in print.

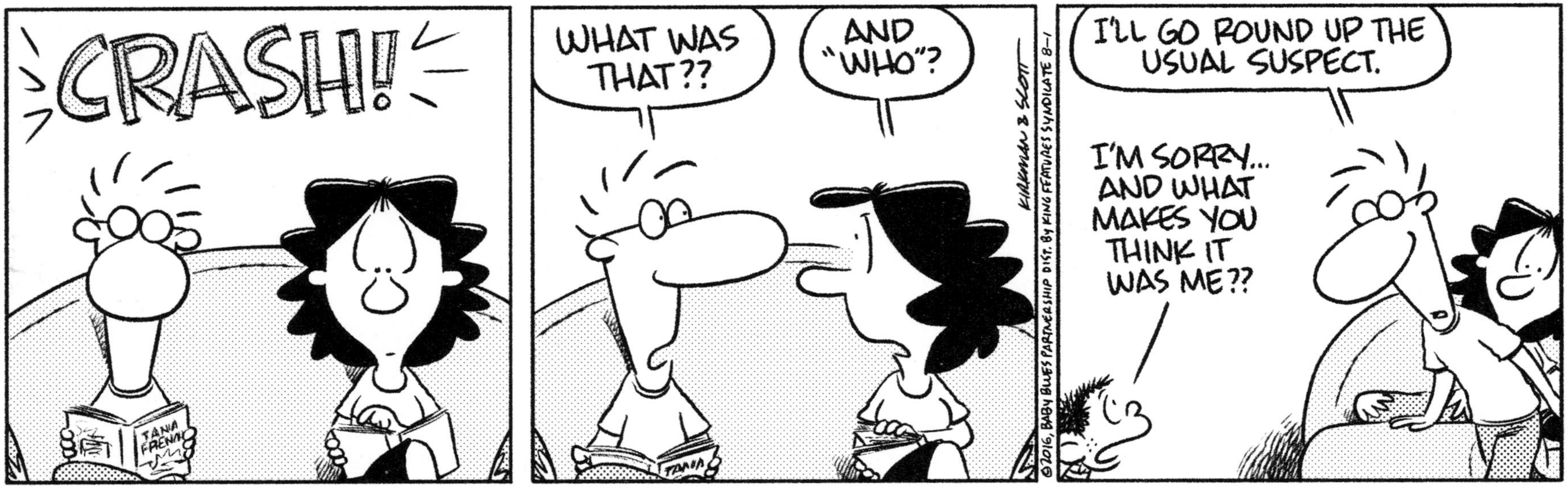
CRASH!
WHAT WAS THAT??
AND "WHO"?
KIRKMAN & SCOTT
©2016, BABY BLUES PARTNERSHIP DIST. BY KING FEATURES SYNDICATE 8-1
I'LL GO ROUND UP THE USUAL SUSPECT.
I'M SORRY... AND WHAT MAKES YOU THINK IT WAS ME??

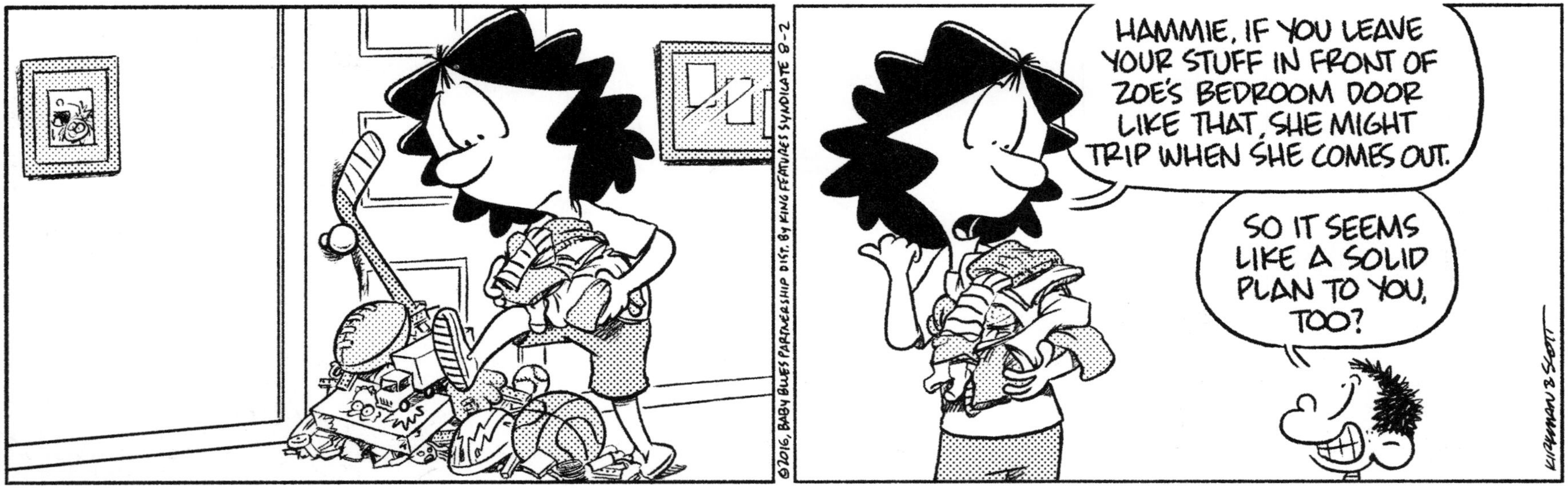
©2016, BABY BLUES PARTNERSHIP DIST. BY KING FEATURES SYNDICATE 8-2
HAMMIE, IF YOU LEAVE YOUR STUFF IN FRONT OF ZOE'S BEDROOM DOOR LIKE THAT, SHE MIGHT TRIP WHEN SHE COMES OUT.
SO IT SEEMS LIKE A SOLID PLAN TO YOU, TOO?
KIRKMAN & SCOTT

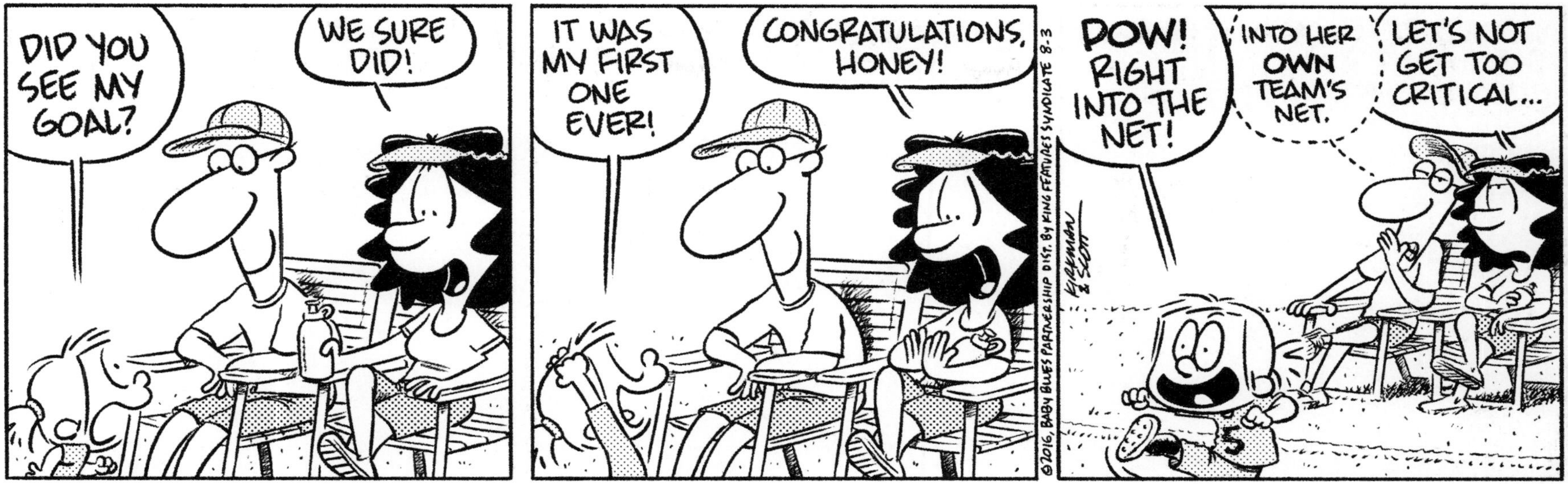
DID YOU SEE MY GOAL?
WE SURE DID!
IT WAS MY FIRST ONE EVER!
CONGRATULATIONS, HONEY!
©2016, BABY BLUES PARTNERSHIP DIST. BY KING FEATURES SYNDICATE 8-3
KIRKMAN & SCOTT
POW! RIGHT INTO THE NET!
INTO HER OWN TEAM'S NET.
LET'S NOT GET TOO CRITICAL...

Jerry: When I was coaching my daughter's soccer team, we celebrated every goal, no matter whose net the ball went into.

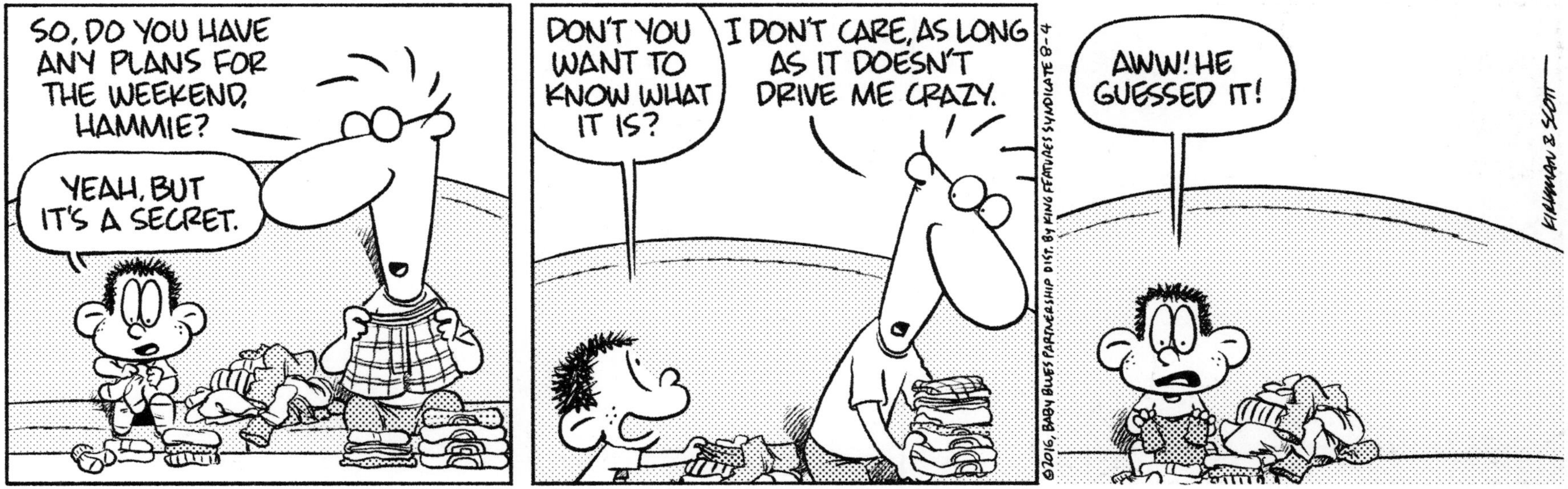
SO, DO YOU HAVE ANY PLANS FOR THE WEEKEND, HAMMIE?
YEAH, BUT IT'S A SECRET.
DON'T YOU WANT TO KNOW WHAT IT IS?
I DON'T CARE, AS LONG AS IT DOESN'T DRIVE ME CRAZY.
©2016, BABY BLUES PARTNERSHIP DIST. BY KING FEATURES SYNDICATE 8-4
AWW! HE GUESSED IT!
KIRKMAN & SCOTT

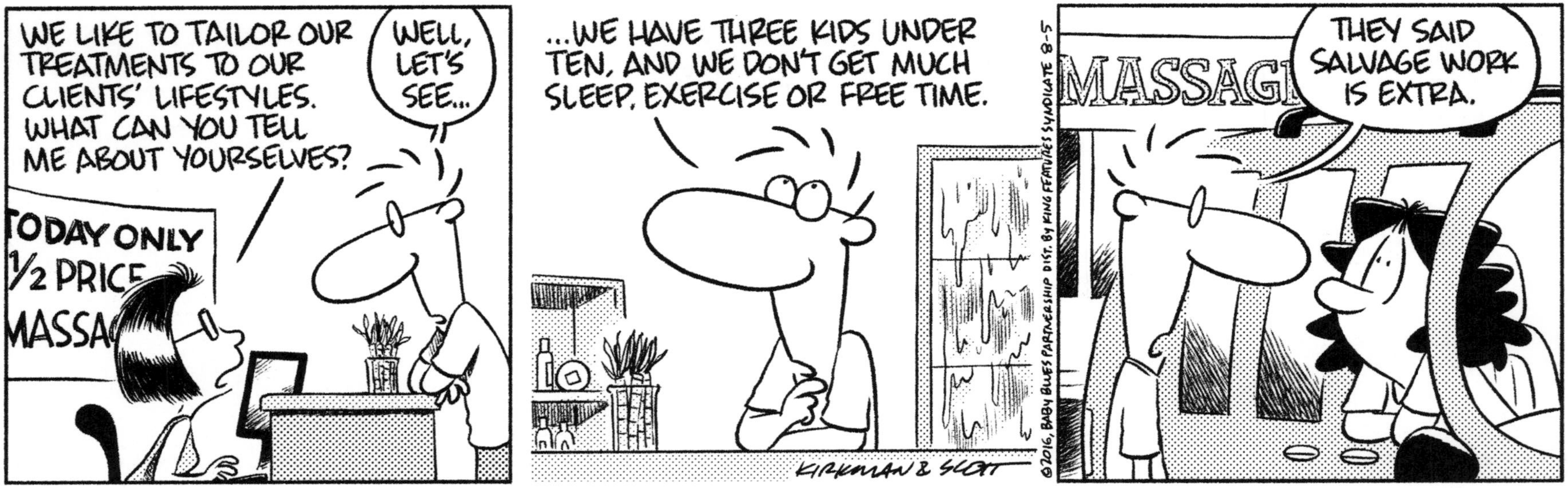
WE LIKE TO TAILOR OUR TREATMENTS TO OUR CLIENTS' LIFESTYLES. WHAT CAN YOU TELL ME ABOUT YOURSELVES?
WELL, LET'S SEE...
TODAY ONLY
1/2 PRICE
...WE HAVE THREE KIDS UNDER TEN, AND WE DON'T GET MUCH SLEEP, EXERCISE OR FREE TIME.
KIRKMAN & SCOTT
©2016, BABY BLUES PARTNERSHIP DIST. BY KING FEATURES SYNDICATE 8-5
MASSAG
THEY SAID SALVAGE WORK IS EXTRA.

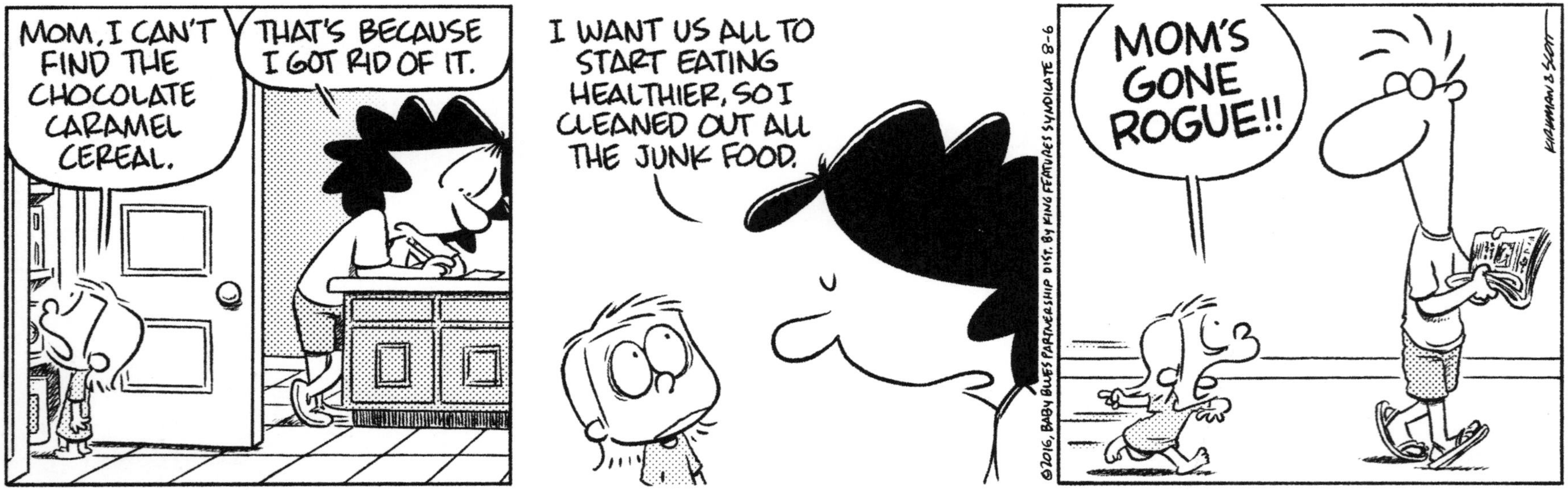
MOM, I CAN'T FIND THE CHOCOLATE CARAMEL CEREAL.
THAT'S BECAUSE I GOT RID OF IT.
I WANT US ALL TO START EATING HEALTHIER, SO I CLEANED OUT ALL THE JUNK FOOD.
©2016, BABY BLUES PARTNERSHIP DIST. BY KING FEATURES SYNDICATE 8-6
MOM'S GONE ROGUE!!
KIRKMAN & SCOTT

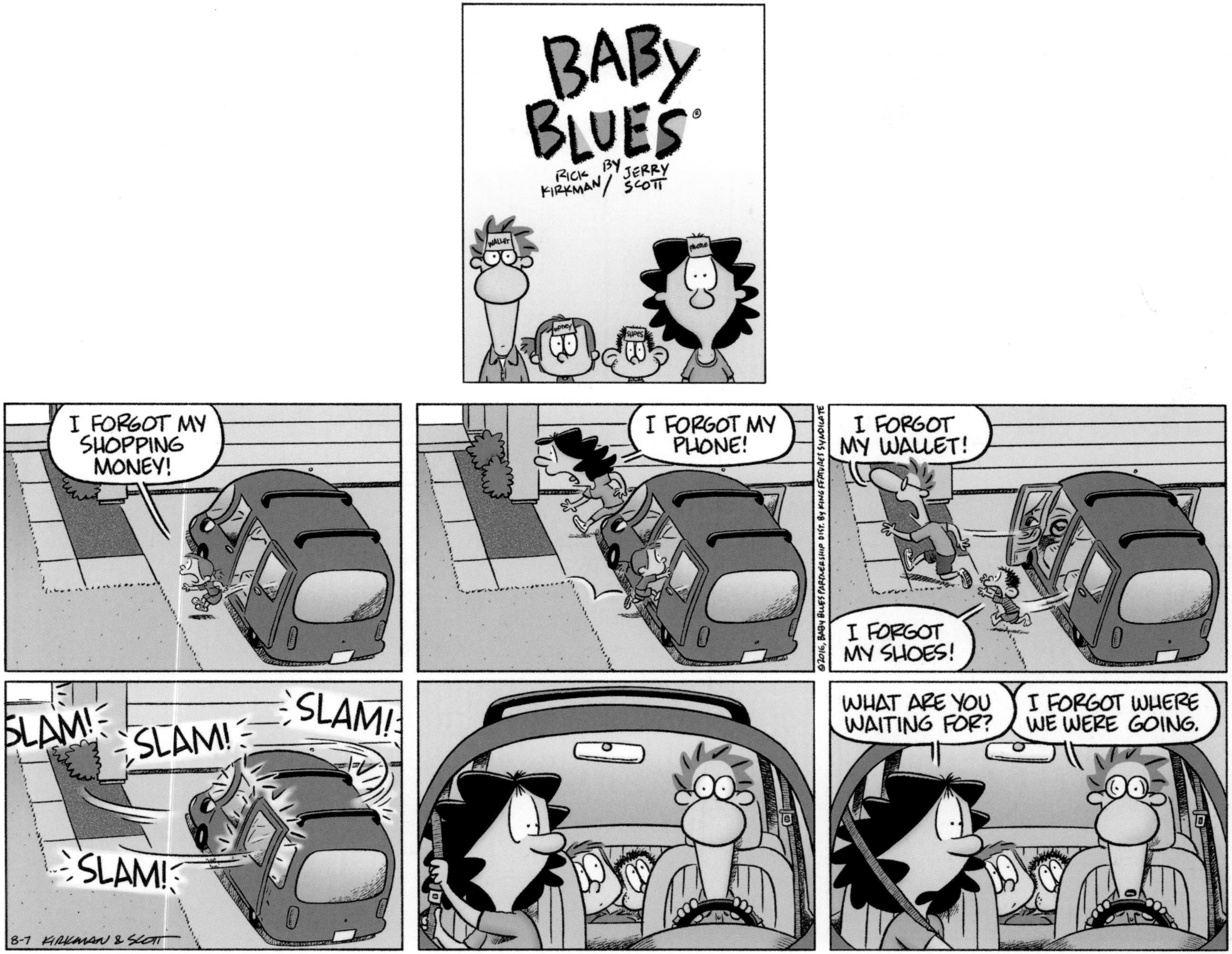
BABY BLUES®
BY RICK KIRKMAN / JERRY SCOTT
I FORGOT MY SHOPPING MONEY!
I FORGOT MY PHONE!
I FORGOT MY WALLET!
I FORGOT MY SHOES!
©2016, BABY BLUES PARTNERSHIP DIST. BY KING FEATURES SYNDICATE
SLAM! SLAM! SLAM! SLAM!
8-7 KIRKMAN & SCOTT
WHAT ARE YOU WAITING FOR?
I FORGOT WHERE WE WERE GOING.

Rick: Unfortunately, inspired by true events.

Jerry: If you were a drone, this is what you would see in my driveway whenever we have to go somewhere.

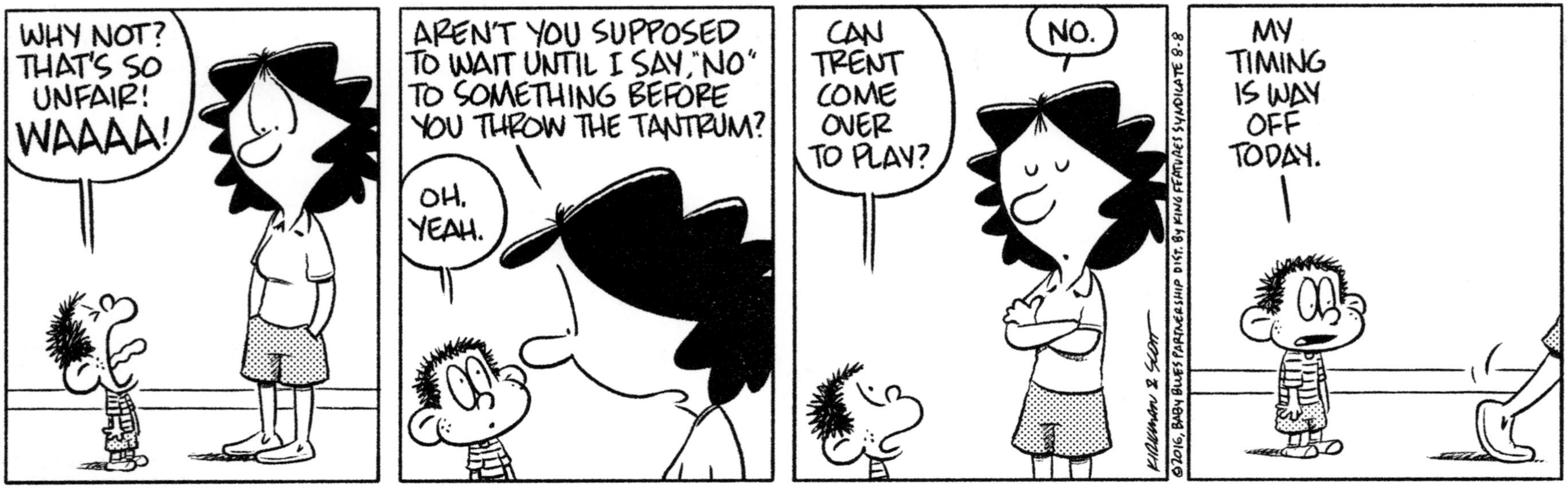
WHY NOT? THAT'S SO UNFAIR! WAAAA!
AREN'T YOU SUPPOSED TO WAIT UNTIL I SAY, "NO" TO SOMETHING BEFORE YOU THROW THE TANTRUM?
OH. YEAH.
CAN TRENT COME OVER TO PLAY?
NO.
MY TIMING IS WAY OFF TODAY.
KIRKMAN & SCOTT
©2016, BABY BLUES PARTNERSHIP DIST. BY KING FEATURES SYNDICATE 8-8

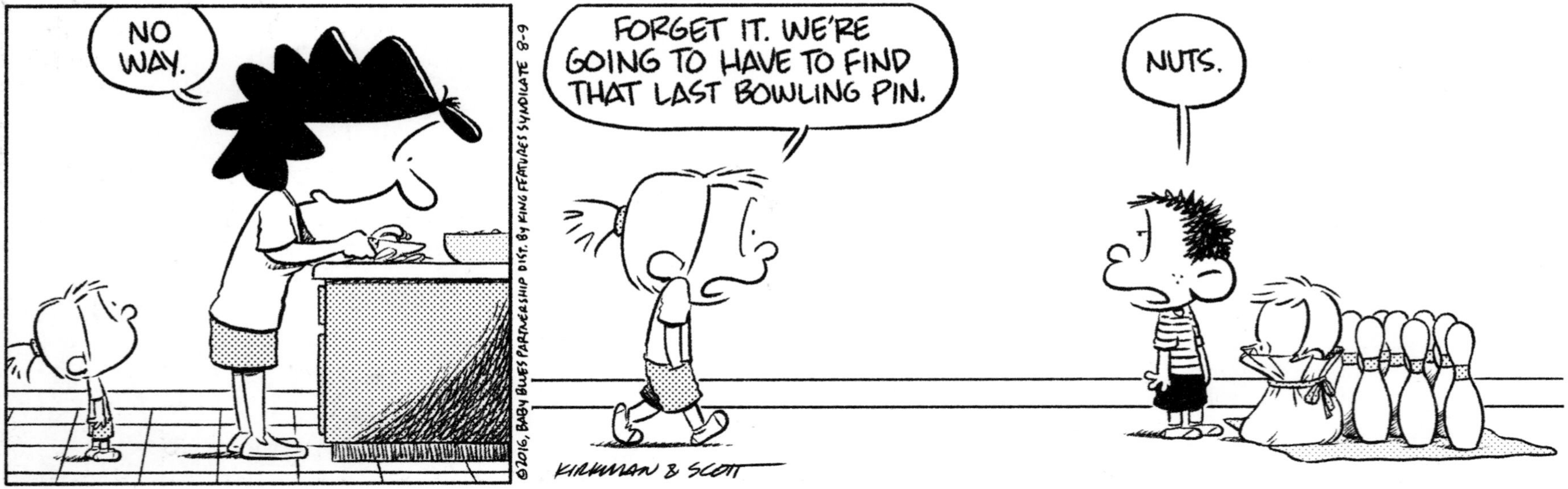
NO WAY.
FORGET IT. WE'RE GOING TO HAVE TO FIND THAT LAST BOWLING PIN.
NUTS.
©2016, BABY BLUES PARTNERSHIP DIST. BY KING FEATURES SYNDICATE 8-9
KIRKMAN & SCOTT

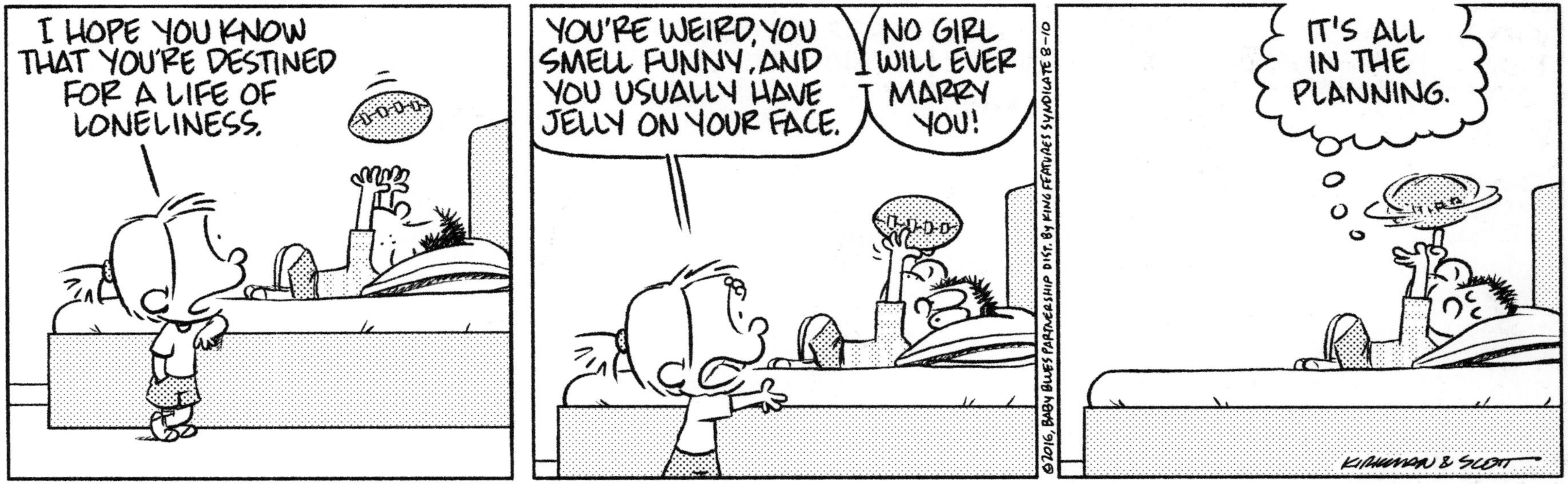
I HOPE YOU KNOW THAT YOU'RE DESTINED FOR A LIFE OF LONELINESS.
YOU'RE WEIRD, YOU SMELL FUNNY, AND YOU USUALLY HAVE JELLY ON YOUR FACE.
NO GIRL WILL EVER MARRY YOU!
©2016, BABY BLUES PARTNERSHIP DIST. BY KING FEATURES SYNDICATE 8-10
IT'S ALL IN THE PLANNING.
KIRKMAN & SCOTT

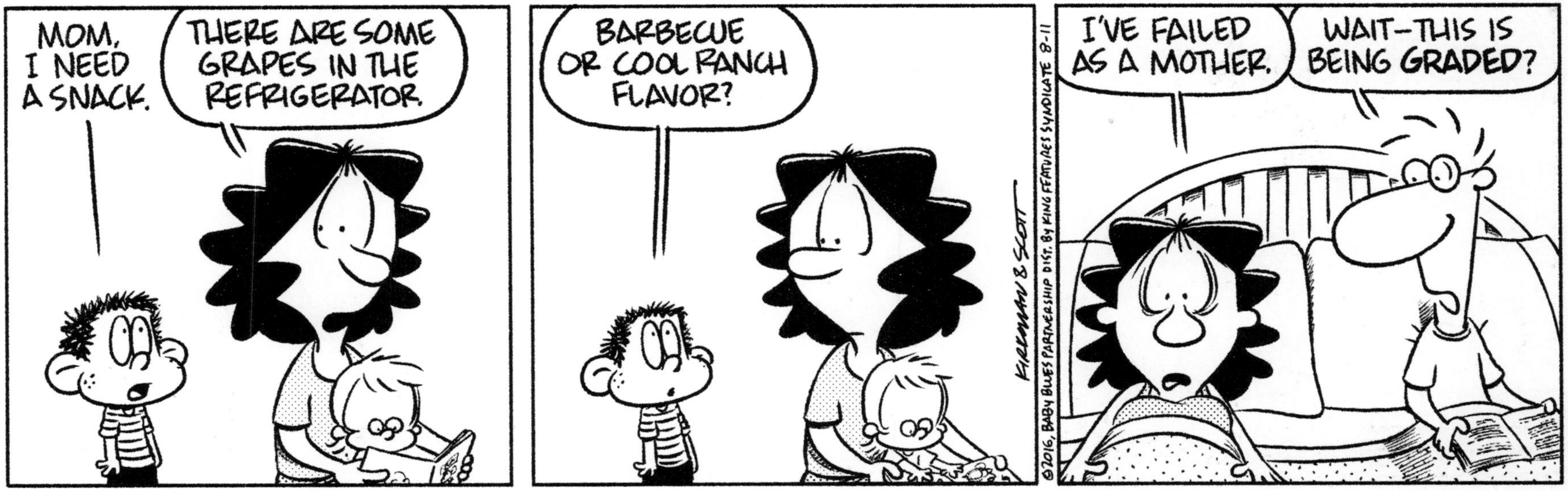
MOM, I NEED A SNACK.
THERE ARE SOME GRAPES IN THE REFRIGERATOR.
BARBECUE OR COOL RANCH FLAVOR?
KIRKMAN & SCOTT
©2016, BABY BLUES PARTNERSHIP DIST. BY KING FEATURES SYNDICATE 8-11
I'VE FAILED AS A MOTHER.
WAIT—THIS IS BEING **GRADED**?

Rick: Personally, I'd go for salt and vinegar.

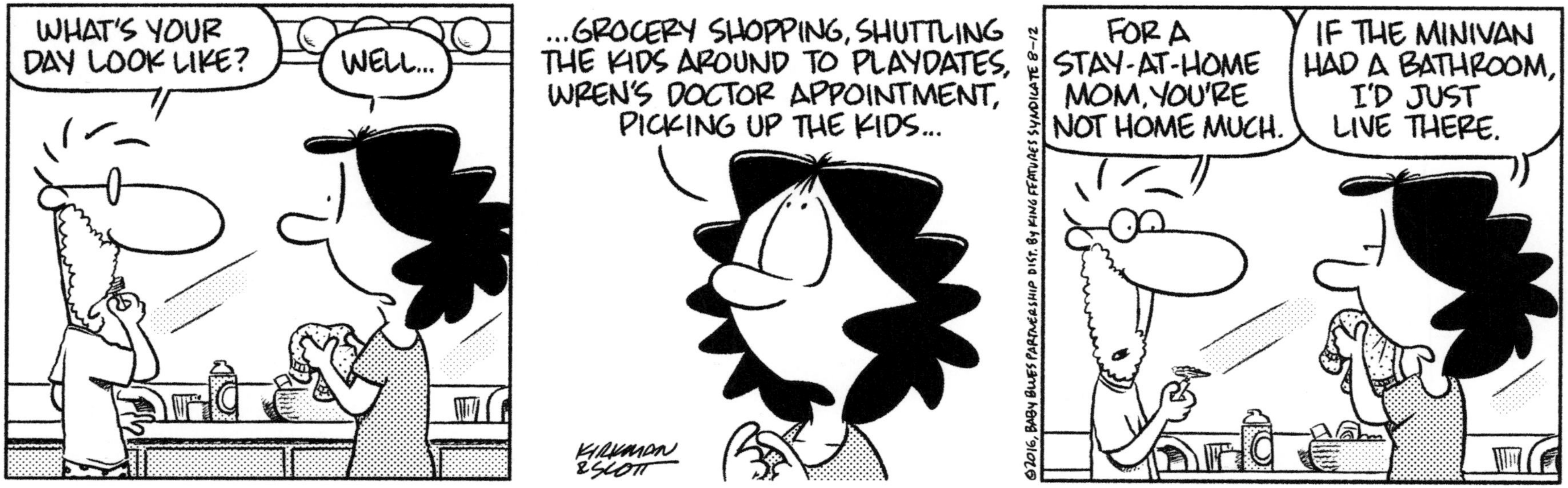
WHAT'S YOUR DAY LOOK LIKE?
WELL...
...GROCERY SHOPPING, SHUTTLING THE KIDS AROUND TO PLAYDATES, WREN'S DOCTOR APPOINTMENT, PICKING UP THE KIDS...
KIRKMAN & SCOTT
©2016, BABY BLUES PARTNERSHIP DIST. BY KING FEATURES SYNDICATE 8-12
FOR A STAY-AT-HOME MOM, YOU'RE NOT HOME MUCH.
IF THE MINIVAN HAD A BATHROOM, I'D JUST LIVE THERE.

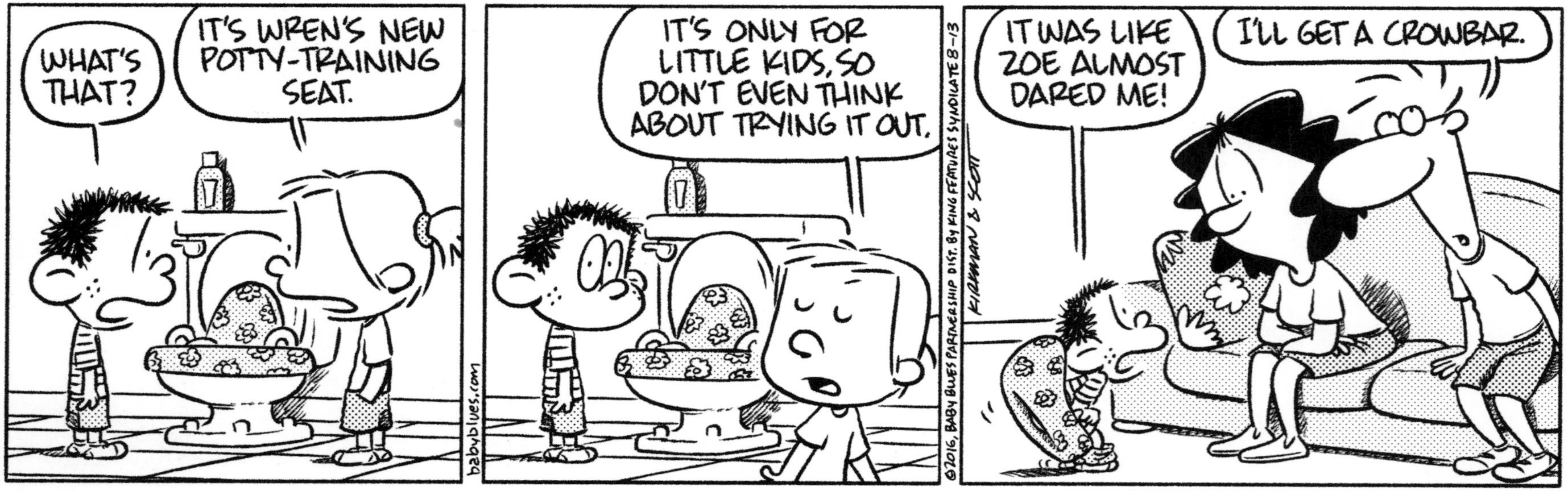
WHAT'S THAT?
IT'S WREN'S NEW POTTY-TRAINING SEAT.
babyblues.com
IT'S ONLY FOR LITTLE KIDS, SO DON'T EVEN THINK ABOUT TRYING IT OUT.
©2016, BABY BLUES PARTNERSHIP DIST. BY KING FEATURES SYNDICATE 8-13
KIRKMAN & SCOTT
IT WAS LIKE ZOE ALMOST DARED ME!
I'LL GET A CROWBAR.

BABY BLUES®
Rick Kirkman & Jerry Scott

I'M GOING NOW, MOM!
©2016, BABY BLUES PARTNERSHIP DIST. BY KING FEATURES SYNDICATE
I HOPE YOU WERE CAREFUL.
MOM, I WORE MY HELMET THE WHOLE TIME!
KIRKMAN & SCOTT 8-14

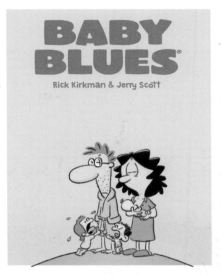

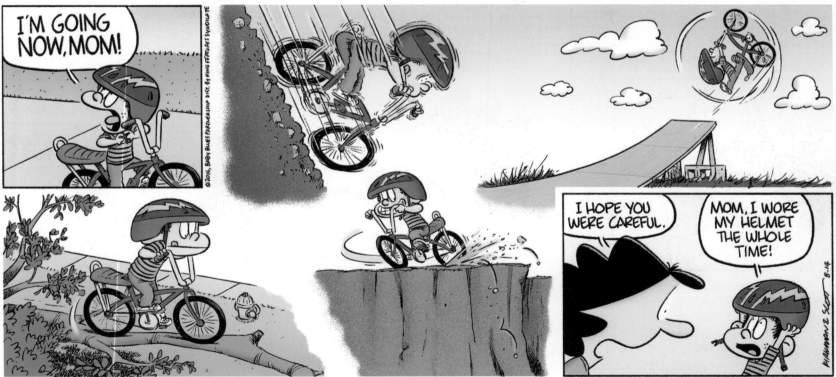

Rick: Five bicycles in one strip. AARRRGGHHH!

Jerry: I tried to get six bikes in there but didn't have room.

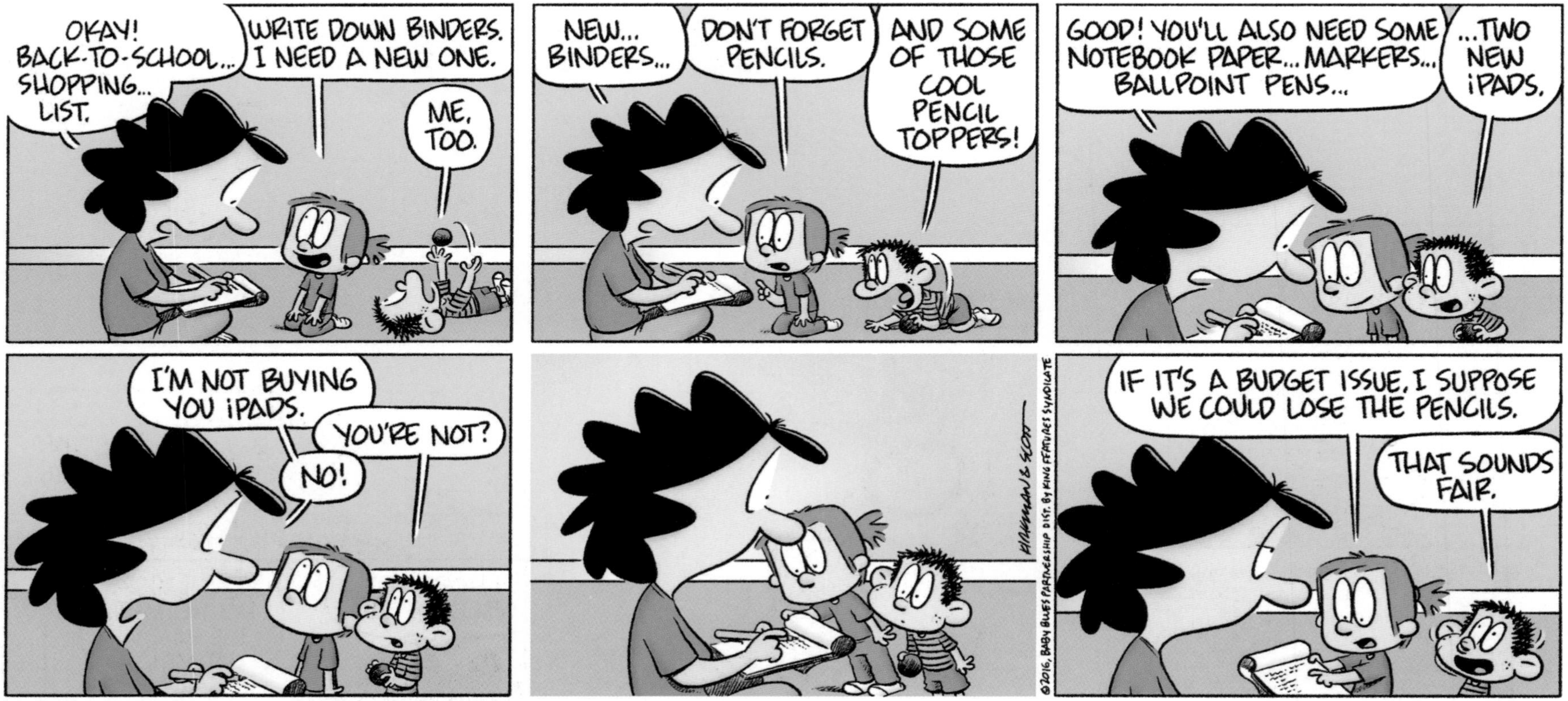
OKAY! BACK-TO-SCHOOL... SHOPPING... LIST.
WRITE DOWN BINDERS. I NEED A NEW ONE.
ME, TOO.
NEW... BINDERS...
DON'T FORGET PENCILS.
AND SOME OF THOSE COOL PENCIL TOPPERS!
GOOD! YOU'LL ALSO NEED SOME NOTEBOOK PAPER... MARKERS... BALLPOINT PENS...
...TWO NEW iPADS.
I'M NOT BUYING YOU iPADS.
YOU'RE NOT?
NO!
IF IT'S A BUDGET ISSUE, I SUPPOSE WE COULD LOSE THE PENCILS.
THAT SOUNDS FAIR.
KIRKMAN & SCOTT
©2016, BABY BLUES PARTNERSHIP DIST. BY KING FEATURES SYNDICATE

Rick: This strip was custom-made for a back-to-school promotional supplement that only ran in some newspapers. Extra credit if you got one of those.

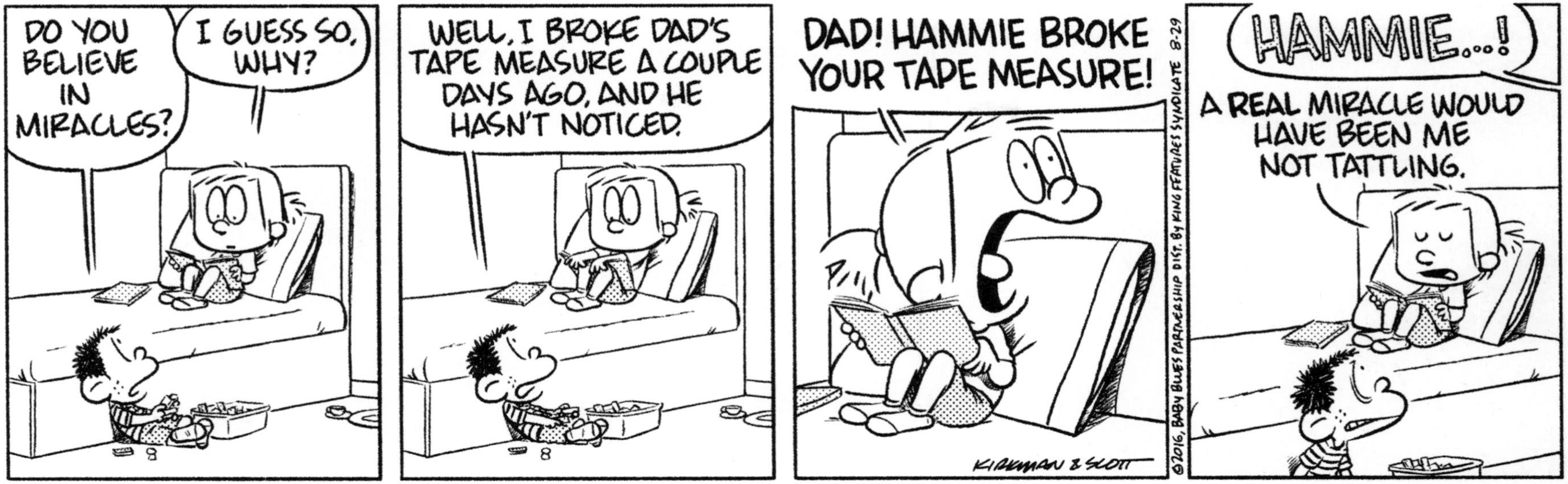
DO YOU BELIEVE IN MIRACLES?
I GUESS SO. WHY?
WELL, I BROKE DAD'S TAPE MEASURE A COUPLE DAYS AGO, AND HE HASN'T NOTICED.
DAD! HAMMIE BROKE YOUR TAPE MEASURE!
8-29
©2016, BABY BLUES PARTNERSHIP DIST. BY KING FEATURES SYNDICATE
KIRKMAN & SCOTT
HAMMIE...!
A REAL MIRACLE WOULD HAVE BEEN ME NOT TATTLING.

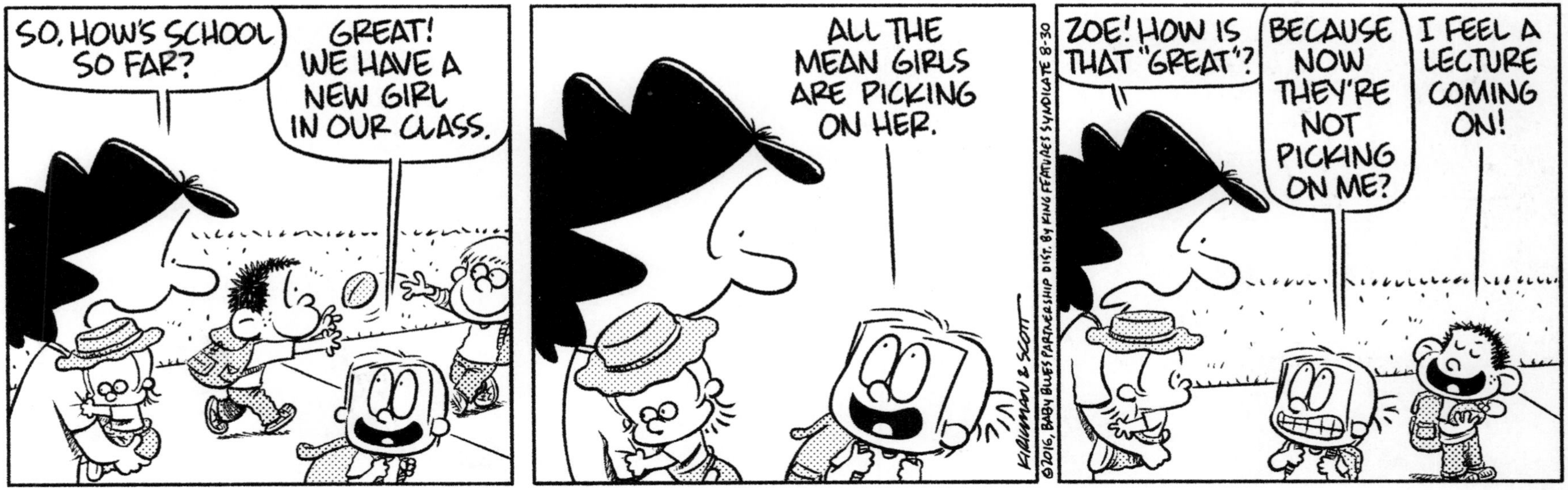
SO, HOW'S SCHOOL SO FAR?
GREAT! WE HAVE A NEW GIRL IN OUR CLASS.
ALL THE MEAN GIRLS ARE PICKING ON HER.
KIRKMAN & SCOTT
©2016, BABY BLUES PARTNERSHIP DIST. BY KING FEATURES SYNDICATE 8-30
ZOE! HOW IS THAT "GREAT"?
BECAUSE NOW THEY'RE NOT PICKING ON ME?
I FEEL A LECTURE COMING ON!

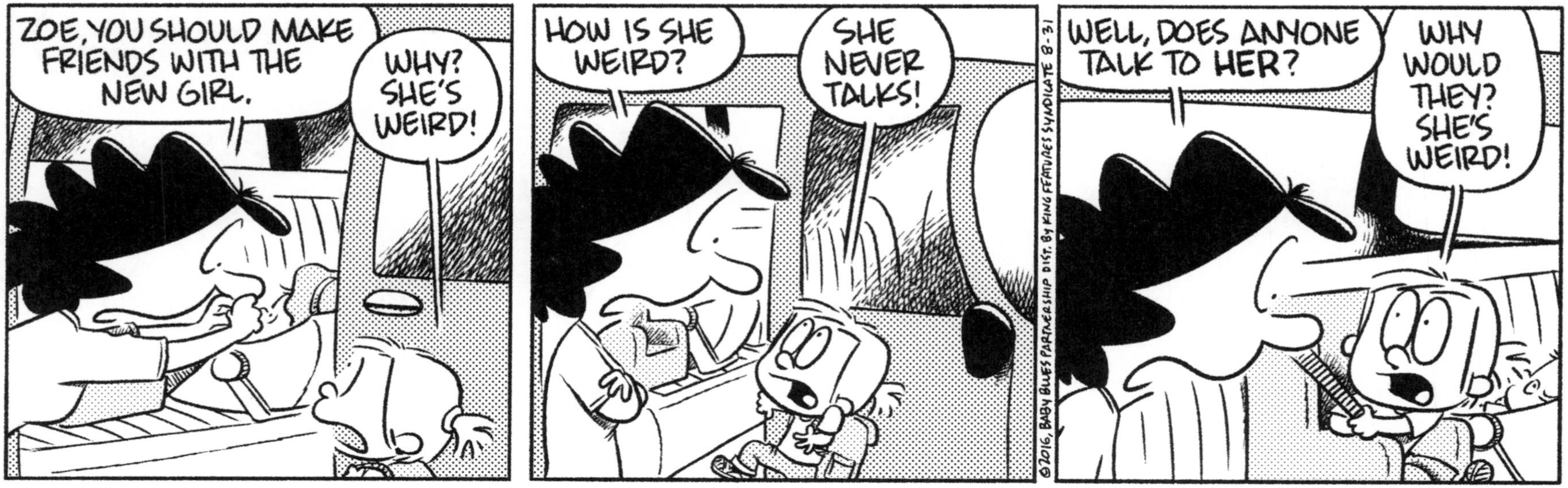
ZOE, YOU SHOULD MAKE FRIENDS WITH THE NEW GIRL.
WHY? SHE'S WEIRD!
HOW IS SHE WEIRD?
SHE NEVER TALKS!
©2016, BABY BLUES PARTNERSHIP DIST. BY KING FEATURES SYNDICATE 8-31
WELL, DOES ANYONE TALK TO HER?
WHY WOULD THEY? SHE'S WEIRD!

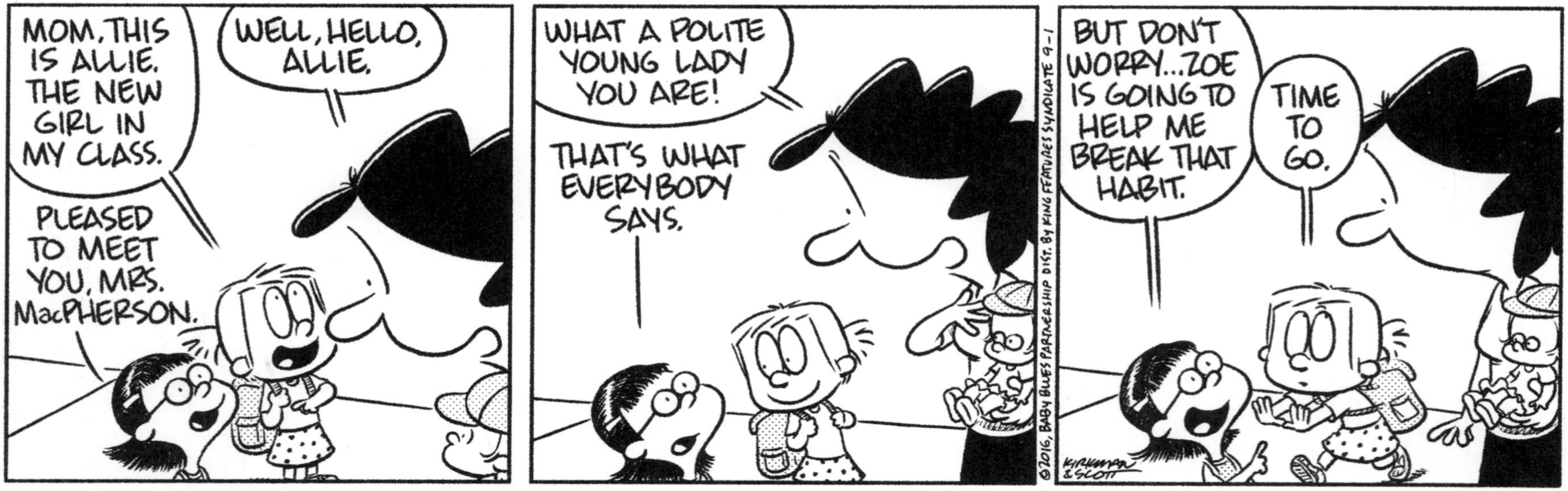
MOM, THIS IS ALLIE. THE NEW GIRL IN MY CLASS.
WELL, HELLO, ALLIE.
PLEASED TO MEET YOU, MRS. MacPHERSON.
WHAT A POLITE YOUNG LADY YOU ARE!
THAT'S WHAT EVERYBODY SAYS.
©2016, BABY BLUES PARTNERSHIP DIST. BY KING FEATURES SYNDICATE 9-1
BUT DON'T WORRY...ZOE IS GOING TO HELP ME BREAK THAT HABIT.
TIME TO GO.
KIRKMAN & SCOTT

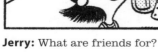

Jerry: What are friends for?

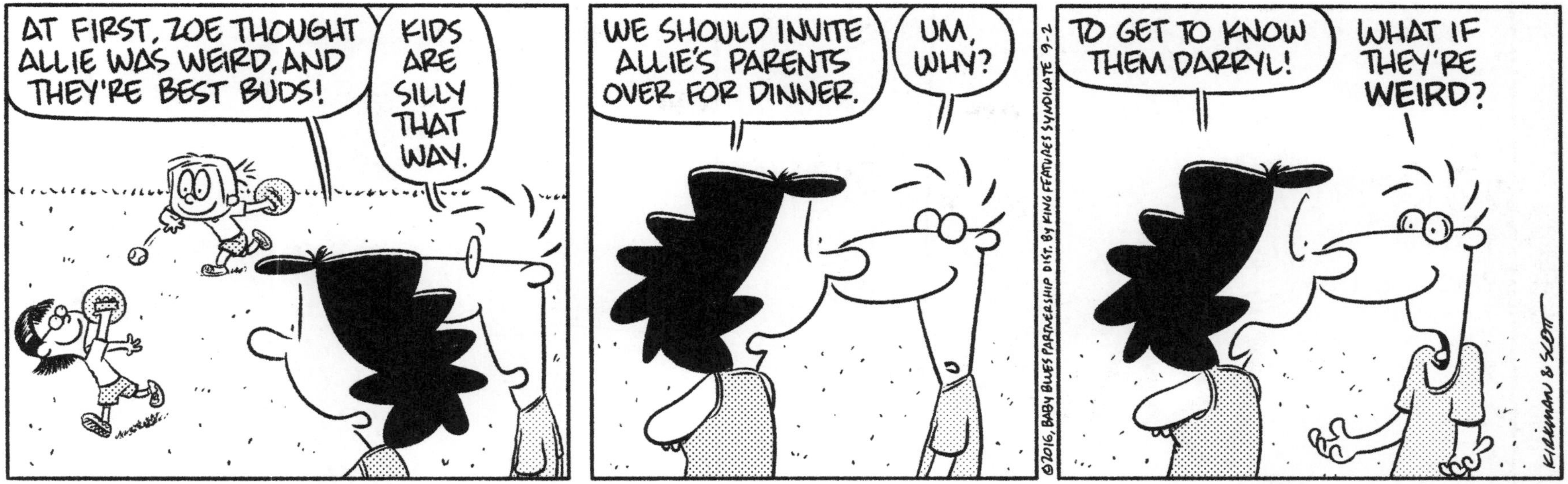
AT FIRST, ZOE THOUGHT ALLIE WAS WEIRD, AND THEY'RE BEST BUDS!
KIDS ARE SILLY THAT WAY.
WE SHOULD INVITE ALLIE'S PARENTS OVER FOR DINNER.
UM, WHY?
©2016, BABY BLUES PARTNERSHIP DIST. BY KING FEATURES SYNDICATE 9-2
TO GET TO KNOW THEM DARRYL!
WHAT IF THEY'RE WEIRD?
KIRKMAN & SCOTT

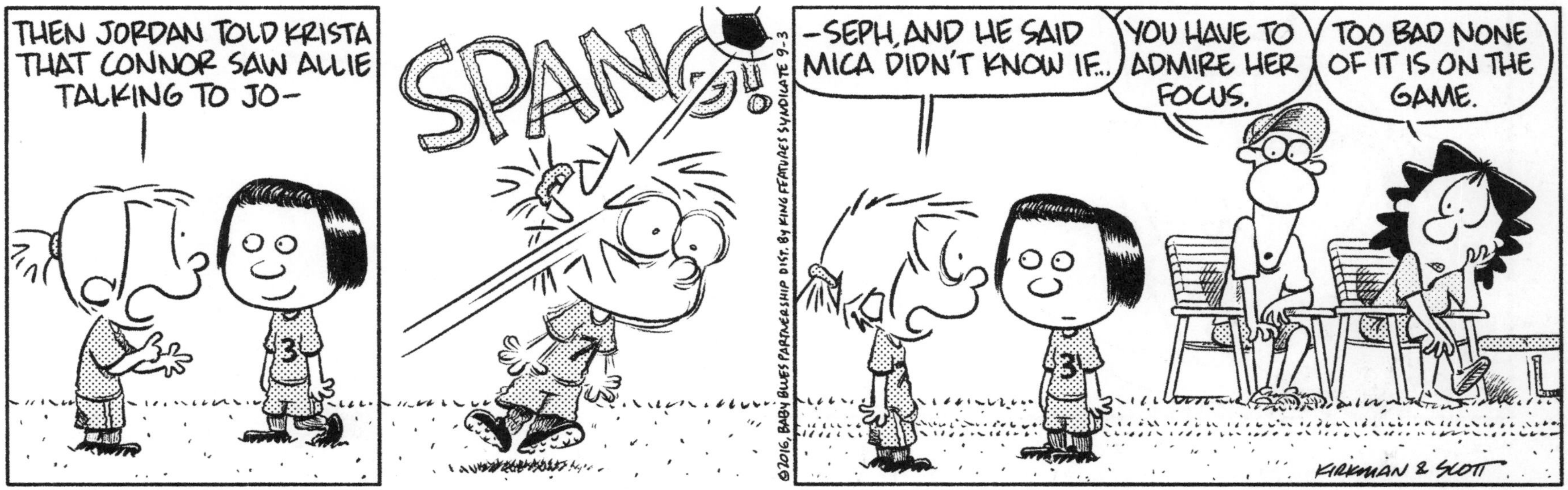
THEN JORDAN TOLD KRISTA THAT CONNOR SAW ALLIE TALKING TO JO—
SPANG!
©2016, BABY BLUES PARTNERSHIP DIST. BY KING FEATURES SYNDICATE 9-3
—SEPH, AND HE SAID MICA DIDN'T KNOW IF...
YOU HAVE TO ADMIRE HER FOCUS.
TOO BAD NONE OF IT IS ON THE GAME.
KIRKMAN & SCOTT

Rick: Yay! SPANG!

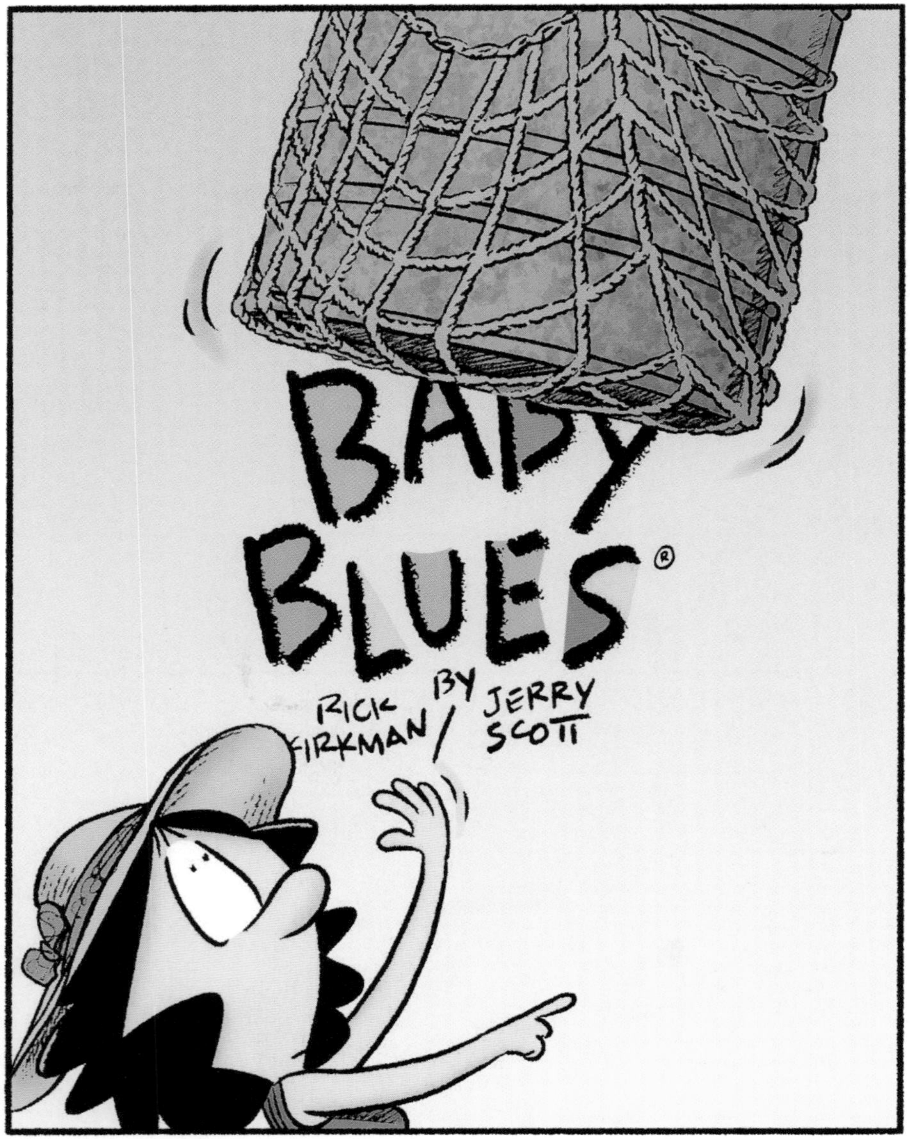

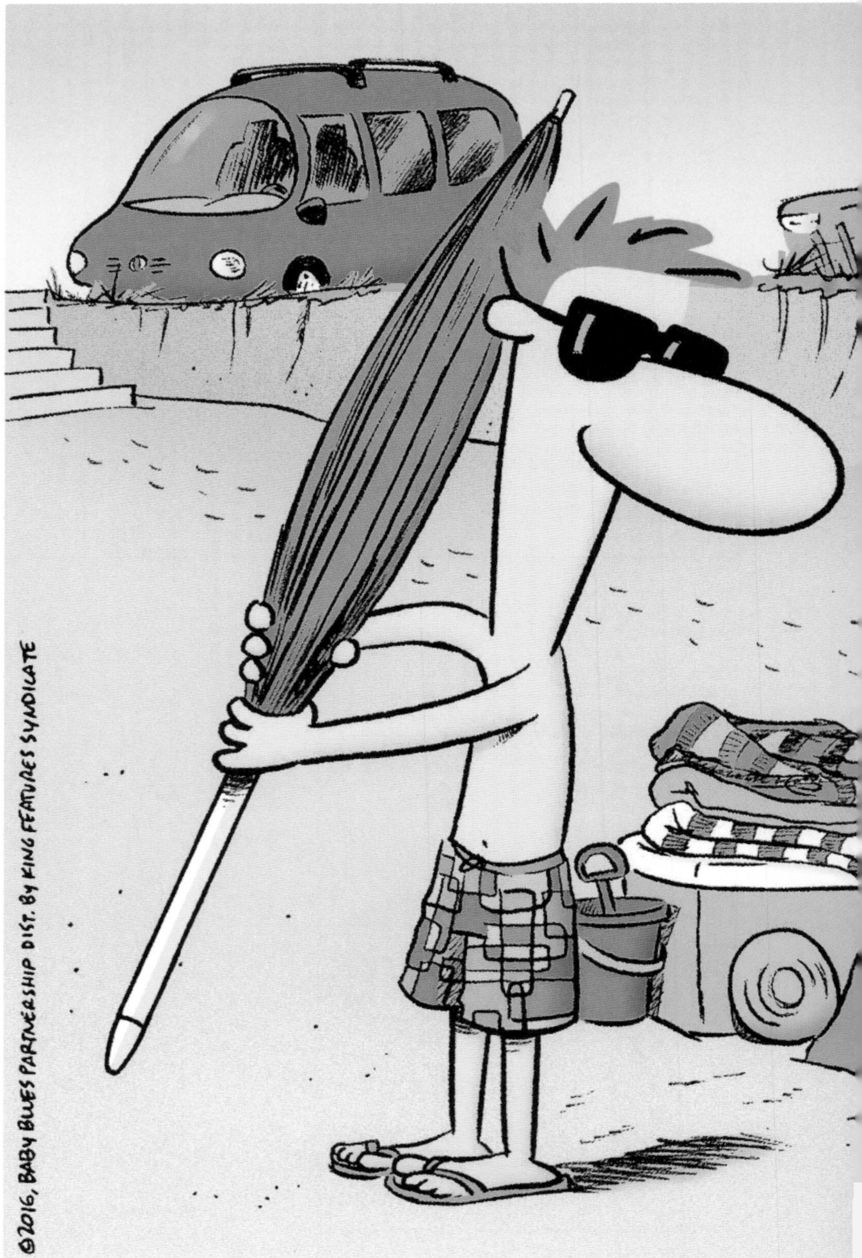

Rick: It's not often we get to have the art this large in a Sunday, but it's always fun to have this much room to use. It even allowed me to go overboard with the rusty barrel coloring. You can even make out all the beach detritus on Hammie.

Jerry: Gotta admire that spork stuck to Hammie's left ear.

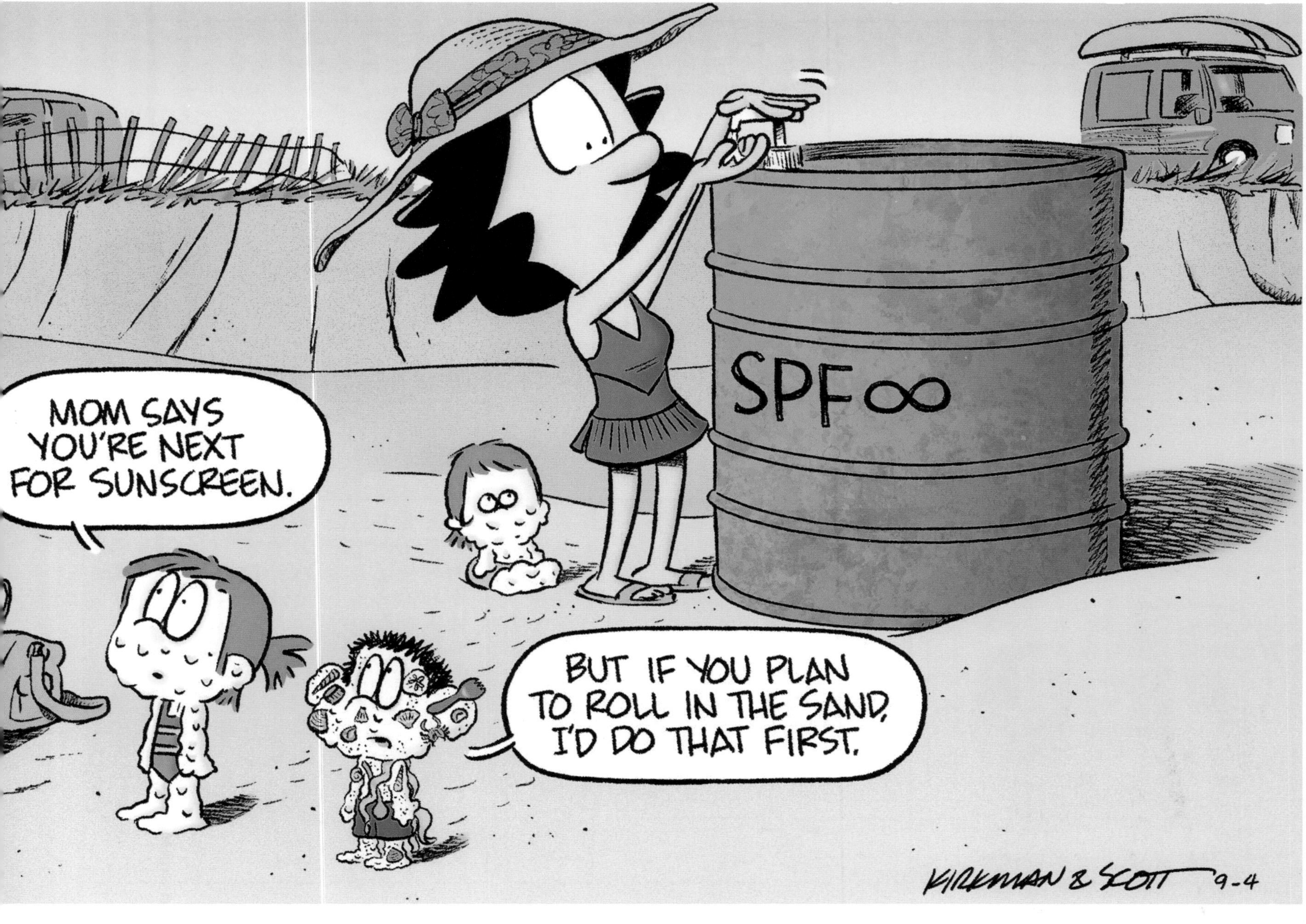
MOM SAYS YOU'RE NEXT FOR SUNSCREEN.
SPF∞
BUT IF YOU PLAN TO ROLL IN THE SAND, I'D DO THAT FIRST.
KIRKMAN & SCOTT 9-4

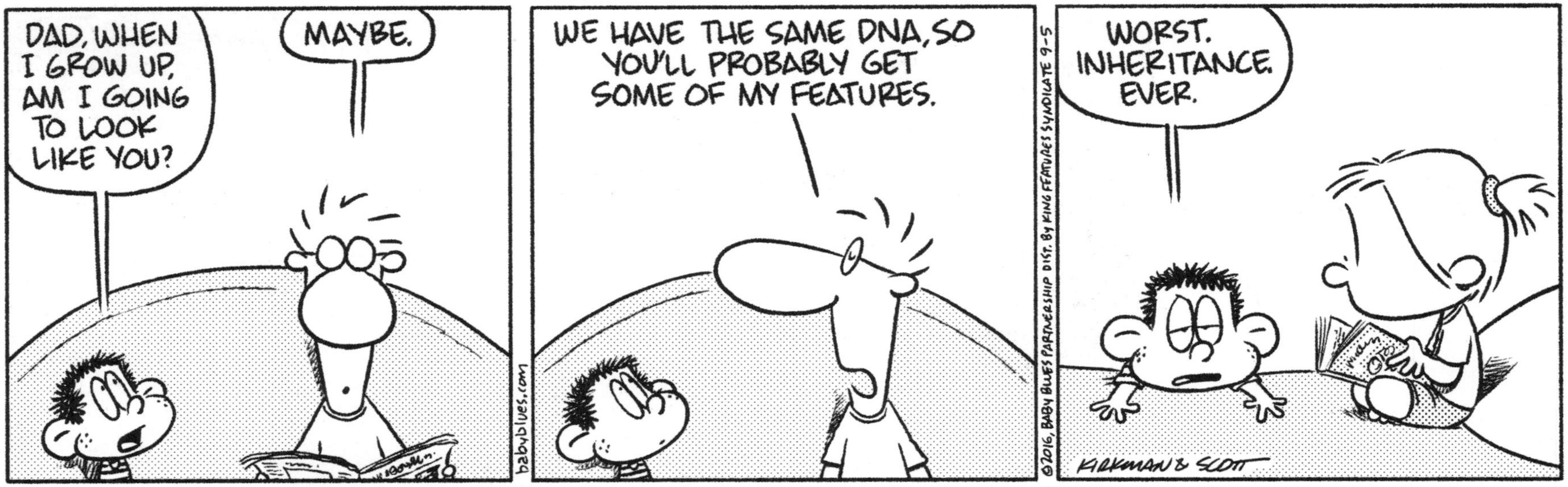
DAD, WHEN I GROW UP, AM I GOING TO LOOK LIKE YOU?
MAYBE.
WE HAVE THE SAME DNA, SO YOU'LL PROBABLY GET SOME OF MY FEATURES.
WORST. INHERITANCE. EVER.
babyblues.com
©2016, BABY BLUES PARTNERSHIP DIST. BY KING FEATURES SYNDICATE 9-5
KIRKMAN & SCOTT

Jerry: Yeah. And thanks for the hairline, Pop.

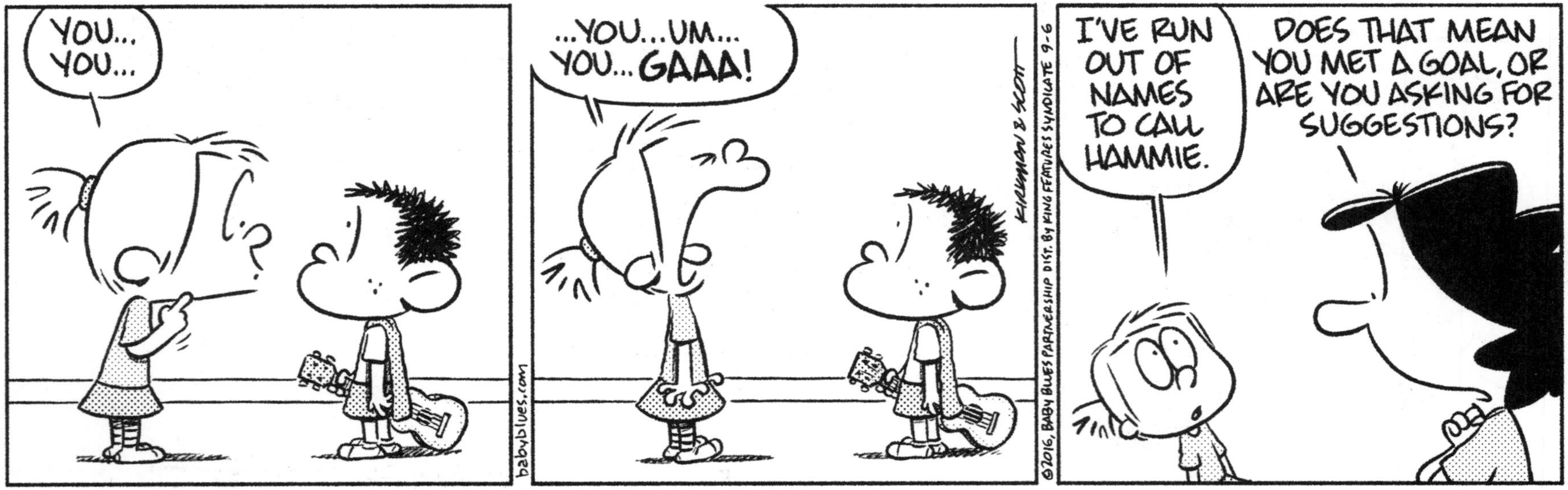
YOU... YOU...
...YOU...UM... YOU...GAAA!
I'VE RUN OUT OF NAMES TO CALL HAMMIE.
DOES THAT MEAN YOU MET A GOAL, OR ARE YOU ASKING FOR SUGGESTIONS?
babyblues.com
©2016, BABY BLUES PARTNERSHIP DIST. BY KING FEATURES SYNDICATE 9-6
KIRKMAN & SCOTT

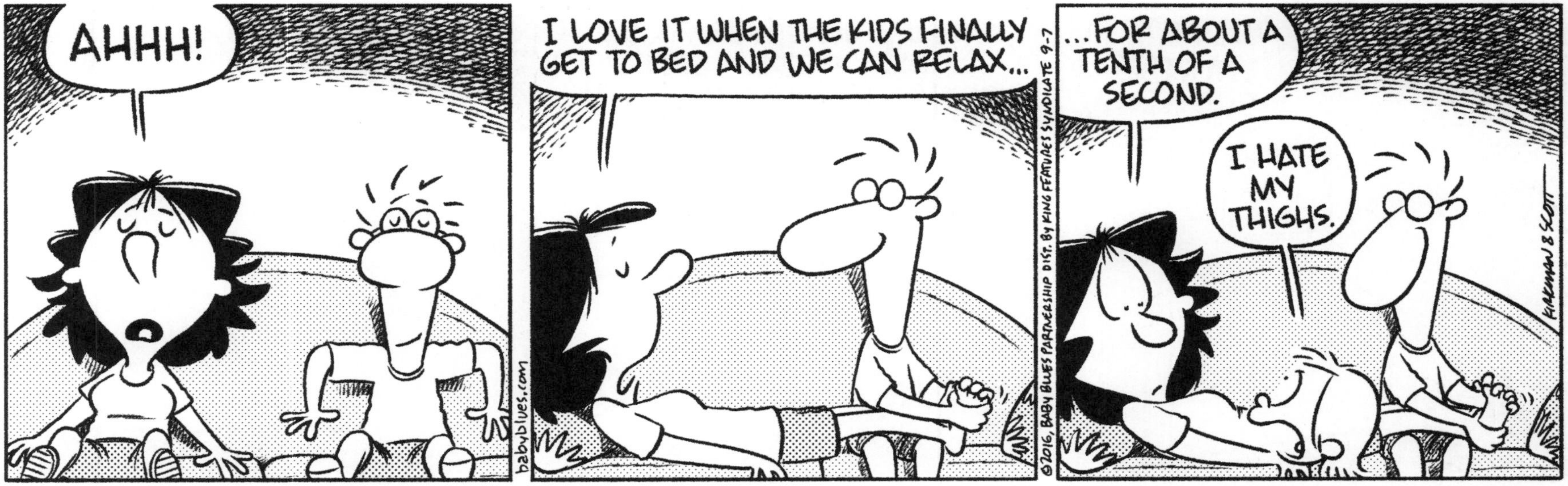
AHHH!
I LOVE IT WHEN THE KIDS FINALLY GET TO BED AND WE CAN RELAX...
...FOR ABOUT A TENTH OF A SECOND.
I HATE MY THIGHS.
babyblues.com
©2016, BABY BLUES PARTNERSHIP DIST. BY KING FEATURES SYNDICATE 9-7
KIRKMAN & SCOTT

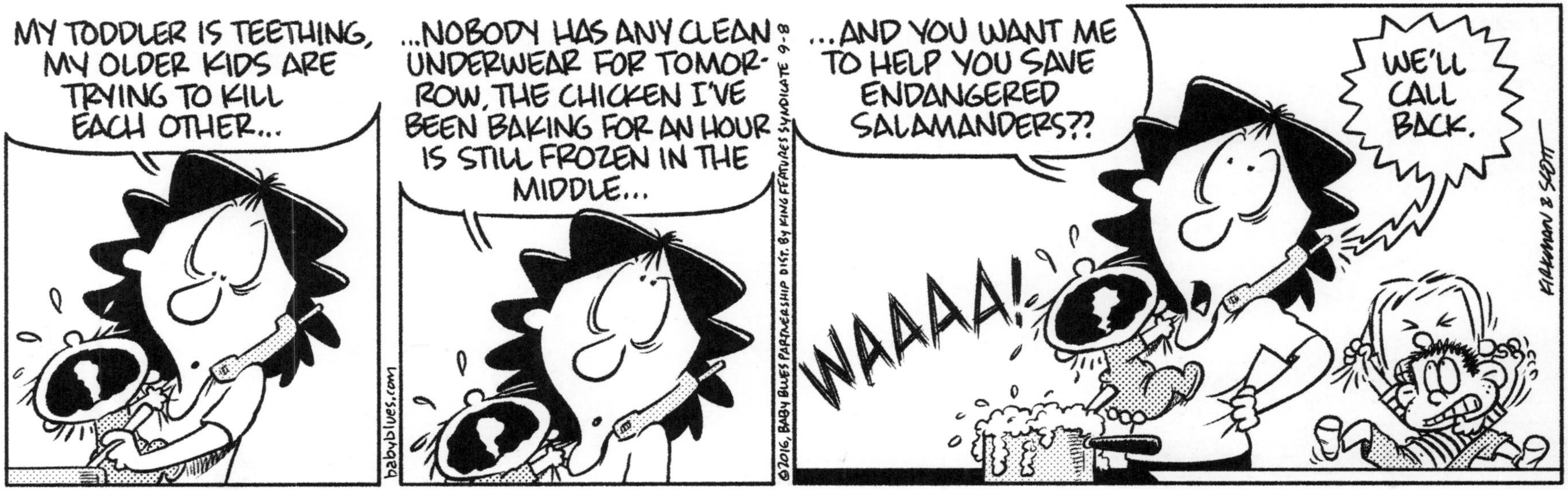
MY TODDLER IS TEETHING, MY OLDER KIDS ARE TRYING TO KILL EACH OTHER...
...NOBODY HAS ANY CLEAN UNDERWEAR FOR TOMORROW, THE CHICKEN I'VE BEEN BAKING FOR AN HOUR IS STILL FROZEN IN THE MIDDLE...
...AND YOU WANT ME TO HELP YOU SAVE ENDANGERED SALAMANDERS??
WE'LL CALL BACK.
WAAAA!
babyblues.com
©2016, BABY BLUES PARTNERSHIP DIST. BY KING FEATURES SYNDICATE 9-8
KIRKMAN & SCOTT

Rick: I feel Wanda's indignation.

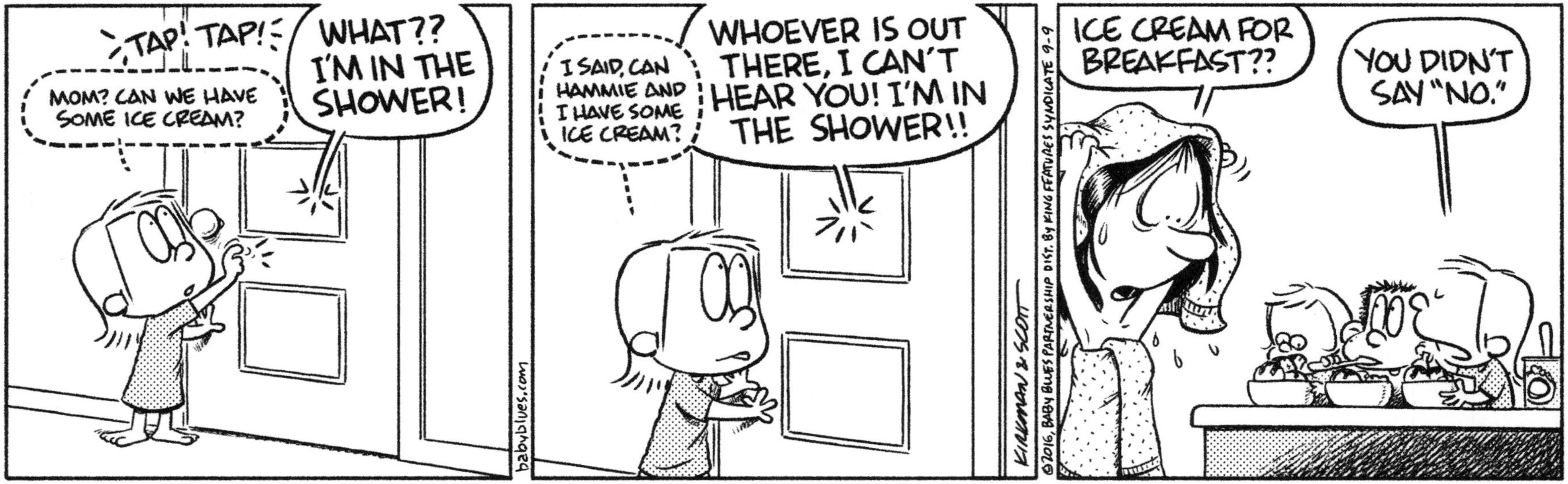
TAP! TAP!
MOM? CAN WE HAVE SOME ICE CREAM?
WHAT?? I'M IN THE SHOWER!
babyblues.com
I SAID, CAN HAMMIE AND I HAVE SOME ICE CREAM?
WHOEVER IS OUT THERE, I CAN'T HEAR YOU! I'M IN THE SHOWER!!
KIRKMAN & SCOTT
© 2016, BABY BLUES PARTNERSHIP DIST. BY KING FEATURES SYNDICATE 9-9
ICE CREAM FOR BREAKFAST??
YOU DIDN'T SAY "NO."

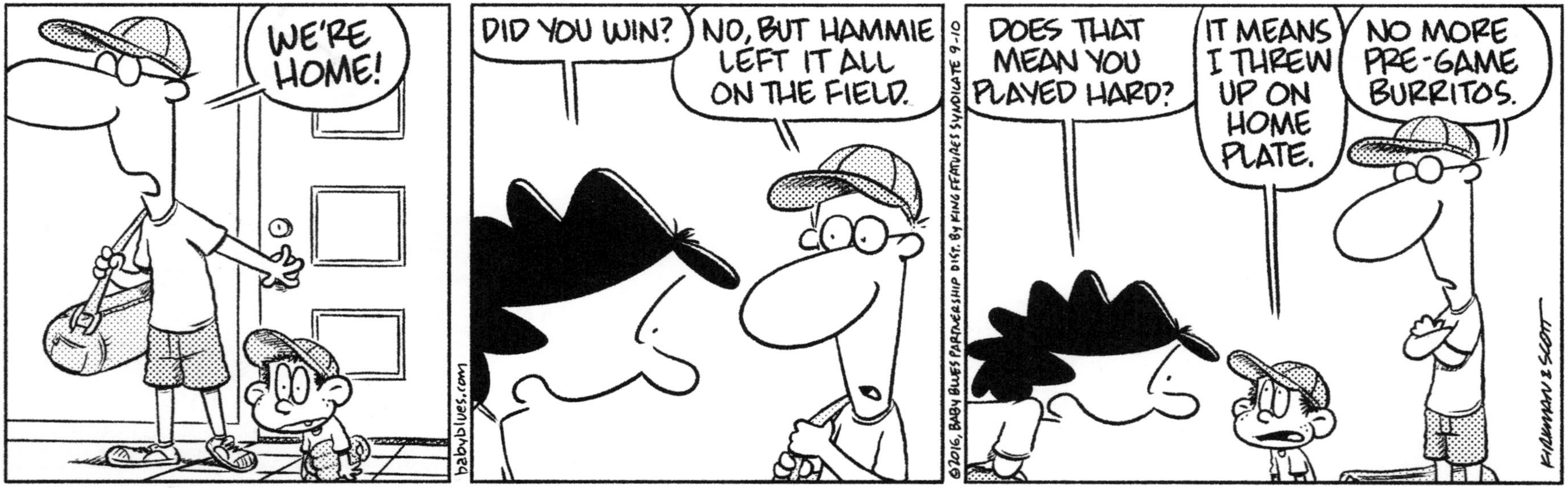
WE'RE HOME!
babyblues.com
DID YOU WIN?
NO, BUT HAMMIE LEFT IT ALL ON THE FIELD.
© 2016, BABY BLUES PARTNERSHIP DIST. BY KING FEATURES SYNDICATE 9-10
DOES THAT MEAN YOU PLAYED HARD?
IT MEANS I THREW UP ON HOME PLATE.
NO MORE PRE-GAME BURRITOS.
KIRKMAN & SCOTT

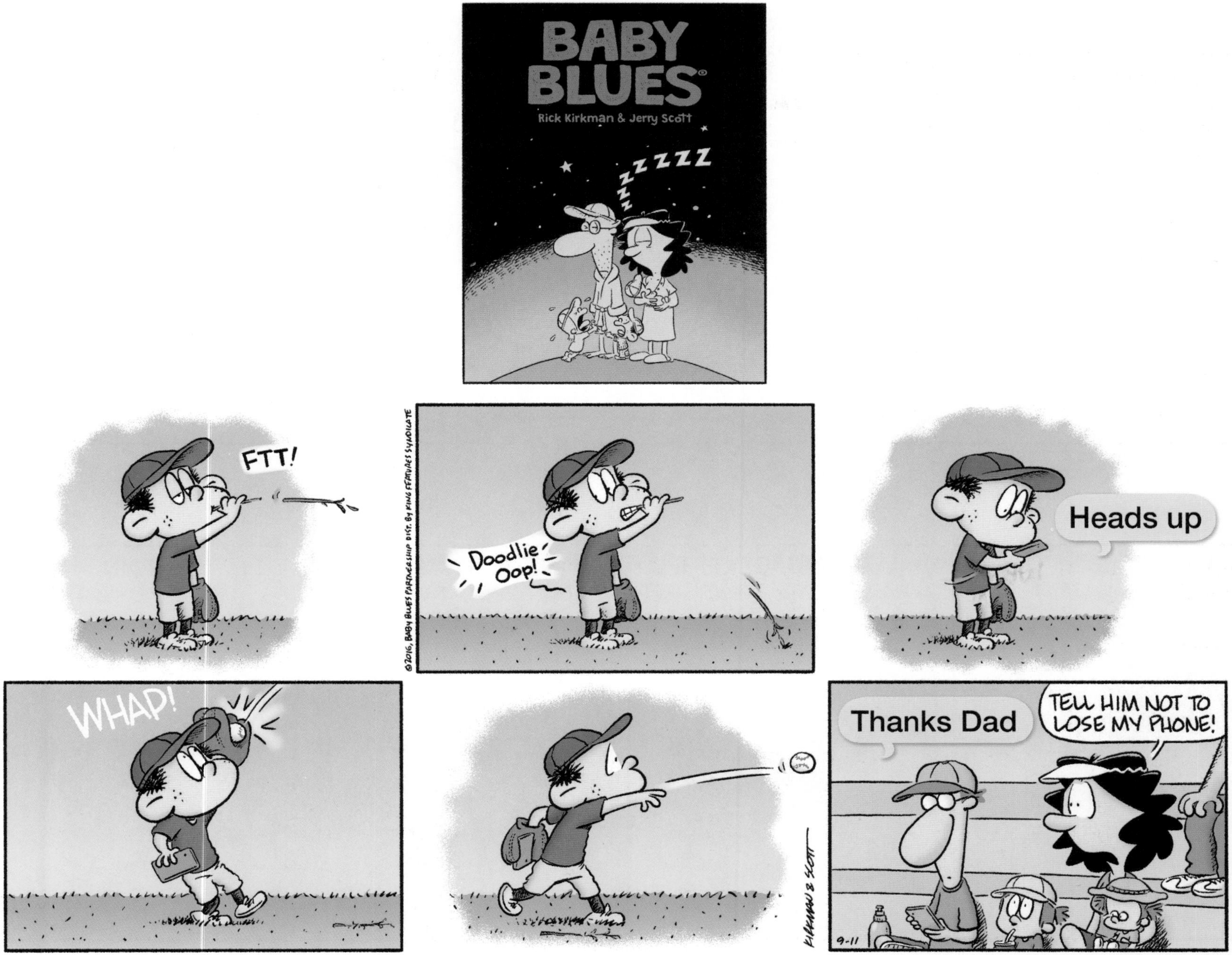
BABY BLUES®
Rick Kirkman & Jerry Scott
ZZZZZ
FTT!
©2016, BABY BLUES PARTNERSHIP DIST. BY KING FEATURES SYNDICATE
Doodlie Oop!
Heads up
WHAP!
KIRKMAN & SCOTT
Thanks Dad
TELL HIM NOT TO LOSE MY PHONE!
9-11

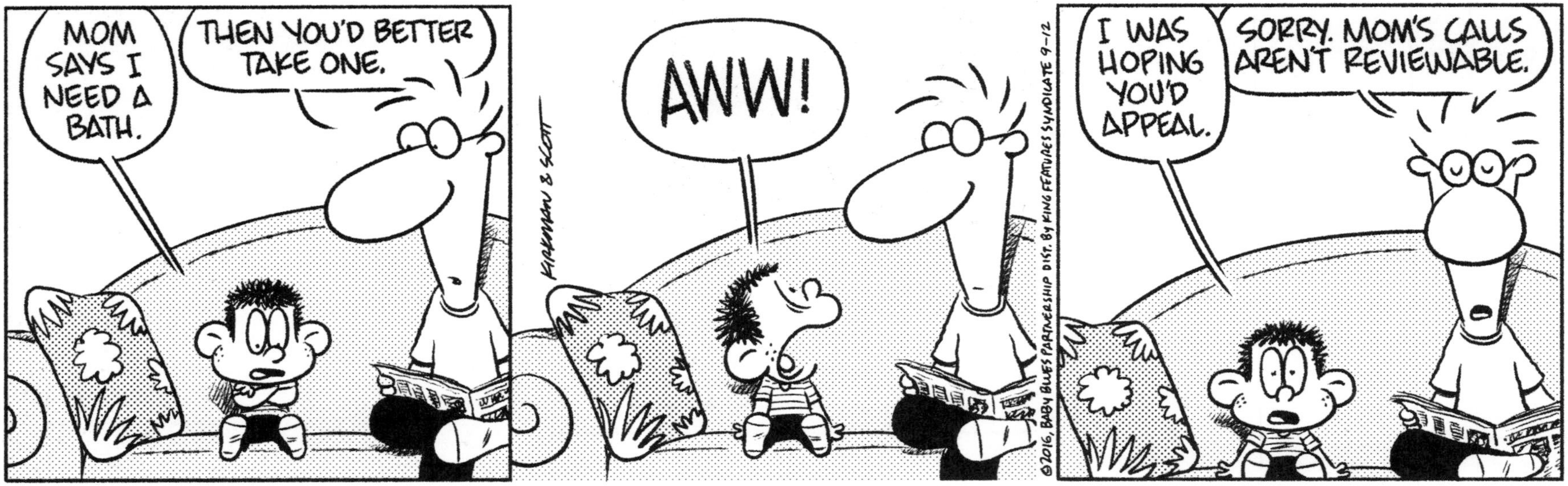
MOM SAYS I NEED A BATH.
THEN YOU'D BETTER TAKE ONE.
AWW!
I WAS HOPING YOU'D APPEAL.
SORRY. MOM'S CALLS AREN'T REVIEWABLE.

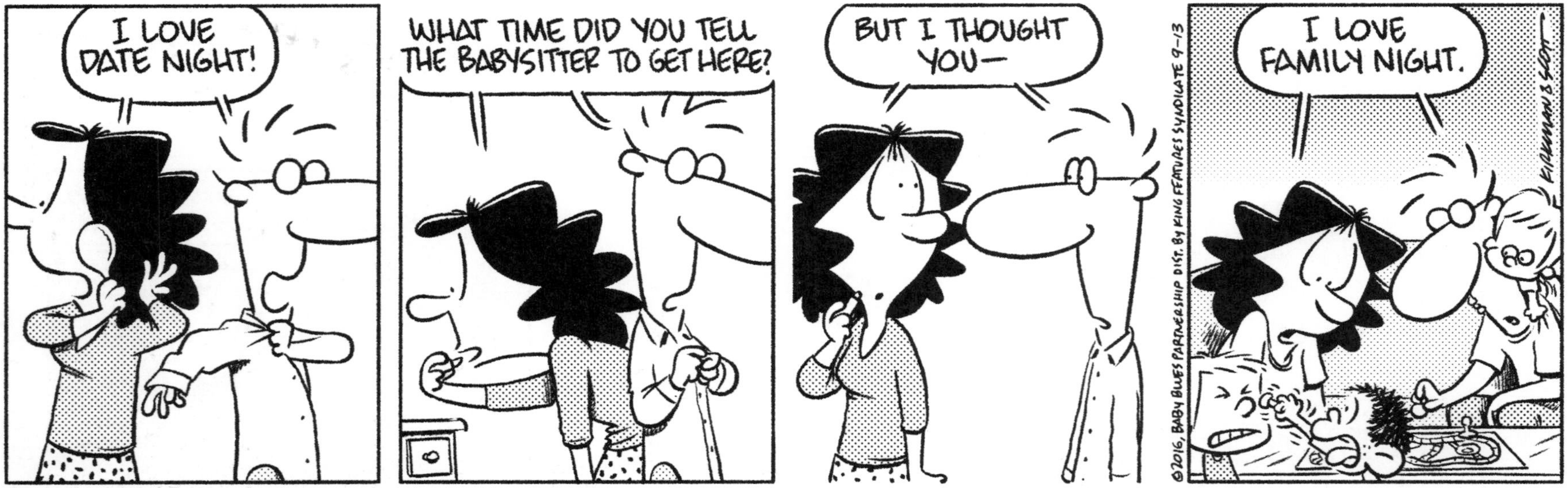
I LOVE DATE NIGHT!
WHAT TIME DID YOU TELL THE BABYSITTER TO GET HERE?
BUT I THOUGHT YOU—
I LOVE FAMILY NIGHT.

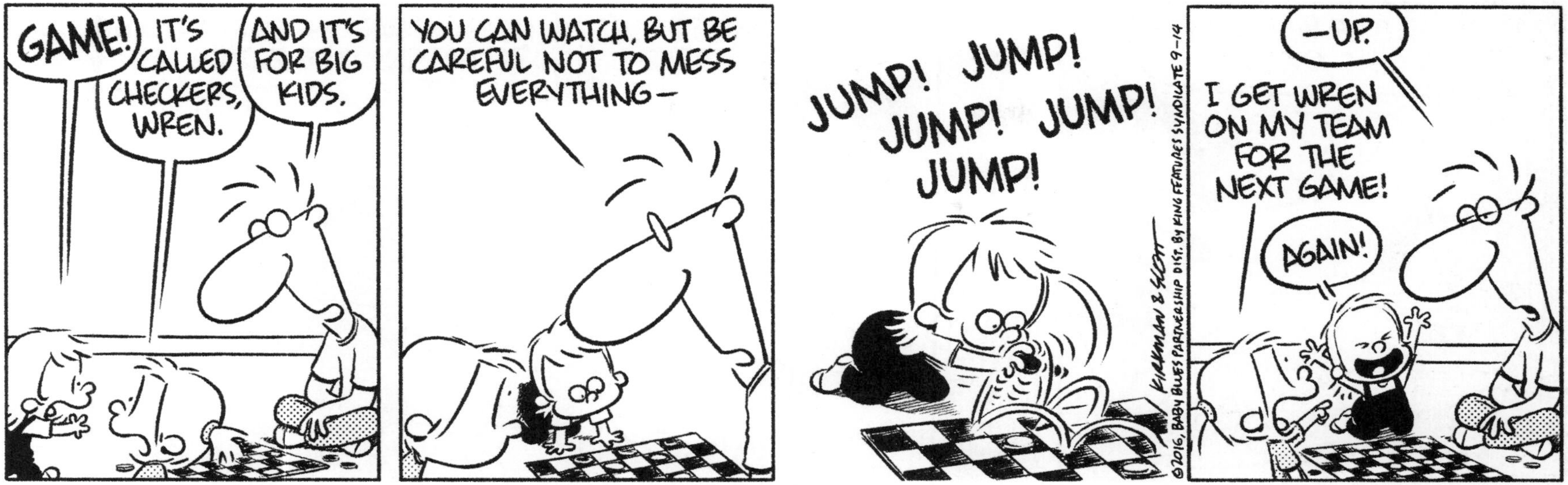
GAME!
IT'S CALLED CHECKERS, WREN.
AND IT'S FOR BIG KIDS.
YOU CAN WATCH, BUT BE CAREFUL NOT TO MESS EVERYTHING—
JUMP! JUMP! JUMP! JUMP! JUMP!
KIRKMAN & SCOTT
©2016, BABY BLUES PARTNERSHIP DIST. BY KING FEATURES SYNDICATE 9-14
—UP.
I GET WREN ON MY TEAM FOR THE NEXT GAME!
AGAIN!

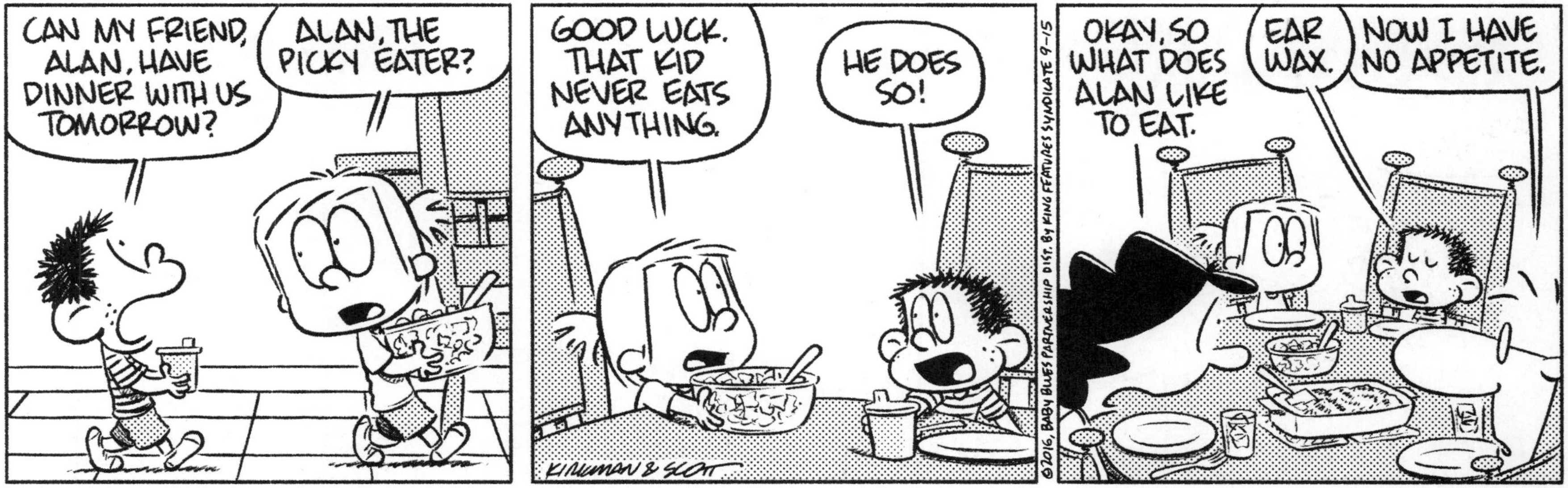
CAN MY FRIEND, ALAN, HAVE DINNER WITH US TOMORROW?
ALAN, THE PICKY EATER?
GOOD LUCK. THAT KID NEVER EATS ANYTHING.
HE DOES SO!
KIRKMAN & SCOTT
©2016, BABY BLUES PARTNERSHIP DIST. BY KING FEATURES SYNDICATE 9-15
OKAY, SO WHAT DOES ALAN LIKE TO EAT.
EAR WAX.
NOW I HAVE NO APPETITE.

Jerry: I wonder if Alan, the earwax eater, knows Eric, the kid who smells like chicken noodle soup, from page 99?

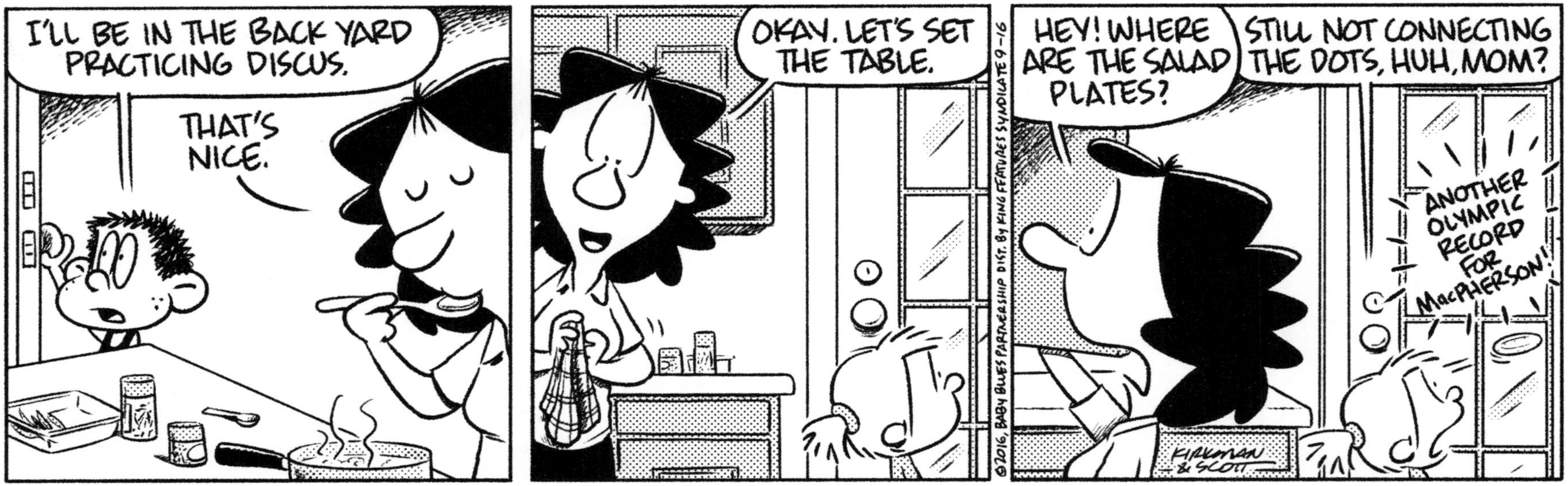
I'LL BE IN THE BACK YARD PRACTICING DISCUS.
THAT'S NICE.
OKAY. LET'S SET THE TABLE.
©2016, BABY BLUES PARTNERSHIP DIST. BY KING FEATURES SYNDICATE 9-16
HEY! WHERE ARE THE SALAD PLATES?
STILL NOT CONNECTING THE DOTS, HUH, MOM?
ANOTHER OLYMPIC RECORD FOR MacPHERSON!
KIRKMAN & SCOTT

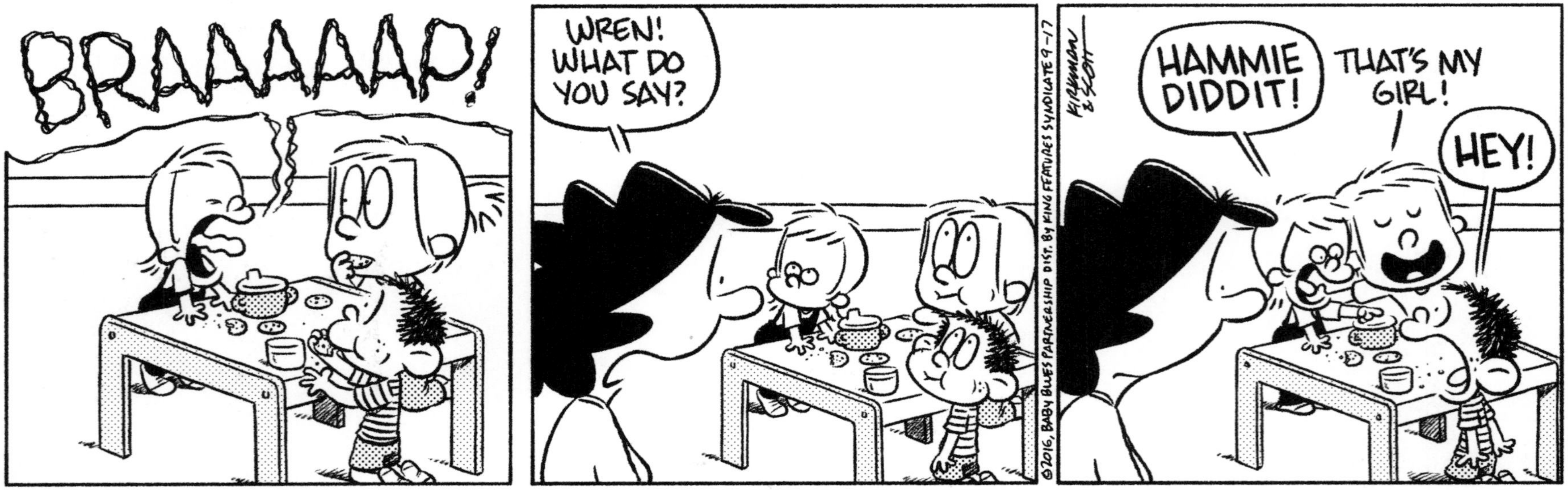
BRAAAAAP!
WREN! WHAT DO YOU SAY?
©2016, BABY BLUES PARTNERSHIP DIST. BY KING FEATURES SYNDICATE 9-17
KIRKMAN & SCOTT
HAMMIE DIDDIT!
THAT'S MY GIRL!
HEY!

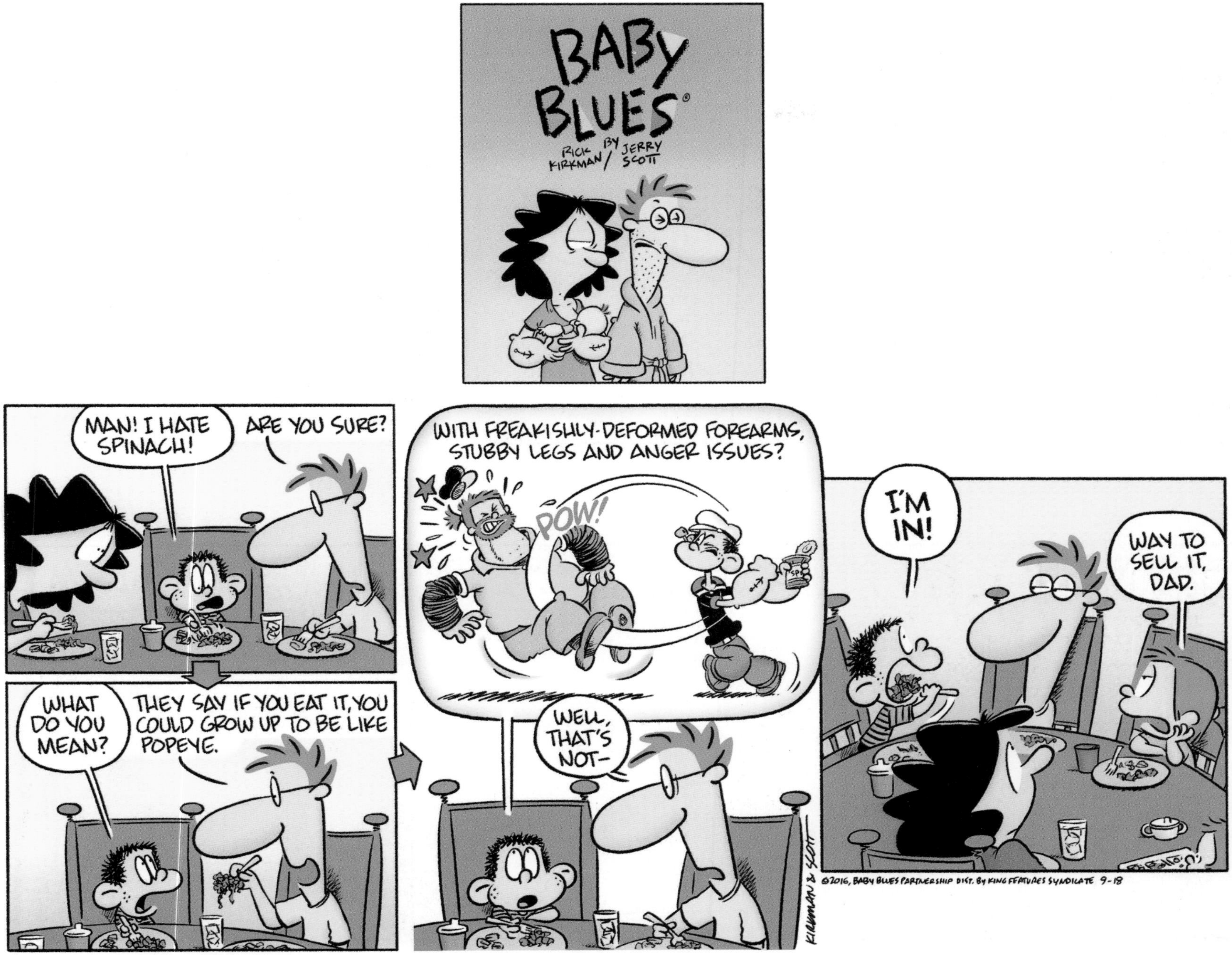
BABY BLUES®
BY RICK KIRKMAN / JERRY SCOTT
MAN! I HATE SPINACH!
ARE YOU SURE?
WHAT DO YOU MEAN?
THEY SAY IF YOU EAT IT, YOU COULD GROW UP TO BE LIKE POPEYE.
WITH FREAKISHLY-DEFORMED FOREARMS, STUBBY LEGS AND ANGER ISSUES?
POW!
WELL, THAT'S NOT-
I'M IN!
WAY TO SELL IT, DAD.
KIRKMAN & SCOTT
©2016, BABY BLUES PARTNERSHIP DIST. BY KING FEATURES SYNDICATE 9-18

Rick: Is Zoe Bluto or Brutus? (I can never keep them straight.)

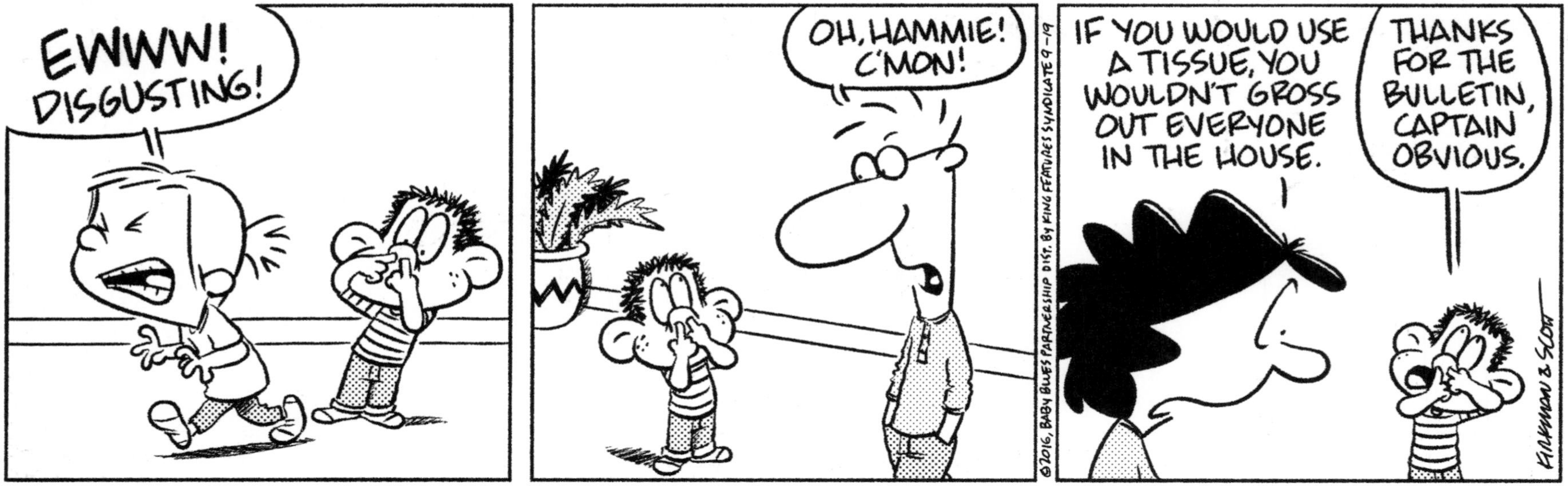
EWWW! DISGUSTING!
OH, HAMMIE! C'MON!
©2016, BABY BLUES PARTNERSHIP DIST. BY KING FEATURES SYNDICATE 9-19
IF YOU WOULD USE A TISSUE, YOU WOULDN'T GROSS OUT EVERYONE IN THE HOUSE.
THANKS FOR THE BULLETIN, CAPTAIN OBVIOUS.
KIRKMAN & SCOTT

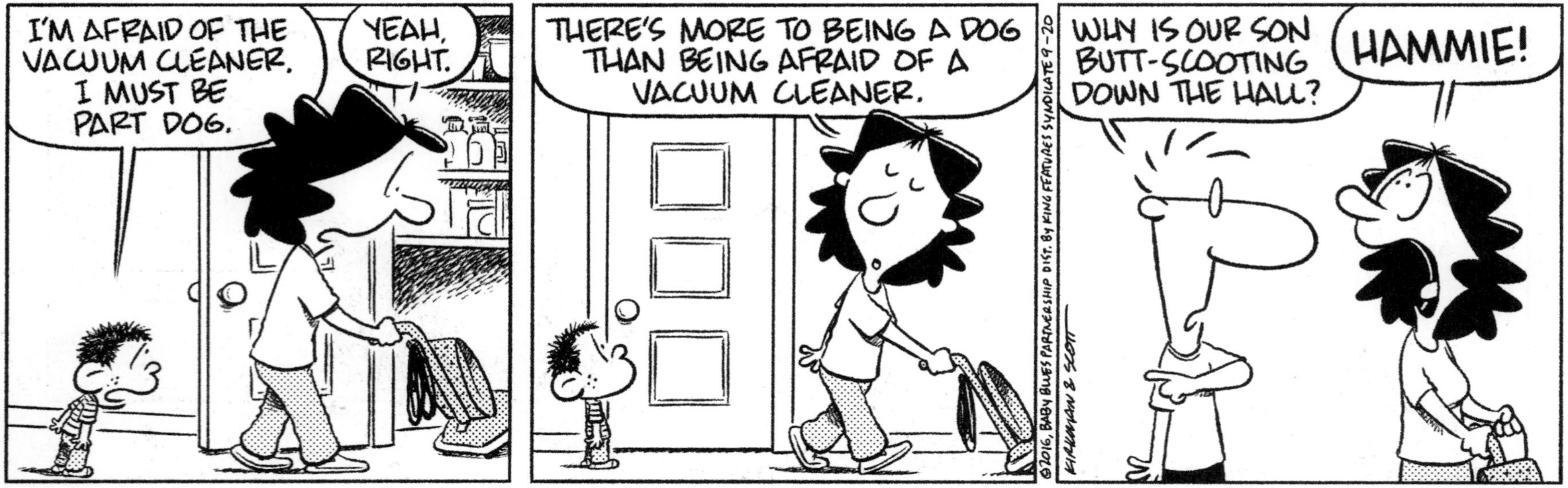
I'M AFRAID OF THE VACUUM CLEANER. I MUST BE PART DOG.
YEAH, RIGHT.
THERE'S MORE TO BEING A DOG THAN BEING AFRAID OF A VACUUM CLEANER.
©2016, BABY BLUES PARTNERSHIP DIST. BY KING FEATURES SYNDICATE 9-20
WHY IS OUR SON BUTT-SCOOTING DOWN THE HALL?
HAMMIE!
KIRKMAN & SCOTT

Rick: Hammie acting like a dog always cracks me up.

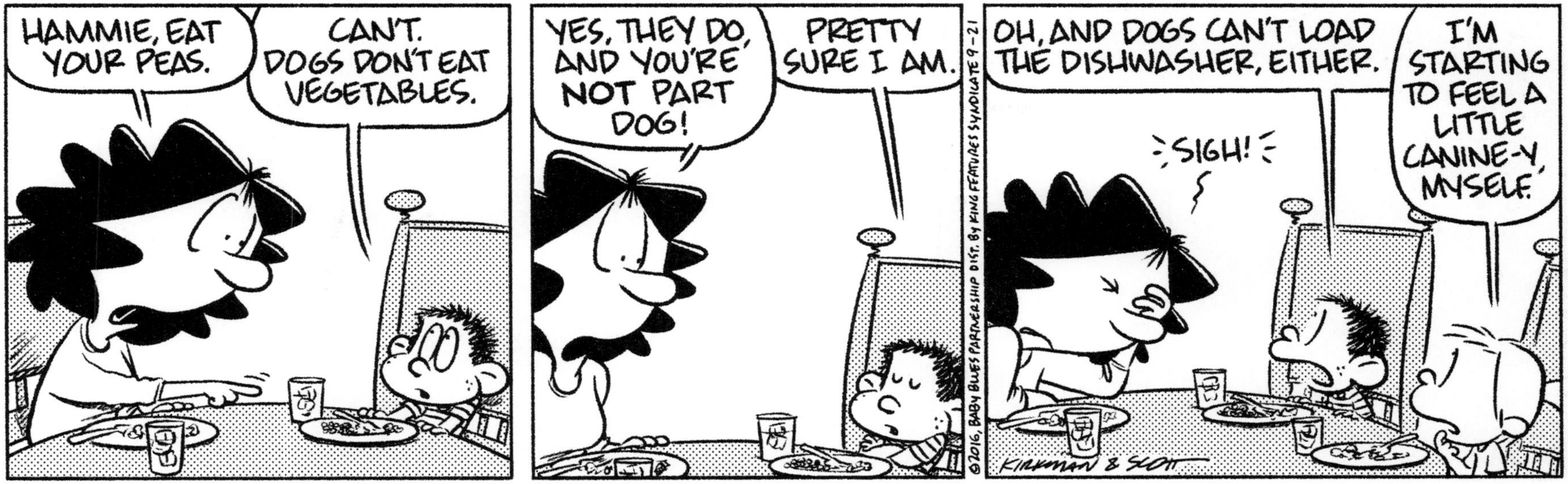
HAMMIE, EAT YOUR PEAS.
CAN'T. DOGS DON'T EAT VEGETABLES.
YES, THEY DO, AND YOU'RE NOT PART DOG!
PRETTY SURE I AM.
©2016, BABY BLUES PARTNERSHIP DIST. BY KING FEATURES SYNDICATE 9-21
OH, AND DOGS CAN'T LOAD THE DISHWASHER, EITHER.
SIGH!
I'M STARTING TO FEEL A LITTLE CANINE-Y, MYSELF.
KIRKMAN & SCOTT

Jerry: Victory comes with a price, I guess.

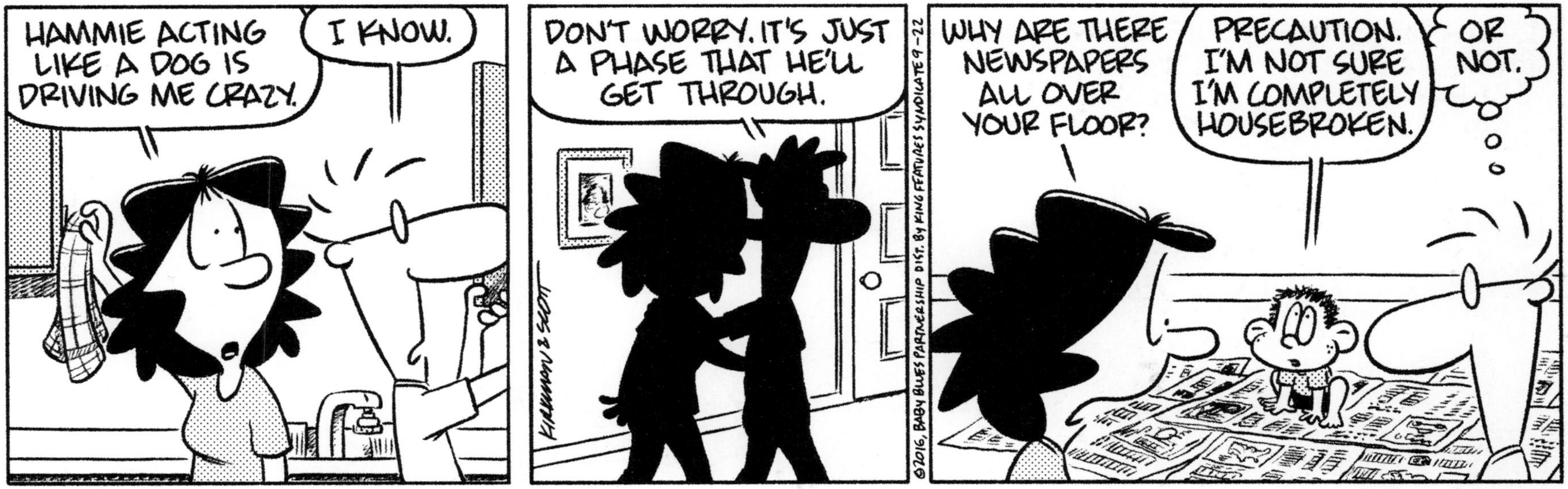
HAMMIE ACTING LIKE A DOG IS DRIVING ME CRAZY.
I KNOW.
KIRKMAN & SCOTT
DON'T WORRY. IT'S JUST A PHASE THAT HE'LL GET THROUGH.
©2016, BABY BLUES PARTNERSHIP DIST. BY KING FEATURES SYNDICATE 9-22
WHY ARE THERE NEWSPAPERS ALL OVER YOUR FLOOR?
PRECAUTION. I'M NOT SURE I'M COMPLETELY HOUSEBROKEN.
OR NOT.

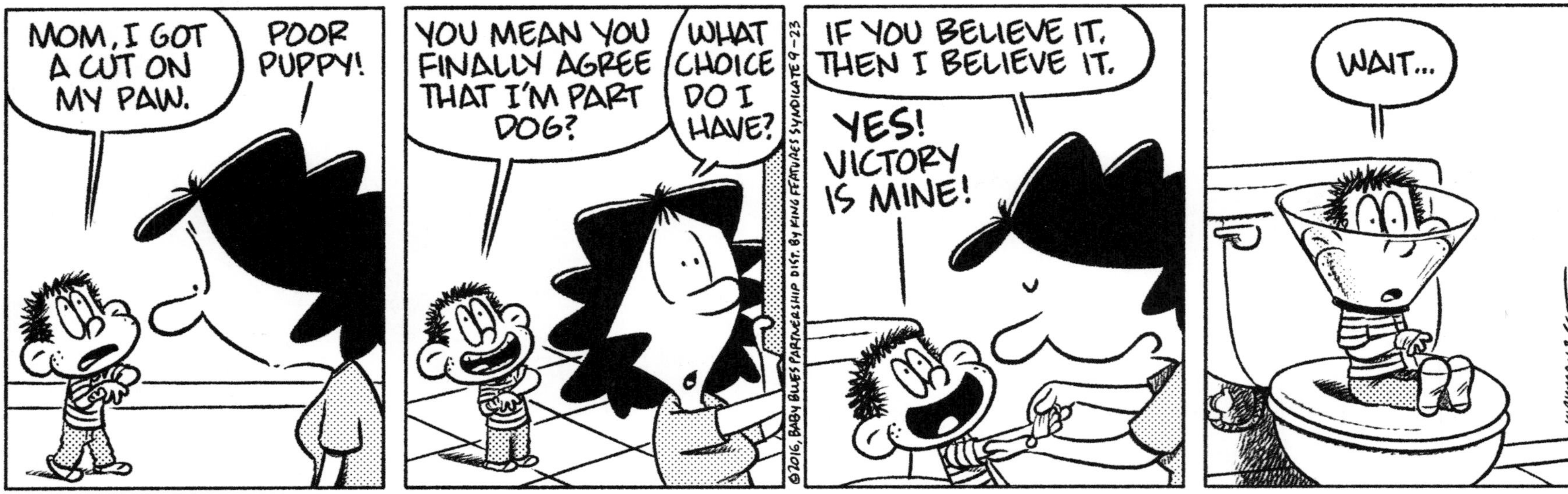
MOM, I GOT A CUT ON MY PAW.
POOR PUPPY!
YOU MEAN YOU FINALLY AGREE THAT I'M PART DOG?
WHAT CHOICE DO I HAVE?
IF YOU BELIEVE IT, THEN I BELIEVE IT.
YES! VICTORY IS MINE!
WAIT...

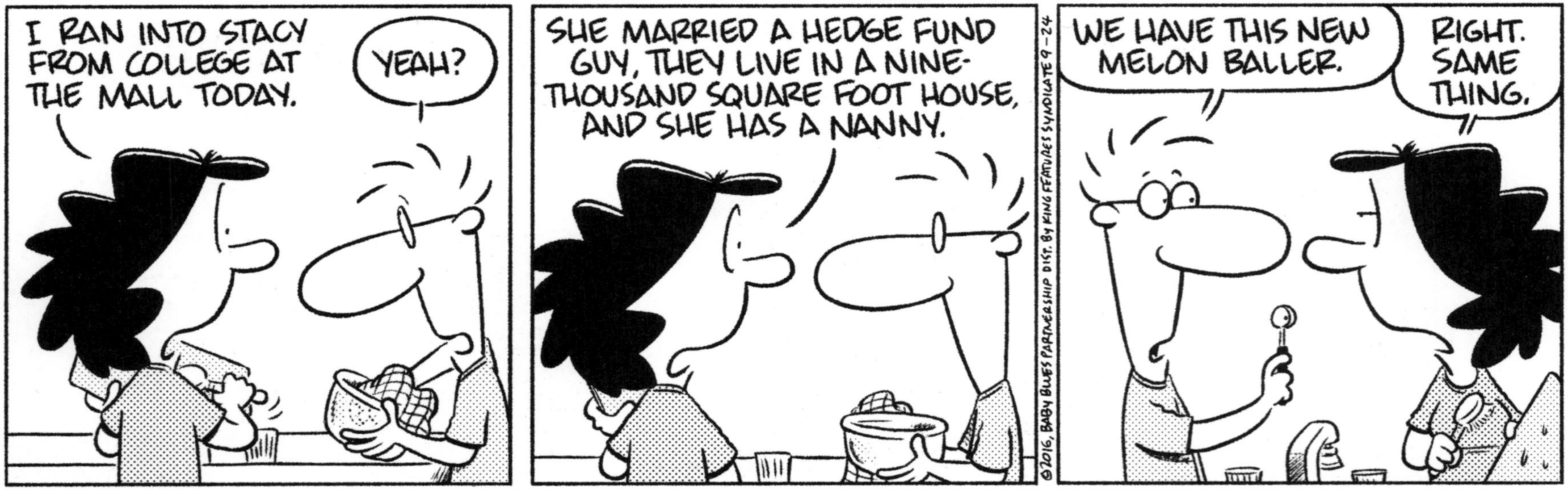
I RAN INTO STACY FROM COLLEGE AT THE MALL TODAY.
YEAH?
SHE MARRIED A HEDGE FUND GUY, THEY LIVE IN A NINE-THOUSAND SQUARE FOOT HOUSE, AND SHE HAS A NANNY.
WE HAVE THIS NEW MELON BALLER.
RIGHT. SAME THING.

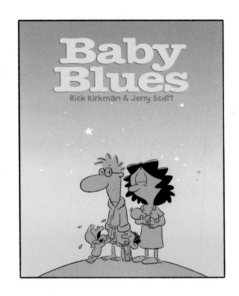

Baby Blues
Rick Kirkman & Jerry Scott

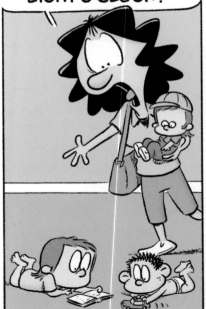

WHAT ARE YOU GUYS DOING?? IT'S ALMOST EIGHT O'CLOCK!
GET DRESSED RIGHT NOW! YOU'RE GOING TO BE LATE FOR SCHOOL!
I CAN'T DECIDE WHAT TO WEAR!
ME NEITHER.
WELL, MAYBE I SHOULD HAVE YOU PICK OUT EACH OTHER'S CLOTHES!
GASP!
MOM! YOU WOULDN'T DARE!
©2016, BABY BLUES PARTNERSHIP DIST. BY KING FEATURES SYNDICATE
WELL, NOW WE KNOW NOT TO USE THE WORDS "MOM" AND "DARE" IN THE SAME SENTENCE.
DON'T TALK TO ME.
KIRKMAN & SCOTT 9-25

Rick: A truly inspired solution.

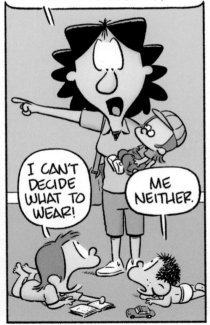

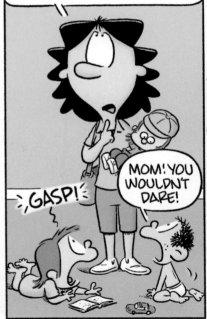

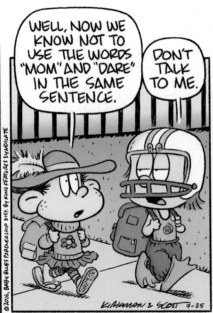

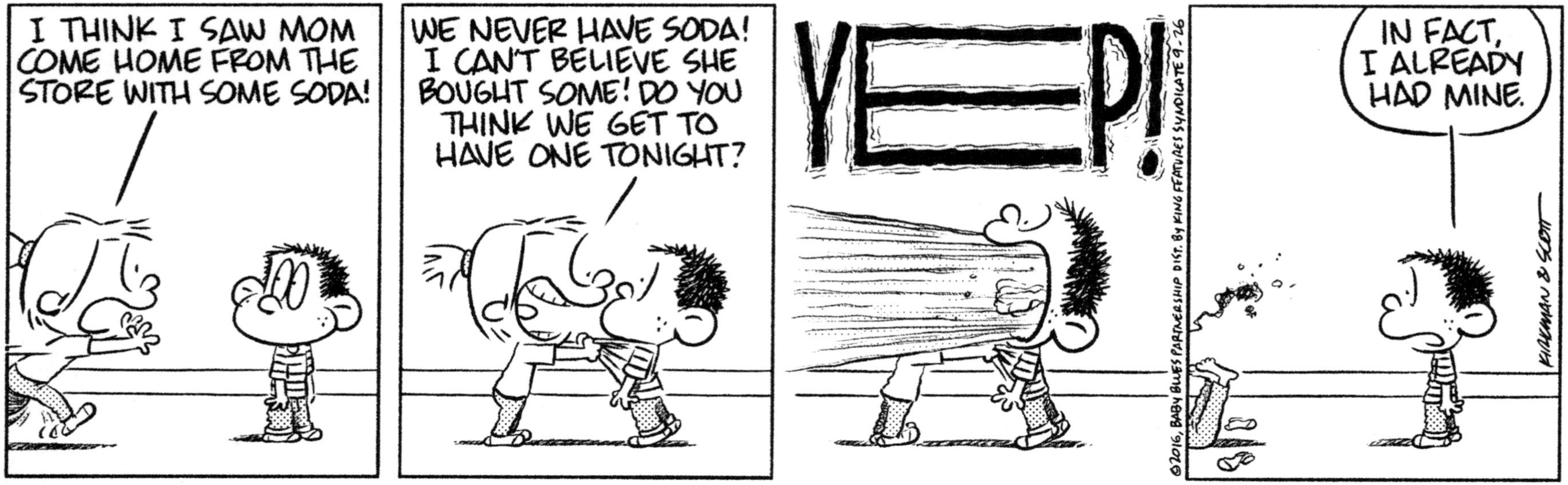
I THINK I SAW MOM COME HOME FROM THE STORE WITH SOME SODA!
WE NEVER HAVE SODA! I CAN'T BELIEVE SHE BOUGHT SOME! DO YOU THINK WE GET TO HAVE ONE TONIGHT?
YEEP!
©2016, BABY BLUES PARTNERSHIP DIST. BY KING FEATURES SYNDICATE 9-26
IN FACT, I ALREADY HAD MINE.
KIRKMAN & SCOTT

Rick: How to make a belch really long *and* big in a small panel? My answer was to stretch out the "E" so I could keep the letters really big without having to squish a string of them together. Obliterating Zoe's head helped, too.

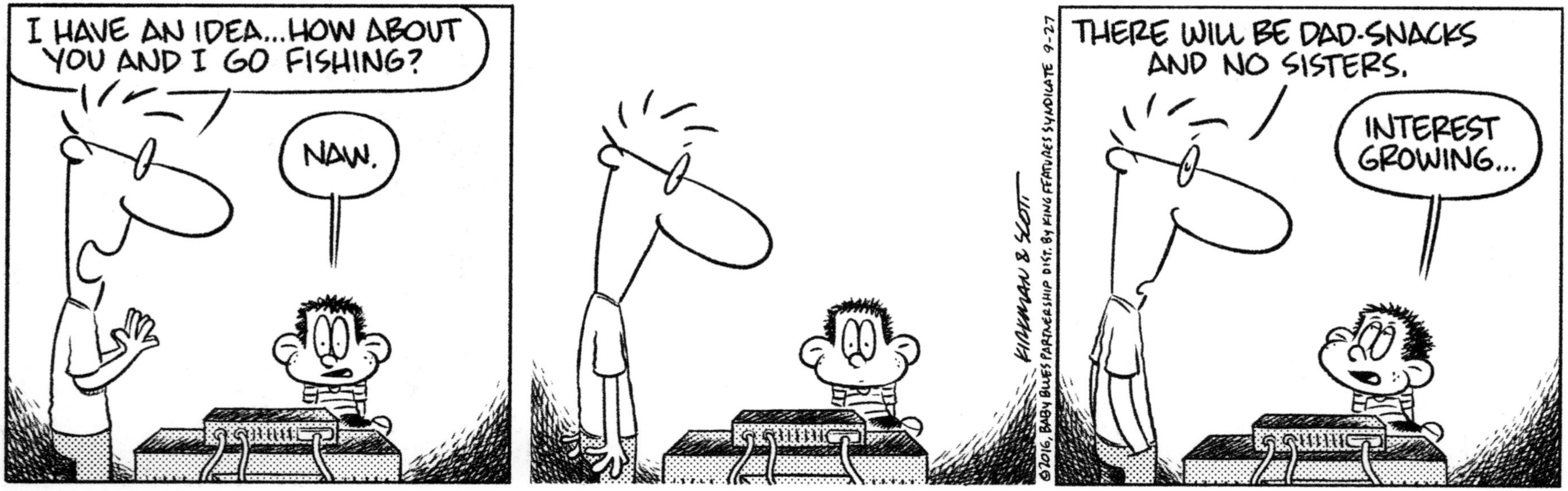
I HAVE AN IDEA...HOW ABOUT YOU AND I GO FISHING?
NAW.
KIRKMAN & SCOTT
©2016, BABY BLUES PARTNERSHIP DIST. BY KING FEATURES SYNDICATE 9-27
THERE WILL BE DAD-SNACKS AND NO SISTERS.
INTEREST GROWING...

Jerry: Darryl knows how to bait the hook.

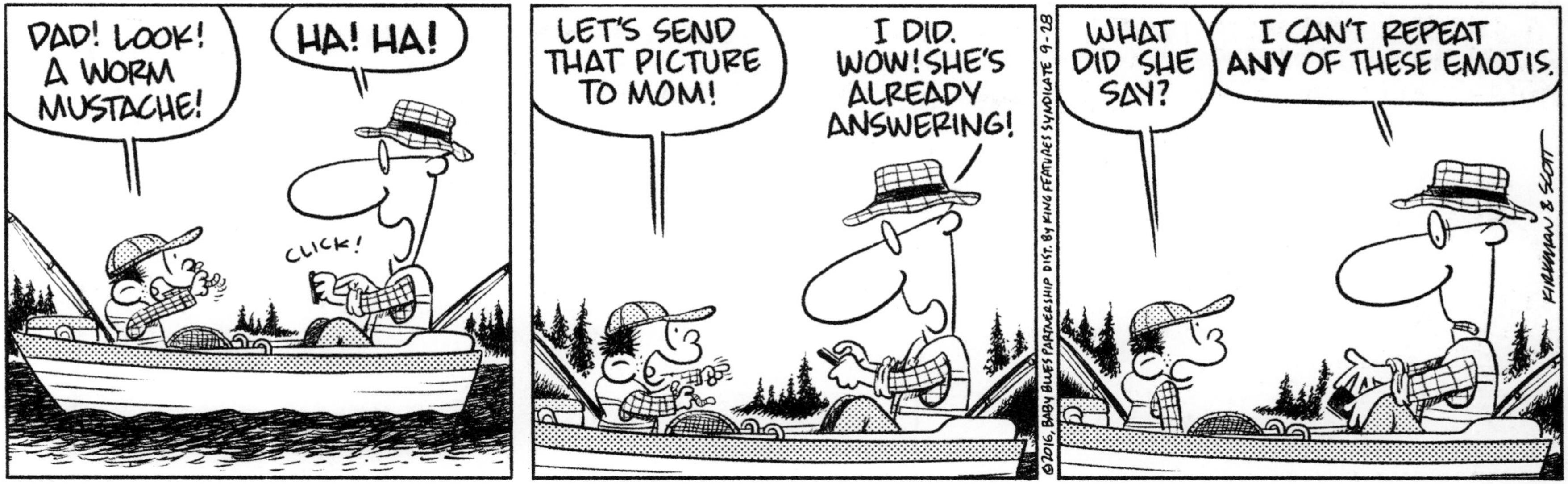
DAD! LOOK! A WORM MUSTACHE!
HA! HA!
CLICK!
LET'S SEND THAT PICTURE TO MOM!
I DID. WOW! SHE'S ALREADY ANSWERING!
© 2016, BABY BLUES PARTNERSHIP DIST. BY KING FEATURES SYNDICATE 9-28
WHAT DID SHE SAY?
I CAN'T REPEAT ANY OF THESE EMOJIS.
KIRKMAN & SCOTT

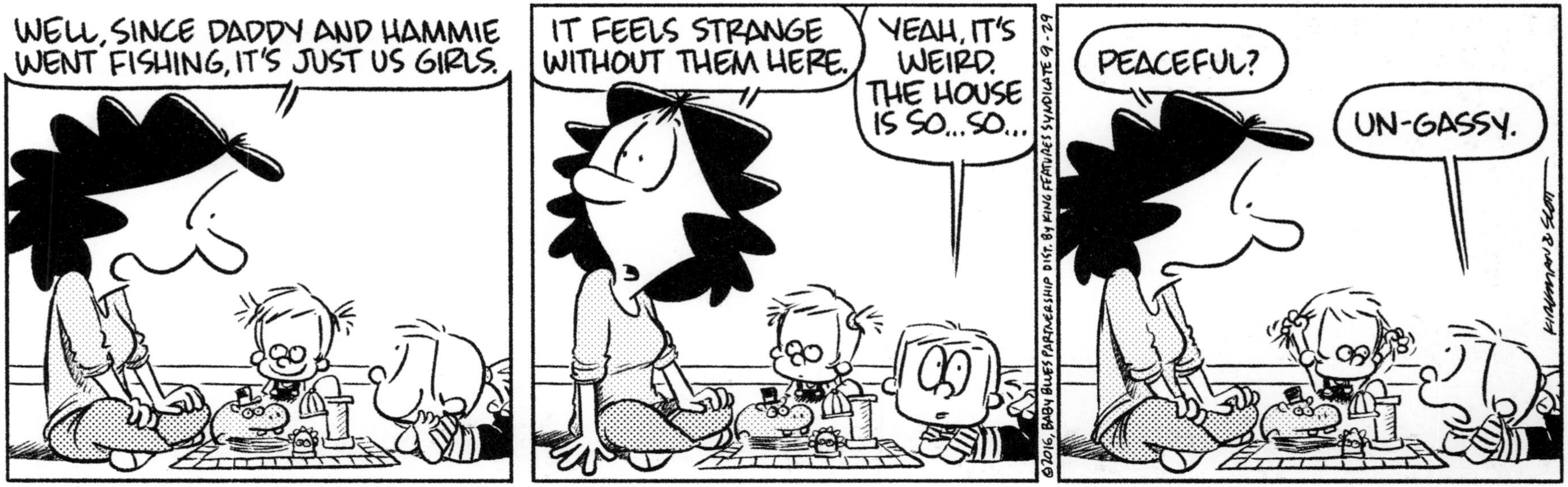
WELL, SINCE DADDY AND HAMMIE WENT FISHING, IT'S JUST US GIRLS.
IT FEELS STRANGE WITHOUT THEM HERE.
YEAH, IT'S WEIRD. THE HOUSE IS SO... SO...
© 2016, BABY BLUES PARTNERSHIP DIST. BY KING FEATURES SYNDICATE 9-29
PEACEFUL?
UN-GASSY.
KIRKMAN & SCOTT

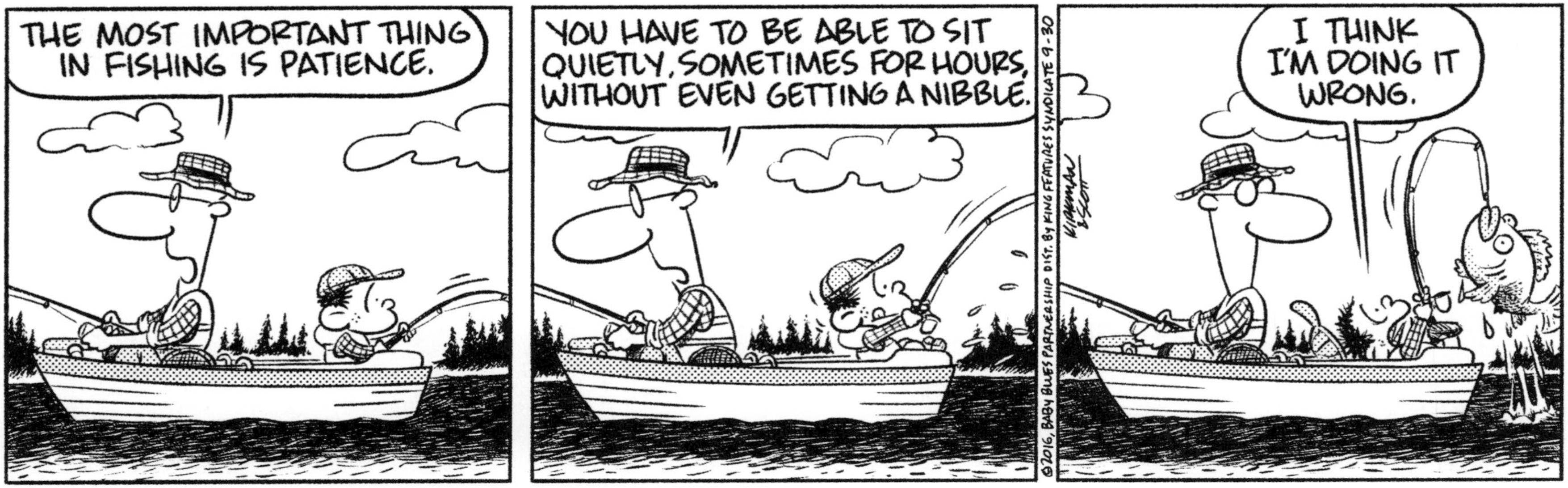
THE MOST IMPORTANT THING IN FISHING IS PATIENCE.
YOU HAVE TO BE ABLE TO SIT QUIETLY, SOMETIMES FOR HOURS, WITHOUT EVEN GETTING A NIBBLE.
©2016, BABY BLUES PARTNERSHIP DIST. BY KING FEATURES SYNDICATE 9-30
KIRKMAN & SCOTT
I THINK I'M DOING IT WRONG.

Jerry: There's something about a father and son fishing together that feels right to me. Especially when the kid gets all the fish.

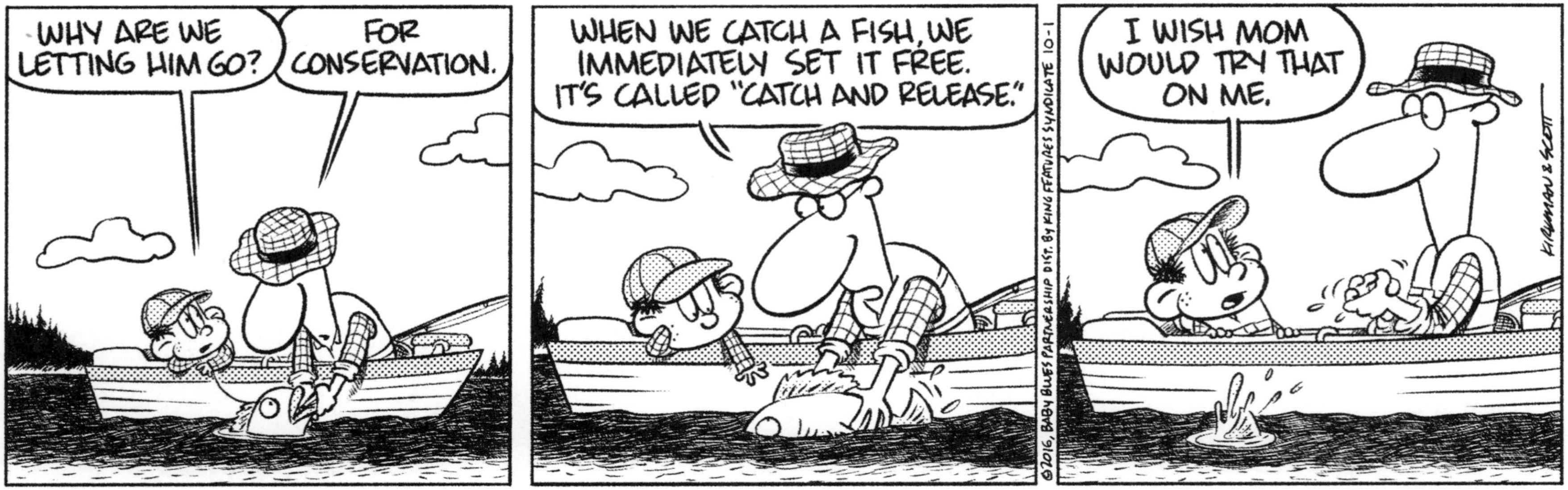
WHY ARE WE LETTING HIM GO?
FOR CONSERVATION.
WHEN WE CATCH A FISH, WE IMMEDIATELY SET IT FREE. IT'S CALLED "CATCH AND RELEASE."
©2016, BABY BLUES PARTNERSHIP DIST. BY KING FEATURES SYNDICATE 10-1
I WISH MOM WOULD TRY THAT ON ME.
KIRKMAN & SCOTT

BABY BLUES®
Rick Kirkman & Jerry Scott
ZZZZZZZ

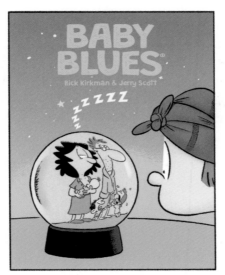

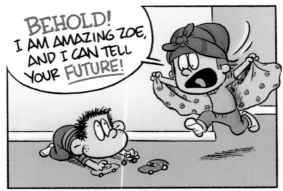

BEHOLD! I AM AMAZING ZOE, AND I CAN TELL YOUR FUTURE!
YEAH, RIGHT.
IT'S TRUE! OBSERVE, AND BE AMAZED!
© 2016, BABY BLUES PARTNERSHIP DIST. BY KING FEATURES SYNDICATE
AMAZING ZOE SEES YOU HEADING FOR A MAJOR TIME-OUT!
HA! YOU'RE WRONG! I HAVEN'T EVEN GOTTEN IN TROUBLE TODAY.
MOM! HAMMIE LAID HIS BIKE DOWN IN THE FLOWER BED AND SMASHED THE HYDRANGEAS!
WHAT??
PRETTY ACCURATE, RIGHT?
YEAH. AND IF I EVER GET OUT OF HERE, YOU WON'T HAVE A FUTURE.
KIRKMAN & SCOTT 10-2

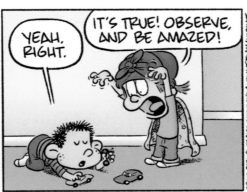

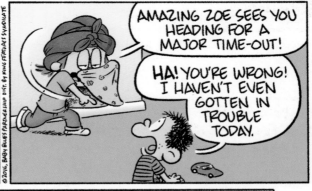

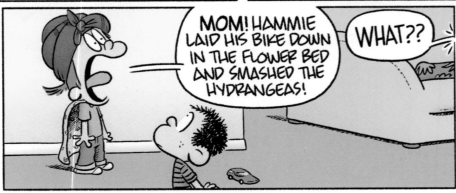

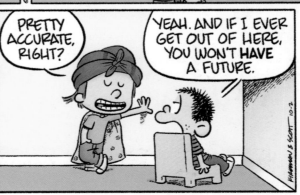

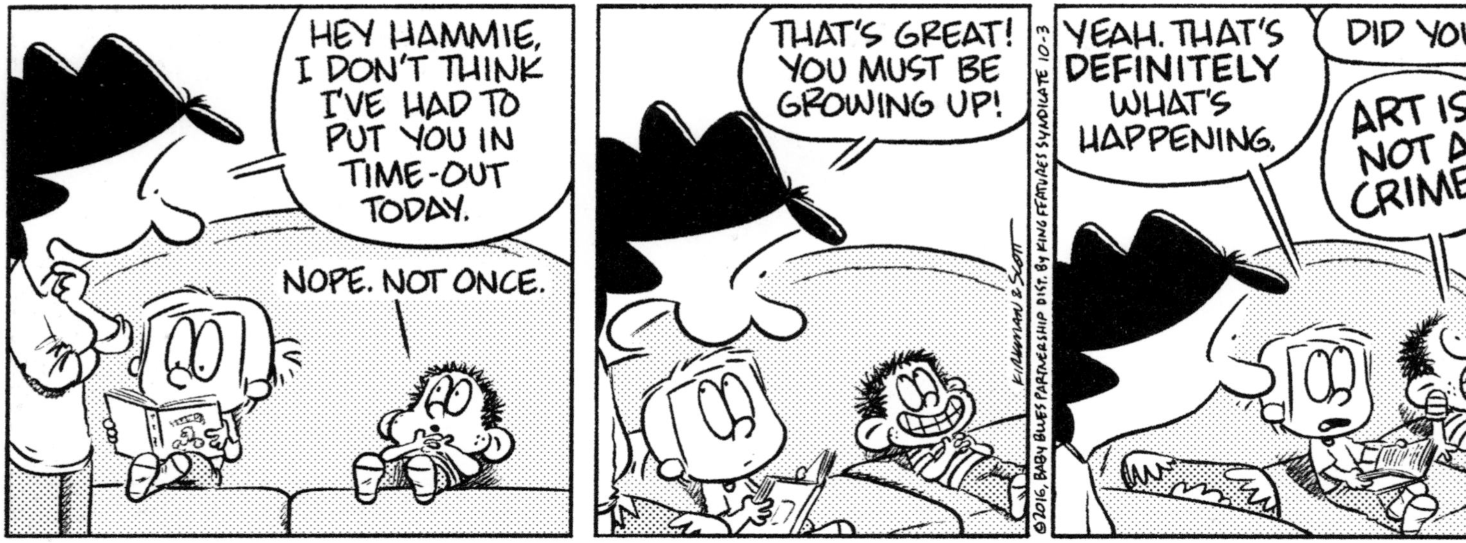
HEY HAMMIE, I DON'T THINK I'VE HAD TO PUT YOU IN TIME-OUT TODAY.
NOPE. NOT ONCE.
THAT'S GREAT! YOU MUST BE GROWING UP!
KIRKMAN & SCOTT
©2016, BABY BLUES PARTNERSHIP DIST. BY KING FEATURES SYNDICATE 10-3
YEAH. THAT'S DEFINITELY WHAT'S HAPPENING.
ART IS NOT A CRIME!
DID YOU DO THIS??

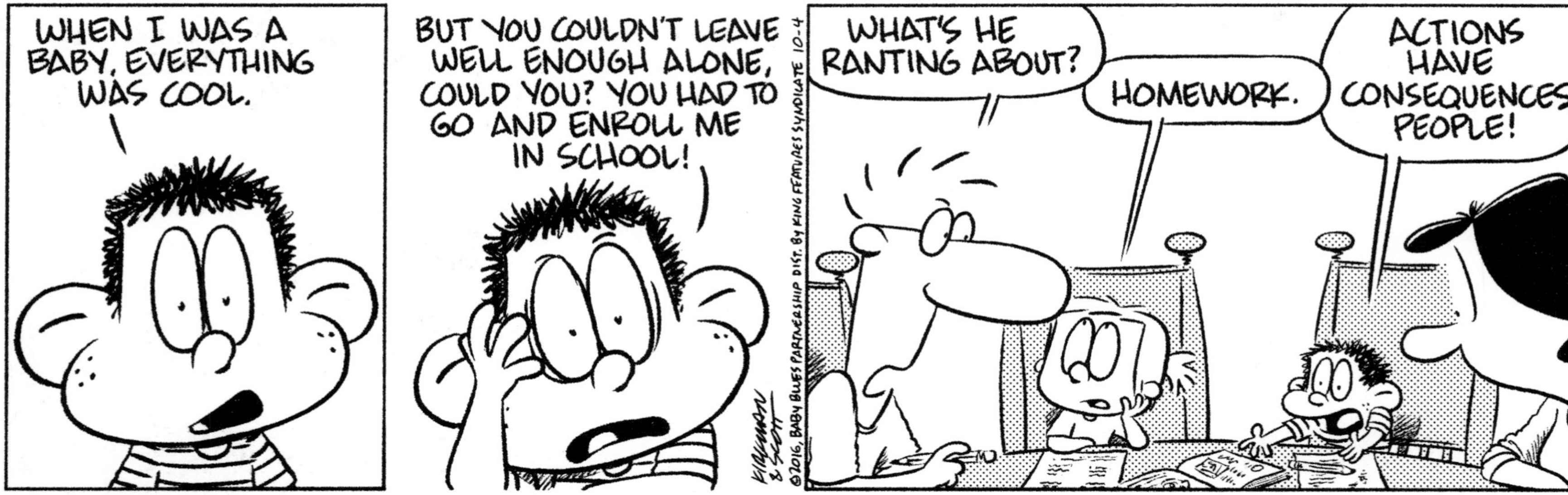
WHEN I WAS A BABY, EVERYTHING WAS COOL.
BUT YOU COULDN'T LEAVE WELL ENOUGH ALONE, COULD YOU? YOU HAD TO GO AND ENROLL ME IN SCHOOL!
KIRKMAN & SCOTT
©2016, BABY BLUES PARTNERSHIP DIST. BY KING FEATURES SYNDICATE 10-4
WHAT'S HE RANTING ABOUT?
HOMEWORK.
ACTIONS HAVE CONSEQUENCES, PEOPLE!

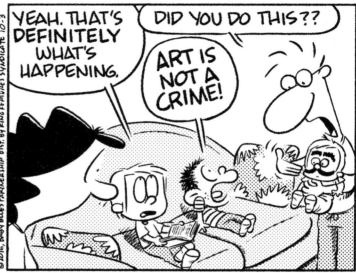

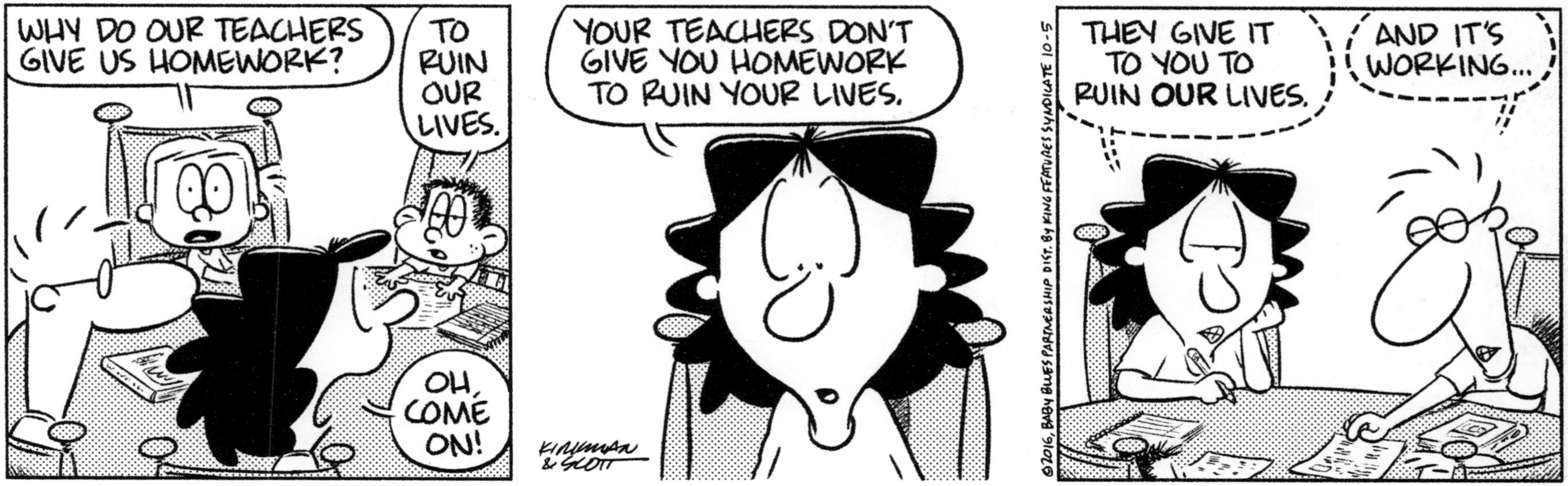
WHY DO OUR TEACHERS GIVE US HOMEWORK?
TO RUIN OUR LIVES.
OH, COME ON!
YOUR TEACHERS DON'T GIVE YOU HOMEWORK TO RUIN YOUR LIVES.
KIRKMAN & SCOTT
©2016, BABY BLUES PARTNERSHIP DIST. BY KING FEATURES SYNDICATE 10-5
THEY GIVE IT TO YOU TO RUIN **OUR** LIVES.
AND IT'S WORKING...

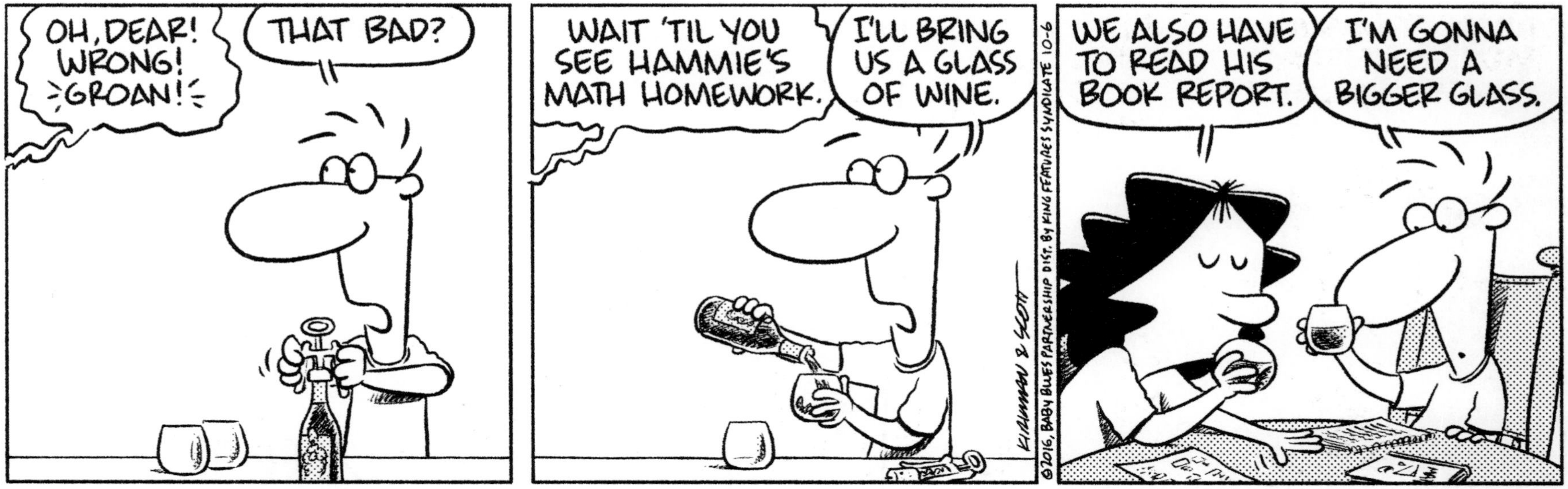
OH, DEAR! WRONG! GROAN!
THAT BAD?
WAIT 'TIL YOU SEE HAMMIE'S MATH HOMEWORK.
I'LL BRING US A GLASS OF WINE.
KIRKMAN & SCOTT
©2016, BABY BLUES PARTNERSHIP DIST. BY KING FEATURES SYNDICATE 10-6
WE ALSO HAVE TO READ HIS BOOK REPORT.
I'M GONNA NEED A BIGGER GLASS.

Jerry: We rarely show Darryl and Wanda drinking . . . just the very occasional beer or glass of wine, and then only for medicinal purposes, like surviving homework.

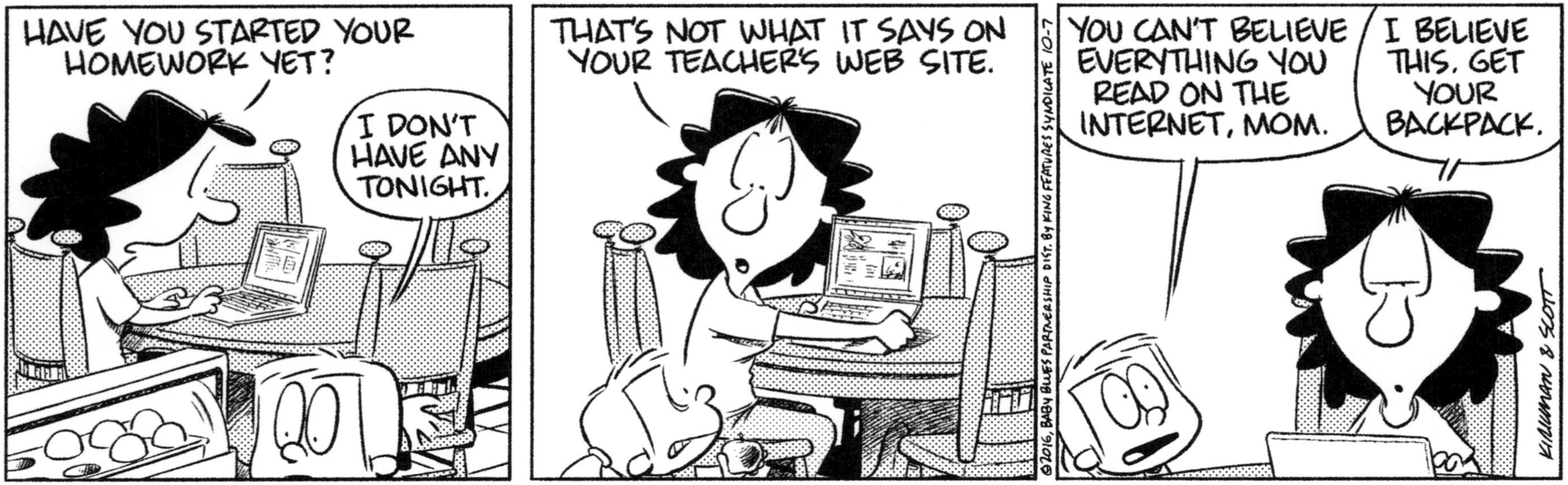
HAVE YOU STARTED YOUR HOMEWORK YET?
I DON'T HAVE ANY TONIGHT.
THAT'S NOT WHAT IT SAYS ON YOUR TEACHER'S WEB SITE.
YOU CAN'T BELIEVE EVERYTHING YOU READ ON THE INTERNET, MOM.
I BELIEVE THIS. GET YOUR BACKPACK.
©2016, BABY BLUES PARTNERSHIP DIST. BY KING FEATURES SYNDICATE 10-7
KIRKMAN & SCOTT

Rick: Nowadays, parents don't even have to work that hard to bust their kids over homework.

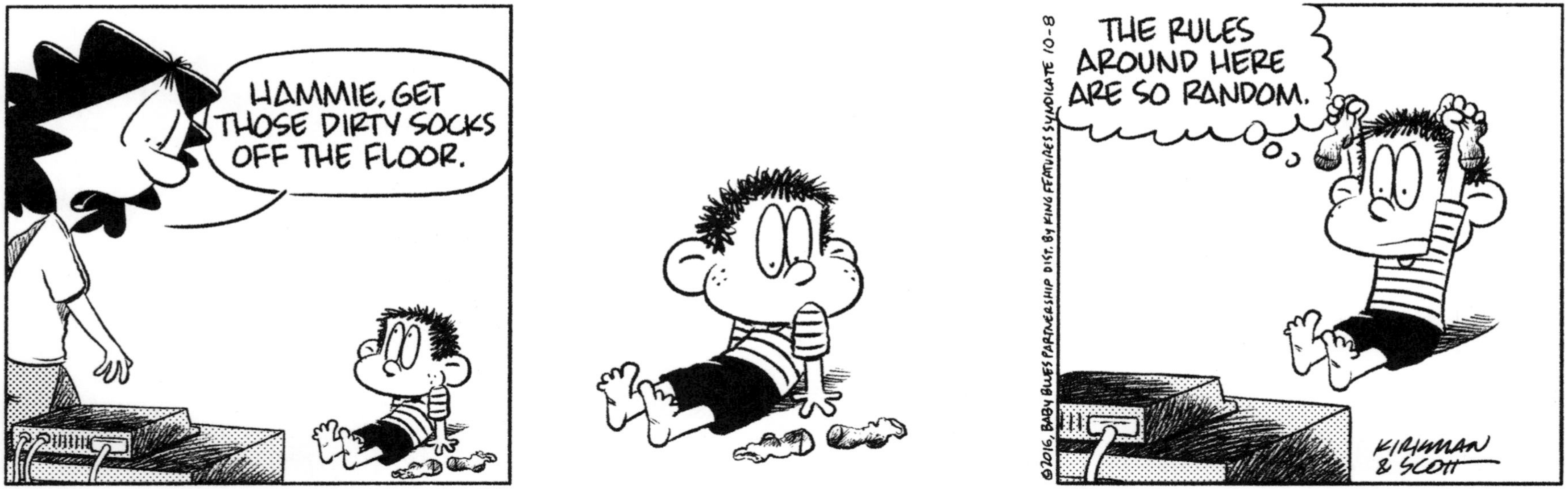
HAMMIE, GET THOSE DIRTY SOCKS OFF THE FLOOR.
THE RULES AROUND HERE ARE SO RANDOM.
©2016, BABY BLUES PARTNERSHIP DIST. BY KING FEATURES SYNDICATE 10-8
KIRKMAN & SCOTT

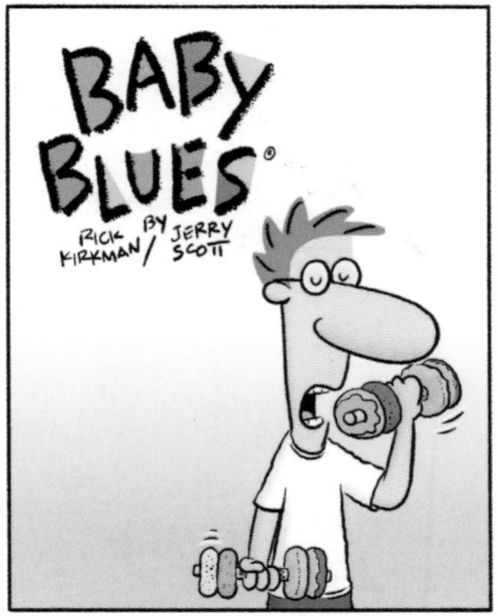
BABY BLUES®
BY RICK KIRKMAN / JERRY SCOTT

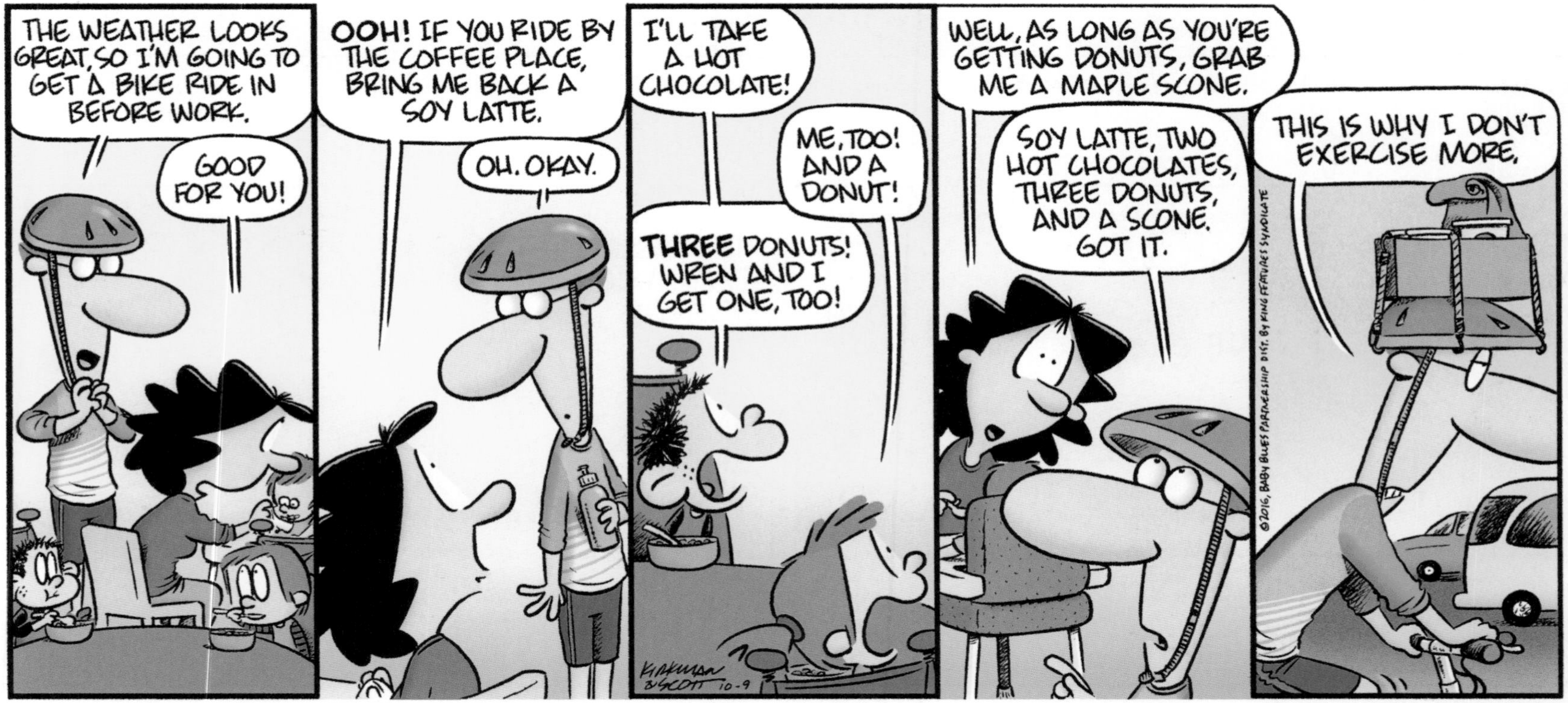
THE WEATHER LOOKS GREAT, SO I'M GOING TO GET A BIKE RIDE IN BEFORE WORK.
GOOD FOR YOU!
OOH! IF YOU RIDE BY THE COFFEE PLACE, BRING ME BACK A SOY LATTE.
OH. OKAY.
I'LL TAKE A HOT CHOCOLATE!
ME, TOO! AND A DONUT!
THREE DONUTS! WREN AND I GET ONE, TOO!
KIRKMAN & SCOTT 10-9
WELL, AS LONG AS YOU'RE GETTING DONUTS, GRAB ME A MAPLE SCONE.
SOY LATTE, TWO HOT CHOCOLATES, THREE DONUTS, AND A SCONE. GOT IT.
THIS IS WHY I DON'T EXERCISE MORE.
©2016, BABY BLUES PARTNERSHIP DIST. BY KING FEATURES SYNDICATE

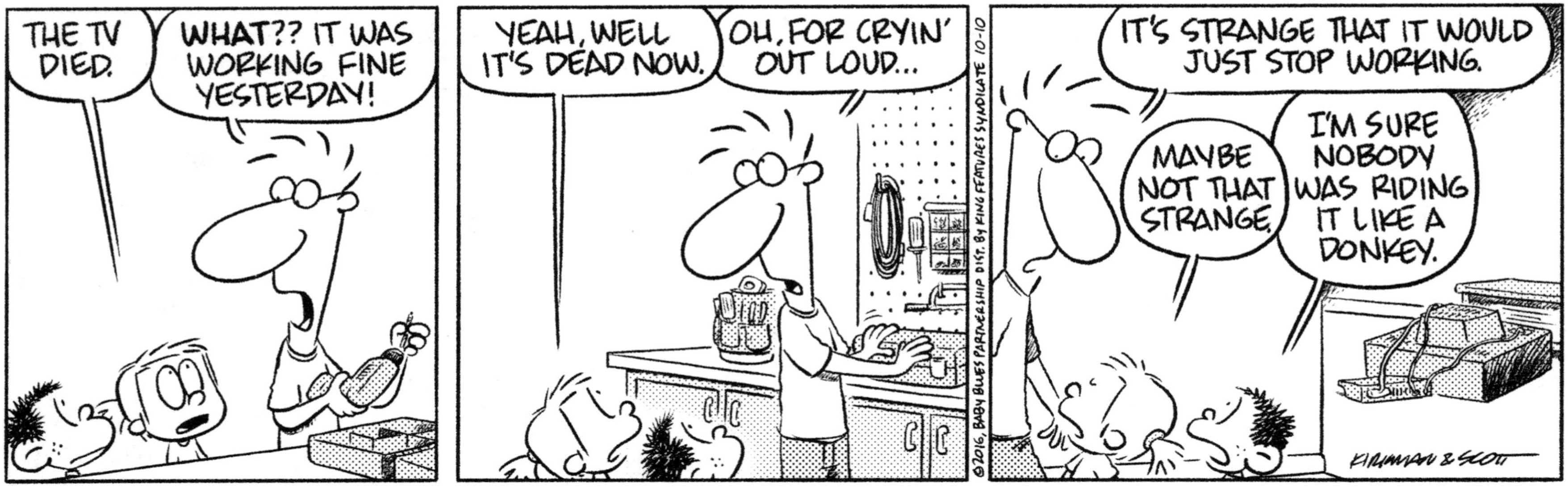
THE TV DIED.
WHAT?? IT WAS WORKING FINE YESTERDAY!
YEAH, WELL IT'S DEAD NOW.
OH, FOR CRYIN' OUT LOUD...
©2016, BABY BLUES PARTNERSHIP DIST. BY KING FEATURES SYNDICATE 10-10
IT'S STRANGE THAT IT WOULD JUST STOP WORKING.
MAYBE NOT THAT STRANGE,
I'M SURE NOBODY WAS RIDING IT LIKE A DONKEY.
KIRKMAN & SCOTT

Jerry: Believe it or not, I worked most of a day coming up with "Riding it like a donkey." No, I will not trade jobs with you.

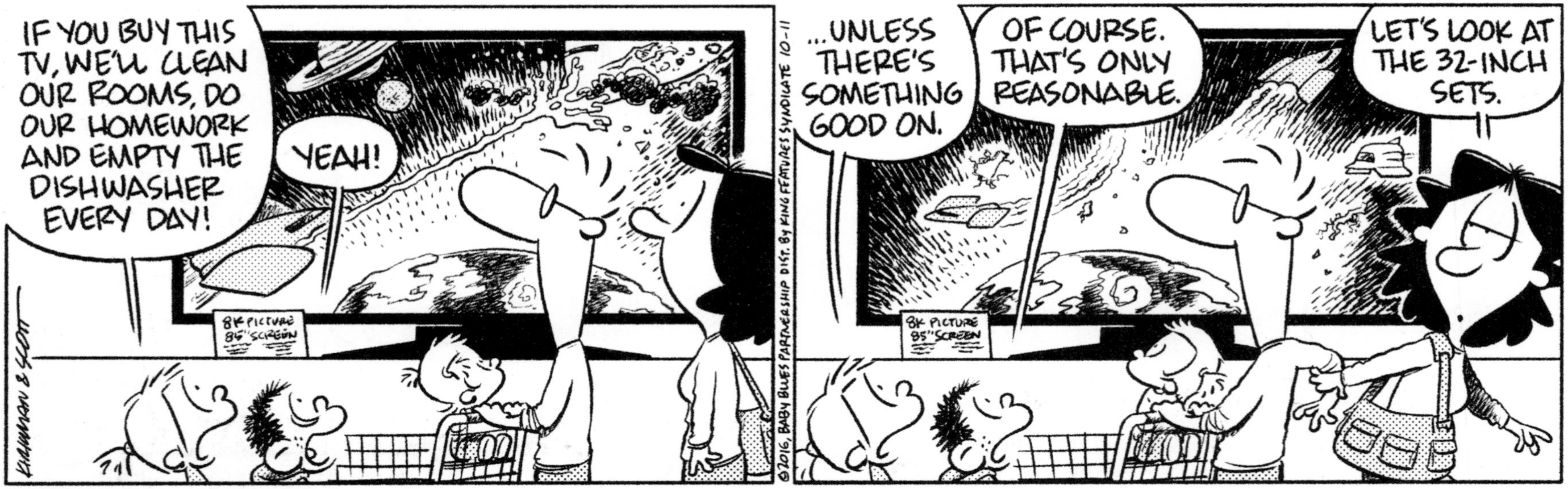
IF YOU BUY THIS TV, WE'LL CLEAN OUR ROOMS, DO OUR HOMEWORK AND EMPTY THE DISHWASHER EVERY DAY!
YEAH!
8K PICTURE 85" SCREEN
KIRKMAN & SCOTT
©2016, BABY BLUES PARTNERSHIP DIST. BY KING FEATURES SYNDICATE 10-11
...UNLESS THERE'S SOMETHING GOOD ON.
OF COURSE. THAT'S ONLY REASONABLE.
LET'S LOOK AT THE 32-INCH SETS.
8K PICTURE 85" SCREEN

Rick: Is it finally going to happen?

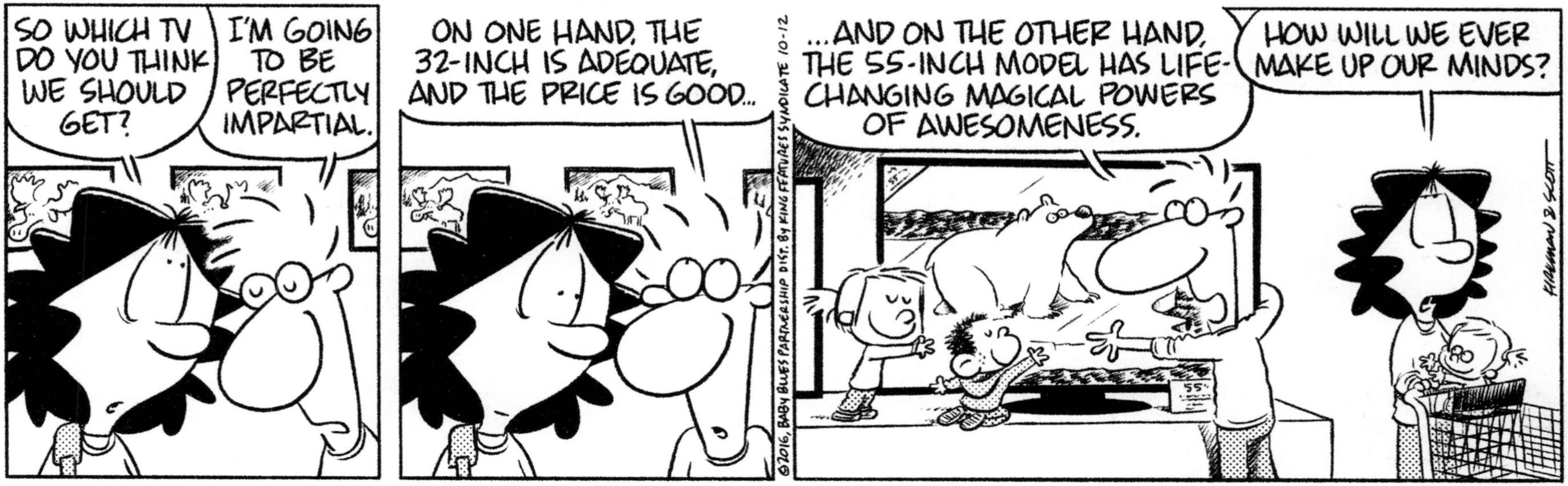
SO WHICH TV DO YOU THINK WE SHOULD GET?
I'M GOING TO BE PERFECTLY IMPARTIAL.
ON ONE HAND, THE 32-INCH IS ADEQUATE, AND THE PRICE IS GOOD...
...AND ON THE OTHER HAND, THE 55-INCH MODEL HAS LIFE-CHANGING MAGICAL POWERS OF AWESOMENESS.
HOW WILL WE EVER MAKE UP OUR MINDS?
©2016, BABY BLUES PARTNERSHIP DIST. BY KING FEATURES SYNDICATE 10-12
KIRKMAN & SCOTT

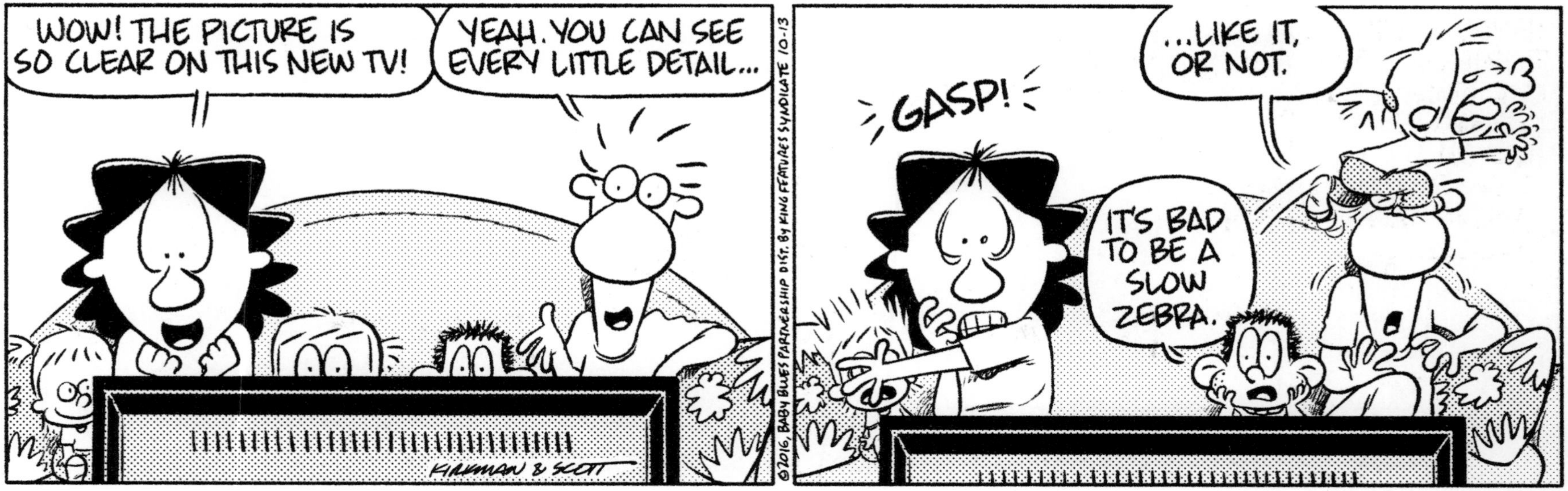
WOW! THE PICTURE IS SO CLEAR ON THIS NEW TV!
YEAH. YOU CAN SEE EVERY LITTLE DETAIL...
GASP!
...LIKE IT, OR NOT.
IT'S BAD TO BE A SLOW ZEBRA.
©2016, BABY BLUES PARTNERSHIP DIST. BY KING FEATURES SYNDICATE 10-13
KIRKMAN & SCOTT

Rick: Yessss! Now the family can be traumatized in high-def.

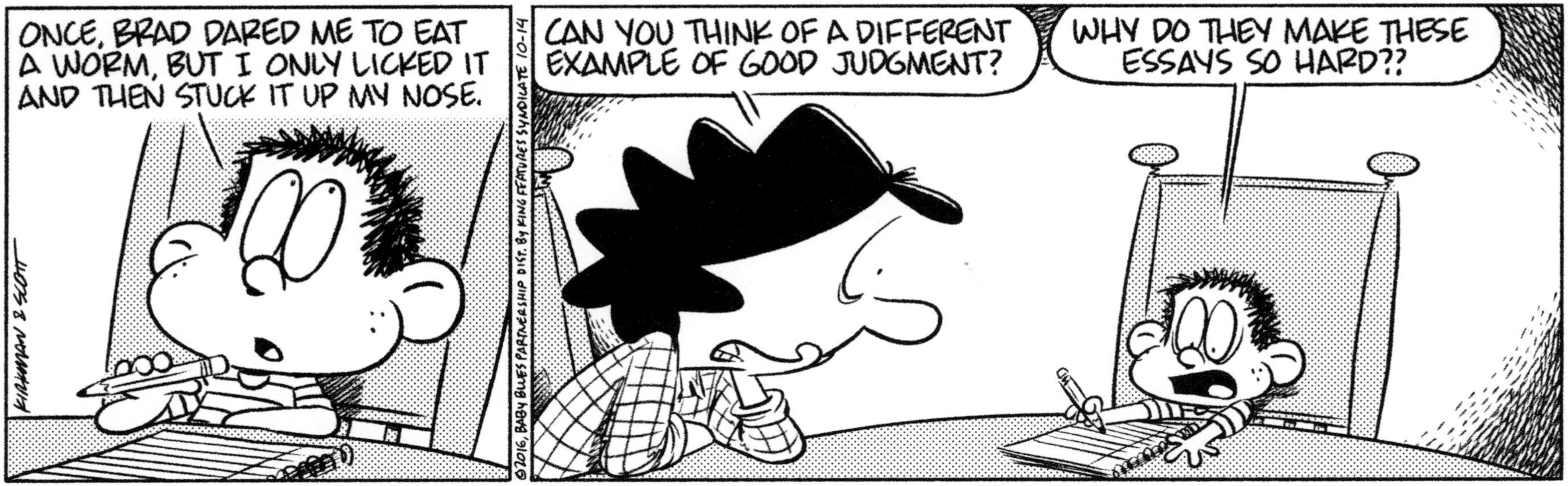
ONCE, BRAD DARED ME TO EAT A WORM, BUT I ONLY LICKED IT AND THEN STUCK IT UP MY NOSE.
KIRKMAN & SCOTT
©2016, BABY BLUES PARTNERSHIP DIST. BY KING FEATURES SYNDICATE 10-14
CAN YOU THINK OF A DIFFERENT EXAMPLE OF GOOD JUDGMENT?
WHY DO THEY MAKE THESE ESSAYS SO HARD??

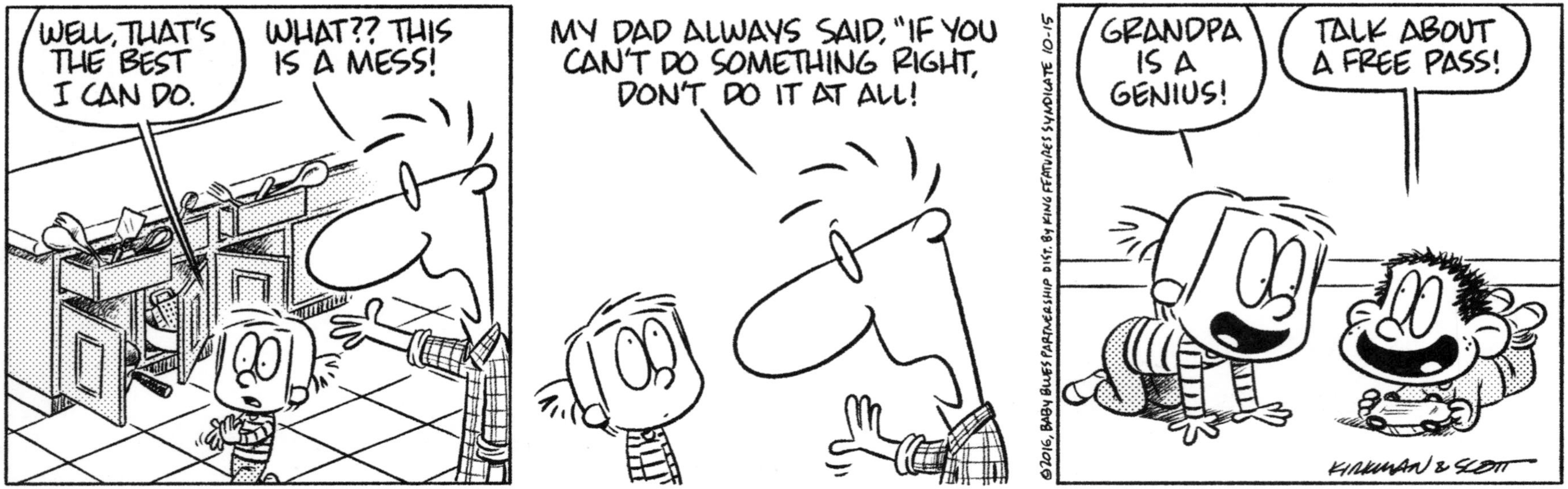
WELL, THAT'S THE BEST I CAN DO.
WHAT?? THIS IS A MESS!
MY DAD ALWAYS SAID, "IF YOU CAN'T DO SOMETHING RIGHT, DON'T DO IT AT ALL!
©2016, BABY BLUES PARTNERSHIP DIST. BY KING FEATURES SYNDICATE 10-15
GRANDPA IS A GENIUS!
TALK ABOUT A FREE PASS!
KIRKMAN & SCOTT

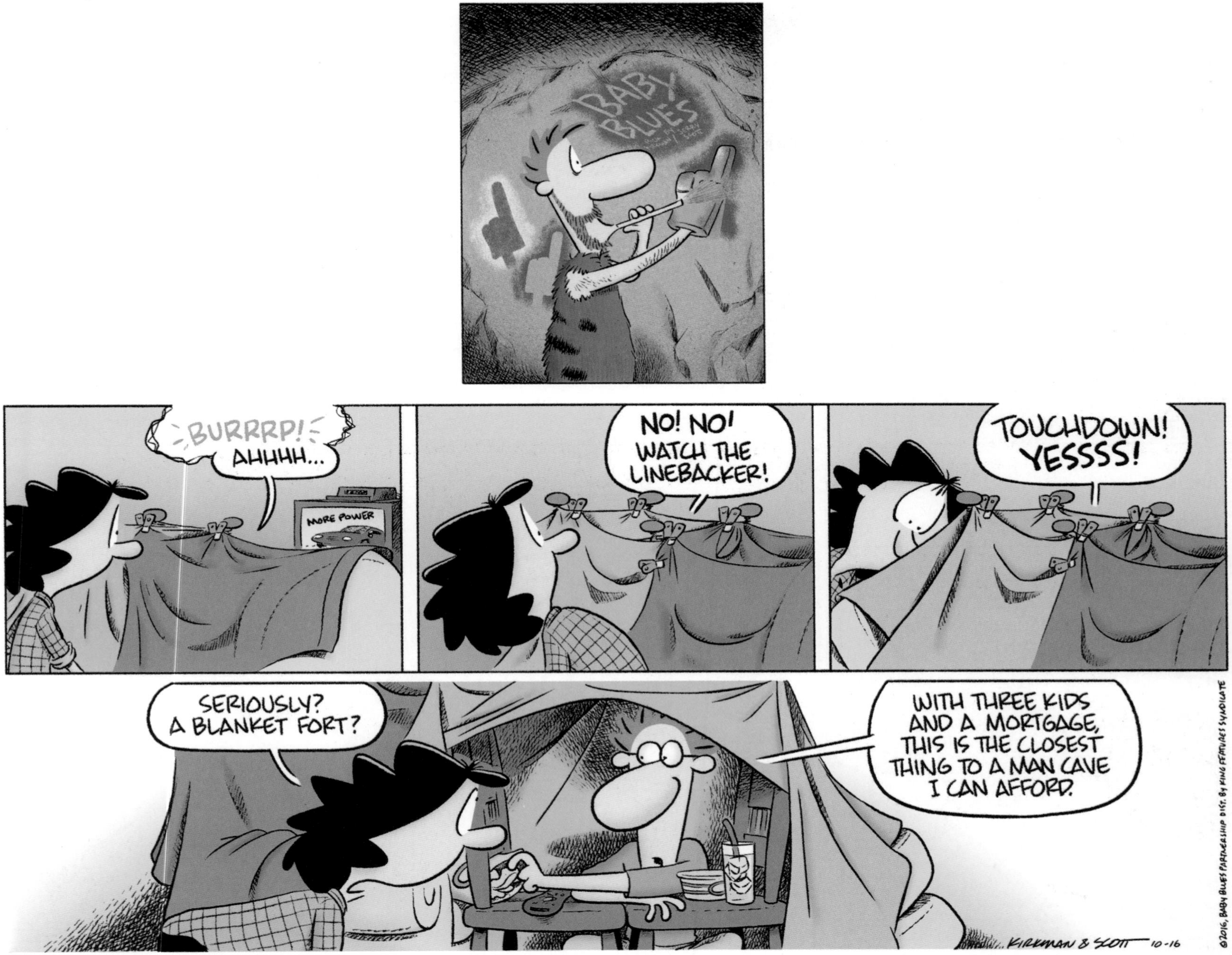
BABY BLUES
BURRRP!
AHHHH...
MORE POWER
NO! NO! WATCH THE LINEBACKER!
TOUCHDOWN! YESSSS!
SERIOUSLY? A BLANKET FORT?
WITH THREE KIDS AND A MORTGAGE, THIS IS THE CLOSEST THING TO A MAN CAVE I CAN AFFORD.
KIRKMAN & SCOTT 10-16
©2016, BABY BLUES PARTNERSHIP DIST. BY KING FEATURES SYNDICATE

Rick: A little Google research into cave painting for the title panel. Here's to cross-hatching, RT.

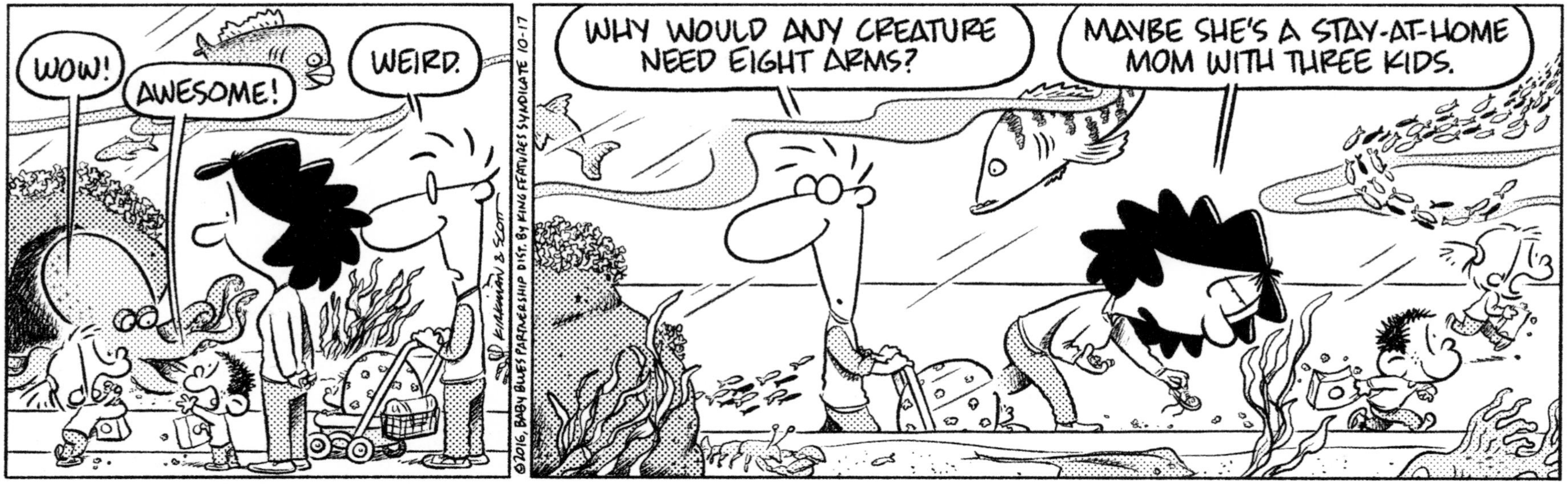
WOW!
AWESOME!
WEIRD.
©2016, BABY BLUES PARTNERSHIP DIST. BY KING FEATURES SYNDICATE 10-17
KIRKMAN & SCOTT
WHY WOULD ANY CREATURE NEED EIGHT ARMS?
MAYBE SHE'S A STAY-AT-HOME MOM WITH THREE KIDS.

Rick: I wonder what the sea creatures think, seeing the MacPhersons from the inside of the aquarium.

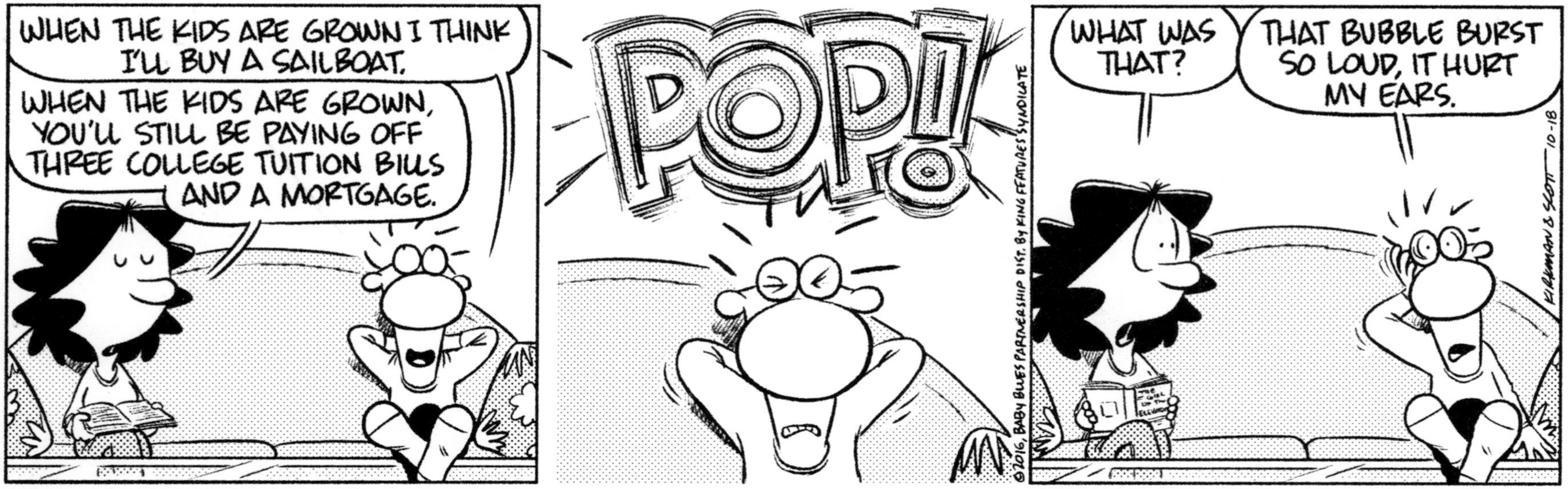
WHEN THE KIDS ARE GROWN I THINK I'LL BUY A SAILBOAT.
WHEN THE KIDS ARE GROWN, YOU'LL STILL BE PAYING OFF THREE COLLEGE TUITION BILLS AND A MORTGAGE.
POP!
©2016, BABY BLUES PARTNERSHIP DIST. BY KING FEATURES SYNDICATE
WHAT WAS THAT?
THAT BUBBLE BURST SO LOUD, IT HURT MY EARS.
KIRKMAN & SCOTT 10-18

Rick: Trying to make lettering look like a sound is one of the small joys of drawing the strip.

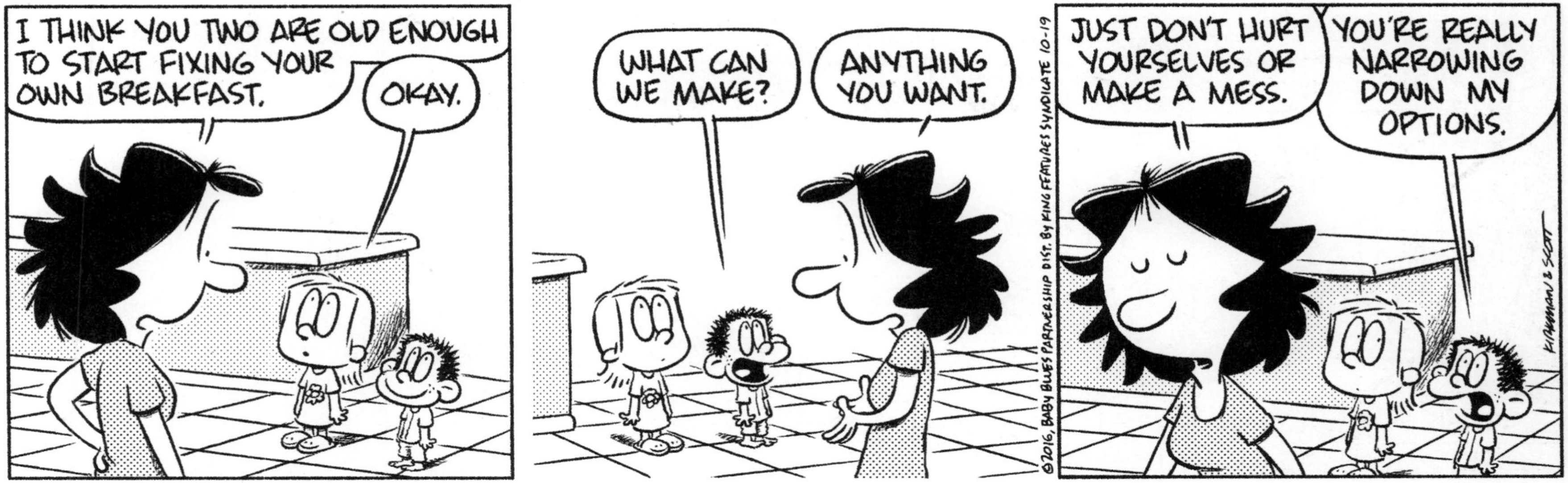
I THINK YOU TWO ARE OLD ENOUGH TO START FIXING YOUR OWN BREAKFAST.
OKAY.
WHAT CAN WE MAKE?
ANYTHING YOU WANT.
©2016, BABY BLUES PARTNERSHIP DIST. BY KING FEATURES SYNDICATE 10-19
JUST DON'T HURT YOURSELVES OR MAKE A MESS.
YOU'RE REALLY NARROWING DOWN MY OPTIONS.
KIRKMAN & SCOTT

Jerry: I love the idea of our kids making their own breakfasts. I also loved the idea of having a full-time maid, but that didn't happen, either.

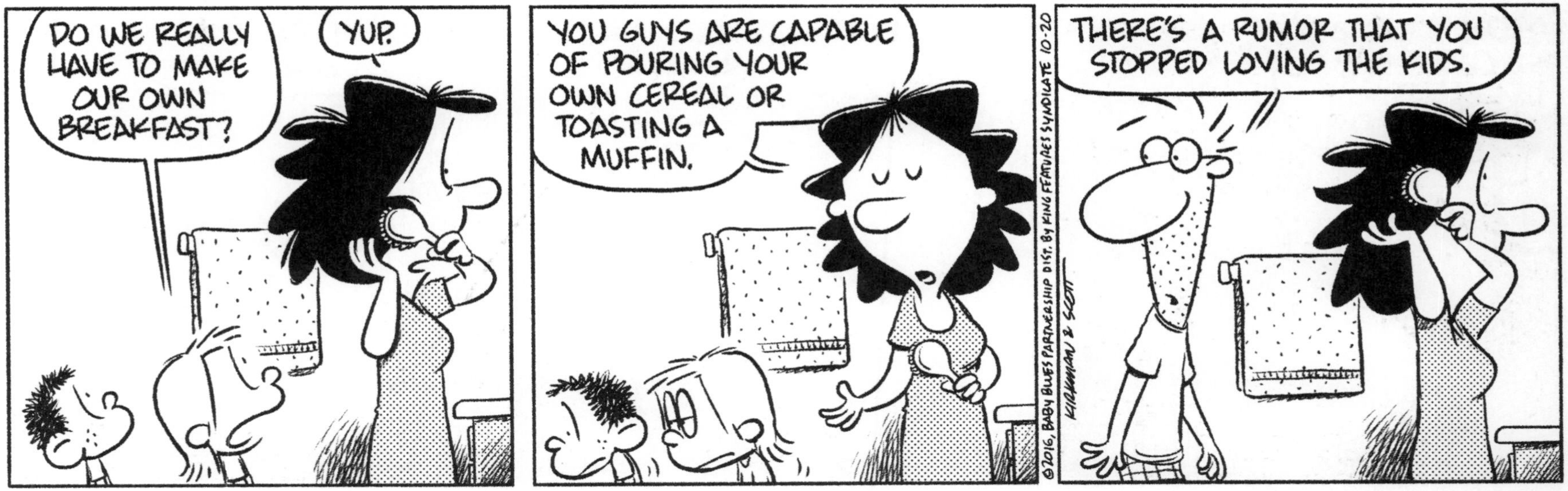
DO WE REALLY HAVE TO MAKE OUR OWN BREAKFAST?
YUP.
YOU GUYS ARE CAPABLE OF POURING YOUR OWN CEREAL OR TOASTING A MUFFIN.
©2016, BABY BLUES PARTNERSHIP DIST. BY KING FEATURES SYNDICATE 10-20
KIRKMAN & SCOTT
THERE'S A RUMOR THAT YOU STOPPED LOVING THE KIDS.

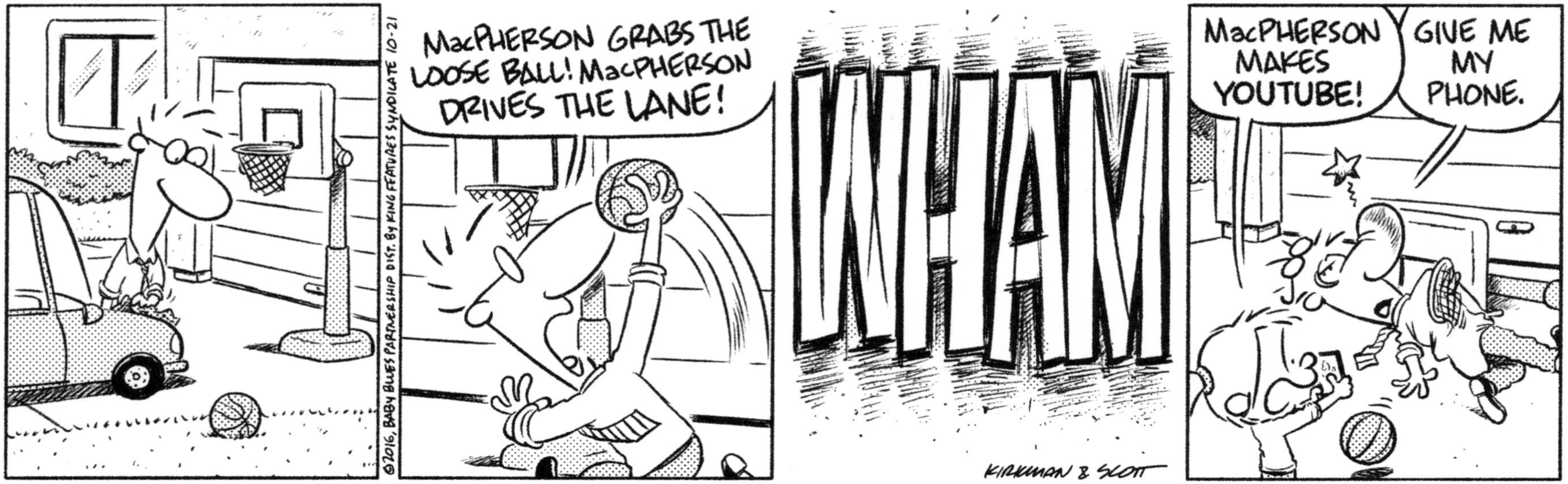
©2016, BABY BLUES PARTNERSHIP DIST. BY KING FEATURES SYNDICATE 10-21
MacPHERSON GRABS THE LOOSE BALL! MacPHERSON DRIVES THE LANE!
WHAM
KIRKMAN & SCOTT
MacPHERSON MAKES YOUTUBE!
GIVE ME MY PHONE.

Rick: Lettering+Sound=Fun. Again.

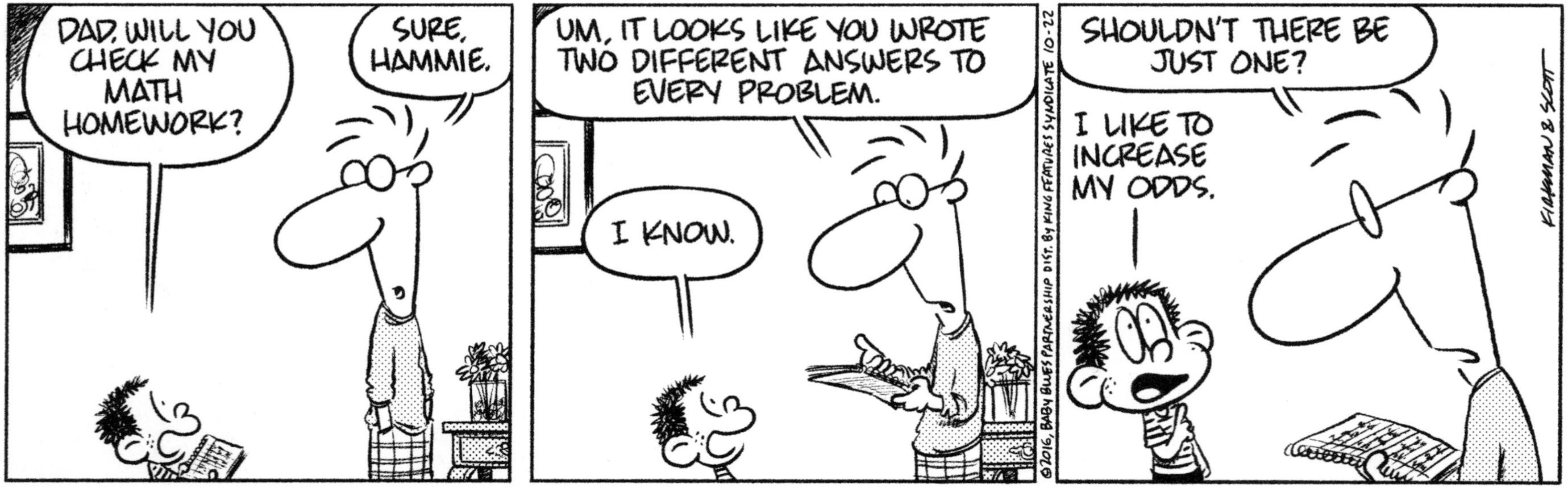
DAD, WILL YOU CHECK MY MATH HOMEWORK?
SURE, HAMMIE.
UM, IT LOOKS LIKE YOU WROTE TWO DIFFERENT ANSWERS TO EVERY PROBLEM.
I KNOW.
©2016, BABY BLUES PARTNERSHIP DIST. BY KING FEATURES SYNDICATE 10-22
SHOULDN'T THERE BE JUST ONE?
I LIKE TO INCREASE MY ODDS.
KIRKMAN & SCOTT

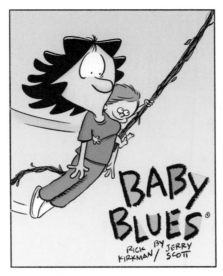

BABY BLUES®
RICK KIRKMAN / BY / JERRY SCOTT

©2016, BABY BLUES PARTNERSHIP DIST. BY KING FEATURES SYNDICATE
HEY, HAVE YOU TWO JUST BEEN KICKIN' BACK ALL DAY?
YEAH. C'MERE. I WANT TO GIVE YOU A "KISS."
KIRKMAN & SCOTT 10-23

Rick: Online, I looked up what Tarzan looked like while carrying Jane through the jungle on a vine. What a rabbit hole of old movie clips.

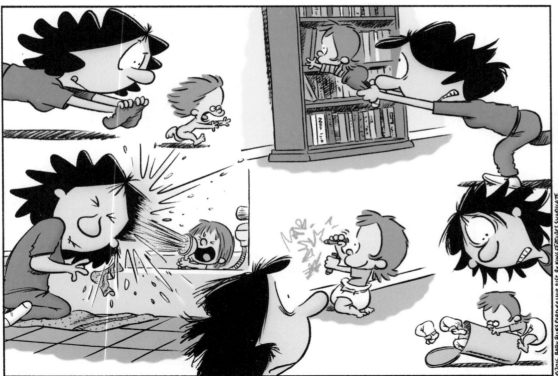

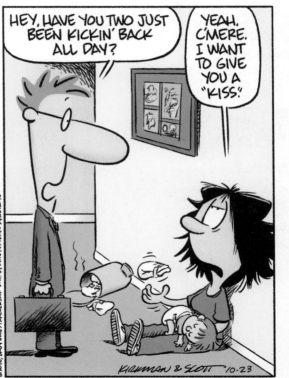

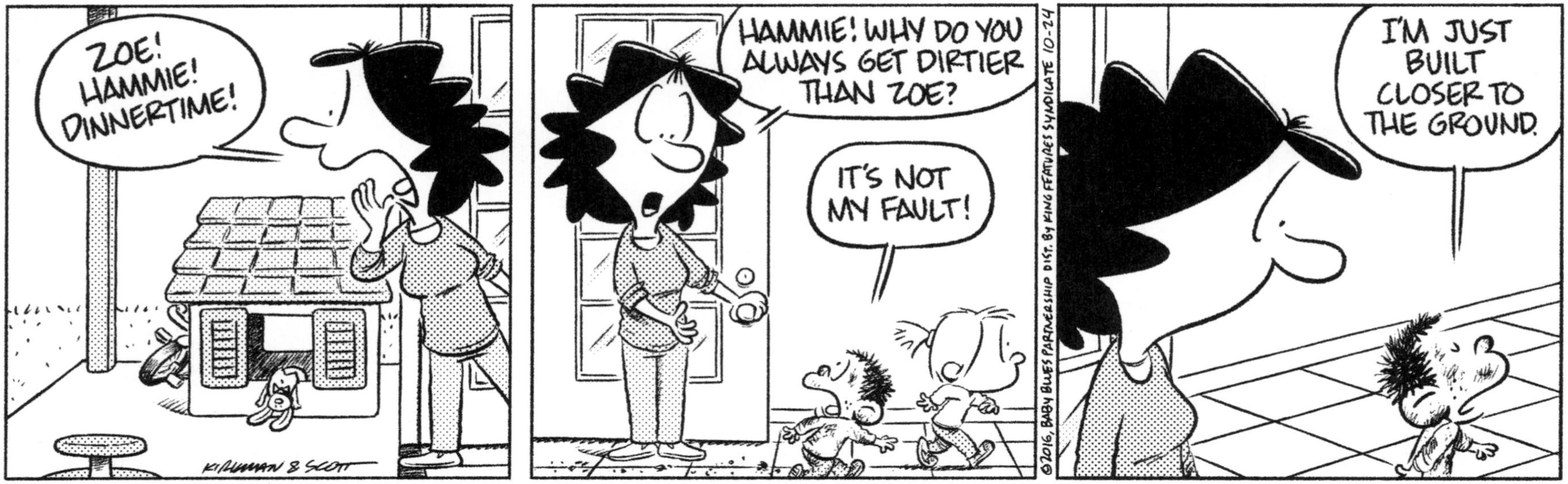
ZOE! HAMMIE! DINNERTIME!
KIRKMAN & SCOTT
HAMMIE! WHY DO YOU ALWAYS GET DIRTIER THAN ZOE?
IT'S NOT MY FAULT!
©2016, BABY BLUES PARTNERSHIP DIST. BY KING FEATURES SYNDICATE 10-24
I'M JUST BUILT CLOSER TO THE GROUND.

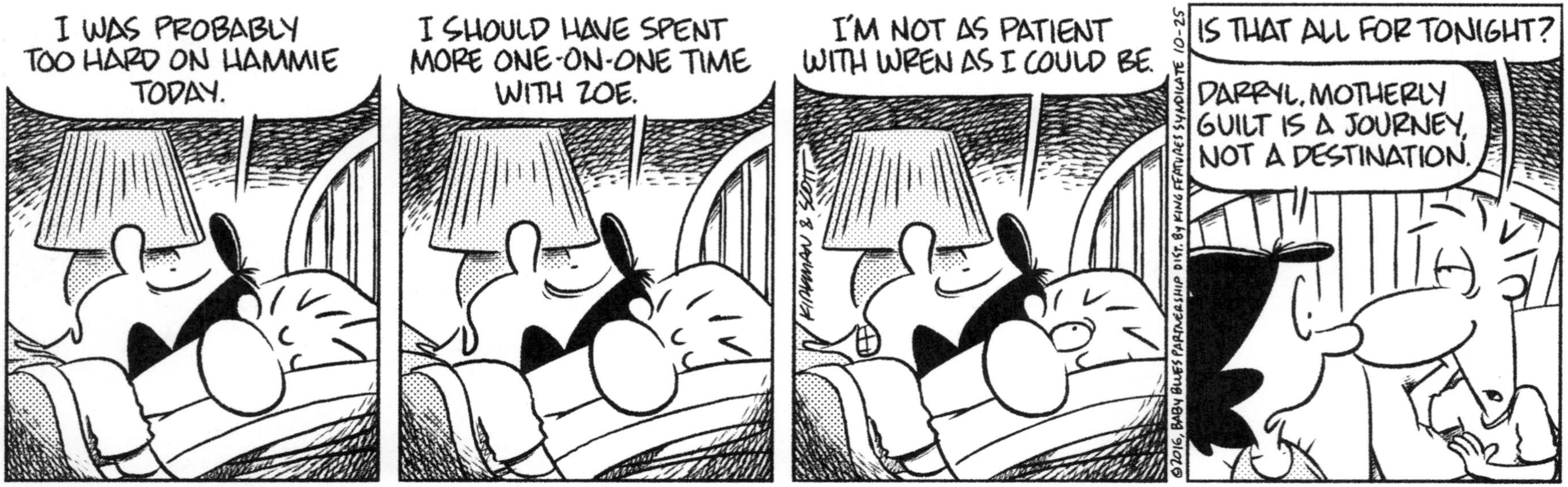
I WAS PROBABLY TOO HARD ON HAMMIE TODAY.
I SHOULD HAVE SPENT MORE ONE-ON-ONE TIME WITH ZOE.
KIRKMAN & SCOTT
I'M NOT AS PATIENT WITH WREN AS I COULD BE.
©2016, BABY BLUES PARTNERSHIP DIST. BY KING FEATURES SYNDICATE 10-25
IS THAT ALL FOR TONIGHT?
DARRYL, MOTHERLY GUILT IS A JOURNEY, NOT A DESTINATION.

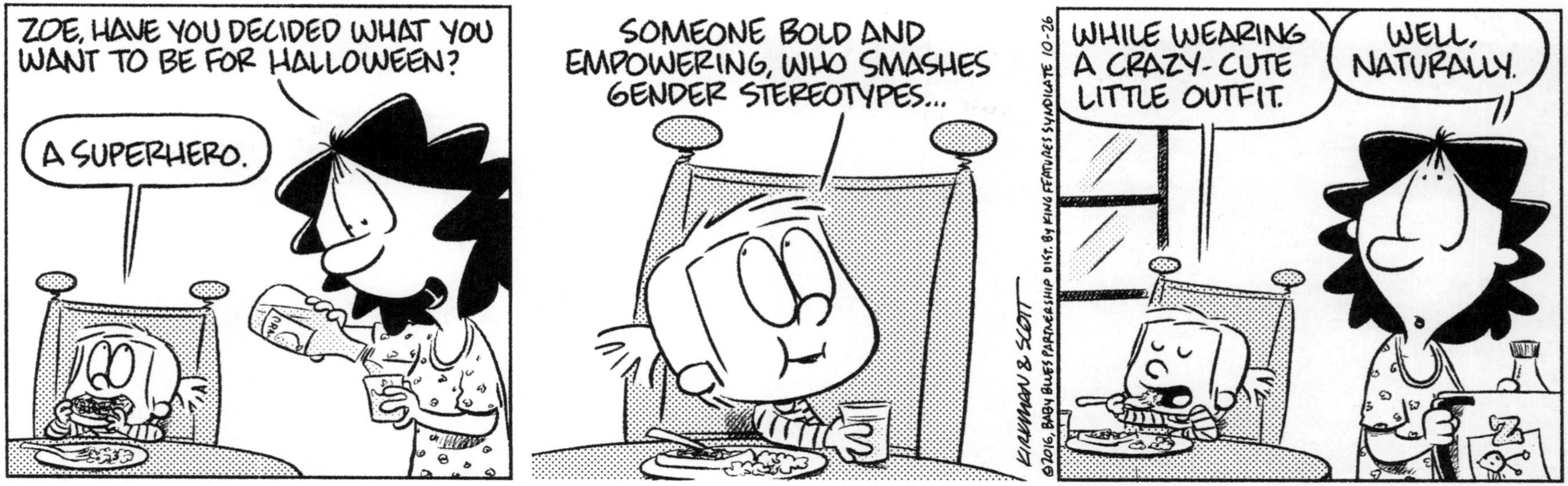
ZOE, HAVE YOU DECIDED WHAT YOU WANT TO BE FOR HALLOWEEN?
A SUPERHERO.
SOMEONE BOLD AND EMPOWERING, WHO SMASHES GENDER STEREOTYPES...
WHILE WEARING A CRAZY-CUTE LITTLE OUTFIT.
WELL, NATURALLY.
KIRKMAN & SCOTT
©2016, BABY BLUES PARTNERSHIP DIST. BY KING FEATURES SYNDICATE 10-26

Rick: Sometimes you have to break barriers one slat at a time.

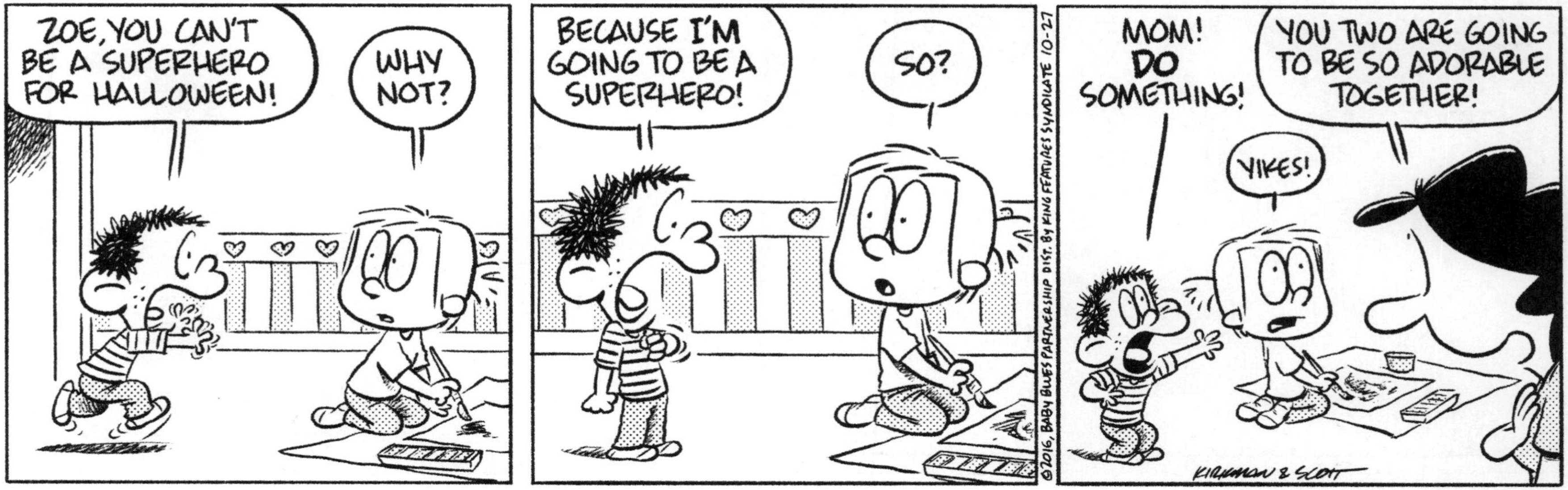
ZOE, YOU CAN'T BE A SUPERHERO FOR HALLOWEEN!
WHY NOT?
BECAUSE I'M GOING TO BE A SUPERHERO!
SO?
MOM! DO SOMETHING!
YOU TWO ARE GOING TO BE SO ADORABLE TOGETHER!
YIKES!
©2016, BABY BLUES PARTNERSHIP DIST. BY KING FEATURES SYNDICATE 10-27
KIRKMAN & SCOTT

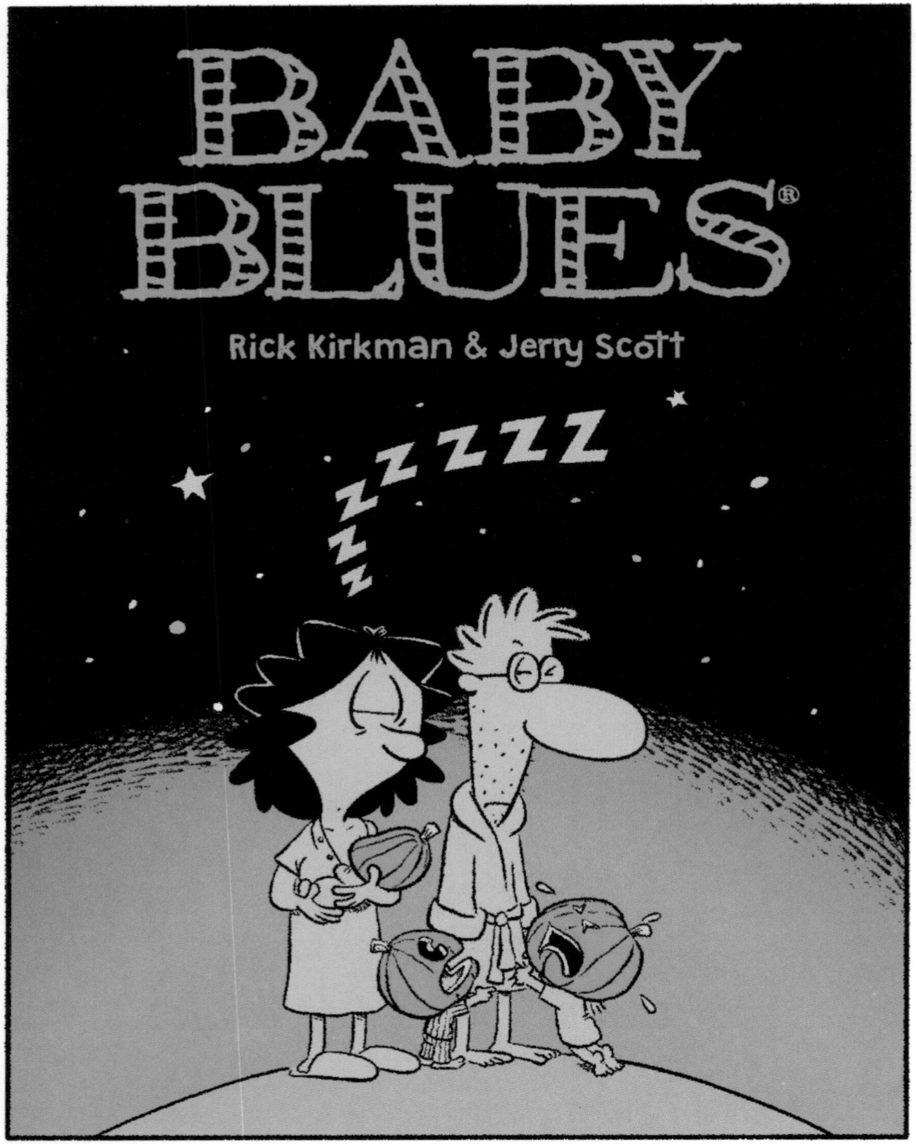
BABY BLUES®
Rick Kirkman & Jerry Scott
ZZZZZZZZZZ

Rick: I may have to try this one for real next Halloween.

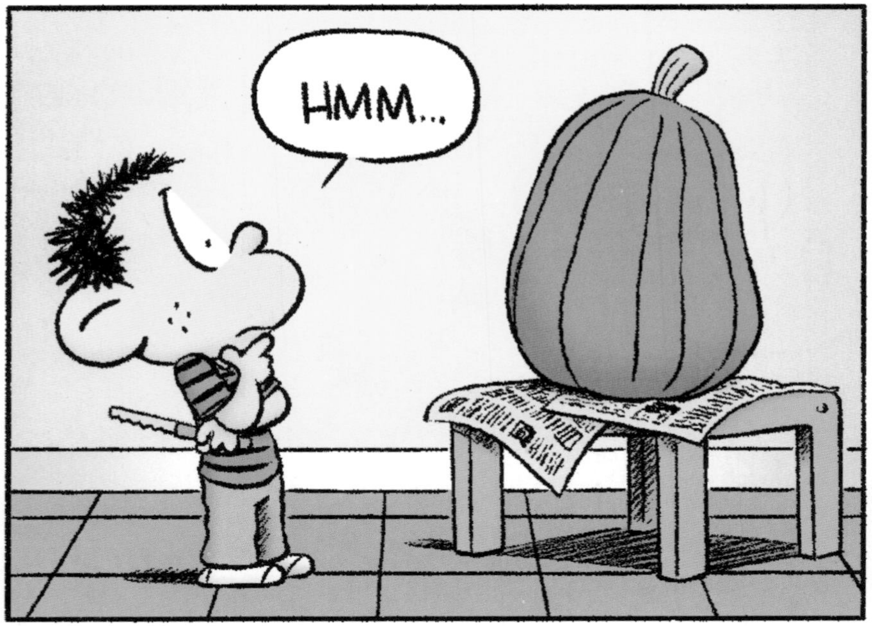
HMM...

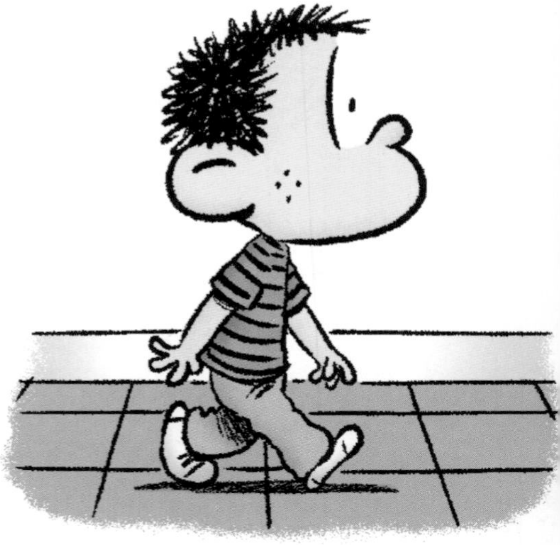

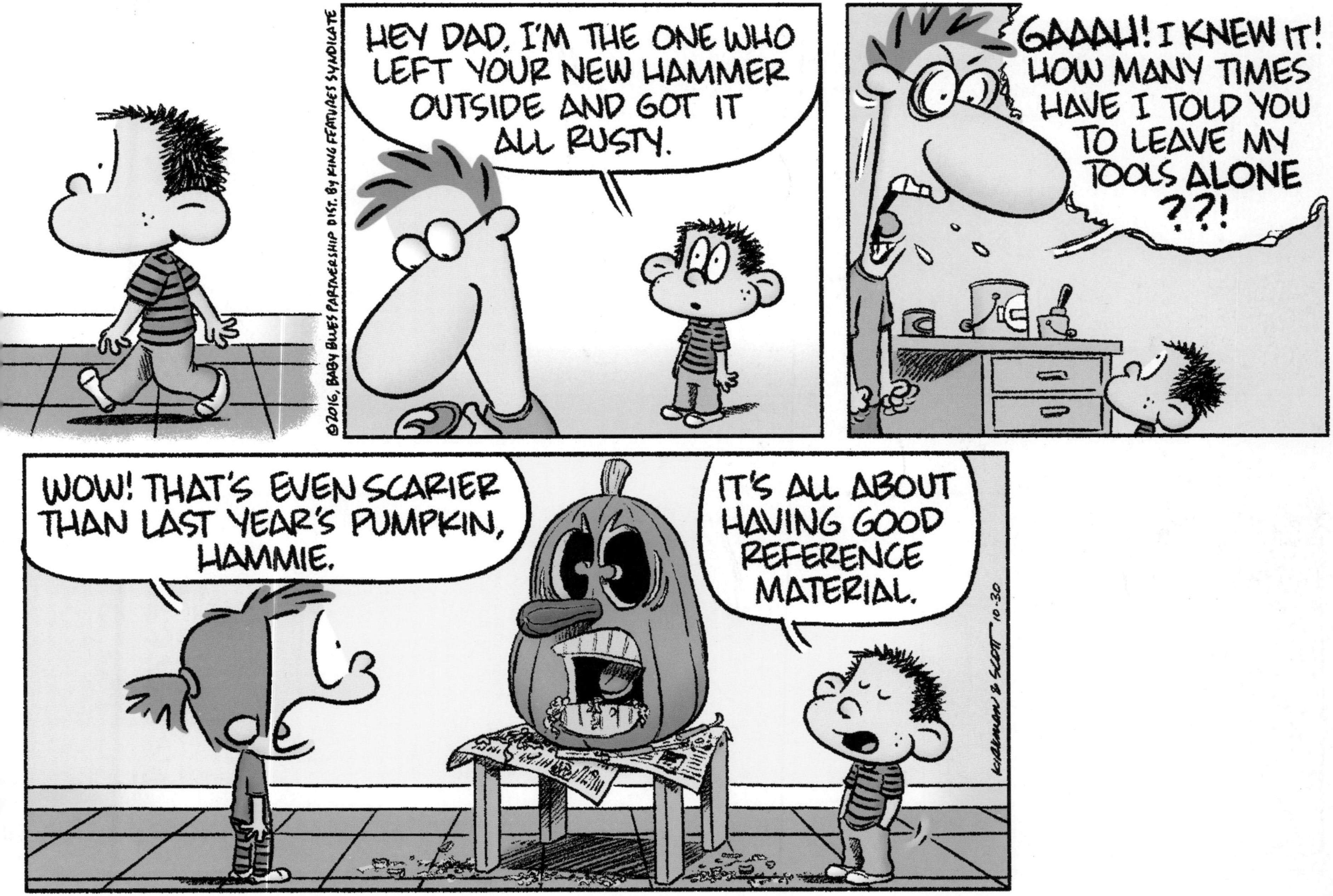
©2016, BABY BLUES PARTNERSHIP DIST. BY KING FEATURES SYNDICATE
HEY DAD, I'M THE ONE WHO LEFT YOUR NEW HAMMER OUTSIDE AND GOT IT ALL RUSTY.
GAAAH! I KNEW IT! HOW MANY TIMES HAVE I TOLD YOU TO LEAVE MY TOOLS ALONE ??!
WOW! THAT'S EVEN SCARIER THAN LAST YEAR'S PUMPKIN, HAMMIE.
IT'S ALL ABOUT HAVING GOOD REFERENCE MATERIAL.
KIRKMAN & SCOTT 10-30

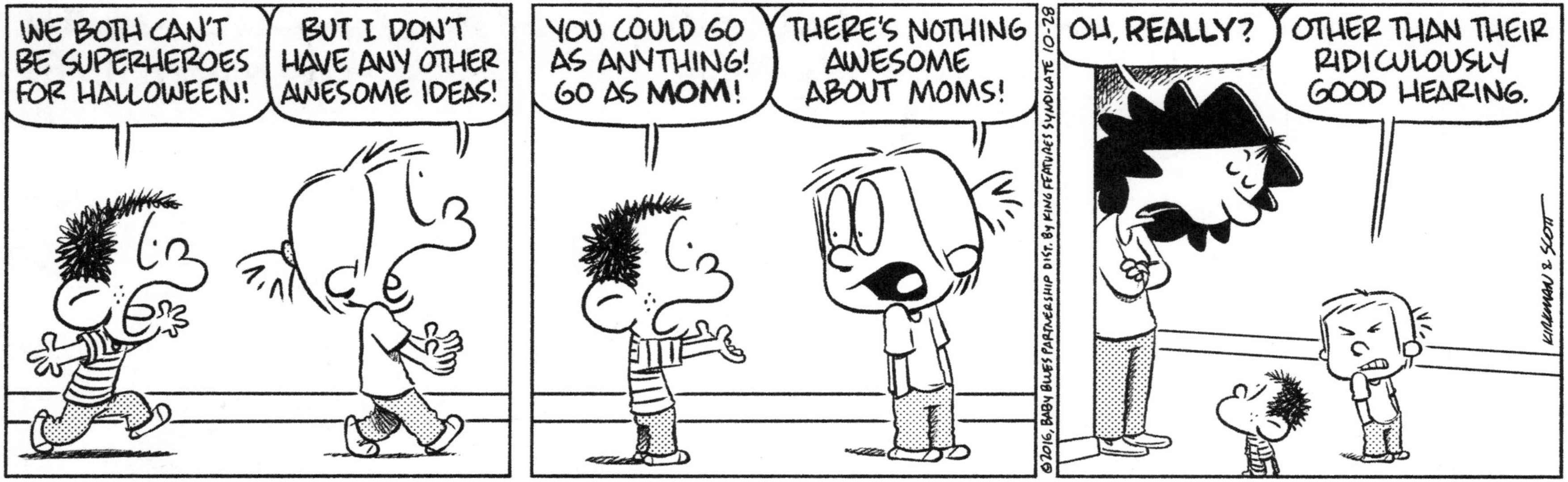
WE BOTH CAN'T BE SUPERHEROES FOR HALLOWEEN!
BUT I DON'T HAVE ANY OTHER AWESOME IDEAS!
YOU COULD GO AS ANYTHING! GO AS **MOM**!
THERE'S NOTHING AWESOME ABOUT MOMS!
©2016, BABY BLUES PARTNERSHIP DIST. BY KING FEATURES SYNDICATE 10-28
OH, **REALLY**?
OTHER THAN THEIR RIDICULOUSLY GOOD HEARING.
KIRKMAN & SCOTT

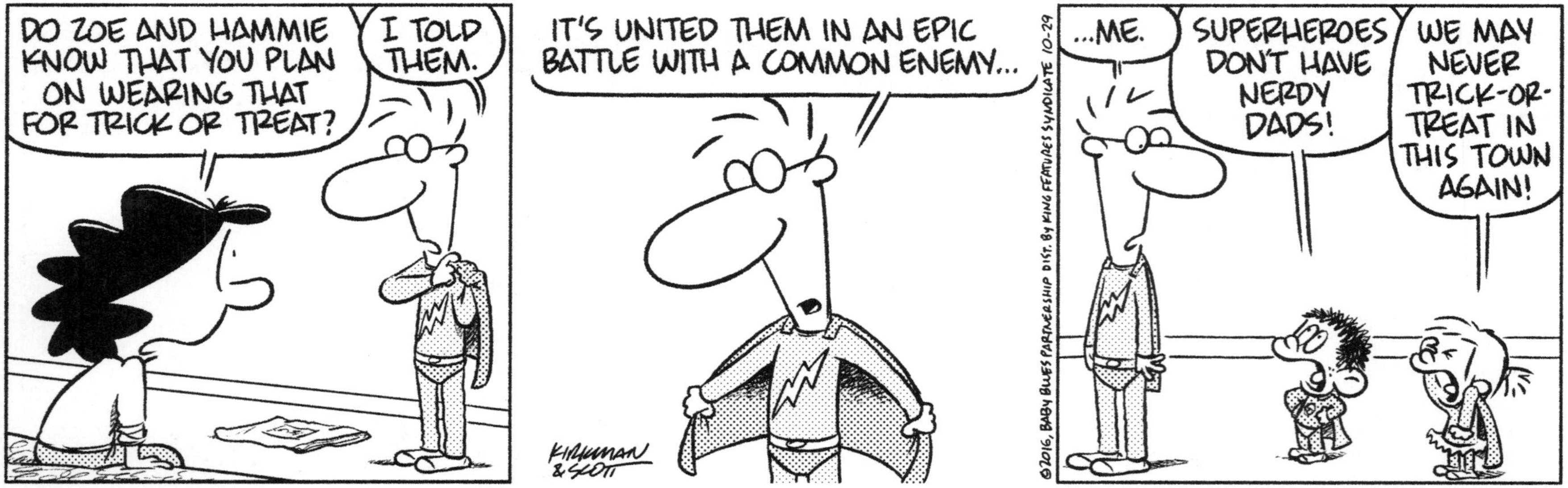
DO ZOE AND HAMMIE KNOW THAT YOU PLAN ON WEARING THAT FOR TRICK OR TREAT?
I TOLD THEM.
IT'S UNITED THEM IN AN EPIC BATTLE WITH A COMMON ENEMY...
KIRKMAN & SCOTT
©2016, BABY BLUES PARTNERSHIP DIST. BY KING FEATURES SYNDICATE 10-29
...ME.
SUPERHEROES DON'T HAVE NERDY DADS!
WE MAY NEVER TRICK-OR-TREAT IN THIS TOWN AGAIN!

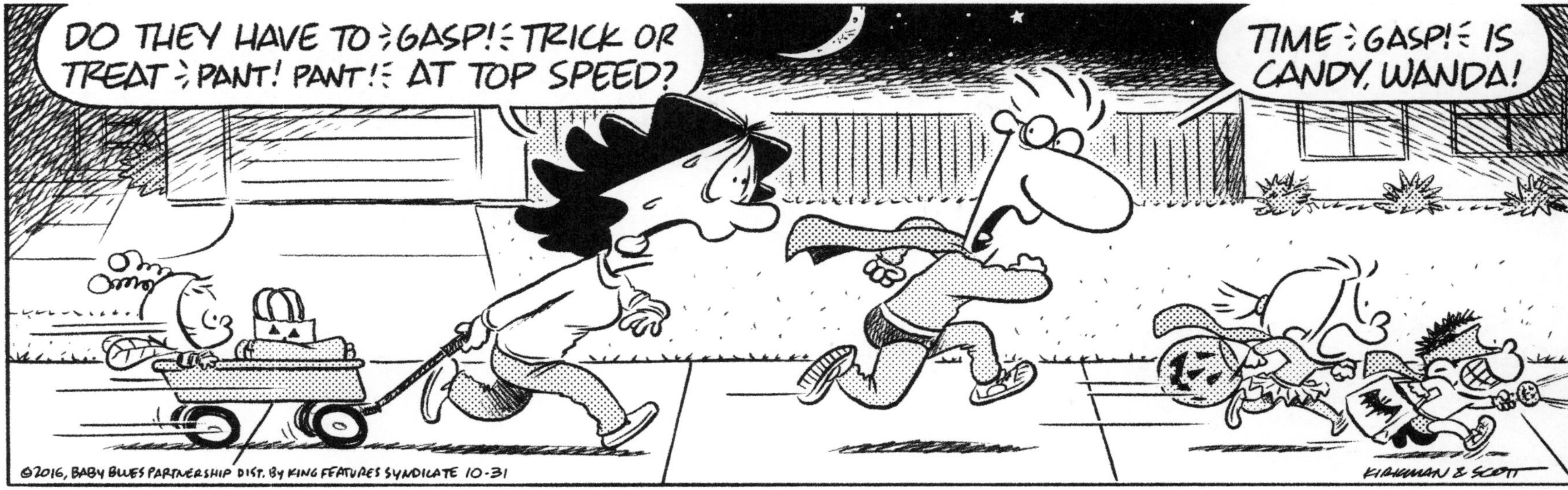
DO THEY HAVE TO -GASP!- TRICK OR TREAT -PANT! PANT!- AT TOP SPEED?
TIME -GASP!- IS CANDY, WANDA!
©2016, BABY BLUES PARTNERSHIP DIST. BY KING FEATURES SYNDICATE 10-31
KIRKMAN & SCOTT

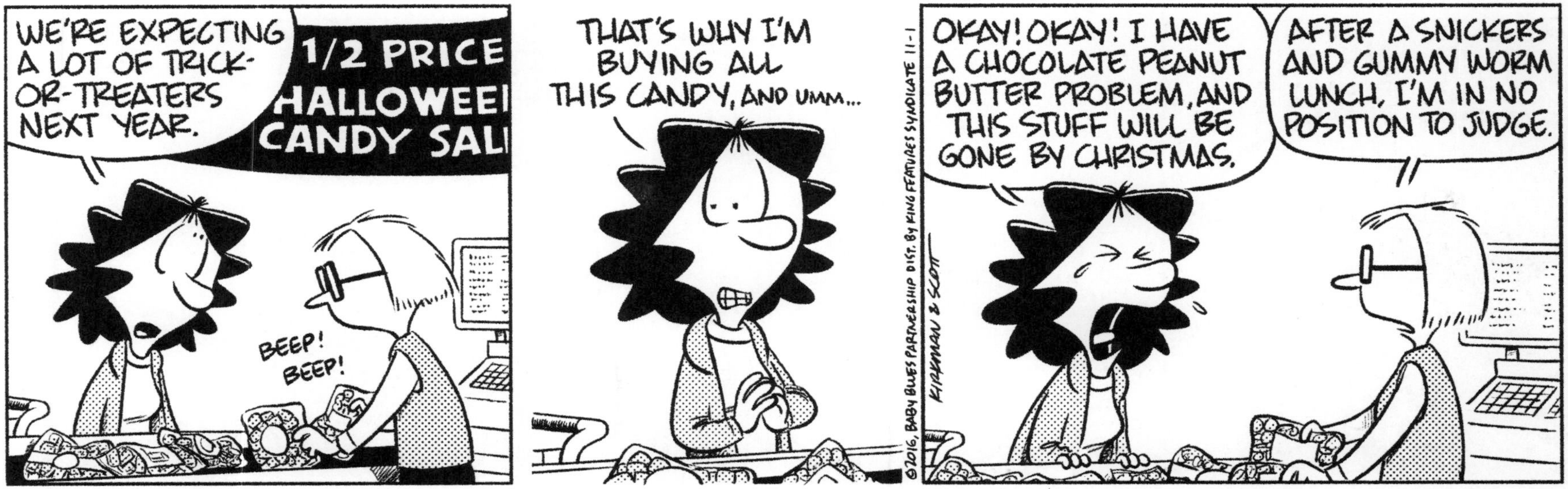
WE'RE EXPECTING A LOT OF TRICK-OR-TREATERS NEXT YEAR.
1/2 PRICE
HALLOWEE
CANDY SAL
BEEP! BEEP!
THAT'S WHY I'M BUYING ALL THIS CANDY, AND UMM...
©2016, BABY BLUES PARTNERSHIP DIST. BY KING FEATURES SYNDICATE 11-1
KIRKMAN & SCOTT
OKAY! OKAY! I HAVE A CHOCOLATE PEANUT BUTTER PROBLEM, AND THIS STUFF WILL BE GONE BY CHRISTMAS.
AFTER A SNICKERS AND GUMMY WORM LUNCH, I'M IN NO POSITION TO JUDGE.

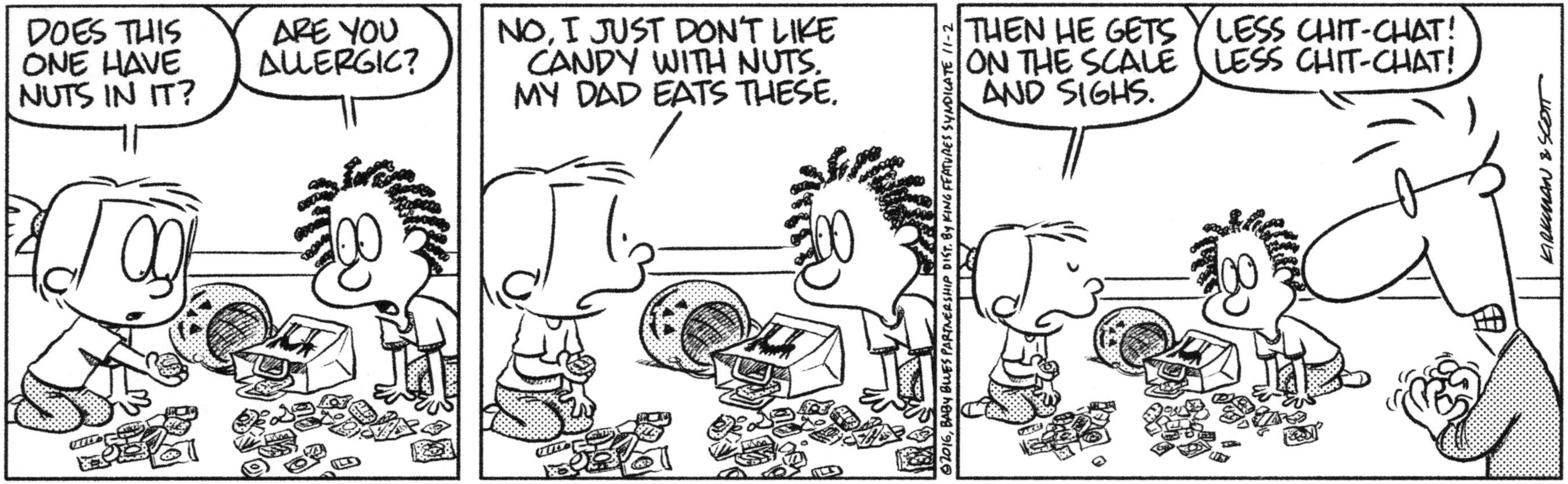
DOES THIS ONE HAVE NUTS IN IT?
ARE YOU ALLERGIC?
NO, I JUST DON'T LIKE CANDY WITH NUTS. MY DAD EATS THESE.
©2016, BABY BLUES PARTNERSHIP DIST. BY KING FEATURES SYNDICATE 11-2
THEN HE GETS ON THE SCALE AND SIGHS.
LESS CHIT-CHAT! LESS CHIT-CHAT!
KIRKMAN & SCOTT

Rick: Keesha's got a new hairstyle!

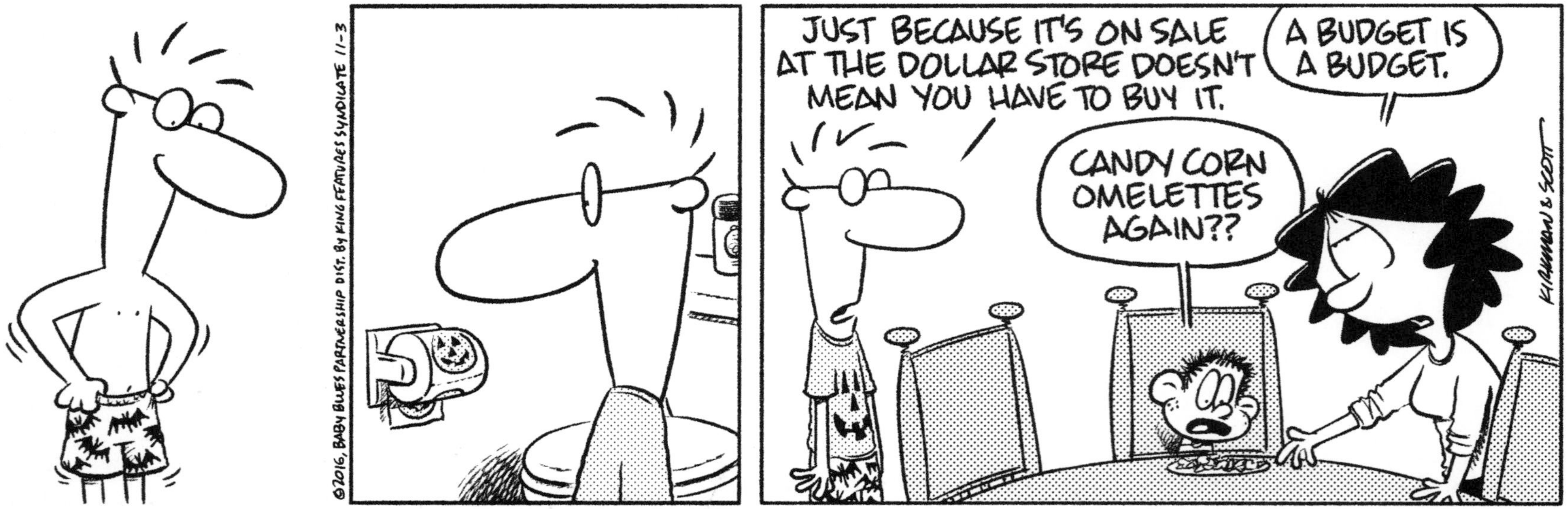
©2016, BABY BLUES PARTNERSHIP DIST. BY KING FEATURES SYNDICATE 11-3
JUST BECAUSE IT'S ON SALE AT THE DOLLAR STORE DOESN'T MEAN YOU HAVE TO BUY IT.
A BUDGET IS A BUDGET.
CANDY CORN OMELETTES AGAIN??
KIRKMAN & SCOTT

Jerry: And a bargain is a bargain.

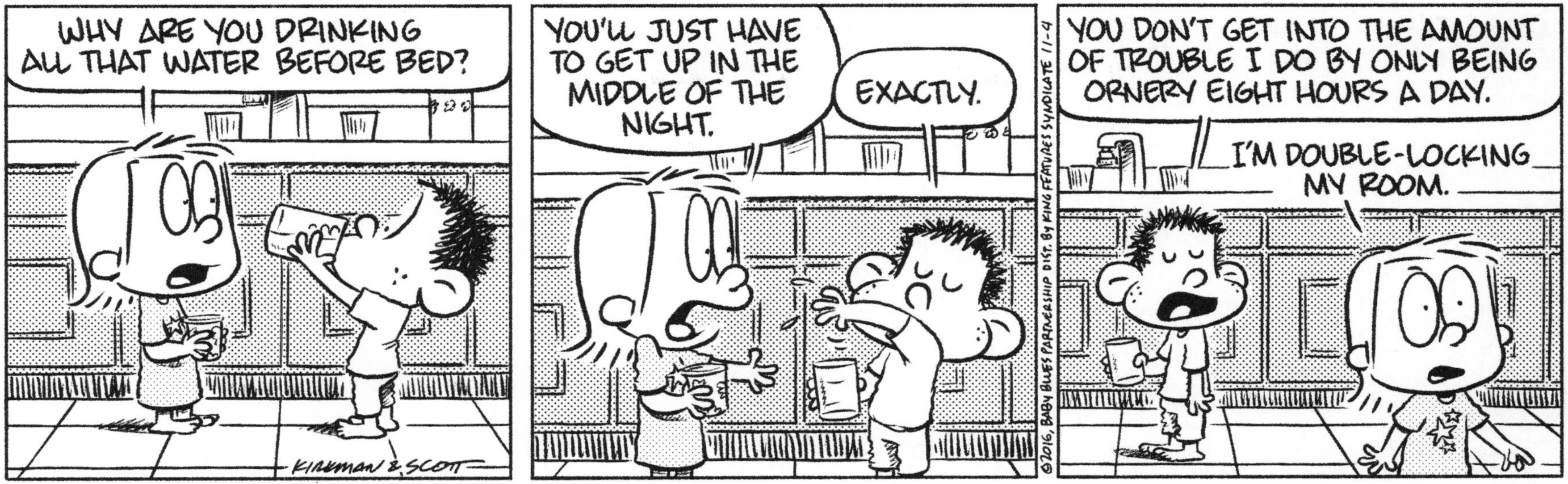
WHY ARE YOU DRINKING ALL THAT WATER BEFORE BED?
KIRKMAN & SCOTT
YOU'LL JUST HAVE TO GET UP IN THE MIDDLE OF THE NIGHT.
EXACTLY.
©2016, BABY BLUES PARTNERSHIP DIST. BY KING FEATURES SYNDICATE 11-4
YOU DON'T GET INTO THE AMOUNT OF TROUBLE I DO BY ONLY BEING ORNERY EIGHT HOURS A DAY.
I'M DOUBLE-LOCKING MY ROOM.

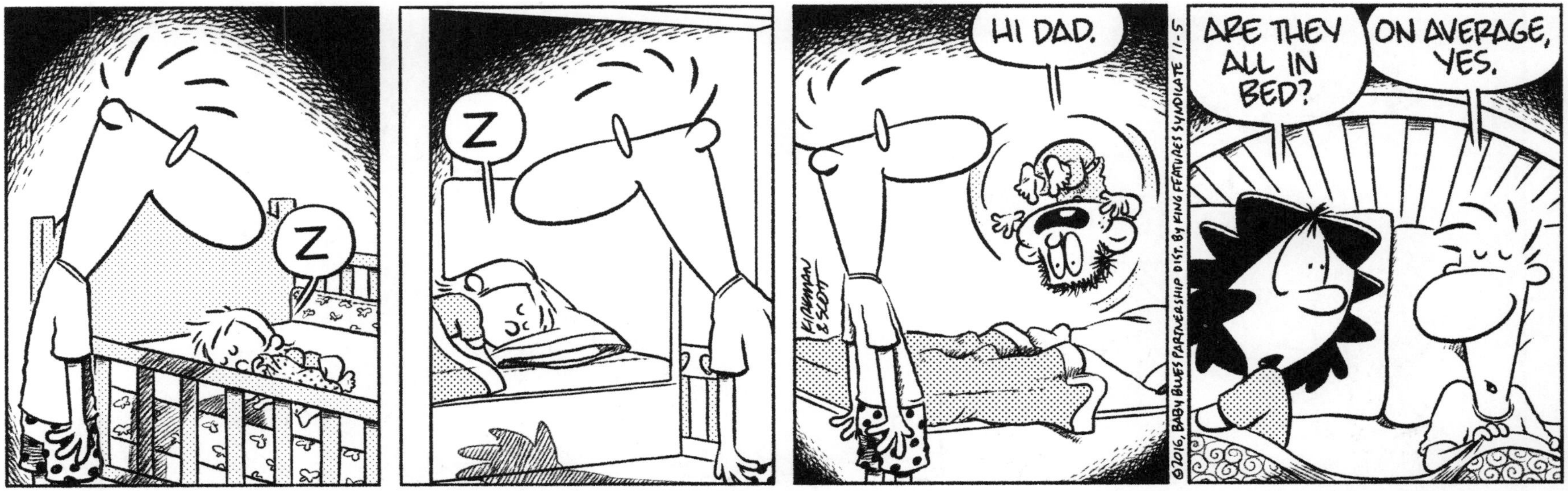
Z
Z
HI DAD.
KIRKMAN & SCOTT
©2016, BABY BLUES PARTNERSHIP DIST. BY KING FEATURES SYNDICATE 11-5
ARE THEY ALL IN BED?
ON AVERAGE, YES.

Jerry: I like how Darryl and Wanda act like real parents, not reacting to every little irritant.

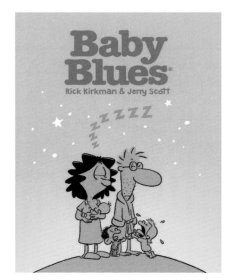

Baby Blues
Rick Kirkman & Jerry Scott
ZZZZZ

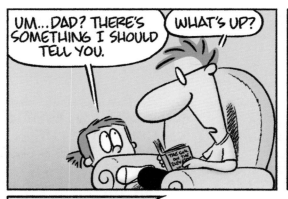

UM... DAD? THERE'S SOMETHING I SHOULD TELL YOU.
WHAT'S UP?
WELL, DO YOU REMEMBER WHEN I SPENT THE DAY WITH AUNT RHONDA LAST SATURDAY?
ZOE, IS SOMETHING WRONG?
WELL, IT'S JUST THAT WHILE WE WE'RE OUT SHOPPING, SHE TOOK ME...
...TO GET THIS TATTOO!
KIRKMAN & SCOTT 11-6
©2016, BABY BLUES PARTNERSHIP DIST. BY KING FEATURES SYNDICATE
THANKS, ZOE, BUT MY HICCUPS WENT AWAY A FEW MINUTES AGO.
THIS BETTER BE A WASHABLE MARKER!
IT SAYS "LAUNDRY MARKER." THAT MEANS WASHABLE, RIGHT?

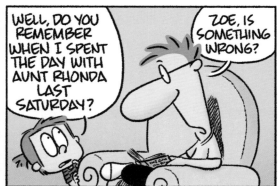

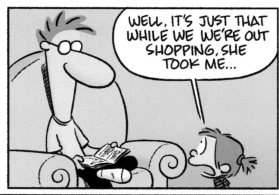

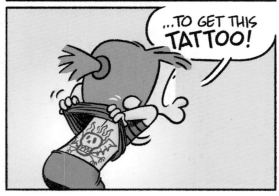

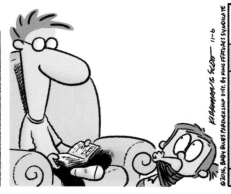

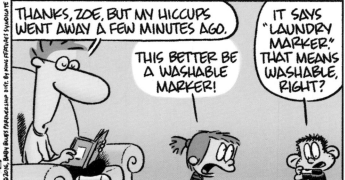

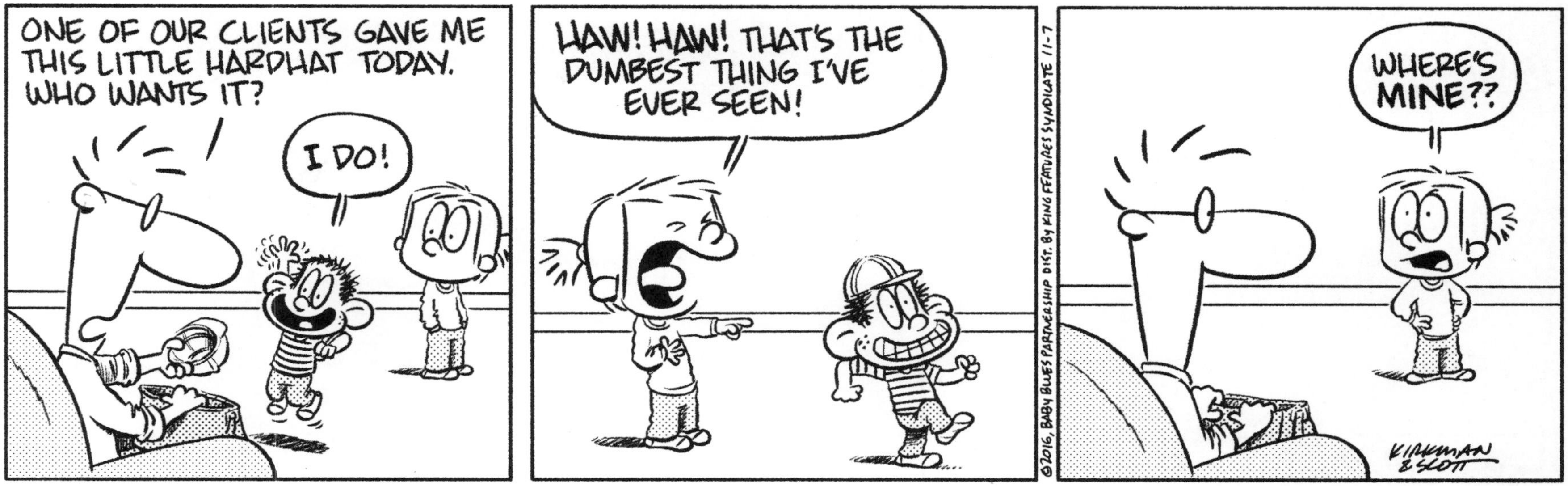
ONE OF OUR CLIENTS GAVE ME THIS LITTLE HARDHAT TODAY. WHO WANTS IT?
I DO!
HAW! HAW! THAT'S THE DUMBEST THING I'VE EVER SEEN!
WHERE'S MINE??
©2016, BABY BLUES PARTNERSHIP DIST. BY KING FEATURES SYNDICATE 11-7
KIRKMAN & SCOTT

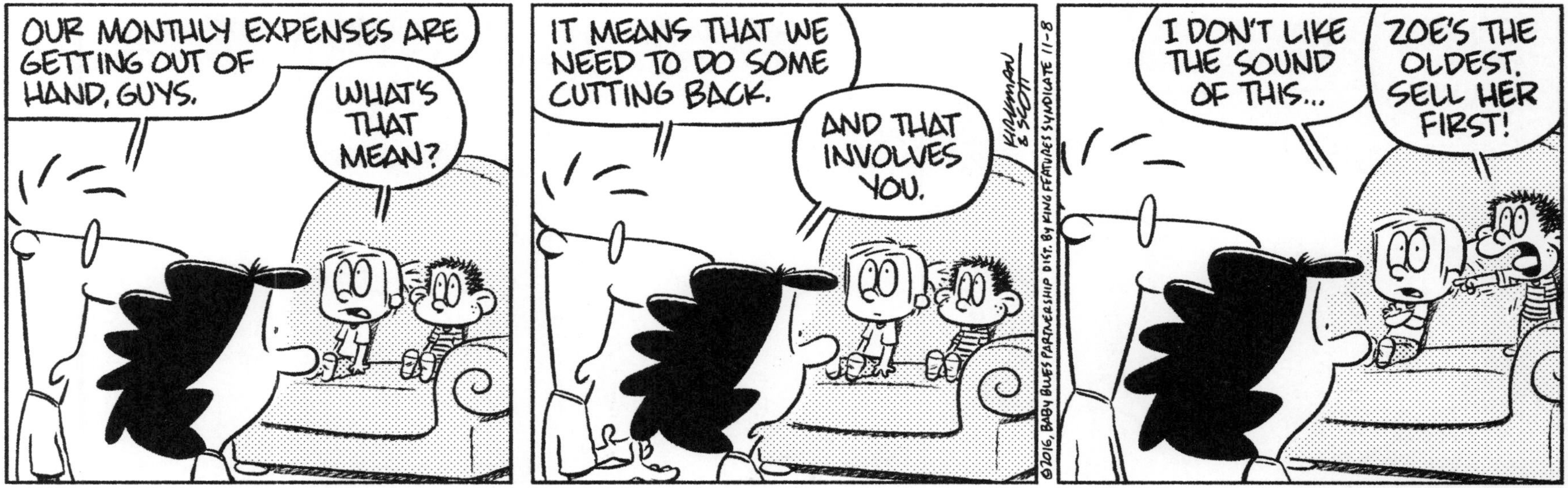
OUR MONTHLY EXPENSES ARE GETTING OUT OF HAND, GUYS.
WHAT'S THAT MEAN?
IT MEANS THAT WE NEED TO DO SOME CUTTING BACK.
AND THAT INVOLVES YOU.
I DON'T LIKE THE SOUND OF THIS...
ZOE'S THE OLDEST. SELL HER FIRST!
KIRKMAN & SCOTT
©2016, BABY BLUES PARTNERSHIP DIST. BY KING FEATURES SYNDICATE 11-8

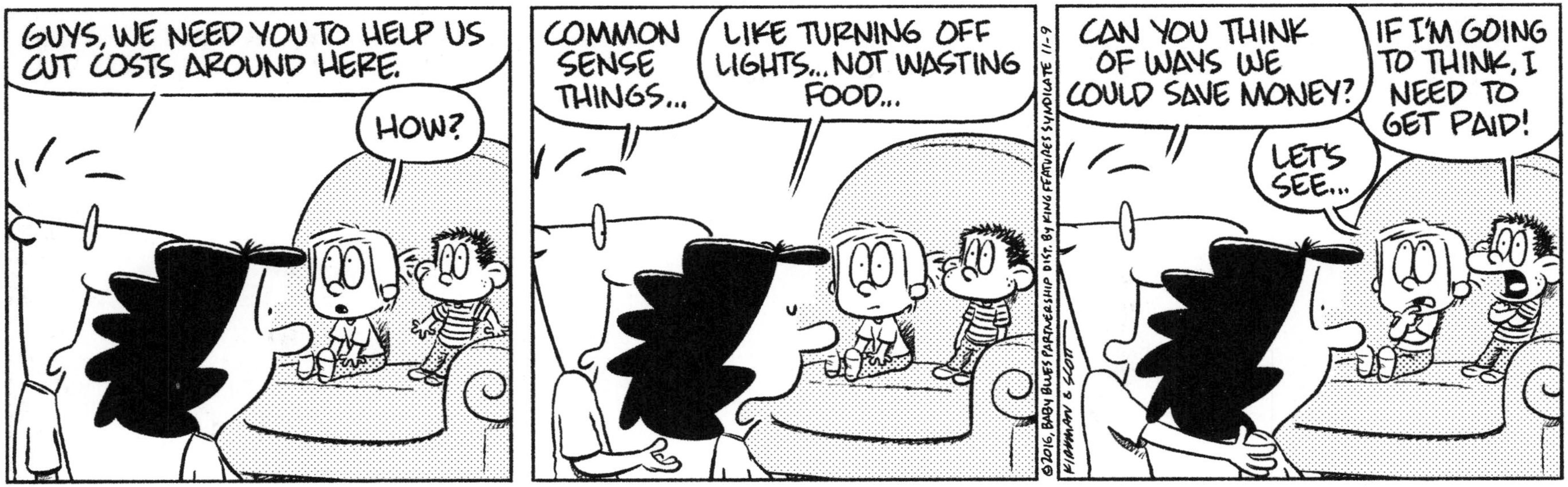
GUYS, WE NEED YOU TO HELP US CUT COSTS AROUND HERE.
HOW?
COMMON SENSE THINGS...
LIKE TURNING OFF LIGHTS... NOT WASTING FOOD...
©2016, BABY BLUES PARTNERSHIP DIST. BY KING FEATURES SYNDICATE 11-9
KIRKMAN & SCOTT
CAN YOU THINK OF WAYS WE COULD SAVE MONEY?
LET'S SEE...
IF I'M GOING TO THINK, I NEED TO GET PAID!

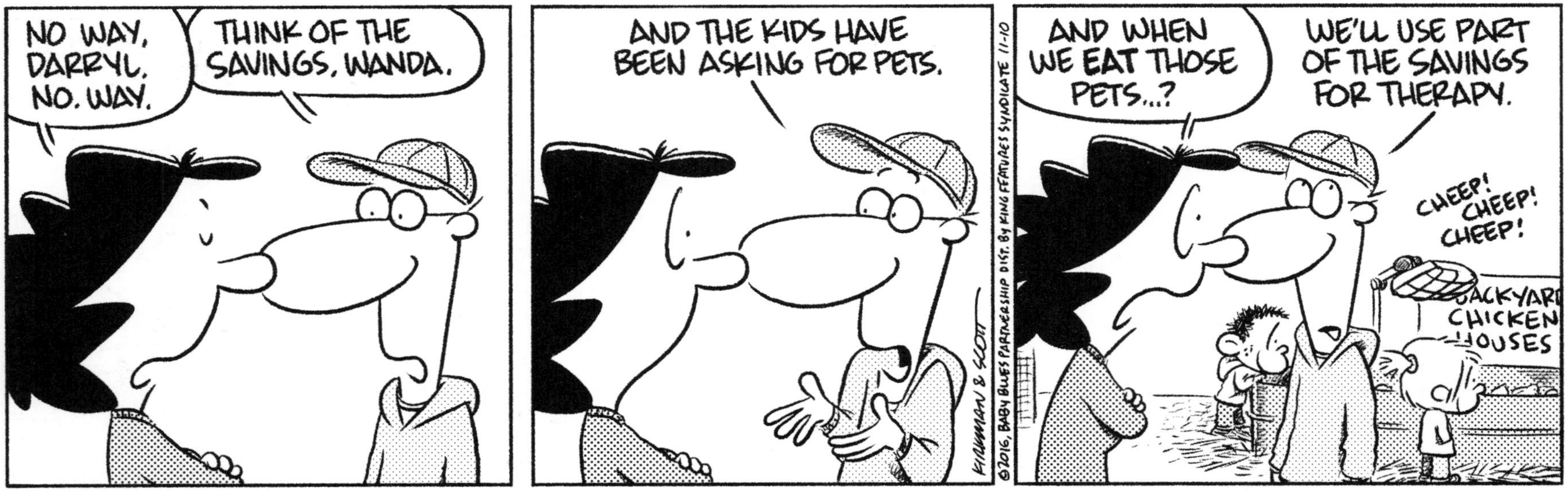
NO WAY, DARRYL. NO. WAY.
THINK OF THE SAVINGS, WANDA.
AND THE KIDS HAVE BEEN ASKING FOR PETS.
©2016, BABY BLUES PARTNERSHIP DIST. BY KING FEATURES SYNDICATE 11-10
KIRKMAN & SCOTT
AND WHEN WE EAT THOSE PETS...?
WE'LL USE PART OF THE SAVINGS FOR THERAPY.
CHEEP! CHEEP! CHEEP!

Jerry: We had backyard chickens when the kids were little. It was a great way to teach responsibility and to get fresh eggs for about six bucks apiece.

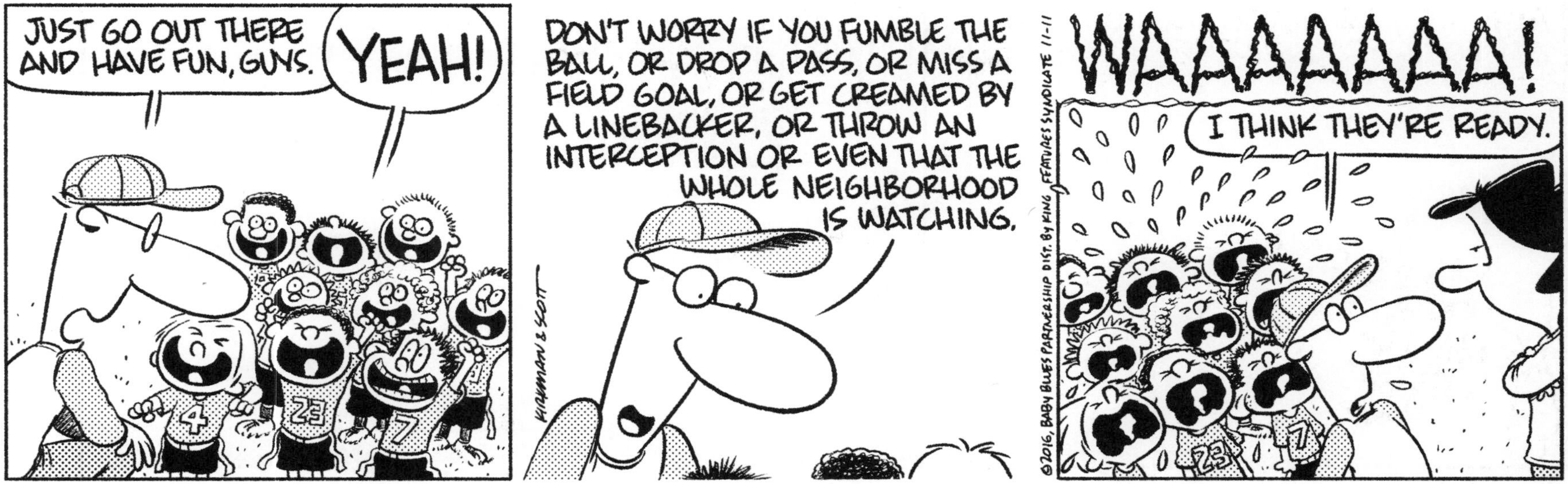
JUST GO OUT THERE AND HAVE FUN, GUYS.
YEAH!
DON'T WORRY IF YOU FUMBLE THE BALL, OR DROP A PASS, OR MISS A FIELD GOAL, OR GET CREAMED BY A LINEBACKER, OR THROW AN INTERCEPTION OR EVEN THAT THE WHOLE NEIGHBORHOOD IS WATCHING.
WAAAAAAA!
I THINK THEY'RE READY.
KIRKMAN & SCOTT
©2016, BABY BLUES PARTNERSHIP DIST. BY KING FEATURES SYNDICATE 11-11

Rick: Vince Lombardi, he's not.

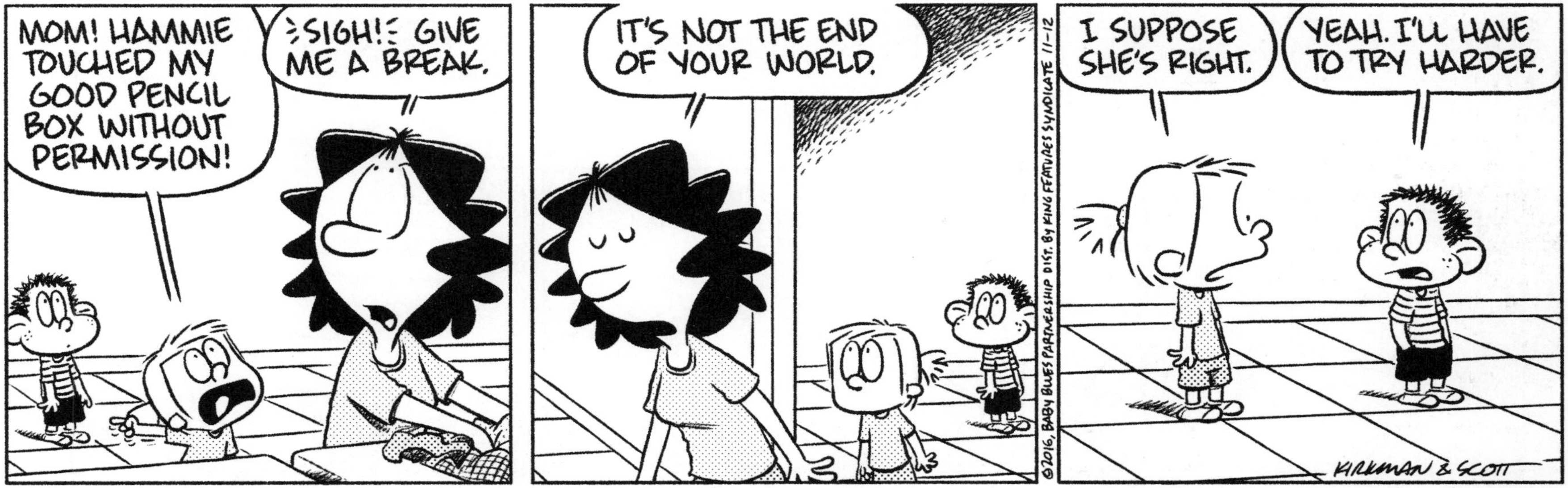
MOM! HAMMIE TOUCHED MY GOOD PENCIL BOX WITHOUT PERMISSION!
SIGH! GIVE ME A BREAK.
IT'S NOT THE END OF YOUR WORLD.
I SUPPOSE SHE'S RIGHT.
YEAH. I'LL HAVE TO TRY HARDER.
©2016, BABY BLUES PARTNERSHIP DIST. BY KING FEATURES SYNDICATE 11-12
KIRKMAN & SCOTT

BABY BLUES®
BY RICK KIRKMAN / JERRY SCOTT
FWEET!
53

TWEET! TWEET! TWEEEEEET!
WHAT'S WITH THE LITTLE YELLOW CLOTH?
PENALTY FLAG. SOMEBODY MUST HAVE DONE SOMETHING WRONG.
11-13
KIRKMAN & SCOTT
SO WHEN SOMEBODY MAKES A MISTAKE, MR. STRIPEY-SHIRT THROWS THAT CLOTH IN THE AIR?
HE'S CALLED A REFEREE, BUT YEAH.
NOW THE REFEREE WILL ANNOUNCE WHAT HAPPENED, AND TELL US WHO DID IT.
HOLDING! OFFENSE! NUMBER 53!
©2016, BABY BLUES PARTNERSHIP DIST. BY KING FEATURES SYNDICATE
SO FOOTBALL IS ABOUT PUBLIC SHAMING?
ARE YOU CAUGHT UP ON HOMEWORK?

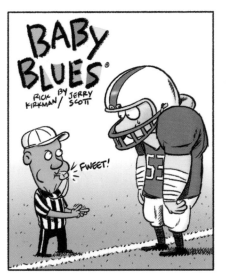

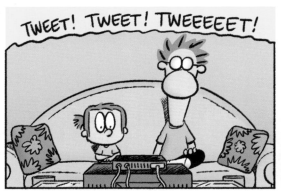

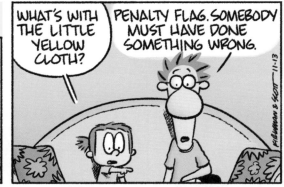

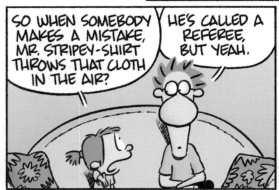

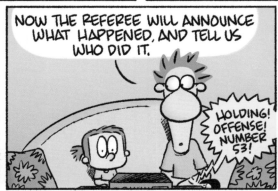

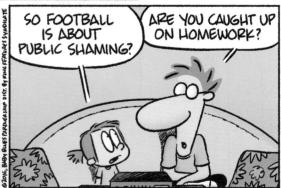

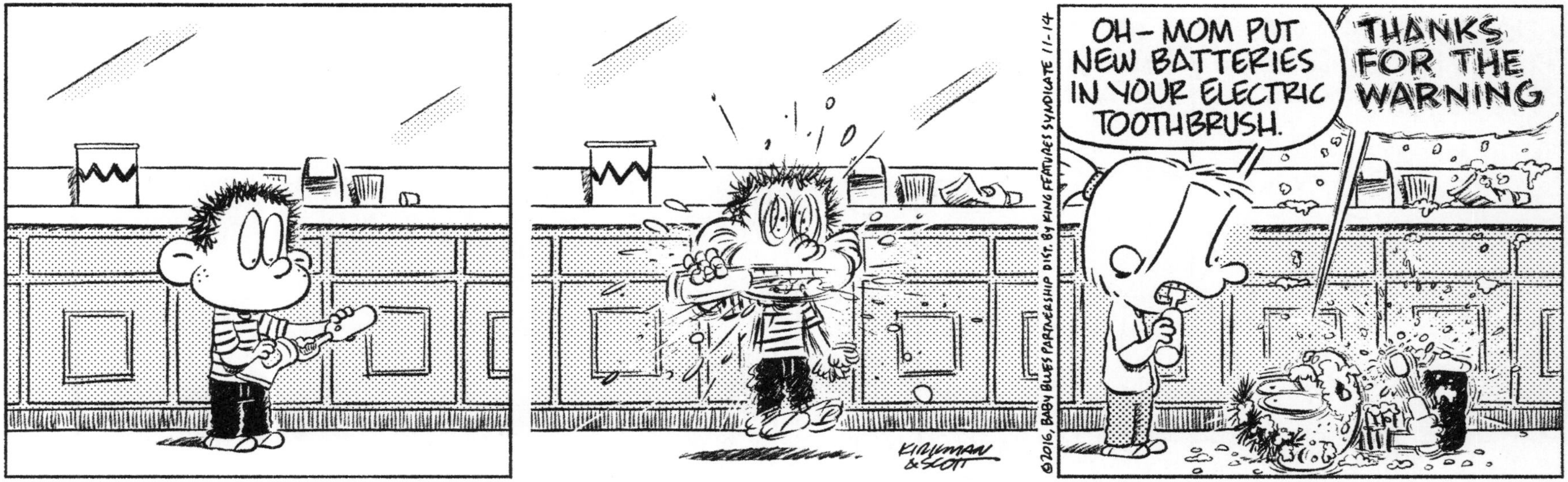
OH–MOM PUT NEW BATTERIES IN YOUR ELECTRIC TOOTHBRUSH.
THANKS FOR THE WARNING
KIRKMAN & SCOTT
©2016, BABY BLUES PARTNERSHIP DIST. BY KING FEATURES SYNDICATE 11-14

Rick: I got a new electric toothbrush, and I wondered what Hammie would look like using it. I drew a sketch and sent it to Jerry, and he came up with this.

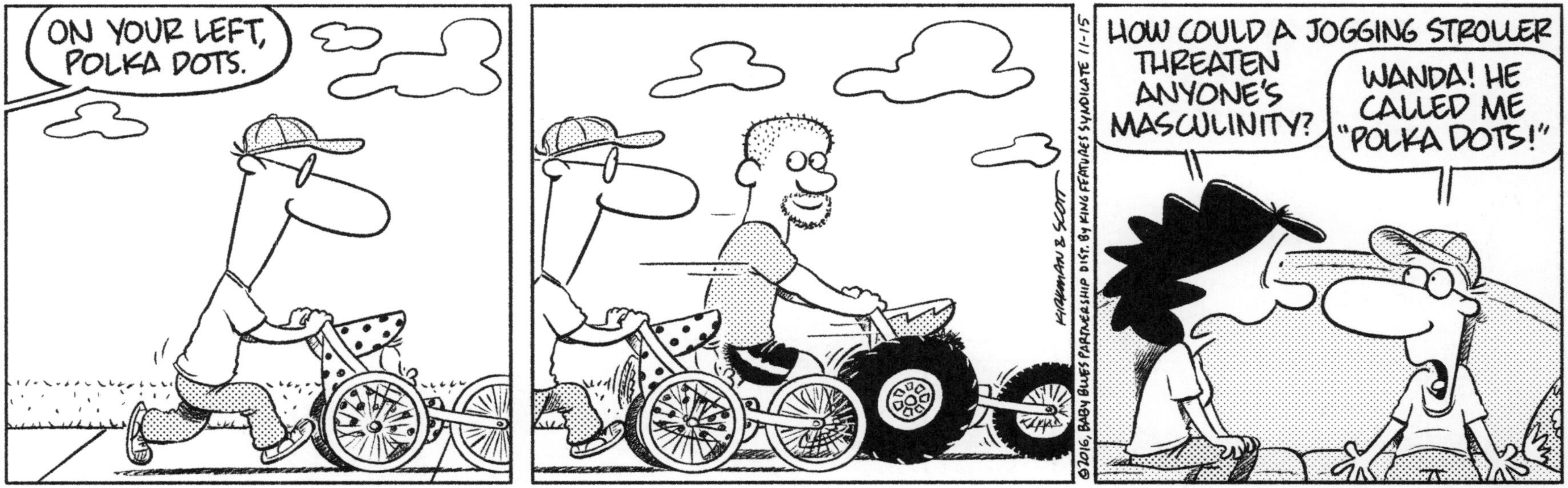
ON YOUR LEFT, POLKA DOTS.
KIRKMAN & SCOTT
©2016, BABY BLUES PARTNERSHIP DIST. BY KING FEATURES SYNDICATE 11-15
HOW COULD A JOGGING STROLLER THREATEN ANYONE'S MASCULINITY?
WANDA! HE CALLED ME "POLKA DOTS!"

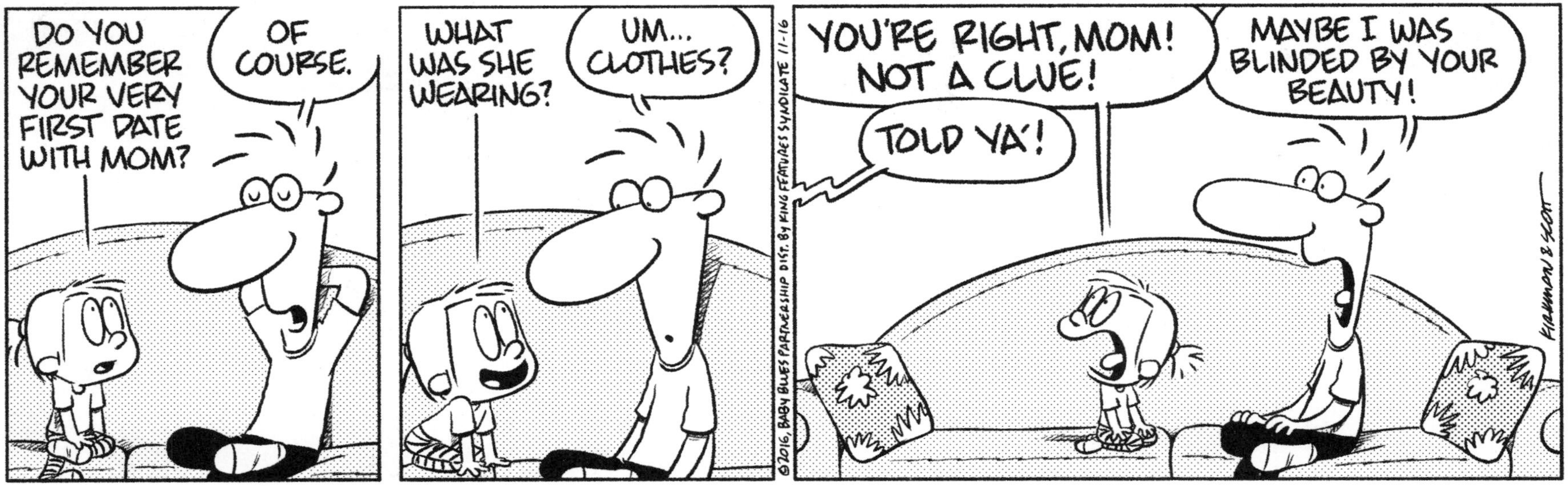
DO YOU REMEMBER YOUR VERY FIRST DATE WITH MOM?
OF COURSE.
WHAT WAS SHE WEARING?
UM... CLOTHES?
©2016, BABY BLUES PARTNERSHIP DIST. BY KING FEATURES SYNDICATE 11-16
YOU'RE RIGHT, MOM! NOT A CLUE!
TOLD YA'!
MAYBE I WAS BLINDED BY YOUR BEAUTY!
KIRKMAN & SCOTT

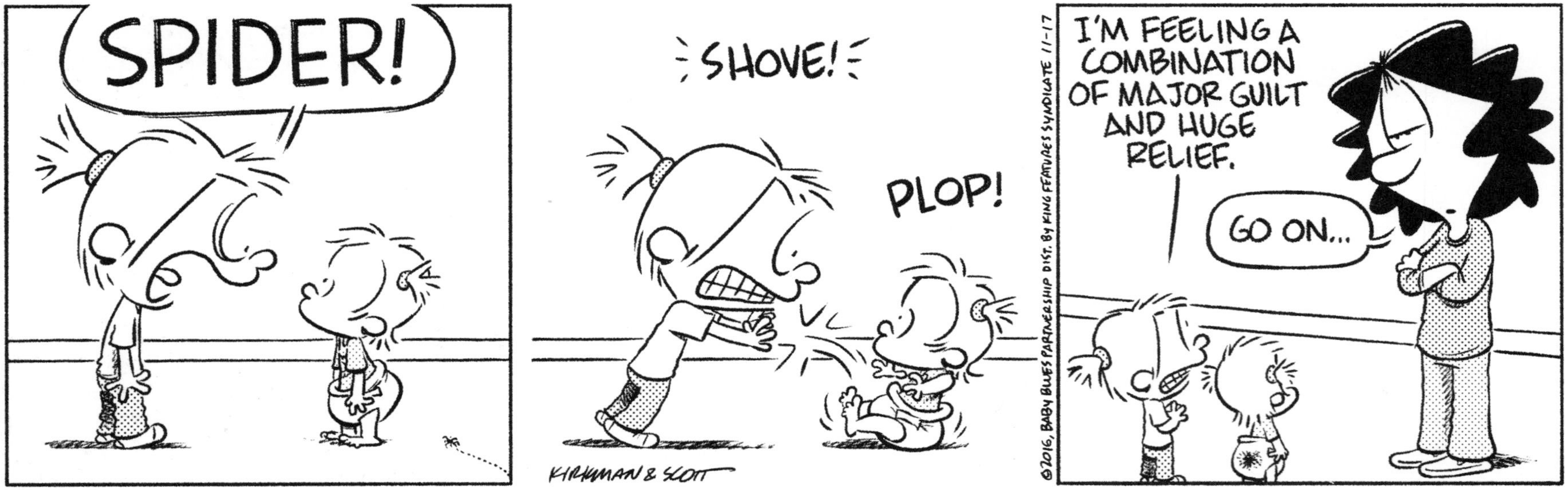
SPIDER!
SHOVE!
PLOP!
KIRKMAN & SCOTT
©2016, BABY BLUES PARTNERSHIP DIST. BY KING FEATURES SYNDICATE 11-17
I'M FEELING A COMBINATION OF MAJOR GUILT AND HUGE RELIEF.
GO ON...

Rick: Improvising is a sign of maturity. Or sometimes sheer terror.

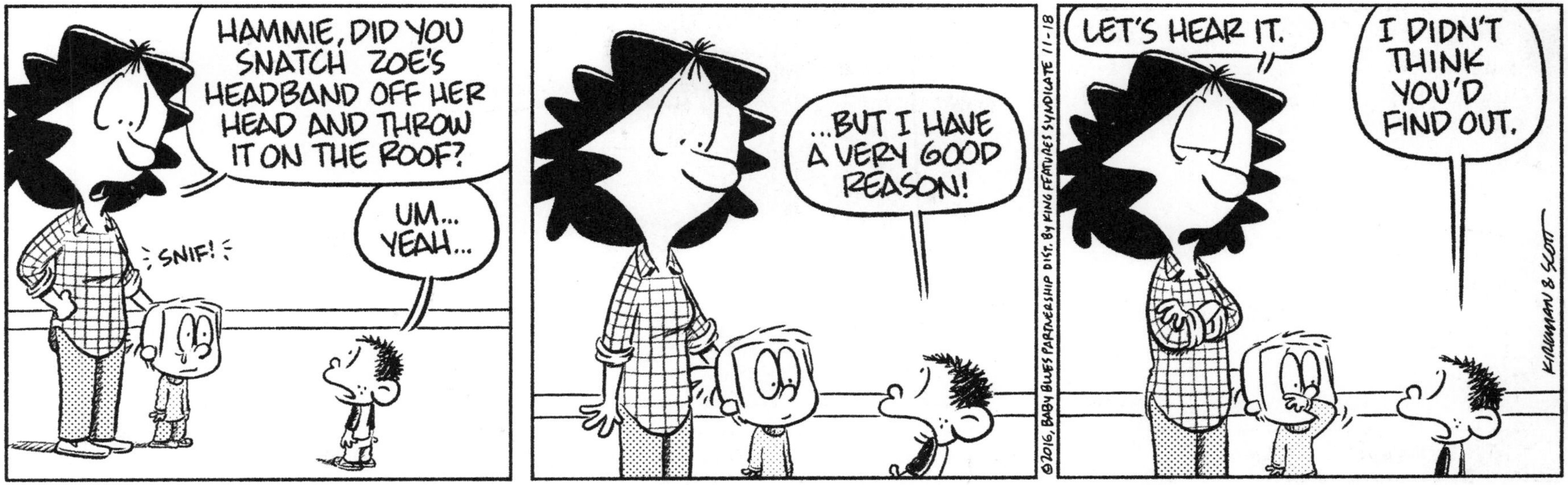
HAMMIE, DID YOU SNATCH ZOE'S HEADBAND OFF HER HEAD AND THROW IT ON THE ROOF?
SNIF!
UM... YEAH...
...BUT I HAVE A VERY GOOD REASON!
©2016, BABY BLUES PARTNERSHIP DIST. BY KING FEATURES SYNDICATE 11-18
LET'S HEAR IT.
I DIDN'T THINK YOU'D FIND OUT.
KIRKMAN & SCOTT

Jerry: The truth will set you free . . . except not really.

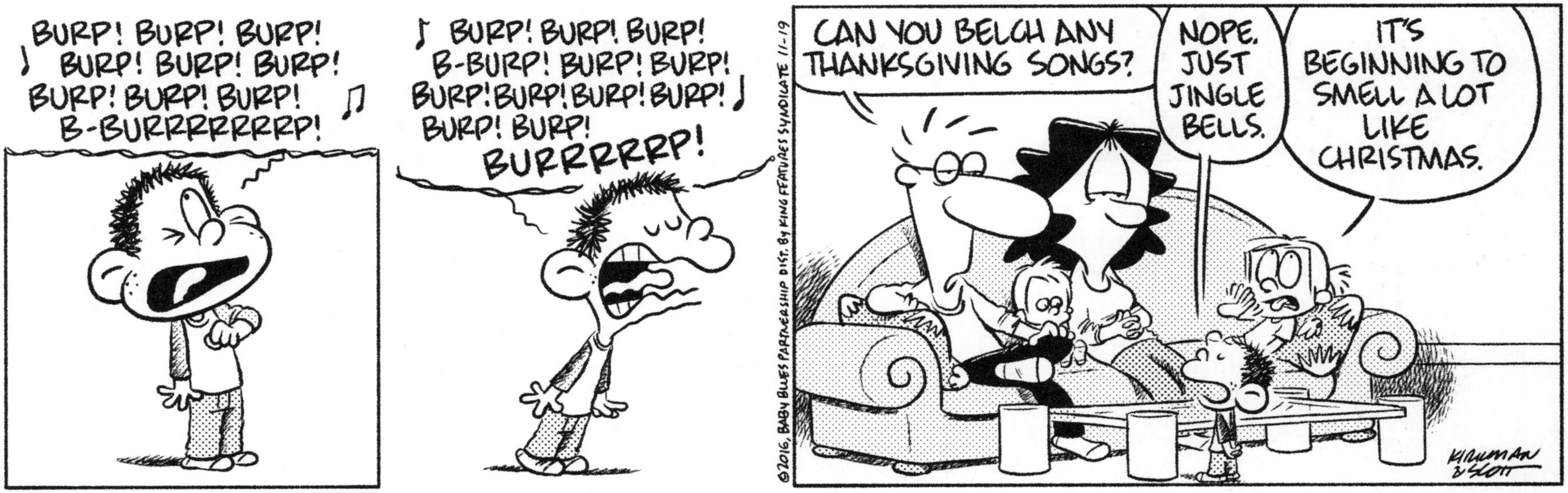
BURP! BURP! BURP! BURP! BURP! BURP! BURP! BURP! BURP! B-BURRRRRRRP!
BURP! BURP! BURP! B-BURP! BURP! BURP! BURP! BURP! BURP! BURP! BURP! BURP! BURRRRRP!
©2016, BABY BLUES PARTNERSHIP DIST. BY KING FEATURES SYNDICATE 11-19
CAN YOU BELCH ANY THANKSGIVING SONGS?
NOPE. JUST JINGLE BELLS.
IT'S BEGINNING TO SMELL A LOT LIKE CHRISTMAS.
KIRKMAN & SCOTT

Baby Blues®
Rick Kirkman & Jerry Scott
ZZZZZZ

HEY MOM! CAN I JUMP IN THE BIG PILE OF LEAVES?
NO!
NO. NO. NO. YOU'LL GET ALL DIRTY AND GROSS, AND I'LL BE VACUUMING LEAF CRUMBS OUT OF THE CARPET FOR A WEEK!
SERIOUSLY?
©2016, BABY BLUES PARTNERSHIP DIST. BY KING FEATURES SYNDICATE
YOU HEARD ME.
OKAY...
KIRKMAN & SCOTT 11-20
PREPARE YOUR DEFENSE.

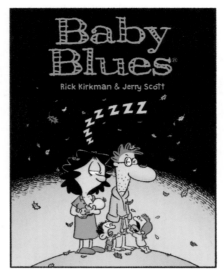

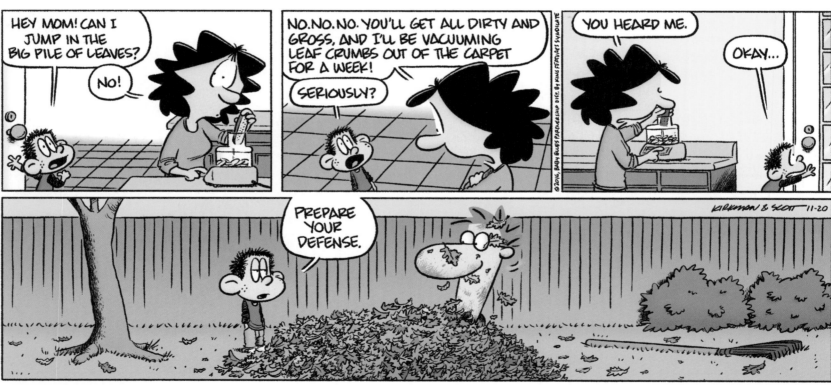

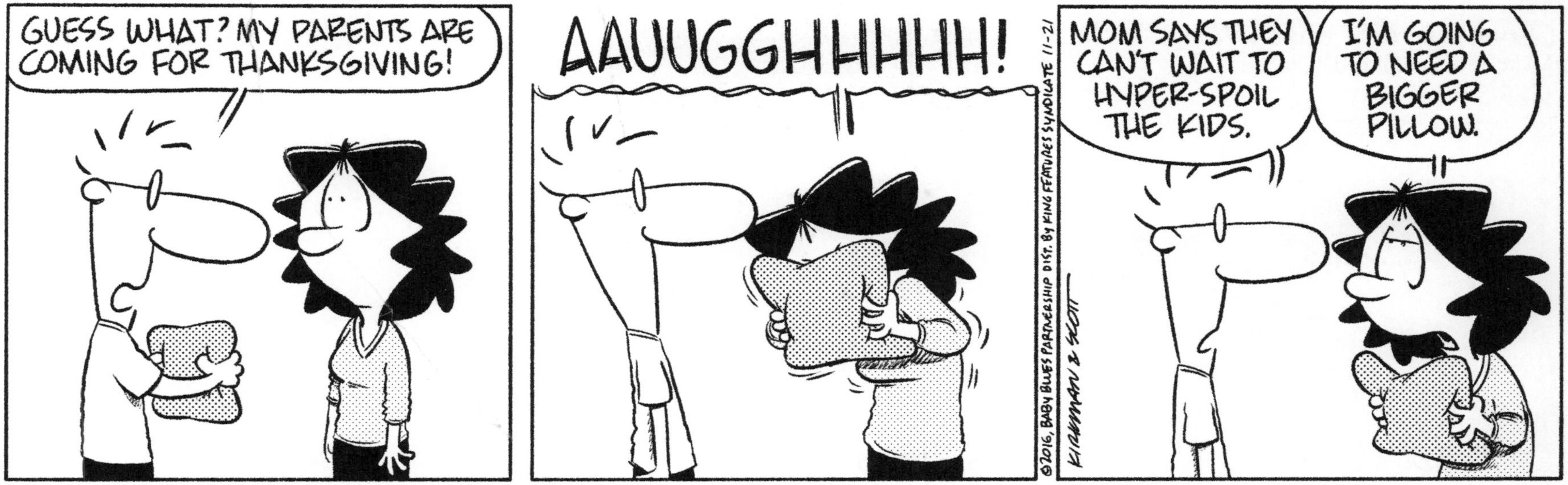
GUESS WHAT? MY PARENTS ARE COMING FOR THANKSGIVING!
AAUUGGHHHHH!
MOM SAYS THEY CAN'T WAIT TO HYPER-SPOIL THE KIDS.
I'M GOING TO NEED A BIGGER PILLOW.
©2016, BABY BLUES PARTNERSHIP DIST. BY KING FEATURES SYNDICATE 11-21
KIRKMAN & SCOTT

Jerry: Cleaning the house for company is how you discover what slobs you really are.

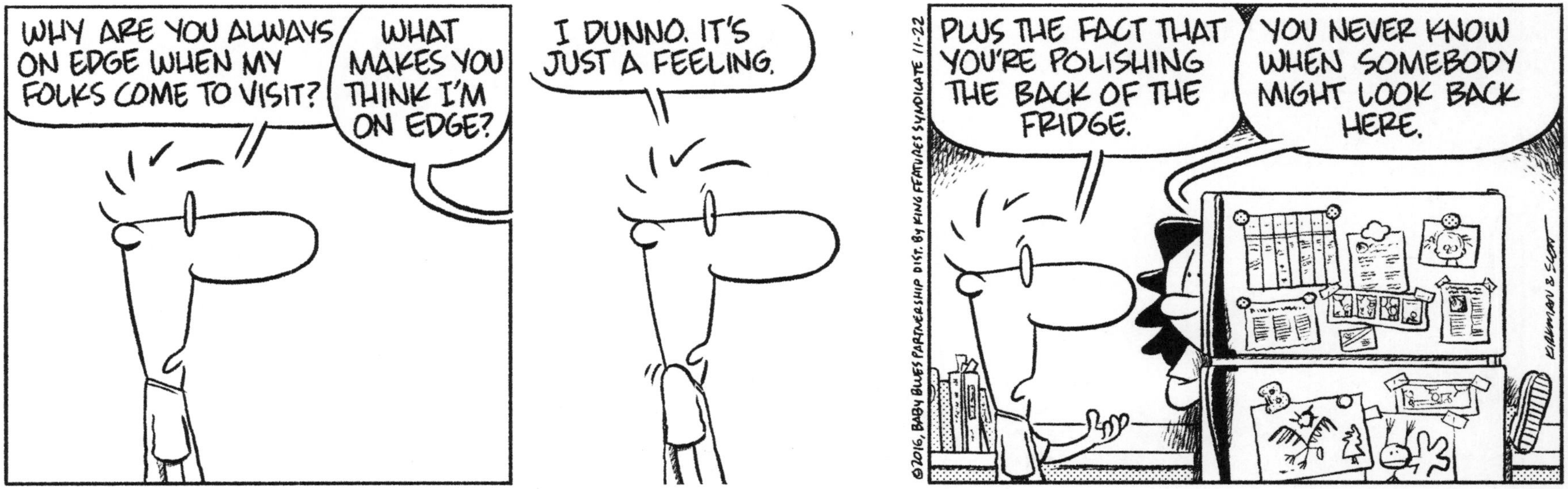
WHY ARE YOU ALWAYS ON EDGE WHEN MY FOLKS COME TO VISIT?
WHAT MAKES YOU THINK I'M ON EDGE?
I DUNNO. IT'S JUST A FEELING.
PLUS THE FACT THAT YOU'RE POLISHING THE BACK OF THE FRIDGE.
YOU NEVER KNOW WHEN SOMEBODY MIGHT LOOK BACK HERE.
©2016, BABY BLUES PARTNERSHIP DIST. BY KING FEATURES SYNDICATE 11-22
KIRKMAN & SCOTT

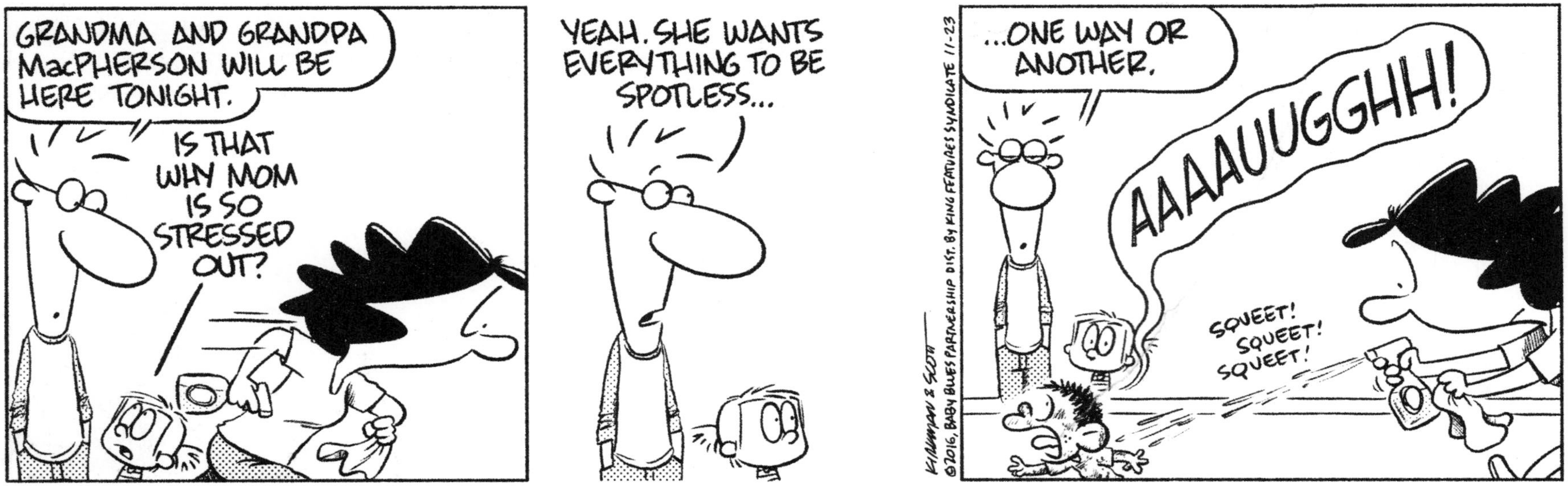
GRANDMA AND GRANDPA MacPHERSON WILL BE HERE TONIGHT.
IS THAT WHY MOM IS SO STRESSED OUT?
YEAH. SHE WANTS EVERYTHING TO BE SPOTLESS...
...ONE WAY OR ANOTHER.
AAAAUUGGHH!
SQUEET! SQUEET! SQUEET!
KIRKMAN & SCOTT
©2016, BABY BLUES PARTNERSHIP DIST. BY KING FEATURES SYNDICATE 11-23

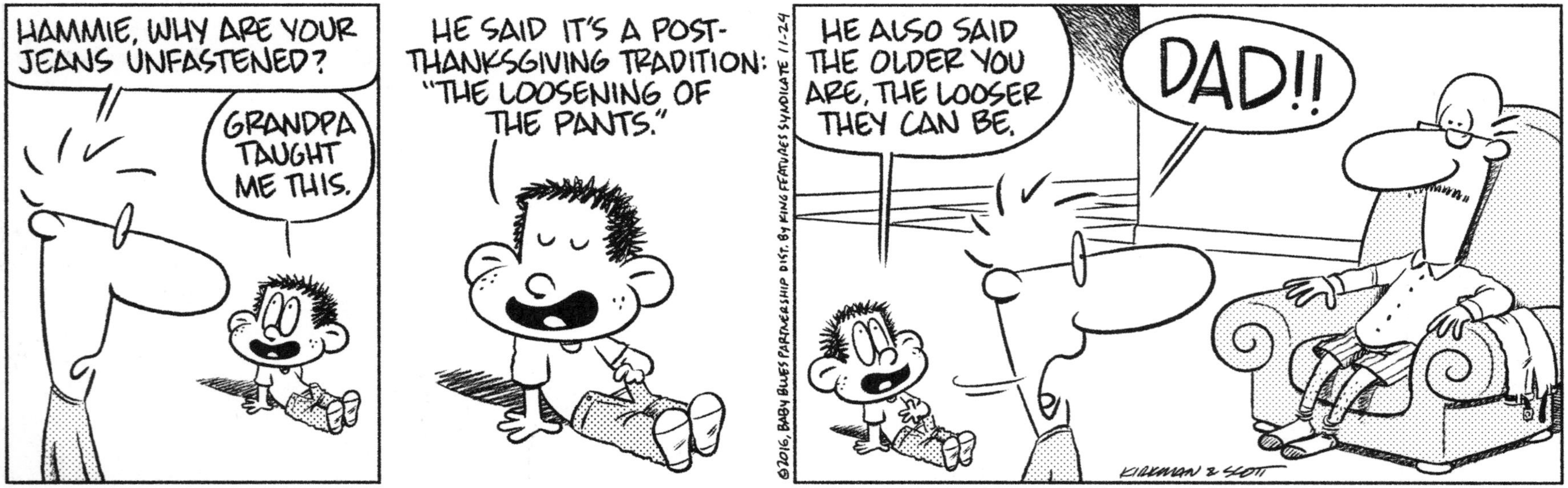
HAMMIE, WHY ARE YOUR JEANS UNFASTENED?
GRANDPA TAUGHT ME THIS.
HE SAID IT'S A POST-THANKSGIVING TRADITION: "THE LOOSENING OF THE PANTS."
©2016, BABY BLUES PARTNERSHIP DIST. BY KING FEATURES SYNDICATE 11-24
HE ALSO SAID THE OLDER YOU ARE, THE LOOSER THEY CAN BE.
DAD!!
KIRKMAN & SCOTT

Rick: Aren't grandparents supposed to pass down their well-earned wisdom?

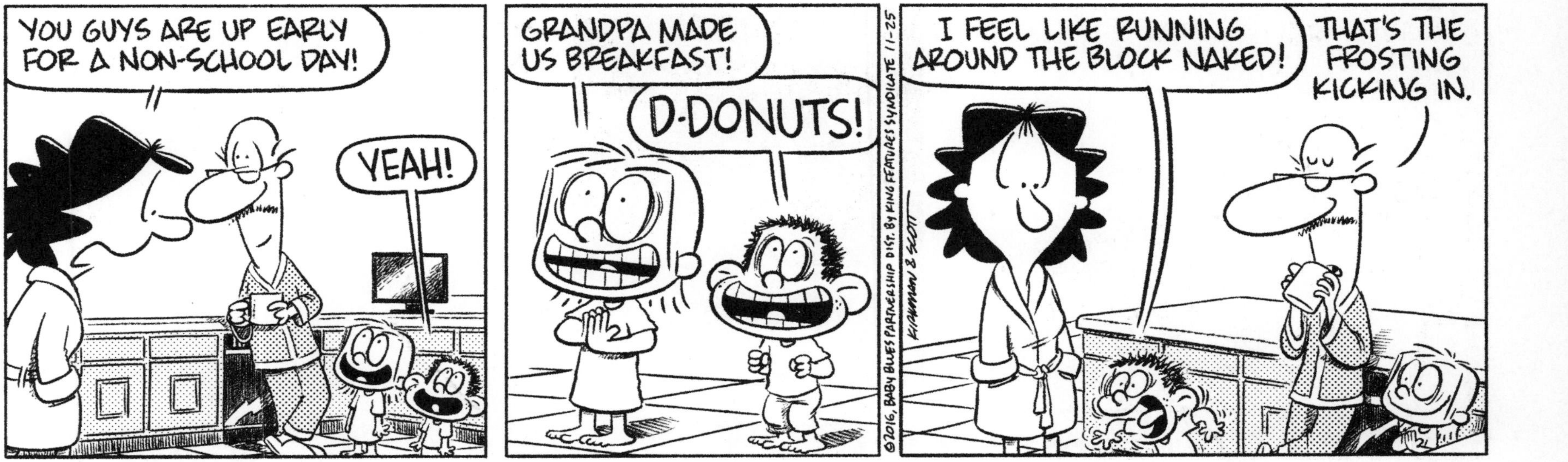
YOU GUYS ARE UP EARLY FOR A NON-SCHOOL DAY!
YEAH!
GRANDPA MADE US BREAKFAST!
D-DONUTS!
©2016, BABY BLUES PARTNERSHIP DIST. BY KING FEATURES SYNDICATE 11-25
KIRKMAN & SCOTT
I FEEL LIKE RUNNING AROUND THE BLOCK NAKED!
THAT'S THE FROSTING KICKING IN.

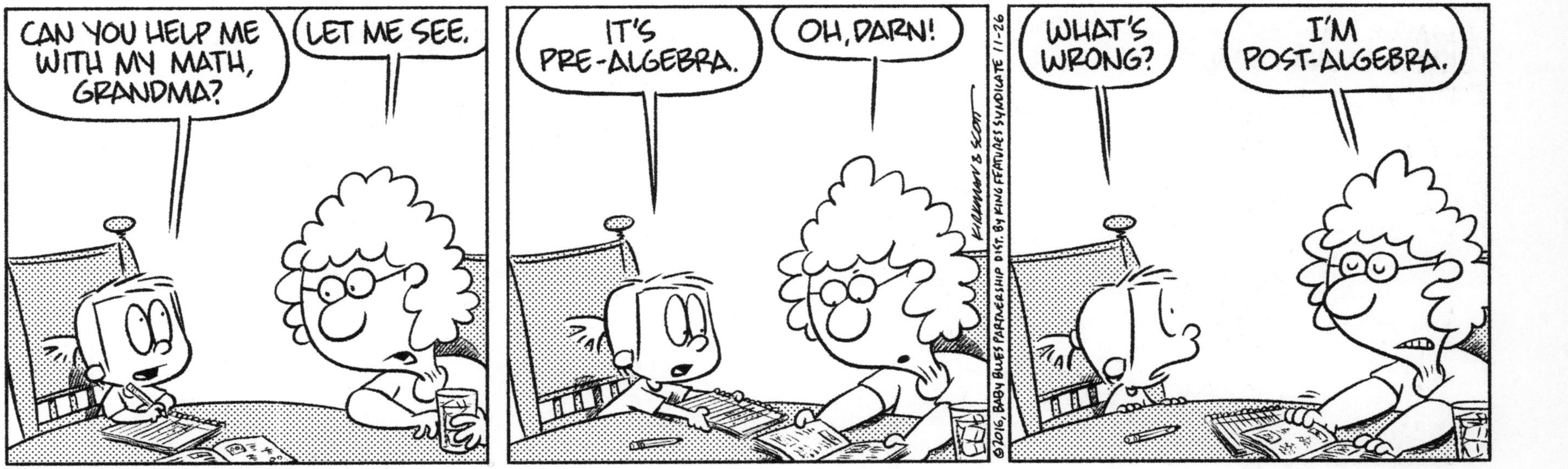
CAN YOU HELP ME WITH MY MATH, GRANDMA?
LET ME SEE.
IT'S PRE-ALGEBRA.
OH, DARN!
©2016, BABY BLUES PARTNERSHIP DIST. BY KING FEATURES SYNDICATE 11-26
KIRKMAN & SCOTT
WHAT'S WRONG?
I'M POST-ALGEBRA.

Rick: Nice save.

BABY BLUES®
Rick Kirkman & Jerry Scott
ZZZZZ

BZZZ
PLING!
PLING!
BZZZ
IT LOOKS LIKE ZOE IS HAVING FUN AT THE MALL.
ADMIT ONE
I DON'T THINK HAMMIE IS, THOUGH.
KIRKMAN & SCOTT 11-27
©2016, BABY BLUES PARTNERSHIP DIST. BY KING FEATURES SYNDICATE
OR WANDA.
SIGH I WONDER IF PEOPLE WILL BE USING WORDS AGAIN BY THE TIME YOU'RE OLD ENOUGH TO TEXT, WREN.

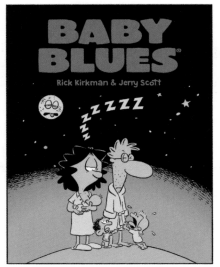

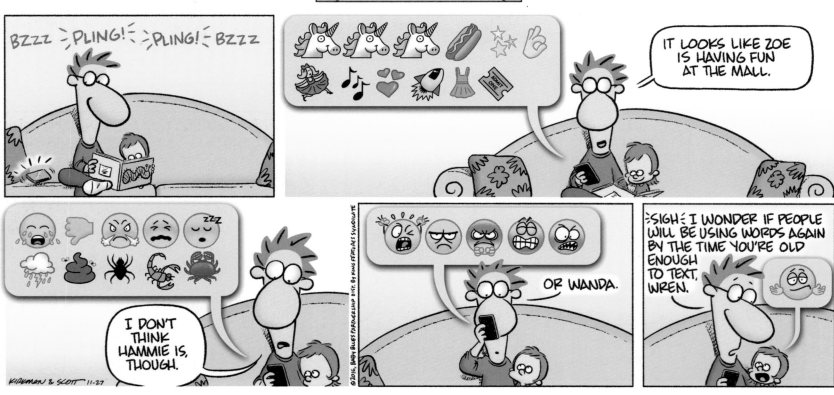

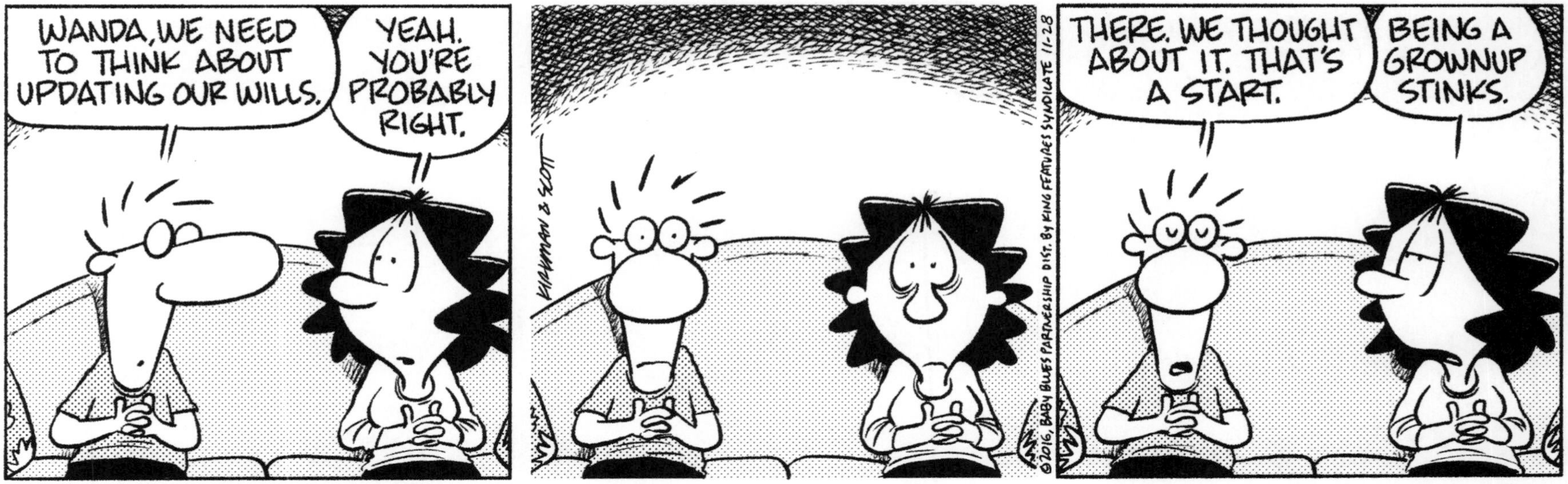
WANDA, WE NEED TO THINK ABOUT UPDATING OUR WILLS.
YEAH. YOU'RE PROBABLY RIGHT.
KIRKMAN & SCOTT
©2016, BABY BLUES PARTNERSHIP DIST. BY KING FEATURES SYNDICATE 11-28
THERE. WE THOUGHT ABOUT IT. THAT'S A START.
BEING A GROWNUP STINKS.

Jerry: A lot of the strip's content comes from real life. Whatever is going on in *Baby Blues* is probably going on in Rick's life or mine . . . but with added funny.

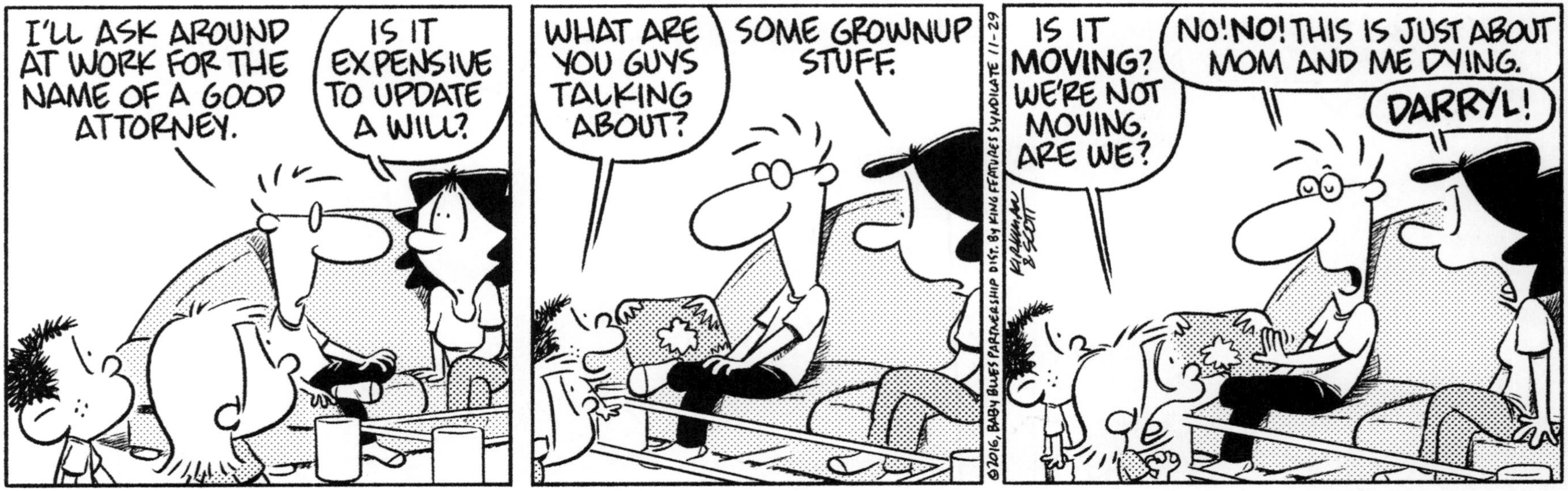
I'LL ASK AROUND AT WORK FOR THE NAME OF A GOOD ATTORNEY.
IS IT EXPENSIVE TO UPDATE A WILL?
WHAT ARE YOU GUYS TALKING ABOUT?
SOME GROWNUP STUFF.
©2016, BABY BLUES PARTNERSHIP DIST. BY KING FEATURES SYNDICATE 11-29
KIRKMAN & SCOTT
IS IT MOVING? WE'RE NOT MOVING, ARE WE?
NO! NO! THIS IS JUST ABOUT MOM AND ME DYING.
DARRYL!

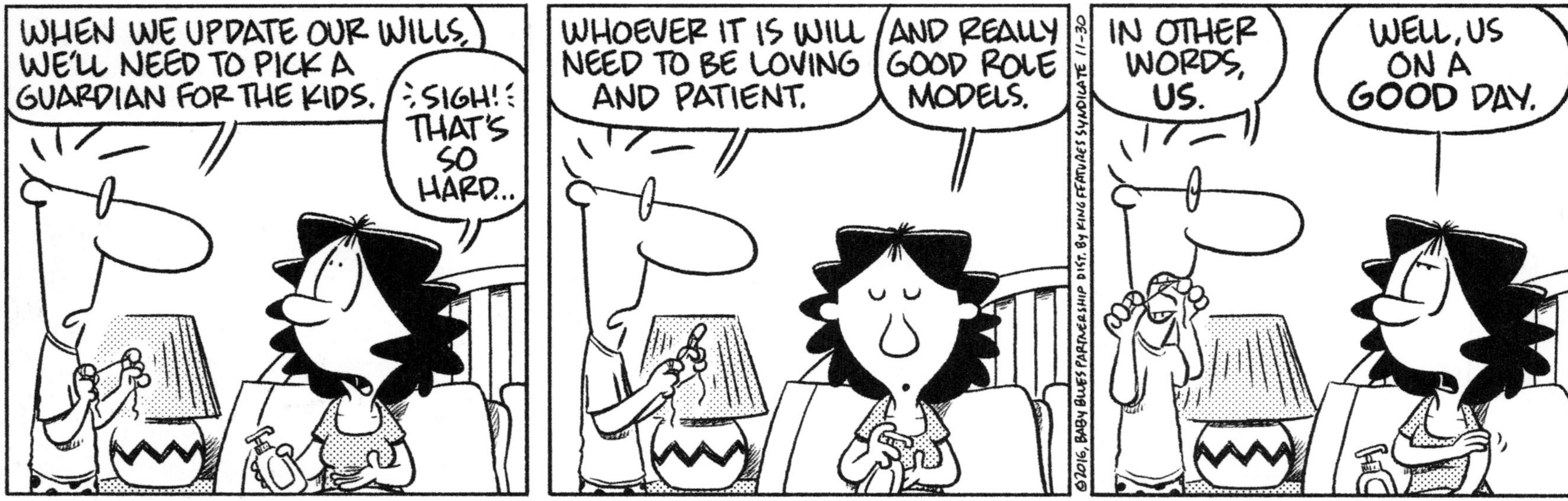
WHEN WE UPDATE OUR WILLS, WE'LL NEED TO PICK A GUARDIAN FOR THE KIDS.
SIGH! THAT'S SO HARD...
WHOEVER IT IS WILL NEED TO BE LOVING AND PATIENT.
AND REALLY GOOD ROLE MODELS.
©2016, BABY BLUES PARTNERSHIP DIST. BY KING FEATURES SYNDICATE 11-30
IN OTHER WORDS, US.
WELL, US ON A GOOD DAY.
KIRKMAN & SCOTT

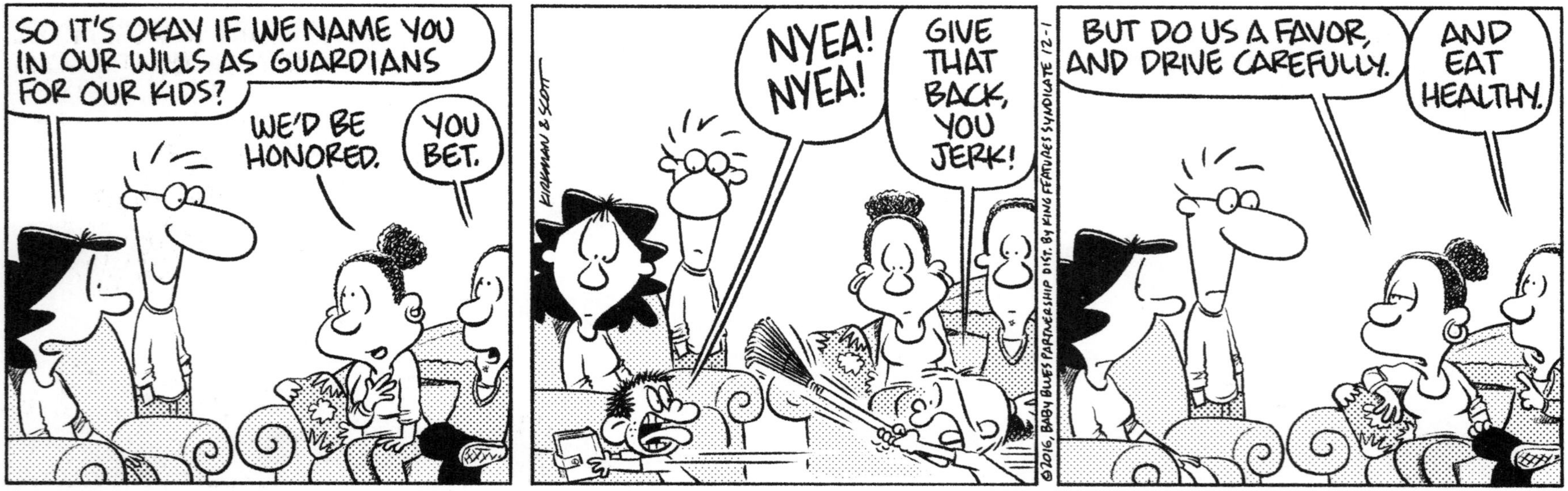
SO IT'S OKAY IF WE NAME YOU IN OUR WILLS AS GUARDIANS FOR OUR KIDS?
WE'D BE HONORED.
YOU BET.
KIRKMAN & SCOTT
NYEA! NYEA!
GIVE THAT BACK, YOU JERK!
©2016, BABY BLUES PARTNERSHIP DIST. BY KING FEATURES SYNDICATE 12-1
BUT DO US A FAVOR, AND DRIVE CAREFULLY.
AND EAT HEALTHY.

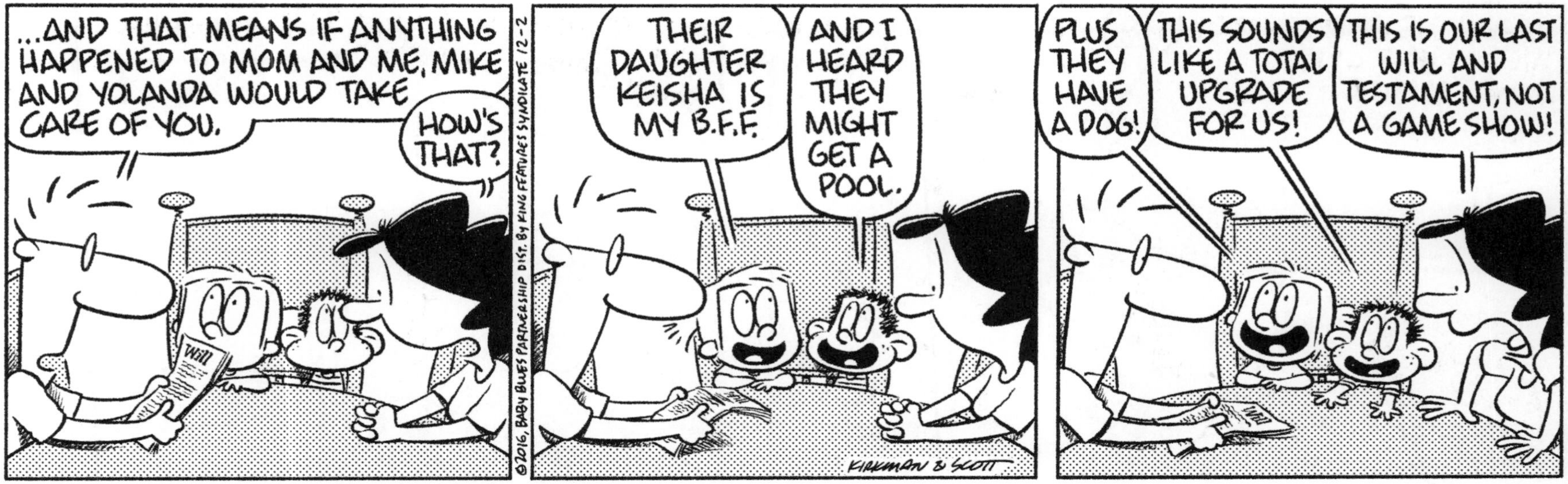
...AND THAT MEANS IF ANYTHING HAPPENED TO MOM AND ME, MIKE AND YOLANDA WOULD TAKE CARE OF YOU.
HOW'S THAT?
©2016, BABY BLUES PARTNERSHIP DIST. BY KING FEATURES SYNDICATE 12-2
THEIR DAUGHTER KEISHA IS MY B.F.F.
AND I HEARD THEY MIGHT GET A POOL.
KIRKMAN & SCOTT
PLUS THEY HAVE A DOG!
THIS SOUNDS LIKE A TOTAL UPGRADE FOR US!
THIS IS OUR LAST WILL AND TESTAMENT, NOT A GAME SHOW!

Rick: Looks like I had a brain cramp spelling Keesha's name. Let's just say she decided on an "alternate spelling."

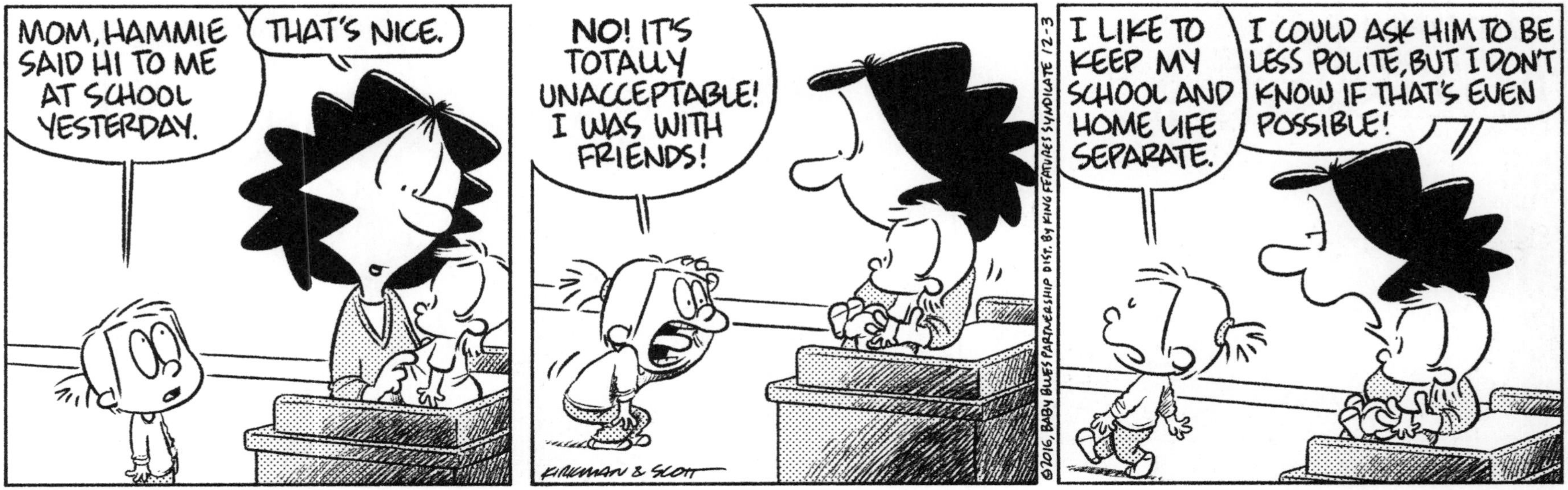
MOM, HAMMIE SAID HI TO ME AT SCHOOL YESTERDAY.
THAT'S NICE.
NO! IT'S TOTALLY UNACCEPTABLE! I WAS WITH FRIENDS!
KIRKMAN & SCOTT
©2016, BABY BLUES PARTNERSHIP DIST. BY KING FEATURES SYNDICATE 12-3
I LIKE TO KEEP MY SCHOOL AND HOME LIFE SEPARATE.
I COULD ASK HIM TO BE LESS POLITE, BUT I DON'T KNOW IF THAT'S EVEN POSSIBLE!

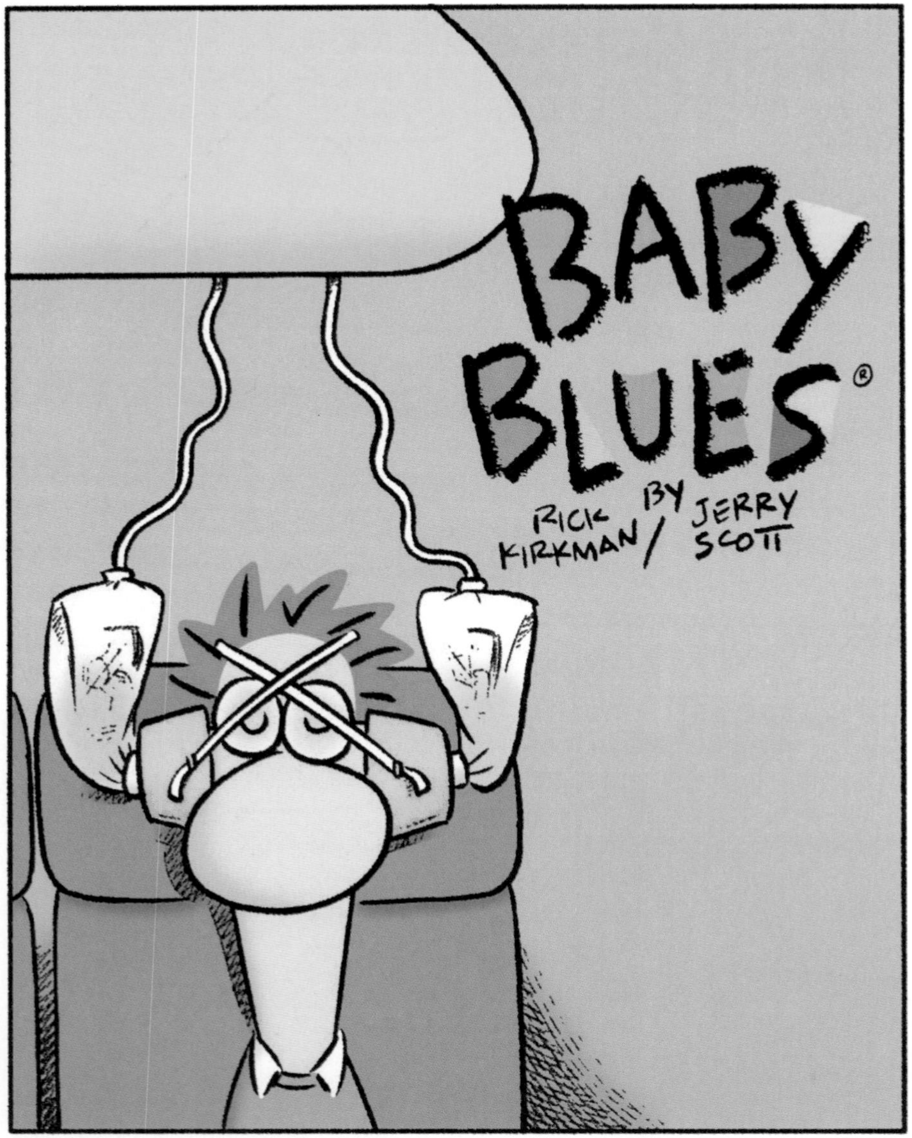
BABY BLUES®
RICK KIRKMAN BY JERRY SCOTT

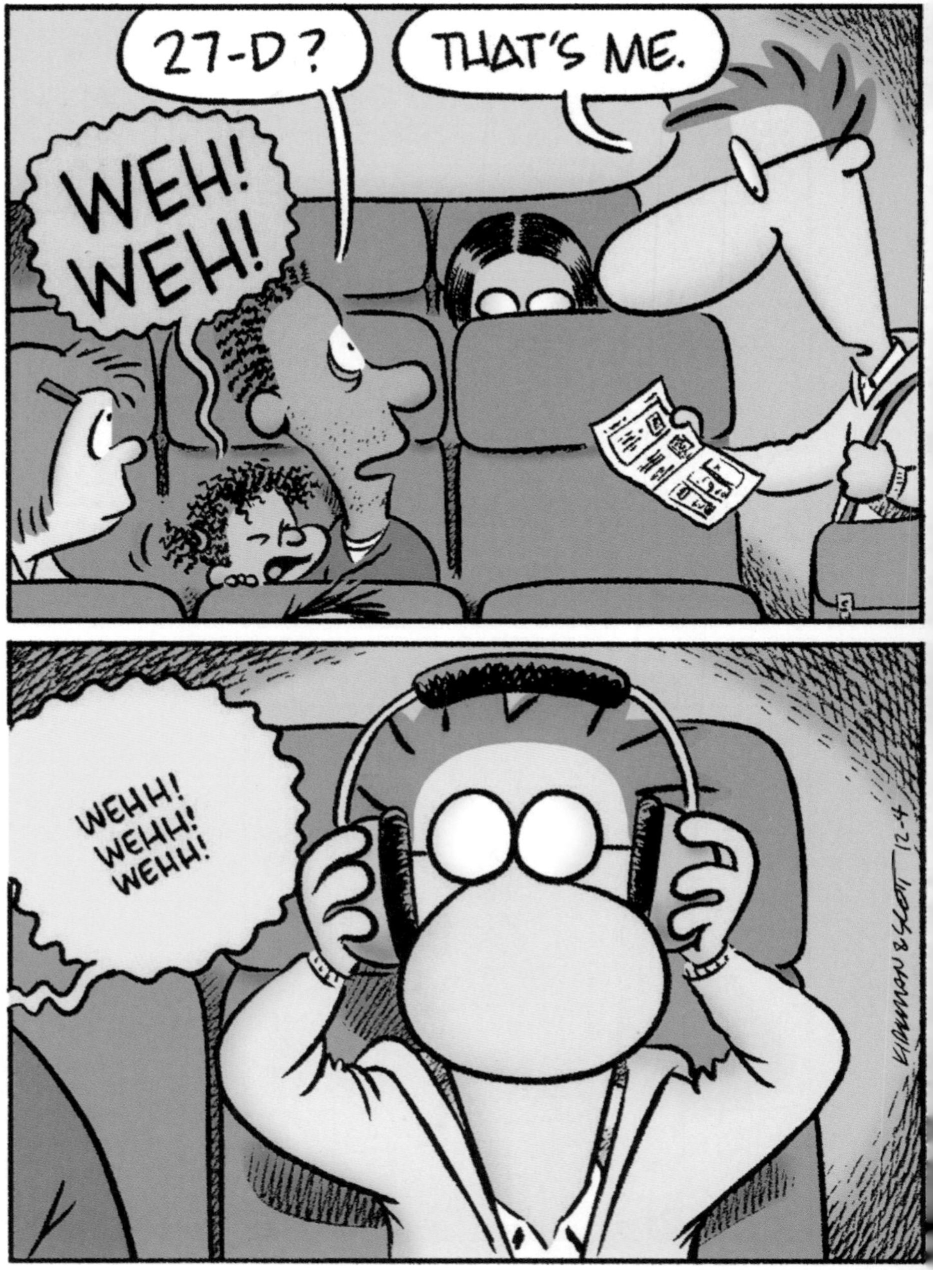
27-D?
THAT'S ME.
WEH! WEH!
WEHH! WEHH! WEHH!

Rick: Guaranteed totally true conversation I had on a plane, up until the Magic Hoodie. That was Jerry's perfect idea. I wonder if anyone ever looks at a strip and realizes they're in it.

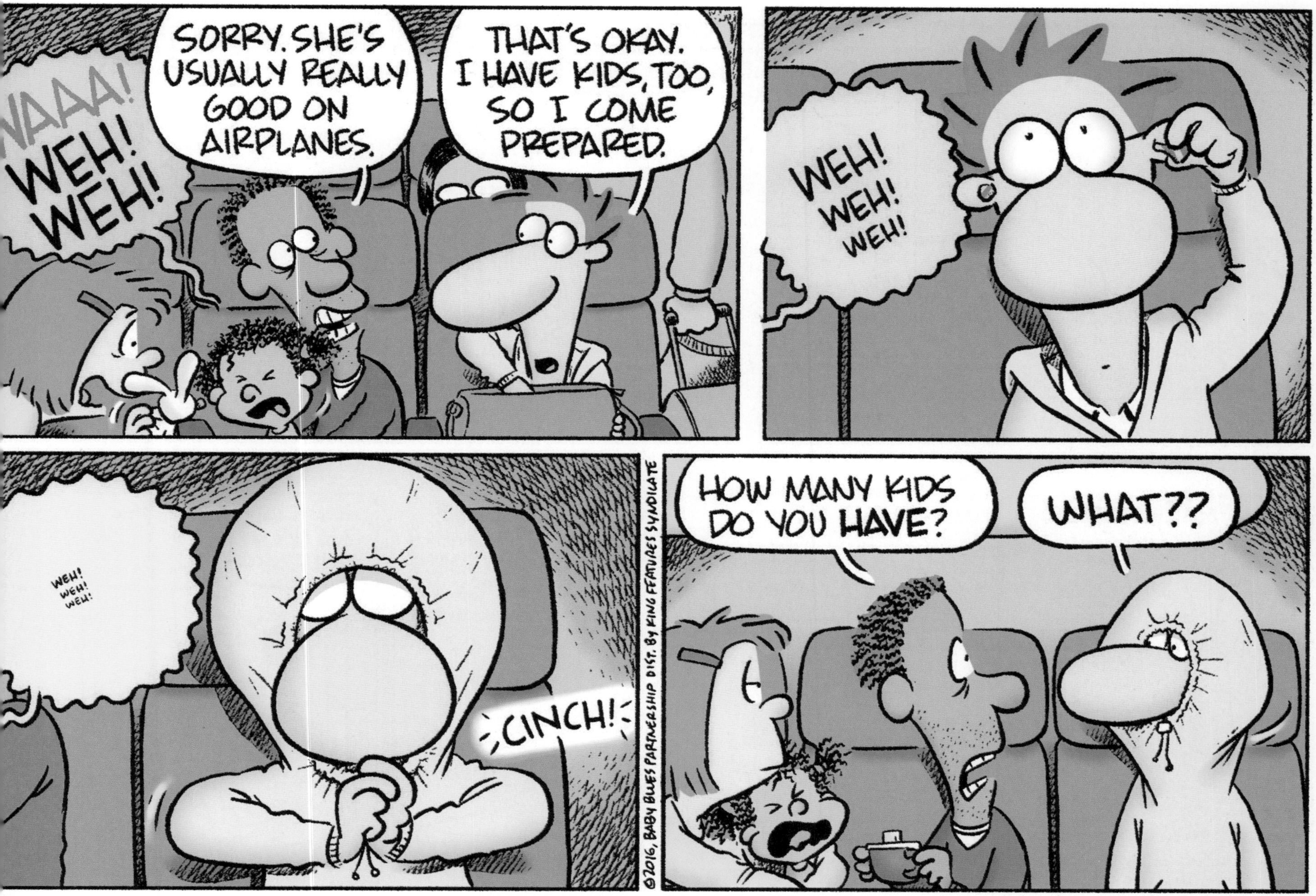
WAAA! WEH! WEH!
SORRY. SHE'S USUALLY REALLY GOOD ON AIRPLANES.
THAT'S OKAY. I HAVE KIDS, TOO, SO I COME PREPARED.
WEH! WEH! WEH!
WEH! WEH! WEH!
CINCH!
©2016, BABY BLUES PARTNERSHIP DIST. BY KING FEATURES SYNDICATE
HOW MANY KIDS DO YOU **HAVE**?
WHAT??

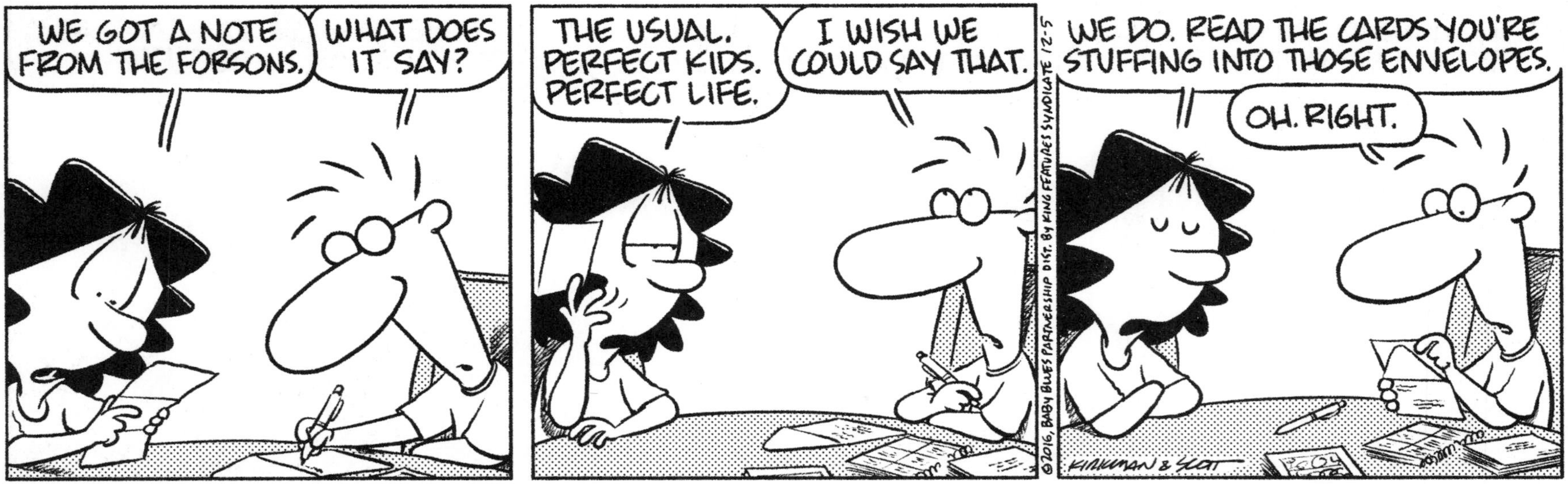
WE GOT A NOTE FROM THE FORSONS.
WHAT DOES IT SAY?
THE USUAL. PERFECT KIDS. PERFECT LIFE.
I WISH WE COULD SAY THAT.
WE DO. READ THE CARDS YOU'RE STUFFING INTO THOSE ENVELOPES.
OH. RIGHT.
©2016, BABY BLUES PARTNERSHIP DIST. BY KING FEATURES SYNDICATE 12-5
KIRKMAN & SCOTT

Rick: The pre-Facebook way to make your friends feel bad about their lives.

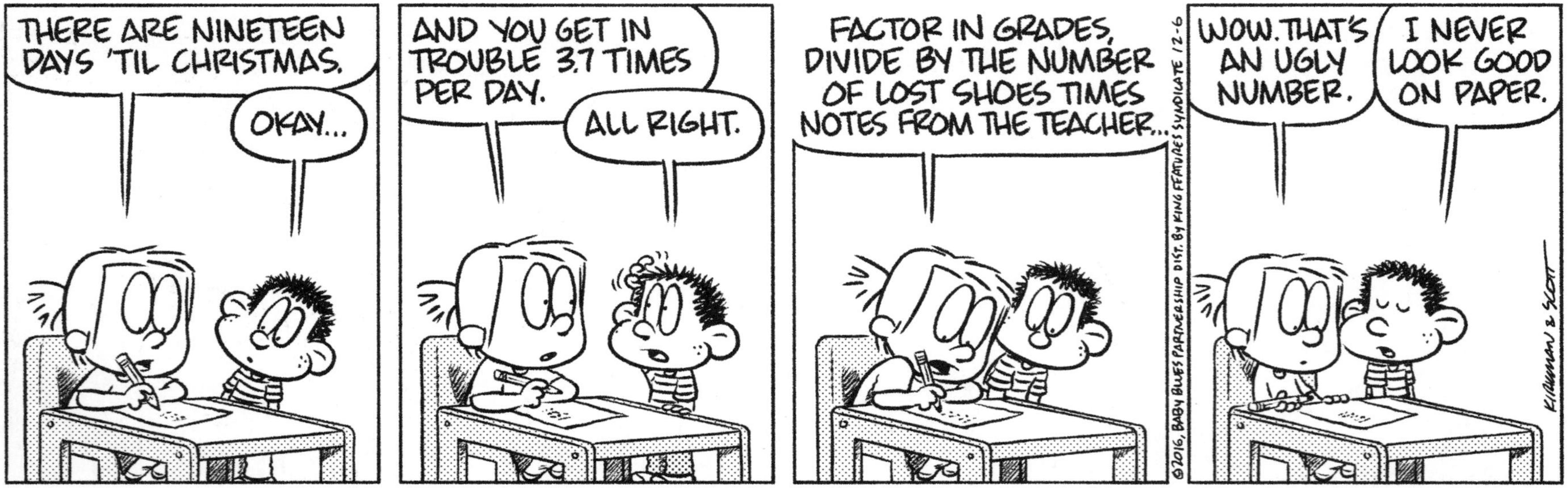
THERE ARE NINETEEN DAYS 'TIL CHRISTMAS.
OKAY...
AND YOU GET IN TROUBLE 3.7 TIMES PER DAY.
ALL RIGHT.
FACTOR IN GRADES, DIVIDE BY THE NUMBER OF LOST SHOES TIMES NOTES FROM THE TEACHER...
WOW. THAT'S AN UGLY NUMBER.
I NEVER LOOK GOOD ON PAPER.
©2016, BABY BLUES PARTNERSHIP DIST. BY KING FEATURES SYNDICATE 12-6
KIRKMAN & SCOTT

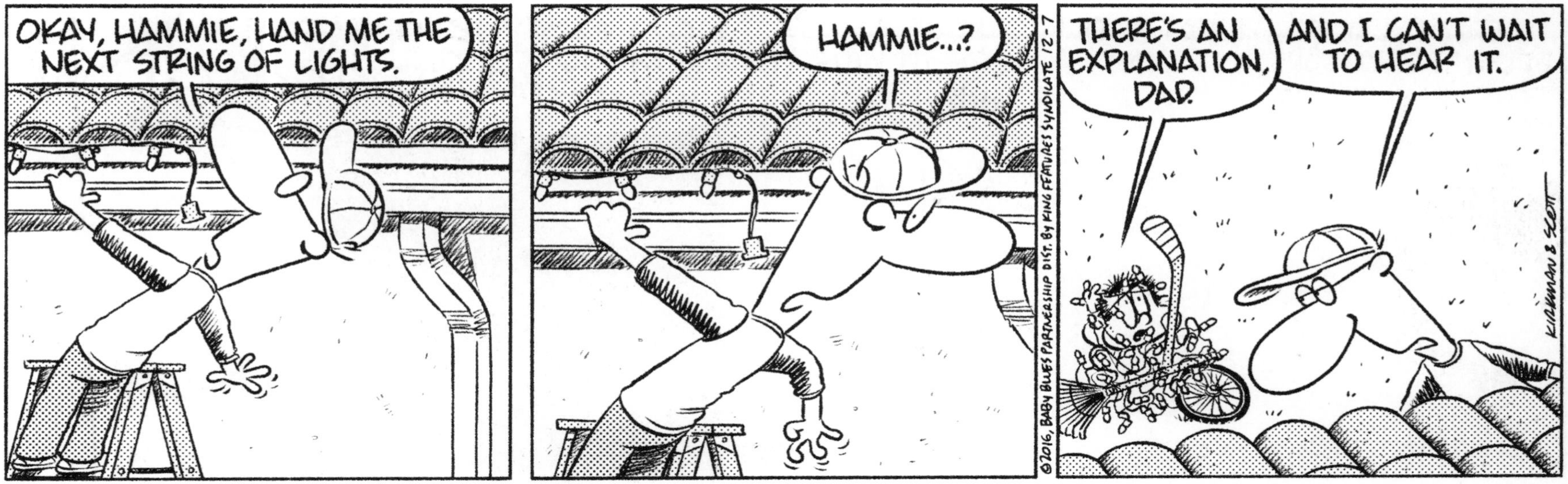
OKAY, HAMMIE, HAND ME THE NEXT STRING OF LIGHTS.
HAMMIE...?
©2016, BABY BLUES PARTNERSHIP DIST. BY KING FEATURES SYNDICATE 12-7
THERE'S AN EXPLANATION, DAD.
AND I CAN'T WAIT TO HEAR IT.
KIRKMAN & SCOTT

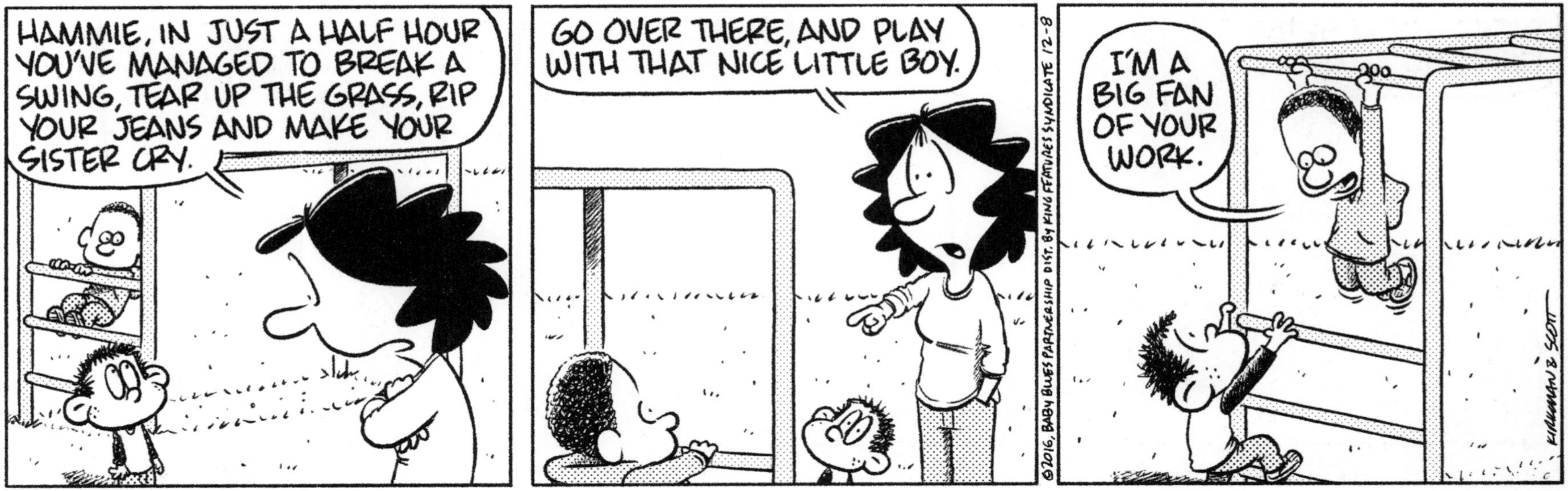
HAMMIE, IN JUST A HALF HOUR YOU'VE MANAGED TO BREAK A SWING, TEAR UP THE GRASS, RIP YOUR JEANS AND MAKE YOUR SISTER CRY.
GO OVER THERE, AND PLAY WITH THAT NICE LITTLE BOY.
©2016, BABY BLUES PARTNERSHIP DIST. BY KING FEATURES SYNDICATE 12-8
I'M A BIG FAN OF YOUR WORK.
KIRKMAN & SCOTT

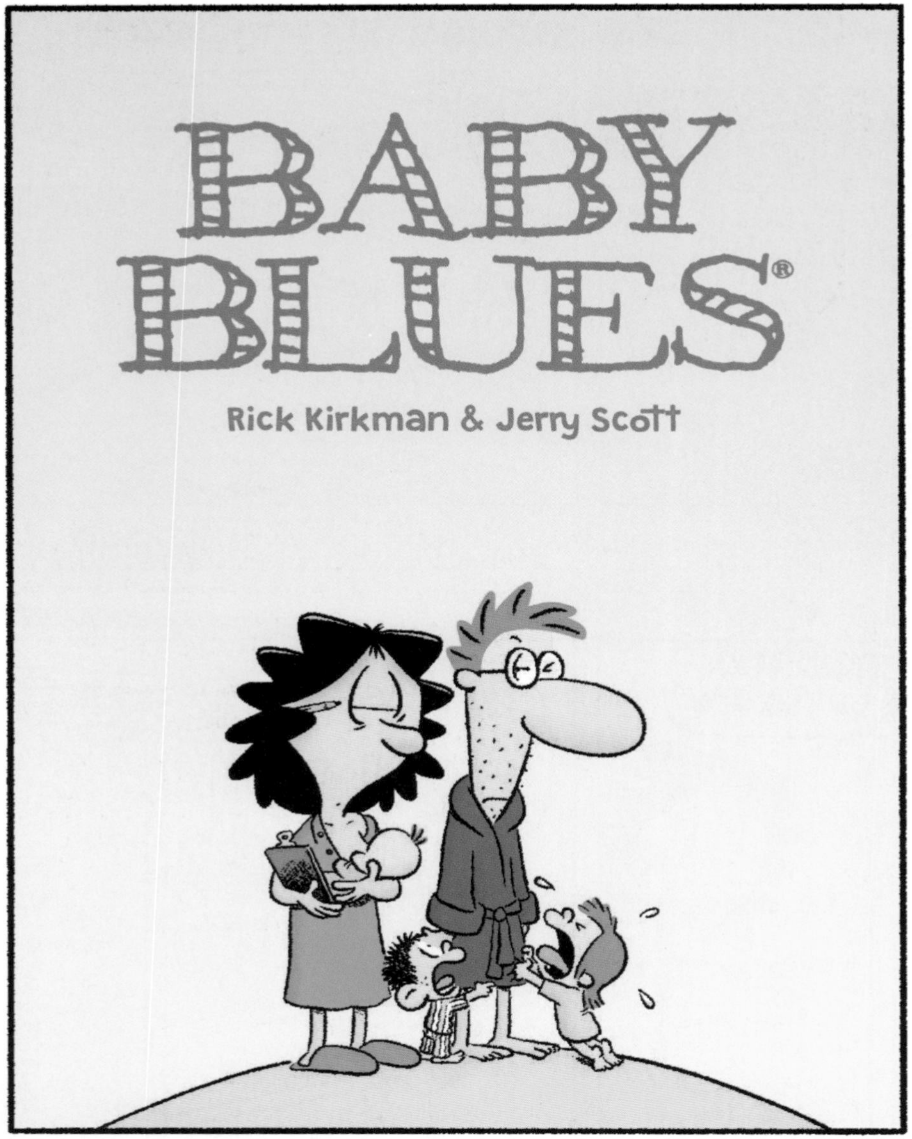
BABY BLUES®
Rick Kirkman & Jerry Scott

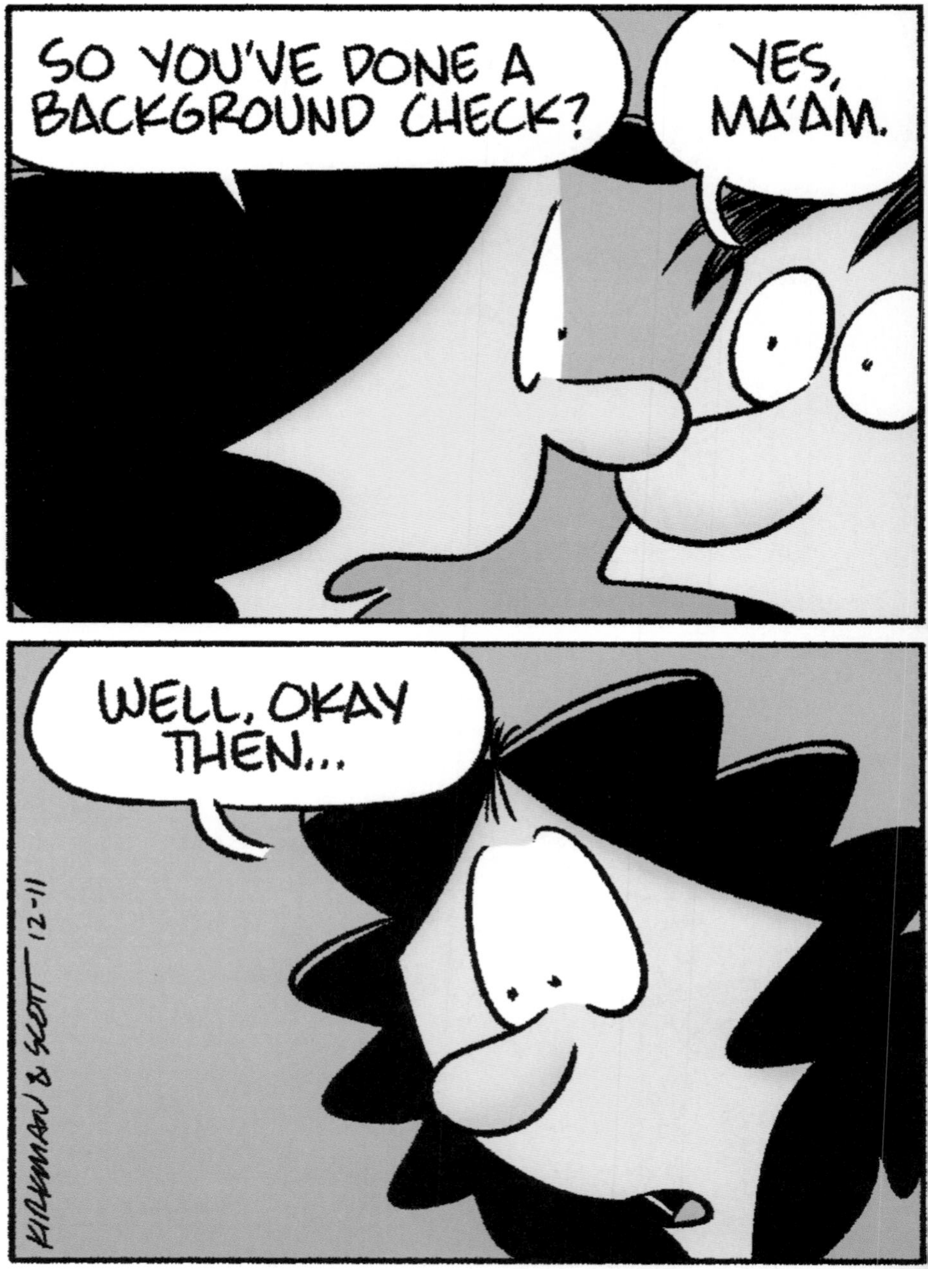
SO YOU'VE DONE A BACKGROUND CHECK?
YES, MA'AM.
WELL, OKAY THEN...
KIRKMAN & SCOTT 12-11

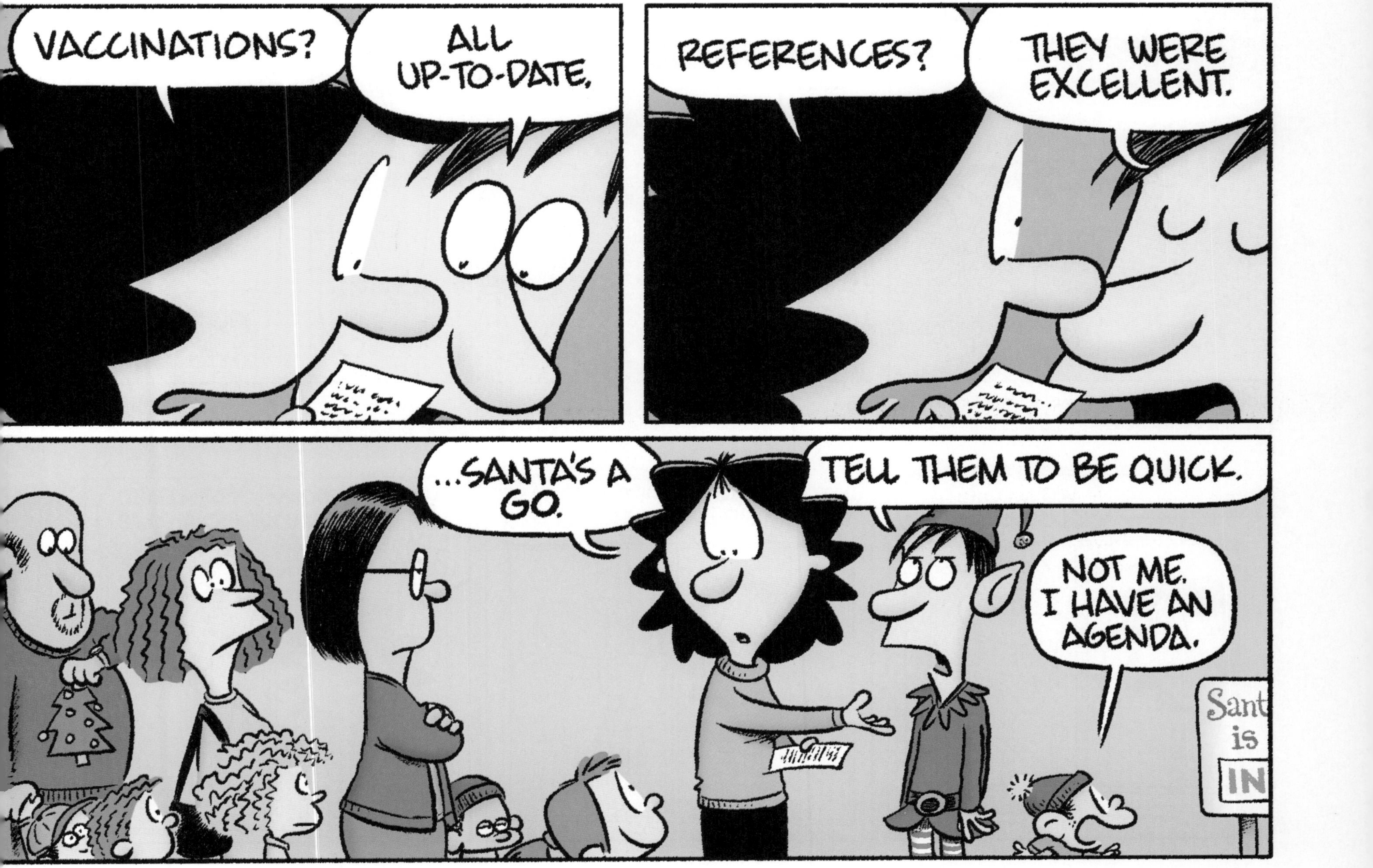
VACCINATIONS?
ALL UP-TO-DATE.
REFERENCES?
THEY WERE EXCELLENT.
...SANTA'S A GO.
TELL THEM TO BE QUICK.
NOT ME. I HAVE AN AGENDA.
Sant
is
IN

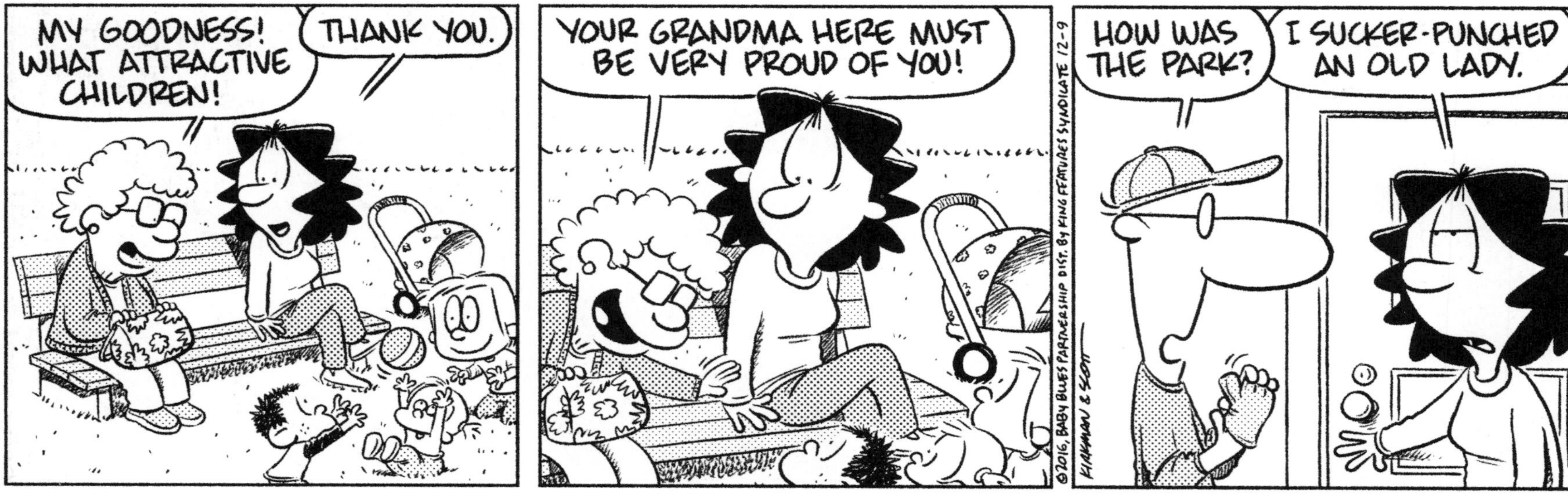
MY GOODNESS! WHAT ATTRACTIVE CHILDREN!
THANK YOU.
YOUR GRANDMA HERE MUST BE VERY PROUD OF YOU!
©2016, BABY BLUES PARTNERSHIP DIST. BY KING FEATURES SYNDICATE 12-9
KIRKMAN & SCOTT
HOW WAS THE PARK?
I SUCKER-PUNCHED AN OLD LADY.

Rick: We do not condone that. But it is a funny line.

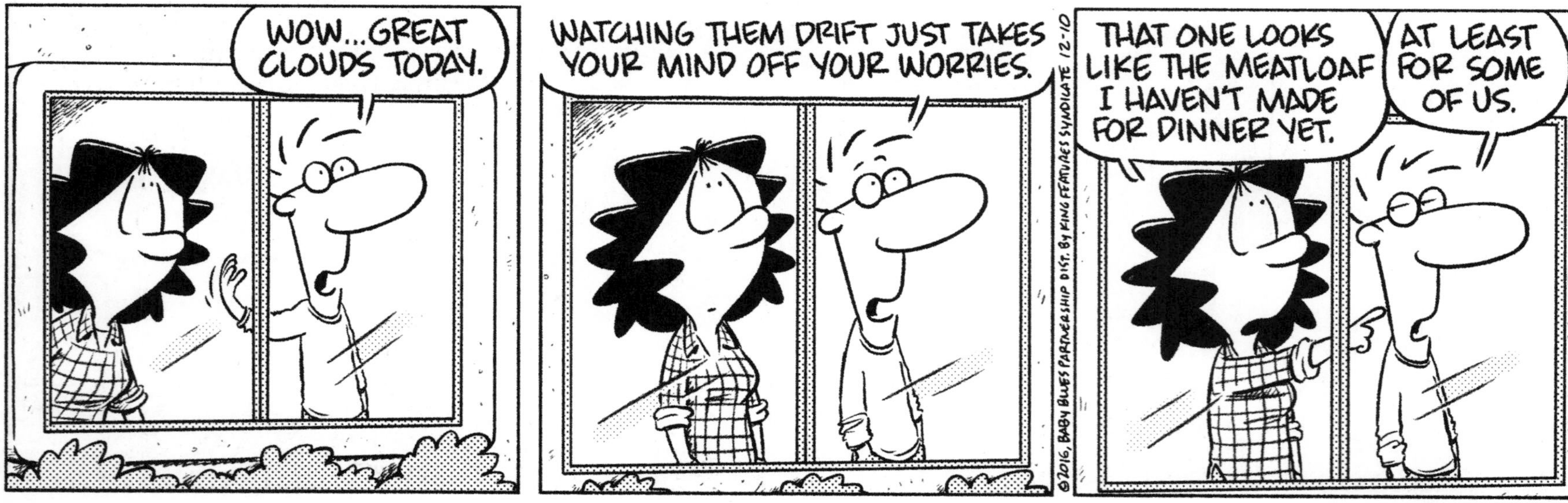
WOW...GREAT CLOUDS TODAY.
WATCHING THEM DRIFT JUST TAKES YOUR MIND OFF YOUR WORRIES.
©2016, BABY BLUES PARTNERSHIP DIST. BY KING FEATURES SYNDICATE 12-10
THAT ONE LOOKS LIKE THE MEATLOAF I HAVEN'T MADE FOR DINNER YET.
AT LEAST FOR SOME OF US.
KIRKMAN & SCOTT

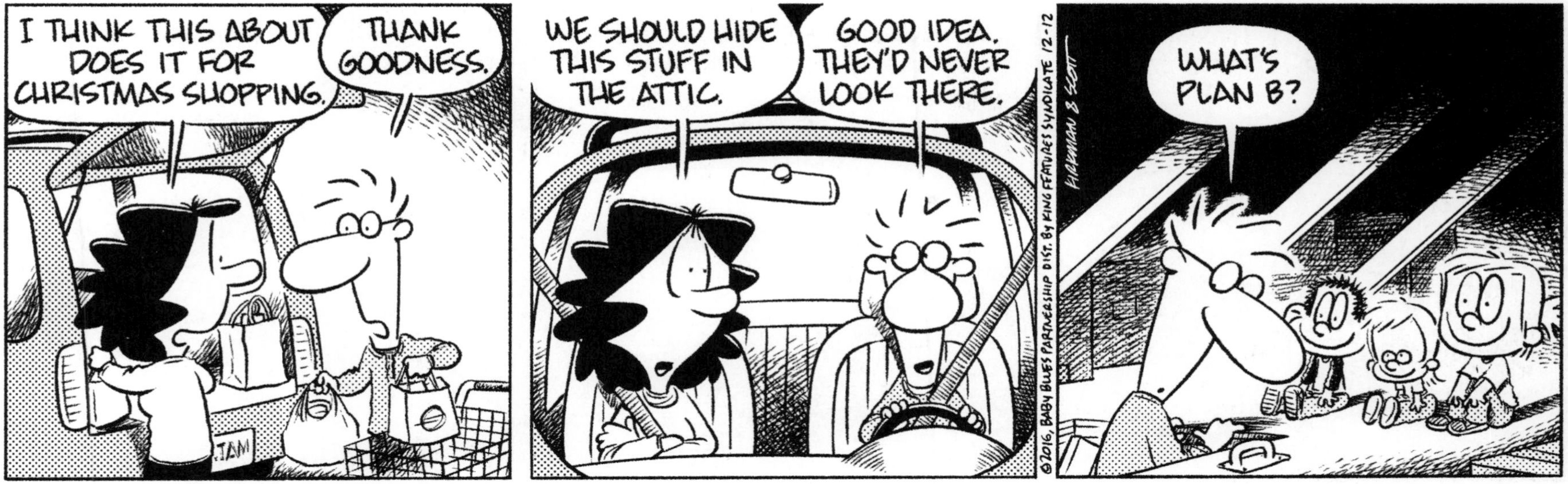
I THINK THIS ABOUT DOES IT FOR CHRISTMAS SHOPPING.
THANK GOODNESS.
WE SHOULD HIDE THIS STUFF IN THE ATTIC.
GOOD IDEA. THEY'D NEVER LOOK THERE.
©2016, BABY BLUES PARTNERSHIP DIST. BY KING FEATURES SYNDICATE 12-12
KIRKMAN & SCOTT
WHAT'S PLAN B?

Jerry: Hiding Christmas presents was not an easy task for my parents, either.

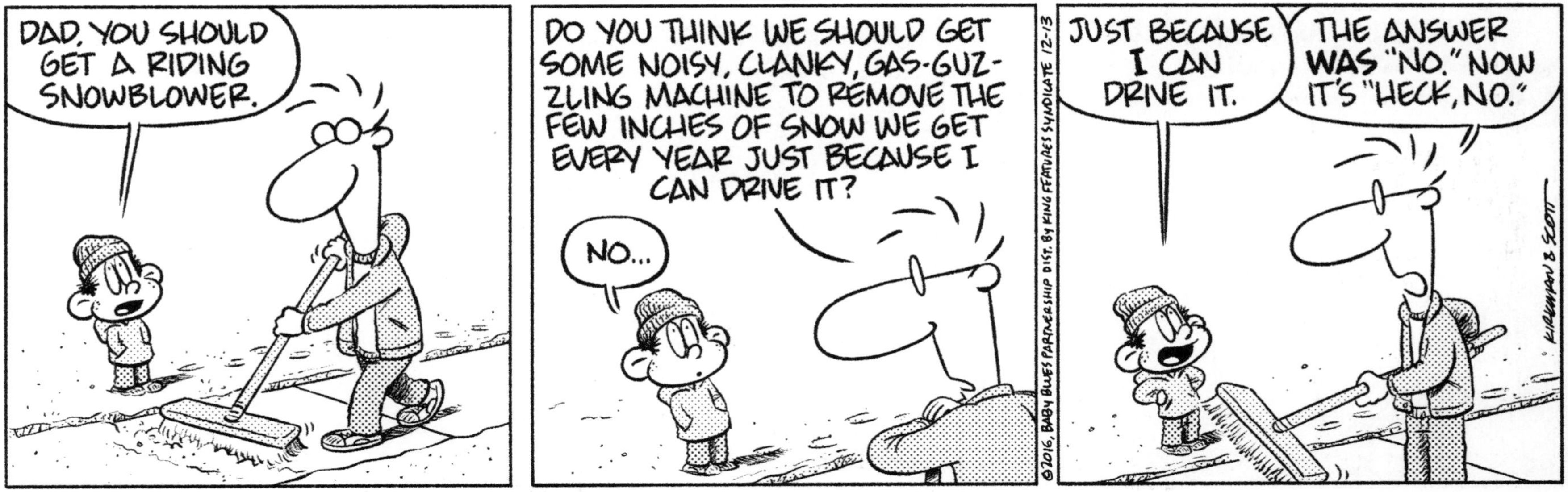
DAD, YOU SHOULD GET A RIDING SNOWBLOWER.
DO YOU THINK WE SHOULD GET SOME NOISY, CLANKY, GAS-GUZZLING MACHINE TO REMOVE THE FEW INCHES OF SNOW WE GET EVERY YEAR JUST BECAUSE I CAN DRIVE IT?
NO...
©2016, BABY BLUES PARTNERSHIP DIST. BY KING FEATURES SYNDICATE 12-13
JUST BECAUSE **I** CAN DRIVE IT.
THE ANSWER **WAS** "NO." NOW IT'S "HECK, NO."
KIRKMAN & SCOTT

Rick: A snowblower in the strange-weather world of the MacPhersons where snow falls on the palm trees and cactuses. Right.

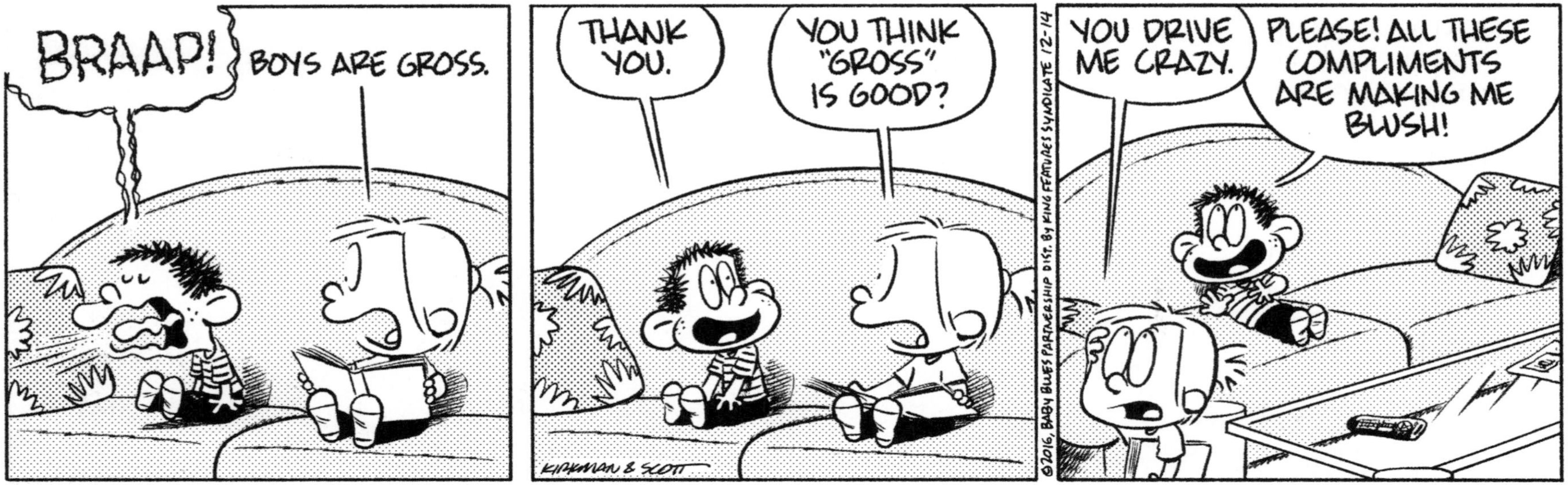
BRAAP!
BOYS ARE GROSS.
THANK YOU.
YOU THINK "GROSS" IS GOOD?
KIRKMAN & SCOTT
©2016, BABY BLUES PARTNERSHIP DIST. BY KING FEATURES SYNDICATE 12-14
YOU DRIVE ME CRAZY.
PLEASE! ALL THESE COMPLIMENTS ARE MAKING ME BLUSH!

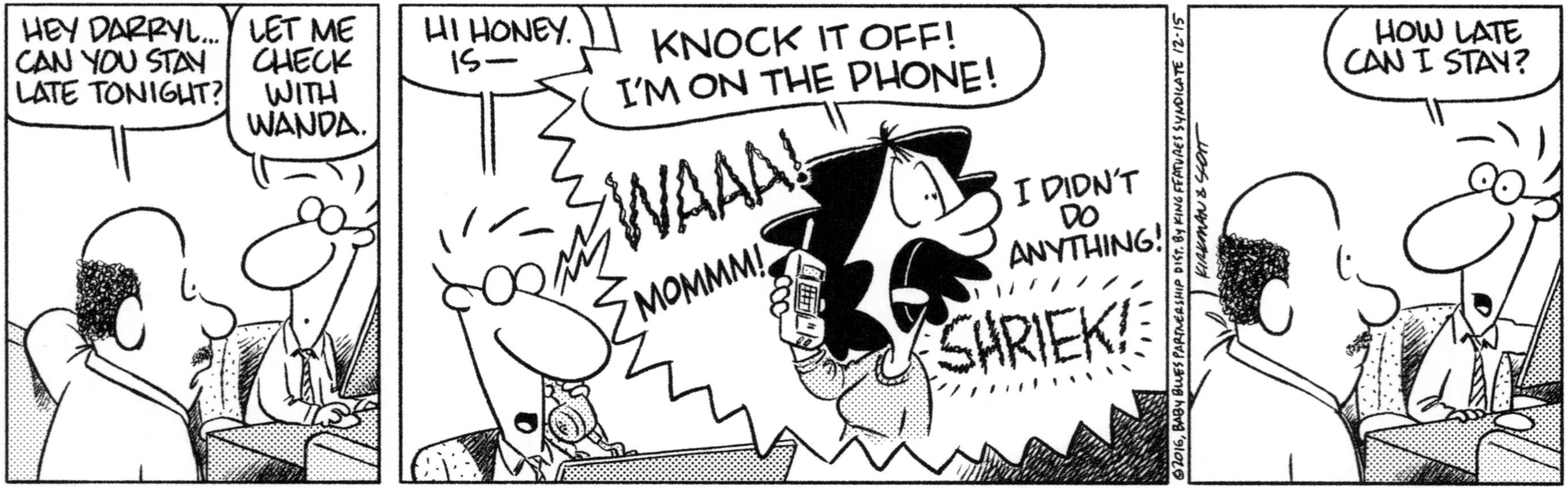
HEY DARRYL... CAN YOU STAY LATE TONIGHT?
LET ME CHECK WITH WANDA.
HI HONEY. IS—
KNOCK IT OFF! I'M ON THE PHONE!
WAAA!
MOMMM!
I DIDN'T DO ANYTHING!
SHRIEK!
©2016, BABY BLUES PARTNERSHIP DIST. BY KING FEATURES SYNDICATE 12-15
KIRKMAN & SCOTT
HOW LATE CAN I STAY?

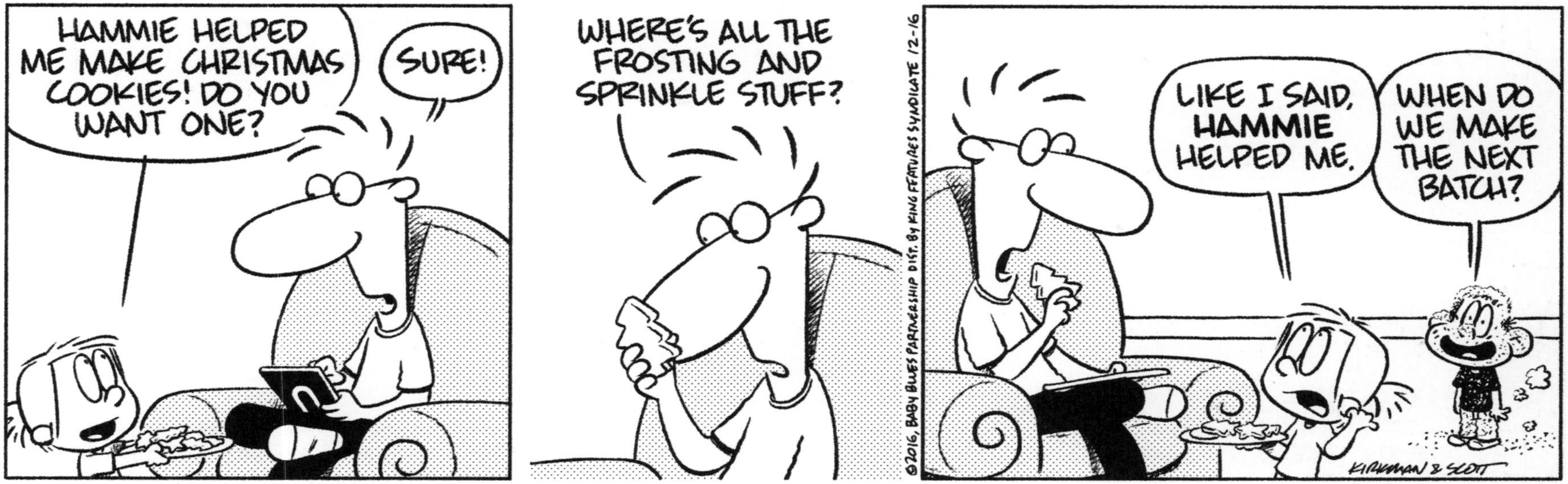
HAMMIE HELPED ME MAKE CHRISTMAS COOKIES! DO YOU WANT ONE?
SURE!
WHERE'S ALL THE FROSTING AND SPRINKLE STUFF?
©2016, BABY BLUES PARTNERSHIP DIST. BY KING FEATURES SYNDICATE 12-16
LIKE I SAID, **HAMMIE** HELPED ME.
WHEN DO WE MAKE THE NEXT BATCH?
KIRKMAN & SCOTT

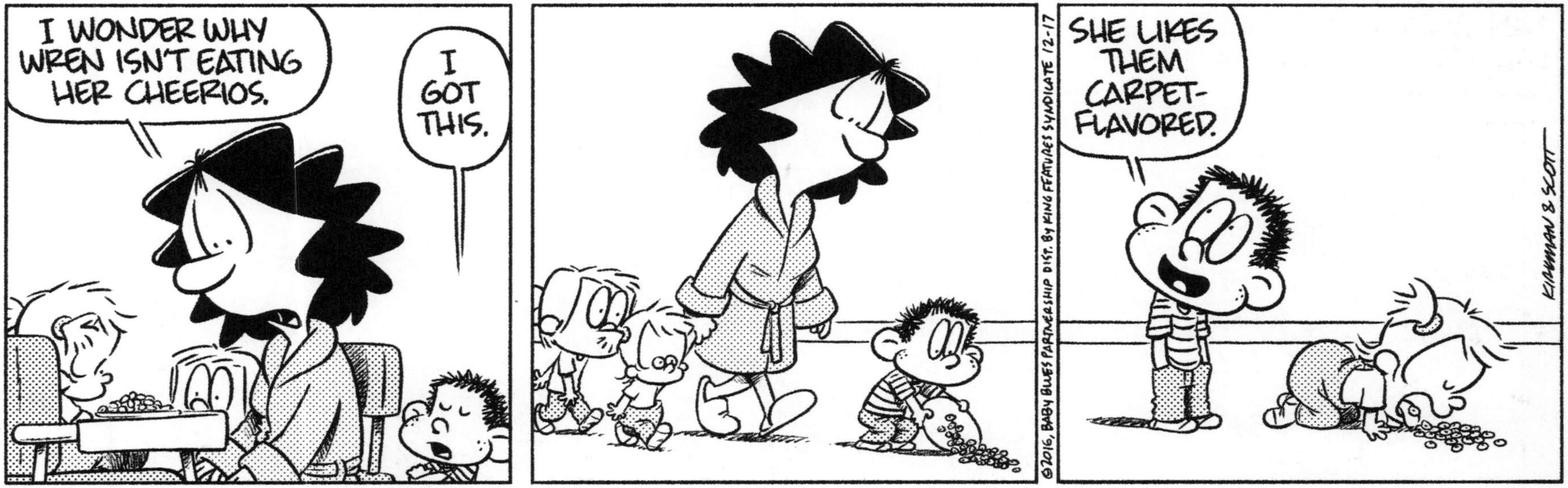
I WONDER WHY WREN ISN'T EATING HER CHEERIOS.
I GOT THIS.
©2016, BABY BLUES PARTNERSHIP DIST. BY KING FEATURES SYNDICATE 12-17
SHE LIKES THEM CARPET-FLAVORED.
KIRKMAN & SCOTT

Rick: By the third child, the five-second rule becomes the ten-Cheerio rule.

Jerry: The position of Wren's right pigtail in the second panel always makes it look like Zoe has a Wilford Brimley-type mustache to me. Now try to unsee it.

Rick: Dang! Why didn't I move Wren to the right? I have a sudden hankering for oatmeal right now.

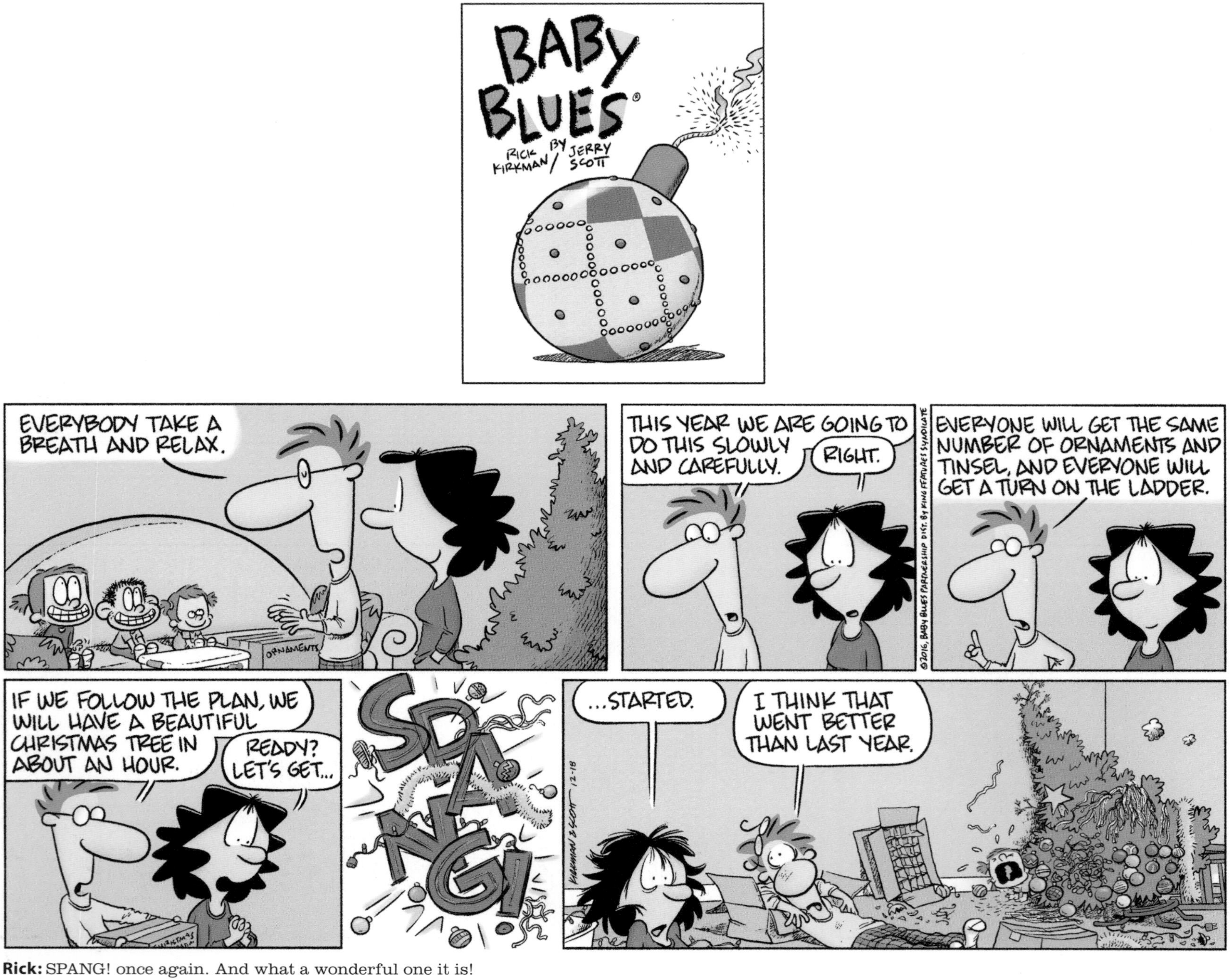
BABY BLUES®
BY RICK KIRKMAN / JERRY SCOTT
EVERYBODY TAKE A BREATH AND RELAX.
ORNAMENTS
THIS YEAR WE ARE GOING TO DO THIS SLOWLY AND CAREFULLY.
RIGHT.
©2016, BABY BLUES PARTNERSHIP DIST. BY KING FEATURES SYNDICATE
EVERYONE WILL GET THE SAME NUMBER OF ORNAMENTS AND TINSEL, AND EVERYONE WILL GET A TURN ON THE LADDER.
IF WE FOLLOW THE PLAN, WE WILL HAVE A BEAUTIFUL CHRISTMAS TREE IN ABOUT AN HOUR.
READY? LET'S GET...
SPANG!
KIRKMAN & SCOTT 12-18
...STARTED.
I THINK THAT WENT BETTER THAN LAST YEAR.

Rick: SPANG! once again. And what a wonderful one it is!

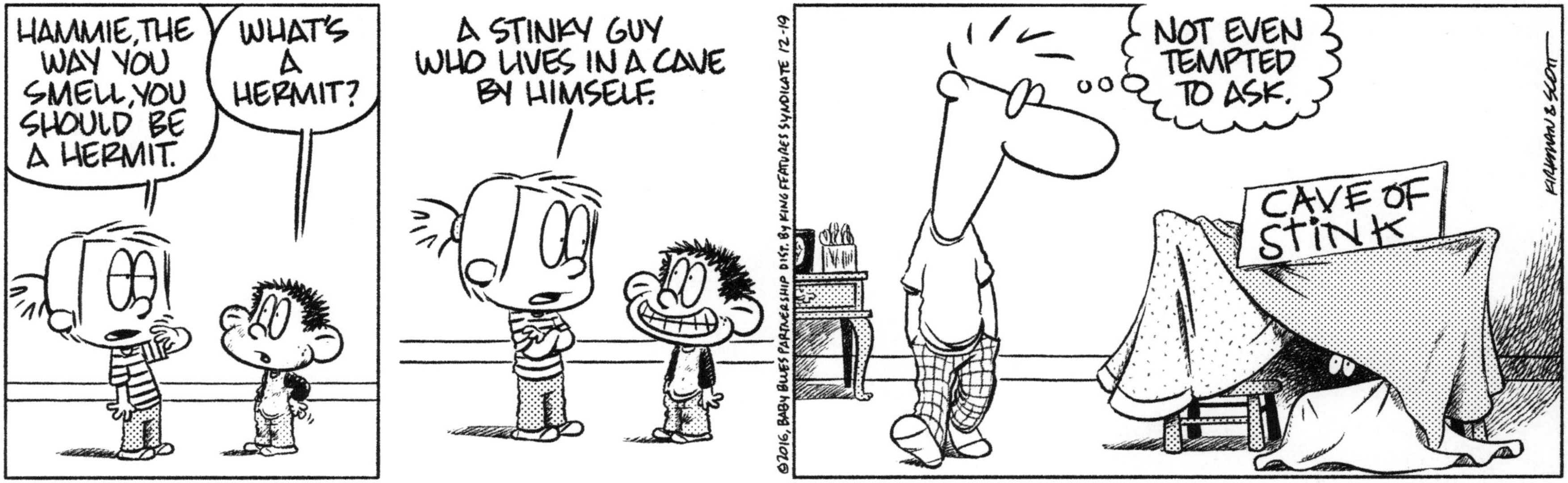
HAMMIE, THE WAY YOU SMELL, YOU SHOULD BE A HERMIT.
WHAT'S A HERMIT?
A STINKY GUY WHO LIVES IN A CAVE BY HIMSELF.
©2016, BABY BLUES PARTNERSHIP DIST. BY KING FEATURES SYNDICATE 12-19
NOT EVEN TEMPTED TO ASK.
CAVE OF STINK
KIRKMAN & SCOTT

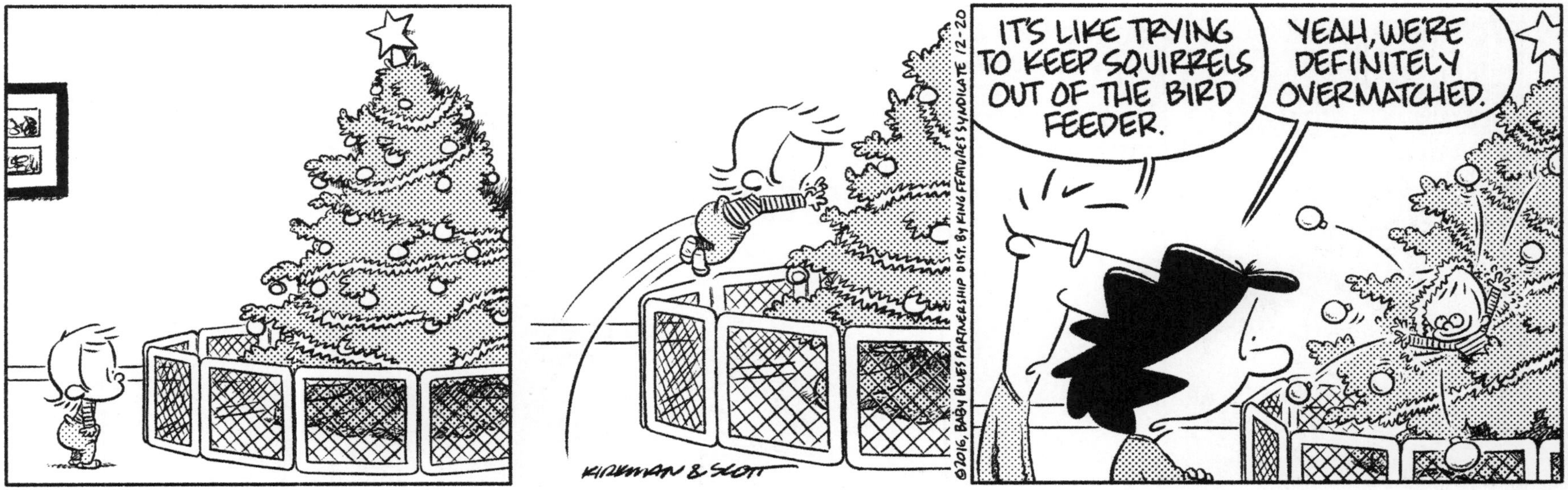
KIRKMAN & SCOTT
©2016, BABY BLUES PARTNERSHIP DIST. BY KING FEATURES SYNDICATE 12-20
IT'S LIKE TRYING TO KEEP SQUIRRELS OUT OF THE BIRD FEEDER.
YEAH, WE'RE DEFINITELY OVERMATCHED.

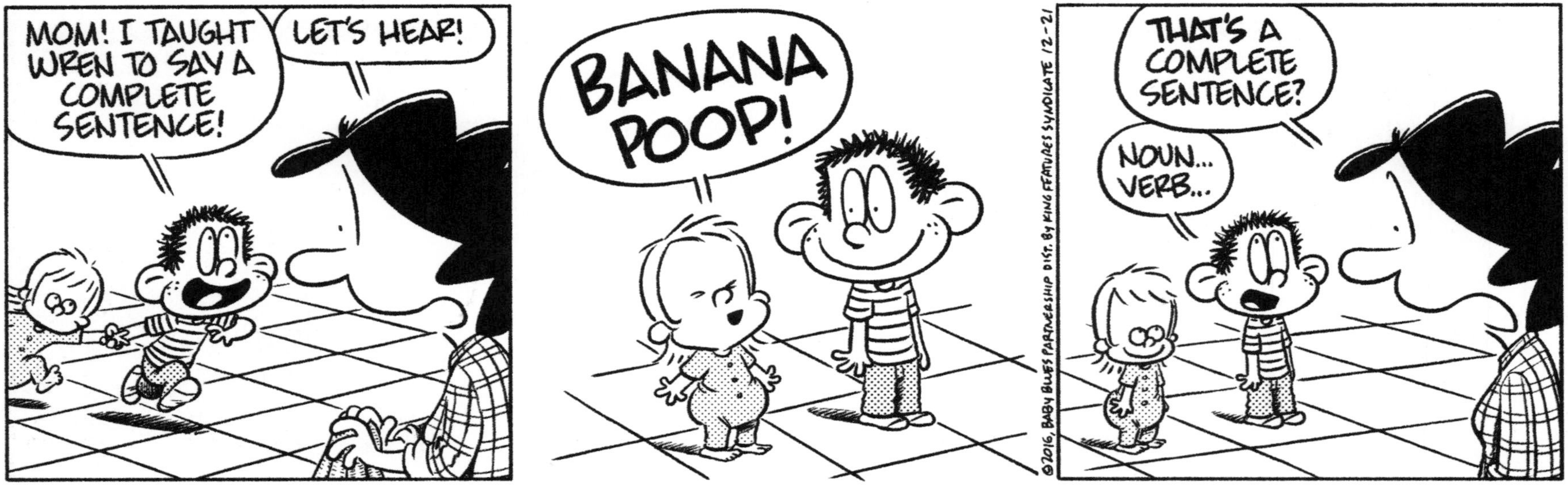
MOM! I TAUGHT WREN TO SAY A COMPLETE SENTENCE!
LET'S HEAR!
BANANA POOP!
©2016, BABY BLUES PARTNERSHIP DIST. BY KING FEATURES SYNDICATE 12-21
THAT'S A COMPLETE SENTENCE?
NOUN... VERB...

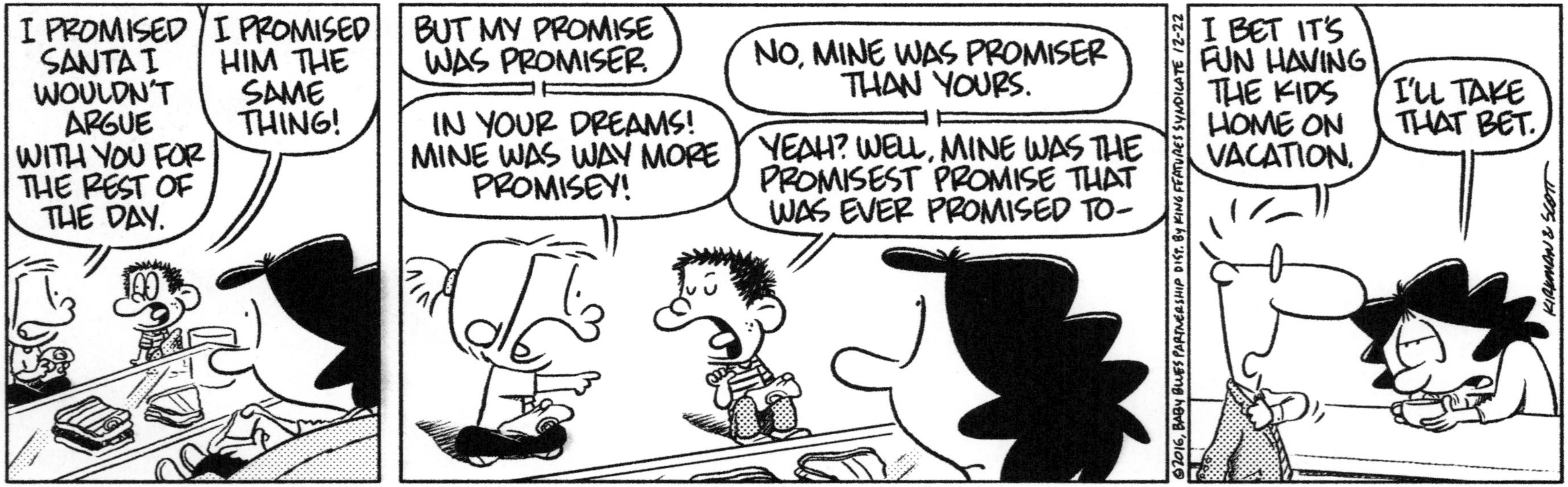
I PROMISED SANTA I WOULDN'T ARGUE WITH YOU FOR THE REST OF THE DAY.
I PROMISED HIM THE SAME THING!
BUT MY PROMISE WAS PROMISER.
IN YOUR DREAMS! MINE WAS WAY MORE PROMISEY!
NO, MINE WAS PROMISER THAN YOURS.
YEAH? WELL, MINE WAS THE PROMISEST PROMISE THAT WAS EVER PROMISED TO-
©2016, BABY BLUES PARTNERSHIP DIST. BY KING FEATURES SYNDICATE 12-22
I BET IT'S FUN HAVING THE KIDS HOME ON VACATION.
I'LL TAKE THAT BET.
KIRKMAN & SCOTT

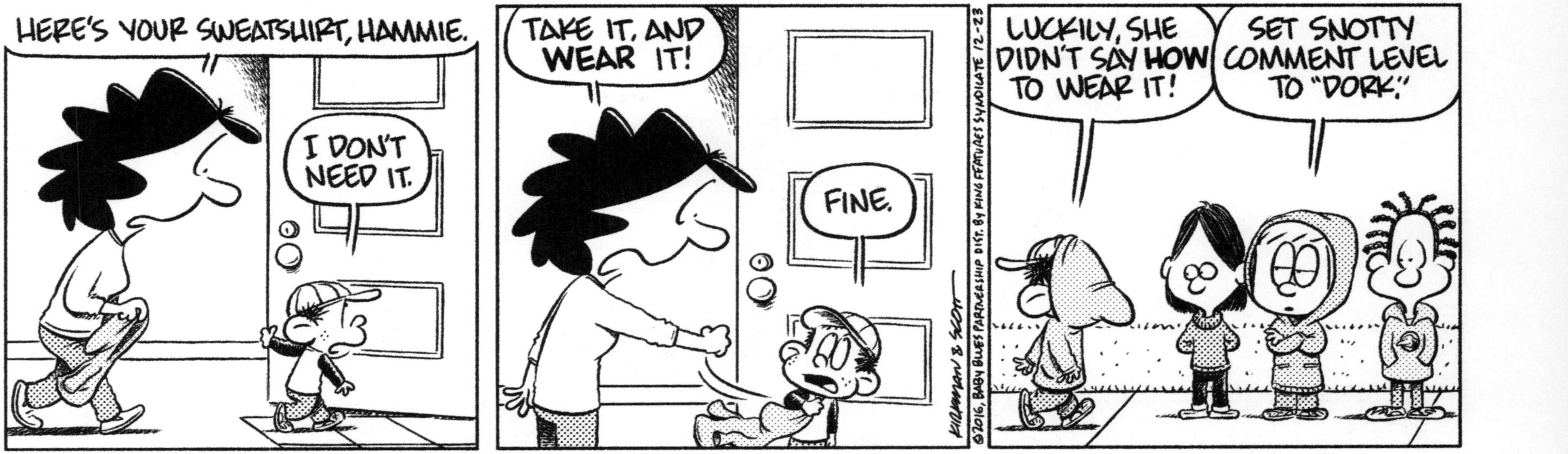
HERE'S YOUR SWEATSHIRT, HAMMIE.
I DON'T NEED IT.
TAKE IT, AND WEAR IT!
FINE.
©2016, BABY BLUES PARTNERSHIP DIST. BY KING FEATURES SYNDICATE 12-23
KIRKMAN & SCOTT
LUCKILY, SHE DIDN'T SAY HOW TO WEAR IT!
SET SNOTTY COMMENT LEVEL TO "DORK."

Jerry: Shields up, Hammie.

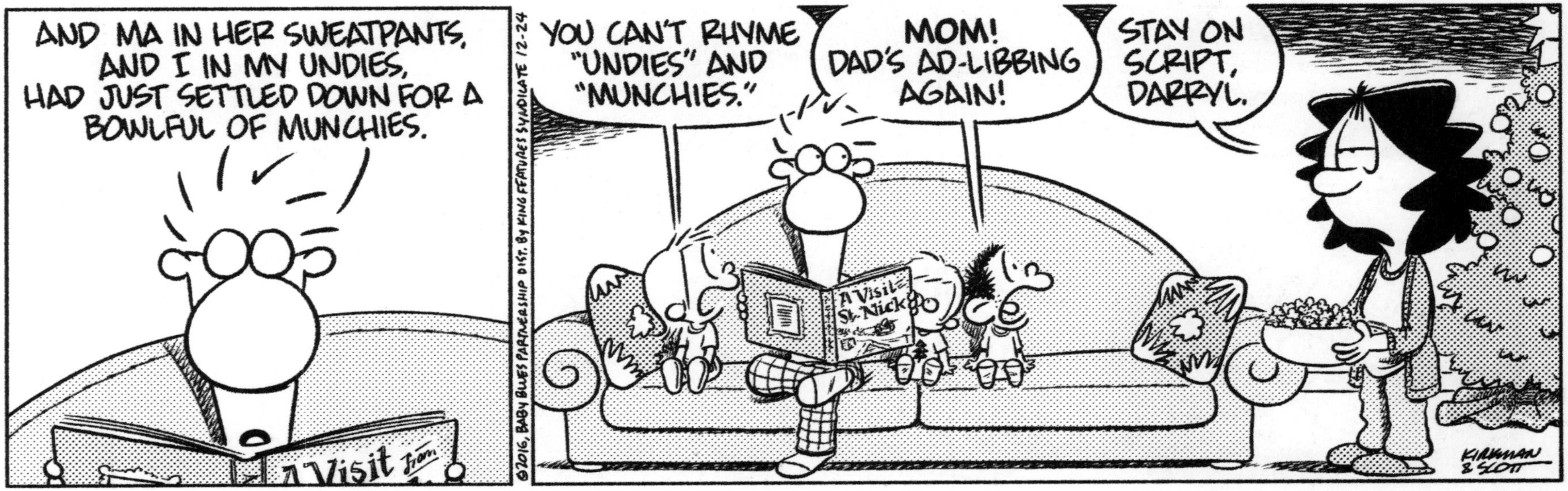
AND MA IN HER SWEATPANTS, AND I IN MY UNDIES, HAD JUST SETTLED DOWN FOR A BOWLFUL OF MUNCHIES.
©2016, BABY BLUES PARTNERSHIP DIST. BY KING FEATURES SYNDICATE 12-24
YOU CAN'T RHYME "UNDIES" AND "MUNCHIES."
MOM! DAD'S AD-LIBBING AGAIN!
STAY ON SCRIPT, DARRYL.
KIRKMAN & SCOTT

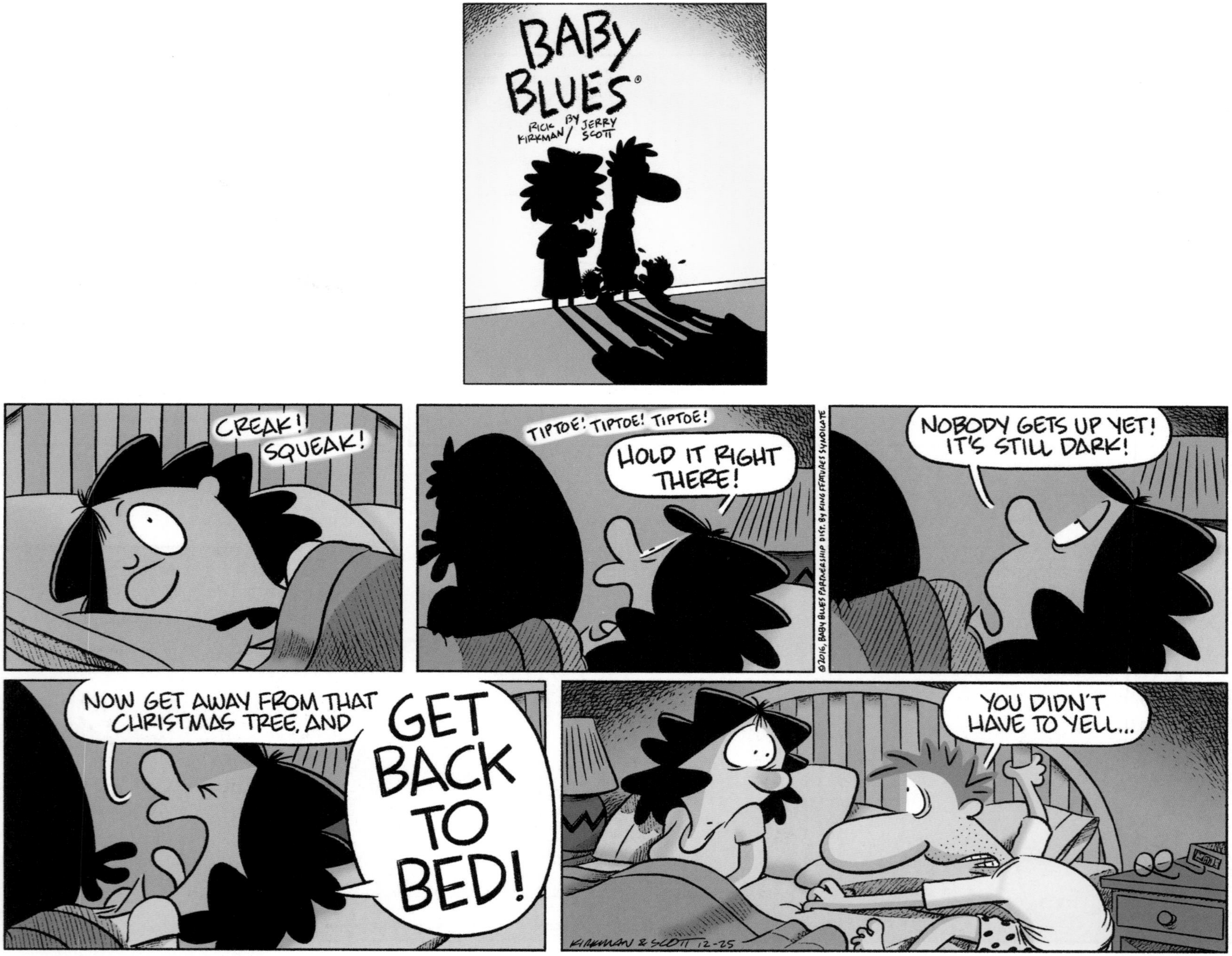
BABY BLUES®
BY RICK KIRKMAN / JERRY SCOTT
CREAK! SQUEAK!
TIPTOE! TIPTOE! TIPTOE!
HOLD IT RIGHT THERE!
©2016, BABY BLUES PARTNERSHIP DIST. BY KING FEATURES SYNDICATE
NOBODY GETS UP YET! IT'S STILL DARK!
NOW GET AWAY FROM THAT CHRISTMAS TREE, AND
GET BACK TO BED!
YOU DIDN'T HAVE TO YELL...
KIRKMAN & SCOTT 12-25

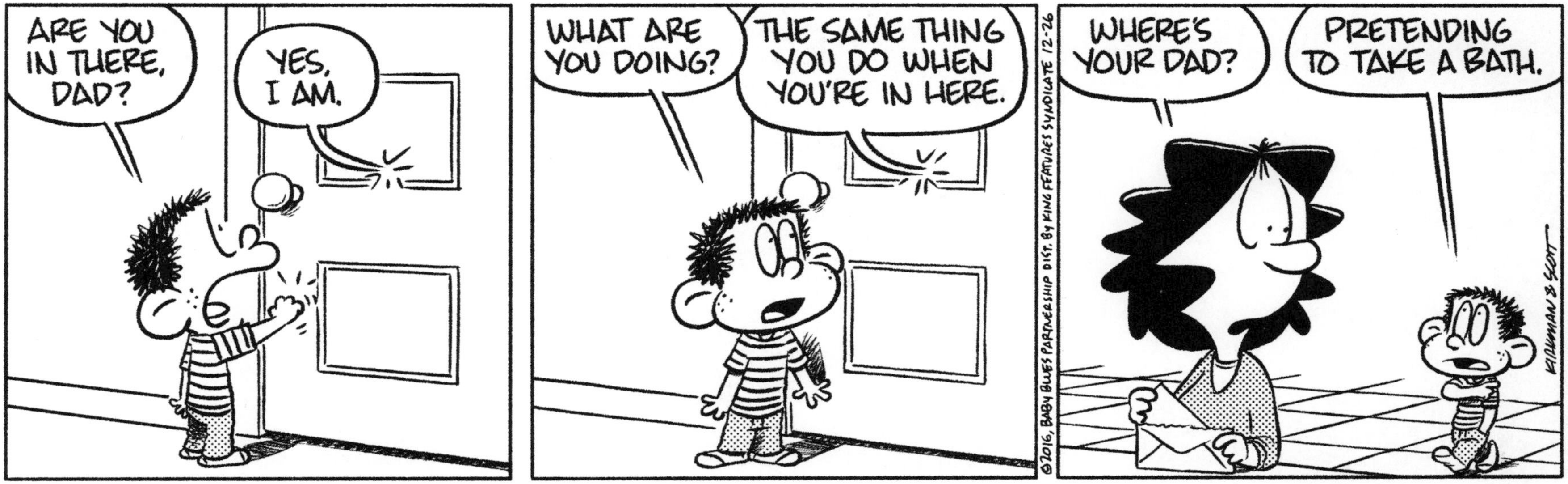
ARE YOU IN THERE, DAD?
YES, I AM.
WHAT ARE YOU DOING?
THE SAME THING YOU DO WHEN YOU'RE IN HERE.
©2016, BABY BLUES PARTNERSHIP DIST. BY KING FEATURES SYNDICATE 12-26
WHERE'S YOUR DAD?
PRETENDING TO TAKE A BATH.
KIRKMAN & SCOTT

Jerry: Bathroom humor doesn't belong in the comics . . . unless you write a comic strip about a family of five. I mean, c'mon!

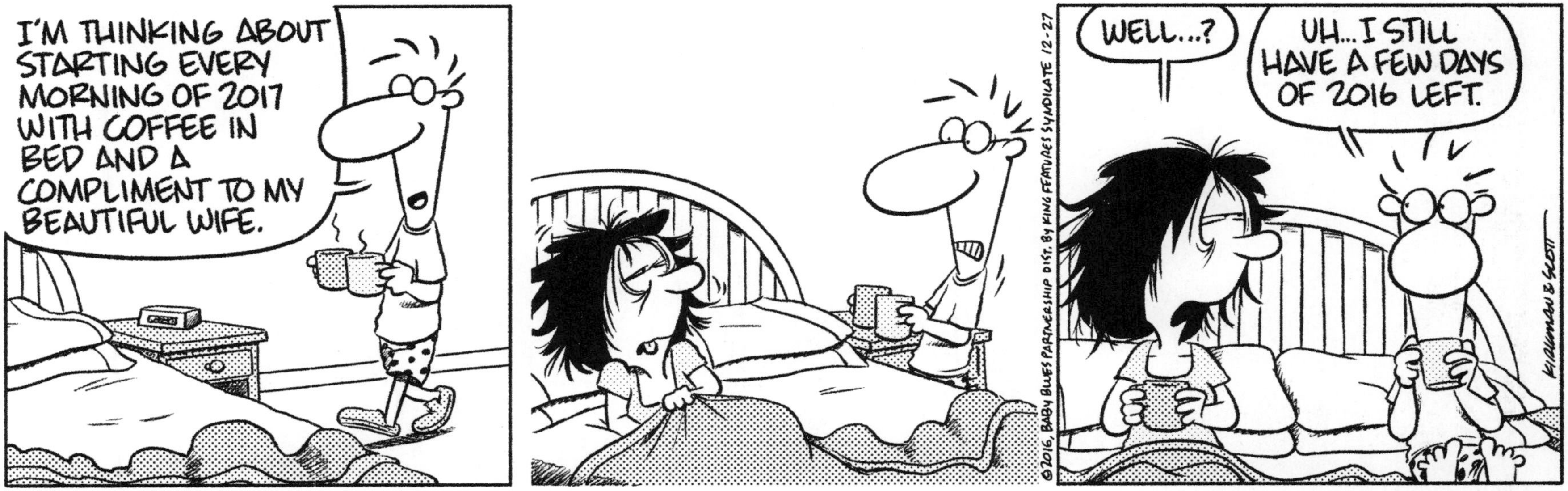
I'M THINKING ABOUT STARTING EVERY MORNING OF 2017 WITH COFFEE IN BED AND A COMPLIMENT TO MY BEAUTIFUL WIFE.
©2016, BABY BLUES PARTNERSHIP DIST. BY KING FEATURES SYNDICATE 12-27
WELL...?
UH... I STILL HAVE A FEW DAYS OF 2016 LEFT.
KIRKMAN & SCOTT

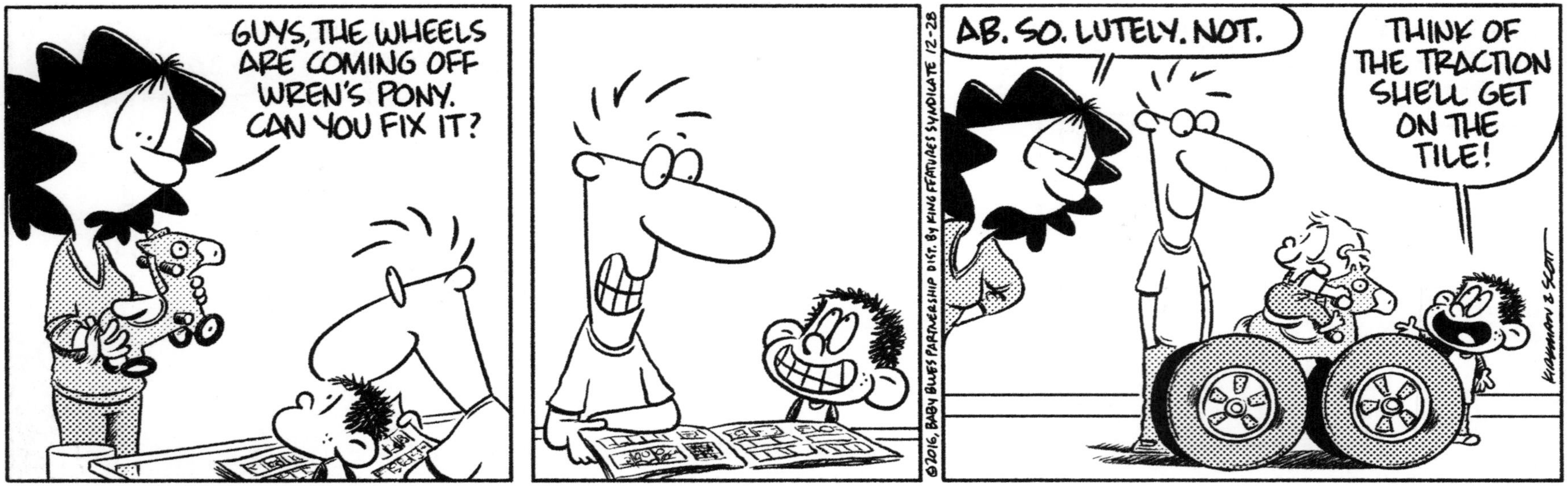
GUYS, THE WHEELS ARE COMING OFF WREN'S PONY. CAN YOU FIX IT?
©2016, BABY BLUES PARTNERSHIP DIST. BY KING FEATURES SYNDICATE 12-28
AB. SO. LUTELY. NOT.
THINK OF THE TRACTION SHE'LL GET ON THE TILE!
KIRKMAN & SCOTT

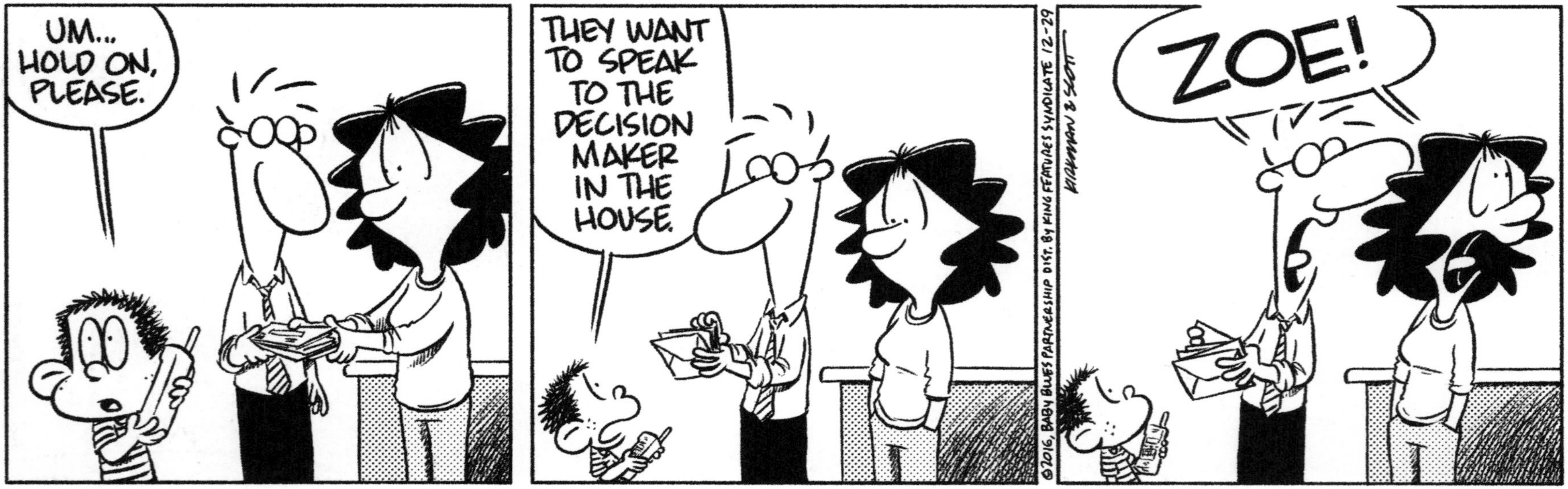
UM... HOLD ON, PLEASE.
THEY WANT TO SPEAK TO THE DECISION MAKER IN THE HOUSE.
©2016, BABY BLUES PARTNERSHIP DIST. BY KING FEATURES SYNDICATE 12-29
KIRKMAN & SCOTT
ZOE!

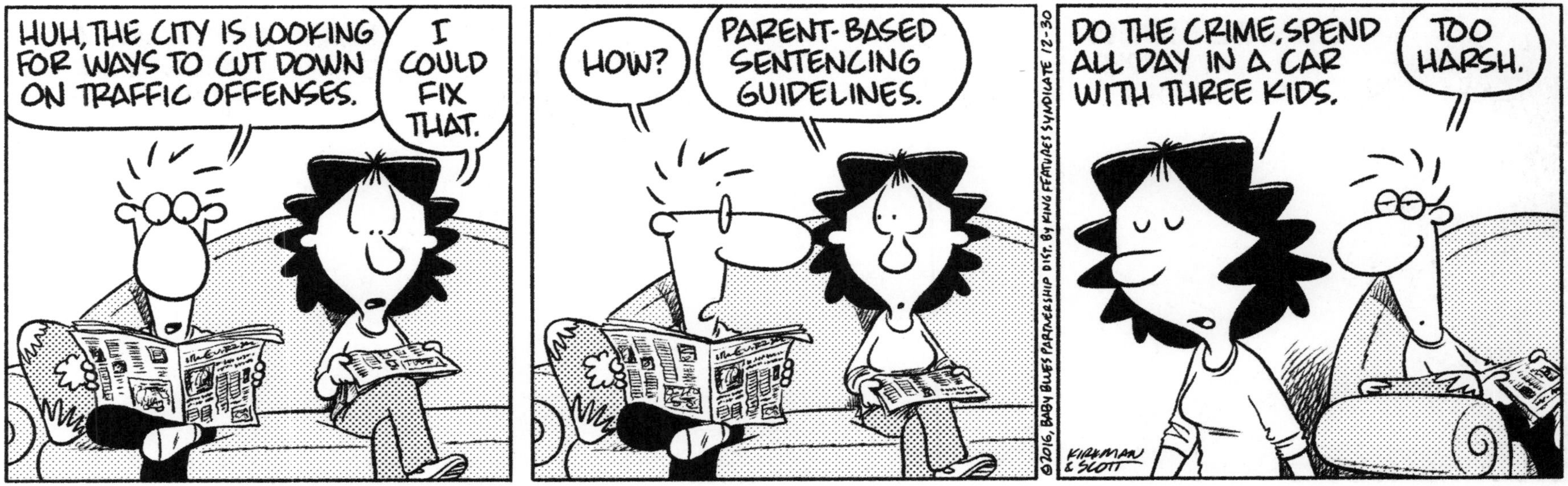
HUH, THE CITY IS LOOKING FOR WAYS TO CUT DOWN ON TRAFFIC OFFENSES.
I COULD FIX THAT.
HOW?
PARENT-BASED SENTENCING GUIDELINES.
©2016, BABY BLUES PARTNERSHIP DIST. BY KING FEATURES SYNDICATE 12-30
DO THE CRIME, SPEND ALL DAY IN A CAR WITH THREE KIDS.
TOO HARSH.
KIRKMAN & SCOTT

Jerry: Any court in the land would define that as cruel and unusual punishment.

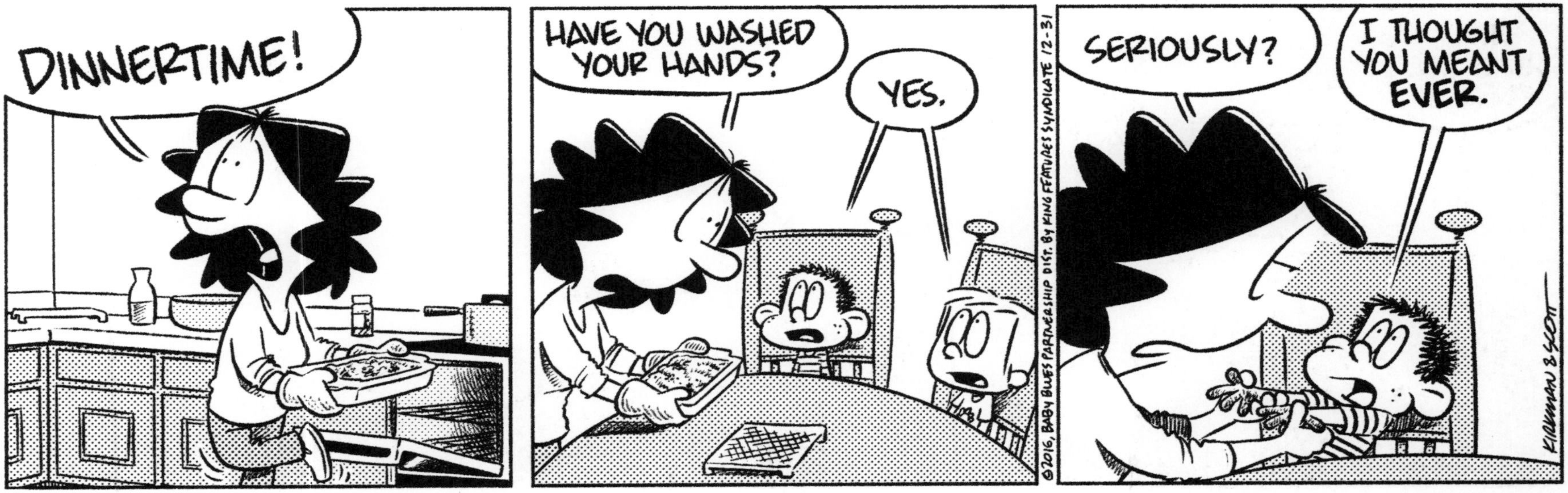
DINNERTIME!
HAVE YOU WASHED YOUR HANDS?
YES.
©2016, BABY BLUES PARTNERSHIP DIST. BY KING FEATURES SYNDICATE 12-31
SERIOUSLY?
I THOUGHT YOU MEANT **EVER**.
KIRKMAN & SCOTT

Baby Blues® is syndicated internationally by King Features Syndicate, Inc.
For information, write King Features Syndicate, Inc.,
300 West Fifty-Seventh Street, New York, New York 10019.

Andrews McMeel Publishing
a division of Andrews McMeel Universal
1130 Walnut Street, Kansas City, Missouri 64106
www.andrewsmcmeel.com

17 18 19 20 21 SDB 10 9 8 7 6 5 4 3 2 1

ISBN: 978-1-4494-8511-5

Library of Congress Control Number: 2017934361

Editor: Dorothy O'Brien
Designer/Art Director: Julie Barnes
Production Manager: Chuck Harper
Production Editor: Amy Strassner
Demand Planner: Sue Eikos

Find *Baby Blues®* on the Web at www.babyblues.com.

ATTENTION: SCHOOLS AND BUSINESSES
Andrews McMeel books are available at quantity discounts with bulk purchase for educational,
business, or sales promotional use. For information, please e-mail the Andrews McMeel Publishing
Special Sales Department: specialsales@amuniversal.com.